2017 U.S. PRODUCT & RETAIL OUTLOOK

NATIONAL EDITION

The 2017 U.S. Product & Retail Outlook report is the leading annual publication that describes over 200 product lines and their sales through 20 retail industries. Published each year in April, the Outlook report provides the most current and accurate estimates of the size of the product lines and their distribution channels.

With over 700 pages, the 2017 U.S. Product & Retail Outlook features:

2016 product line sales totals for each retail industry

2017 forecast product line sales totals for each retail industry

5-year trend product line sales totals for each retail industry

Product line sales by 7 company size categories (by employee size of company)

Summary tables showing matrix of product line sales by retail industry

Industry definitions and descriptions

The Outlook report is available for purchase in either PDF, spreadsheet (Excel) or print format edition.

The 2017 U.S. Product & Retail Outlook report is an essential reference tool for industry researchers, market analysts, CEOs and leading industry executives.

Copyright © 2017 By C. Barnes & Co.

Printed in USA

TABLE OF CONTENTS

2017 U.S. PRODUCT & RETAIL OUTLOOK

TABLE OF CONTENTS

TABLE OF CONTENTS

2017 U.S. PRODUCT & RETAIL OUTLOOK

TABLE OF CONTENTS

2017 U.S. PRODUCT & RETAIL OUTLOOK

TABLE OF CONTENTS

TABLE OF CONTENTS

TABLE OF CONTENTS

2017 U.S. Product & Retail Outlook

USERS' GUIDE

The Barnes Reports are the leading publications on U.S. industries and estimates and forecasts on sales and employment demographics. As a way of making the most of this information, we have included a few suggestions and tips to aid you in processing and using this information.

Managers, planners, and market researchers use this information for a variety of activities:
- Sizing markets and segments – You can estimate the size of the regional markets you sell in and your company's market penetration into that market. You can do the same with the market segments in which you participate.
- Sales territory potential – You can estimate your market penetration and also the market potential in any regional area or market segment.
- Sales forecasting – With the estimates on the size of the industry, market researchers supporting a sales force can then estimate and forecast the future size of the industry.
- Advertising strategies – You can use this information for forecasting and estimating sales potential and target advertising campaigns.
- Competitive analysis – You will use the information to locate your possible competitors (if it is not already known), to estimate their size, growth and strengths and weaknesses and to see what market segments in which they participate.

We recognize that many managers today are asked to provide detailed analysis of their markets, sales territories, distribution channels, and product placements. We have organized these reports in a logical format making your market analysis and research tasks easy to accomplish.

Printed in USA

SUMMARY OF PRODUCT LINES SALES BY INDUSTRY

SALES (MILLIONS OF U.S. DOLLARS)

Main Category	Sub Category	U.S. Industry	Year			
			2015	2016	2017	2018
Grocery Foods	--	Home centers	10	11	11	12
Grocery Foods	--	Hardware stores	88	93	97	102
Grocery Foods	--	Supermarkets & grocery stores	409,078	406,514	406,566	407,411
Grocery Foods	--	Beer, wine, & liquor stores	1,924	2,056	2,201	2,360
Grocery Foods	--	Pharmacies & drug stores	5,757	6,225	6,693	7,205
Grocery Foods	--	Gas stations w/ conven. stores	49,389	54,118	59,030	64,353
Grocery Foods	--	Men's clothing stores	0	0	0	0
Grocery Foods	--	Women's clothing stores	1	1	1	1
Grocery Foods	--	Family clothing stores	7	7	8	8
Grocery Foods	--	CD, tape & record stores	1	1	1	1
Grocery Foods	--	Department stores	5,652	5,652	5,678	5,719
Grocery Foods	--	Warehouse clubs & supercntrs	198,486	219,384	238,278	253,052
Grocery Foods	--	Office supply/stationery stores	1	1	1	1
Grocery Foods	--	Electronic shopping & mail-order	4,683	5,288	5,977	6,609
Grocery Foods	--	Book stores	45	45	45	45
	Meat, Fish & Poultry	Supermarkets & grocery stores	71,422	70,975	70,984	71,131
	Meat, Fish & Poultry	Beer, wine, & liquor stores	109	117	125	134
	Meat, Fish & Poultry	Warehouse clubs & supercntrs	25,624	28,322	30,761	32,669
	Produce	Supermarkets & grocery stores	56,355	56,002	56,009	56,125
	Produce	Beer, wine, & liquor stores	11	12	13	14
	Produce	Warehouse clubs & supercntrs	18,677	20,643	22,421	23,811
	Frozen Foods	Supermarkets & grocery stores	31,879	31,679	31,683	31,749
	Frozen Foods	Beer, wine, & liquor stores	33	35	38	41
	Frozen Foods	Warehouse clubs & supercntrs	20,695	22,874	24,844	26,384
	Dairy Products	Supermarkets & grocery stores	48,679	48,374	48,381	48,481
	Dairy Products	Beer, wine, & liquor stores	138	148	158	169
	Dairy Products	Gas stations w/ conven. stores	5,670	6,213	6,777	7,388
	Dairy Products	Warehouse clubs & supercntrs	16,073	17,766	19,296	20,492

SUMMARY OF PRODUCT LINES SALES BY INDUSTRY

SALES (MILLIONS OF U.S. DOLLARS)

Main Category	Sub Category	U.S. Industry	Year			
			2015	2016	2017	2018
	In-Store Bakery Prod.	Supermarkets & grocery stores	9,126	9,069	9,070	9,089
	In-Store Bakery Prod.	Beer, wine, & liquor stores	20	22	23	25
	In-Store Bakery Prod.	Warehouse clubs & supercntrs	4,784	5,287	5,743	6,099
	Bakery-Off Premises	Supermarkets & grocery stores	15,289	15,193	15,195	15,227
	Bakery-Off Premises	Beer, wine, & liquor stores	76	81	87	93
	Bakery-Off Premises	Gas stations w/ conven. stores	2,047	2,243	2,447	2,667
	Bakery-Off Premises	Warehouse clubs & supercntrs	6,229	6,885	7,478	7,941
	Delicatessen Items	Supermarkets & grocery stores	20,422	20,294	20,296	20,339
	Delicatessen Items	Beer, wine, & liquor stores	75	81	86	93
	Delicatessen Items	Warehouse clubs & supercntrs	6,465	7,145	7,761	8,242
	Soft Drinks	Supermarkets & grocery stores	16,260	16,158	16,160	16,194
	Soft Drinks	Beer, wine, & liquor stores	777	830	889	953
	Soft Drinks	Pharmacies & drug stores	1,725	1,865	2,005	2,158
	Soft Drinks	Gas stations w/ conven. stores	15,329	16,796	18,321	19,973
	Soft Drinks	Warehouse clubs & supercntrs	14,509	16,037	17,418	18,498
	Soft Drinks	Electronic shopping & mail-order	483	545	616	681
	Soft Drinks	Book stores	5	5	5	5
	Candy	Supermarkets & grocery stores	5,393	5,359	5,360	5,371
	Candy	Beer, wine, & liquor stores	200	214	229	245
	Candy	Gas stations w/ conven. stores	6,210	6,805	7,422	8,092
	Candy	Warehouse clubs & supercntrs	14,231	15,729	17,083	18,143
	All Other Foods	Supermarkets & grocery stores	134,252	133,411	133,428	133,706
	All Other Foods	Beer, wine, & liquor stores	483	516	553	593
	All Other Foods	Warehouse clubs & supercntrs	71,199	78,695	85,473	90,772
	All Other Foods	Gas stations w/ conven. stores	20,134	22,061	24,063	26,234
	All Other Foods	Pharmacies & drug stores	4,032	4,360	4,688	5,046
	All Other Foods	Electronic shopping & mail-order	4,200	4,743	5,361	5,928
	All Other Foods	Book stores	40	40	40	41

SUMMARY OF PRODUCT LINES SALES BY INDUSTRY

SALES (MILLIONS OF U.S. DOLLARS)

Main Category	Sub Category	U.S. Industry	Year			
			2015	2016	2017	2018
Beer, Wine, Liquor	--	Supermarkets & grocery stores	19,178	19,058	19,060	19,100
Beer, Wine, Liquor	--	Beer, wine, & liquor stores	37,312	39,868	42,683	45,773
Beer, Wine, Liquor	--	Pharmacies & drug stores	1,973	2,133	2,294	2,469
Beer, Wine, Liquor	--	Gas stations w/ conven. stores	15,795	17,308	18,878	20,581
Beer, Wine, Liquor	--	Department stores	10	10	10	10
Beer, Wine, Liquor	--	Warehouse clubs & supercntrs	8,992	9,939	10,795	11,464
Beer, Wine, Liquor	--	Electronic shopping & mail-order	699	789	892	986
Beer, Wine, Liquor	--	Book stores	1	1	1	1
	Liquor	Supermarkets & grocery stores	3,741	3,718	3,718	3,726
	Liquor	Beer, wine, & liquor stores	15,786	16,867	18,058	19,365
	Liquor	Gas stations w/ conven. stores	530	580	633	690
	Liquor	Warehouse clubs & supercntrs	931	1,029	1,117	1,186
	Wine	Supermarkets & grocery stores	6,323	6,283	6,284	6,297
	Wine	Beer, wine, & liquor stores	10,846	11,588	12,407	13,305
	Wine	Gas stations w/ conven. stores	814	892	973	1,060
	Wine	Warehouse clubs & supercntrs	3,915	4,327	4,699	4,991
	Beer	Supermarkets & grocery stores	9,114	9,057	9,058	9,077
	Beer	Beer, wine, & liquor stores	10,681	11,412	12,218	13,103
	Beer	Gas stations w/ conven. stores	14,452	15,835	17,273	18,830
	Beer	Warehouse clubs & supercntrs	4,147	4,584	4,978	5,287

SUMMARY OF PRODUCT LINES SALES BY INDUSTRY

SALES (MILLIONS OF U.S. DOLLARS)

Main Category	Sub Category	U.S. Industry	Year			
			2015	2016	2017	2018
Drugs, Health/Beauty	--	Home centers	26	27	29	30
Drugs, Health/Beauty	--	Hardware stores	2	2	2	2
Drugs, Health/Beauty	--	Supermarkets & grocery stores	50,327	50,012	50,018	50,122
Drugs, Health/Beauty	--	Beer, wine, & liquor stores	135	144	154	165
Drugs, Health/Beauty	--	Pharmacies & drug stores	164,390	177,753	191,124	205,722
Drugs, Health/Beauty	--	Gas stations w/ conven. stores	1,814	1,988	2,168	2,364
Drugs, Health/Beauty	--	Men's clothing stores	1	1	1	1
Drugs, Health/Beauty	--	Women's clothing stores	890	957	1,017	1,083
Drugs, Health/Beauty	--	Family clothing stores	679	719	762	810
Drugs, Health/Beauty	--	Department stores	17,668	17,667	17,749	17,877
Drugs, Health/Beauty	--	Warehouse clubs & supercntrs	63,120	69,765	75,774	80,472
Drugs, Health/Beauty	--	Office supply/stationery stores	0	0	0	0
Drugs, Health/Beauty	--	Electronic shopping & mail-order	97,596	110,199	124,575	137,735
Drugs, Health/Beauty	--	Book stores	6	6	6	6
	Prescriptions	Supermarkets & grocery stores	25,716	25,555	25,559	25,612
	Prescriptions	Beer, wine, & liquor stores	7	7	8	8
	Prescriptions	Pharmacies & drug stores	138,167	149,398	160,636	172,906
	Prescriptions	Department stores	5,084	5,084	5,108	5,145
	Prescriptions	Warehouse clubs & supercntrs	19,650	21,719	23,590	25,052
	Prescriptions	Electronic shopping & mail-order	75,583	85,344	96,477	106,669
	Nonprescriptn. Meds	Supermarkets & grocery stores	3,768	3,745	3,745	3,753
	Nonprescriptn. Meds	Beer, wine, & liquor stores	29	31	33	36
	Nonprescriptn. Meds	Pharmacies & drug stores	10,892	11,778	12,664	13,631
	Nonprescriptn. Meds	Department stores	873	873	877	884
	Nonprescriptn. Meds	Warehouse clubs & supercntrs	6,823	7,541	8,190	8,698
	Nonprescriptn. Meds	Electronic shopping & mail-order	1,859	2,100	2,373	2,624

SUMMARY OF PRODUCT LINES SALES BY INDUSTRY

SALES (MILLIONS OF U.S. DOLLARS)

Main Category	Sub Category	U.S. Industry	Year			
			2015	2016	2017	2018
	Vitamins Supplemts.	Supermarkets & grocery stores	3,024	3,005	3,006	3,012
	Vitamins Supplemts.	Beer, wine, & liquor stores	9	10	11	12
	Vitamins Supplemts.	Pharmacies & drug stores	2,070	2,238	2,406	2,590
	Vitamins Supplemts.	Department stores	672	672	676	680
	Vitamins Supplemts.	Warehouse clubs & supercntrs	4,507	4,982	5,411	5,746
	Vitamins Supplemts.	Electronic shopping & mail-order	11,111	12,545	14,182	15,680
	Health Aids	Supermarkets & grocery stores	2,861	2,843	2,844	2,850
	Health Aids	Beer, wine, & liquor stores	16	17	18	19
	Health Aids	Pharmacies & drug stores	3,522	3,808	4,094	4,407
	Health Aids	Department Stores	566	566	568	572
	Health Aids	Warehouse clubs & supercntrs	5,217	5,766	6,263	6,651
	Health Aids	Electronic shopping & mail-order	3,909	4,413	4,989	5,516
	Cosmetics	Supermarkets & grocery stores	2,542	2,526	2,526	2,532
	Cosmetics	Beer, wine, & liquor stores	47	50	54	58
	Cosmetics	Pharmacies & drug stores	4,073	4,404	4,736	5,097
	Cosmetics	Department Stores	5,903	5,902	5,930	5,972
	Cosmetics	Warehouse clubs & supercntrs	5,757	6,363	6,911	7,339
	Cosmetics	Electronic shopping & mail-order	4,182	4,722	5,338	5,902
	Other Hygiene Needs	Supermarkets & grocery stores	12,415	12,337	12,339	12,364
	Other Hygiene Needs	Beer, wine, & liquor stores	27	29	31	33
	Other Hygiene Needs	Pharmacies & drug stores	5,591	6,046	6,501	6,997
	Other Hygiene Needs	Department Stores	4,570	4,569	4,591	4,624
	Other Hygiene Needs	Warehouse clubs & supercntrs	21,166	23,395	25,409	26,985
	Other Hygiene Needs	Electronic shopping & mail-order	737	832	941	1,040
	Hearing Aids	Pharmacies & drug stores	75	81	87	94
	Hearing Aids	Electronic shopping & mail-order	215	243	274	303

SUMMARY OF PRODUCT LINES SALES BY INDUSTRY

SALES (MILLIONS OF U.S. DOLLARS)

Main Category	Sub Category	U.S. Industry	Year			
			2015	2016	2017	2018
Soaps & Cleaners	--	Home centers	1,540	1,635	1,719	1,810
Soaps & Cleaners	--	Hardware stores	207	219	229	240
Soaps & Cleaners	--	Supermarkets & grocery stores	13,949	13,862	13,864	13,893
Soaps & Cleaners	--	Beer, wine, & liquor stores	72	77	82	88
Soaps & Cleaners	--	Pharmacies & drug stores	922	997	1,073	1,154
Soaps & Cleaners	--	Gas stations w/ conven. stores	573	628	685	746
Soaps & Cleaners	--	Women's clothing stores	0	0	0	0
Soaps & Cleaners	--	Department stores	2,424	2,424	2,435	2,452
Soaps & Cleaners	--	Warehouse Clubs & Superctrs.	16,185	17,889	19,430	20,635
Soaps & Cleaners	--	Office Supplies & Stationery	2	2	2	2
Soaps & Cleaners	--	Electronic Shopping/Mail-Order	277	312	353	390
Paper Products	--	Hardware stores	1	1	1	1
Paper Products	--	Supermarkets & grocery stores	14,325	14,235	14,237	14,266
Paper Products	--	Beer, wine, & liquor stores	44	47	50	54
Paper Products	--	Pharmacies & drug stores	739	799	859	925
Paper Products	--	Gas stations w/ conven. stores	701	768	837	913
Paper Products	--	Family clothing stores	0	0	0	0
Paper Products	--	Prerecorded Tapes/CDs Stores	0	0	0	0
Paper Products	--	Department stores	1,884	1,884	1,893	1,907
Paper Products	--	Warehouse clubs & supercntrs	14,543	16,074	17,459	18,541
Paper Products	--	Office Supplies & Stationery	22	22	21	21
Paper Products	--	Electronic Shopping/Mail-Order	1,709	1,930	2,181	2,412
Paper Products	--	Book Stores	2	2	2	2

SUMMARY OF PRODUCT LINES SALES BY INDUSTRY

SALES (MILLIONS OF U.S. DOLLARS)

Main Category	Sub Category	U.S. Industry	Year			
			2015	2016	2017	2018
Men's Wear	--	Home centers	84	89	93	98
Men's Wear	--	Hardware stores	44	47	49	51
Men's Wear	--	Men's clothing stores	7,380	7,604	7,872	8,161
Men's Wear	--	Women's clothing stores	1,425	1,531	1,627	1,733
Men's Wear	--	Family clothing stores	28,475	30,138	31,969	33,977
Men's Wear	--	CD, tape & record stores	1	1	1	1
Men's Wear	--	Department stores	11,867	11,866	11,921	12,007
Men's Wear	--	Warehouse clubs & supercntrs	13,059	14,434	15,678	16,649
Men's Wear	--	Electronic shopping & mail-order	7,645	8,632	9,758	10,789
Men's Wear	--	Book stores	131	131	132	133
	Coats/Jackets	Men's clothing stores	336	347	359	372
	Coats/Jackets	Women's clothing stores	103	110	117	125
	Coats/Jackets	Family clothing stores	1,806	1,911	2,027	2,155
	Coats/Jackets	Department stores	547	547	550	554
	Coats/Jackets	Warehouse clubs & supercntrs	801	886	962	1,021
	Suits/Formal Wear	Men's clothing stores	1,594	1,642	1,700	1,762
	Suits/Formal Wear	Women's clothing stores	44	47	50	54
	Suits/Formal Wear	Family clothing stores	1,047	1,108	1,175	1,249
	Suits/Formal Wear	Department stores	521	521	523	527
	Sport Coats/Blazers	Men's clothing stores	609	627	650	673
	Sport Coats/Blazers	Women's clothing stores	36	39	41	44
	Sport Coats/Blazers	Family clothing stores	623	659	699	743
	Sport Coats/Blazers	Department stores	181	181	182	183
	Dress Slacks	Men's clothing stores	590	608	629	652
	Dress Slacks	Women's clothing stores	65	70	74	79
	Dress Slacks	Family clothing stores	1,681	1,779	1,887	2,005
	Dress Slacks	Department stores	275	275	276	278
	Casual Slacks/Jeans	Men's clothing stores	965	995	1,030	1,068
	Casual Slacks/Jeans	Women's clothing stores	314	337	359	382
	Casual Slacks/Jeans	Family clothing stores	5,963	6,312	6,695	7,116
	Casual Slacks/Jeans	Department stores	3,054	3,053	3,068	3,090
	Casual Slacks/Jeans	Warehouse clubs & supercntrs	3,444	3,807	4,134	4,391
	Work Uniforms	Men's clothing stores	100	103	107	111
	Work Uniforms	Family clothing stores	823	872	924	983
	Work Uniforms	Department stores	110	110	110	111

2017 U.S. PRODUCT & RETAIL OUTLOOK

SUMMARY OF PRODUCT LINES SALES BY INDUSTRY

SALES (MILLIONS OF U.S. DOLLARS)

Main Category	Sub Category	U.S. Industry	Year			
			2015	2016	2017	2018
	Dress Shirts	Men's clothing stores	554	571	591	613
	Dress Shirts	Women's clothing stores	90	97	103	109
	Dress Shirts	Family clothing stores	2,037	2,156	2,287	2,430
	Dress Shirts	Department stores	524	524	527	530
	Sport Shirts/T-Shirts	Men's clothing stores	1,081	1,114	1,153	1,196
	Sport Shirts/T-Shirts	Women's clothing stores	459	493	524	558
	Sport Shirts/T-Shirts	Family clothing stores	6,719	7,111	7,543	8,017
	Sport Shirts/T-Shirts	Department stores	2,692	2,692	2,705	2,724
	Sport Shirts/T-Shirts	Warehouse clubs & supercntrs	2,306	2,548	2,768	2,939
	Sweaters	Men's clothing stores	252	259	268	278
	Sweaters	Women's clothing stores	96	104	110	117
	Sweaters	Family clothing stores	1,982	2,098	2,225	2,365
	Sweaters	Department stores	385	385	387	390
	Sweaters	Warehouse clubs & supercntrs	507	561	609	647
	Socks/Underwear	Men's clothing stores	165	170	176	182
	Socks/Underwear	Women's clothing stores	54	59	62	66
	Socks/Underwear	Family clothing stores	1,387	1,468	1,557	1,655
	Socks/Underwear	Department stores	1,478	1,478	1,485	1,496
	Socks/Underwear	Warehouse clubs & supercntrs	2,459	2,717	2,951	3,134
	Sports Apparel	Men's clothing stores	330	340	352	365
	Sports Apparel	Women's clothing stores	33	36	38	41
	Sports Apparel	Family clothing stores	971	1,028	1,090	1,159
	Sports Apparel	Department stores	687	686	690	695
	Sports Apparel	Warehouse clubs & supercntrs	1,317	1,455	1,581	1,679
	Accessories	Men's clothing stores	635	654	677	702
	Accessories	Women's clothing stores	116	124	132	141
	Accessories	Family clothing stores	1,891	2,002	2,123	2,257
	Accessories	Department stores	698	698	701	706
	Accessories	Warehouse clubs & supercntrs	572	632	687	729
	Custom-made	Men's clothing stores	83	86	89	92
	Sweats/Warm-ups	Men's clothing stores	85	88	91	94
	Sweats/Warm-ups	Family clothing stores	1,518	1,607	1,705	1,812
	Sweats/Warm-ups	Department stores	716	715	719	724
	Sweats/Warm-ups	Warehouse clubs & supercntrs	1,064	1,176	1,277	1,356

SUMMARY OF PRODUCT LINES SALES BY INDUSTRY

SALES (MILLIONS OF U.S. DOLLARS)

Main Category	Sub Category	U.S. Industry	Year			
			2015	2016	2017	2018
Women's Wear	--	Home centers	56	60	63	66
Women's Wear	--	Supermarkets & grocery stores	142	141	141	142
Women's Wear	--	Pharmacies & drug stores	173	187	201	216
Women's Wear	--	Men's clothing stores	183	188	195	202
Women's Wear	--	Women's clothing stores	41,304	44,385	47,175	50,229
Women's Wear	--	Family clothing stores	46,722	49,449	52,454	55,749
Women's Wear	--	Department stores	23,959	23,957	24,069	24,242
Women's Wear	--	Warehouse clubs & supercntrs	17,298	19,119	20,766	22,053
Women's Wear	--	Electronic shopping & mail-order	26,288	29,682	33,554	37,099
Women's Wear	--	Book stores	67	67	67	68
	Fur Garments	Women's clothing stores	56	61	64	69
	Fur Garments	Family clothing stores	62	65	69	73
	Dresses	Women's clothing stores	5,008	5,382	5,720	6,090
	Dresses	Family clothing stores	3,058	3,237	3,433	3,649
	Dresses	Department stores	1,825	1,825	1,833	1,846
	Dresses	Warehouse clubs & supercntrs	643	711	772	820
	Coats/Outerwear	Women's clothing stores	1,898	2,040	2,168	2,308
	Coats/Outerwear	Family clothing stores	2,302	2,436	2,584	2,746
	Coats/Outerwear	Department stores	959	959	963	970
	Coats/Outerwear	Warehouse clubs & supercntrs	456	504	548	582
	Suits/Blazers	Men's clothing stores	29	29	30	32
	Suits/Blazers	Women's clothing stores	2,895	3,111	3,307	3,521
	Suits/Blazers	Family clothing stores	4,143	4,385	4,651	4,943
	Suits/Blazers	Department stores	3,611	3,610	3,627	3,653
	Suits/Blazers	Warehouse clubs & supercntrs	191	211	230	244
	Slacks/Jeans	Men's clothing stores	43	44	45	47
	Slacks/Jeans	Women's clothing stores	11,113	11,941	12,692	13,514
	Slacks/Jeans	Family clothing stores	9,142	9,676	10,264	10,908
	Slacks/Jeans	Department stores	3,600	3,600	3,616	3,642
	Slacks/Jeans	Warehouse clubs & supercntrs	4,510	4,985	5,414	5,750
	Shirts/Sweaters	Men's clothing stores	48	49	51	53
	Shirts/Sweaters	Women's clothing stores	14,563	15,649	16,633	17,709
	Shirts/Sweaters	Family clothing stores	15,011	15,887	16,852	17,911
	Shirts/Sweaters	Department stores	3,508	3,508	3,524	3,550
	Shirts/Sweaters	Warehouse clubs & supercntrs	3,574	3,950	4,290	4,556

SUMMARY OF PRODUCT LINES SALES BY INDUSTRY

SALES (MILLIONS OF U.S. DOLLARS)

Main Category	Sub Category	U.S. Industry	Year			
			2015	2016	2017	2018
	Sports Apparel	Women's clothing stores	556	598	635	677
	Sports Apparel	Family clothing stores	1,349	1,428	1,515	1,610
	Sports Apparel	Department stores	2,759	2,758	2,771	2,791
	Sports Apparel	Warehouse clubs & supercntrs	1,190	1,315	1,429	1,517
	Hosiery/Socks	Women's clothing stores	382	411	436	465
	Hosiery/Socks	Family clothing stores	1,072	1,134	1,203	1,279
	Hosiery/Socks	Department stores	739	739	742	748
	Hosiery/Socks	Warehouse clubs & supercntrs	1,304	1,442	1,566	1,663
	Bras/Panties	Women's clothing stores	647	695	739	787
	Bras/Panties	Family clothing stores	1,637	1,733	1,838	1,953
	Bras/Panties	Department stores	3,032	3,032	3,046	3,068
	Bras/Panties	Warehouse clubs & supercntrs	2,243	2,479	2,692	2,859
	Lingerie/Sleepwear	Women's clothing stores	1,023	1,099	1,169	1,244
	Lingerie/Sleepwear	Family clothing stores	1,377	1,458	1,546	1,643
	Lingerie/Sleepwear	Department stores	1,653	1,653	1,661	1,673
	Lingerie/Sleepwear	Warehouse clubs & supercntrs	1,679	1,856	2,016	2,141
	Hats/Wigs	Women's clothing stores	83	89	95	101
	Hats/Wigs	Family clothing stores	773	818	867	922
	Accessories/Bags	Women's clothing stores	2,193	2,357	2,505	2,667
	Accessories/Bags	Family clothing stores	4,263	4,512	4,786	5,087
	Accessories/Bags	Department stores	1,978	1,977	1,987	2,001
	Accessories/Bags	Warehouse clubs & supercntrs	1,108	1,225	1,331	1,413
	Custom-made	Women's clothing stores	14	16	17	18
	Custom-made	Family clothing stores	295	312	331	352
	Sweat Tops/Pants	Women's clothing stores	595	639	680	724
	Sweat Tops/Pants	Family clothing stores	2,075	2,196	2,330	2,476
	Sweat Tops/Pants	Department stores	80	80	81	81
	Uniforms/Misc.	Men's clothing stores	17	18	19	19
	Uniforms/Misc.	Women's clothing stores	276	297	316	336
	Uniforms/Misc.	Family clothing stores	164	173	184	195
	Uniforms/Misc.	Department stores	185	185	186	187
	Uniforms/Misc.	Warehouse clubs & supercntrs	308	341	370	393

SUMMARY OF PRODUCT LINES SALES BY INDUSTRY

SALES (MILLIONS OF U.S. DOLLARS)

Main Category	Sub Category	U.S. Industry	Year			
			2015	2016	2017	2018
Children's Wear	--	Supermarkets & grocery stores	55	55	55	55
Children's Wear	--	Pharmacies & drug stores	28	30	32	34
Children's Wear	--	Men's clothing stores	106	109	113	117
Children's Wear	--	Women's clothing stores	260	279	297	316
Children's Wear	--	Family clothing stores	11,575	12,251	12,995	13,812
Children's Wear	--	Department stores	8,677	8,677	8,717	8,780
Children's Wear	--	Warehouse clubs & supercntrs	12,410	13,717	14,898	15,822
Children's Wear	--	Electronic shopping & mail-order	3,299	3,725	4,211	4,655
Children's Wear	--	Book stores	9	9	9	9
	Boys' Clothing	Men's clothing stores	76	79	82	85
	Boys' Clothing	Women's clothing stores	54	57	61	65
	Boys' Clothing	Family clothing stores	4,194	4,439	4,709	5,005
	Boys' Clothing	Department stores	2,691	2,690	2,703	2,722
	Boys' Clothing	Warehouse clubs & supercntrs	3,034	3,354	3,643	3,868
	Girls' Clothing	Men's clothing stores	25	26	27	28
	Girls' Clothing	Women's clothing stores	121	130	138	147
	Girls' Clothing	Family clothing stores	4,500	4,763	5,052	5,369
	Girls' Clothing	Department stores	2,584	2,584	2,596	2,614
	Girls' Clothing	Warehouse clubs & supercntrs	2,841	3,140	3,410	3,622
	Infants' & Toddlers'	Men's clothing stores	4	4	5	5
	Infants' & Toddlers'	Women's clothing stores	85	92	97	104
	Infants' & Toddlers'	Family clothing stores	2,881	3,049	3,234	3,438
	Infants' & Toddlers'	Department stores	3,403	3,403	3,419	3,443
	Infants' & Toddlers'	Warehouse clubs & supercntrs	6,535	7,223	7,846	8,332

SUMMARY OF PRODUCT LINES SALES BY INDUSTRY

SALES (MILLIONS OF U.S. DOLLARS)

Main Category	Sub Category	U.S. Industry	Year			
			2015	2016	2017	2018
Footwear Products	--	Hardware stores	29	30	32	33
Footwear Products	--	Supermarkets & grocery stores	36	36	36	36
Footwear Products	--	Pharmacies & drug stores	202	218	234	252
Footwear Products	--	Men's clothing stores	362	373	387	401
Footwear Products	--	Women's clothing stores	1,437	1,544	1,641	1,747
Footwear Products	--	Family clothing stores	5,816	6,156	6,530	6,940
Footwear Products	--	Department stores	5,045	5,045	5,068	5,105
Footwear Products	--	Warehouse clubs & supercntrs	4,443	4,911	5,334	5,664
Footwear Products	--	Electronic shopping & mail-order	5,699	6,435	7,275	8,043
	Men's Footwear	Men's clothing stores	283	292	302	313
	Men's Footwear	Women's clothing stores	29	31	33	35
	Men's Footwear	Family clothing stores	1,131	1,197	1,270	1,350
	Men's Footwear	Department stores	914	914	918	925
	Women's Footwear	Men's clothing stores	13	14	14	15
	Women's Footwear	Women's clothing stores	1,373	1,476	1,568	1,670
	Women's Footwear	Family clothing stores	2,542	2,690	2,854	3,033
	Women's Footwear	Department stores	2,554	2,554	2,566	2,585
	Children's Footwear	Family clothing stores	457	484	513	545
	Children's Footwear	Department stores	463	463	465	469
	Men's Sneakers	Men's clothing stores	59	61	63	65
	Men's Sneakers	Family clothing stores	841	890	945	1,004
	Men's Sneakers	Department stores	504	504	506	510
	Women's Sneakers	Women's clothing stores	22	23	25	26
	Women's Sneakers	Family clothing stores	647	685	726	772
	Women's Sneakers	Department stores	501	501	503	507
	Children's Sneakers	Family clothing stores	180	191	202	215
	Children's Sneakers	Department stores	96	96	97	98
	Footwear Access.	Family clothing stores	18	19	20	21
	Footwear Access.	Department stores	12	12	12	12

SUMMARY OF PRODUCT LINES SALES BY INDUSTRY

SALES (MILLIONS OF U.S. DOLLARS)

Main Category	Sub Category	U.S. Industry	Year			
			2015	2016	2017	2018
Household Appliances	--	Home centers	7,192	7,635	8,024	8,450
Household Appliances	--	Hardware stores	400	423	443	465
Household Appliances	--	Supermarkets & grocery stores	7	7	7	7
Household Appliances	--	Department stores	5,081	5,081	5,105	5,141
Household Appliances	--	Warehouse clubs & supercntrs	5,964	6,592	7,159	7,603
Household Appliances	--	Electronic shopping & mail-order	2,104	2,375	2,685	2,969
	Kitchen Appliances	Department stores	3,444	3,444	3,460	3,485
	Kitchen Appliances	Warehouse clubs & supercntrs	1,944	2,149	2,334	2,479
	Laundry Appliances	Warehouse clubs & supercntrs	135	149	162	172
	Other Appliances	Department stores	1,637	1,637	1,645	1,657
	Other Appliances	Warehouse clubs & supercntrs	3,885	4,294	4,664	4,953
Small Appliances	--	Home centers	576	612	643	677
Small Appliances	--	Hardware stores	308	326	341	358
Small Appliances	--	Supermarkets & grocery stores	193	192	192	192
Small Appliances	--	Beer, Wine & Liquor Stores	0	0	0	0
Small Appliances	--	Pharmacies & Drug Stores	902	975	1,049	1,129
Small Appliances	--	Women's Clothing Stores	2	2	2	2
Small Appliances	--	Family Clothing Stores	1	1	1	1
Small Appliances	--	Department Stores	1,909	1,908	1,917	1,931
Small Appliances	--	Warehouse clubs & supercntrs	6,166	6,815	7,402	7,861
Small Appliances	--	Electronic Shopping/Mail-Order	1,275	1,440	1,628	1,799

SUMMARY OF PRODUCT LINES SALES BY INDUSTRY

SALES (MILLIONS OF U.S. DOLLARS)

Main Category	Sub Category	U.S. Industry	Year			
			2015	2016	2017	2018
TVs & Video Equip	--	Home centers	5	6	6	6
TVs & Video Equip	--	Hardware stores	30	32	34	35
TVs & Video Equip	--	Supermarkets & grocery stores	5	5	5	5
TVs & Video Equip	--	Pharmacies & drug stores	200	217	233	251
TVs & Video Equip	--	Women's clothing stores	1	1	1	1
TVs & Video Equip	--	Family clothing stores	13	14	15	16
TVs & Video Equip	--	Prerecorded Tape/CD Stores	435	391	367	344
TVs & Video Equip	--	Department stores	3,890	3,890	3,908	3,936
TVs & Video Equip	--	Warehouse clubs & supercntrs	13,834	15,290	16,607	17,637
TVs & Video Equip	--	Office supply/stationery stores	2	2	2	2
TVs & Video Equip	--	Electronic shopping & mail-order	8,373	9,454	10,687	11,816
TVs & Video Equip	--	Book stores	360	361	363	367
	Televisions	Prerecorded Tape/CD Stores	0	0	0	0
	Televisions	Department stores	1,491	1,491	1,498	1,509
	Televisions	Warehouse clubs & supercntrs	6,229	6,884	7,477	7,941
	Televisions	Electronic shopping & mail-order	965	1,090	1,232	1,362
	Video Recorders	Prerecorded Tape/CD Stores	25	22	21	20
	Video Tapes/Discs	Prerecorded Tape/CD Stores	410	369	346	324
	Other Video Equip	Department stores	2,399	2,399	2,410	2,428
	Other Video Equip	Warehouse clubs & supercntrs	7,605	8,406	9,130	9,696
	Other Video Equip	Electronic shopping & mail-order	7,408	8,364	9,456	10,454

SUMMARY OF PRODUCT LINES SALES BY INDUSTRY

SALES (MILLIONS OF U.S. DOLLARS)

Main Category	Sub Category	U.S. Industry	Year			
			2015	2016	2017	2018
Audio Equipment	--	Home centers	12	12	13	14
Audio Equipment	--	Hardware stores	20	21	22	23
Audio Equipment	--	Supermarkets & grocery stores	364	361	362	362
Audio Equipment	--	Beer, wine, & liquor stores	0	0	0	1
Audio Equipment	--	Pharmacies & drug stores	666	720	774	833
Audio Equipment	--	Gas stations w/ conven. stores	2	2	3	3
Audio Equipment	--	Prerecorded Tape/CD Stores	1,257	1,129	1,058	993
Audio Equipment	--	Department stores	3,246	3,246	3,261	3,284
Audio Equipment	--	Warehouse clubs & supercntrs	12,235	13,524	14,688	15,599
Audio Equipment	--	Office supply/stationery stores	4	4	4	4
Audio Equipment	--	Electronic shopping & mail-order	12,107	13,670	15,453	17,086
Audio Equipment	--	Book stores	654	655	660	666
	Stereos & Compon.	Prerecorded Tape/CD Stores	9	8	8	7
	Stereos & Compon.	Department stores	1,635	1,635	1,642	1,654
	Stereos & Compon.	Warehouse clubs & supercntrs	5,423	5,994	6,510	6,914
	Stereos & Compon.	Electronic shopping & mail-order	3,334	3,765	4,256	4,705
	Pianos	Prerecorded Tape/CD Stores	0	0	0	0
	Musical Instruments	Prerecorded Tape/CD Stores	1	0	0	0
	Tapes & CDs	Prerecorded Tape/CD Stores	1,241	1,116	1,045	981
	Tapes & CDs	Department stores	1,611	1,611	1,618	1,630
	Tapes & CDs	Warehouse clubs & supercntrs	6,712	7,419	8,058	8,558
	Tapes & CDs	Electronic shopping & mail-order	4,309	4,865	5,500	6,081
	Sheet Music	Prerecorded Tape/CD Stores	5	5	4	4
	Other Musical Items	Department stores	0	0	0	0
	Other Musical Items	Warehouse clubs & supercntrs	100	111	120	128
	Other Musical Items	Electronic shopping & mail-order	4,464	5,040	5,698	6,299

SUMMARY OF PRODUCT LINES SALES BY INDUSTRY

SALES (MILLIONS OF U.S. DOLLARS)

Main Category	Sub Category	U.S. Industry	Year			
			2015	2016	2017	2018
Furniture	--	Home centers	2,873	3,050	3,205	3,376
Furniture	--	Hardware stores	330	349	365	383
Furniture	--	Supermarkets & grocery stores	6	6	6	6
Furniture	--	Men's clothing stores	0	0	0	0
Furniture	--	Women's clothing stores	32	34	36	38
Furniture	--	Family clothing stores	26	27	29	31
Furniture	--	Department stores	2,673	2,673	2,685	2,705
Furniture	--	Warehouse clubs & supercntrs	6,983	7,718	8,383	8,902
Furniture	--	Office supply/stationery stores	1,339	1,321	1,291	1,265
Furniture	--	Electronic shopping & mail-order	5,897	6,659	7,527	8,322
	Upholstered Furn.	Department stores	370	370	372	375
	Upholstered Furn.	Warehouse clubs & supercntrs	249	275	299	317
	Sleep Sofas/Futons	Department stores	40	40	40	40
	Sleep Sofas/Futons	Warehouse clubs & supercntrs	196	217	236	250
	Mattresses	Department stores	326	326	327	329
	Mattresses	Warehouse clubs & supercntrs	1,681	1,858	2,018	2,143
	Home Furniture	Department stores	619	619	622	626
	Home Furniture	Warehouse clubs & supercntrs	574	634	689	731
	Office Furniture	Department stores	1,318	1,318	1,324	1,334
	Office Furniture	Warehouse clubs & supercntrs	4,283	4,734	5,142	5,461

SUMMARY OF PRODUCT LINES SALES BY INDUSTRY

SALES (MILLIONS OF U.S. DOLLARS)

Main Category	Sub Category	U.S. Industry	Year			
			2015	2016	2017	2018
Flooring & Coverings	--	Home centers	9,314	9,887	10,391	10,943
Flooring & Coverings	--	Hardware stores	75	79	83	87
Flooring & Coverings	--	Supermarkets & grocery stores	0	0	0	0
Flooring & Coverings	--	Women's clothing stores	0	0	0	0
Flooring & Coverings	--	Department stores	422	422	424	427
Flooring & Coverings	--	Warehouse clubs & supercntrs	86	95	103	109
Flooring & Coverings	--	Electronic shopping & mail-order	1,019	1,150	1,300	1,438
	Soft Floor Coverings	Home centers	3,310	3,513	3,692	3,888
	Soft Floor Coverings	Hardware stores	28	30	31	32
	Soft Floor Coverings	Department stores	411	411	413	416
	Soft Floor Coverings	Warehouse clubs & supercntrs	79	88	95	101
	Hardwood Flooring	Home centers	522	554	582	613
	Hardwood Flooring	Hardware stores	8	9	9	10
	Hardwood Flooring	Department stores	7	7	7	7
	Other Hard Flooring	Home centers	5,482	5,820	6,116	6,441
	Other Hard Flooring	Hardware stores	38	41	43	45
	Other Hard Flooring	Department stores	4	4	4	4
	Other Hard Flooring	Warehouse clubs & supercntrs	6	7	7	8

SUMMARY OF PRODUCT LINES SALES BY INDUSTRY

SALES (MILLIONS OF U.S. DOLLARS)

Main Category	Sub Category	U.S. Industry	Year			
			2015	2016	2017	2018
Hardware & Software	--	Home centers	614	651	685	721
Hardware & Software	--	Hardware stores	4	4	5	5
Hardware & Software	--	Supermarkets & grocery stores	0	0	0	0
Hardware & Software	--	Prerecorded Tapes/CDs Stores	20	18	17	16
Hardware & Software	--	Department stores	577	577	579	584
Hardware & Software	--	Warehouse clubs & supercntrs	8,658	9,569	10,393	11,038
Hardware & Software	--	Office supply/stationery stores	1,914	1,888	1,845	1,808
Hardware & Software	--	Electronic shopping & mail-order	64,355	72,665	82,145	90,823
Hardware & Software	--	Book stores	89	90	90	91
	Computers & Equip.	Department stores	425	425	427	430
	Computers & Equip.	Warehouse clubs & supercntrs	5,886	6,506	7,066	7,504
	Computers & Equip.	Electronic shopping & mail-order	59,381	67,050	75,796	83,804
	Computers & Equip.	Book stores	43	44	44	44
	Software	Department stores	152	152	152	154
	Software	Warehouse clubs & supercntrs	2,772	3,063	3,327	3,533
	Software	Electronic shopping & mail-order	4,973	5,616	6,348	7,019
	Software	Book stores	46	46	46	47

SUMMARY OF PRODUCT LINES SALES BY INDUSTRY

SALES (MILLIONS OF U.S. DOLLARS)

Main Category	Sub Category	U.S. Industry	Year			
			2015	2016	2017	2018
Kitchenware/Furnishing	--	Home centers	3,993	4,238	4,454	4,691
Kitchenware/Furnishing	--	Hardware stores	436	462	483	507
Kitchenware/Furnishing	--	Supermarkets & grocery stores	1,827	1,816	1,816	1,820
Kitchenware/Furnishing	--	Beer, wine, & liquor stores	36	38	41	44
Kitchenware/Furnishing	--	Pharmacies & drug stores	562	608	653	703
Kitchenware/Furnishing	--	Gas stations w/ conven. stores	3	3	4	4
Kitchenware/Furnishing	--	Men's clothing stores	14	15	15	16
Kitchenware/Furnishing	--	Women's clothing stores	130	139	148	158
Kitchenware/Furnishing	--	Family clothing stores	4,213	4,459	4,730	5,028
Kitchenware/Furnishing	--	Prerecorded Tapes/CDs Stores	1	1	1	1
Kitchenware/Furnishing	--	Department stores	5,314	5,314	5,338	5,377
Kitchenware/Furnishing	--	Warehouse clubs & supercntrs	10,131	11,198	12,163	12,917
Kitchenware/Furnishing	--	Office supply/stationery stores	10	10	9	9
Kitchenware/Furnishing	--	Electronic shopping & mail-order	17,654	19,934	22,535	24,915
Kitchenware/Furnishing	--	Book stores	64	64	64	65
	Cookware	Department stores	1,452	1,452	1,459	1,470
	Cookware	Warehouse clubs & supercntrs	4,254	4,702	5,106	5,423
	Dinnerware	Department stores	1,334	1,334	1,340	1,350
	Dinnerware	Warehouse clubs & supercntrs	1,031	1,139	1,237	1,314
	Decorative Access.	Department stores	1,367	1,367	1,373	1,383
	Decorative Access.	Warehouse clubs & supercntrs	3,005	3,321	3,607	3,831
	Other Kitchenware	Department stores	1,160	1,160	1,166	1,174
	Other Kitchenware	Warehouse clubs & supercntrs	1,842	2,036	2,212	2,349
	Giftware	Office supply/stationery stores	8	7	7	7
	Giftware	Book stores	44	45	45	45
	Other Furnishings	Office supply/stationery stores	2	2	2	2
	Other Furnishings	Book stores	19	19	19	19

SUMMARY OF PRODUCT LINES SALES BY INDUSTRY

SALES (MILLIONS OF U.S. DOLLARS)

Main Category	Sub Category	U.S. Industry	Year			
			2015	2016	2017	2018
Jewelry & Watches	--	Hardware stores	1	1	1	1
Jewelry & Watches	--	Supermarkets & grocery stores	190	189	189	189
Jewelry & Watches	--	Beer, wine, & liquor stores	10	11	12	12
Jewelry & Watches	--	Pharmacies & drug stores	241	260	280	301
Jewelry & Watches	--	Gas stations w/ conven. stores	5	5	6	6
Jewelry & Watches	--	Men's clothing stores	10	10	11	11
Jewelry & Watches	--	Women's clothing stores	1,218	1,309	1,391	1,481
Jewelry & Watches	--	Family clothing stores	1,401	1,482	1,572	1,671
Jewelry & Watches	--	Prerecorded Tapes/CDs Stores	4	4	3	3
Jewelry & Watches	--	Department stores	3,362	3,362	3,377	3,402
Jewelry & Watches	--	Warehouse clubs & supercntrs	5,741	6,346	6,892	7,320
Jewelry & Watches	--	Office supply/stationery stores	2	2	2	2
Jewelry & Watches	--	Electronic shopping & mail-order	14,850	16,767	18,955	20,957
Jewelry & Watches	--	Book stores	19	19	19	20
	Gold Jewelry	Department stores	537	537	540	544
	Gold Jewelry	Warehouse clubs & supercntrs	1,580	1,746	1,897	2,014
	Diamond Jewelry	Department stores	972	972	977	984
	Diamond Jewelry	Warehouse clubs & supercntrs	1,430	1,581	1,717	1,824
	Other Fine Jewelry	Department stores	1,852	1,852	1,861	1,874
	Other Fine Jewelry	Warehouse clubs & supercntrs	2,731	3,018	3,278	3,481
	Costume Jewelry	Men's clothing stores	5	5	5	6
	Costume Jewelry	Women's clothing stores	1,050	1,128	1,199	1,277
	Costume Jewelry	Family clothing stores	523	554	587	624
	Other Jewelry	Men's clothing stores	5	5	5	5
	Other Jewelry	Women's clothing stores	168	181	192	204
	Other Jewelry	Family clothing stores	877	928	985	1,047

SUMMARY OF PRODUCT LINES SALES BY INDUSTRY

SALES (MILLIONS OF U.S. DOLLARS)

Main Category	Sub Category	U.S. Industry	Year			
			2015	2016	2017	2018
Books	--	Hardware stores	1	1	1	1
Books	--	Supermarkets & grocery stores	904	898	898	900
Books	--	Beer, wine, & liquor stores	3	3	4	4
Books	--	Pharmacies & drug stores	214	231	248	267
Books	--	Gas stations w/ conven. stores	92	101	110	120
Books	--	Women's clothing stores	1	1	1	1
Books	--	Prerecorded Tapes/CDs Stores	48	43	40	38
Books	--	Department stores	385	385	386	389
Books	--	Warehouse clubs & supercntrs	5,590	6,178	6,710	7,126
Books	--	Office supply/stationery stores	31	31	30	30
Books	--	Electronic shopping & mail-order	13,363	15,088	17,057	18,859
Books	--	Book stores	8,217	8,230	8,297	8,371
	Trade Books	Book stores	4,372	4,379	4,414	4,454
	Paperbacks	Book stores	266	266	268	271
	Religious	Book stores	508	509	513	518
	General Reference	Book stores	68	68	69	69
	Textbooks	Book stores	2,716	2,721	2,743	2,767
	Professional Books	Book stores	82	82	82	83
	Other Books	Book stores	206	206	208	209

SUMMARY OF PRODUCT LINES SALES BY INDUSTRY

SALES (MILLIONS OF U.S. DOLLARS)

Main Category	Sub Category	U.S. Industry	Year			
			2015	2016	2017	2018
Toys & Games	--	Home centers	7	7	7	8
Toys & Games	--	Hardware stores	73	77	81	85
Toys & Games	--	Supermarkets & grocery stores	472	469	469	470
Toys & Games	--	Beer, wine, & liquor stores	4	5	5	5
Toys & Games	--	Pharmacies & drug stores	677	732	787	847
Toys & Games	--	Gas stations w/ conven. stores	13	15	16	17
Toys & Games	--	Men's clothing stores	1	1	1	1
Toys & Games	--	Women's clothing stores	6	6	6	7
Toys & Games	--	Family clothing stores	2,238	2,369	2,513	2,671
Toys & Games	--	CD, tape & record stores	59	53	50	47
Toys & Games	--	Department stores	4,555	4,554	4,576	4,609
Toys & Games	--	Warehouse clubs & supercntrs	15,506	17,138	18,614	19,768
Toys & Games	--	Office supply/stationery stores	16	16	15	15
Toys & Games	--	Electronic shopping & mail-order	8,362	9,441	10,673	11,801
Toys & Games	--	Book stores	26	26	26	26
	Toys	Pharmacies & drug stores	597	645	694	746
	Toys	Department stores	3,064	3,064	3,078	3,100
	Toys	Electronic shopping & mail-order	4,342	4,903	5,542	6,128
	Games	Pharmacies & drug stores	26	28	30	32
	Games	Department stores	1,487	1,487	1,494	1,505
	Games	Electronic shopping & mail-order	1,078	1,218	1,376	1,522
	Hobby Goods	Pharmacies & drug stores	54	59	63	68
	Hobby Goods	Department stores	4	4	4	4
	Hobby Goods	Electronic shopping & mail-order	2,941	3,321	3,754	4,151

SUMMARY OF PRODUCT LINES SALES BY INDUSTRY

SALES (MILLIONS OF U.S. DOLLARS)

Main Category	Sub Category	U.S. Industry	Year			
			2015	2016	2017	2018
Sporting Goods	--	Home centers	149	158	166	175
Sporting Goods	--	Hardware stores	197	209	218	229
Sporting Goods	--	Supermarkets & grocery stores	92	91	91	91
Sporting Goods	--	Beer, wine, & liquor stores	10	11	12	12
Sporting Goods	--	Pharmacies & drug stores	30	32	34	37
Sporting Goods	--	Gas stations w/ conven. stores	210	230	251	273
Sporting Goods	--	Men's clothing stores	12	12	13	13
Sporting Goods	--	Women's clothing stores	3	3	3	4
Sporting Goods	--	Family clothing stores	156	166	176	187
Sporting Goods	--	Department stores	2,909	2,909	2,922	2,943
Sporting Goods	--	Warehouse clubs & supercntrs	11,492	12,702	13,795	14,651
Sporting Goods	--	Office supply/stationery stores	1	1	1	1
Sporting Goods	--	Electronic shopping & mail-order	14,409	16,270	18,393	20,336
	Exercise Equip.	Department stores	600	600	602	607
	Exercise Equip.	Warehouse clubs & supercntrs	2,253	2,490	2,705	2,873
	Firearms	Department stores	456	456	458	462
	Firearms	Warehouse clubs & supercntrs	2,583	2,855	3,100	3,293
	Fishing Equip.	Department stores	251	251	252	254
	Fishing Equip.	Warehouse clubs & supercntrs	1,462	1,616	1,755	1,864
	Camping Equip.	Department stores	621	621	624	629
	Camping Equip.	Warehouse clubs & supercntrs	1,685	1,862	2,023	2,148
	Bicycles	Department stores	393	393	394	397
	Bicycles	Warehouse clubs & supercntrs	1,523	1,683	1,828	1,941
	Boats	Department stores	72	72	73	73
	Boats	Warehouse clubs & supercntrs	585	647	703	746
	Boats	Electronic shopping & mail-order	1,132	1,279	1,445	1,598
	Other Sporting Equip.	Electronic shopping & mail-order	13,277	14,992	16,947	18,738
	Other Sporting Equip.	Department stores	516	515	518	522
	Other Sporting Equip.	Warehouse clubs & supercntrs	1,401	1,548	1,681	1,786

SUMMARY OF PRODUCT LINES SALES BY INDUSTRY

SALES (MILLIONS OF U.S. DOLLARS)

Main Category	Sub Category	U.S. Industry	Year			
			2015	2016	2017	2018
Hardware	--	Home centers	44,475	47,214	49,619	52,254
Hardware	--	Hardware stores	11,196	11,858	12,411	13,022
Hardware	--	Supermarkets & grocery stores	568	565	565	566
Hardware	--	Beer, wine, & liquor stores	0	0	1	1
Hardware	--	Pharmacies & drug stores	279	302	325	350
Hardware	--	Gas stations w/ conven. stores	416	456	497	542
Hardware	--	Men's clothing stores	0	0	0	0
Hardware	--	Department stores	2,853	2,853	2,866	2,887
Hardware	--	Warehouse clubs & supercntrs	8,942	9,883	10,734	11,400
Hardware	--	Office supply/stationery stores	0	0	0	0
Hardware	--	Electronic shopping & mail-order	3,201	3,615	4,086	4,518
	General Hardware	Home centers	7,088	7,524	7,908	8,328
	General Hardware	Hardware stores	3,521	3,729	3,903	4,095
	Tools & Equip.	Home centers	11,911	12,645	13,289	13,995
	Tools & Equip.	Hardware stores	3,914	4,146	4,339	4,553
	Plumbing Supplies	Home centers	12,416	13,180	13,852	14,587
	Plumbing Supplies	Hardware stores	1,938	2,053	2,149	2,255
	Wiring Supplies	Home centers	2,132	2,263	2,379	2,505
	Wiring Supplies	Hardware stores	498	527	552	579
	Welding Supplies	Home centers	14	14	15	16
	Welding Supplies	Hardware stores	73	77	81	85
	Electrical Supplies	Home centers	10,915	11,587	12,177	12,824
	Electrical Supplies	Hardware stores	1,252	1,326	1,387	1,456

SUMMARY OF PRODUCT LINES SALES BY INDUSTRY

SALES (MILLIONS OF U.S. DOLLARS)

Main Category	Sub Category	U.S. Industry	Year			
			2015	2016	2017	2018
Lawn & Garden	--	Home centers	18,440	19,576	20,573	21,666
Lawn & Garden	--	Hardware stores	2,999	3,176	3,324	3,488
Lawn & Garden	--	Supermarkets & grocery stores	4,045	4,020	4,021	4,029
Lawn & Garden	--	Beer, wine, & liquor stores	1	1	1	1
Lawn & Garden	--	Pharmacies & drug stores	248	268	288	310
Lawn & Garden	--	Gas stations w/ conven. stores	129	141	154	168
Lawn & Garden	--	Department stores	2,574	2,573	2,585	2,604
Lawn & Garden	--	Warehouse clubs & supercntrs	12,281	13,574	14,743	15,657
Lawn & Garden	--	Electronic shopping & mail-order	4,691	5,297	5,988	6,621
	Cut Flowers	Home centers	2	2	2	3
	Cut Flowers	Hardware stores	20	21	22	23
	Cut Flowers	Department stores	15	15	15	15
	Cut Flowers	Warehouse clubs & supercntrs	2,081	2,300	2,498	2,653
	Indoor Plants	Home centers	987	1,047	1,101	1,159
	Indoor Plants	Hardware stores	42	44	47	49
	Indoor Plants	Department stores	90	90	91	91
	Indoor Plants	Warehouse clubs & supercntrs	571	632	686	729
	Outdoor Plants	Home centers	4,541	4,821	5,067	5,336
	Outdoor Plants	Hardware stores	201	213	223	233
	Outdoor Plants	Department stores	479	479	481	484
	Outdoor Plants	Warehouse clubs & supercntrs	1,828	2,020	2,194	2,330
	Fertilizers	Home centers	3,548	3,766	3,958	4,168
	Fertilizers	Hardware stores	479	508	531	557
	Fertilizers	Department stores	254	254	255	257
	Fertilizers	Warehouse clubs & supercntrs	1,684	1,861	2,021	2,146
	Lawn Tools	Home centers	1,564	1,660	1,745	1,837
	Lawn Tools	Hardware stores	523	554	580	608
	Lawn Tools	Department stores	53	53	54	54
	Lawn Tools	Warehouse clubs & supercntrs	381	421	457	486
	Lawn Machinery	Home centers	4,177	4,434	4,660	4,907
	Lawn Machinery	Hardware stores	773	819	857	899
	Lawn Machinery	Department stores	1,054	1,053	1,058	1,066
	Lawn Machinery	Warehouse clubs & supercntrs	4,014	4,437	4,819	5,118

Sales (Millions of U.S. Dollars)

Main Category	Sub Category	U.S. Industry	Year			
			2015	2016	2017	2018
	Farm Machinery	Home Centers	80	84	89	94
	Farm Machinery	Hardware Stores	124	132	138	145
	Farm Machinery	Department Stores	4	4	4	4
	Other Farm Supplies	Home Centers	34	36	38	40
	Other Farm Supplies	Hardware Stores	370	392	410	430
	Other Farm Supplies	Department Stores	6	6	6	6
	Other Farm Supplies	Warehouse clubs & supercntrs	18	20	21	23
	Other Lawn Supplies	Home Centers	3,508	3,724	3,914	4,122
	Other Lawn Supplies	Hardware Stores	467	495	518	543
	Other Lawn Supplies	Department Stores	619	619	622	627
	Other Lawn Supplies	Warehouse clubs & supercntrs	1,705	1,884	2,046	2,173

SUMMARY OF PRODUCT LINES SALES BY INDUSTRY

SALES (MILLIONS OF U.S. DOLLARS)

Main Category	Sub Category	U.S. Industry	Year			
			2015	2016	2017	2018
Lumber & Bldg Mat.	--	Home centers	52,759	56,008	58,862	61,988
Lumber & Bldg Mat.	--	Hardware stores	1,348	1,428	1,495	1,568
Lumber & Bldg Mat.	--	Gas stations w/ conven. stores	2	2	3	3
Lumber & Bldg Mat.	--	Department stores	4	4	4	4
Lumber & Bldg Mat.	--	Warehouse clubs & supercntrs	41	45	49	52
Lumber & Bldg Mat.	--	Electronic shopping & mail-order	571	645	729	806
	Nontreated Lumber	Home centers	4,103	4,356	4,578	4,821
	Nontreated Lumber	Hardware stores	126	133	140	146
	Treated Lumber	Home centers	4,246	4,507	4,737	4,988
	Treated Lumber	Hardware stores	81	86	90	95
	Bldg. Boards	Home centers	1,677	1,780	1,870	1,970
	Bldg. Boards	Hardware stores	51	54	57	60
	Gypsum	Home centers	3,072	3,262	3,428	3,610
	Gypsum	Hardware stores	45	47	50	52
	Engin'd. Wood Prod.	Home centers	352	374	393	414
	Engin'd. Wood Prod.	Hardware stores	5	5	5	5
	Structural Panels	Home centers	3,096	3,287	3,454	3,637
	Structural Panels	Hardware stores	40	43	44	47
	Other Panel Prods.	Home centers	2,991	3,176	3,337	3,515
	Other Panel Prods.	Hardware stores	45	48	50	53
	Bldg. Components	Home centers	273	290	305	321
	Bldg. Components	Hardware stores	8	9	9	10
	Connectors	Home centers	347	368	387	407
	Connectors	Hardware stores	31	33	34	36
	Steel Studs	Home centers	131	139	146	154
	Steel Studs	Hardware stores	6	6	6	6
	Doors & Moulding	Home centers	7,639	8,110	8,523	8,975
	Doors & Moulding	Hardware stores	95	101	106	111
	Windows & Skylights	Home centers	4,475	4,751	4,993	5,258
	Windows & Skylights	Hardware stores	44	47	49	52
	Glass	Home centers	242	257	270	284
	Glass	Hardware stores	84	89	93	97
	Masonry Supplies	Home centers	2,357	2,502	2,630	2,769
	Masonry Supplies	Hardware stores	162	172	180	189

SUMMARY OF PRODUCT LINES SALES BY INDUSTRY

SALES (MILLIONS OF U.S. DOLLARS)

Main Category	Sub Category	U.S. Industry	Year			
			2015	2016	2017	2018
	Insulation Products	Home centers	1,197	1,271	1,336	1,407
	Insulation Products	Hardware stores	57	60	63	66
	Siding & Exter. Trim	Home centers	664	705	741	781
	Siding & Exter. Trim	Hardware stores	15	15	16	17
	Roofing Supplies	Home centers	2,062	2,189	2,300	2,422
	Roofing Supplies	Hardware stores	59	62	65	68
	Ceilings	Home centers	416	442	465	489
	Ceilings	Hardware stores	9	10	10	11
	Kitchen & Cabinets	Home centers	8,500	9,024	9,483	9,987
	Kitchen & Cabinets	Hardware stores	119	126	132	139
	Heating & HVAC	Home centers	2,117	2,247	2,362	2,487
	Heating & HVAC	Hardware stores	127	135	141	148
	Refrigeration	Home centers	6	6	7	7
	Refrigeration	Hardware stores	13	14	15	15
	Other Bldg. Supplies	Home centers	2,796	2,968	3,119	3,285
	Other Bldg. Supplies	Hardware stores	126	133	139	146

SUMMARY OF PRODUCT LINES SALES BY INDUSTRY

SALES (MILLIONS OF U.S. DOLLARS)

Main Category	Sub Category	U.S. Industry	Year			
			2015	2016	2017	2018
Paint & Wallpaper	--	Home centers	11,429	12,133	12,751	13,428
Paint & Wallpaper	--	Hardware stores	2,354	2,493	2,609	2,738
Paint & Wallpaper	--	Supermarkets & grocery stores	0	0	0	0
Paint & Wallpaper	--	Gas stations w/ conven. stores	0	0	0	0
Paint & Wallpaper	--	Department stores	507	507	509	513
Paint & Wallpaper	--	Warehouse clubs & supercntrs	1,895	2,094	2,274	2,415
Paint & Wallpaper	--	Electronic shopping & mail-order	22	25	29	32
	Interior Paint	Home centers	4,271	4,534	4,765	5,018
	Interior Paint	Hardware stores	775	821	860	902
	Exterior Paint	Home centers	1,298	1,378	1,448	1,525
	Exterior Paint	Hardware stores	500	530	555	582
	Stains & Varnishes	Home centers	1,089	1,156	1,215	1,279
	Stains & Varnishes	Hardware stores	257	272	284	298
	Painting Equipment	Home centers	2,029	2,154	2,264	2,384
	Painting Equipment	Hardware stores	495	524	548	575
	Painting Supplies	Home centers	2,742	2,911	3,060	3,222
	Painting Supplies	Hardware stores	327	346	363	380

SUMMARY OF PRODUCT LINES SALES BY INDUSTRY

SALES (MILLIONS OF U.S. DOLLARS)

Main Category	Sub Category	U.S. Industry	Year			
			2015	2016	2017	2018
Gasoline & Fuels	--	Home centers	2	2	2	2
Gasoline & Fuels	--	Hardware stores	27	29	30	32
Gasoline & Fuels	--	Supermarkets & grocery stores	3,284	3,263	3,264	3,270
Gasoline & Fuels	--	Beer, wine, & liquor stores	108	116	124	133
Gasoline & Fuels	--	Gas stations w/ conven. stores	268,906	294,653	321,393	350,379
Gasoline & Fuels	--	Department stores	10	10	10	10
Gasoline & Fuels	--	Warehouse clubs & supercntrs	307	339	368	391
Gasoline & Fuels	--	Electronic shopping & mail-order	4	4	5	5
	Unleaded Regular	Gas stations w/ conven. stores	183,574	201,151	219,405	239,193
	Unleaded Mid-Grade	Gas stations w/ conven. stores	38,620	42,318	46,158	50,321
	Unleaded Premium	Gas stations w/ conven. stores	29,735	32,582	35,539	38,744
	Leaded Gasoline	Gas stations w/ conven. stores	576	631	688	750
	Diesel Fuel	Gas stations w/ conven. stores	14,989	16,424	17,915	19,530
	Other Fuels	Gas stations w/ conven. stores	1,412	1,547	1,688	1,840
Tires & Other Parts	--	Home centers	138	146	154	162
Tires & Other Parts	--	Hardware stores	163	173	181	190
Tires & Other Parts	--	Supermarkets & grocery stores	38	38	38	38
Tires & Other Parts	--	Beer, wine, & liquor stores	0	0	0	0
Tires & Other Parts	--	Pharmacies & drug stores	22	24	26	28
Tires & Other Parts	--	Gas stations w/ conven. stores	2,110	2,312	2,522	2,749
Tires & Other Parts	--	Department stores	1,286	1,286	1,292	1,301
Tires & Other Parts	--	Warehouse clubs & supercntrs	9,421	10,413	11,310	12,011
Tires & Other Parts	--	Electronic shopping & mail-order	9,441	10,660	12,050	13,324
	Tires & Tubes	Gas stations w/ conven. stores	422	463	505	550
	Tires & Tubes	Department stores	152	152	153	154
	Tires & Tubes	Warehouse clubs & supercntrs	3,943	4,358	4,734	5,027
	Auto Parts	Department stores	970	970	974	981
	Auto Parts	Warehouse clubs & supercntrs	4,102	4,534	4,924	5,230
	Auto Parts	Gas stations w/ conven. stores	881	965	1,053	1,148
	Batteries	Gas stations w/ conven. stores	93	102	111	121
	Batteries	Department stores	164	164	164	166
	Batteries	Warehouse clubs & supercntrs	1,376	1,521	1,652	1,754
	Auto Accessories	Gas stations w/ conven. stores	174	191	208	227
	Other Auto Parts	Gas stations w/ conven. stores	540	591	645	703

SUMMARY OF PRODUCT LINES SALES BY INDUSTRY

SALES (MILLIONS OF U.S. DOLLARS)

Main Category	Sub Category	U.S. Industry	Year			
			2015	2016	2017	2018
Pets & Pet Foods	--	Home centers	476	505	531	559
Pets & Pet Foods	--	Hardware stores	114	120	126	132
Pets & Pet Foods	--	Supermarkets & grocery stores	5,091	5,059	5,059	5,070
Pets & Pet Foods	--	Beer, wine, & liquor stores	9	10	10	11
Pets & Pet Foods	--	Pharmacies & drug stores	211	228	245	264
Pets & Pet Foods	--	Gas stations w/ conven. stores	291	319	348	379
Pets & Pet Foods	--	Department Stores	1,447	1,447	1,454	1,464
Pets & Pet Foods	--	Warehouse Clubs & Superctrs	9,527	10,530	11,437	12,146
Pets & Pet Foods	--	Electronic Shopping/Mail-Order	1,480	1,671	1,889	2,088
Pets & Pet Foods	--	Book Stores	1	1	1	1
	Stationery Products	Supermarkets & grocery stores	248	246	246	247
	Stationery Products	Beer, wine, & liquor stores	3	3	3	3
	Stationery Products	Pharmacies & drug stores	325	352	378	407
	Stationery Products	Department stores	395	395	396	399
	Stationery Products	Warehouse clubs & supercntrs	2,152	2,379	2,584	2,744
	Stationery Products	Office supply/stationery stores	1,536	1,515	1,480	1,451
	Stationery Products	Electronic shopping & mail-order	3,723	4,203	4,752	5,254
	Stationery Products	Book stores	63	63	64	64
	Office Paper	Supermarkets & grocery stores	57	57	57	57
	Office Paper	Beer, wine, & liquor stores	0	0	0	0
	Office Paper	Pharmacies & drug stores	100	108	116	125
	Office Paper	Department stores	347	347	349	351
	Office Paper	Warehouse clubs & supercntrs	2,070	2,288	2,485	2,639
	Office Paper	Office supply/stationery stores	2,982	2,941	2,875	2,817
	Office Paper	Elcctronic shopping & mail-order	3,268	3,690	4,172	4,612
	Office Paper	Book stores	21	21	22	22
	Office Supplies	Supermarkets & grocery stores	463	460	460	461
	Office Supplies	Beer, wine, & liquor stores	4	5	5	5
	Office Supplies	Pharmacies & drug stores	597	645	694	747
	Office Supplies	Department stores	456	456	458	461
	Office Supplies	Warehouse clubs & supercntrs	4,788	5,292	5,748	6,104
	Office Supplies	Office supply/stationery stores	4,220	4,162	4,068	3,986
	Office Supplies	Electronic shopping & mail-order	12,596	14,222	16,078	17,776
	Office Supplies	Book stores	125	126	127	128

SUMMARY OF PRODUCT LINES SALES BY INDUSTRY

SALES (MILLIONS OF U.S. DOLLARS)

Main Category	Sub Category	U.S. Industry	Year			
			2015	2016	2017	2018
	Office Equipment	Pharmacies & drug stores	13	14	15	16
	Office Equipment	Department stores	172	172	173	174
	Office Equipment	Warehouse clubs & supercntrs	753	833	904	960
	Office Equipment	Office supply/stationery stores	1,952	1,925	1,881	1,843
	Office Equipment	Electronic shopping & mail-order	2,313	2,612	2,953	3,265
	Office Equipment	Book stores	3	3	3	3
	Greeting Cards	Supermarkets & grocery stores	1,498	1,489	1,489	1,492
	Greeting Cards	Beer, wine, & liquor stores	4	4	4	5
	Greeting Cards	Warehouse clubs & supercntrs	1,707	1,846	1,985	2,137
	Greeting Cards	Pharmacies & drug stores	683	683	686	691
	Greeting Cards	Department stores	1,921	2,123	2,306	2,449
	Greeting Cards	Office supply/stationery stores	39	39	38	37
	Greeting Cards	Electronic shopping & mail-order	315	356	402	445
	Greeting Cards	Book stores	164	164	165	167
	Magazine/Newpaper	Supermarkets & grocery stores	2,146	2,132	2,133	2,137
	Magazine/Newpaper	Beer, wine, & liquor stores	52	56	60	64
	Magazine/Newpaper	Pharmacies & drug stores	339	367	394	424
	Magazine/Newpaper	Gas stations w/ conven. stores	1,720	1,885	2,056	2,241
	Magazine/Newpaper	Prerecorded Tape & CDs stores	17	15	14	14
	Magazine/Newpaper	Department stores	300	300	302	304
	Magazine/Newpaper	Warehouse clubs & supercntrs	1,203	1,330	1,444	1,534
	Magazine/Newpaper	Office supply/stationery stores	6	6	6	5
	Magazine/Newpaper	Electronic shopping & mail-order	2,434	2,748	3,107	3,435
	Magazine/Newpaper	Office supply/stationery stores	386	387	390	394

SUMMARY OF PRODUCT LINES SALES BY INDUSTRY

SALES (MILLIONS OF U.S. DOLLARS)

Main Category	Sub Category	U.S. Industry	Year			
			2015	2016	2017	2018
Souvenirs & Novelty	--	Supermarkets & grocery stores	506	502	502	503
Souvenirs & Novelty	--	Beer, wine, & liquor stores	24	26	28	30
Souvenirs & Novelty	--	Pharmacies & drug stores	328	355	382	411
Souvenirs & Novelty	--	Men's clothing stores	13	13	14	14
Souvenirs & Novelty	--	Women's clothing stores	28	31	33	35
Souvenirs & Novelty	--	Family clothing stores	282	298	316	336
Souvenirs & Novelty	--	Department stores	484	484	486	490
Souvenirs & Novelty	--	Warehouse Clubs & Superctrs	822	908	987	1,048
Souvenirs & Novelty	--	Office Supplies/Stationery Store	15	15	14	14
Souvenirs & Novelty	--	Electronic Shopping/Mail-Order	5,092	5,749	6,499	7,186
Souvenirs & Novelty	--	Book Stores	305	306	308	311

INDUSTRY: HOME CENTERS INDUSTRY (NAICS 44411)
PRODUCT LINE: GROCERY FOODS (Main Category)

NAICS 44411: Home Centers. This industry comprises establishments known as home centers primarily engaged in retailing a general line of new home repair and improvement materials and supplies, such as lumber, plumbing goods, electrical goods, tools, housewares, hardware, and lawn and garden supplies, with no one merchandise line predominating. The merchandise lines are normally arranged in separate departments.

5-YEAR TREND — ESTIMATED INDUSTRY SALES ($MILLIONS)

Year	Employee Size of Establishment									Total Industry Sales
	1-4 Emps.	5-9 Emps.	10-19 Emps.	20-49 Emps.	50-99 Emps.	100-249 Emps.	250-499 Emps.	500-999 Emps.	Unknown Emps.	
2014	0.0	0.0	0.1	0.2	0.1	8.9	0.8	0.0	0.0	10.2
2015	0.0	0.0	0.1	0.2	0.1	9.2	0.8	0.0	0.0	10.6
2016	0.0	0.0	0.1	0.2	0.1	9.5	0.8	0.0	0.0	10.9
2017	0.0	0.0	0.1	0.2	0.2	10.0	0.9	0.0	0.0	11.4
2018	0.0	0.0	0.1	0.2	0.2	10.5	0.9	0.0	0.0	12.0

INDUSTRY: HARDWARE STORES (NAICS 44413)
PRODUCT LINE: GROCERY FOODS (Main Category)

NAICS 44413: Hardware Stores. Establishments primarily engaged in the retail sale of a number of basic hardware lines, such as tools, builders' hardware, paint and glass, housewares and household appliances, and cutlery.

5-YEAR TREND — ESTIMATED INDUSTRY SALES ($MILLIONS)

Year	Employee Size of Establishment									Total Industry Sales
	1-4 Emps.	5-9 Emps.	10-19 Emps.	20-49 Emps.	50-99 Emps.	100-249 Emps.	250-499 Emps.	500-999 Emps.	Unknown Emps.	
2014	7.8	12.5	25.1	35.1	6.4	1.5	0.4	0.0	0.7	89.6
2015	8.0	12.8	25.6	35.8	6.6	1.5	0.4	0.0	0.7	91.3
2016	8.1	13.0	26.0	36.4	6.7	1.6	0.4	0.0	0.7	92.8
2017	8.5	13.6	27.2	38.1	7.0	1.6	0.5	0.0	0.7	97.2
2018	8.9	14.3	28.5	40.0	7.3	1.7	0.5	0.0	0.8	102.0

INDUSTRY: SUPERMARKETS & GROCERY STORES (NAICS 44511)
PRODUCT LINE: GROCERY FOODS (Main Category)

NAICS 44511: Grocery Stores Industry. This industry comprises establishments generally known as supermarkets and grocery stores primarily engaged in retailing a general line of food, such as canned and frozen foods; fresh fruits and vegetables; and fresh and prepared meats, fish, and poultry. Included in this industry are delicatessen-type establishments primarily engaged in retailing a general line of food.

5-YEAR TREND — ESTIMATED INDUSTRY SALES ($MILLIONS)

Year	Employee Size of Establishment									Total
	1-4 Emps.	5-9 Emps.	10-19 Emps.	20-49 Emps.	50-99 Emps.	100-249 Emps.	250-499 Emps.	500-999 Emps.	Unknown Emps.	Industry Sales
2014	5,976	4,473	11,341	37,049	89,866	204,936	59,079	8,145	1,131	421,996
2015	5,873	4,395	11,145	36,406	88,308	201,381	58,054	8,004	1,111	414,677
2016	5,757	4,309	10,925	35,689	86,569	197,417	56,911	7,846	1,089	406,514
2017	5,758	4,309	10,927	35,694	86,581	197,445	56,920	7,842	1,090	406,566
2018	5,770	4,318	10,950	35,769	86,763	197,859	57,039	7,851	1,092	407,411

INDUSTRY: BEER & WINE & LIQUOR STORES (NAICS 44531)
PRODUCT LINE: GROCERY FOODS (Main Category)

NAICS 44531: Beer & Wine & Liquor Stores. Establishments primarily engaged in the retail sale of packaged alcoholic beverages, such as ale, beer, wine, and liquor, for consumption off the premises. Stores selling prepared drinks for consumption on the premises are classified in SIC 5813.

5-YEAR TREND — ESTIMATED INDUSTRY SALES ($MILLIONS)

Year	Employee Size of Establishment									Total
	1-4 Emps.	5-9 Emps.	10-19 Emps.	20-49 Emps.	50-99 Emps.	100-249 Emps.	250-499 Emps.	500-999 Emps.	Unknown Emps.	Industry Sales
2014	527.7	512.5	429.4	313.4	41.1	30.2	0.1	15.7	29.6	1,899.8
2015	549.9	534.0	447.4	326.5	42.9	31.5	0.1	16.4	30.9	1,979.6
2016	571.0	554.5	464.6	339.1	44.5	32.7	0.1	17.0	32.1	2,055.5
2017	611.3	593.7	497.4	363.0	47.6	35.0	0.1	18.2	34.3	2,200.7
2018	655.6	636.7	533.4	389.3	51.1	37.6	0.1	19.5	36.8	2,360.0

INDUSTRY: PHARMACIES & DRUG STORES (NAICS 44611)
PRODUCT LINE: GROCERY FOODS (Main Category)

NAICS 44611 Pharmacies and Drug Stores – This industry comprises establishments known as pharmacies and drug stores engaged in retailing prescription or nonprescription drugs and medicines.

5-YEAR TREND – ESTIMATED INDUSTRY SALES ($MILLIONS)

Year	Employee Size of Establishment									Total Industry Sales
	1-4 Emps.	5-9 Emps.	10-19 Emps.	20-49 Emps.	50-99 Emps.	100-249 Emps.	250-499 Emps.	500-999 Emps.	Unknown Emps.	
2014	116.9	291.8	1,232.5	3,483.0	327.2	128.5	39.8	16.0	9.8	5,645.5
2015	123.0	307.1	1,297.0	3,665.3	344.3	135.2	41.9	16.9	10.3	5,941.0
2016	128.9	321.8	1,359.0	3,840.7	360.8	141.7	43.9	17.7	10.8	6,225.1
2017	138.6	346.0	1,461.3	4,129.9	387.9	152.4	47.2	18.5	11.6	6,693.4
2018	149.2	372.5	1,573.1	4,445.7	417.6	164.0	50.8	19.2	12.5	7,204.6

INDUSTRY: GAS STATIONS WITH CONVENIENCE STORES (NAICS 44711)
PRODUCT LINE: GROCERY FOODS (Main Category)

NAICS 44711: Gas Stations with Convenience Stores. This industry comprises establishments primarily engaged in selling gasoline and lubricating oils. These establishments frequently sell other merchandise, such as tires, batteries, and other automobile parts, or perform minor repair work. Gasoline stations combined with other activities, such as grocery stores, convenience stores, or carwashes, are classified according to the primary activity.

5-YEAR TREND – ESTIMATED INDUSTRY SALES ($MILLIONS)

Year	Employee Size of Establishment									Total Industry Sales
	1-4 Emps.	5-9 Emps.	10-19 Emps.	20-49 Emps.	50-99 Emps.	100-249 Emps.	250-499 Emps.	500-999 Emps.	Unknown Emps.	
2014	4,225	11,372	18,404	11,321	991	620	87	2	48	47,070
2015	4,545	12,235	19,801	12,180	1,067	667	94	2	51	50,641
2016	4,857	13,075	21,160	13,016	1,140	712	100	3	55	54,118
2017	5,298	14,261	23,080	14,198	1,243	777	109	3	60	59,030
2018	5,776	15,548	25,162	15,478	1,355	847	119	3	65	64,353

INDUSTRY: DEPARTMENT STORES (NAICS 45211)
PRODUCT LINE: GROCERY FOODS (Main Category)

NAICS 45211: Department Stores Industry . This industry comprises establishments known as department stores primarily engaged in retailing a wide range of the following new products with no one merchandise line predominating: apparel, furniture, appliances and home furnishings; and selected additional items, such as paint, hardware, toiletries, cosmetics, photographic equipment, jewelry, toys, and sporting goods. Merchandise lines are normally arranged in separate departments.

5-YEAR TREND — ESTIMATED INDUSTRY SALES ($MILLIONS)

Year	Employee Size of Establishment									Total Industry Sales
	1-4 Emps.	5-9 Emps.	10-19 Emps.	20-49 Emps.	50-99 Emps.	100-249 Emps.	250-499 Emps.	500-999 Emps.	Unknown Emps.	
2014	0	0	1	48	916	3,037	1,332	178	8	5,520
2015	0	0	1	49	927	3,076	1,350	181	8	5,592
2016	0	0	1	49	937	3,109	1,364	183	8	5,652
2017	0	0	1	50	942	3,124	1,370	184	8	5,678
2018	0	0	1	50	949	3,146	1,380	185	8	5,719

INDUSTRY: WAREHOUSE CLUBS & SUPERCENTERS (NAICS 45291)
PRODUCT LINE: GROCERY FOODS (Main Category)

NAICS 45291: Warehouse Clubs and Superstores This industry comprises establishments known as warehouse clubs, superstores or supercenters primarily engaged in retailing a general line of groceries in combination with general lines of new merchandise, such as apparel, furniture, and appliances.

5-YEAR TREND — ESTIMATED INDUSTRY SALES ($MILLIONS)

Year	Employee Size of Establishment									Total Industry Sales
	1-4 Emps.	5-9 Emps.	10-19 Emps.	20-49 Emps.	50-99 Emps.	100-249 Emps.	250-499 Emps.	500-999 Emps.	Unknown Emps.	
2014	9	0	2	88	111	13,675	60,456	1,597	19	75,958
2015	10	0	2	91	115	14,175	62,667	1,656	20	78,735
2016	10	0	2	94	119	14,648	64,756	1,711	20	81,360
2017	11	0	2	102	129	15,909	70,333	1,858	22	88,367
2018	12	0	2	109	137	16,896	74,694	1,973	23	93,846

INDUSTRY: OFFICE SUPPLIES & STATIONERY STORES (NAICS 45321)
PRODUCT LINE: GROCERY FOODS (Main Category)

NAICS 45321: Office Supplies and Stationery Stores . This industry comprises establishments primarily engaged in one or more of the following: (1) retailing new stationery, school supplies, and office supplies; (2) selling a combination of new office equipment, furniture, and supplies; and (3) selling new office equipment, furniture, and supplies in combination with selling new computers.

5-YEAR TREND — ESTIMATED INDUSTRY SALES ($MILLIONS)

Year	Employee Size of Establishment									Total
	1-4 Emps.	5-9 Emps.	10-19 Emps.	20-49 Emps.	50-99 Emps.	100-249 Emps.	250-499 Emps.	500-999 Emps.	Unknown Emps.	Industry Sales
2014	2.1	1.6	8.4	23.6	0.6	0.6	0.0	0.0	0.4	37.2
2015	2.1	1.6	8.4	23.6	0.6	0.6	0.0	0.0	0.4	37.3
2016	2.1	1.6	8.4	23.6	0.6	0.6	0.0	0.0	0.4	37.2
2017	2.1	1.5	8.2	23.0	0.6	0.6	0.0	0.0	0.4	36.4
2018	2.0	1.5	8.0	22.6	0.5	0.5	0.0	0.0	0.4	35.6

INDUSTRY: ELECTRONIC SHOPPING & MAIL-ORDER (NAICS 45411)
PRODUCT LINE: GROCERY FOODS (Main Category)

NAICS 45411: Electronic Shopping and Mail-Order Houses This industry comprises establishments primarily engaged in retailing all types of merchandise by means of mail or by electronic media, such as interactive television or computer. Included in this industry are establishments primarily engaged in retailing from catalogue showrooms of mail-order houses.

5-YEAR TREND — ESTIMATED INDUSTRY SALES ($MILLIONS)

Year	Employee Size of Establishment									Total
	1-4 Emps.	5-9 Emps.	10-19 Emps.	20-49 Emps.	50-99 Emps.	100-249 Emps.	250-499 Emps.	500-999 Emps.	Unknown Emps.	Industry Sales
2014	1,429.4	758.9	1,126.9	1,823.2	1,311.4	2,556.7	3,740.8	4,738.6	216.2	17,702.0
2015	1,524.7	809.5	1,202.1	1,944.8	1,398.9	2,727.2	3,990.3	5,054.8	230.6	18,883.0
2016	1,617.3	858.6	1,275.0	2,062.8	1,483.7	2,892.7	4,232.4	5,361.5	244.6	20,028.7
2017	1,840.3	977.1	1,450.9	2,347.3	1,688.4	3,291.7	4,816.2	5,951.4	278.3	22,641.4
2018	2,044.0	1,085.2	1,611.5	2,607.1	1,875.3	3,656.0	5,349.3	6,495.8	309.1	25,033.3

INDUSTRY: BOOK STORES (NAICS 451211)
PRODUCT LINE: GROCERY FOODS (Main Category)

NAICS 451211: Book Stores. This industry comprises establishments primarily engaged in the retail sale of new books and magazines. Establishments primarily engaged in the retail sale of used books are classified in 5932.

5-YEAR TREND — ESTIMATED INDUSTRY SALES ($MILLIONS)

Year	Employee Size of Establishment									Total Industry Sales
	1-4 Emps.	5-9 Emps.	10-19 Emps.	20-49 Emps.	50-99 Emps.	100-249 Emps.	250-499 Emps.	500-999 Emps.	Unknown Emps.	
2014	49.1	75.1	155.4	406.9	183.7	72.4	13.2	48.7	25.2	1,029.7
2015	51.8	79.2	163.8	429.1	193.7	76.3	13.9	51.3	26.6	1,085.8
2016	54.4	83.1	172.0	450.5	203.3	80.1	14.6	53.9	27.9	1,139.8
2017	54.8	83.7	173.2	453.7	204.8	80.7	14.7	55.3	28.1	1,149.1
2018	55.2	84.4	174.6	457.4	206.5	81.4	14.8	56.8	28.3	1,159.4

INDUSTRY: SUPERMARKETS & GROCERY STORES (NAICS 44511)
PRODUCT LINE: MEAT, FISH & POULTRY (Sub Category)

NAICS 44511: Grocery Stores Industry. This industry comprises establishments generally known as supermarkets and grocery stores primarily engaged in retailing a general line of food, such as canned and frozen foods; fresh fruits and vegetables; and fresh and prepared meats, fish, and poultry. Included in this industry are delicatessen-type establishments primarily engaged in retailing a general line of food.

5-YEAR TREND — ESTIMATED INDUSTRY SALES ($MILLIONS)

Year	Employee Size of Establishment									Total Industry Sales
	1-4 Emps.	5-9 Emps.	10-19 Emps.	20-49 Emps.	50-99 Emps.	100-249 Emps.	250-499 Emps.	500-999 Emps.	Unknown Emps.	
2014	2	2	4	14	33	75	22	3	0	154
2015	2	2	4	13	32	74	21	3	0	152
2016	2	2	4	13	32	72	21	3	0	149
2017	2	2	4	13	32	72	21	3	0	149
2018	2	2	4	13	32	72	21	3	0	149

INDUSTRY: WAREHOUSE CLUBS & SUPERCENTERS (NAICS 45291)
PRODUCT LINE: MEAT, FISH & POULTRY (Sub Category)

NAICS 45291: Warehouse Clubs and Superstores This industry comprises establishments known as warehouse clubs, superstores or supercenters primarily engaged in retailing a general line of groceries in combination with general lines of new merchandise, such as apparel, furniture, and appliances.

5-YEAR TREND — ESTIMATED INDUSTRY SALES ($MILLIONS)

Year	Employee Size of Establishment									Total
	1-4 Emps.	5-9 Emps.	10-19 Emps.	20-49 Emps.	50-99 Emps.	100-249 Emps.	250-499 Emps.	500-999 Emps.	Unknown Emps.	Industry Sales
2014	3.3	0.1	0.6	30.6	38.6	4,760.5	21,045.5	556.0	6.5	26,441.7
2015	3.4	0.1	0.6	31.7	40.0	4,934.5	21,814.9	576.4	6.8	27,408.4
2016	3.5	0.1	0.6	32.8	41.3	5,099.1	22,542.2	595.6	7.0	28,322.2
2017	3.8	0.1	0.7	35.6	44.9	5,538.2	24,483.7	646.9	7.6	30,761.5
2018	4.1	0.1	0.7	37.8	47.6	5,881.6	26,001.7	687.0	8.1	32,668.7

INDUSTRY: SUPERMARKETS & GROCERY STORES (NAICS 44511)
PRODUCT LINE: PRODUCE, FRESH & PREPACKAGED (Sub Category)

NAICS 44511: Grocery Stores Industry. This industry comprises establishments generally known as supermarkets and grocery stores primarily engaged in retailing a general line of food, such as canned and frozen foods; fresh fruits and vegetables; and fresh and prepared meats, fish, and poultry. Included in this industry are delicatessen-type establishments primarily engaged in retailing a general line of food.

5-YEAR TREND — ESTIMATED INDUSTRY SALES ($MILLIONS)

Year	Employee Size of Establishment									Total
	1-4 Emps.	5-9 Emps.	10-19 Emps.	20-49 Emps.	50-99 Emps.	100-249 Emps.	250-499 Emps.	500-999 Emps.	Unknown Emps.	Industry Sales
2014	823.3	616.2	1,562.4	5,103.8	12,380.0	28,232.1	8,138.8	1,122.1	155.8	58,134.4
2015	809.0	605.5	1,535.3	5,015.3	12,165.3	27,742.4	7,997.6	1,102.6	153.1	57,126.1
2016	793.1	593.6	1,505.1	4,916.6	11,925.8	27,196.3	7,840.2	1,080.9	150.1	56,001.6
2017	793.2	593.7	1,505.3	4,917.3	11,927.5	27,200.1	7,841.3	1,080.3	150.1	56,008.7
2018	794.9	594.9	1,508.4	4,927.6	11,952.5	27,257.1	7,857.7	1,081.6	150.4	56,125.2

INDUSTRY: WAREHOUSE CLUBS & SUPERCENTERS (NAICS 45291)
PRODUCT LINE: PRODUCE, FRESH & PREPACKAGED (Sub Category)

NAICS 45291: Warehouse Clubs and Superstores This industry comprises establishments known as warehouse clubs, superstores or supercenters primarily engaged in retailing a general line of groceries in combination with general lines of new merchandise, such as apparel, furniture, and appliances.

5-YEAR TREND — ESTIMATED INDUSTRY SALES ($MILLIONS)

Year	1-4 Emps.	5-9 Emps.	10-19 Emps.	20-49 Emps.	50-99 Emps.	100-249 Emps.	250-499 Emps.	500-999 Emps.	Unknown Emps.	Total Industry Sales
2014	2.4	0.1	0.4	22.3	28.1	3,469.8	15,339.5	405.3	4.8	19,272.6
2015	2.5	0.1	0.4	23.1	29.1	3,596.6	15,900.3	420.1	4.9	19,977.3
2016	2.6	0.1	0.4	23.9	30.1	3,716.6	16,430.5	434.1	5.1	20,643.3
2017	2.8	0.1	0.5	25.9	32.7	4,036.7	17,845.5	471.5	5.6	22,421.2
2018	3.0	0.1	0.5	27.6	34.7	4,286.9	18,951.9	500.7	5.9	23,811.3

INDUSTRY: SUPERMARKETS & GROCERY STORES (NAICS 44511)
PRODUCT LINE: FROZEN FOODS (Sub Category)

NAICS 44511: Grocery Stores Industry. This industry comprises establishments generally known as supermarkets and grocery stores primarily engaged in retailing a general line of food, such as canned and frozen foods; fresh fruits and vegetables; and fresh and prepared meats, fish, and poultry. Included in this industry are delicatessen-type establishments primarily engaged in retailing a general line of food.

5-YEAR TREND — ESTIMATED INDUSTRY SALES ($MILLIONS)

Year	1-4 Emps.	5-9 Emps.	10-19 Emps.	20-49 Emps.	50-99 Emps.	100-249 Emps.	250-499 Emps.	500-999 Emps.	Unknown Emps.	Total Industry Sales
2014	466	349	884	2,887	7,003	15,970	4,604	635	88	32,885
2015	458	343	868	2,837	6,882	15,693	4,524	624	87	32,315
2016	449	336	851	2,781	6,746	15,384	4,435	611	85	31,679
2017	449	336	852	2,782	6,747	15,387	4,436	611	85	31,683
2018	450	337	853	2,787	6,761	15,419	4,445	612	85	31,749

INDUSTRY: WAREHOUSE CLUBS & SUPERCENTERS (NAICS 45291)
PRODUCT LINE: FROZEN FOODS (Sub Category)

NAICS 45291: Warehouse Clubs and Superstores This industry comprises establishments known as warehouse clubs, superstores or supercenters primarily engaged in retailing a general line of groceries in combination with general lines of new merchandise, such as apparel, furniture, and appliances.

5-YEAR TREND – ESTIMATED INDUSTRY SALES ($MILLIONS)

Year	Employee Size of Establishment									Total Industry Sales
	1-4 Emps.	5-9 Emps.	10-19 Emps.	20-49 Emps.	50-99 Emps.	100-249 Emps.	250-499 Emps.	500-999 Emps.	Unknown Emps.	
2014	2.7	0.1	0.5	24.7	31.1	3,844.7	16,997.1	449.1	5.3	21,355.3
2015	2.8	0.1	0.5	25.6	32.3	3,985.3	17,618.5	465.5	5.5	22,136.0
2016	2.8	0.1	0.5	26.5	33.4	4,118.2	18,206.0	481.0	5.7	22,874.1
2017	3.1	0.1	0.5	28.8	36.2	4,472.9	19,773.9	522.4	6.2	24,844.1
2018	3.3	0.1	0.6	30.5	38.5	4,750.2	20,999.9	554.8	6.5	26,384.4

INDUSTRY: SUPERMARKETS & GROCERY STORES (NAICS 44511)
PRODUCT LINE: DAIRY PRODUCTS (Sub Category)

NAICS 44511: Grocery Stores Industry. This industry comprises establishments generally known as supermarkets and grocery stores primarily engaged in retailing a general line of food, such as canned and frozen foods; fresh fruits and vegetables; and fresh and prepared meats, fish, and poultry. Included in this industry are delicatessen-type establishments primarily engaged in retailing a general line of food.

5-YEAR TREND – ESTIMATED INDUSTRY SALES ($MILLIONS)

Year	Employee Size of Establishment									Total Industry Sales
	1-4 Emps.	5-9 Emps.	10-19 Emps.	20-49 Emps.	50-99 Emps.	100-249 Emps.	250-499 Emps.	500-999 Emps.	Unknown Emps.	
2014	711	532	1,350	4,409	10,694	24,387	7,030	969	135	50,217
2015	699	523	1,326	4,332	10,508	23,964	6,908	952	132	49,346
2016	685	513	1,300	4,247	10,302	23,492	6,772	934	130	48,374
2017	685	513	1,300	4,248	10,303	23,496	6,773	933	130	48,381
2018	687	514	1,303	4,256	10,325	23,545	6,788	934	130	48,481

INDUSTRY: GASOLINE STATIONS W/ CONVEN. STORES (NAICS 44771)
PRODUCT LINE: DAIRY PRODUCTS (Sub Category)

NAICS 44711: Gas Stations with Convenience Stores. This industry comprises establishments primarily engaged in selling gasoline and lubricating oils. These establishments frequently sell other merchandise, such as tires, batteries, and other automobile parts, or perform minor repair work. Gasoline stations combined with other activities, such as grocery stores, convenience stores, or carwashes, are classified according to the primary activity.

5-YEAR TREND — ESTIMATED INDUSTRY SALES ($MILLIONS)

Year	Employee Size of Establishment									Total Industry Sales
	1-4 Emps.	5-9 Emps.	10-19 Emps.	20-49 Emps.	50-99 Emps.	100-249 Emps.	250-499 Emps.	500-999 Emps.	Unknown Emps.	
2014	485.0	1,305.5	2,112.8	1,299.7	113.8	71.1	10.0	0.3	5.5	5,403.7
2015	521.8	1,404.6	2,273.1	1,398.3	122.5	76.5	10.7	0.3	5.9	5,813.6
2016	557.6	1,501.0	2,429.2	1,494.3	130.9	81.8	11.5	0.3	6.3	6,212.8
2017	608.2	1,637.2	2,649.6	1,629.9	142.7	89.2	12.5	0.3	6.9	6,776.6
2018	663.1	1,784.9	2,888.6	1,776.9	155.6	97.2	13.7	0.3	7.5	7,387.8

INDUSTRY: WAREHOUSE CLUBS & SUPERCENTERS (NAICS 45291)
PRODUCT LINE: DAIRY PRODUCTS (Sub Category)

NAICS 45291: Warehouse Clubs and Superstores This industry comprises establishments known as warehouse clubs, superstores or supercenters primarily engaged in retailing a general line of groceries in combination with general lines of new merchandise, such as apparel, furniture, and appliances.

5-YEAR TREND — ESTIMATED INDUSTRY SALES ($MILLIONS)

Year	Employee Size of Establishment									Total Industry Sales
	1-4 Emps.	5-9 Emps.	10-19 Emps.	20-49 Emps.	50-99 Emps.	100-249 Emps.	250-499 Emps.	500-999 Emps.	Unknown Emps.	
2014	2.1	0.1	0.4	19.2	24.2	2,986.1	13,201.3	348.8	4.1	16,586.2
2015	2.1	0.1	0.4	19.9	25.1	3,095.3	13,683.9	361.5	4.3	17,192.6
2016	2.2	0.1	0.4	20.6	25.9	3,198.5	14,140.2	373.6	4.4	17,765.8
2017	2.4	0.1	0.4	22.3	28.1	3,474.0	15,358.0	405.8	4.8	19,295.9
2018	2.5	0.1	0.4	23.7	29.9	3,689.4	16,310.2	430.9	5.1	20,492.2

INDUSTRY: SUPERMARKETS & GROCERY STORES (NAICS 44511)
PRODUCT LINE: IN-STORE BAKED GOODS (Sub Category)

NAICS 44511: Grocery Stores Industry. This industry comprises establishments generally known as supermarkets and grocery stores primarily engaged in retailing a general line of food, such as canned and frozen foods; fresh fruits and vegetables; and fresh and prepared meats, fish, and poultry. Included in this industry are delicatessen-type establishments primarily engaged in retailing a general line of food.

5-YEAR TREND — ESTIMATED INDUSTRY SALES ($MILLIONS)

Year	Employee Size of Establishment									Total Industry Sales
	1-4 Emps.	5-9 Emps.	10-19 Emps.	20-49 Emps.	50-99 Emps.	100-249 Emps.	250-499 Emps.	500-999 Emps.	Unknown Emps.	
2014	133	100	253	827	2,005	4,572	1,318	182	25	9,414
2015	131	98	249	812	1,970	4,493	1,295	179	25	9,251
2016	128	96	244	796	1,931	4,404	1,270	175	24	9,069
2017	128	96	244	796	1,932	4,405	1,270	175	24	9,070
2018	129	96	244	798	1,936	4,414	1,272	175	24	9,089

INDUSTRY: WAREHOUSE CLUBS & SUPERCENTERS (NAICS 45291)
PRODUCT LINE: IN-STORE BAKED GOODS (Sub Category)

NAICS 45291: Warehouse Clubs and Superstores This industry comprises establishments known as warehouse clubs, superstores or supercenters primarily engaged in retailing a general line of groceries in combination with general lines of new merchandise, such as apparel, furniture, and appliances.

5-YEAR TREND — ESTIMATED INDUSTRY SALES ($MILLIONS)

Year	Employee Size of Establishment									Total Industry Sales
	1-4 Emps.	5-9 Emps.	10-19 Emps.	20-49 Emps.	50-99 Emps.	100-249 Emps.	250-499 Emps.	500-999 Emps.	Unknown Emps.	
2014	0.6	0.0	0.1	5.7	7.2	888.7	3,928.8	103.8	1.2	4,936.2
2015	0.6	0.0	0.1	5.9	7.5	921.2	4,072.5	107.6	1.3	5,116.7
2016	0.7	0.0	0.1	6.1	7.7	951.9	4,208.3	111.2	1.3	5,287.3
2017	0.7	0.0	0.1	6.6	8.4	1,033.9	4,570.7	120.8	1.4	5,742.6
2018	0.8	0.0	0.1	7.1	8.9	1,098.0	4,854.1	128.2	1.5	6,098.7

INDUSTRY: SUPERMARKETS & GROCERY STORES (NAICS 44511)
PRODUCT LINE: BAKED GOODS-OFF PREMISES (Sub Category)

NAICS 44511: Grocery Stores Industry. This industry comprises establishments generally known as supermarkets and grocery stores primarily engaged in retailing a general line of food, such as canned and frozen foods; fresh fruits and vegetables; and fresh and prepared meats, fish, and poultry. Included in this industry are delicatessen-type establishments primarily engaged in retailing a general line of food.

5-YEAR TREND – ESTIMATED INDUSTRY SALES ($MILLIONS)

Year	Employee Size of Establishment									Total
	1-4 Emps.	5-9 Emps.	10-19 Emps.	20-49 Emps.	50-99 Emps.	100-249 Emps.	250-499 Emps.	500-999 Emps.	Unknown Emps.	Industry Sales
2014	223	167	424	1,385	3,359	7,659	2,208	304	42	15,772
2015	219	164	417	1,361	3,301	7,527	2,170	299	42	15,499
2016	215	161	408	1,334	3,236	7,378	2,127	293	41	15,193
2017	215	161	408	1,334	3,236	7,380	2,127	293	41	15,195
2018	216	161	409	1,337	3,243	7,395	2,132	293	41	15,227

INDUSTRY: GASOLINE STATIONS W/ CONVEN. STORES (NAICS 44711)
PRODUCT LINE: BAKED GOODS-OFF PREMISES (Sub Category)

NAICS 44711: Gas Stations with Convenience Stores. This industry comprises establishments primarily engaged in selling gasoline and lubricating oils. These establishments frequently sell other merchandise, such as tires, batteries, and other automobile parts, or perform minor repair work. Gasoline stations combined with other activities, such as grocery stores, convenience stores, or carwashes, are classified according to the primary activity.

5-YEAR TREND – ESTIMATED INDUSTRY SALES ($MILLIONS)

Year	Employee Size of Establishment									Total
	1-4 Emps.	5-9 Emps.	10-19 Emps.	20-49 Emps.	50-99 Emps.	100-249 Emps.	250-499 Emps.	500-999 Emps.	Unknown Emps.	Industry Sales
2014	175.1	471.3	762.8	469.2	41.1	25.7	3.6	0.1	2.0	1,950.9
2015	188.4	507.1	820.7	504.8	44.2	27.6	3.9	0.1	2.1	2,098.9
2016	201.3	541.9	877.0	539.5	47.2	29.5	4.1	0.1	2.3	2,243.1
2017	219.6	591.1	956.6	588.5	51.5	32.2	4.5	0.1	2.5	2,446.6
2018	239.4	644.4	1,042.9	641.5	56.2	35.1	4.9	0.1	2.7	2,667.3

INDUSTRY: WAREHOUSE CLUBS & SUPERCENTERS (NAICS 45291)

PRODUCT LINE: BAKED GOODS-OFF PREMISE (Sub Category)

NAICS 45291: Warehouse Clubs and Superstores This industry comprises establishments known as warehouse clubs, superstores or supercenters primarily engaged in retailing a general line of groceries in combination with general lines of new merchandise, such as apparel, furniture, and appliances.

5-YEAR TREND – ESTIMATED INDUSTRY SALES ($MILLIONS)

Year	Employee Size of Establishment									Total Industry Sales
	1-4 Emps.	5-9 Emps.	10-19 Emps.	20-49 Emps.	50-99 Emps.	100-249 Emps.	250-499 Emps.	500-999 Emps.	Unknown Emps.	
2014	0.8	0.0	0.1	7.4	9.4	1,157.2	5,115.9	135.2	1.6	6,427.6
2015	0.8	0.0	0.1	7.7	9.7	1,199.5	5,302.9	140.1	1.7	6,662.6
2016	0.9	0.0	0.1	8.0	10.0	1,239.5	5,479.7	144.8	1.7	6,884.8
2017	0.9	0.0	0.2	8.7	10.9	1,346.3	5,951.7	157.2	1.9	7,477.7
2018	1.0	0.0	0.2	9.2	11.6	1,429.7	6,320.7	167.0	2.0	7,941.3

INDUSTRY: SUPERMARKETS & GROCERY STORES (NAICS 44511)

PRODUCT LINE: DELICATESSEN FOODS (Sub Category)

NAICS 44511: Grocery Stores Industry. This industry comprises establishments generally known as supermarkets and grocery stores primarily engaged in retailing a general line of food, such as canned and frozen foods; fresh fruits and vegetables; and fresh and prepared meats, fish, and poultry. Included in this industry are delicatessen-type establishments primarily engaged in retailing a general line of food.

5-YEAR TREND – ESTIMATED INDUSTRY SALES ($MILLIONS)

Year	Employee Size of Establishment									Total Industry Sales
	1-4 Emps.	5-9 Emps.	10-19 Emps.	20-49 Emps.	50-99 Emps.	100-249 Emps.	250-499 Emps.	500-999 Emps.	Unknown Emps.	
2014	298	223	566	1,850	4,486	10,231	2,949	407	56	21,067
2015	293	219	556	1,817	4,408	10,053	2,898	400	55	20,701
2016	287	215	545	1,782	4,322	9,855	2,841	392	54	20,294
2017	287	215	545	1,782	4,322	9,857	2,842	391	54	20,296
2018	288	216	547	1,786	4,331	9,877	2,847	392	55	20,339

INDUSTRY: WAREHOUSE CLUBS & SUPERCENTERS (NAICS 45291)
PRODUCT LINE: DELICATESSEN FOODS (Sub Category)

NAICS 45291: Warehouse Clubs and Superstores This industry comprises establishments known as warehouse clubs, superstores or supercenters primarily engaged in retailing a general line of groceries in combination with general lines of new merchandise, such as apparel, furniture, and appliances.

5-YEAR TREND – ESTIMATED INDUSTRY SALES ($MILLIONS)

Year	Employee Size of Establishment									Total
	1-4 Emps.	5-9 Emps.	10-19 Emps.	20-49 Emps.	50-99 Emps.	100-249 Emps.	250-499 Emps.	500-999 Emps.	Unknown Emps.	Industry Sales
2014	0.8	0.0	0.1	7.7	9.7	1,201.0	5,309.5	140.3	1.7	6,670.9
2015	0.9	0.0	0.1	8.0	10.1	1,244.9	5,503.7	145.4	1.7	6,914.8
2016	0.9	0.0	0.2	8.3	10.4	1,286.4	5,687.2	150.3	1.8	7,145.4
2017	1.0	0.0	0.2	9.0	11.3	1,397.2	6,177.0	163.2	1.9	7,760.8
2018	1.0	0.0	0.2	9.5	12.0	1,483.9	6,559.9	173.3	2.0	8,241.9

INDUSTRY: SUPERMARKETS & GROCERY STORES (NAICS 44511)
PRODUCT LINE: SOFT DRINKS (Sub Category)

NAICS 44511: Grocery Stores Industry. This industry comprises establishments generally known as supermarkets and grocery stores primarily engaged in retailing a general line of food, such as canned and frozen foods; fresh fruits and vegetables; and fresh and prepared meats, fish, and poultry. Included in this industry are delicatessen-type establishments primarily engaged in retailing a general line of food.

5-YEAR TREND – ESTIMATED INDUSTRY SALES ($MILLIONS)

Year	Employee Size of Establishment									Total
	1-4 Emps.	5-9 Emps.	10-19 Emps.	20-49 Emps.	50-99 Emps.	100-249 Emps.	250-499 Emps.	500-999 Emps.	Unknown Emps.	Industry Sales
2014	238	178	451	1,473	3,572	8,146	2,348	324	45	16,773
2015	233	175	443	1,447	3,510	8,004	2,308	318	44	16,482
2016	229	171	434	1,419	3,441	7,847	2,262	312	43	16,158
2017	229	171	434	1,419	3,441	7,848	2,262	312	43	16,160
2018	229	172	435	1,422	3,449	7,864	2,267	312	43	16,194

INDUSTRY: BEER, WINE & LIQUOR STORES (NAICS 44531)
PRODUCT LINE: SOFT DRINKS (Sub Category)

NAICS 44531: Beer & Wine & Liquor Stores. Establishments primarily engaged in the retail sale of packaged alcoholic beverages, such as ale, beer, wine, and liquor, for consumption off the premises. Stores selling prepared drinks for consumption on the premises are classified in SIC 5813.

5-Year Trend — Estimated Industry Sales ($Millions)

Year	Employee Size of Establishment									Total Industry Sales
	1-4 Emps.	5-9 Emps.	10-19 Emps.	20-49 Emps.	50-99 Emps.	100-249 Emps.	250-499 Emps.	500-999 Emps.	Unknown Emps.	
2014	213.1	206.9	173.4	126.5	16.6	12.2	0.0	6.3	12.0	767.1
2015	222.0	215.6	180.7	131.8	17.3	12.7	0.0	6.6	12.5	799.3
2016	230.6	223.9	187.6	136.9	18.0	13.2	0.0	6.9	12.9	830.0
2017	246.8	239.7	200.8	146.6	19.2	14.1	0.0	7.3	13.9	888.6
2018	264.7	257.1	215.4	157.2	20.6	15.2	0.0	7.9	14.9	952.9

INDUSTRY: PHARMACIES & DRUG STORES (NAICS 44611)
PRODUCT LINE: SOFT DRINKS (Sub Category)

NAICS 44611 Pharmacies and Drug Stores – This industry comprises establishments known as pharmacies and drug stores engaged in retailing prescription or nonprescription drugs and medicines.

5-Year Trend — Estimated Industry Sales ($Millions)

Year	Employee Size of Establishment									Total Industry Sales
	1-4 Emps.	5-9 Emps.	10-19 Emps.	20-49 Emps.	50-99 Emps.	100-249 Emps.	250-499 Emps.	500-999 Emps.	Unknown Emps.	
2014	35.0	87.4	369.2	1,043.5	98.0	38.5	11.9	4.8	2.9	1,691.4
2015	36.8	92.0	388.6	1,098.1	103.1	40.5	12.6	5.1	3.1	1,779.9
2016	38.6	96.4	407.1	1,150.6	108.1	42.5	13.2	5.3	3.2	1,865.0
2017	41.5	103.7	437.8	1,237.3	116.2	45.6	14.1	5.5	3.5	2,005.3
2018	44.7	111.6	471.3	1,331.9	125.1	49.1	15.2	5.8	3.7	2,158.5

INDUSTRY: GAS STATIONS W/ CONVEN. STORES (NAICS 44711)
PRODUCT LINE: SOFT DRINKS (Sub Category)

NAICS 44711: Gas Stations with Convenience Stores. This industry comprises establishments primarily engaged in selling gasoline and lubricating oils. These establishments frequently sell other merchandise, such as tires, batteries, and other automobile parts, or perform minor repair work. Gasoline stations combined with other activities, such as grocery stores, convenience stores, or carwashes, are classified according to the primary activity.

5-Year Trend – Estimated Industry Sales ($Millions)

Year	Employee Size of Establishment									Total Industry Sales
	1-4 Emps.	5-9 Emps.	10-19 Emps.	20-49 Emps.	50-99 Emps.	100-249 Emps.	250-499 Emps.	500-999 Emps.	Unknown Emps.	
2014	1,311.2	3,529.5	5,712.1	3,513.7	307.7	192.3	27.0	0.7	14.8	14,609.0
2015	1,410.6	3,797.3	6,145.4	3,780.3	331.0	206.9	29.1	0.7	16.0	15,717.3
2016	1,507.5	4,058.0	6,567.4	4,039.8	353.8	221.1	31.1	0.8	17.1	16,796.4
2017	1,644.3	4,426.2	7,163.4	4,406.4	385.9	241.2	33.9	0.8	18.6	18,320.7
2018	1,792.6	4,825.4	7,809.4	4,803.9	420.7	262.9	36.9	0.9	20.3	19,973.1

INDUSTRY: WAREHOUSE CLUBS & SUPERCENTERS (NAICS 45291)
PRODUCT LINE: SOFT DRINKS (Sub Category)

NAICS 45291: Warehouse Clubs and Superstores This industry comprises establishments known as warehouse clubs, superstores or supercenters primarily engaged in retailing a general line of groceries in combination with general lines of new merchandise, such as apparel, furniture, and appliances.

5-Year Trend – Estimated Industry Sales ($Millions)

Year	Employee Size of Establishment									Total Industry Sales
	1-4 Emps.	5-9 Emps.	10-19 Emps.	20-49 Emps.	50-99 Emps.	100-249 Emps.	250-499 Emps.	500-999 Emps.	Unknown Emps.	
2014	1.9	0.1	0.3	17.3	21.8	2,695.5	11,916.6	314.9	3.7	14,972.2
2015	1.9	0.1	0.3	18.0	22.6	2,794.1	12,352.3	326.4	3.8	15,519.5
2016	2.0	0.1	0.3	18.6	23.4	2,887.3	12,764.2	337.2	4.0	16,037.0
2017	2.2	0.1	0.4	20.2	25.4	3,135.9	13,863.5	366.3	4.3	17,418.2
2018	2.3	0.1	0.4	21.4	27.0	3,330.3	14,723.0	389.0	4.6	18,498.1

INDUSTRY: SUPERMARKETS & GROCERY STORES (NAICS 44511)
PRODUCT LINE: CANDY (Sub Category)

NAICS 44511: Grocery Stores Industry. This industry comprises establishments generally known as supermarkets and grocery stores primarily engaged in retailing a general line of food, such as canned and frozen foods; fresh fruits and vegetables; and fresh and prepared meats, fish, and poultry. Included in this industry are delicatessen-type establishments primarily engaged in retailing a general line of food.

5-YEAR TREND — ESTIMATED INDUSTRY SALES ($MILLIONS)

Year	Employee Size of Establishment									Total Industry Sales
	1-4 Emps.	5-9 Emps.	10-19 Emps.	20-49 Emps.	50-99 Emps.	100-249 Emps.	250-499 Emps.	500-999 Emps.	Unknown Emps.	
2014	78.8	59.0	149.5	488.4	1,184.7	2,701.7	778.9	107.4	14.9	5,563.3
2015	77.4	57.9	146.9	480.0	1,164.2	2,654.9	765.3	105.5	14.7	5,466.8
2016	75.9	56.8	144.0	470.5	1,141.3	2,602.6	750.3	103.4	14.4	5,359.2
2017	75.9	56.8	144.1	470.6	1,141.4	2,603.0	750.4	103.4	14.4	5,359.9
2018	76.1	56.9	144.4	471.6	1,143.8	2,608.4	752.0	103.5	14.4	5,371.0

INDUSTRY: GAS STATIONS W/ CONVEN. STORES (NAICS 44711)
PRODUCT LINE: CANDY (Sub Category)

NAICS 44711: Gas Stations with Convenience Stores. This industry comprises establishments primarily engaged in selling gasoline and lubricating oils. These establishments frequently sell other merchandise, such as tires, batteries, and other automobile parts, or perform minor repair work. Gasoline stations combined with other activities, such as grocery stores, convenience stores, or carwashes, are classified according to the primary activity.

5-YEAR TREND — ESTIMATED INDUSTRY SALES ($MILLIONS)

Year	Employee Size of Establishment									Total Industry Sales
	1-4 Emps.	5-9 Emps.	10-19 Emps.	20-49 Emps.	50-99 Emps.	100-249 Emps.	250-499 Emps.	500-999 Emps.	Unknown Emps.	
2014	531.2	1,429.9	2,314.1	1,423.5	124.7	77.9	10.9	0.3	6.0	5,918.5
2015	571.5	1,538.4	2,489.7	1,531.5	134.1	83.8	11.8	0.3	6.5	6,367.5
2016	610.7	1,644.0	2,660.6	1,636.7	143.3	89.6	12.6	0.3	6.9	6,804.7
2017	666.1	1,793.2	2,902.1	1,785.2	156.3	97.7	13.7	0.3	7.5	7,422.3
2018	726.2	1,954.9	3,163.8	1,946.2	170.4	106.5	15.0	0.4	8.2	8,091.7

INDUSTRY: WAREHOUSE CLUBS & GROCERY STORES (NAICS 45291)
PRODUCT LINE: CANDY (Sub Category)

NAICS 45291: Warehouse Clubs and Superstores This industry comprises establishments known as warehouse clubs, superstores or supercenters primarily engaged in retailing a general line of groceries in combination with general lines of new merchandise, such as apparel, furniture, and appliances.

5-YEAR TREND – ESTIMATED INDUSTRY SALES ($MILLIONS)

Year	Employee Size of Establishment									Total Industry Sales
	1-4 Emps.	5-9 Emps.	10-19 Emps.	20-49 Emps.	50-99 Emps.	100-249 Emps.	250-499 Emps.	500-999 Emps.	Unknown Emps.	
2014	1.8	0.1	0.3	17.0	21.4	2,643.7	11,687.6	308.8	3.6	14,684.4
2015	1.9	0.1	0.3	17.6	22.2	2,740.4	12,114.9	320.1	3.8	15,221.3
2016	2.0	0.1	0.3	18.2	22.9	2,831.8	12,518.9	330.8	3.9	15,728.8
2017	2.1	0.1	0.4	19.8	24.9	3,075.7	13,597.1	359.2	4.2	17,083.4
2018	2.3	0.1	0.4	21.0	26.5	3,266.3	14,440.1	381.5	4.5	18,142.6

INDUSTRY: SUPERMARKETS & GROCERY STORES (NAICS 44511)
PRODUCT LINE: ALL OTHER FOODS (Sub Category)

NAICS 44511: Grocery Stores Industry. This industry comprises establishments generally known as supermarkets and grocery stores primarily engaged in retailing a general line of food, such as canned and frozen foods; fresh fruits and vegetables; and fresh and prepared meats, fish, and poultry. Included in this industry are delicatessen-type establishments primarily engaged in retailing a general line of food.

5-YEAR TREND – ESTIMATED INDUSTRY SALES ($MILLIONS)

Year	Employee Size of Establishment									Total Industry Sales
	1-4 Emps.	5-9 Emps.	10-19 Emps.	20-49 Emps.	50-99 Emps.	100-249 Emps.	250-499 Emps.	500-999 Emps.	Unknown Emps.	
2014	1,961	1,468	3,722	12,159	29,493	67,256	19,389	2,673	371	138,492
2015	1,927	1,442	3,657	11,948	28,981	66,090	19,052	2,627	365	136,090
2016	1,889	1,414	3,585	11,713	28,411	64,789	18,677	2,575	358	133,411
2017	1,890	1,414	3,586	11,714	28,415	64,798	18,680	2,574	358	133,428
2018	1,894	1,417	3,594	11,739	28,474	64,934	18,719	2,577	358	133,706

INDUSTRY: BEER, WINE & LIQUOR STORES (NAICS 44531)
PRODUCT LINE: ALL OTHER FOODS (Sub Category)

NAICS 44531: Beer & Wine & Liquor Stores. Establishments primarily engaged in the retail sale of packaged alcoholic beverages, such as ale, beer, wine, and liquor, for consumption off the premises. Stores selling prepared drinks for consumption on the premises are classified in SIC 5813.

5-YEAR TREND – ESTIMATED INDUSTRY SALES ($MILLIONS)

Year	Employee Size of Establishment									Total Industry Sales
	1-4 Emps.	5-9 Emps.	10-19 Emps.	20-49 Emps.	50-99 Emps.	100-249 Emps.	250-499 Emps.	500-999 Emps.	Unknown Emps.	
2014	132.5	128.7	107.8	78.7	10.3	7.6	0.0	3.9	7.4	477.2
2015	138.1	134.1	112.4	82.0	10.8	7.9	0.0	4.1	7.8	497.2
2016	143.4	139.3	116.7	85.2	11.2	8.2	0.0	4.3	8.1	516.3
2017	153.5	149.1	124.9	91.2	12.0	8.8	0.0	4.6	8.6	552.7
2018	164.7	159.9	134.0	97.8	12.8	9.4	0.0	4.9	9.2	592.8

INDUSTRY: WAREHOUSE CLUBS & SUPERCENTERS (NAICS 45291)
PRODUCT LINE: ALL OTHER FOODS (Sub Category)

NAICS 45291: Warehouse Clubs and Superstores This industry comprises establishments known as warehouse clubs, superstores or supercenters primarily engaged in retailing a general line of groceries in combination with general lines of new merchandise, such as apparel, furniture, and appliances.

5-YEAR TREND – ESTIMATED INDUSTRY SALES ($MILLIONS)

Year	Employee Size of Establishment									Total Industry Sales
	1-4 Emps.	5-9 Emps.	10-19 Emps.	20-49 Emps.	50-99 Emps.	100-249 Emps.	250-499 Emps.	500-999 Emps.	Unknown Emps.	
2014	9	0	2	85	107	13,227	58,476	1,545	18	73,470
2015	9	0	2	88	111	13,711	60,614	1,602	19	76,156
2016	10	0	2	91	115	14,168	62,635	1,655	19	78,695
2017	11	0	2	99	125	15,388	68,030	1,797	21	85,473
2018	11	0	2	105	132	16,342	72,248	1,909	22	90,772

INDUSTRY: GAS STATIONS W/ CONVEN. STORES (NAICS 44711)
PRODUCT LINE: ALL OTHER FOODS (Sub Category)

NAICS 44711: Gas Stations with Convenience Stores. This industry comprises establishments primarily engaged in selling gasoline and lubricating oils. These establishments frequently sell other merchandise, such as tires, batteries, and other automobile parts, or perform minor repair work. Gasoline stations combined with other activities, such as grocery stores, convenience stores, or carwashes, are classified according to the primary activity.

5-YEAR TREND – ESTIMATED INDUSTRY SALES ($MILLIONS)

Year	Employee Size of Establishment									Total Industry Sales
	1-4 Emps.	5-9 Emps.	10-19 Emps.	20-49 Emps.	50-99 Emps.	100-249 Emps.	250-499 Emps.	500-999 Emps.	Unknown Emps.	
2014	1,722.1	4,635.8	7,502.6	4,615.1	404.2	252.6	35.5	0.9	19.5	19,188.2
2015	1,852.8	4,987.5	8,071.8	4,965.2	434.8	271.7	38.2	1.0	21.0	20,644.0
2016	1,980.0	5,330.0	8,625.9	5,306.1	464.7	290.4	40.8	1.0	22.4	22,061.3
2017	2,159.7	5,813.7	9,408.8	5,787.7	506.8	316.8	44.5	1.1	24.5	24,063.4
2018	2,354.5	6,338.0	10,257.3	6,309.6	552.6	345.3	48.5	1.2	26.7	26,233.7

INDUSTRY: PHARMACIES & DRUG STORES (NAICS 44611)
PRODUCT LINE: ALL OTHER FOODS (Sub Category)

NAICS 44611 Pharmacies and Drug Stores – This industry comprises establishments known as pharmacies and drug stores engaged in retailing prescription or nonprescription drugs and medicines.

5-YEAR TREND – ESTIMATED INDUSTRY SALES ($MILLIONS)

Year	Employee Size of Establishment									Total Industry Sales
	1-4 Emps.	5-9 Emps.	10-19 Emps.	20-49 Emps.	50-99 Emps.	100-249 Emps.	250-499 Emps.	500-999 Emps.	Unknown Emps.	
2014	81.9	204.4	863.2	2,439.5	229.2	90.0	27.9	11.2	6.8	3,954.1
2015	86.1	215.1	908.4	2,567.2	241.1	94.7	29.4	11.8	7.2	4,161.1
2016	90.3	225.4	951.8	2,690.0	252.7	99.2	30.8	12.4	7.6	4,360.1
2017	97.1	242.3	1,023.5	2,892.6	271.7	106.7	33.1	12.9	8.1	4,688.1
2018	104.5	260.9	1,101.8	3,113.8	292.5	114.9	35.6	13.5	8.7	5,046.2

INDUSTRY: ELECTRONIC SHOPPING & MAIL-ORDER (NAICS 45411)
PRODUCT LINE: ALL OTHER FOODS (Sub Category)

NAICS 45411: Electronic Shopping and Mail-Order Houses This industry comprises establishments primarily engaged in retailing all types of merchandise by means of mail or by electronic media, such as interactive television or computer. Included in this industry are establishments primarily engaged in retailing from catalogue showrooms of mail-order houses.

5-Year Trend — Estimated Industry Sales ($Millions)

Year	Employee Size of Establishment									Total
	1-4 Emps.	5-9 Emps.	10-19 Emps.	20-49 Emps.	50-99 Emps.	100-249 Emps.	250-499 Emps.	500-999 Emps.	Unknown Emps.	Industry Sales
2014	338.5	179.7	266.9	431.7	310.5	605.4	885.8	1,122.1	51.2	4,191.8
2015	361.1	191.7	284.7	460.5	331.3	645.8	944.9	1,197.0	54.6	4,471.5
2016	383.0	203.3	301.9	488.5	351.3	685.0	1,002.2	1,269.6	57.9	4,742.7
2017	435.8	231.4	343.6	555.8	399.8	779.5	1,140.5	1,409.3	65.9	5,361.4
2018	484.0	257.0	381.6	617.4	444.1	865.7	1,266.7	1,538.2	73.2	5,927.8

INDUSTRY: SUPERMARKETS & GROCERY STORES (NAICS 44511)
PRODUCT LINE: BEER, WINE & LIQUOR (Main Category)

NAICS 44511: Grocery Stores Industry. This industry comprises establishments generally known as supermarkets and grocery stores primarily engaged in retailing a general line of food, such as canned and frozen foods; fresh fruits and vegetables; and fresh and prepared meats, fish, and poultry. Included in this industry are delicatessen-type establishments primarily engaged in retailing a general line of food.

5-Year Trend — Estimated Industry Sales ($Millions)

Year	Employee Size of Establishment									Total
	1-4 Emps.	5-9 Emps.	10-19 Emps.	20-49 Emps.	50-99 Emps.	100-249 Emps.	250-499 Emps.	500-999 Emps.	Unknown Emps.	Industry Sales
2014	280	210	532	1,737	4,213	9,608	2,770	382	53	19,784
2015	275	206	522	1,707	4,140	9,441	2,722	375	52	19,441
2016	270	202	512	1,673	4,058	9,255	2,668	368	51	19,058
2017	270	202	512	1,673	4,059	9,256	2,668	368	51	19,060
2018	271	202	513	1,677	4,068	9,276	2,674	368	51	19,100

| INDUSTRY: BEER, WINE & LIQUOR STORES (NAICS 44531) |
| PRODUCT LINE: BEER, WINE & LIQUOR (Main Category) |

NAICS 44531: Beer & Wine & Liquor Stores. Establishments primarily engaged in the retail sale of packaged alcoholic beverages, such as ale, beer, wine, and liquor, for consumption off the premises. Stores selling prepared drinks for consumption on the premises are classified in SIC 5813.

5-YEAR TREND – ESTIMATED INDUSTRY SALES ($MILLIONS)

Year	Employee Size of Establishment									Total
	1-4 Emps.	5-9 Emps.	10-19 Emps.	20-49 Emps.	50-99 Emps.	100-249 Emps.	250-499 Emps.	500-999 Emps.	Unknown Emps.	Industry Sales
2014	10,236	9,940	8,328	6,078	798	586	2	305	575	36,847
2015	10,665	10,358	8,678	6,333	831	611	2	318	599	38,394
2016	11,075	10,755	9,011	6,576	863	634	2	330	622	39,868
2017	11,857	11,515	9,647	7,041	924	679	2	353	666	42,683
2018	12,715	12,348	10,346	7,550	991	728	2	378	714	45,773

| INDUSTRY: PHARMACIES & DRUG STORES (NAICS 44611) |
| PRODUCT LINE: BEER, WINE & LIQUOR (Main Category) |

NAICS 44611 Pharmacies and Drug Stores – This industry comprises establishments known as pharmacies and drug stores engaged in retailing prescription or nonprescription drugs and medicines.

5-YEAR TREND – ESTIMATED INDUSTRY SALES ($MILLIONS)

Year	Employee Size of Establishment									Total
	1-4 Emps.	5-9 Emps.	10-19 Emps.	20-49 Emps.	50-99 Emps.	100-249 Emps.	250-499 Emps.	500-999 Emps.	Unknown Emps.	Industry Sales
2014	40.1	100.0	422.4	1,193.7	112.1	44.0	13.6	5.5	3.4	1,934.8
2015	42.2	105.2	444.5	1,256.1	118.0	46.3	14.4	5.8	3.5	2,036.0
2016	44.2	110.3	465.7	1,316.2	123.6	48.6	15.0	6.1	3.7	2,133.4
2017	47.5	118.6	500.8	1,415.3	132.9	52.2	16.2	6.3	4.0	2,293.9
2018	51.1	127.6	539.1	1,523.6	143.1	56.2	17.4	6.6	4.3	2,469.1

INDUSTRY: GASOLINE STATIONS W/ CONVEN. STORES (NAICS 44711)
PRODUCT LINE: BEER, WINE & LIQUOR (Main Category)

NAICS 44711: Gas Stations with Convenience Stores. This industry comprises establishments primarily engaged in selling gasoline and lubricating oils. These establishments frequently sell other merchandise, such as tires, batteries, and other automobile parts, or perform minor repair work. Gasoline stations combined with other activities, such as grocery stores, convenience stores, or carwashes, are classified according to the primary activity.

5-YEAR TREND – ESTIMATED INDUSTRY SALES ($MILLIONS)

Year	Employee Size of Establishment									Total Industry Sales
	1-4 Emps.	5-9 Emps.	10-19 Emps.	20-49 Emps.	50-99 Emps.	100-249 Emps.	250-499 Emps.	500-999 Emps.	Unknown Emps.	
2014	1,351.1	3,636.9	5,885.9	3,620.6	317.1	198.2	27.8	0.7	15.3	15,053.6
2015	1,453.6	3,912.8	6,332.5	3,895.3	341.1	213.2	29.9	0.8	16.5	16,195.6
2016	1,553.4	4,181.5	6,767.2	4,162.8	364.5	227.8	32.0	0.8	17.6	17,307.6
2017	1,694.3	4,560.9	7,381.4	4,540.6	397.6	248.5	34.9	0.9	19.2	18,878.3
2018	1,847.1	4,972.3	8,047.1	4,950.1	433.5	270.9	38.0	0.9	20.9	20,580.9

INDUSTRY: WAREHOUSE CLUBS & SUPERCENTERS (NAICS 45291)
PRODUCT LINE: BEER, WINE & LIQUOR (Main Category)

NAICS 45291: Warehouse Clubs and Superstores This industry comprises establishments known as warehouse clubs, superstores or supercenters primarily engaged in retailing a general line of groceries in combination with general lines of new merchandise, such as apparel, furniture, and appliances.

Year	Employee Size of Establishment									Total Industry Sales
	1-4 Emps.	5-9 Emps.	10-19 Emps.	20-49 Emps.	50-99 Emps.	100-249 Emps.	250-499 Emps.	500-999 Emps.	Unknown Emps.	
2014	1.2	0.0	0.2	10.7	13.5	1,670.6	7,385.3	195.1	2.3	9,279.0
2015	1.2	0.0	0.2	11.1	14.0	1,731.6	7,655.4	202.3	2.4	9,618.2
2016	1.2	0.0	0.2	11.5	14.5	1,789.4	7,910.6	209.0	2.5	9,938.9
2017	1.3	0.0	0.2	12.5	15.7	1,943.5	8,591.9	227.0	2.7	10,794.9
2018	1.4	0.0	0.2	13.3	16.7	2,064.0	9,124.6	241.1	2.8	11,464.2

INDUSTRY: ELECTRONIC SHOPPING & MAIL ORDER (NAICS 45411)
PRODUCT LINE: BEER, WINE & LIQUOR (Main Category)

NAICS 45411: Electronic Shopping and Mail-Order Houses This industry comprises establishments primarily engaged in retailing all types of merchandise by means of mail or by electronic media, such as interactive television or computer. Included in this industry are establishments primarily engaged in retailing from catalogue showrooms of mail-order houses.

5-YEAR TREND — ESTIMATED INDUSTRY SALES ($MILLIONS)

Year	Employee Size of Establishment									Total Industry Sales
	1-4 Emps.	5-9 Emps.	10-19 Emps.	20-49 Emps.	50-99 Emps.	100-249 Emps.	250-499 Emps.	500-999 Emps.	Unknown Emps.	
2014	56.3	29.9	44.4	71.8	51.7	100.7	147.4	186.7	8.5	697.4
2015	60.1	31.9	47.4	76.6	55.1	107.4	157.2	199.1	9.1	744.0
2016	63.7	33.8	50.2	81.3	58.5	114.0	166.7	211.2	9.6	789.1
2017	72.5	38.5	57.2	92.5	66.5	129.7	189.7	234.5	11.0	892.0
2018	80.5	42.8	63.5	102.7	73.9	144.0	210.8	255.9	12.2	986.3

INDUSTRY: SUPERMARKETS & GROCERY STORES (NAICS 44511)
PRODUCT LINE: LIQUOR, BRANDIES & LIQUEURS (Sub Category)

NAICS 44511: Grocery Stores Industry. This industry comprises establishments generally known as supermarkets and grocery stores primarily engaged in retailing a general line of food, such as canned and frozen foods; fresh fruits and vegetables; and fresh and prepared meats, fish, and poultry. Included in this industry are delicatessen-type establishments primarily engaged in retailing a general line of food.

5-YEAR TREND — ESTIMATED INDUSTRY SALES ($MILLIONS)

Year	Employee Size of Establishment									Total Industry Sales
	1-4 Emps.	5-9 Emps.	10-19 Emps.	20-49 Emps.	50-99 Emps.	100-249 Emps.	250-499 Emps.	500-999 Emps.	Unknown Emps.	
2014	54.7	40.9	103.7	338.8	821.9	1,874.3	540.3	74.5	10.3	3,859.5
2015	53.7	40.2	101.9	333.0	807.6	1,841.8	531.0	73.2	10.2	3,792.5
2016	52.7	39.4	99.9	326.4	791.7	1,805.5	520.5	71.8	10.0	3,717.9
2017	52.7	39.4	99.9	326.5	791.9	1,805.8	520.6	71.7	10.0	3,718.4
2018	52.8	39.5	100.1	327.1	793.5	1,809.6	521.7	71.8	10.0	3,726.1

INDUSTRY: BEER, WINE & LIQUOR STORES (NAICS 44531)
PRODUCT LINE: LIQUOR, BRANDIES & LIQUEURS (Sub Category)

NAICS 44531: Beer & Wine & Liquor Stores. Establishments primarily engaged in the retail sale of packaged alcoholic beverages, such as ale, beer, wine, and liquor, for consumption off the premises. Stores selling prepared drinks for consumption on the premises are classified in SIC 5813.

5-YEAR TREND – ESTIMATED INDUSTRY SALES ($MILLIONS)

Year	Employee Size of Establishment									Total Industry Sales
	1-4 Emps.	5-9 Emps.	10-19 Emps.	20-49 Emps.	50-99 Emps.	100-249 Emps.	250-499 Emps.	500-999 Emps.	Unknown Emps.	
2014	4,330.4	4,205.4	3,523.4	2,571.4	337.5	248.0	0.7	129.0	243.2	15,589.0
2015	4,512.2	4,382.0	3,671.3	2,679.3	351.6	258.5	0.7	134.4	253.4	16,243.5
2016	4,685.4	4,550.1	3,812.2	2,782.2	365.1	268.4	0.8	139.6	263.1	16,866.9
2017	5,016.3	4,871.5	4,081.5	2,978.7	390.9	287.3	0.8	149.3	281.7	18,058.1
2018	5,379.5	5,224.2	4,377.0	3,194.3	419.2	308.1	0.9	160.0	302.1	19,365.4

INDUSTRY: GASOLINE STATIONS W/ CONVEN. STORES (NAICS 44711)
PRODUCT LINE: LIQUOR, BRANDIES & LIQUEURS (Sub Category)

NAICS 44711: Gas Stations with Convenience Stores. This industry comprises establishments primarily engaged in selling gasoline and lubricating oils. These establishments frequently sell other merchandise, such as tires, batteries, and other automobile parts, or perform minor repair work. Gasoline stations combined with other activities, such as grocery stores, convenience stores, or carwashes, are classified according to the primary activity.

5-YEAR TREND – ESTIMATED INDUSTRY SALES ($MILLIONS)

Year	Employee Size of Establishment									Total Industry Sales
	1-4 Emps.	5-9 Emps.	10-19 Emps.	20-49 Emps.	50-99 Emps.	100-249 Emps.	250-499 Emps.	500-999 Emps.	Unknown Emps.	
2014	45.3	122.0	197.4	121.4	10.6	6.6	0.9	0.0	0.5	504.9
2015	48.8	131.2	212.4	130.6	11.4	7.2	1.0	0.0	0.6	543.2
2016	52.1	140.2	227.0	139.6	12.2	7.6	1.1	0.0	0.6	580.5
2017	56.8	153.0	247.6	152.3	13.3	8.3	1.2	0.0	0.6	633.2
2018	62.0	166.8	269.9	166.0	14.5	9.1	1.3	0.0	0.7	690.3

INDUSTRY: WAREHOUSE CLUBS & SUPERCENTERS (NAICS 45291)
PRODUCT LINE: LIQUOR, BRANDIES & LIQUEURS (Sub Category)

NAICS 45291: Warehouse Clubs and Superstores This industry comprises establishments known as warehouse clubs, superstores or supercenters primarily engaged in retailing a general line of groceries in combination with general lines of new merchandise, such as apparel, furniture, and appliances.

5-YEAR TREND — ESTIMATED INDUSTRY SALES ($MILLIONS)

Year	Employee Size of Establishment									Total Industry Sales
	1-4 Emps.	5-9 Emps.	10-19 Emps.	20-49 Emps.	50-99 Emps.	100-249 Emps.	250-499 Emps.	500-999 Emps.	Unknown Emps.	
2014	0.1	0.0	0.0	1.1	1.4	172.9	764.3	20.2	0.2	960.2
2015	0.1	0.0	0.0	1.2	1.5	179.2	792.2	20.9	0.2	995.3
2016	0.1	0.0	0.0	1.2	1.5	185.2	818.6	21.6	0.3	1,028.5
2017	0.1	0.0	0.0	1.3	1.6	201.1	889.1	23.5	0.3	1,117.1
2018	0.1	0.0	0.0	1.4	1.7	213.6	944.2	24.9	0.3	1,186.3

INDUSTRY: SUPERMARKETS & GROCERY STORES (NAICS 44511)
PRODUCT LINE: WINE PRODUCTS (Sub Category)

NAICS 44511: Grocery Stores Industry. This industry comprises establishments generally known as supermarkets and grocery stores primarily engaged in retailing a general line of food, such as canned and frozen foods; fresh fruits and vegetables; and fresh and prepared meats, fish, and poultry. Included in this industry are delicatessen-type establishments primarily engaged in retailing a general line of food.

5-YEAR TREND — ESTIMATED INDUSTRY SALES ($MILLIONS)

Year	Employee Size of Establishment									Total Industry Sales
	1-4 Emps.	5-9 Emps.	10-19 Emps.	20-49 Emps.	50-99 Emps.	100-249 Emps.	250-499 Emps.	500-999 Emps.	Unknown Emps.	
2014	92	69	175	573	1,389	3,168	913	126	17	6,523
2015	91	68	172	563	1,365	3,113	897	124	17	6,409
2016	89	67	169	552	1,338	3,051	880	121	17	6,283
2017	89	67	169	552	1,338	3,052	880	121	17	6,284
2018	89	67	169	553	1,341	3,058	882	121	17	6,297

INDUSTRY: BEER, WINE & LIQUOR STORES (NAICS 44531)
PRODUCT LINE: WINE PRODUCTS (Sub Category)

NAICS 44531: Beer & Wine & Liquor Stores. Establishments primarily engaged in the retail sale of packaged alcoholic beverages, such as ale, beer, wine, and liquor, for consumption off the premises. Stores selling prepared drinks for consumption on the premises are classified in SIC 5813.

5-YEAR TREND – ESTIMATED INDUSTRY SALES ($MILLIONS)

Year	Employee Size of Establishment									Total
	1-4 Emps.	5-9 Emps.	10-19 Emps.	20-49 Emps.	50-99 Emps.	100-249 Emps.	250-499 Emps.	500-999 Emps.	Unknown Emps.	Industry Sales
2014	2,975.2	2,889.3	2,420.8	1,766.7	231.9	170.4	0.5	88.6	167.1	10,710.4
2015	3,100.1	3,010.7	2,522.4	1,840.9	241.6	177.6	0.5	92.3	174.1	11,160.2
2016	3,219.1	3,126.2	2,619.2	1,911.5	250.9	184.4	0.5	95.9	180.8	11,588.4
2017	3,446.5	3,347.0	2,804.2	2,046.5	268.6	197.4	0.6	102.6	193.6	12,406.9
2018	3,696.0	3,589.3	3,007.2	2,194.7	288.0	211.7	0.6	110.0	207.6	13,305.1

INDUSTRY: GASOLINE STATIONS W/ CONVEN. STORES (NAICS 44711)
PRODUCT LINE: WINE PRODUCTS (Sub Category)

NAICS 44711: Gas Stations with Convenience Stores. This industry comprises establishments primarily engaged in selling gasoline and lubricating oils. These establishments frequently sell other merchandise, such as tires, batteries, and other automobile parts, or perform minor repair work. Gasoline stations combined with other activities, such as grocery stores, convenience stores, or carwashes, are classified according to the primary activity.

5-YEAR TREND – ESTIMATED INDUSTRY SALES ($MILLIONS)

Year	Employee Size of Establishment									Total
	1-4 Emps.	5-9 Emps.	10-19 Emps.	20-49 Emps.	50-99 Emps.	100-249 Emps.	250-499 Emps.	500-999 Emps.	Unknown Emps.	Industry Sales
2014	69.6	187.4	303.2	186.5	16.3	10.2	1.4	0.0	0.8	775.5
2015	74.9	201.6	326.2	200.7	17.6	11.0	1.5	0.0	0.8	834.4
2016	80.0	215.4	348.6	214.5	18.8	11.7	1.6	0.0	0.9	891.7
2017	87.3	235.0	380.3	233.9	20.5	12.8	1.8	0.0	1.0	972.6
2018	95.2	256.2	414.6	255.0	22.3	14.0	2.0	0.0	1.1	1,060.3

INDUSTRY: WAREHOUSE CLUBS & SUPERCENTERS (NAICS 45291)
PRODUCT LINE: WINE PRODUCTS (Sub Category)

NAICS 45291: Warehouse Clubs and Superstores This industry comprises establishments known as warehouse clubs, superstores or supercenters primarily engaged in retailing a general line of groceries in combination with general lines of new merchandise, such as apparel, furniture, and appliances.

5-YEAR TREND – ESTIMATED INDUSTRY SALES ($MILLIONS)

Year	Employee Size of Establishment									Total Industry Sales
	1-4 Emps.	5-9 Emps.	10-19 Emps.	20-49 Emps.	50-99 Emps.	100-249 Emps.	250-499 Emps.	500-999 Emps.	Unknown Emps.	
2014	0.5	0.0	0.1	4.7	5.9	727.3	3,215.1	84.9	1.0	4,039.5
2015	0.5	0.0	0.1	4.8	6.1	753.8	3,332.7	88.1	1.0	4,187.2
2016	0.5	0.0	0.1	5.0	6.3	779.0	3,443.8	91.0	1.1	4,326.8
2017	0.6	0.0	0.1	5.4	6.9	846.1	3,740.4	98.8	1.2	4,699.4
2018	0.6	0.0	0.1	5.8	7.3	898.5	3,972.3	104.9	1.2	4,990.8

INDUSTRY: SUPERMARKETS & GROCERY STORES (NAICS 44511)
PRODUCT LINE: BEER & ALE PRODUCTS (Sub Category)

NAICS 44511: Grocery Stores Industry. This industry comprises establishments generally known as supermarkets and grocery stores primarily engaged in retailing a general line of food, such as canned and frozen foods; fresh fruits and vegetables; and fresh and prepared meats, fish, and poultry. Included in this industry are delicatessen-type establishments primarily engaged in retailing a general line of food.

5-YEAR TREND – ESTIMATED INDUSTRY SALES ($MILLIONS)

Year	Employee Size of Establishment									Total Industry Sales
	1-4 Emps.	5-9 Emps.	10-19 Emps.	20-49 Emps.	50-99 Emps.	100-249 Emps.	250-499 Emps.	500-999 Emps.	Unknown Emps.	
2014	133	100	253	825	2,002	4,566	1,316	181	25	9,402
2015	131	98	248	811	1,967	4,487	1,293	178	25	9,239
2016	128	96	243	795	1,929	4,398	1,268	175	24	9,057
2017	128	96	243	795	1,929	4,399	1,268	175	24	9,058
2018	129	96	244	797	1,933	4,408	1,271	175	24	9,077

INDUSTRY: BEER, WINE & LIQUOR STORES (NAICS 44531)
PRODUCT LINE: BEER & ALE PRODUCTS (Sub Category)

NAICS 44531: Beer & Wine & Liquor Stores. Establishments primarily engaged in the retail sale of packaged alcoholic beverages, such as ale, beer, wine, and liquor, for consumption off the premises. Stores selling prepared drinks for consumption on the premises are classified in SIC 5813.

5-YEAR TREND — ESTIMATED INDUSTRY SALES ($MILLIONS)

Year	Employee Size of Establishment									Total Industry Sales
	1-4 Emps.	5-9 Emps.	10-19 Emps.	20-49 Emps.	50-99 Emps.	100-249 Emps.	250-499 Emps.	500-999 Emps.	Unknown Emps.	
2014	2,930.0	2,845.4	2,384.0	1,739.8	228.3	167.8	0.5	87.3	164.5	10,547.6
2015	3,053.0	2,964.9	2,484.1	1,812.9	237.9	174.9	0.5	90.9	171.5	10,990.5
2016	3,170.2	3,078.7	2,579.4	1,882.4	247.0	181.6	0.5	94.4	178.0	11,412.3
2017	3,394.1	3,296.1	2,761.6	2,015.4	264.5	194.4	0.5	101.0	190.6	12,218.3
2018	3,639.8	3,534.8	2,961.5	2,161.3	283.6	208.5	0.6	108.3	204.4	13,102.8

INDUSTRY: GASOLINE STATIONS W/ CONVEN. STORES (NAICS 44711)
PRODUCT LINE: BEER & ALE PRODUCTS (Sub Category)

NAICS 44711: Gas Stations with Convenience Stores. This industry comprises establishments primarily engaged in selling gasoline and lubricating oils. These establishments frequently sell other merchandise, such as tires, batteries, and other automobile parts, or perform minor repair work. Gasoline stations combined with other activities, such as grocery stores, convenience stores, or carwashes, are classified according to the primary activity.

5-YEAR TREND — ESTIMATED INDUSTRY SALES ($MILLIONS)

Year	Employee Size of Establishment									Total Industry Sales
	1-4 Emps.	5-9 Emps.	10-19 Emps.	20-49 Emps.	50-99 Emps.	100-249 Emps.	250-499 Emps.	500-999 Emps.	Unknown Emps.	
2014	1,236.1	3,327.5	5,385.3	3,312.7	290.1	181.3	25.5	0.6	14.0	13,773.1
2015	1,329.9	3,580.0	5,793.8	3,564.0	312.1	195.1	27.4	0.7	15.1	14,818.1
2016	1,421.2	3,825.8	6,191.6	3,808.7	333.5	208.5	29.3	0.7	16.1	15,835.5
2017	1,550.2	4,173.0	6,753.5	4,154.3	363.8	227.4	31.9	0.8	17.6	17,272.5
2018	1,690.0	4,549.4	7,362.6	4,529.0	396.6	247.9	34.8	0.9	19.1	18,830.3

INDUSTRY: WAREHOUSE CLUBS & SUPERCENTERS (NAICS 45291)
PRODUCT LINE: BEER & ALE PRODUCTS (Sub Category)

NAICS 45291: Warehouse Clubs and Superstores This industry comprises establishments known as warehouse clubs, superstores or supercenters primarily engaged in retailing a general line of groceries in combination with general lines of new merchandise, such as apparel, furniture, and appliances.

5-YEAR TREND – ESTIMATED INDUSTRY SALES ($MILLIONS)

Year	Employee Size of Establishment									Total Industry Sales
	1-4 Emps.	5-9 Emps.	10-19 Emps.	20-49 Emps.	50-99 Emps.	100-249 Emps.	250-499 Emps.	500-999 Emps.	Unknown Emps.	
2014	1	0	0	5	6	770	3,406	90	1	4,279
2015	1	0	0	5	6	799	3,531	93	1	4,436
2016	1	0	0	5	7	825	3,648	96	1	4,584
2017	1	0	0	6	7	896	3,962	105	1	4,978
2018	1	0	0	6	8	952	4,208	111	1	5,287

INDUSTRY: SUPERMARKETS & GROCERY STORES (NAICS 44511)
PRODUCT LINE: DRUGS & HEALTH/BEAUTY AIDS (Main Category)

NAICS 44511: Grocery Stores Industry. This industry comprises establishments generally known as supermarkets and grocery stores primarily engaged in retailing a general line of food, such as canned and frozen foods; fresh fruits and vegetables; and fresh and prepared meats, fish, and poultry. Included in this industry are delicatessen-type establishments primarily engaged in retailing a general line of food.

5-YEAR TREND – ESTIMATED INDUSTRY SALES ($MILLIONS)

Year	Employee Size of Establishment									Total Industry Sales
	1-4 Emps.	5-9 Emps.	10-19 Emps.	20-49 Emps.	50-99 Emps.	100-249 Emps.	250-499 Emps.	500-999 Emps.	Unknown Emps.	
2014	735	550	1,395	4,558	11,056	25,212	7,268	1,002	139	51,916
2015	723	541	1,371	4,479	10,864	24,775	7,142	985	137	51,016
2016	708	530	1,344	4,391	10,650	24,287	7,002	965	134	50,012
2017	708	530	1,344	4,391	10,652	24,291	7,003	965	134	50,018
2018	710	531	1,347	4,401	10,674	24,342	7,017	966	134	50,122

INDUSTRY: BEER, WINE & LIQUOR STORES (NAICS 44531)
PRODUCT LINE: DRUGS & HEALTH/BEAUTY AIDS (Main Category)

NAICS 44531: Beer & Wine & Liquor Stores. Establishments primarily engaged in the retail sale of packaged alcoholic beverages, such as ale, beer, wine, and liquor, for consumption off the premises. Stores selling prepared drinks for consumption on the premises are classified in SIC 5813.

5-YEAR TREND — ESTIMATED INDUSTRY SALES ($MILLIONS)

Year	Employee Size of Establishment									Total Industry Sales
	1-4 Emps.	5-9 Emps.	10-19 Emps.	20-49 Emps.	50-99 Emps.	100-249 Emps.	250-499 Emps.	500-999 Emps.	Unknown Emps.	
2014	37.0	35.9	30.1	22.0	2.9	2.1	0.0	1.1	2.1	133.1
2015	38.5	37.4	31.3	22.9	3.0	2.2	0.0	1.1	2.2	138.7
2016	40.0	38.8	32.5	23.7	3.1	2.3	0.0	1.2	2.2	144.0
2017	42.8	41.6	34.8	25.4	3.3	2.5	0.0	1.3	2.4	154.2
2018	45.9	44.6	37.4	27.3	3.6	2.6	0.0	1.4	2.6	165.3

INDUSTRY: PHARMACIES & DRUG STORES (NAICS 44611)
PRODUCT LINE: DRUGS & HEALTH/BEAUTY AIDS (Main Category)

NAICS 44611 Pharmacies and Drug Stores – This industry comprises establishments known as pharmacies and drug stores engaged in retailing prescription or nonprescription drugs and medicines.

5-YEAR TREND — ESTIMATED INDUSTRY SALES ($MILLIONS)

Year	Employee Size of Establishment									Total Industry Sales
	1-4 Emps.	5-9 Emps.	10-19 Emps.	20-49 Emps.	50-99 Emps.	100-249 Emps.	250-499 Emps.	500-999 Emps.	Unknown Emps.	
2014	3,337	8,332	35,192	99,455	9,342	3,669	1,137	458	279	161,202
2015	3,512	8,768	37,033	104,660	9,831	3,861	1,197	482	294	169,639
2016	3,680	9,188	38,805	109,666	10,301	4,046	1,254	505	308	177,753
2017	3,957	9,880	41,727	117,925	11,077	4,351	1,348	528	331	191,124
2018	4,260	10,635	44,918	126,944	11,924	4,683	1,452	549	356	205,722

INDUSTRY: GASOLINE STATIONS W/ CONVEN. STORES (NAICS 44711)
PRODUCT LINE: DRUGS & HEALTH/BEAUTY AIDS (Main Category)

NAICS 44711: Gas Stations with Convenience Stores. This industry comprises establishments primarily engaged in selling gasoline and lubricating oils. These establishments frequently sell other merchandise, such as tires, batteries, and other automobile parts, or perform minor repair work. Gasoline stations combined with other activities, such as grocery stores, convenience stores, or carwashes, are classified according to the primary activity.

5-YEAR TREND — ESTIMATED INDUSTRY SALES ($MILLIONS)

Year	Employee Size of Establishment									Total Industry Sales
	1-4 Emps.	5-9 Emps.	10-19 Emps.	20-49 Emps.	50-99 Emps.	100-249 Emps.	250-499 Emps.	500-999 Emps.	Unknown Emps.	
2014	155.2	417.7	676.1	415.9	36.4	22.8	3.2	0.1	1.8	1,729.1
2015	167.0	449.4	727.4	447.4	39.2	24.5	3.4	0.1	1.9	1,860.3
2016	178.4	480.3	777.3	478.1	41.9	26.2	3.7	0.1	2.0	1,988.0
2017	194.6	523.9	847.8	521.5	45.7	28.5	4.0	0.1	2.2	2,168.4
2018	212.2	571.1	924.3	568.6	49.8	31.1	4.4	0.1	2.4	2,364.0

INDUSTRY: WOMEN'S CLOTHING STORES (NAICS 44812)
PRODUCT LINE: DRUGS & HEALTH/BEAUTY AIDS (Main Category)

NAICS 44812: Women's Clothing Stores . This industry comprises establishments primarily engaged in retailing a general line of new women's, misses' and juniors' clothing, including maternity wear. These establishments may provide basic alterations, such as hemming, taking in or letting out seams, or lengthening or shortening sleeves.

5-YEAR TREND — ESTIMATED INDUSTRY SALES ($MILLIONS)

Year	Employee Size of Establishment									Total Industry Sales
	1-4 Emps.	5-9 Emps.	10-19 Emps.	20-49 Emps.	50-99 Emps.	100-249 Emps.	250-499 Emps.	500-999 Emps.	Unknown Emps.	
2014	55.5	125.9	308.5	211.2	65.9	64.1	24.0	21.8	12.9	889.9
2015	57.7	130.8	320.4	219.4	68.5	66.6	24.9	22.6	13.4	924.3
2016	59.7	135.4	331.7	227.1	70.9	69.0	25.8	23.4	13.8	956.9
2017	63.5	144.0	352.7	241.5	75.4	73.3	27.5	24.6	14.7	1,017.0
2018	67.6	153.3	375.6	257.2	80.3	78.1	29.2	25.8	15.7	1,082.8

INDUSTRY: DEPARTMENT STORES (NAICS 45211)
PRODUCT LINE: DRUGS & HEALTH/BEAUTY AIDS (Main Category)

NAICS 45211: Department Stores Industry . This industry comprises establishments known as department stores primarily engaged in retailing a wide range of the following new products with no one merchandise line predominating: apparel, furniture, appliances and home furnishings; and selected additional items, such as paint, hardware, toiletries, cosmetics, photographic equipment, jewelry, toys, and sporting goods. Merchandise lines are normally arranged in separate departments.

5-YEAR TREND — ESTIMATED INDUSTRY SALES ($MILLIONS)

Year	Employee Size of Establishment									Total
	1-4 Emps.	5-9 Emps.	10-19 Emps.	20-49 Emps.	50-99 Emps.	100-249 Emps.	250-499 Emps.	500-999 Emps.	Unknown Emps.	Industry Sales
2014	1	0	2	151	2,862	9,493	4,165	558	24	17,256
2015	1	0	2	153	2,899	9,616	4,218	565	24	17,479
2016	1	0	2	154	2,930	9,719	4,264	571	25	17,667
2017	1	0	2	155	2,944	9,764	4,283	574	25	17,749
2018	1	0	2	156	2,965	9,834	4,314	578	25	17,877

INDUSTRY: WAREHOUSE CLUBS & SUPERCENTERS (NAICS 45291)
PRODUCT LINE: DRUGS & HEALTH/BEAUTY AIDS (Main Category)

NAICS 45291: Warehouse Clubs and Superstores This industry comprises establishments known as warehouse clubs, superstores or supercenters primarily engaged in retailing a general line of groceries in combination with general lines of new merchandise, such as apparel, furniture, and appliances.

5-YEAR TREND — ESTIMATED INDUSTRY SALES ($MILLIONS)

Year	Employee Size of Establishment									Total
	1-4 Emps.	5-9 Emps.	10-19 Emps.	20-49 Emps.	50-99 Emps.	100-249 Emps.	250-499 Emps.	500-999 Emps.	Unknown Emps.	Industry Sales
2014	8	0	1	75	95	11,726	51,841	1,370	16	65,133
2015	8	0	1	78	98	12,155	53,736	1,420	17	67,514
2016	9	0	1	81	102	12,560	55,528	1,467	17	69,765
2017	9	0	2	88	110	13,642	60,310	1,593	19	75,774
2018	10	0	2	93	117	14,488	64,049	1,692	20	80,472

INDUSTRY: ELECTRONIC SHOPPING & MAIL ORDER (NAICS 45411)
PRODUCT LINE: DRUGS & HEALTH/BEAUTY AIDS (Main Category)

NAICS 45411: Electronic Shopping and Mail-Order Houses This industry comprises establishments primarily engaged in retailing all types of merchandise by means of mail or by electronic media, such as interactive television or computer. Included in this industry are establishments primarily engaged in retailing from catalogue showrooms of mail-order houses.

5-YEAR TREND — ESTIMATED INDUSTRY SALES ($MILLIONS)

Year	Employee Size of Establishment									Total Industry Sales
	1-4 Emps.	5-9 Emps.	10-19 Emps.	20-49 Emps.	50-99 Emps.	100-249 Emps.	250-499 Emps.	500-999 Emps.	Unknown Emps.	
2014	7,865	4,175	6,200	10,031	7,215	14,067	20,582	26,072	1,189	97,398
2015	8,389	4,454	6,614	10,700	7,697	15,006	21,955	27,812	1,269	103,896
2016	8,898	4,724	7,015	11,350	8,164	15,916	23,287	29,499	1,346	110,199
2017	10,125	5,376	7,983	12,915	9,290	18,111	26,499	32,745	1,531	124,575
2018	11,246	5,971	8,867	14,345	10,318	20,116	29,432	35,740	1,701	137,735

INDUSTRY: SUPERMARKETS & GROCERY STORES (NAICS 44511)
PRODUCT LINE: PRESCRIPTIONS (Sub Category)

NAICS 44511: Grocery Stores Industry. This industry comprises establishments generally known as supermarkets and grocery stores primarily engaged in retailing a general line of food, such as canned and frozen foods; fresh fruits and vegetables; and fresh and prepared meats, fish, and poultry. Included in this industry are delicatessen-type establishments primarily engaged in retailing a general line of food.

5-YEAR TREND — ESTIMATED INDUSTRY SALES ($MILLIONS)

Year	Employee Size of Establishment									Total Industry Sales
	1-4 Emps.	5-9 Emps.	10-19 Emps.	20-49 Emps.	50-99 Emps.	100-249 Emps.	250-499 Emps.	500-999 Emps.	Unknown Emps.	
2014	376	281	713	2,329	5,649	12,883	3,714	512	71	26,529
2015	369	276	701	2,289	5,551	12,660	3,650	503	70	26,068
2016	362	271	687	2,244	5,442	12,411	3,578	493	68	25,555
2017	362	271	687	2,244	5,443	12,412	3,578	493	68	25,559
2018	363	271	688	2,249	5,454	12,438	3,586	494	69	25,612

INDUSTRY: PHARMACIES & DRUG STORES (NAICS 44611)
PRODUCT LINE: PRESCRIPTIONS (Sub Category)

NAICS 44611 Pharmacies and Drug Stores – This industry comprises establishments known as pharmacies and drug stores engaged in retailing prescription or nonprescription drugs and medicines.

5-YEAR TREND – ESTIMATED INDUSTRY SALES ($MILLIONS)

Year	Employee Size of Establishment									Total Industry Sales
	1-4 Emps.	5-9 Emps.	10-19 Emps.	20-49 Emps.	50-99 Emps.	100-249 Emps.	250-499 Emps.	500-999 Emps.	Unknown Emps.	
2014	2,805	7,003	29,578	83,591	7,852	3,084	956	385	235	135,488
2015	2,952	7,370	31,126	87,965	8,263	3,245	1,006	405	247	142,579
2016	3,093	7,722	32,615	92,173	8,658	3,401	1,054	424	259	149,398
2017	3,326	8,304	35,071	99,114	9,310	3,657	1,133	443	278	160,636
2018	3,580	8,939	37,753	106,694	10,022	3,936	1,220	462	299	172,906

INDUSTRY: DEPARTMENT STORES (NAICS 45211)
PRODUCT LINE: PRESCRIPTIONS (Sub Category)

NAICS 45211: Department Stores Industry . This industry comprises establishments known as department stores primarily engaged in retailing a wide range of the following new products with no one merchandise line predominating: apparel, furniture, appliances and home furnishings; and selected additional items, such as paint, hardware, toiletries, cosmetics, photographic equipment, jewelry, toys, and sporting goods. Merchandise lines are normally arranged in separate departments.

5-YEAR TREND – ESTIMATED INDUSTRY SALES ($MILLIONS)

Year	Employee Size of Establishment									Total Industry Sales
	1-4 Emps.	5-9 Emps.	10-19 Emps.	20-49 Emps.	50-99 Emps.	100-249 Emps.	250-499 Emps.	500-999 Emps.	Unknown Emps.	
2014	0	0	1	43	824	2,732	1,198	160	7	4,966
2015	0	0	1	44	834	2,767	1,214	163	7	5,030
2016	0	0	1	44	843	2,797	1,227	164	7	5,084
2017	0	0	1	45	847	2,810	1,233	165	7	5,108
2018	0	0	1	45	853	2,830	1,242	166	7	5,145

INDUSTRY: WAREHOUSE CLUBS & SUPERCENTERS (NAICS 45291)
PRODUCT LINE: PRESCRIPTIONS (Sub Category)

NAICS 45291: Warehouse Clubs and Superstores This industry comprises establishments known as warehouse clubs, superstores or supercenters primarily engaged in retailing a general line of groceries in combination with general lines of new merchandise, such as apparel, furniture, and appliances.

5-YEAR TREND – ESTIMATED INDUSTRY SALES ($MILLIONS)

Year	Employee Size of Establishment									Total
	1-4 Emps.	5-9 Emps.	10-19 Emps.	20-49 Emps.	50-99 Emps.	100-249 Emps.	250-499 Emps.	500-999 Emps.	Unknown Emps.	Industry Sales
2014	2.5	0.1	0.4	23.5	29.6	3,650.6	16,138.8	426.4	5.0	20,276.9
2015	2.6	0.1	0.4	24.3	30.6	3,784.1	16,728.8	442.0	5.2	21,018.2
2016	2.7	0.1	0.5	25.1	31.7	3,910.2	17,286.6	456.7	5.4	21,719.0
2017	2.9	0.1	0.5	27.3	34.4	4,247.0	18,775.4	496.1	5.8	23,589.6
2018	3.1	0.1	0.5	29.0	36.5	4,510.3	19,939.5	526.8	6.2	25,052.1

INDUSTRY: ELECTRONIC SHOPPING & MAIL ORDER (NAICS 45411)
PRODUCT LINE: PRESCRIPTIONS (Sub Category)

NAICS 45411: Electronic Shopping and Mail-Order Houses This industry comprises establishments primarily engaged in retailing all types of merchandise by means of mail or by electronic media, such as interactive television or computer. Included in this industry are establishments primarily engaged in retailing from catalogue showrooms of mail-order houses.

5-YEAR TREND – ESTIMATED INDUSTRY SALES ($MILLIONS)

Year	Employee Size of Establishment									Total
	1-4 Emps.	5-9 Emps.	10-19 Emps.	20-49 Emps.	50-99 Emps.	100-249 Emps.	250-499 Emps.	500-999 Emps.	Unknown Emps.	Industry Sales
2014	6,091	3,234	4,802	7,769	5,588	10,894	15,940	20,192	921	75,429
2015	6,497	3,449	5,122	8,287	5,961	11,621	17,003	21,539	983	80,462
2016	6,891	3,659	5,433	8,790	6,322	12,326	18,035	22,846	1,042	85,344
2017	7,842	4,163	6,182	10,002	7,194	14,026	20,522	25,359	1,186	96,477
2018	8,710	4,624	6,867	11,109	7,991	15,579	22,794	27,679	1,317	106,669

INDUSTRY: SUPERMARKETS & GROCERY STORES (NAICS 44511)
PRODUCT LINE: NON-PRESCRIPTION MEDICINES (Sub Category)

NAICS 44511: Grocery Stores Industry. This industry comprises establishments generally known as supermarkets and grocery stores primarily engaged in retailing a general line of food, such as canned and frozen foods; fresh fruits and vegetables; and fresh and prepared meats, fish, and poultry. Included in this industry are delicatessen-type establishments primarily engaged in retailing a general line of food.

5-YEAR TREND — ESTIMATED INDUSTRY SALES ($MILLIONS)

Year	Employee Size of Establishment									Total Industry Sales
	1-4 Emps.	5-9 Emps.	10-19 Emps.	20-49 Emps.	50-99 Emps.	100-249 Emps.	250-499 Emps.	500-999 Emps.	Unknown Emps.	
2014	55.1	41.2	104.5	341.3	827.8	1,887.7	544.2	75.0	10.4	3,887.2
2015	54.1	40.5	102.7	335.4	813.4	1,855.0	534.8	73.7	10.2	3,819.8
2016	53.0	39.7	100.6	328.7	797.4	1,818.5	524.2	72.3	10.0	3,744.6
2017	53.0	39.7	100.7	328.8	797.5	1,818.7	524.3	72.2	10.0	3,745.0
2018	53.2	39.8	100.9	329.5	799.2	1,822.6	525.4	72.3	10.1	3,752.8

INDUSTRY: PHARMACIES & DRUG STORES (NAICS 44611)
PRODUCT LINE: NON-PRESCRIPTION MEDICINES (Sub Category)

NAICS 44611 Pharmacies and Drug Stores – This industry comprises establishments known as pharmacies and drug stores engaged in retailing prescription or nonprescription drugs and medicines.

5-YEAR TREND — ESTIMATED INDUSTRY SALES ($MILLIONS)

Year	Employee Size of Establishment									Total Industry Sales
	1-4 Emps.	5-9 Emps.	10-19 Emps.	20-49 Emps.	50-99 Emps.	100-249 Emps.	250-499 Emps.	500-999 Emps.	Unknown Emps.	
2014	221.1	552.1	2,331.8	6,589.8	619.0	243.1	75.3	30.3	18.5	10,681.1
2015	232.7	581.0	2,453.8	6,934.7	651.4	255.8	79.3	31.9	19.5	11,240.0
2016	243.8	608.8	2,571.2	7,266.4	682.5	268.1	83.1	33.5	20.4	11,777.7
2017	262.2	654.6	2,764.8	7,813.6	733.9	288.3	89.3	35.0	21.9	12,663.6
2018	282.3	704.7	2,976.2	8,411.1	790.1	310.3	96.2	36.4	23.6	13,630.9

INDUSTRY: DEPARTMENT STORES (NAICS 45211)
PRODUCT LINE: NON-PRESCRIPTION MEDICINES (Sub Category)

NAICS 45211: Department Stores Industry . This industry comprises
establishments known as department stores primarily engaged in retailing
a wide range of the following new products with no one merchandise line
predominating: apparel, furniture, appliances and home furnishings; and
selected additional items, such as paint, hardware, toiletries, cosmetics,
photographic equipment, jewelry, toys, and sporting goods. Merchandise lines
are normally arranged in separate departments.

5-YEAR TREND – ESTIMATED INDUSTRY SALES ($MILLIONS)

Year	Employee Size of Establishment									Total
	1-4 Emps.	5-9 Emps.	10-19 Emps.	20-49 Emps.	50-99 Emps.	100-249 Emps.	250-499 Emps.	500-999 Emps.	Unknown Emps.	Industry Sales
2014	0.1	0.0	0.1	7.5	141.5	469.3	205.9	27.6	1.2	853.1
2015	0.1	0.0	0.1	7.5	143.3	475.4	208.5	27.9	1.2	864.1
2016	0.1	0.0	0.1	7.6	144.9	480.5	210.8	28.2	1.2	873.4
2017	0.1	0.0	0.1	7.7	145.5	482.7	211.8	28.4	1.2	877.5
2018	0.1	0.0	0.1	7.7	146.6	486.2	213.3	28.6	1.2	883.8

INDUSTRY: WAREHOUSE CLUBS & SUPERCENTERS (NAICS 45291)
PRODUCT LINE: NON-PRESCRIPTION MEDICINES (Sub Category)

NAICS 45291: Warehouse Clubs and Superstores This industry
comprises establishments known as warehouse clubs, superstores or
supercenters primarily engaged in retailing a general line of groceries
in combination with general lines of new merchandise, such as apparel,
furniture, and appliances.

5-YEAR TREND – ESTIMATED INDUSTRY SALES ($MILLIONS)

Year	Employee Size of Establishment									Total
	1-4 Emps.	5-9 Emps.	10-19 Emps.	20-49 Emps.	50-99 Emps.	100-249 Emps.	250-499 Emps.	500-999 Emps.	Unknown Emps.	Industry Sales
2014	0.9	0.0	0.2	8.1	10.3	1,267.5	5,603.4	148.0	1.7	7,040.2
2015	0.9	0.0	0.2	8.4	10.6	1,313.8	5,808.3	153.5	1.8	7,297.6
2016	0.9	0.0	0.2	8.7	11.0	1,357.6	6,001.9	158.6	1.9	7,540.9
2017	1.0	0.0	0.2	9.5	11.9	1,474.6	6,518.9	172.2	2.0	8,190.3
2018	1.1	0.0	0.2	10.1	12.7	1,566.0	6,923.0	182.9	2.2	8,698.1

INDUSTRY: ELECTRONIC SHOPPING & MAIL ORDER (NAICS 45411)
PRODUCT LINE: NON-PRESCRIPTION MEDICINES (Sub Category)

NAICS 45411: Electronic Shopping and Mail-Order Houses This industry comprises establishments primarily engaged in retailing all types of merchandise by means of mail or by electronic media, such as interactive television or computer. Included in this industry are establishments primarily engaged in retailing from catalogue showrooms of mail-order houses.

5-YEAR TREND — ESTIMATED INDUSTRY SALES ($MILLIONS)

Year	Employee Size of Establishment									Total
	1-4 Emps.	5-9 Emps.	10-19 Emps.	20-49 Emps.	50-99 Emps.	100-249 Emps.	250-499 Emps.	500-999 Emps.	Unknown Emps.	Industry Sales
2014	149.8	79.6	118.1	191.1	137.5	268.0	392.1	496.7	22.7	1,855.7
2015	159.8	84.9	126.0	203.9	146.6	285.9	418.3	529.9	24.2	1,979.5
2016	169.5	90.0	133.7	216.2	155.5	303.2	443.7	562.0	25.6	2,099.6
2017	192.9	102.4	152.1	246.1	177.0	345.1	504.9	623.9	29.2	2,373.5
2018	214.3	113.8	168.9	273.3	196.6	383.3	560.8	680.9	32.4	2,624.2

INDUSTRY: SUPERMARKETS & GROCERY STORES (NAICS 44511)
PRODUCT LINE: VITAMINS, MINERALS & SUPPLEMENTS (Sub Category)

NAICS 44511: Grocery Stores Industry. This industry comprises establishments generally known as supermarkets and grocery stores primarily engaged in retailing a general line of food, such as canned and frozen foods; fresh fruits and vegetables; and fresh and prepared meats, fish, and poultry. Included in this industry are delicatessen-type establishments primarily engaged in retailing a general line of food.

5-YEAR TREND — ESTIMATED INDUSTRY SALES ($MILLIONS)

Year	Employee Size of Establishment									Total
	1-4 Emps.	5-9 Emps.	10-19 Emps.	20-49 Emps.	50-99 Emps.	100-249 Emps.	250-499 Emps.	500-999 Emps.	Unknown Emps.	Industry Sales
2014	44.2	33.1	83.8	273.9	664.4	1,515.1	436.8	60.2	8.4	3,119.7
2015	43.4	32.5	82.4	269.1	652.8	1,488.8	429.2	59.2	8.2	3,065.6
2016	42.6	31.9	80.8	263.8	640.0	1,459.5	420.7	58.0	8.1	3,005.3
2017	42.6	31.9	80.8	263.9	640.1	1,459.7	420.8	58.0	8.1	3,005.7
2018	42.7	31.9	80.9	264.4	641.4	1,462.7	421.7	58.0	8.1	3,011.9

INDUSTRY: PHARMACIES & DRUG STORES (NAICS 44611)
PRODUCT LINE: VITAMINS, MINERALS & SUPPLEMENTS (Sub Category)

NAICS 44611 Pharmacies and Drug Stores – This industry comprises
establishments known as pharmacies and drug stores engaged in retailing
prescription or nonprescription drugs and medicines.

5-YEAR TREND – ESTIMATED INDUSTRY SALES ($MILLIONS)

Year	Employee Size of Establishment									Total
	1-4 Emps.	5-9 Emps.	10-19 Emps.	20-49 Emps.	50-99 Emps.	100-249 Emps.	250-499 Emps.	500-999 Emps.	Unknown Emps.	Industry Sales
2014	42.0	104.9	443.1	1,252.2	117.6	46.2	14.3	5.8	3.5	2,029.7
2015	44.2	110.4	466.3	1,317.8	123.8	48.6	15.1	6.1	3.7	2,135.9
2016	46.3	115.7	488.6	1,380.8	129.7	50.9	15.8	6.4	3.9	2,238.1
2017	49.8	124.4	525.4	1,484.8	139.5	54.8	17.0	6.6	4.2	2,406.4
2018	53.6	133.9	565.6	1,598.3	150.1	59.0	18.3	6.9	4.5	2,590.2

INDUSTRY: DEPARTMENT STORES (NAICS 45211)
PRODUCT LINE: VITAMINS, MINERALS & SUPPLEMENTS (Sub Category)

NAICS 45211: Department Stores Industry . This industry comprises
establishments known as department stores primarily engaged in retailing
a wide range of the following new products with no one merchandise line
predominating: apparel, furniture, appliances and home furnishings; and
selected additional items, such as paint, hardware, toiletries, cosmetics,
photographic equipment, jewelry, toys, and sporting goods. Merchandise lines
are normally arranged in separate departments.

5-YEAR TREND – ESTIMATED INDUSTRY SALES ($MILLIONS)

Year	Employee Size of Establishment									Total
	1-4 Emps.	5-9 Emps.	10-19 Emps.	20-49 Emps.	50-99 Emps.	100-249 Emps.	250-499 Emps.	500-999 Emps.	Unknown Emps.	Industry Sales
2014	0.0	0.0	0.1	5.7	108.9	361.3	158.5	21.2	0.9	656.8
2015	0.0	0.0	0.1	5.8	110.3	366.0	160.6	21.5	0.9	665.3
2016	0.0	0.0	0.1	5.9	111.5	369.9	162.3	21.7	0.9	672.4
2017	0.0	0.0	0.1	5.9	112.0	371.6	163.0	21.9	0.9	675.6
2018	0.1	0.0	0.1	5.9	112.9	374.3	164.2	22.0	1.0	680.4

INDUSTRY: WAREHOUSE CLUBS & SUPERCENTERS (NAICS 45291)
PRODUCT LINE: VITAMINS, MINERALS & SUPPLEMENTS (Sub Category)

NAICS 45291: Warehouse Clubs and Superstores This industry comprises establishments known as warehouse clubs, superstores or supercenters primarily engaged in retailing a general line of groceries in combination with general lines of new merchandise, such as apparel, furniture, and appliances.

5-Year Trend – Estimated Industry Sales ($Millions)

Year	Employee Size of Establishment									Total
	1-4 Emps.	5-9 Emps.	10-19 Emps.	20-49 Emps.	50-99 Emps.	100-249 Emps.	250-499 Emps.	500-999 Emps.	Unknown Emps.	Industry Sales
2014	0.6	0.0	0.1	5.4	6.8	837.4	3,701.9	97.8	1.2	4,651.1
2015	0.6	0.0	0.1	5.6	7.0	868.0	3,837.3	101.4	1.2	4,821.2
2016	0.6	0.0	0.1	5.8	7.3	896.9	3,965.2	104.8	1.2	4,981.9
2017	0.7	0.0	0.1	6.3	7.9	974.2	4,306.7	113.8	1.3	5,411.0
2018	0.7	0.0	0.1	6.7	8.4	1,034.6	4,573.7	120.8	1.4	5,746.5

INDUSTRY: ELECTRONIC SHOPPING & MAIL ORDER (NAICS 45411)
PRODUCT LINE: VITAMINS, MINERALS & SUPPLEMENTS (Sub Category)

NAICS 45411: Electronic Shopping and Mail-Order Houses This industry comprises establishments primarily engaged in retailing all types of merchandise by means of mail or by electronic media, such as interactive television or computer. Included in this industry are establishments primarily engaged in retailing from catalogue showrooms of mail-order houses.

5-Year Trend – Estimated Industry Sales ($Millions)

Year	Employee Size of Establishment									Total
	1-4 Emps.	5-9 Emps.	10-19 Emps.	20-49 Emps.	50-99 Emps.	100-249 Emps.	250-499 Emps.	500-999 Emps.	Unknown Emps.	Industry Sales
2014	895.3	475.3	705.9	1,142.0	821.4	1,601.4	2,343.1	2,968.2	135.4	11,088.1
2015	955.1	507.1	753.0	1,218.2	876.2	1,708.3	2,499.5	3,166.2	144.4	11,827.9
2016	1,013.0	537.8	798.7	1,292.1	929.4	1,811.9	2,651.1	3,358.3	153.2	12,545.5
2017	1,152.7	612.0	908.8	1,470.3	1,057.6	2,061.8	3,016.7	3,727.8	174.3	14,182.1
2018	1,280.3	679.7	1,009.4	1,633.0	1,174.6	2,290.0	3,350.7	4,068.8	193.6	15,680.3

INDUSTRY: SUPERMARKETS & GROCERY STORES (NAICS 44511)
PRODUCT LINE: HEALTH AIDS/FIRST-AID PRODUCTS (Sub Category)

NAICS 44511: Grocery Stores Industry. This industry comprises establishments generally known as supermarkets and grocery stores primarily engaged in retailing a general line of food, such as canned and frozen foods; fresh fruits and vegetables; and fresh and prepared meats, fish, and poultry. Included in this industry are delicatessen-type establishments primarily engaged in retailing a general line of food.

5-YEAR TREND – ESTIMATED INDUSTRY SALES ($MILLIONS)

Year	Employee Size of Establishment									Total Industry Sales
	1-4 Emps.	5-9 Emps.	10-19 Emps.	20-49 Emps.	50-99 Emps.	100-249 Emps.	250-499 Emps.	500-999 Emps.	Unknown Emps.	
2014	41.8	31.3	79.3	259.1	628.6	1,433.5	413.2	57.0	7.9	2,951.7
2015	41.1	30.7	78.0	254.6	617.7	1,408.6	406.1	56.0	7.8	2,900.5
2016	40.3	30.1	76.4	249.6	605.5	1,380.9	398.1	54.9	7.6	2,843.4
2017	40.3	30.1	76.4	249.7	605.6	1,381.1	398.1	54.9	7.6	2,843.8
2018	40.4	30.2	76.6	250.2	606.9	1,384.0	399.0	54.9	7.6	2,849.7

INDUSTRY: PHARMACIES & DRUG STORES (NAICS 44611)
PRODUCT LINE: HEALTH AIDS/FIRST-AID PRODUCTS (Sub Category)

NAICS 44611 Pharmacies and Drug Stores – This industry comprises establishments known as pharmacies and drug stores engaged in retailing prescription or nonprescription drugs and medicines.

5-YEAR TREND – ESTIMATED INDUSTRY SALES ($MILLIONS)

Year	Employee Size of Establishment									Total Industry Sales
	1-4 Emps.	5-9 Emps.	10-19 Emps.	20-49 Emps.	50-99 Emps.	100-249 Emps.	250-499 Emps.	500-999 Emps.	Unknown Emps.	
2014	71.5	178.5	753.9	2,130.5	200.1	78.6	24.4	9.8	6.0	3,453.2
2015	75.2	187.8	793.3	2,242.0	210.6	82.7	25.6	10.3	6.3	3,634.0
2016	78.8	196.8	831.3	2,349.2	220.7	86.7	26.9	10.8	6.6	3,807.8
2017	84.8	211.6	893.9	2,526.2	237.3	93.2	28.9	11.3	7.1	4,094.2
2018	91.3	227.8	962.2	2,719.4	255.4	100.3	31.1	11.8	7.6	4,406.9

INDUSTRY: DEPARTMENT STORES (NAICS 45211)
PRODUCT LINE: HEALTH AIDS/FIRST-AID PRODUCTS (Sub Category)

NAICS 45211: Department Stores Industry . This industry comprises establishments known as department stores primarily engaged in retailing a wide range of the following new products with no one merchandise line predominating: apparel, furniture, appliances and home furnishings; and selected additional items, such as paint, hardware, toiletries, cosmetics, photographic equipment, jewelry, toys, and sporting goods. Merchandise lines are normally arranged in separate departments.

5-YEAR TREND – ESTIMATED INDUSTRY SALES ($MILLIONS)

Year	Employee Size of Establishment									Total Industry Sales
	1-4 Emps.	5-9 Emps.	10-19 Emps.	20-49 Emps.	50-99 Emps.	100-249 Emps.	250-499 Emps.	500-999 Emps.	Unknown Emps.	
2014	0.0	0.0	0.1	4.8	91.6	303.9	133.3	17.9	0.8	552.4
2015	0.0	0.0	0.1	4.9	92.8	307.8	135.0	18.1	0.8	559.6
2016	0.0	0.0	0.1	4.9	93.8	311.1	136.5	18.3	0.8	565.6
2017	0.0	0.0	0.1	5.0	94.2	312.6	137.1	18.4	0.8	568.2
2018	0.0	0.0	0.1	5.0	94.9	314.8	138.1	18.5	0.8	572.3

INDUSTRY: WAREHOUSE CLUBS & SUPERCENTERS (NAICS 45291)
PRODUCT LINE: HEALTH AIDS/FIRST-AID PRODUCTS (Sub Category)

NAICS 45291: Warehouse Clubs and Superstores This industry comprises establishments known as warehouse clubs, superstores or supercenters primarily engaged in retailing a general line of groceries in combination with general lines of new merchandise, such as apparel, furniture, and appliances.

5-YEAR TREND – ESTIMATED INDUSTRY SALES ($MILLIONS)

Year	Employee Size of Establishment									Total Industry Sales
	1-4 Emps.	5-9 Emps.	10-19 Emps.	20-49 Emps.	50-99 Emps.	100-249 Emps.	250-499 Emps.	500-999 Emps.	Unknown Emps.	
2014	0.7	0.0	0.1	6.2	7.9	969.2	4,284.7	113.2	1.3	5,383.4
2015	0.7	0.0	0.1	6.5	8.1	1,004.6	4,441.4	117.3	1.4	5,580.2
2016	0.7	0.0	0.1	6.7	8.4	1,038.1	4,589.5	121.3	1.4	5,766.2
2017	0.8	0.0	0.1	7.2	9.1	1,127.5	4,984.7	131.7	1.6	6,262.8
2018	0.8	0.0	0.1	7.7	9.7	1,197.5	5,293.8	139.9	1.6	6,651.1

INDUSTRY: ELECTRONIC SHOPPING & MAIL ORDER (NAICS 45411)
PRODUCT LINE: HEALTH AIDS/FIRST-AID PRODUCTS (Sub Category)

NAICS 45411: Electronic Shopping and Mail-Order Houses This industry comprises establishments primarily engaged in retailing all types of merchandise by means of mail or by electronic media, such as interactive television or computer. Included in this industry are establishments primarily engaged in retailing from catalogue showrooms of mail-order houses.

5-YEAR TREND — ESTIMATED INDUSTRY SALES ($MILLIONS)

Year	Employee Size of Establishment									Total Industry Sales
	1-4 Emps.	5-9 Emps.	10-19 Emps.	20-49 Emps.	50-99 Emps.	100-249 Emps.	250-499 Emps.	500-999 Emps.	Unknown Emps.	
2014	315.0	167.2	248.3	401.7	289.0	563.4	824.3	1,044.2	47.6	3,900.7
2015	336.0	178.4	264.9	428.5	308.3	601.0	879.3	1,113.9	50.8	4,161.0
2016	356.4	189.2	281.0	454.5	327.0	637.4	932.6	1,181.4	53.9	4,413.4
2017	405.5	215.3	319.7	517.2	372.0	725.3	1,061.3	1,311.4	61.3	4,989.2
2018	450.4	239.1	355.1	574.5	413.2	805.6	1,178.7	1,431.4	68.1	5,516.3

INDUSTRY: SUPERMARKETS & GROCERY STORES (NAICS 44511)
PRODUCT LINE: COSMETICS/PERFUMES PRODUCTS (Sub Category)

NAICS 44511: Grocery Stores Industry. This industry comprises establishments generally known as supermarkets and grocery stores primarily engaged in retailing a general line of food, such as canned and frozen foods; fresh fruits and vegetables; and fresh and prepared meats, fish, and poultry. Included in this industry are delicatessen-type establishments primarily engaged in retailing a general line of food.

5-YEAR TREND — ESTIMATED INDUSTRY SALES ($MILLIONS)

Year	Employee Size of Establishment									Total Industry Sales
	1-4 Emps.	5-9 Emps.	10-19 Emps.	20-49 Emps.	50-99 Emps.	100-249 Emps.	250-499 Emps.	500-999 Emps.	Unknown Emps.	
2014	37.1	27.8	70.5	230.2	558.4	1,273.5	367.1	50.6	7.0	2,622.3
2015	36.5	27.3	69.3	226.2	548.8	1,251.4	360.8	49.7	6.9	2,576.9
2016	35.8	26.8	67.9	221.8	538.0	1,226.8	353.7	48.8	6.8	2,526.1
2017	35.8	26.8	67.9	221.8	538.0	1,227.0	353.7	48.7	6.8	2,526.5
2018	35.9	26.8	68.0	222.3	539.2	1,229.5	354.4	48.8	6.8	2,531.7

INDUSTRY: PHARMACIES & DRUG STORES (NAICS 44611)
PRODUCT LINE: COSMETICS/PERFUMES PRODUCTS (Sub Category)

NAICS 44611 Pharmacies and Drug Stores – This industry comprises
establishments known as pharmacies and drug stores engaged in retailing
prescription or nonprescription drugs and medicines.

5-YEAR TREND – ESTIMATED INDUSTRY SALES ($MILLIONS)

Year	Employee Size of Establishment									Total Industry Sales
	1-4 Emps.	5-9 Emps.	10-19 Emps.	20-49 Emps.	50-99 Emps.	100-249 Emps.	250-499 Emps.	500-999 Emps.	Unknown Emps.	
2014	82.7	206.5	872.0	2,464.3	231.5	90.9	28.2	11.3	6.9	3,994.3
2015	87.0	217.3	917.6	2,593.3	243.6	95.7	29.7	11.9	7.3	4,203.3
2016	91.2	227.7	961.5	2,717.3	255.2	100.3	31.1	12.5	7.6	4,404.4
2017	98.1	244.8	1,033.9	2,921.9	274.5	107.8	33.4	13.1	8.2	4,735.7
2018	105.6	263.5	1,113.0	3,145.4	295.5	116.0	36.0	13.6	8.8	5,097.4

INDUSTRY: DEPARTMENT STORES (NAICS 45211)
PRODUCT LINE: COSMETICS/PERFUMES PRODUCTS (Sub Category)

NAICS 45211: Department Stores Industry . This industry comprises
establishments known as department stores primarily engaged in retailing
a wide range of the following new products with no one merchandise line
predominating: apparel, furniture, appliances and home furnishings; and
selected additional items, such as paint, hardware, toiletries, cosmetics,
photographic equipment, jewelry, toys, and sporting goods. Merchandise lines
are normally arranged in separate departments.

5-YEAR TREND – ESTIMATED INDUSTRY SALES ($MILLIONS)

Year	Employee Size of Establishment									Total Industry Sales
	1-4 Emps.	5-9 Emps.	10-19 Emps.	20-49 Emps.	50-99 Emps.	100-249 Emps.	250-499 Emps.	500-999 Emps.	Unknown Emps.	
2014	0	0	1	50	956	3,171	1,391	186	8	5,765
2015	0	0	1	51	969	3,212	1,409	189	8	5,839
2016	0	0	1	52	979	3,247	1,424	191	8	5,902
2017	0	0	1	52	983	3,262	1,431	192	8	5,930
2018	0	0	1	52	991	3,285	1,441	193	8	5,972

INDUSTRY: WAREHOUSE CLUBS & SUPERCENTERS (NAICS 45291)
PRODUCT LINE: COSMETICS/PERFUMES PRODUCTS (Sub Category)

NAICS 45291: Warehouse Clubs and Superstores This industry comprises establishments known as warehouse clubs, superstores or supercenters primarily engaged in retailing a general line of groceries in combination with general lines of new merchandise, such as apparel, furniture, and appliances.

5-YEAR TREND – ESTIMATED INDUSTRY SALES ($MILLIONS)

Year	Employee Size of Establishment									Total Industry Sales
	1-4 Emps.	5-9 Emps.	10-19 Emps.	20-49 Emps.	50-99 Emps.	100-249 Emps.	250-499 Emps.	500-999 Emps.	Unknown Emps.	
2014	0.7	0.0	0.1	6.9	8.7	1,069.5	4,728.0	124.9	1.5	5,940.3
2015	0.8	0.0	0.1	7.1	9.0	1,108.6	4,900.8	129.5	1.5	6,157.4
2016	0.8	0.0	0.1	7.4	9.3	1,145.5	5,064.2	133.8	1.6	6,362.7
2017	0.9	0.0	0.1	8.0	10.1	1,244.2	5,500.4	145.3	1.7	6,910.7
2018	0.9	0.0	0.2	8.5	10.7	1,321.3	5,841.4	154.3	1.8	7,339.2

INDUSTRY: ELECTRONIC SHOPPING & MAIL ORDER (NAICS 45411)
PRODUCT LINE: COSMETICS/PERFUMES PRODUCTS (Sub Category)

NAICS 45411: Electronic Shopping and Mail-Order Houses This industry comprises establishments primarily engaged in retailing all types of merchandise by means of mail or by electronic media, such as interactive television or computer. Included in this industry are establishments primarily engaged in retailing from catalogue showrooms of mail-order houses.

5-YEAR TREND – ESTIMATED INDUSTRY SALES ($MILLIONS)

Year	Employee Size of Establishment									Total Industry Sales
	1-4 Emps.	5-9 Emps.	10-19 Emps.	20-49 Emps.	50-99 Emps.	100-249 Emps.	250-499 Emps.	500-999 Emps.	Unknown Emps.	
2014	337.0	178.9	265.7	429.9	309.2	602.8	882.0	1,117.2	51.0	4,173.6
2015	359.5	190.9	283.4	458.5	329.8	643.0	940.8	1,191.8	54.4	4,452.1
2016	381.3	202.4	300.6	486.3	349.8	682.0	997.9	1,264.1	57.7	4,722.2
2017	433.9	230.4	342.1	553.4	398.1	776.1	1,135.5	1,403.2	65.6	5,338.2
2018	481.9	255.9	379.9	614.7	442.1	862.0	1,261.2	1,531.5	72.9	5,902.2

INDUSTRY: SUPERMARKETS & GROCERY STORES (NAICS 44511)
PRODUCT LINE: HYGIENIC/DEORDANTS/HAIR PRODUCTS (Sub Category)

NAICS 44511: Grocery Stores Industry. This industry comprises establishments generally known as supermarkets and grocery stores primarily engaged in retailing a general line of food, such as canned and frozen foods; fresh fruits and vegetables; and fresh and prepared meats, fish, and poultry. Included in this industry are delicatessen-type establishments primarily engaged in retailing a general line of food.

5-YEAR TREND — ESTIMATED INDUSTRY SALES ($MILLIONS)

Year	Employee Size of Establishment									Total Industry Sales
	1-4 Emps.	5-9 Emps.	10-19 Emps.	20-49 Emps.	50-99 Emps.	100-249 Emps.	250-499 Emps.	500-999 Emps.	Unknown Emps.	
2014	181	136	344	1,124	2,727	6,219	1,793	247	34	12,807
2015	178	133	338	1,105	2,680	6,112	1,762	243	34	12,585
2016	175	131	332	1,083	2,627	5,991	1,727	238	33	12,337
2017	175	131	332	1,083	2,628	5,992	1,727	238	33	12,339
2018	175	131	332	1,086	2,633	6,005	1,731	238	33	12,364

INDUSTRY: PHARMACIES & DRUG STORES (NAICS 44611)
PRODUCT LINE: HYGIENIC/DEORDANTS/HAIR PRODUCTS (Sub Category)

NAICS 44611 Pharmacies and Drug Stores – This industry comprises establishments known as pharmacies and drug stores engaged in retailing prescription or nonprescription drugs and medicines.

5-YEAR TREND — ESTIMATED INDUSTRY SALES ($MILLIONS)

Year	Employee Size of Establishment									Total Industry Sales
	1-4 Emps.	5-9 Emps.	10-19 Emps.	20-49 Emps.	50-99 Emps.	100-249 Emps.	250-499 Emps.	500-999 Emps.	Unknown Emps.	
2014	113.5	283.4	1,197.0	3,382.8	317.8	124.8	38.7	15.6	9.5	5,483.0
2015	119.5	298.2	1,259.6	3,559.8	334.4	131.3	40.7	16.4	10.0	5,769.9
2016	125.2	312.5	1,319.9	3,730.1	350.4	137.6	42.7	17.2	10.5	6,045.9
2017	134.6	336.0	1,419.3	4,011.0	376.8	148.0	45.9	17.9	11.3	6,500.7
2018	144.9	361.7	1,527.8	4,317.8	405.6	159.3	49.4	18.7	12.1	6,997.2

INDUSTRY: DEPARTMENT STORES (NAICS 45211)
PRODUCT LINE: HYGIENIC/DEORDANTS/HAIR PRODUCTS (Sub Category)

NAICS 45211: Department Stores Industry . This industry comprises
establishments known as department stores primarily engaged in retailing
a wide range of the following new products with no one merchandise line
predominating: apparel, furniture, appliances and home furnishings; and
selected additional items, such as paint, hardware, toiletries, cosmetics,
photographic equipment, jewelry, toys, and sporting goods. Merchandise lines
are normally arranged in separate departments.

5-YEAR TREND — ESTIMATED INDUSTRY SALES ($MILLIONS)

Year	Employee Size of Establishment									Total
	1-4 Emps.	5-9 Emps.	10-19 Emps.	20-49 Emps.	50-99 Emps.	100-249 Emps.	250-499 Emps.	500-999 Emps.	Unknown Emps.	Industry Sales
2014	0.3	0.1	0.5	39.0	740.3	2,455.2	1,077.1	144.2	6.3	4,463.0
2015	0.3	0.1	0.5	39.5	749.8	2,486.9	1,091.0	146.1	6.3	4,520.6
2016	0.3	0.1	0.5	39.9	757.9	2,513.7	1,102.8	147.7	6.4	4,569.3
2017	0.3	0.1	0.5	40.1	761.4	2,525.3	1,107.9	148.5	6.4	4,590.6
2018	0.3	0.1	0.5	40.4	766.9	2,543.5	1,115.8	149.6	6.5	4,623.6

INDUSTRY: WAREHOUSE CLUBS & SUPERSTORES (NAICS 45291)
PRODUCT LINE: HYGIENIC/DEORDANTS/HAIR PRODUCTS (Sub Category)

NAICS 45291: Warehouse Clubs and Superstores This industry
comprises establishments known as warehouse clubs, superstores or
supercenters primarily engaged in retailing a general line of groceries
in combination with general lines of new merchandise, such as apparel,
furniture, and appliances.

5-YEAR TREND — ESTIMATED INDUSTRY SALES ($MILLIONS)

Year	Employee Size of Establishment									Total
	1-4 Emps.	5-9 Emps.	10-19 Emps.	20-49 Emps.	50-99 Emps.	100-249 Emps.	250-499 Emps.	500-999 Emps.	Unknown Emps.	Industry Sales
2014	2.7	0.1	0.5	25.3	31.8	3,932.2	17,383.9	459.3	5.4	21,841.2
2015	2.8	0.1	0.5	26.2	33.0	4,076.0	18,019.4	476.1	5.6	22,639.8
2016	2.9	0.1	0.5	27.1	34.1	4,211.9	18,620.2	492.0	5.8	23,394.6
2017	3.2	0.1	0.5	29.4	37.1	4,574.6	20,223.9	534.3	6.3	25,409.4
2018	3.4	0.1	0.6	31.2	39.4	4,858.3	21,477.8	567.5	6.7	26,984.8

INDUSTRY: ELECTRONIC SHOPPING & MAIL ORDER (NAICS 45411)
PRODUCT LINE: DRUGS & HEALTH/BEAUTY AIDS (Main Category)

NAICS 45411: Electronic Shopping and Mail-Order Houses This industry comprises establishments primarily engaged in retailing all types of merchandise by means of mail or by electronic media, such as interactive television or computer. Included in this industry are establishments primarily engaged in retailing from catalogue showrooms of mail-order houses.

5-YEAR TREND – ESTIMATED INDUSTRY SALES ($MILLIONS)

Year	Employee Size of Establishment									Total Industry Sales
	1-4 Emps.	5-9 Emps.	10-19 Emps.	20-49 Emps.	50-99 Emps.	100-249 Emps.	250-499 Emps.	500-999 Emps.	Unknown Emps.	
2014	59.4	31.5	46.8	75.8	54.5	106.2	155.4	196.9	9.0	735.6
2015	63.4	33.6	50.0	80.8	58.1	113.3	165.8	210.0	9.6	784.6
2016	67.2	35.7	53.0	85.7	61.7	120.2	175.9	222.8	10.2	832.2
2017	76.5	40.6	60.3	97.5	70.2	136.8	200.1	247.3	11.6	940.8
2018	84.9	45.1	67.0	108.3	77.9	151.9	222.3	269.9	12.8	1,040.2

INDUSTRY: PHARMACIES & DRUG STORES (NAICS 44611)
PRODUCT LINE: HEARING AIDS & SUPPLIES (Sub Category)

NAICS 44611 Pharmacies and Drug Stores – This industry comprises establishments known as pharmacies and drug stores engaged in retailing prescription or nonprescription drugs and medicines.

5-YEAR TREND – ESTIMATED INDUSTRY SALES ($MILLIONS)

Year	Employee Size of Establishment									Total Industry Sales
	1-4 Emps.	5-9 Emps.	10-19 Emps.	20-49 Emps.	50-99 Emps.	100-249 Emps.	250-499 Emps.	500-999 Emps.	Unknown Emps.	
2014	1.5	3.8	16.0	45.2	4.2	1.7	0.5	0.2	0.1	73.3
2015	1.6	4.0	16.8	47.6	4.5	1.8	0.5	0.2	0.1	77.1
2016	1.7	4.2	17.6	49.8	4.7	1.8	0.6	0.2	0.1	80.8
2017	1.8	4.5	19.0	53.6	5.0	2.0	0.6	0.2	0.2	86.9
2018	1.9	4.8	20.4	57.7	5.4	2.1	0.7	0.2	0.2	93.5

INDUSTRY: ELECTRONIC SHOPPING & MAIL ORDER (NAICS 45411)
PRODUCT LINE: HEARING AIDS & SUPPLIES (Sub Category)

NAICS 45411: Electronic Shopping and Mail-Order Houses This industry comprises establishments primarily engaged in retailing all types of merchandise by means of mail or by electronic media, such as interactive television or computer. Included in this industry are establishments primarily engaged in retailing from catalogue showrooms of mail-order houses.

5-YEAR TREND – ESTIMATED INDUSTRY SALES ($MILLIONS)

Year	Employee Size of Establishment									Total Industry Sales
	1-4 Emps.	5-9 Emps.	10-19 Emps.	20-49 Emps.	50-99 Emps.	100-249 Emps.	250-499 Emps.	500-999 Emps.	Unknown Emps.	
2014	17.3	9.2	13.7	22.1	15.9	31.0	45.3	57.4	2.6	214.4
2015	18.5	9.8	14.6	23.6	16.9	33.0	48.3	61.2	2.8	228.8
2016	19.6	10.4	15.4	25.0	18.0	35.0	51.3	65.0	3.0	242.6
2017	22.3	11.8	17.6	28.4	20.5	39.9	58.3	72.1	3.4	274.3
2018	24.8	13.1	19.5	31.6	22.7	44.3	64.8	78.7	3.7	303.3

INDUSTRY: HOME CENTERS INDUSTRY (NAICS 44411)
PRODUCT LINE: SOAPS & CLEANERS (Main Category)

NAICS 44411: Home Centers. This industry comprises establishments known as home centers primarily engaged in retailing a general line of new home repair and improvement materials and supplies, such as lumber, plumbing goods, electrical goods, tools, housewares, hardware, and lawn and garden supplies, with no one merchandise line predominating. The merchandise lines are normally arranged in separate departments.

5-YEAR TREND – ESTIMATED INDUSTRY SALES ($MILLIONS)

Year	Employee Size of Establishment									Total Industry Sales
	1-4 Emps.	5-9 Emps.	10-19 Emps.	20-49 Emps.	50-99 Emps.	100-249 Emps.	250-499 Emps.	500-999 Emps.	Unknown Emps.	
2014	2.7	5.4	14.0	28.0	20.5	1,344.4	118.9	2.2	0.9	1,537.0
2015	2.8	5.6	14.5	28.9	21.2	1,388.7	122.8	2.3	1.0	1,587.7
2016	2.9	5.7	14.9	29.8	21.9	1,430.3	126.5	2.3	1.0	1,635.3
2017	3.0	6.0	15.7	31.3	23.0	1,503.2	132.9	2.5	1.0	1,718.7
2018	3.2	6.3	16.5	33.0	24.2	1,583.1	140.0	2.6	1.1	1,809.9

INDUSTRY: HARDWARE STORES (NAICS 44413)
PRODUCT LINE: SOAPS & CLEANERS (Main Category)

NAICS 44413: Hardware Stores. Establishments primarily engaged in the retail sale of a number of basic hardware lines, such as tools, builders' hardware, paint and glass, housewares and household appliances, and cutlery.

5-YEAR TREND — ESTIMATED INDUSTRY SALES ($MILLIONS)

Year	Employee Size of Establishment									Total Industry Sales
	1-4 Emps.	5-9 Emps.	10-19 Emps.	20-49 Emps.	50-99 Emps.	100-249 Emps.	250-499 Emps.	500-999 Emps.	Unknown Emps.	
2014	18.4	29.6	59.2	82.8	15.2	3.6	1.0	0.0	1.6	211.3
2015	18.8	30.1	60.3	84.4	15.5	3.6	1.0	0.1	1.6	215.3
2016	19.1	30.6	61.3	85.8	15.7	3.7	1.0	0.1	1.6	218.9
2017	20.0	32.1	64.1	89.8	16.4	3.9	1.1	0.1	1.7	229.1
2018	21.0	33.6	67.3	94.2	17.2	4.0	1.1	0.1	1.8	240.4

INDUSTRY: SUPERMARKETS INDUSTRY (NAICS 44511)
PRODUCT LINE: SOAPS & CLEANERS (Main Category)

NAICS 44511: Grocery Stores Industry. This industry comprises establishments generally known as supermarkets and grocery stores primarily engaged in retailing a general line of food, such as canned and frozen foods; fresh fruits and vegetables; and fresh and prepared meats, fish, and poultry. Included in this industry are delicatessen-type establishments primarily engaged in retailing a general line of food.

5-YEAR TREND — ESTIMATED INDUSTRY SALES ($MILLIONS)

Year	Employee Size of Establishment									Total Industry Sales
	1-4 Emps.	5-9 Emps.	10-19 Emps.	20-49 Emps.	50-99 Emps.	100-249 Emps.	250-499 Emps.	500-999 Emps.	Unknown Emps.	
2014	203.8	152.5	386.7	1,263.3	3,064.4	6,988.2	2,014.6	277.8	38.6	14,389.9
2015	200.3	149.9	380.0	1,241.4	3,011.3	6,867.0	1,979.6	272.9	37.9	14,140.3
2016	196.3	146.9	372.5	1,217.0	2,952.0	6,731.8	1,940.7	267.6	37.1	13,862.0
2017	196.3	147.0	372.6	1,217.2	2,952.4	6,732.8	1,940.9	267.4	37.2	13,863.7
2018	196.8	147.3	373.4	1,219.7	2,958.6	6,746.9	1,945.0	267.7	37.2	13,892.6

INDUSTRY: BEER, WINE & LIQUOR STORES INDUSTRY (NAICS 44531)
PRODUCT LINE: SOAPS & CLEANERS (Main Category)

NAICS 44531: Beer & Wine & Liquor Stores. Establishments primarily engaged in the retail sale of packaged alcoholic beverages, such as ale, beer, wine, and liquor, for consumption off the premises. Stores selling prepared drinks for consumption on the premises are classified in SIC 5813.

5-YEAR TREND – ESTIMATED INDUSTRY SALES ($MILLIONS)

Year	Employee Size of Establishment									Total Industry Sales
	1-4 Emps.	5-9 Emps.	10-19 Emps.	20-49 Emps.	50-99 Emps.	100-249 Emps.	250-499 Emps.	500-999 Emps.	Unknown Emps.	
2014	19.7	19.2	16.0	11.7	1.5	1.1	0.0	0.6	1.1	71.0
2015	20.5	20.0	16.7	12.2	1.6	1.2	0.0	0.6	1.2	74.0
2016	21.3	20.7	17.4	12.7	1.7	1.2	0.0	0.6	1.2	76.8
2017	22.8	22.2	18.6	13.6	1.8	1.3	0.0	0.7	1.3	82.2
2018	24.5	23.8	19.9	14.5	1.9	1.4	0.0	0.7	1.4	88.2

INDUSTRY: PHARMACIES & DRUG STORES INDUSTRY (NAICS 44611)
PRODUCT LINE: SOAPS & CLEANERS (Main Category)

NAICS 44611 Pharmacies and Drug Stores – This industry comprises establishments known as pharmacies and drug stores engaged in retailing prescription or nonprescription drugs and medicines.

5-YEAR TREND – ESTIMATED INDUSTRY SALES ($MILLIONS)

Year	Employee Size of Establishment									Total Industry Sales
	1-4 Emps.	5-9 Emps.	10-19 Emps.	20-49 Emps.	50-99 Emps.	100-249 Emps.	250-499 Emps.	500-999 Emps.	Unknown Emps.	
2014	18.7	46.8	197.5	558.1	52.4	20.6	6.4	2.6	1.6	904.6
2015	19.7	49.2	207.8	587.3	55.2	21.7	6.7	2.7	1.6	952.0
2016	20.7	51.6	217.8	615.4	57.8	22.7	7.0	2.8	1.7	997.5
2017	22.2	55.4	234.2	661.8	62.2	24.4	7.6	3.0	1.9	1,072.5
2018	23.9	59.7	252.1	712.4	66.9	26.3	8.1	3.1	2.0	1,154.4

INDUSTRY: GAS STATIONS W/CONVENIENCE STORES (NAICS 44711)
PRODUCT LINE: SOAPS & CLEANERS (Main Category)

NAICS 44711: Gas Stations with Convenience Stores. This industry comprises establishments primarily engaged in selling gasoline and lubricating oils. These establishments frequently sell other merchandise, such as tires, batteries, and other automobile parts, or perform minor repair work. Gasoline stations combined with other activities, such as grocery stores, convenience stores, or carwashes, are classified according to the primary activity.

5-YEAR TREND – ESTIMATED INDUSTRY SALES ($MILLIONS)

Year	Employee Size of Establishment									Total Industry Sales
	1-4 Emps.	5-9 Emps.	10-19 Emps.	20-49 Emps.	50-99 Emps.	100-249 Emps.	250-499 Emps.	500-999 Emps.	Unknown Emps.	
2014	49.0	131.9	213.5	131.3	11.5	7.2	1.0	0.0	0.6	545.9
2015	52.7	141.9	229.7	141.3	12.4	7.7	1.1	0.0	0.6	587.4
2016	56.3	151.6	245.4	151.0	13.2	8.3	1.2	0.0	0.6	627.7
2017	61.4	165.4	267.7	164.7	14.4	9.0	1.3	0.0	0.7	684.6
2018	67.0	180.3	291.8	179.5	15.7	9.8	1.4	0.0	0.8	746.4

INDUSTRY: DEPARTMENT STORES INDUSTRY (NAICS 45211)
PRODUCT LINE: SOAPS & CLEANERS (Main Category)

NAICS 45211: Department Stores Industry . This industry comprises establishments known as department stores primarily engaged in retailing a wide range of the following new products with no one merchandise line predominating: apparel, furniture, appliances and home furnishings; and selected additional items, such as paint, hardware, toiletries, cosmetics, photographic equipment, jewelry, toys, and sporting goods. Merchandise lines are normally arranged in separate departments.

5-YEAR TREND – ESTIMATED INDUSTRY SALES ($MILLIONS)

Year	Employee Size of Establishment									Total Industry Sales
	1-4 Emps.	5-9 Emps.	10-19 Emps.	20-49 Emps.	50-99 Emps.	100-249 Emps.	250-499 Emps.	500-999 Emps.	Unknown Emps.	
2014	0.2	0.1	0.3	20.7	392.6	1,302.3	571.3	76.5	3.3	2,367.3
2015	0.2	0.1	0.3	20.9	397.7	1,319.1	578.7	77.5	3.4	2,397.8
2016	0.2	0.1	0.3	21.2	402.0	1,333.3	584.9	78.3	3.4	2,423.7
2017	0.2	0.1	0.3	21.3	403.9	1,339.5	587.6	78.8	3.4	2,434.9
2018	0.2	0.1	0.3	21.4	406.8	1,349.1	591.9	79.4	3.4	2,452.5

INDUSTRY: WAREHOUSE CLUBS & SUPERCENTERS (NAICS 45291)
PRODUCT LINE: SOAPS & CLEANERS (Main Category)

NAICS 45291: Warehouse Clubs and Superstores This industry comprises establishments known as warehouse clubs, superstores or supercenters primarily engaged in retailing a general line of groceries in combination with general lines of new merchandise, such as apparel, furniture, and appliances.

5-YEAR TREND — ESTIMATED INDUSTRY SALES ($MILLIONS)

Year	Employee Size of Establishment									Total Industry Sales
	1-4 Emps.	5-9 Emps.	10-19 Emps.	20-49 Emps.	50-99 Emps.	100-249 Emps.	250-499 Emps.	500-999 Emps.	Unknown Emps.	
2014	2.1	0.1	0.4	19.3	24.4	3,006.9	13,293.0	351.2	4.1	16,701.4
2015	2.2	0.1	0.4	20.0	25.2	3,116.8	13,779.0	364.1	4.3	17,312.0
2016	2.2	0.1	0.4	20.7	26.1	3,220.7	14,238.4	376.2	4.4	17,889.2
2017	2.4	0.1	0.4	22.5	28.3	3,498.1	15,464.7	408.6	4.8	19,429.9
2018	2.6	0.1	0.4	23.9	30.1	3,715.0	16,423.5	433.9	5.1	20,634.5

INDUSTRY: ELECTRONIC SHOPPING & MAIL-ORDER (NAICS 45411)
PRODUCT LINE: SOAPS & CLEANERS (Main Category)

NAICS 45411: Electronic Shopping and Mail-Order Houses This industry comprises establishments primarily engaged in retailing all types of merchandise by means of mail or by electronic media, such as interactive television or computer. Included in this industry are establishments primarily engaged in retailing from catalogue showrooms of mail-order houses.

5-YEAR TREND — ESTIMATED INDUSTRY SALES ($MILLIONS)

Year	Employee Size of Establishment									Total Industry Sales
	1-4 Emps.	5-9 Emps.	10-19 Emps.	20-49 Emps.	50-99 Emps.	100-249 Emps.	250-499 Emps.	500-999 Emps.	Unknown Emps.	
2014	22.3	11.8	17.6	28.4	20.5	39.9	58.3	73.9	3.4	276.1
2015	23.8	12.6	18.7	30.3	21.8	42.5	62.2	78.8	3.6	294.5
2016	25.2	13.4	19.9	32.2	23.1	45.1	66.0	83.6	3.8	312.3
2017	28.7	15.2	22.6	36.6	26.3	51.3	75.1	92.8	4.3	353.1
2018	31.9	16.9	25.1	40.7	29.2	57.0	83.4	101.3	4.8	390.4

INDUSTRY: SUPERMARKETS INDUSTRY (NAICS 44511)
PRODUCT LINE: PAPER & TISSUE PRODUCTS (Main Category)

NAICS 44511: Grocery Stores Industry. This industry comprises establishments generally known as supermarkets and grocery stores primarily engaged in retailing a general line of food, such as canned and frozen foods; fresh fruits and vegetables; and fresh and prepared meats, fish, and poultry. Included in this industry are delicatessen-type establishments primarily engaged in retailing a general line of food.

5-YEAR TREND — ESTIMATED INDUSTRY SALES ($MILLIONS)

Year	Employee Size of Establishment									Total Industry Sales
	1-4 Emps.	5-9 Emps.	10-19 Emps.	20-49 Emps.	50-99 Emps.	100-249 Emps.	250-499 Emps.	500-999 Emps.	Unknown Emps.	
2014	209.3	156.6	397.1	1,297.3	3,146.8	7,176.2	2,068.8	285.2	39.6	14,776.9
2015	205.6	153.9	390.2	1,274.8	3,092.2	7,051.7	2,032.9	280.3	38.9	14,520.6
2016	201.6	150.9	382.6	1,249.7	3,031.4	6,912.9	1,992.9	274.8	38.1	14,234.8
2017	201.6	150.9	382.6	1,249.9	3,031.8	6,913.9	1,993.1	274.6	38.2	14,236.6
2018	202.1	151.2	383.4	1,252.5	3,038.2	6,928.4	1,997.3	274.9	38.2	14,266.2

INDUSTRY: BEER, WINE & LIQUOR STORES (NAICS 44531)
PRODUCT LINE: PAPER & TISSUE PRODUCTS (Main Category)

NAICS 44531: Beer & Wine & Liquor Stores. Establishments primarily engaged in the retail sale of packaged alcoholic beverages, such as ale, beer, wine, and liquor, for consumption off the premises. Stores selling prepared drinks for consumption on the premises are classified in SIC 5813.

5-YEAR TREND — ESTIMATED INDUSTRY SALES ($MILLIONS)

Year	Employee Size of Establishment									Total Industry Sales
	1-4 Emps.	5-9 Emps.	10-19 Emps.	20-49 Emps.	50-99 Emps.	100-249 Emps.	250-499 Emps.	500-999 Emps.	Unknown Emps.	
2014	12.0	11.7	9.8	7.1	0.9	0.7	0.0	0.4	0.7	43.2
2015	12.5	12.2	10.2	7.4	1.0	0.7	0.0	0.4	0.7	45.1
2016	13.0	12.6	10.6	7.7	1.0	0.7	0.0	0.4	0.7	46.8
2017	13.9	13.5	11.3	8.3	1.1	0.8	0.0	0.4	0.8	50.1
2018	14.9	14.5	12.1	8.9	1.2	0.9	0.0	0.4	0.8	53.7

INDUSTRY: PHARMACIES & DRUG STORES INDUSTRY (NAICS 44611)
PRODUCT LINE: PAPER & TISSUE PRODUCTS (Main Category)

NAICS 44611 Pharmacies and Drug Stores – This industry comprises establishments known as pharmacies and drug stores engaged in retailing prescription or nonprescription drugs and medicines.

5-YEAR TREND – ESTIMATED INDUSTRY SALES ($MILLIONS)

Year	Employee Size of Establishment									Total Industry Sales
	1-4 Emps.	5-9 Emps.	10-19 Emps.	20-49 Emps.	50-99 Emps.	100-249 Emps.	250-499 Emps.	500-999 Emps.	Unknown Emps.	
2014	15.0	37.5	158.2	447.1	42.0	16.5	5.1	2.1	1.3	724.8
2015	15.8	39.4	166.5	470.5	44.2	17.4	5.4	2.2	1.3	762.7
2016	16.5	41.3	174.5	493.1	46.3	18.2	5.6	2.3	1.4	799.2
2017	17.8	44.4	187.6	530.2	49.8	19.6	6.1	2.4	1.5	859.3
2018	19.2	47.8	201.9	570.7	53.6	21.1	6.5	2.5	1.6	924.9

INDUSTRY: GAS STATIONS W/CONVENIENCE STORES (NAICS 44711)
PRODUCT LINE: PAPER & TISSUE PRODUCTS (Main Category)

NAICS 44711: Gas Stations with Convenience Stores. This industry comprises establishments primarily engaged in selling gasoline and lubricating oils. These establishments frequently sell other merchandise, such as tires, batteries, and other automobile parts, or perform minor repair work. Gasoline stations combined with other activities, such as grocery stores, convenience stores, or carwashes, are classified according to the primary activity.

5-YEAR TREND – ESTIMATED INDUSTRY SALES ($MILLIONS)

Year	Employee Size of Establishment									Total Industry Sales
	1-4 Emps.	5-9 Emps.	10-19 Emps.	20-49 Emps.	50-99 Emps.	100-249 Emps.	250-499 Emps.	500-999 Emps.	Unknown Emps.	
2014	59.9	161.3	261.0	160.6	14.1	8.8	1.2	0.0	0.7	667.6
2015	64.5	173.5	280.8	172.8	15.1	9.5	1.3	0.0	0.7	718.3
2016	68.9	185.4	300.1	184.6	16.2	10.1	1.4	0.0	0.8	767.6
2017	75.1	202.3	327.4	201.4	17.6	11.0	1.5	0.0	0.9	837.2
2018	81.9	220.5	356.9	219.5	19.2	12.0	1.7	0.0	0.9	912.8

INDUSTRY: DEPARTMENT STORES INDUSTRY (NAICS 45211)
PRODUCT LINE: PAPER & TISSUE PRODUCTS (Main Category)

NAICS 45211: Department Stores Industry . This industry comprises establishments known as department stores primarily engaged in retailing a wide range of the following new products with no one merchandise line predominating: apparel, furniture, appliances and home furnishings; and selected additional items, such as paint, hardware, toiletries, cosmetics, photographic equipment, jewelry, toys, and sporting goods. Merchandise lines are normally arranged in separate departments.

5-YEAR TREND — ESTIMATED INDUSTRY SALES ($MILLIONS)

Year	Employee Size of Establishment									Total Industry Sales
	1-4 Emps.	5-9 Emps.	10-19 Emps.	20-49 Emps.	50-99 Emps.	100-249 Emps.	250-499 Emps.	500-999 Emps.	Unknown Emps.	
2014	0.1	0.0	0.2	16.1	305.2	1,012.4	444.1	59.5	2.6	1,840.3
2015	0.1	0.0	0.2	16.3	309.2	1,025.5	449.9	60.2	2.6	1,864.1
2016	0.1	0.0	0.2	16.5	312.5	1,036.5	454.7	60.9	2.6	1,884.1
2017	0.1	0.0	0.2	16.5	314.0	1,041.3	456.8	61.2	2.7	1,892.9
2018	0.1	0.0	0.2	16.7	316.2	1,048.8	460.1	61.7	2.7	1,906.5

INDUSTRY: WAREHOUSE CLUBS & SUPERCENTERS (NAICS 45291)
PRODUCT LINE: PAPER & TISSUE PRODUCTS (Main Category)

NAICS 45291: Warehouse Clubs and Superstores This industry comprises establishments known as warehouse clubs, superstores or supercenters primarily engaged in retailing a general line of groceries in combination with general lines of new merchandise, such as apparel, furniture, and appliances.

5-YEAR TREND — ESTIMATED INDUSTRY SALES ($MILLIONS)

Year	Employee Size of Establishment									Total Industry Sales
	1-4 Emps.	5-9 Emps.	10-19 Emps.	20-49 Emps.	50-99 Emps.	100-249 Emps.	250-499 Emps.	500-999 Emps.	Unknown Emps.	
2014	1.9	0.1	0.3	17.4	21.9	2,701.8	11,944.5	315.6	3.7	15,007.1
2015	1.9	0.1	0.3	18.0	22.7	2,800.6	12,381.2	327.1	3.9	15,555.8
2016	2.0	0.1	0.3	18.6	23.4	2,894.0	12,794.0	338.0	4.0	16,074.5
2017	2.2	0.1	0.4	20.2	25.5	3,143.2	13,895.9	367.1	4.3	17,458.9
2018	2.3	0.1	0.4	21.5	27.0	3,338.1	14,757.4	389.9	4.6	18,541.3

INDUSTRY: OFFICE SUPPLIES & STATIONERY STORES (NAICS 45321)
PRODUCT LINE: PAPER & TISSUE PRODUCTS (Main Category)

NAICS 45321: Office Supplies and Stationery Stores . This industry comprises establishments primarily engaged in one or more of the following: (1) retailing new stationery, school supplies, and office supplies; (2) selling a combination of new office equipment, furniture, and supplies; and (3) selling new office equipment, furniture, and supplies in combination with selling new computers.

5-YEAR TREND – ESTIMATED INDUSTRY SALES ($MILLIONS)

Year	Employee Size of Establishment									Total Industry Sales
	1-4 Emps.	5-9 Emps.	10-19 Emps.	20-49 Emps.	50-99 Emps.	100-249 Emps.	250-499 Emps.	500-999 Emps.	Unknown Emps.	
2014	1.2	0.9	4.8	13.6	0.3	0.3	0.0	0.0	0.3	21.5
2015	1.2	0.9	4.8	13.6	0.3	0.3	0.0	0.0	0.3	21.5
2016	1.2	0.9	4.8	13.6	0.3	0.3	0.0	0.0	0.3	21.5
2017	1.2	0.9	4.7	13.3	0.3	0.3	0.0	0.0	0.2	21.0
2018	1.2	0.9	4.6	13.0	0.3	0.3	0.0	0.0	0.2	20.6

INDUSTRY: ELECTRONIC SHOPPING & MAIL-ORDER (NAICS 45411)
PRODUCT LINE: PAPER & TISSUE PRODUCTS (Main Category)

NAICS 45411: Electronic Shopping and Mail-Order Houses This industry comprises establishments primarily engaged in retailing all types of merchandise by means of mail or by electronic media, such as interactive television or computer. Included in this industry are establishments primarily engaged in retailing from catalogue showrooms of mail-order houses.

5-YEAR TREND – ESTIMATED INDUSTRY SALES ($MILLIONS)

Year	Employee Size of Establishment									Total Industry Sales
	1-4 Emps.	5-9 Emps.	10-19 Emps.	20-49 Emps.	50-99 Emps.	100-249 Emps.	250-499 Emps.	500-999 Emps.	Unknown Emps.	
2014	137.7	73.1	108.6	175.6	126.3	246.3	360.4	456.5	20.8	1,705.4
2015	146.9	78.0	115.8	187.4	134.8	262.7	384.4	487.0	22.2	1,819.2
2016	155.8	82.7	122.8	198.7	142.9	278.7	407.7	516.5	23.6	1,929.5
2017	177.3	94.1	139.8	226.1	162.7	317.1	464.0	573.3	26.8	2,181.3
2018	196.9	104.5	155.3	251.2	180.7	352.2	515.3	625.8	29.8	2,411.7

INDUSTRY: HARDWARE STORES (NAICS 44413)
PRODUCT LINE: MEN'S WEAR (Main Category)

NAICS 44413: Hardware Stores. Establishments primarily engaged in the retail sale of a number of basic hardware lines, such as tools, builders' hardware, paint and glass, housewares and household appliances, and cutlery.

5-YEAR TREND – ESTIMATED INDUSTRY SALES ($MILLIONS)

Year	Employee Size of Establishment									Total Industry Sales
	1-4 Emps.	5-9 Emps.	10-19 Emps.	20-49 Emps.	50-99 Emps.	100-249 Emps.	250-499 Emps.	500-999 Emps.	Unknown Emps.	
2014	3.9	6.3	12.6	17.6	3.2	0.8	0.2	0.0	0.3	45.0
2015	4.0	6.4	12.8	18.0	3.3	0.8	0.2	0.0	0.3	45.8
2016	4.1	6.5	13.0	18.3	3.3	0.8	0.2	0.0	0.3	46.6
2017	4.3	6.8	13.6	19.1	3.5	0.8	0.2	0.0	0.4	48.7
2018	4.5	7.2	14.3	20.0	3.7	0.9	0.2	0.0	0.4	51.1

INDUSTRY: MEN'S CLOTHING STORES (NAICS 44811)
PRODUCT LINE: MEN'S WEAR (Main Category)

NAICS 44811: Men's Clothing Stores. This industry comprises establishments primarily engaged in retailing a general line of new men's and boys' clothing. These establishments may provide basic alterations, such as hemming, taking in or letting out seams, or lengthening or shortening sleeves.

5-YEAR TREND – ESTIMATED INDUSTRY SALES ($MILLIONS)

Year	Employee Size of Establishment									Total Industry Sales
	1-4 Emps.	5-9 Emps.	10-19 Emps.	20-49 Emps.	50-99 Emps.	100-249 Emps.	250-499 Emps.	500-999 Emps.	Unknown Emps.	
2014	769	1,148	2,680	1,562	399	200	84	4	128	6,976
2015	805	1,201	2,803	1,634	417	209	88	5	134	7,297
2016	839	1,252	2,921	1,703	435	218	92	5	140	7,604
2017	868	1,296	3,024	1,763	450	226	95	5	144	7,872
2018	900	1,343	3,135	1,828	467	234	99	5	150	8,161

INDUSTRY: WOMEN'S CLOTHING STORES (NAICS 44812)
PRODUCT LINE: MEN'S WEAR (Main Category)

NAICS 44812: Women's Clothing Stores . This industry comprises establishments primarily engaged in retailing a general line of new women's, misses' and juniors' clothing, including maternity wear. These establishments may provide basic alterations, such as hemming, taking in or letting out seams, or lengthening or shortening sleeves.

5-YEAR TREND — ESTIMATED INDUSTRY SALES ($MILLIONS)

| Year | Employee Size of Establishment | | | | | | | | | Total Industry Sales |
	1-4 Emps.	5-9 Emps.	10-19 Emps.	20-49 Emps.	50-99 Emps.	100-249 Emps.	250-499 Emps.	500-999 Emps.	Unknown Emps.	
2014	88.9	201.5	493.6	338.0	105.5	102.6	38.4	34.8	20.6	1,423.9
2015	92.3	209.3	512.7	351.0	109.6	106.6	39.9	36.2	21.4	1,478.8
2016	95.5	216.6	530.7	363.4	113.4	110.3	41.3	37.5	22.1	1,530.9
2017	101.6	230.3	564.3	386.3	120.6	117.3	43.9	39.3	23.5	1,627.2
2018	108.2	245.3	601.0	411.5	128.4	125.0	46.8	41.2	25.1	1,732.5

INDUSTRY: FAMILY CLOTHING STORES (NAICS 44814)
PRODUCT LINE: MEN'S WEAR (Main Category)

NAICS 44814: Family Clothing Stores . This industry comprises establishments primarily engaged in retailing a general line of new clothing for men, women, and children, without specializing in sales for an individual gender or age group. These establishments may provide basic alterations, such as hemming, taking in or letting out seams, or lengthening or shortening sleeves.

5-YEAR TREND — ESTIMATED INDUSTRY SALES ($MILLIONS)

| Year | Employee Size of Establishment | | | | | | | | | Total Industry Sales |
	1-4 Emps.	5-9 Emps.	10-19 Emps.	20-49 Emps.	50-99 Emps.	100-249 Emps.	250-499 Emps.	500-999 Emps.	Unknown Emps.	
2014	381	683	2,939	9,010	9,450	2,357	2,330	923	103	28,176
2015	394	707	3,044	9,332	9,788	2,442	2,414	956	107	29,185
2016	407	730	3,144	9,637	10,108	2,522	2,492	988	110	30,138
2017	432	775	3,335	10,223	10,723	2,675	2,644	1,045	117	31,969
2018	459	824	3,545	10,866	11,397	2,843	2,810	1,108	124	33,977

INDUSTRY: DEPARTMENT STORES (NAICS 45211)
PRODUCT LINE: MEN'S WEAR (Main Category)

NAICS 45211: Department Stores Industry . This industry comprises
establishments known as department stores primarily engaged in retailing
a wide range of the following new products with no one merchandise line
predominating: apparel, furniture, appliances and home furnishings; and
selected additional items, such as paint, hardware, toiletries, cosmetics,
photographic equipment, jewelry, toys, and sporting goods. Merchandise lines
are normally arranged in separate departments.

5-YEAR TREND – ESTIMATED INDUSTRY SALES ($MILLIONS)

| Year | Employee Size of Establishment | | | | | | | | | Total |
	1-4 Emps.	5-9 Emps.	10-19 Emps.	20-49 Emps.	50-99 Emps.	100-249 Emps.	250-499 Emps.	500-999 Emps.	Unknown Emps.	Industry Sales
2014	1	0	1	101	1,922	6,376	2,797	375	16	11,590
2015	1	0	1	103	1,947	6,458	2,833	379	16	11,740
2016	1	0	1	104	1,968	6,528	2,864	384	17	11,866
2017	1	0	1	104	1,977	6,558	2,877	386	17	11,921
2018	1	0	1	105	1,992	6,605	2,898	389	17	12,007

INDUSTRY: WAREHOUSE CLUBS & SUPERCENTERS (NAICS 45291)
PRODUCT LINE: MEN'S WEAR (Main Category)

NAICS 45291: Warehouse Clubs and Superstores This industry
comprises establishments known as warehouse clubs, superstores or
supercenters primarily engaged in retailing a general line of groceries
in combination with general lines of new merchandise, such as apparel,
furniture, and appliances.

5-YEAR TREND – ESTIMATED INDUSTRY SALES ($MILLIONS)

| Year | Employee Size of Establishment | | | | | | | | | Total |
	1-4 Emps.	5-9 Emps.	10-19 Emps.	20-49 Emps.	50-99 Emps.	100-249 Emps.	250-499 Emps.	500-999 Emps.	Unknown Emps.	Industry Sales
2014	1.7	0.1	0.3	15.6	19.7	2,426.2	10,725.8	283.4	3.3	13,475.9
2015	1.7	0.1	0.3	16.2	20.4	2,514.9	11,117.9	293.7	3.5	13,968.6
2016	1.8	0.1	0.3	16.7	21.0	2,598.7	11,488.6	303.5	3.6	14,434.4
2017	1.9	0.1	0.3	18.1	22.9	2,822.5	12,478.1	329.7	3.9	15,677.5
2018	2.1	0.1	0.4	19.3	24.3	2,997.5	13,251.7	350.1	4.1	16,649.5

INDUSTRY: ELECTRONIC SHOPPING & MAIL ORDER (NAICS 45411)
PRODUCT LINE: MEN'S WEAR (Main Category)

NAICS 45411: Electronic Shopping and Mail-Order Houses This industry comprises establishments primarily engaged in retailing all types of merchandise by means of mail or by electronic media, such as interactive television or computer. Included in this industry are establishments primarily engaged in retailing from catalogue showrooms of mail-order houses.

5-YEAR TREND — ESTIMATED INDUSTRY SALES ($MILLIONS)

Year	Employee Size of Establishment									Total Industry Sales
	1-4 Emps.	5-9 Emps.	10-19 Emps.	20-49 Emps.	50-99 Emps.	100-249 Emps.	250-499 Emps.	500-999 Emps.	Unknown Emps.	
2014	616.0	327.1	485.7	785.7	565.2	1,101.9	1,612.2	2,042.2	93.2	7,629.1
2015	657.1	348.9	518.1	838.2	602.9	1,175.4	1,719.7	2,178.5	99.4	8,138.1
2016	697.0	370.1	549.5	889.0	639.5	1,246.7	1,824.1	2,310.7	105.4	8,631.9
2017	793.1	421.1	625.3	1,011.6	727.7	1,418.6	2,075.6	2,564.9	119.9	9,757.9
2018	880.9	467.7	694.5	1,123.6	808.2	1,575.7	2,305.4	2,799.5	133.2	10,788.7

INDUSTRY: BOOK STORES (NAICS 451211)
PRODUCT LINE: MEN'S WEAR (Main Category)

NAICS 451211: Book Stores. This industry comprises establishments primarily engaged in the retail sale of new books and magazines. Establishments primarily engaged in the retail sale of used books are classified in 5932.

5-YEAR TREND — ESTIMATED INDUSTRY SALES ($MILLIONS)

Year	Employee Size of Establishment									Total Industry Sales
	1-4 Emps.	5-9 Emps.	10-19 Emps.	20-49 Emps.	50-99 Emps.	100-249 Emps.	250-499 Emps.	500-999 Emps.	Unknown Emps.	
2014	5.7	8.6	17.9	46.8	21.1	8.3	1.5	5.6	2.9	118.5
2015	6.0	9.1	18.9	49.4	22.3	8.8	1.6	5.9	3.1	124.9
2016	6.3	9.6	19.8	51.8	23.4	9.2	1.7	6.2	3.2	131.1
2017	6.3	9.6	19.9	52.2	23.6	9.3	1.7	6.4	3.2	132.2
2018	6.4	9.7	20.1	52.6	23.8	9.4	1.7	6.5	3.3	133.4

INDUSTRY: MEN'S CLOTHING STORES (NAICS 44811)
PRODUCT LINE: MEN'S OVERCOATS & OUTERWEAR (Sub Category)

NAICS 44811: Men's Clothing Stores. This industry comprises establishments primarily engaged in retailing a general line of new men's and boys' clothing. These establishments may provide basic alterations, such as hemming, taking in or letting out seams, or lengthening or shortening sleeves.

5-YEAR TREND – ESTIMATED INDUSTRY SALES ($MILLIONS)

Year	Employee Size of Establishment									Total Industry Sales
	1-4 Emps.	5-9 Emps.	10-19 Emps.	20-49 Emps.	50-99 Emps.	100-249 Emps.	250-499 Emps.	500-999 Emps.	Unknown Emps.	
2014	35.1	52.3	122.2	71.2	18.2	9.1	3.8	0.2	5.8	318.0
2015	36.7	54.7	127.8	74.5	19.0	9.5	4.0	0.2	6.1	332.6
2016	38.2	57.0	133.2	77.6	19.8	9.9	4.2	0.2	6.4	346.6
2017	39.6	59.1	137.8	80.4	20.5	10.3	4.3	0.2	6.6	358.8
2018	41.0	61.2	142.9	83.3	21.3	10.7	4.5	0.2	6.8	372.0

INDUSTRY: WOMEN'S CLOTHING STORES (NAICS 44812)
PRODUCT LINE: MEN'S OVERCOATS & OUTERWEAR (Sub Category)

NAICS 44812: Women's Clothing Stores . This industry comprises establishments primarily engaged in retailing a general line of new women's, misses' and juniors' clothing, including maternity wear. These establishments may provide basic alterations, such as hemming, taking in or letting out seams, or lengthening or shortening sleeves.

5-YEAR TREND – ESTIMATED INDUSTRY SALES ($MILLIONS)

Year	Employee Size of Establishment									Total Industry Sales
	1-4 Emps.	5-9 Emps.	10-19 Emps.	20-49 Emps.	50-99 Emps.	100-249 Emps.	250-499 Emps.	500-999 Emps.	Unknown Emps.	
2014	6.4	14.5	35.6	24.4	7.6	7.4	2.8	2.5	1.5	102.6
2015	6.7	15.1	37.0	25.3	7.9	7.7	2.9	2.6	1.5	106.6
2016	6.9	15.6	38.3	26.2	8.2	8.0	3.0	2.7	1.6	110.4
2017	7.3	16.6	40.7	27.8	8.7	8.5	3.2	2.8	1.7	117.3
2018	7.8	17.7	43.3	29.7	9.3	9.0	3.4	3.0	1.8	124.9

INDUSTRY: FAMILY CLOTHING STORES (NAICS 44814)
PRODUCT LINE: MEN'S OVERCOATS & OUTERWEAR (Sub Category)

NAICS 44814: Family Clothing Stores . This industry comprises establishments primarily engaged in retailing a general line of new clothing for men, women, and children, without specializing in sales for an individual gender or age group. These establishments may provide basic alterations, such as hemming, taking in or letting out seams, or lengthening or shortening sleeves.

5-YEAR TREND — ESTIMATED INDUSTRY SALES ($MILLIONS)

Year	Employee Size of Establishment									Total Industry Sales
	1-4 Emps.	5-9 Emps.	10-19 Emps.	20-49 Emps.	50-99 Emps.	100-249 Emps.	250-499 Emps.	500-999 Emps.	Unknown Emps.	
2014	24.1	43.3	186.4	571.4	599.3	149.5	147.8	58.6	6.5	1,786.8
2015	25.0	44.9	193.1	591.8	620.7	154.9	153.1	60.7	6.8	1,850.8
2016	25.8	46.3	199.4	611.1	641.0	159.9	158.1	62.6	7.0	1,911.2
2017	27.4	49.1	211.5	648.3	680.0	169.6	167.7	66.3	7.4	2,027.4
2018	29.1	52.2	224.8	689.1	722.8	180.3	178.2	70.3	7.9	2,154.7

INDUSTRY: DEPARTMENT STORES (NAICS 45211)
PRODUCT LINE: MEN'S OVERCOATS & OUTERWEAR (Sub Category)

NAICS 45211: Department Stores Industry . This industry comprises establishments known as department stores primarily engaged in retailing a wide range of the following new products with no one merchandise line predominating: apparel, furniture, appliances and home furnishings; and selected additional items, such as paint, hardware, toiletries, cosmetics, photographic equipment, jewelry, toys, and sporting goods. Merchandise lines are normally arranged in separate departments.

5-YEAR TREND — ESTIMATED INDUSTRY SALES ($MILLIONS)

Year	Employee Size of Establishment									Total Industry Sales
	1-4 Emps.	5-9 Emps.	10-19 Emps.	20-49 Emps.	50-99 Emps.	100-249 Emps.	250-499 Emps.	500-999 Emps.	Unknown Emps.	
2014	0.0	0.0	0.1	4.7	88.6	293.9	129.0	17.3	0.7	534.3
2015	0.0	0.0	0.1	4.7	89.8	297.7	130.6	17.5	0.8	541.2
2016	0.0	0.0	0.1	4.8	90.7	300.9	132.0	17.7	0.8	547.0
2017	0.0	0.0	0.1	4.8	91.2	302.3	132.6	17.8	0.8	549.6
2018	0.0	0.0	0.1	4.8	91.8	304.5	133.6	17.9	0.8	553.5

INDUSTRY: WAREHOUSE CLUBS & SUPERCENTERS (NAICS 45291)
PRODUCT LINE: MEN'S OVERCOATS & OUTERWEAR (Sub Category)

NAICS 45291: Warehouse Clubs and Superstores This industry comprises establishments known as warehouse clubs, superstores or supercenters primarily engaged in retailing a general line of groceries in combination with general lines of new merchandise, such as apparel, furniture, and appliances.

5-YEAR TREND – ESTIMATED INDUSTRY SALES ($MILLIONS)

Year	Employee Size of Establishment									Total Industry Sales
	1-4 Emps.	5-9 Emps.	10-19 Emps.	20-49 Emps.	50-99 Emps.	100-249 Emps.	250-499 Emps.	500-999 Emps.	Unknown Emps.	
2014	0.1	0.0	0.0	1.0	1.2	148.8	658.0	17.4	0.2	826.7
2015	0.1	0.0	0.0	1.0	1.2	154.3	682.1	18.0	0.2	856.9
2016	0.1	0.0	0.0	1.0	1.3	159.4	704.8	18.6	0.2	885.5
2017	0.1	0.0	0.0	1.1	1.4	173.2	765.5	20.2	0.2	961.8
2018	0.1	0.0	0.0	1.2	1.5	183.9	813.0	21.5	0.3	1,021.4

INDUSTRY: MEN'S CLOTHING STORES (NAICS 44811)
PRODUCT LINE: MEN'S SUITS & FORMAL WEAR (Sub Category)

NAICS 44811: Men's Clothing Stores. This industry comprises establishments primarily engaged in retailing a general line of new men's and boys' clothing. These establishments may provide basic alterations, such as hemming, taking in or letting out seams, or lengthening or shortening sleeves.

5-YEAR TREND – ESTIMATED INDUSTRY SALES ($MILLIONS)

Year	Employee Size of Establishment									Total Industry Sales
	1-4 Emps.	5-9 Emps.	10-19 Emps.	20-49 Emps.	50-99 Emps.	100-249 Emps.	250-499 Emps.	500-999 Emps.	Unknown Emps.	
2014	75.5	112.6	262.9	153.2	39.1	19.6	8.3	0.4	12.6	684.3
2015	78.9	117.8	275.0	160.3	40.9	20.5	8.7	0.5	13.1	715.7
2016	82.3	122.8	286.5	167.0	42.7	21.4	9.0	0.5	13.7	745.8
2017	85.2	127.1	296.6	172.9	44.2	22.2	9.3	0.5	14.2	772.1
2018	88.3	131.7	307.5	179.3	45.8	23.0	9.7	0.5	14.7	800.5

INDUSTRY: FAMILY CLOTHING STORES (NAICS 44814)
PRODUCT LINE: MEN'S SUITS & FORMAL WEAR (Sub Category)

NAICS 44814: Family Clothing Stores . This industry comprises establishments primarily engaged in retailing a general line of new clothing for men, women, and children, without specializing in sales for an individual gender or age group. These establishments may provide basic alterations, such as hemming, taking in or letting out seams, or lengthening or shortening sleeves.

5-YEAR TREND — ESTIMATED INDUSTRY SALES ($MILLIONS)

Year	Employee Size of Establishment									Total Industry Sales
	1-4 Emps.	5-9 Emps.	10-19 Emps.	20-49 Emps.	50-99 Emps.	100-249 Emps.	250-499 Emps.	500-999 Emps.	Unknown Emps.	
2014	14.0	25.1	108.0	331.1	347.3	86.6	85.6	33.9	3.8	1,035.6
2015	14.5	26.0	111.9	343.0	359.8	89.7	88.7	35.2	3.9	1,072.7
2016	15.0	26.8	115.5	354.2	371.5	92.7	91.6	36.3	4.0	1,107.7
2017	15.9	28.5	122.6	375.7	394.1	98.3	97.2	38.4	4.3	1,175.0
2018	16.9	30.3	130.3	399.4	418.9	104.5	103.3	40.7	4.6	1,248.8

INDUSTRY: DEPARTMENT STORES (NAICS 45211)
PRODUCT LINE: MEN'S SUITS & FORMAL WEAR (Sub Category)

NAICS 45211: Department Stores Industry . This industry comprises establishments known as department stores primarily engaged in retailing a wide range of the following new products with no one merchandise line predominating: apparel, furniture, appliances and home furnishings; and selected additional items, such as paint, hardware, toiletries, cosmetics, photographic equipment, jewelry, toys, and sporting goods. Merchandise lines are normally arranged in separate departments.

5-YEAR TREND — ESTIMATED INDUSTRY SALES ($MILLIONS)

Year	Employee Size of Establishment									Total Industry Sales
	1-4 Emps.	5-9 Emps.	10-19 Emps.	20-49 Emps.	50-99 Emps.	100-249 Emps.	250-499 Emps.	500-999 Emps.	Unknown Emps.	
2014	0.0	0.0	0.1	4.4	84.4	279.9	122.8	16.4	0.7	508.7
2015	0.0	0.0	0.1	4.5	85.5	283.5	124.4	16.7	0.7	515.3
2016	0.0	0.0	0.1	4.6	86.4	286.5	125.7	16.8	0.7	520.9
2017	0.0	0.0	0.1	4.6	86.8	287.9	126.3	16.9	0.7	523.3
2018	0.0	0.0	0.1	4.6	87.4	289.9	127.2	17.1	0.7	527.1

INDUSTRY: MEN'S CLOTHING STORES (NAICS 44811)
PRODUCT LINE: MEN'S SPORT COATS & BLAZERS (Sub Category)

NAICS 44811: Men's Clothing Stores. This industry comprises establishments primarily engaged in retailing a general line of new men's and boys' clothing. These establishments may provide basic alterations, such as hemming, taking in or letting out seams, or lengthening or shortening sleeves.

5-YEAR TREND – ESTIMATED INDUSTRY SALES ($MILLIONS)

Year	Employee Size of Establishment									Total Industry Sales
	1-4 Emps.	5-9 Emps.	10-19 Emps.	20-49 Emps.	50-99 Emps.	100-249 Emps.	250-499 Emps.	500-999 Emps.	Unknown Emps.	
2014	63.5	94.7	221.1	128.9	32.9	16.5	7.0	0.4	10.6	575.6
2015	66.4	99.1	231.3	134.8	34.4	17.3	7.3	0.4	11.0	602.1
2016	69.2	103.3	241.0	140.5	35.9	18.0	7.6	0.4	11.5	627.4
2017	71.6	106.9	249.5	145.5	37.2	18.6	7.9	0.4	11.9	649.5
2018	74.3	110.8	258.7	150.8	38.5	19.3	8.1	0.4	12.4	673.4

INDUSTRY: FAMILY CLOTHING STORES (NAICS 44814)
PRODUCT LINE: MEN'S SPORT COATS & BLAZERS (Sub Category)

NAICS 44814: Family Clothing Stores . This industry comprises establishments primarily engaged in retailing a general line of new clothing for men, women, and children, without specializing in sales for an individual gender or age group. These establishments may provide basic alterations, such as hemming, taking in or letting out seams, or lengthening or shortening sleeves.

5-YEAR TREND – ESTIMATED INDUSTRY SALES ($MILLIONS)

Year	Employee Size of Establishment									Total Industry Sales
	1-4 Emps.	5-9 Emps.	10-19 Emps.	20-49 Emps.	50-99 Emps.	100-249 Emps.	250-499 Emps.	500-999 Emps.	Unknown Emps.	
2014	8.3	14.9	64.3	197.0	206.6	51.5	50.9	20.2	2.3	616.1
2015	8.6	15.5	66.6	204.0	214.0	53.4	52.8	20.9	2.3	638.1
2016	8.9	16.0	68.7	210.7	221.0	55.1	54.5	21.6	2.4	658.9
2017	9.4	16.9	72.9	223.5	234.4	58.5	57.8	22.9	2.6	699.0
2018	10.0	18.0	77.5	237.6	249.2	62.2	61.4	24.2	2.7	742.9

INDUSTRY: DEPARTMENT STORES (NAICS 45211)
PRODUCT LINE: MEN'S SPORT COATS & BLAZERS (Sub Category)

NAICS 45211: Department Stores Industry . This industry comprises establishments known as department stores primarily engaged in retailing a wide range of the following new products with no one merchandise line predominating: apparel, furniture, appliances and home furnishings; and selected additional items, such as paint, hardware, toiletries, cosmetics, photographic equipment, jewelry, toys, and sporting goods. Merchandise lines are normally arranged in separate departments.

5-YEAR TREND – ESTIMATED INDUSTRY SALES ($MILLIONS)

Year	Employee Size of Establishment									Total
	1-4 Emps.	5-9 Emps.	10-19 Emps.	20-49 Emps.	50-99 Emps.	100-249 Emps.	250-499 Emps.	500-999 Emps.	Unknown Emps.	Industry Sales
2014	0.0	0.0	0.0	1.5	29.3	97.3	42.7	5.7	0.2	176.9
2015	0.0	0.0	0.0	1.6	29.7	98.6	43.3	5.8	0.3	179.2
2016	0.0	0.0	0.0	1.6	30.0	99.7	43.7	5.9	0.3	181.1
2017	0.0	0.0	0.0	1.6	30.2	100.1	43.9	5.9	0.3	182.0
2018	0.0	0.0	0.0	1.6	30.4	100.8	44.2	5.9	0.3	183.3

INDUSTRY: MEN'S CLOTHING STORES (NAICS 44811)
PRODUCT LINE: MEN'S DRESS SLACKS (Sub Category)

NAICS 44811: Men's Clothing Stores. This industry comprises establishments primarily engaged in retailing a general line of new men's and boys' clothing. These establishments may provide basic alterations, such as hemming, taking in or letting out seams, or lengthening or shortening sleeves.

5-YEAR TREND – ESTIMATED INDUSTRY SALES ($MILLIONS)

Year	Employee Size of Establishment									Total
	1-4 Emps.	5-9 Emps.	10-19 Emps.	20-49 Emps.	50-99 Emps.	100-249 Emps.	250-499 Emps.	500-999 Emps.	Unknown Emps.	Industry Sales
2014	61.5	91.8	214.3	124.9	31.9	16.0	6.7	0.4	10.2	557.7
2015	64.3	96.0	224.1	130.7	33.4	16.7	7.1	0.4	10.7	583.4
2016	67.1	100.1	233.6	136.2	34.8	17.4	7.3	0.4	11.2	607.9
2017	69.4	103.6	241.8	140.9	36.0	18.1	7.6	0.4	11.5	629.4
2018	72.0	107.4	250.7	146.1	37.3	18.7	7.9	0.4	12.0	652.5

INDUSTRY: WOMEN'S CLOTHING STORES (NAICS 44812)
PRODUCT LINE: MEN'S DRESS SLACKS (Sub Category)

NAICS 44812: Women's Clothing Stores . This industry comprises establishments primarily engaged in retailing a general line of new women's, misses' and juniors' clothing, including maternity wear. These establishments may provide basic alterations, such as hemming, taking in or letting out seams, or lengthening or shortening sleeves.

5-YEAR TREND – ESTIMATED INDUSTRY SALES ($MILLIONS)

Year	Employee Size of Establishment									Total Industry Sales
	1-4 Emps.	5-9 Emps.	10-19 Emps.	20-49 Emps.	50-99 Emps.	100-249 Emps.	250-499 Emps.	500-999 Emps.	Unknown Emps.	
2014	4.0	9.2	22.5	15.4	4.8	4.7	1.7	1.6	0.9	64.8
2015	4.2	9.5	23.3	16.0	5.0	4.8	1.8	1.6	1.0	67.3
2016	4.3	9.9	24.1	16.5	5.2	5.0	1.9	1.7	1.0	69.6
2017	4.6	10.5	25.7	17.6	5.5	5.3	2.0	1.8	1.1	74.0
2018	4.9	11.2	27.3	18.7	5.8	5.7	2.1	1.9	1.1	78.8

INDUSTRY: FAMILY CLOTHING STORES (NAICS 44814)
PRODUCT LINE: MEN'S DRESS SLACKS (Sub Category)

NAICS 44814: Family Clothing Stores . This industry comprises establishments primarily engaged in retailing a general line of new clothing for men, women, and children, without specializing in sales for an individual gender or age group. These establishments may provide basic alterations, such as hemming, taking in or letting out seams, or lengthening or shortening sleeves.

5-YEAR TREND – ESTIMATED INDUSTRY SALES ($MILLIONS)

Year	Employee Size of Establishment									Total Industry Sales
	1-4 Emps.	5-9 Emps.	10-19 Emps.	20-49 Emps.	50-99 Emps.	100-249 Emps.	250-499 Emps.	500-999 Emps.	Unknown Emps.	
2014	22.5	40.3	173.5	531.8	557.7	139.1	137.5	54.5	6.1	1,663.0
2015	23.3	41.7	179.7	550.8	577.7	144.1	142.4	56.5	6.3	1,722.5
2016	24.0	43.1	185.6	568.8	596.6	148.8	147.1	58.3	6.5	1,778.8
2017	25.5	45.7	196.8	603.4	632.9	157.9	156.1	61.7	6.9	1,886.8
2018	27.1	48.6	209.2	641.3	672.7	167.8	165.9	65.4	7.3	2,005.4

INDUSTRY: DEPARTMENT STORES (NAICS 45211)
PRODUCT LINE: MEN'S DRESS SLACKS (Sub Category)

NAICS 45211: Department Stores Industry . This industry comprises establishments known as department stores primarily engaged in retailing a wide range of the following new products with no one merchandise line predominating: apparel, furniture, appliances and home furnishings; and selected additional items, such as paint, hardware, toiletries, cosmetics, photographic equipment, jewelry, toys, and sporting goods. Merchandise lines are normally arranged in separate departments.

5-YEAR TREND – ESTIMATED INDUSTRY SALES ($MILLIONS)

Year	Employee Size of Establishment									Total
	1-4 Emps.	5-9 Emps.	10-19 Emps.	20-49 Emps.	50-99 Emps.	100-249 Emps.	250-499 Emps.	500-999 Emps.	Unknown Emps.	Industry Sales
2014	0.0	0.0	0.0	0.1	1.4	4.5	2.0	0.3	0.0	8.2
2015	0.0	0.0	0.0	0.1	1.4	4.6	2.0	0.3	0.0	8.3
2016	0.0	0.0	0.0	0.1	1.4	4.6	2.0	0.3	0.0	8.4
2017	0.0	0.0	0.0	0.1	1.4	4.6	2.0	0.3	0.0	8.4
2018	0.0	0.0	0.0	0.1	1.4	4.7	2.0	0.3	0.0	8.5

INDUSTRY: MEN'S CLOTHING STORES (NAICS 44811)
PRODUCT LINE: MEN'S CASUAL SLACKS & JEANS (Sub Category)

NAICS 44811: Men's Clothing Stores. This industry comprises establishments primarily engaged in retailing a general line of new men's and boys' clothing. These establishments may provide basic alterations, such as hemming, taking in or letting out seams, or lengthening or shortening sleeves.

5-YEAR TREND – ESTIMATED INDUSTRY SALES ($MILLIONS)

Year	Employee Size of Establishment									Total
	1-4 Emps.	5-9 Emps.	10-19 Emps.	20-49 Emps.	50-99 Emps.	100-249 Emps.	250-499 Emps.	500-999 Emps.	Unknown Emps.	Industry Sales
2014	100.7	150.2	350.6	204.4	52.2	26.2	11.0	0.6	16.7	912.6
2015	105.3	157.1	366.7	213.8	54.6	27.4	11.5	0.6	17.5	954.6
2016	109.7	163.7	382.1	222.8	56.9	28.5	12.0	0.6	18.2	994.7
2017	113.6	169.5	395.6	230.6	58.9	29.5	12.4	0.7	18.9	1,029.8
2018	117.8	175.7	410.1	239.1	61.1	30.6	12.9	0.7	19.6	1,067.6

INDUSTRY: WOMEN'S CLOTHING STORES (NAICS 44812)
PRODUCT LINE: MEN'S CASUAL SLACKS & JEANS (Sub Category)

NAICS 44812: Women's Clothing Stores . This industry comprises establishments primarily engaged in retailing a general line of new women's, misses' and juniors' clothing, including maternity wear. These establishments may provide basic alterations, such as hemming, taking in or letting out seams, or lengthening or shortening sleeves.

5-YEAR TREND — ESTIMATED INDUSTRY SALES ($MILLIONS)

Year	Employee Size of Establishment									Total Industry Sales
	1-4 Emps.	5-9 Emps.	10-19 Emps.	20-49 Emps.	50-99 Emps.	100-249 Emps.	250-499 Emps.	500-999 Emps.	Unknown Emps.	
2014	19.6	44.4	108.8	74.5	23.3	22.6	8.5	7.7	4.5	313.9
2015	20.3	46.1	113.0	77.4	24.2	23.5	8.8	8.0	4.7	326.0
2016	21.1	47.8	117.0	80.1	25.0	24.3	9.1	8.3	4.9	337.5
2017	22.4	50.8	124.4	85.2	26.6	25.9	9.7	8.7	5.2	358.7
2018	23.8	54.1	132.5	90.7	28.3	27.5	10.3	9.1	5.5	381.9

INDUSTRY: FAMILY CLOTHING STORES (NAICS 44814)
PRODUCT LINE: MEN'S CASUAL SLACKS & JEANS (Sub Category)

NAICS 44814: Family Clothing Stores . This industry comprises establishments primarily engaged in retailing a general line of new clothing for men, women, and children, without specializing in sales for an individual gender or age group. These establishments may provide basic alterations, such as hemming, taking in or letting out seams, or lengthening or shortening sleeves.

5-YEAR TREND — ESTIMATED INDUSTRY SALES ($MILLIONS)

Year	Employee Size of Establishment									Total Industry Sales
	1-4 Emps.	5-9 Emps.	10-19 Emps.	20-49 Emps.	50-99 Emps.	100-249 Emps.	250-499 Emps.	500-999 Emps.	Unknown Emps.	
2014	79.7	143.0	615.5	1,886.8	1,979.0	493.7	488.0	193.4	21.6	5,900.7
2015	82.6	148.1	637.6	1,954.4	2,049.9	511.4	505.5	200.3	22.3	6,112.0
2016	85.3	153.0	658.4	2,018.2	2,116.8	528.1	522.0	206.8	23.1	6,311.5
2017	90.5	162.3	698.5	2,141.0	2,245.6	560.2	553.7	218.9	24.5	6,695.1
2018	96.2	172.5	742.4	2,275.7	2,386.8	595.5	588.5	232.1	26.0	7,115.7

INDUSTRY: DEPARTMENT STORES (NAICS 45211)
PRODUCT LINE: MEN'S CASUAL SLACKS & JEANS (Sub Category)

NAICS 45211: Department Stores Industry . This industry comprises establishments known as department stores primarily engaged in retailing a wide range of the following new products with no one merchandise line predominating: apparel, furniture, appliances and home furnishings; and selected additional items, such as paint, hardware, toiletries, cosmetics, photographic equipment, jewelry, toys, and sporting goods. Merchandise lines are normally arranged in separate departments.

5-YEAR TREND — ESTIMATED INDUSTRY SALES ($MILLIONS)

Year	Employee Size of Establishment									Total Industry Sales
	1-4 Emps.	5-9 Emps.	10-19 Emps.	20-49 Emps.	50-99 Emps.	100-249 Emps.	250-499 Emps.	500-999 Emps.	Unknown Emps.	
2014	6.6	13.1	34.0	68.0	49.9	3,265.8	288.8	5.3	2.3	3,733.9
2015	6.8	13.5	35.2	70.2	51.6	3,373.6	298.4	5.5	2.4	3,857.1
2016	7.0	13.9	36.2	72.3	53.1	3,474.7	307.3	5.7	2.4	3,972.8
2017	7.4	14.6	38.1	76.0	55.8	3,651.8	323.0	6.0	2.5	4,175.2
2018	7.8	15.4	40.1	80.1	58.8	3,845.7	340.1	6.3	2.7	4,396.9

INDUSTRY: WAREHOUSE CLUBS & SUPERCENTERS (NAICS 45291)
PRODUCT LINE: MEN'S CASUAL SLACKS & JEANS (Sub Category)

NAICS 45291: Warehouse Clubs and Superstores This industry comprises establishments known as warehouse clubs, superstores or supercenters primarily engaged in retailing a general line of groceries in combination with general lines of new merchandise, such as apparel, furniture, and appliances.

5-YEAR TREND — ESTIMATED INDUSTRY SALES ($MILLIONS)

Year	Employee Size of Establishment									Total Industry Sales
	1-4 Emps.	5-9 Emps.	10-19 Emps.	20-49 Emps.	50-99 Emps.	100-249 Emps.	250-499 Emps.	500-999 Emps.	Unknown Emps.	
2014	0.4	0.0	0.1	4.1	5.2	639.8	2,828.6	74.7	0.9	3,553.8
2015	0.5	0.0	0.1	4.3	5.4	663.2	2,932.0	77.5	0.9	3,683.8
2016	0.5	0.0	0.1	4.4	5.6	685.3	3,029.7	80.0	0.9	3,806.6
2017	0.5	0.0	0.1	4.8	6.0	744.4	3,290.7	86.9	1.0	4,134.4
2018	0.5	0.0	0.1	5.1	6.4	790.5	3,494.7	92.3	1.1	4,390.8

INDUSTRY: MEN'S CLOTHING STORES (NAICS 44811)
PRODUCT LINE: MEN'S WORK UNIFORMS (Sub Category)

NAICS 44811: Men's Clothing Stores. This industry comprises establishments primarily engaged in retailing a general line of new men's and boys' clothing. These establishments may provide basic alterations, such as hemming, taking in or letting out seams, or lengthening or shortening sleeves.

5-YEAR TREND — ESTIMATED INDUSTRY SALES ($MILLIONS)

Year	Employee Size of Establishment									Total Industry Sales
	1-4 Emps.	5-9 Emps.	10-19 Emps.	20-49 Emps.	50-99 Emps.	100-249 Emps.	250-499 Emps.	500-999 Emps.	Unknown Emps.	
2014	10.4	15.6	36.4	21.2	5.4	2.7	1.1	0.1	1.7	94.7
2015	10.9	16.3	38.1	22.2	5.7	2.8	1.2	0.1	1.8	99.1
2016	11.4	17.0	39.7	23.1	5.9	3.0	1.2	0.1	1.9	103.2
2017	11.8	17.6	41.1	23.9	6.1	3.1	1.3	0.1	2.0	106.9
2018	12.2	18.2	42.6	24.8	6.3	3.2	1.3	0.1	2.0	110.8

INDUSTRY: FAMILY CLOTHING STORES (NAICS 44814)
PRODUCT LINE: MEN'S WORK UNIFORMS (Sub Category)

NAICS 44814: Family Clothing Stores . This industry comprises establishments primarily engaged in retailing a general line of new clothing for men, women, and children, without specializing in sales for an individual gender or age group. These establishments may provide basic alterations, such as hemming, taking in or letting out seams, or lengthening or shortening sleeves.

5-YEAR TREND — ESTIMATED INDUSTRY SALES ($MILLIONS)

Year	Employee Size of Establishment									Total Industry Sales
	1-4 Emps.	5-9 Emps.	10-19 Emps.	20-49 Emps.	50-99 Emps.	100-249 Emps.	250-499 Emps.	500-999 Emps.	Unknown Emps.	
2014	11.0	19.7	85.0	260.5	273.3	68.2	67.4	26.7	3.0	814.8
2015	11.4	20.5	88.0	269.9	283.0	70.6	69.8	27.7	3.1	844.0
2016	11.8	21.1	90.9	278.7	292.3	72.9	72.1	28.6	3.2	871.5
2017	12.5	22.4	96.4	295.6	310.1	77.4	76.5	30.2	3.4	924.5
2018	13.3	23.8	102.5	314.2	329.6	82.2	81.3	32.0	3.6	982.5

INDUSTRY: MEN'S CLOTHING STORES (NAICS 44811)
PRODUCT LINE: MEN'S DRESS SHIRTS (Sub Category)

NAICS 44811: Men's Clothing Stores. This industry comprises establishments primarily engaged in retailing a general line of new men's and boys' clothing. These establishments may provide basic alterations, such as hemming, taking in or letting out seams, or lengthening or shortening sleeves.

5-YEAR TREND — ESTIMATED INDUSTRY SALES ($MILLIONS)

Year	Employee Size of Establishment									Total Industry Sales
	1-4 Emps.	5-9 Emps.	10-19 Emps.	20-49 Emps.	50-99 Emps.	100-249 Emps.	250-499 Emps.	500-999 Emps.	Unknown Emps.	
2014	57.8	86.3	201.3	117.4	30.0	15.0	6.3	0.3	9.6	524.0
2015	60.5	90.2	210.6	122.8	31.4	15.7	6.6	0.4	10.1	548.1
2016	63.0	94.0	219.4	127.9	32.7	16.4	6.9	0.4	10.5	571.2
2017	65.2	97.3	227.2	132.4	33.8	17.0	7.1	0.4	10.8	591.3
2018	67.6	100.9	235.5	137.3	35.1	17.6	7.4	0.4	11.2	613.0

INDUSTRY: FAMILY CLOTHING STORES (NAICS 44814)
PRODUCT LINE: MEN'S DRESS SHIRTS (Sub Category)

NAICS 44814: Family Clothing Stores . This industry comprises establishments primarily engaged in retailing a general line of new clothing for men, women, and children, without specializing in sales for an individual gender or age group. These establishments may provide basic alterations, such as hemming, taking in or letting out seams, or lengthening or shortening sleeves.

5-YEAR TREND — ESTIMATED INDUSTRY SALES ($MILLIONS)

Year	Employee Size of Establishment									Total Industry Sales
	1-4 Emps.	5-9 Emps.	10-19 Emps.	20-49 Emps.	50-99 Emps.	100-249 Emps.	250-499 Emps.	500-999 Emps.	Unknown Emps.	
2014	27.2	48.8	210.2	644.4	675.9	168.6	166.7	66.1	7.4	2,015.4
2015	28.2	50.6	217.8	667.5	700.1	174.7	172.6	68.4	7.6	2,087.5
2016	29.1	52.2	224.9	689.3	723.0	180.4	178.3	70.6	7.9	2,155.7
2017	30.9	55.4	238.6	731.2	767.0	191.3	189.1	74.8	8.4	2,286.7
2018	32.9	58.9	253.6	777.2	815.2	203.4	201.0	79.3	8.9	2,430.3

INDUSTRY: DEPARTMENT STORES (NAICS 45211)
PRODUCT LINE: MEN'S DRESS SHIRTS (Sub Category)

NAICS 45211: Department Stores Industry . This industry comprises establishments known as department stores primarily engaged in retailing a wide range of the following new products with no one merchandise line predominating: apparel, furniture, appliances and home furnishings; and selected additional items, such as paint, hardware, toiletries, cosmetics, photographic equipment, jewelry, toys, and sporting goods. Merchandise lines are normally arranged in separate departments.

5-YEAR TREND – ESTIMATED INDUSTRY SALES ($MILLIONS)

Year	Employee Size of Establishment									Total
	1-4 Emps.	5-9 Emps.	10-19 Emps.	20-49 Emps.	50-99 Emps.	100-249 Emps.	250-499 Emps.	500-999 Emps.	Unknown Emps.	Industry Sales
2014	0.0	0.0	0.1	4.5	84.9	281.6	123.6	16.5	0.7	511.9
2015	0.0	0.0	0.1	4.5	86.0	285.3	125.1	16.8	0.7	518.5
2016	0.0	0.0	0.1	4.6	86.9	288.3	126.5	16.9	0.7	524.1
2017	0.0	0.0	0.1	4.6	87.3	289.7	127.1	17.0	0.7	526.6
2018	0.0	0.0	0.1	4.6	88.0	291.8	128.0	17.2	0.7	530.4

INDUSTRY: MEN'S CLOTHING STORES (NAICS 44811)
PRODUCT LINE: MEN'S SPORT SHIRTS & T-SHIRTS (Sub Category)

NAICS 44811: Men's Clothing Stores. This industry comprises establishments primarily engaged in retailing a general line of new men's and boys' clothing. These establishments may provide basic alterations, such as hemming, taking in or letting out seams, or lengthening or shortening sleeves.

5-YEAR TREND – ESTIMATED INDUSTRY SALES ($MILLIONS)

Year	Employee Size of Establishment									Total
	1-4 Emps.	5-9 Emps.	10-19 Emps.	20-49 Emps.	50-99 Emps.	100-249 Emps.	250-499 Emps.	500-999 Emps.	Unknown Emps.	Industry Sales
2014	112.7	168.2	392.7	228.9	58.5	29.3	12.4	0.7	18.8	1,022.0
2015	117.9	176.0	410.7	239.4	61.2	30.7	12.9	0.7	19.6	1,069.1
2016	122.9	183.4	428.0	249.5	63.7	32.0	13.5	0.7	20.4	1,114.0
2017	127.2	189.8	443.1	258.3	66.0	33.1	13.9	0.7	21.2	1,153.3
2018	131.9	196.8	459.3	267.8	68.4	34.3	14.5	0.8	21.9	1,195.6

INDUSTRY: WOMEN'S CLOTHING STORES (NAICS 44812)
PRODUCT LINE: MEN'S SPORT SHIRTS & T-SHIRTS (Sub Category)

NAICS 44812: Women's Clothing Stores . This industry comprises establishments primarily engaged in retailing a general line of new women's, misses' and juniors' clothing, including maternity wear. These establishments may provide basic alterations, such as hemming, taking in or letting out seams, or lengthening or shortening sleeves.

5-YEAR TREND – ESTIMATED INDUSTRY SALES ($MILLIONS)

Year	Employee Size of Establishment									Total Industry Sales
	1-4 Emps.	5-9 Emps.	10-19 Emps.	20-49 Emps.	50-99 Emps.	100-249 Emps.	250-499 Emps.	500-999 Emps.	Unknown Emps.	
2014	28.6	64.9	159.0	108.9	34.0	33.1	12.4	11.2	6.6	458.7
2015	29.7	67.4	165.2	113.1	35.3	34.3	12.9	11.7	6.9	476.4
2016	30.8	69.8	171.0	117.1	36.5	35.5	13.3	12.1	7.1	493.2
2017	32.7	74.2	181.8	124.5	38.8	37.8	14.2	12.7	7.6	524.2
2018	34.9	79.0	193.6	132.6	41.4	40.3	15.1	13.3	8.1	558.2

INDUSTRY: FAMILY CLOTHING STORES (NAICS 44814)
PRODUCT LINE: MEN'S SPORT SHIRTS & T-SHIRTS (Sub Category)

NAICS 44814: Family Clothing Stores . This industry comprises establishments primarily engaged in retailing a general line of new clothing for men, women, and children, without specializing in sales for an individual gender or age group. These establishments may provide basic alterations, such as hemming, taking in or letting out seams, or lengthening or shortening sleeves.

5-YEAR TREND – ESTIMATED INDUSTRY SALES ($MILLIONS)

Year	Employee Size of Establishment									Total Industry Sales
	1-4 Emps.	5-9 Emps.	10-19 Emps.	20-49 Emps.	50-99 Emps.	100-249 Emps.	250-499 Emps.	500-999 Emps.	Unknown Emps.	
2014	89.8	161.1	693.5	2,125.8	2,229.7	556.2	549.8	217.9	24.3	6,648.1
2015	93.1	166.9	718.3	2,201.9	2,309.5	576.2	569.5	225.7	25.2	6,886.2
2016	96.1	172.3	741.8	2,273.8	2,384.9	595.0	588.1	233.0	26.0	7,111.0
2017	101.9	182.8	786.9	2,412.2	2,530.0	631.2	623.8	246.7	27.6	7,543.1
2018	108.4	194.3	836.4	2,563.9	2,689.2	670.9	663.1	261.5	29.3	8,017.0

INDUSTRY: DEPARTMENT STORES (NAICS 45211)
PRODUCT LINE: MEN'S SPORT SHIRTS & T-SHIRTS (Sub Category)

NAICS 45211: Department Stores Industry . This industry comprises establishments known as department stores primarily engaged in retailing a wide range of the following new products with no one merchandise line predominating: apparel, furniture, appliances and home furnishings; and selected additional items, such as paint, hardware, toiletries, cosmetics, photographic equipment, jewelry, toys, and sporting goods. Merchandise lines are normally arranged in separate departments.

5-YEAR TREND — ESTIMATED INDUSTRY SALES ($MILLIONS)

Year	Employee Size of Establishment									Total
	1-4 Emps.	5-9 Emps.	10-19 Emps.	20-49 Emps.	50-99 Emps.	100-249 Emps.	250-499 Emps.	500-999 Emps.	Unknown Emps.	Industry Sales
2014	0.2	0.1	0.3	23.0	436.1	1,446.6	634.6	85.0	3.7	2,629.5
2015	0.2	0.1	0.3	23.3	441.8	1,465.2	642.8	86.1	3.7	2,663.5
2016	0.2	0.1	0.3	23.5	446.5	1,481.0	649.7	87.0	3.8	2,692.1
2017	0.2	0.1	0.3	23.6	448.6	1,487.9	652.7	87.5	3.8	2,704.7
2018	0.2	0.1	0.3	23.8	451.8	1,498.6	657.4	88.1	3.8	2,724.2

INDUSTRY: WAREHOUSE CLUBS & SUPERCENTERS (NAICS 45291)
PRODUCT LINE: MEN'S SPORT SHIRTS & T-SHIRTS (Sub Category)

NAICS 45291: Warehouse Clubs and Superstores This industry comprises establishments known as warehouse clubs, superstores or supercenters primarily engaged in retailing a general line of groceries in combination with general lines of new merchandise, such as apparel, furniture, and appliances.

5-YEAR TREND — ESTIMATED INDUSTRY SALES ($MILLIONS)

Year	Employee Size of Establishment									Total
	1-4 Emps.	5-9 Emps.	10-19 Emps.	20-49 Emps.	50-99 Emps.	100-249 Emps.	250-499 Emps.	500-999 Emps.	Unknown Emps.	Industry Sales
2014	0.3	0.0	0.1	2.8	3.5	428.3	1,893.6	50.0	0.6	2,379.1
2015	0.3	0.0	0.1	2.9	3.6	444.0	1,962.8	51.9	0.6	2,466.1
2016	0.3	0.0	0.1	2.9	3.7	458.8	2,028.3	53.6	0.6	2,548.3
2017	0.3	0.0	0.1	3.2	4.0	498.3	2,202.9	58.2	0.7	2,767.8
2018	0.4	0.0	0.1	3.4	4.3	529.2	2,339.5	61.8	0.7	2,939.4

INDUSTRY: MEN'S CLOTHING STORES (NAICS 44811)
PRODUCT LINE: MEN'S SWEATERS (Sub Category)

NAICS 44811: Men's Clothing Stores. This industry comprises establishments primarily engaged in retailing a general line of new men's and boys' clothing. These establishments may provide basic alterations, such as hemming, taking in or letting out seams, or lengthening or shortening sleeves.

5-YEAR TREND — ESTIMATED INDUSTRY SALES ($MILLIONS)

Year	Employee Size of Establishment									Total
	1-4 Emps.	5-9 Emps.	10-19 Emps.	20-49 Emps.	50-99 Emps.	100-249 Emps.	250-499 Emps.	500-999 Emps.	Unknown Emps.	Industry Sales
2014	26.2	39.2	91.4	53.3	13.6	6.8	2.9	0.2	4.4	237.9
2015	27.4	41.0	95.6	55.7	14.2	7.1	3.0	0.2	4.6	248.8
2016	28.6	42.7	99.6	58.1	14.8	7.4	3.1	0.2	4.8	259.3
2017	29.6	44.2	103.1	60.1	15.4	7.7	3.2	0.2	4.9	268.4
2018	30.7	45.8	106.9	62.3	15.9	8.0	3.4	0.2	5.1	278.3

INDUSTRY: FAMILY CLOTHING STORES (NAICS 44814)
PRODUCT LINE: MEN'S SWEATERS (Sub Category)

NAICS 44814: Family Clothing Stores . This industry comprises establishments primarily engaged in retailing a general line of new clothing for men, women, and children, without specializing in sales for an individual gender or age group. These establishments may provide basic alterations, such as hemming, taking in or letting out seams, or lengthening or shortening sleeves.

5-YEAR TREND — ESTIMATED INDUSTRY SALES ($MILLIONS)

Year	Employee Size of Establishment									Total
	1-4 Emps.	5-9 Emps.	10-19 Emps.	20-49 Emps.	50-99 Emps.	100-249 Emps.	250-499 Emps.	500-999 Emps.	Unknown Emps.	Industry Sales
2014	26.5	47.5	204.6	627.1	657.8	164.1	162.2	64.3	7.2	1,961.2
2015	27.5	49.2	211.9	649.6	681.3	170.0	168.0	66.6	7.4	2,031.5
2016	28.4	50.8	218.8	670.8	703.6	175.5	173.5	68.8	7.7	2,097.8
2017	30.1	53.9	232.1	711.6	746.4	186.2	184.0	72.8	8.1	2,225.3
2018	32.0	57.3	246.7	756.4	793.3	197.9	195.6	77.1	8.6	2,365.0

INDUSTRY: DEPARTMENT STORES (NAICS 45211)
PRODUCT LINE: MEN'S SWEATERS (Sub Category)

NAICS 45211: Department Stores Industry . This industry comprises establishments known as department stores primarily engaged in retailing a wide range of the following new products with no one merchandise line predominating: apparel, furniture, appliances and home furnishings; and selected additional items, such as paint, hardware, toiletries, cosmetics, photographic equipment, jewelry, toys, and sporting goods. Merchandise lines are normally arranged in separate departments.

5-YEAR TREND — ESTIMATED INDUSTRY SALES ($MILLIONS)

Year	Employee Size of Establishment									Total Industry Sales
	1-4 Emps.	5-9 Emps.	10-19 Emps.	20-49 Emps.	50-99 Emps.	100-249 Emps.	250-499 Emps.	500-999 Emps.	Unknown Emps.	
2014	0.0	0.0	0.0	3.3	62.4	207.0	90.8	12.2	0.5	376.3
2015	0.0	0.0	0.0	3.3	63.2	209.7	92.0	12.3	0.5	381.1
2016	0.0	0.0	0.0	3.4	63.9	211.9	93.0	12.5	0.5	385.3
2017	0.0	0.0	0.0	3.4	64.2	212.9	93.4	12.5	0.5	387.0
2018	0.0	0.0	0.0	3.4	64.7	214.5	94.1	12.6	0.5	389.8

INDUSTRY: MEN'S CLOTHING STORES (NAICS 44811)
PRODUCT LINE: MEN'S SOCKS & UNDERWEAR (Sub Category)

NAICS 44811: Men's Clothing Stores. This industry comprises establishments primarily engaged in retailing a general line of new men's and boys' clothing. These establishments may provide basic alterations, such as hemming, taking in or letting out seams, or lengthening or shortening sleeves.

5-YEAR TREND — ESTIMATED INDUSTRY SALES ($MILLIONS)

Year	Employee Size of Establishment									Total Industry Sales
	1-4 Emps.	5-9 Emps.	10-19 Emps.	20-49 Emps.	50-99 Emps.	100-249 Emps.	250-499 Emps.	500-999 Emps.	Unknown Emps.	
2014	17.2	25.7	59.9	34.9	8.9	4.5	1.9	0.1	2.9	155.8
2015	18.0	26.8	62.6	36.5	9.3	4.7	2.0	0.1	3.0	163.0
2016	18.7	28.0	65.3	38.0	9.7	4.9	2.1	0.1	3.1	169.9
2017	19.4	28.9	67.6	39.4	10.1	5.0	2.1	0.1	3.2	175.9
2018	20.1	30.0	70.0	40.8	10.4	5.2	2.2	0.1	3.3	182.3

INDUSTRY: FAMILY CLOTHING STORES (NAICS 44814)
PRODUCT LINE: MEN'S SOCKS & UNDERWEAR (Sub Category)

NAICS 44814: Family Clothing Stores . This industry comprises
establishments primarily engaged in retailing a general line of new clothing
for men, women, and children, without specializing in sales for an individual
gender or age group. These establishments may provide basic alterations,
such as hemming, taking in or letting out seams, or lengthening or shortening sleeves.

5-YEAR TREND — ESTIMATED INDUSTRY SALES ($MILLIONS)

Year	Employee Size of Establishment									Total Industry Sales
	1-4 Emps.	5-9 Emps.	10-19 Emps.	20-49 Emps.	50-99 Emps.	100-249 Emps.	250-499 Emps.	500-999 Emps.	Unknown Emps.	
2014	18.5	33.3	143.1	438.7	460.2	114.8	113.5	45.0	5.0	1,372.1
2015	19.2	34.4	148.3	454.4	476.6	118.9	117.5	46.6	5.2	1,421.2
2016	19.8	35.6	153.1	469.3	492.2	122.8	121.4	48.1	5.4	1,467.6
2017	21.0	37.7	162.4	497.8	522.2	130.3	128.8	50.9	5.7	1,556.8
2018	22.4	40.1	172.6	529.2	555.0	138.5	136.9	54.0	6.0	1,654.6

INDUSTRY: DEPARTMENT STORES (NAICS 45211)
PRODUCT LINE: MEN'S SOCKS & UNDERWEAR (Sub Category)

NAICS 45211: Department Stores Industry . This industry comprises
establishments known as department stores primarily engaged in retailing
a wide range of the following new products with no one merchandise line
predominating: apparel, furniture, appliances and home furnishings; and
selected additional items, such as paint, hardware, toiletries, cosmetics,
photographic equipment, jewelry, toys, and sporting goods. Merchandise lines
are normally arranged in separate departments.

5-YEAR TREND — ESTIMATED INDUSTRY SALES ($MILLIONS)

Year	Employee Size of Establishment									Total Industry Sales
	1-4 Emps.	5-9 Emps.	10-19 Emps.	20-49 Emps.	50-99 Emps.	100-249 Emps.	250-499 Emps.	500-999 Emps.	Unknown Emps.	
2014	0.1	0.0	0.2	12.6	239.5	794.3	348.4	46.7	2.0	1,443.8
2015	0.1	0.0	0.2	12.8	242.6	804.5	352.9	47.3	2.0	1,462.4
2016	0.1	0.0	0.2	12.9	245.2	813.2	356.7	47.8	2.1	1,478.2
2017	0.1	0.0	0.2	13.0	246.3	816.9	358.4	48.0	2.1	1,485.0
2018	0.1	0.0	0.2	13.1	248.1	822.8	361.0	48.4	2.1	1,495.7

INDUSTRY: WAREHOUSE CLUBS & SUPERCENTERS (NAICS 45291)
PRODUCT LINE: MEN'S SOCKS & UNDERWEAR (Sub Category)

NAICS 45291: Warehouse Clubs and Superstores This industry comprises establishments known as warehouse clubs, superstores or supercenters primarily engaged in retailing a general line of groceries in combination with general lines of new merchandise, such as apparel, furniture, and appliances.

5-YEAR TREND — ESTIMATED INDUSTRY SALES ($MILLIONS)

Year	Employee Size of Establishment									Total Industry Sales
	1-4 Emps.	5-9 Emps.	10-19 Emps.	20-49 Emps.	50-99 Emps.	100-249 Emps.	250-499 Emps.	500-999 Emps.	Unknown Emps.	
2014	0.3	0.0	0.1	2.9	3.7	456.7	2,019.2	53.4	0.6	2,537.0
2015	0.3	0.0	0.1	3.0	3.8	473.4	2,093.1	55.3	0.7	2,629.7
2016	0.3	0.0	0.1	3.1	4.0	489.2	2,162.8	57.1	0.7	2,717.4
2017	0.4	0.0	0.1	3.4	4.3	531.4	2,349.1	62.1	0.7	2,951.4
2018	0.4	0.0	0.1	3.6	4.6	564.3	2,494.8	65.9	0.8	3,134.4

INDUSTRY: MEN'S CLOTHING STORES (NAICS 44811)
PRODUCT LINE: MEN'S SPORTS APPAREL (Sub Category)

NAICS 44811: Men's Clothing Stores. This industry comprises establishments primarily engaged in retailing a general line of new men's and boys' clothing. These establishments may provide basic alterations, such as hemming, taking in or letting out seams, or lengthening or shortening sleeves.

5-YEAR TREND — ESTIMATED INDUSTRY SALES ($MILLIONS)

Year	Employee Size of Establishment									Total Industry Sales
	1-4 Emps.	5-9 Emps.	10-19 Emps.	20-49 Emps.	50-99 Emps.	100-249 Emps.	250-499 Emps.	500-999 Emps.	Unknown Emps.	
2014	34.5	51.4	120.0	70.0	17.9	9.0	3.8	0.2	5.7	312.4
2015	36.0	53.8	125.5	73.2	18.7	9.4	3.9	0.2	6.0	326.7
2016	37.6	56.0	130.8	76.2	19.5	9.8	4.1	0.2	6.2	340.5
2017	38.9	58.0	135.4	78.9	20.2	10.1	4.3	0.2	6.5	352.5
2018	40.3	60.1	140.4	81.8	20.9	10.5	4.4	0.2	6.7	365.4

| INDUSTRY: FAMILY CLOTHING STORES (NAICS 44814) |
| PRODUCT LINE: MEN'S SPORTS APPAREL (Sub Category) |

NAICS 44814: Family Clothing Stores . This industry comprises establishments primarily engaged in retailing a general line of new clothing for men, women, and children, without specializing in sales for an individual gender or age group. These establishments may provide basic alterations, such as hemming, taking in or letting out seams, or lengthening or shortening sleeves.

5-YEAR TREND — ESTIMATED INDUSTRY SALES ($MILLIONS)

| Year | Employee Size of Establishment | | | | | | | | | Total Industry Sales |
	1-4 Emps.	5-9 Emps.	10-19 Emps.	20-49 Emps.	50-99 Emps.	100-249 Emps.	250-499 Emps.	500-999 Emps.	Unknown Emps.	
2014	13.0	23.3	100.2	307.3	322.3	80.4	79.5	31.5	3.5	960.9
2015	13.5	24.1	103.8	318.3	333.8	83.3	82.3	32.6	3.6	995.3
2016	13.9	24.9	107.2	328.7	344.7	86.0	85.0	33.7	3.8	1,027.8
2017	14.7	26.4	113.7	348.7	365.7	91.2	90.2	35.7	4.0	1,090.3
2018	15.7	28.1	120.9	370.6	388.7	97.0	95.8	37.8	4.2	1,158.8

| INDUSTRY: DEPARTMENT STORES (NAICS 45211) |
| PRODUCT LINE: MEN'S SPORTS APPAREL (Sub Category) |

NAICS 45211: Department Stores Industry . This industry comprises establishments known as department stores primarily engaged in retailing a wide range of the following new products with no one merchandise line predominating: apparel, furniture, appliances and home furnishings; and selected additional items, such as paint, hardware, toiletries, cosmetics, photographic equipment, jewelry, toys, and sporting goods. Merchandise lines are normally arranged in separate departments.

5-YEAR TREND — ESTIMATED INDUSTRY SALES ($MILLIONS)

| Year | Employee Size of Establishment | | | | | | | | | Total Industry Sales |
	1-4 Emps.	5-9 Emps.	10-19 Emps.	20-49 Emps.	50-99 Emps.	100-249 Emps.	250-499 Emps.	500-999 Emps.	Unknown Emps.	
2014	0.0	0.0	0.1	5.9	111.2	368.9	161.8	21.7	0.9	670.5
2015	0.0	0.0	0.1	5.9	112.6	373.6	163.9	22.0	1.0	679.2
2016	0.1	0.0	0.1	6.0	113.9	377.6	165.7	22.2	1.0	686.5
2017	0.1	0.0	0.1	6.0	114.4	379.4	166.4	22.3	1.0	689.7
2018	0.1	0.0	0.1	6.1	115.2	382.1	167.6	22.5	1.0	694.6

INDUSTRY: MEN'S CLOTHING STORES (NAICS 44811)
PRODUCT LINE: MEN'S ACCESSORIES (Sub Category)

NAICS 44811: Men's Clothing Stores. This industry comprises establishments primarily engaged in retailing a general line of new men's and boys' clothing. These establishments may provide basic alterations, such as hemming, taking in or letting out seams, or lengthening or shortening sleeves.

5-YEAR TREND — ESTIMATED INDUSTRY SALES ($MILLIONS)

Year	Employee Size of Establishment									Total Industry Sales
	1-4 Emps.	5-9 Emps.	10-19 Emps.	20-49 Emps.	50-99 Emps.	100-249 Emps.	250-499 Emps.	500-999 Emps.	Unknown Emps.	
2014	66.2	98.7	230.5	134.3	34.3	17.2	7.3	0.4	11.0	599.9
2015	69.2	103.3	241.1	140.5	35.9	18.0	7.6	0.4	11.5	627.5
2016	72.1	107.6	251.2	146.4	37.4	18.8	7.9	0.4	12.0	653.9
2017	74.7	111.4	260.0	151.6	38.7	19.4	8.2	0.4	12.4	676.9
2018	77.4	115.5	269.6	157.2	40.1	20.1	8.5	0.5	12.9	701.7

INDUSTRY: FAMILY CLOTHING STORES (NAICS 44814)
PRODUCT LINE: MEN'S ACCESSORIES (Sub Category)

NAICS 44814: Family Clothing Stores . This industry comprises establishments primarily engaged in retailing a general line of new clothing for men, women, and children, without specializing in sales for an individual gender or age group. These establishments may provide basic alterations, such as hemming, taking in or letting out seams, or lengthening or shortening sleeves.

5-YEAR TREND — ESTIMATED INDUSTRY SALES ($MILLIONS)

Year	Employee Size of Establishment									Total Industry Sales
	1-4 Emps.	5-9 Emps.	10-19 Emps.	20-49 Emps.	50-99 Emps.	100-249 Emps.	250-499 Emps.	500-999 Emps.	Unknown Emps.	
2014	25.3	45.3	195.2	598.4	627.6	156.6	154.8	61.3	6.8	1,871.3
2015	26.2	47.0	202.2	619.8	650.1	162.2	160.3	63.5	7.1	1,938.3
2016	27.1	48.5	208.8	640.0	671.3	167.5	165.5	65.6	7.3	2,001.6
2017	28.7	51.5	221.5	679.0	712.1	177.7	175.6	69.4	7.8	2,123.2
2018	30.5	54.7	235.4	721.7	756.9	188.8	186.6	73.6	8.3	2,256.6

INDUSTRY: DEPARTMENT STORES (NAICS 45211)
PRODUCT LINE: MEN'S ACCESSORIES (Sub Category)

NAICS 45211: Department Stores Industry . This industry comprises establishments known as department stores primarily engaged in retailing a wide range of the following new products with no one merchandise line predominating: apparel, furniture, appliances and home furnishings; and selected additional items, such as paint, hardware, toiletries, cosmetics, photographic equipment, jewelry, toys, and sporting goods. Merchandise lines are normally arranged in separate departments.

5-YEAR TREND – ESTIMATED INDUSTRY SALES ($MILLIONS)

Year	Employee Size of Establishment									Total Industry Sales
	1-4 Emps.	5-9 Emps.	10-19 Emps.	20-49 Emps.	50-99 Emps.	100-249 Emps.	250-499 Emps.	500-999 Emps.	Unknown Emps.	
2014	0.1	0.0	0.1	6.0	113.0	374.9	164.5	22.0	1.0	681.6
2015	0.1	0.0	0.1	6.0	114.5	379.8	166.6	22.3	1.0	690.4
2016	0.1	0.0	0.1	6.1	115.7	383.9	168.4	22.6	1.0	697.8
2017	0.1	0.0	0.1	6.1	116.3	385.6	169.2	22.7	1.0	701.0
2018	0.1	0.0	0.1	6.2	117.1	388.4	170.4	22.8	1.0	706.1

INDUSTRY: MEN'S CLOTHING STORES (NAICS 44811)
PRODUCT LINE: MEN'S CUSTOM-MADE GARMENTS Category)

NAICS 44811: Men's Clothing Stores. This industry comprises establishments primarily engaged in retailing a general line of new men's and boys' clothing. These establishments may provide basic alterations, such as hemming, taking in or letting out seams, or lengthening or shortening sleeves.

5-YEAR TREND – ESTIMATED INDUSTRY SALES ($MILLIONS)

Year	Employee Size of Establishment									Total Industry Sales
	1-4 Emps.	5-9 Emps.	10-19 Emps.	20-49 Emps.	50-99 Emps.	100-249 Emps.	250-499 Emps.	500-999 Emps.	Unknown Emps.	
2014	8.7	12.9	30.2	17.6	4.5	2.3	0.9	0.1	1.4	78.5
2015	9.1	13.5	31.6	18.4	4.7	2.4	1.0	0.1	1.5	82.1
2016	9.4	14.1	32.9	19.2	4.9	2.5	1.0	0.1	1.6	85.6
2017	9.8	14.6	34.0	19.8	5.1	2.5	1.1	0.1	1.6	88.6
2018	10.1	15.1	35.3	20.6	5.3	2.6	1.1	0.1	1.7	91.8

INDUSTRY: MEN'S CLOTHING STORES (NAICS 44811)
PRODUCT LINE: MEN'S SWEAT TOPS & PANTS (Sub Category)

NAICS 44811: Men's Clothing Stores. This industry comprises establishments primarily engaged in retailing a general line of new men's and boys' clothing. These establishments may provide basic alterations, such as hemming, taking in or letting out seams, or lengthening or shortening sleeves.

5-YEAR TREND — ESTIMATED INDUSTRY SALES ($MILLIONS)

Year	Employee Size of Establishment									Total
	1-4 Emps.	5-9 Emps.	10-19 Emps.	20-49 Emps.	50-99 Emps.	100-249 Emps.	250-499 Emps.	500-999 Emps.	Unknown Emps.	Industry Sales
2014	8.9	13.3	31.0	18.1	4.6	2.3	1.0	0.1	1.5	80.7
2015	9.3	13.9	32.4	18.9	4.8	2.4	1.0	0.1	1.5	84.4
2016	9.7	14.5	33.8	19.7	5.0	2.5	1.1	0.1	1.6	87.9
2017	10.0	15.0	35.0	20.4	5.2	2.6	1.1	0.1	1.7	91.0
2018	10.4	15.5	36.2	21.1	5.4	2.7	1.1	0.1	1.7	94.4

INDUSTRY: FAMILY CLOTHING STORES (NAICS 44814)
PRODUCT LINE: MEN'S SWEAT TOPS & PANTS (Sub Category)

NAICS 44814: Family Clothing Stores . This industry comprises establishments primarily engaged in retailing a general line of new clothing for men, women, and children, without specializing in sales for an individual gender or age group. These establishments may provide basic alterations, such as hemming, taking in or letting out seams, or lengthening or shortening sleeves.

5-YEAR TREND — ESTIMATED INDUSTRY SALES ($MILLIONS)

Year	Employee Size of Establishment									Total
	1-4 Emps.	5-9 Emps.	10-19 Emps.	20-49 Emps.	50-99 Emps.	100-249 Emps.	250-499 Emps.	500-999 Emps.	Unknown Emps.	Industry Sales
2014	20.3	36.4	156.7	480.4	503.9	125.7	124.2	49.2	5.5	1,502.4
2015	21.0	37.7	162.3	497.6	521.9	130.2	128.7	51.0	5.7	1,556.2
2016	21.7	38.9	167.6	513.8	538.9	134.5	132.9	52.7	5.9	1,607.0
2017	23.0	41.3	177.8	545.1	571.7	142.6	141.0	55.7	6.2	1,704.6
2018	24.5	43.9	189.0	579.4	607.7	151.6	149.8	59.1	6.6	1,811.7

INDUSTRY: DEPARTMENT STORES (NAICS 45211)
PRODUCT LINE: MEN'S SWEAT TOPS & PANTS (Sub Category)

NAICS 45211: Department Stores Industry . This industry comprises establishments known as department stores primarily engaged in retailing a wide range of the following new products with no one merchandise line predominating: apparel, furniture, appliances and home furnishings; and selected additional items, such as paint, hardware, toiletries, cosmetics, photographic equipment, jewelry, toys, and sporting goods. Merchandise lines are normally arranged in separate departments.

5-YEAR TREND – ESTIMATED INDUSTRY SALES ($MILLIONS)

Year	1-4 Emps.	5-9 Emps.	10-19 Emps.	20-49 Emps.	50-99 Emps.	100-249 Emps.	250-499 Emps.	500-999 Emps.	Unknown Emps.	Total Industry Sales
2014	0.1	0.0	0.1	6.1	115.9	384.4	168.7	22.6	1.0	698.8
2015	0.1	0.0	0.1	6.2	117.4	389.4	170.8	22.9	1.0	707.8
2016	0.1	0.0	0.1	6.3	118.7	393.6	172.7	23.1	1.0	715.5
2017	0.1	0.0	0.1	6.3	119.2	395.4	173.5	23.3	1.0	718.8
2018	0.1	0.0	0.1	6.3	120.1	398.3	174.7	23.4	1.0	724.0

INDUSTRY: MEN'S CLOTHING STORES (NAICS 44811)
PRODUCT LINE: WOMEN'S WEAR (Main Category)

NAICS 44811: Men's Clothing Stores. This industry comprises establishments primarily engaged in retailing a general line of new men's and boys' clothing. These establishments may provide basic alterations, such as hemming, taking in or letting out seams, or lengthening or shortening sleeves.

5-YEAR TREND – ESTIMATED INDUSTRY SALES ($MILLIONS)

Year	1-4 Emps.	5-9 Emps.	10-19 Emps.	20-49 Emps.	50-99 Emps.	100-249 Emps.	250-499 Emps.	500-999 Emps.	Unknown Emps.	Total Industry Sales
2014	19.1	28.4	66.4	38.7	9.9	5.0	2.1	0.1	3.2	172.8
2015	19.9	29.8	69.4	40.5	10.3	5.2	2.2	0.1	3.3	180.8
2016	20.8	31.0	72.4	42.2	10.8	5.4	2.3	0.1	3.5	188.4
2017	21.5	32.1	74.9	43.7	11.2	5.6	2.4	0.1	3.6	195.0
2018	22.3	33.3	77.7	45.3	11.6	5.8	2.4	0.1	3.7	202.2

INDUSTRY: WOMEN'S CLOTHING STORES (NAICS 44812)
PRODUCT LINE: WOMEN'S WEAR (Main Category)

NAICS 44812: Women's Clothing Stores . This industry comprises establishments primarily engaged in retailing a general line of new women's, misses' and juniors' clothing, including maternity wear. These establishments may provide basic alterations, such as hemming, taking in or letting out seams, or lengthening or shortening sleeves.

5-YEAR TREND – ESTIMATED INDUSTRY SALES ($MILLIONS)

Year	Employee Size of Establishment									Total Industry Sales
	1-4 Emps.	5-9 Emps.	10-19 Emps.	20-49 Emps.	50-99 Emps.	100-249 Emps.	250-499 Emps.	500-999 Emps.	Unknown Emps.	
2014	2,576	5,842	14,311	9,798	3,058	2,975	1,114	1,010	596	41,281
2015	2,675	6,067	14,863	10,176	3,176	3,090	1,157	1,049	620	42,874
2016	2,770	6,281	15,387	10,535	3,288	3,199	1,198	1,086	641	44,385
2017	2,945	6,678	16,359	11,201	3,496	3,401	1,274	1,140	682	47,175
2018	3,136	7,113	17,425	11,930	3,724	3,623	1,357	1,196	726	50,229

INDUSTRY: FAMILY CLOTHING STORES (NAICS 44814)
PRODUCT LINE: WOMEN'S WEAR (Main Category)

NAICS 44814: Family Clothing Stores . This industry comprises establishments primarily engaged in retailing a general line of new clothing for men, women, and children, without specializing in sales for an individual gender or age group. These establishments may provide basic alterations, such as hemming, taking in or letting out seams, or lengthening or shortening sleeves.

5-YEAR TREND – ESTIMATED INDUSTRY SALES ($MILLIONS)

Year	Employee Size of Establishment									Total Industry Sales
	1-4 Emps.	5-9 Emps.	10-19 Emps.	20-49 Emps.	50-99 Emps.	100-249 Emps.	250-499 Emps.	500-999 Emps.	Unknown Emps.	
2014	625	1,120	4,822	14,783	15,505	3,868	3,823	1,515	169	46,230
2015	647	1,160	4,995	15,312	16,060	4,007	3,960	1,569	175	47,886
2016	668	1,198	5,158	15,812	16,584	4,137	4,089	1,621	181	49,449
2017	709	1,271	5,472	16,774	17,593	4,389	4,338	1,715	192	52,454
2018	754	1,351	5,816	17,829	18,700	4,665	4,611	1,818	204	55,749

INDUSTRY: DEPARTMENT STORES (NAICS 45211)
PRODUCT LINE: WOMEN'S WEAR (Main Category)

NAICS 45211: Department Stores Industry . This industry comprises establishments known as department stores primarily engaged in retailing a wide range of the following new products with no one merchandise line predominating: apparel, furniture, appliances and home furnishings; and selected additional items, such as paint, hardware, toiletries, cosmetics, photographic equipment, jewelry, toys, and sporting goods. Merchandise lines are normally arranged in separate departments.

5-YEAR TREND – ESTIMATED INDUSTRY SALES ($MILLIONS)

Year	Employee Size of Establishment									Total
	1-4 Emps.	5-9 Emps.	10-19 Emps.	20-49 Emps.	50-99 Emps.	100-249 Emps.	250-499 Emps.	500-999 Emps.	Unknown Emps.	Industry Sales
2014	1.7	0.6	2.6	204.4	3,881.2	12,872.9	5,647.4	756.3	32.8	23,399.9
2015	1.7	0.6	2.6	207.1	3,931.3	13,039.1	5,720.3	766.0	33.2	23,701.9
2016	1.8	0.6	2.6	209.3	3,973.6	13,179.5	5,781.9	774.3	33.6	23,957.2
2017	1.8	0.6	2.6	210.3	3,992.0	13,240.3	5,808.6	778.7	33.7	24,068.6
2018	1.8	0.6	2.7	211.8	4,020.7	13,335.8	5,850.4	784.4	34.0	24,242.1

INDUSTRY: WAREHOUSE CLUBS & SUPERCENTERS (NAICS 45291)
PRODUCT LINE: WOMEN'S WEAR (Main Category)

NAICS 45291: Warehouse Clubs and Superstores This industry comprises establishments known as warehouse clubs, superstores or supercenters primarily engaged in retailing a general line of groceries in combination with general lines of new merchandise, such as apparel, furniture, and appliances.

5-YEAR TREND – ESTIMATED INDUSTRY SALES ($MILLIONS)

Year	Employee Size of Establishment									Total
	1-4 Emps.	5-9 Emps.	10-19 Emps.	20-49 Emps.	50-99 Emps.	100-249 Emps.	250-499 Emps.	500-999 Emps.	Unknown Emps.	Industry Sales
2014	2.2	0.1	0.4	20.7	26.0	3,213.6	14,207.0	375.4	4.4	17,849.8
2015	2.3	0.1	0.4	21.4	27.0	3,331.1	14,726.4	389.1	4.6	18,502.4
2016	2.4	0.1	0.4	22.1	27.9	3,442.2	15,217.4	402.1	4.7	19,119.3
2017	2.6	0.1	0.4	24.0	30.3	3,738.6	16,528.0	436.7	5.1	20,765.9
2018	2.7	0.1	0.5	25.5	32.2	3,970.4	17,552.8	463.8	5.5	22,053.4

INDUSTRY: ELECTRONIC SHOPPING & MAIL ORDER (NAICS 45411)
PRODUCT LINE: WOMEN'S WEAR (Main Category)

NAICS 45411: Electronic Shopping and Mail-Order Houses This industry comprises establishments primarily engaged in retailing all types of merchandise by means of mail or by electronic media, such as interactive television or computer. Included in this industry are establishments primarily engaged in retailing from catalogue showrooms of mail-order houses.

5-YEAR TREND – ESTIMATED INDUSTRY SALES ($MILLIONS)

Year	Employee Size of Establishment									Total Industry Sales
	1-4 Emps.	5-9 Emps.	10-19 Emps.	20-49 Emps.	50-99 Emps.	100-249 Emps.	250-499 Emps.	500-999 Emps.	Unknown Emps.	
2014	2,118	1,125	1,670	2,702	1,943	3,789	5,544	7,023	320	26,234
2015	2,260	1,200	1,782	2,882	2,073	4,042	5,914	7,491	342	27,984
2016	2,397	1,272	1,890	3,057	2,199	4,287	6,272	7,946	362	29,682
2017	2,727	1,448	2,150	3,479	2,502	4,878	7,138	8,820	412	33,554
2018	3,029	1,608	2,388	3,864	2,779	5,418	7,928	9,627	458	37,099

INDUSTRY: BOOK STORES (NAICS 451211)
PRODUCT LINE: WOMEN'S WEAR (Main Category)

NAICS 451211: Book Stores. This industry comprises establishments primarily engaged in the retail sale of new books and magazines. Establishments primarily engaged in the retail sale of used books are classified in 5932.

5-YEAR TREND – ESTIMATED INDUSTRY SALES ($MILLIONS)

Year	Employee Size of Establishment									Total Industry Sales
	1-4 Emps.	5-9 Emps.	10-19 Emps.	20-49 Emps.	50-99 Emps.	100-249 Emps.	250-499 Emps.	500-999 Emps.	Unknown Emps.	
2014	2.9	4.4	9.1	23.9	10.8	4.2	0.8	2.9	1.5	60.4
2015	3.0	4.6	9.6	25.2	11.4	4.5	0.8	3.0	1.6	63.6
2016	3.2	4.9	10.1	26.4	11.9	4.7	0.9	3.2	1.6	66.8
2017	3.2	4.9	10.2	26.6	12.0	4.7	0.9	3.2	1.6	67.4
2018	3.2	4.9	10.2	26.8	12.1	4.8	0.9	3.3	1.7	68.0

INDUSTRY: WOMEN'S CLOTHING STORES (NAICS 44812)
PRODUCT LINE: FURS (Sub Category)

NAICS 44812: Women's Clothing Stores . This industry comprises establishments primarily engaged in retailing a general line of new women's, misses' and juniors' clothing, including maternity wear. These establishments may provide basic alterations, such as hemming, taking in or letting out seams, or lengthening or shortening sleeves.

5-YEAR TREND – ESTIMATED INDUSTRY SALES ($MILLIONS)

Year	Employee Size of Establishment									Total Industry Sales
	1-4 Emps.	5-9 Emps.	10-19 Emps.	20-49 Emps.	50-99 Emps.	100-249 Emps.	250-499 Emps.	500-999 Emps.	Unknown Emps.	
2014	3.5	8.0	19.5	13.4	4.2	4.1	1.5	1.4	0.8	56.4
2015	3.7	8.3	20.3	13.9	4.3	4.2	1.6	1.4	0.8	58.5
2016	3.8	8.6	21.0	14.4	4.5	4.4	1.6	1.5	0.9	60.6
2017	4.0	9.1	22.3	15.3	4.8	4.6	1.7	1.6	0.9	64.4
2018	4.3	9.7	23.8	16.3	5.1	4.9	1.9	1.6	1.0	68.6

INDUSTRY: WOMEN'S CLOTHING STORES (NAICS 44812)
PRODUCT LINE: DRESSES (Sub Category)

NAICS 44812: Women's Clothing Stores . This industry comprises establishments primarily engaged in retailing a general line of new women's, misses' and juniors' clothing, including maternity wear. These establishments may provide basic alterations, such as hemming, taking in or letting out seams, or lengthening or shortening sleeves.

5-YEAR TREND – ESTIMATED INDUSTRY SALES ($MILLIONS)

Year	Employee Size of Establishment									Total Industry Sales
	1-4 Emps.	5-9 Emps.	10-19 Emps.	20-49 Emps.	50-99 Emps.	100-249 Emps.	250-499 Emps.	500-999 Emps.	Unknown Emps.	
2014	312.3	708.3	1,735.2	1,188.0	370.8	360.7	135.1	122.5	72.3	5,005.4
2015	324.4	735.7	1,802.2	1,233.9	385.1	374.7	140.3	127.2	75.1	5,198.6
2016	335.8	761.6	1,865.7	1,277.4	398.7	387.9	145.3	131.7	77.8	5,381.8
2017	357.0	809.7	1,983.6	1,358.1	423.9	412.4	154.4	138.2	82.7	5,720.0
2018	380.3	862.4	2,112.8	1,446.5	451.5	439.2	164.5	145.0	88.1	6,090.3

INDUSTRY: FAMILY CLOTHING STORES (NAICS 44814)
PRODUCT LINE: DRESSES (Sub Category)

NAICS 44814: Family Clothing Stores . This industry comprises establishments primarily engaged in retailing a general line of new clothing for men, women, and children, without specializing in sales for an individual gender or age group. These establishments may provide basic alterations, such as hemming, taking in or letting out seams, or lengthening or shortening sleeves.

5-YEAR TREND — ESTIMATED INDUSTRY SALES ($MILLIONS)

Year	Employee Size of Establishment									Total Industry Sales
	1-4 Emps.	5-9 Emps.	10-19 Emps.	20-49 Emps.	50-99 Emps.	100-249 Emps.	250-499 Emps.	500-999 Emps.	Unknown Emps.	
2014	40.9	73.3	315.6	967.6	1,014.8	253.2	250.2	99.2	11.1	3,025.9
2015	42.4	76.0	326.9	1,002.2	1,051.2	262.2	259.2	102.7	11.5	3,134.3
2016	43.7	78.4	337.6	1,034.9	1,085.5	270.8	267.7	106.1	11.8	3,236.6
2017	46.4	83.2	358.2	1,097.9	1,151.5	287.3	283.9	112.3	12.6	3,433.2
2018	49.3	88.4	380.7	1,167.0	1,224.0	305.3	301.8	119.0	13.3	3,648.9

INDUSTRY: DEPARTMENT STORES (NAICS 45211)
PRODUCT LINE: DRESSES (Sub Category)

NAICS 45211: Department Stores Industry . This industry comprises establishments known as department stores primarily engaged in retailing a wide range of the following new products with no one merchandise line predominating: apparel, furniture, appliances and home furnishings; and selected additional items, such as paint, hardware, toiletries, cosmetics, photographic equipment, jewelry, toys, and sporting goods. Merchandise lines are normally arranged in separate departments.

5-YEAR TREND — ESTIMATED INDUSTRY SALES ($MILLIONS)

Year	Employee Size of Establishment									Total Industry Sales
	1-4 Emps.	5-9 Emps.	10-19 Emps.	20-49 Emps.	50-99 Emps.	100-249 Emps.	250-499 Emps.	500-999 Emps.	Unknown Emps.	
2014	0.1	0.0	0.2	15.6	295.6	980.5	430.1	57.6	2.5	1,782.3
2015	0.1	0.0	0.2	15.8	299.4	993.1	435.7	58.3	2.5	1,805.3
2016	0.1	0.0	0.2	15.9	302.7	1,003.8	440.4	59.0	2.6	1,824.7
2017	0.1	0.0	0.2	16.0	304.1	1,008.5	442.4	59.3	2.6	1,833.2
2018	0.1	0.0	0.2	16.1	306.2	1,015.7	445.6	59.7	2.6	1,846.4

INDUSTRY: WAREHOUSE CLUBS & SUPERCENTERS (NAICS 45291)
PRODUCT LINE: DRESSES (Sub Category)

NAICS 45291: Warehouse Clubs and Superstores This industry comprises establishments known as warehouse clubs, superstores or supercenters primarily engaged in retailing a general line of groceries in combination with general lines of new merchandise, such as apparel, furniture, and appliances.

5-YEAR TREND – ESTIMATED INDUSTRY SALES ($MILLIONS)

Year	Employee Size of Establishment									Total Industry Sales
	1-4 Emps.	5-9 Emps.	10-19 Emps.	20-49 Emps.	50-99 Emps.	100-249 Emps.	250-499 Emps.	500-999 Emps.	Unknown Emps.	
2014	0.1	0.0	0.0	0.8	1.0	119.5	528.2	14.0	0.2	663.6
2015	0.1	0.0	0.0	0.8	1.0	123.8	547.5	14.5	0.2	687.8
2016	0.1	0.0	0.0	0.8	1.0	128.0	565.7	14.9	0.2	710.8
2017	0.1	0.0	0.0	0.9	1.1	139.0	614.4	16.2	0.2	772.0
2018	0.1	0.0	0.0	0.9	1.2	147.6	652.5	17.2	0.2	819.9

INDUSTRY: WOMEN'S CLOTHING STORES (NAICS 44812)
PRODUCT LINE: COATS & OUTERWEAR (Sub Category)

NAICS 44812: Women's Clothing Stores . This industry comprises establishments primarily engaged in retailing a general line of new women's, misses' and juniors' clothing, including maternity wear. These establishments may provide basic alterations, such as hemming, taking in or letting out seams, or lengthening or shortening sleeves.

5-YEAR TREND – ESTIMATED INDUSTRY SALES ($MILLIONS)

Year	Employee Size of Establishment									Total Industry Sales
	1-4 Emps.	5-9 Emps.	10-19 Emps.	20-49 Emps.	50-99 Emps.	100-249 Emps.	250-499 Emps.	500-999 Emps.	Unknown Emps.	
2014	118.4	268.4	657.6	450.2	140.5	136.7	51.2	46.4	27.4	1,897.0
2015	122.9	278.8	683.0	467.6	146.0	142.0	53.2	48.2	28.5	1,970.2
2016	127.3	288.6	707.1	484.1	151.1	147.0	55.0	49.9	29.5	2,039.6
2017	135.3	306.9	751.7	514.7	160.6	156.3	58.5	52.4	31.3	2,167.8
2018	144.1	326.8	800.7	548.2	171.1	166.5	62.3	54.9	33.4	2,308.1

INDUSTRY: FAMILY CLOTHING STORES (NAICS 44814)
PRODUCT LINE: COATS & OUTERWEAR (Sub Category)

NAICS 44814: Family Clothing Stores . This industry comprises establishments primarily engaged in retailing a general line of new clothing for men, women, and children, without specializing in sales for an individual gender or age group. These establishments may provide basic alterations, such as hemming, taking in or letting out seams, or lengthening or shortening sleeves.

5-YEAR TREND — ESTIMATED INDUSTRY SALES ($MILLIONS)

Year	Employee Size of Establishment									Total Industry Sales
	1-4 Emps.	5-9 Emps.	10-19 Emps.	20-49 Emps.	50-99 Emps.	100-249 Emps.	250-499 Emps.	500-999 Emps.	Unknown Emps.	
2014	30.8	55.2	237.6	728.3	763.8	190.6	188.3	74.6	8.3	2,277.6
2015	31.9	57.2	246.1	754.3	791.2	197.4	195.1	77.3	8.6	2,359.1
2016	32.9	59.0	254.1	779.0	817.0	203.8	201.5	79.8	8.9	2,436.1
2017	34.9	62.6	269.6	826.4	866.7	216.2	213.7	84.5	9.4	2,584.2
2018	37.1	66.6	286.5	878.4	921.3	229.8	227.2	89.6	10.0	2,746.5

INDUSTRY: DEPARTMENT STORES (NAICS 45211)
PRODUCT LINE: COATS & OUTERWEAR (Sub Category)

NAICS 45211: Department Stores Industry . **This industry comprises** establishments known as department stores primarily engaged in retailing a wide range of the following new products with no one merchandise line predominating: apparel, furniture, appliances and home furnishings; and selected additional items, such as paint, hardware, toiletries, cosmetics, photographic equipment, jewelry, toys, and sporting goods. Merchandise lines are normally arranged in separate departments.

5-YEAR TREND — ESTIMATED INDUSTRY SALES ($MILLIONS)

Year	Employee Size of Establishment									Total Industry Sales
	1-4 Emps.	5-9 Emps.	10-19 Emps.	20-49 Emps.	50-99 Emps.	100-249 Emps.	250-499 Emps.	500-999 Emps.	Unknown Emps.	
2014	0.1	0.0	0.1	8.2	155.3	515.1	226.0	30.3	1.3	936.4
2015	0.1	0.0	0.1	8.3	157.3	521.8	228.9	30.7	1.3	948.5
2016	0.1	0.0	0.1	8.4	159.0	527.4	231.4	31.0	1.3	958.7
2017	0.1	0.0	0.1	8.4	159.7	529.8	232.4	31.2	1.3	963.2
2018	0.1	0.0	0.1	8.5	160.9	533.7	234.1	31.4	1.4	970.1

INDUSTRY: MEN'S CLOTHING STORES (NAICS 44811)
PRODUCT LINE: SUITS & BLAZERS (Sub Category)

NAICS 44811: Men's Clothing Stores. This industry comprises establishments primarily engaged in retailing a general line of new men's and boys' clothing. These establishments may provide basic alterations, such as hemming, taking in or letting out seams, or lengthening or shortening sleeves.

5-YEAR TREND — ESTIMATED INDUSTRY SALES ($MILLIONS)

Year	Employee Size of Establishment									Total
	1-4 Emps.	5-9 Emps.	10-19 Emps.	20-49 Emps.	50-99 Emps.	100-249 Emps.	250-499 Emps.	500-999 Emps.	Unknown Emps.	Industry Sales
2014	3.0	4.4	10.4	6.0	1.5	0.8	0.3	0.0	0.5	27.0
2015	3.1	4.6	10.8	6.3	1.6	0.8	0.3	0.0	0.5	28.2
2016	3.2	4.8	11.3	6.6	1.7	0.8	0.4	0.0	0.5	29.4
2017	3.4	5.0	11.7	6.8	1.7	0.9	0.4	0.0	0.6	30.4
2018	3.5	5.2	12.1	7.1	1.8	0.9	0.4	0.0	0.6	31.5

INDUSTRY: WOMEN'S CLOTHING STORES (NAICS 44812)
PRODUCT LINE: SUITS & BLAZERS (Sub Category)

NAICS 44812: Women's Clothing Stores . This industry comprises establishments primarily engaged in retailing a general line of new women's, misses' and juniors' clothing, including maternity wear. These establishments may provide basic alterations, such as hemming, taking in or letting out seams, or lengthening or shortening sleeves.

5-YEAR TREND — ESTIMATED INDUSTRY SALES ($MILLIONS)

Year	Employee Size of Establishment									Total
	1-4 Emps.	5-9 Emps.	10-19 Emps.	20-49 Emps.	50-99 Emps.	100-249 Emps.	250-499 Emps.	500-999 Emps.	Unknown Emps.	Industry Sales
2014	180.6	409.5	1,003.1	686.8	214.4	208.5	78.1	70.8	41.8	2,893.6
2015	187.5	425.3	1,041.8	713.3	222.6	216.6	81.1	73.6	43.4	3,005.3
2016	194.1	440.3	1,078.5	738.4	230.5	224.2	84.0	76.1	45.0	3,111.2
2017	206.4	468.1	1,146.7	785.1	245.0	238.4	89.3	79.9	47.8	3,306.7
2018	219.8	498.6	1,221.4	836.2	261.0	253.9	95.1	83.8	50.9	3,520.8

INDUSTRY: FAMILY CLOTHING STORES (NAICS 44814)
PRODUCT LINE: SUITS & BLAZERS (Sub Category)

NAICS 44814: Family Clothing Stores . This industry comprises establishments primarily engaged in retailing a general line of new clothing for men, women, and children, without specializing in sales for an individual gender or age group. These establishments may provide basic alterations, such as hemming, taking in or letting out seams, or lengthening or shortening sleeves.

5-YEAR TREND — ESTIMATED INDUSTRY SALES ($MILLIONS)

Year	Employee Size of Establishment									Total Industry Sales
	1-4 Emps.	5-9 Emps.	10-19 Emps.	20-49 Emps.	50-99 Emps.	100-249 Emps.	250-499 Emps.	500-999 Emps.	Unknown Emps.	
2014	55.4	99.3	427.6	1,310.7	1,374.8	343.0	339.0	134.3	15.0	4,099.1
2015	57.4	102.9	442.9	1,357.7	1,424.0	355.2	351.1	139.2	15.5	4,245.9
2016	59.3	106.3	457.4	1,402.0	1,470.5	366.8	362.6	143.7	16.0	4,384.5
2017	62.9	112.7	485.2	1,487.3	1,560.0	389.2	384.7	152.1	17.0	4,651.0
2018	66.8	119.8	515.7	1,580.9	1,658.1	413.7	408.9	161.2	18.1	4,943.1

INDUSTRY: DEPARTMENT STORES (NAICS 45211)
PRODUCT LINE: SUITS & BLAZERS (Sub Category)

NAICS 45211: Department Stores Industry . This industry comprises establishments known as department stores primarily engaged in retailing a wide range of the following new products with no one merchandise line predominating: apparel, furniture, appliances and home furnishings; and selected additional items, such as paint, hardware, toiletries, cosmetics, photographic equipment, jewelry, toys, and sporting goods. Merchandise lines are normally arranged in separate departments.

5-YEAR TREND — ESTIMATED INDUSTRY SALES ($MILLIONS)

Year	Employee Size of Establishment									Total Industry Sales
	1-4 Emps.	5-9 Emps.	10-19 Emps.	20-49 Emps.	50-99 Emps.	100-249 Emps.	250-499 Emps.	500-999 Emps.	Unknown Emps.	
2014	0	0	0	31	585	1,940	851	114	5	3,526
2015	0	0	0	31	592	1,965	862	115	5	3,572
2016	0	0	0	32	599	1,986	871	117	5	3,610
2017	0	0	0	32	602	1,995	875	117	5	3,627
2018	0	0	0	32	606	2,010	882	118	5	3,653

INDUSTRY: MEN'S CLOTHING STORES (NAICS 44811)
PRODUCT LINE: SLACKS & JEANS & SKIRTS (Sub Category)

NAICS 44811: Men's Clothing Stores. This industry comprises establishments primarily engaged in retailing a general line of new men's and boys' clothing. These establishments may provide basic alterations, such as hemming, taking in or letting out seams, or lengthening or shortening sleeves.

5-YEAR TREND — ESTIMATED INDUSTRY SALES ($MILLIONS)

Year	Employee Size of Establishment									Total Industry Sales
	1-4 Emps.	5-9 Emps.	10-19 Emps.	20-49 Emps.	50-99 Emps.	100-249 Emps.	250-499 Emps.	500-999 Emps.	Unknown Emps.	
2014	4.4	6.6	15.5	9.0	2.3	1.2	0.5	0.0	0.7	40.3
2015	4.7	6.9	16.2	9.4	2.4	1.2	0.5	0.0	0.8	42.2
2016	4.8	7.2	16.9	9.8	2.5	1.3	0.5	0.0	0.8	43.9
2017	5.0	7.5	17.5	10.2	2.6	1.3	0.5	0.0	0.8	45.5
2018	5.2	7.8	18.1	10.6	2.7	1.4	0.6	0.0	0.9	47.2

INDUSTRY: WOMEN'S CLOTHING STORES (NAICS 44812)
PRODUCT LINE: SLACKS & JEANS & SKIRTS (Sub Category)

NAICS 44812: Women's Clothing Stores . This industry comprises establishments primarily engaged in retailing a general line of new women's, misses' and juniors' clothing, including maternity wear. These establishments may provide basic alterations, such as hemming, taking in or letting out seams, or lengthening or shortening sleeves.

5-YEAR TREND — ESTIMATED INDUSTRY SALES ($MILLIONS)

Year	Employee Size of Establishment									Total Industry Sales
	1-4 Emps.	5-9 Emps.	10-19 Emps.	20-49 Emps.	50-99 Emps.	100-249 Emps.	250-499 Emps.	500-999 Emps.	Unknown Emps.	
2014	693.0	1,571.7	3,850.3	2,636.1	822.8	800.5	299.8	271.8	160.5	11,106.4
2015	719.8	1,632.3	3,998.9	2,737.9	854.5	831.4	311.3	282.3	166.7	11,535.0
2016	745.2	1,689.8	4,139.8	2,834.3	884.7	860.6	322.3	292.3	172.6	11,941.5
2017	792.2	1,796.6	4,401.4	3,013.4	940.6	915.0	342.7	306.6	183.5	12,692.0
2018	843.8	1,913.6	4,688.0	3,209.7	1,001.8	974.6	365.0	321.7	195.4	13,513.7

INDUSTRY: FAMILY CLOTHING STORES (NAICS 44814)
PRODUCT LINE: SLACKS & JEANS & SKIRTS (Sub Category)

NAICS 44814: Family Clothing Stores . This industry comprises establishments primarily engaged in retailing a general line of new clothing for men, women, and children, without specializing in sales for an individual gender or age group. These establishments may provide basic alterations, such as hemming, taking in or letting out seams, or lengthening or shortening sleeves.

5-YEAR TREND — ESTIMATED INDUSTRY SALES ($MILLIONS)

Year	Employee Size of Establishment									Total
	1-4 Emps.	5-9 Emps.	10-19 Emps.	20-49 Emps.	50-99 Emps.	100-249 Emps.	250-499 Emps.	500-999 Emps.	Unknown Emps.	Industry Sales
2014	122.3	219.2	943.6	2,892.5	3,033.8	756.9	748.1	296.5	33.1	9,045.9
2015	126.6	227.1	977.4	2,996.1	3,142.5	784.0	774.9	307.1	34.3	9,369.9
2016	130.8	234.5	1,009.3	3,093.9	3,245.0	809.6	800.2	317.1	35.4	9,675.7
2017	138.7	248.8	1,070.7	3,282.2	3,442.5	858.8	848.9	335.6	37.5	10,263.7
2018	147.4	264.4	1,138.1	3,488.6	3,659.1	912.8	902.3	355.8	39.9	10,908.4

INDUSTRY: DEPARTMENT STORES (NAICS 45211)
PRODUCT LINE: SLACKS & JEANS & SKIRTS (Sub Category)

NAICS 45211: Department Stores Industry . **This industry comprises** establishments known as department stores primarily engaged in retailing a wide range of the following new products with no one merchandise line predominating: apparel, furniture, appliances and home furnishings; and selected additional items, such as paint, hardware, toiletries, cosmetics, photographic equipment, jewelry, toys, and sporting goods. Merchandise lines are normally arranged in separate departments.

5-YEAR TREND — ESTIMATED INDUSTRY SALES ($MILLIONS)

Year	Employee Size of Establishment									Total
	1-4 Emps.	5-9 Emps.	10-19 Emps.	20-49 Emps.	50-99 Emps.	100-249 Emps.	250-499 Emps.	500-999 Emps.	Unknown Emps.	Industry Sales
2014	0	0	0	31	583	1,934	849	114	5	3,516
2015	0	0	0	31	591	1,959	859	115	5	3,561
2016	0	0	0	31	597	1,980	869	116	5	3,600
2017	0	0	0	32	600	1,989	873	117	5	3,616
2018	0	0	0	32	604	2,004	879	118	5	3,642

INDUSTRY: WAREHOUSE CLUBS & SUPERCENTERS (NAICS 45291)
PRODUCT LINE: SLACKS & JEANS & SKIRTS (Sub Category)

NAICS 45291: Warehouse Clubs and Superstores This industry comprises establishments known as warehouse clubs, superstores or supercenters primarily engaged in retailing a general line of groceries in combination with general lines of new merchandise, such as apparel, furniture, and appliances.

5-YEAR TREND — ESTIMATED INDUSTRY SALES ($MILLIONS)

Year	Employee Size of Establishment									Total Industry Sales
	1-4 Emps.	5-9 Emps.	10-19 Emps.	20-49 Emps.	50-99 Emps.	100-249 Emps.	250-499 Emps.	500-999 Emps.	Unknown Emps.	
2014	0.6	0.0	0.1	5.4	6.8	837.8	3,703.9	97.9	1.2	4,653.7
2015	0.6	0.0	0.1	5.6	7.0	868.5	3,839.4	101.4	1.2	4,823.8
2016	0.6	0.0	0.1	5.8	7.3	897.4	3,967.4	104.8	1.2	4,984.6
2017	0.7	0.0	0.1	6.3	7.9	974.7	4,309.1	113.8	1.3	5,413.9
2018	0.7	0.0	0.1	6.7	8.4	1,035.1	4,576.2	120.9	1.4	5,749.6

INDUSTRY: MEN'S CLOTHING STORES (NAICS 44811)
PRODUCT LINE: SHIRTS & SWEATERS (Sub Category)

NAICS 44811: Men's Clothing Stores. This industry comprises establishments primarily engaged in retailing a general line of new men's and boys' clothing. These establishments may provide basic alterations, such as hemming, taking in or letting out seams, or lengthening or shortening sleeves.

5-YEAR TREND — ESTIMATED INDUSTRY SALES ($MILLIONS)

Year	Employee Size of Establishment									Total Industry Sales
	1-4 Emps.	5-9 Emps.	10-19 Emps.	20-49 Emps.	50-99 Emps.	100-249 Emps.	250-499 Emps.	500-999 Emps.	Unknown Emps.	
2014	5.0	7.4	17.4	10.1	2.6	1.3	0.5	0.0	0.8	45.2
2015	5.2	7.8	18.2	10.6	2.7	1.4	0.6	0.0	0.9	47.3
2016	5.4	8.1	18.9	11.0	2.8	1.4	0.6	0.0	0.9	49.3
2017	5.6	8.4	19.6	11.4	2.9	1.5	0.6	0.0	0.9	51.0
2018	5.8	8.7	20.3	11.8	3.0	1.5	0.6	0.0	1.0	52.9

INDUSTRY: WOMEN'S CLOTHING STORES (NAICS 44812)
PRODUCT LINE: SHIRTS & SWEATERS (Sub Category)

NAICS 44812: Women's Clothing Stores . This industry comprises establishments primarily engaged in retailing a general line of new women's, misses' and juniors' clothing, including maternity wear. These establishments may provide basic alterations, such as hemming, taking in or letting out seams, or lengthening or shortening sleeves.

5-YEAR TREND — ESTIMATED INDUSTRY SALES ($MILLIONS)

Year	Employee Size of Establishment									Total Industry Sales
	1-4 Emps.	5-9 Emps.	10-19 Emps.	20-49 Emps.	50-99 Emps.	100-249 Emps.	250-499 Emps.	500-999 Emps.	Unknown Emps.	
2015	908	2,060	5,046	3,455	1,078	1,049	393	356	210	14,555
2016	943	2,139	5,240	3,588	1,120	1,089	408	370	218	15,116
2017	977	2,215	5,425	3,714	1,159	1,128	422	383	226	15,649
2018	1,038	2,354	5,768	3,949	1,233	1,199	449	402	240	16,633
2018	1,106	2,508	6,144	4,206	1,313	1,277	478	422	256	17,709

INDUSTRY: FAMILY CLOTHING STORES (NAICS 44814)
PRODUCT LINE: SHIRTS & SWEATERS (Sub Category)

NAICS 44814: Family Clothing Stores . This industry comprises establishments primarily engaged in retailing a general line of new clothing for men, women, and children, without specializing in sales for an individual gender or age group. These establishments may provide basic alterations, such as hemming, taking in or letting out seams, or lengthening or shortening sleeves.

5-YEAR TREND — ESTIMATED INDUSTRY SALES ($MILLIONS)

Year	Employee Size of Establishment									Total Industry Sales
	1-4 Emps.	5-9 Emps.	10-19 Emps.	20-49 Emps.	50-99 Emps.	100-249 Emps.	250-499 Emps.	500-999 Emps.	Unknown Emps.	
2015	200.7	359.9	1,549.4	4,749.3	4,981.4	1,242.7	1,228.3	486.8	54.3	14,852.8
2016	207.9	372.8	1,604.9	4,919.4	5,159.7	1,287.2	1,272.3	504.2	56.2	15,384.7
2017	214.7	385.0	1,657.2	5,080.0	5,328.2	1,329.2	1,313.8	520.7	58.1	15,886.9
2018	227.8	408.4	1,758.1	5,389.1	5,652.4	1,410.1	1,393.8	551.1	61.6	16,852.3
2018	242.1	434.1	1,868.7	5,728.1	6,008.0	1,498.8	1,481.4	584.2	65.5	17,911.0

INDUSTRY: DEPARTMENT STORES (NAICS 45211)
PRODUCT LINE: SHIRTS & SWEATERS (Sub Category)

NAICS 45211: Department Stores Industry . This industry comprises establishments known as department stores primarily engaged in retailing a wide range of the following new products with no one merchandise line predominating: apparel, furniture, appliances and home furnishings; and selected additional items, such as paint, hardware, toiletries, cosmetics, photographic equipment, jewelry, toys, and sporting goods. Merchandise lines are normally arranged in separate departments.

5-YEAR TREND — ESTIMATED INDUSTRY SALES ($MILLIONS)

Year	Employee Size of Establishment									Total Industry Sales
	1-4 Emps.	5-9 Emps.	10-19 Emps.	20-49 Emps.	50-99 Emps.	100-249 Emps.	250-499 Emps.	500-999 Emps.	Unknown Emps.	
2015	0	0	0	30	568	1,885	827	111	5	3,426
2016	0	0	0	30	576	1,909	838	112	5	3,471
2017	0	0	0	31	582	1,930	847	113	5	3,508
2018	0	0	0	31	585	1,939	851	114	5	3,524
2018	0	0	0	31	589	1,953	857	115	5	3,550

INDUSTRY: WAREHOUSE CLUBS & SUPERSTORES (NAICS 45291)
PRODUCT LINE: SHIRTS & SWEATERS (Sub Category)

NAICS 45291: Warehouse Clubs and Superstores This industry comprises establishments known as warehouse clubs, superstores or supercenters primarily engaged in retailing a general line of groceries in combination with general lines of new merchandise, such as apparel, furniture, and appliances.

5-YEAR TREND — ESTIMATED INDUSTRY SALES ($MILLIONS)

Year	Employee Size of Establishment									Total Industry Sales
	1-4 Emps.	5-9 Emps.	10-19 Emps.	20-49 Emps.	50-99 Emps.	100-249 Emps.	250-499 Emps.	500-999 Emps.	Unknown Emps.	
2015	0.5	0.0	0.1	4.3	5.4	663.9	2,935.1	77.5	0.9	3,687.7
2016	0.5	0.0	0.1	4.4	5.6	688.2	3,042.4	80.4	0.9	3,822.5
2017	0.5	0.0	0.1	4.6	5.8	711.1	3,143.8	83.1	1.0	3,949.9
2018	0.5	0.0	0.1	5.0	6.3	772.4	3,414.6	90.2	1.1	4,290.1
2018	0.6	0.0	0.1	5.3	6.6	820.3	3,626.3	95.8	1.1	4,556.1

INDUSTRY: WOMEN'S CLOTHING STORES (NAICS 44812)
PRODUCT LINE: SPORTS APPAREL (Sub Category)

NAICS 44812: Women's Clothing Stores . This industry comprises establishments primarily engaged in retailing a general line of new women's, misses' and juniors' clothing, including maternity wear. These establishments may provide basic alterations, such as hemming, taking in or letting out seams, or lengthening or shortening sleeves.

5-YEAR TREND — ESTIMATED INDUSTRY SALES ($MILLIONS)

Year	Employee Size of Establishment									Total Industry Sales
	1-4 Emps.	5-9 Emps.	10-19 Emps.	20-49 Emps.	50-99 Emps.	100-249 Emps.	250-499 Emps.	500-999 Emps.	Unknown Emps.	
2015	34.7	78.7	192.8	132.0	41.2	40.1	15.0	13.6	8.0	556.1
2016	36.0	81.7	200.2	137.1	42.8	41.6	15.6	14.1	8.3	577.5
2017	37.3	84.6	207.3	141.9	44.3	43.1	16.1	14.6	8.6	597.9
2018	39.7	90.0	220.4	150.9	47.1	45.8	17.2	15.4	9.2	635.4
2018	42.2	95.8	234.7	160.7	50.2	48.8	18.3	16.1	9.8	676.6

INDUSTRY: FAMILY CLOTHING STORES (NAICS 44814)
PRODUCT LINE: SPORTS APPAREL (Sub Category)

NAICS 44814: Family Clothing Stores . This industry comprises establishments primarily engaged in retailing a general line of new clothing for men, women, and children, without specializing in sales for an individual gender or age group. These establishments may provide basic alterations, such as hemming, taking in or letting out seams, or lengthening or shortening sleeves.

5-YEAR TREND — ESTIMATED INDUSTRY SALES ($MILLIONS)

Year	Employee Size of Establishment									Total Industry Sales
	1-4 Emps.	5-9 Emps.	10-19 Emps.	20-49 Emps.	50-99 Emps.	100-249 Emps.	250-499 Emps.	500-999 Emps.	Unknown Emps.	
2015	18.0	32.4	139.3	427.0	447.8	111.7	110.4	43.8	4.9	1,335.2
2016	18.7	33.5	144.3	442.2	463.8	115.7	114.4	45.3	5.1	1,383.0
2017	19.3	34.6	149.0	456.7	479.0	119.5	118.1	46.8	5.2	1,428.2
2018	20.5	36.7	158.0	484.5	508.1	126.8	125.3	49.5	5.5	1,515.0
2018	21.8	39.0	168.0	514.9	540.1	134.7	133.2	52.5	5.9	1,610.1

INDUSTRY: DEPARTMENT STORES (NAICS 45211)
PRODUCT LINE: SPORTS APPAREL (Sub Category)

NAICS 45211: Department Stores Industry . This industry comprises establishments known as department stores primarily engaged in retailing a wide range of the following new products with no one merchandise line predominating: apparel, furniture, appliances and home furnishings; and selected additional items, such as paint, hardware, toiletries, cosmetics, photographic equipment, jewelry, toys, and sporting goods. Merchandise lines are normally arranged in separate departments.

5-YEAR TREND – ESTIMATED INDUSTRY SALES ($MILLIONS)

Year	Employee Size of Establishment									Total Industry Sales
	1-4 Emps.	5-9 Emps.	10-19 Emps.	20-49 Emps.	50-99 Emps.	100-249 Emps.	250-499 Emps.	500-999 Emps.	Unknown Emps.	
2015	0.2	0.1	0.3	23.5	446.9	1,482.1	650.2	87.1	3.8	2,694.2
2016	0.2	0.1	0.3	23.8	452.6	1,501.3	658.6	88.2	3.8	2,728.9
2017	0.2	0.1	0.3	24.1	457.5	1,517.4	665.7	89.1	3.9	2,758.3
2018	0.2	0.1	0.3	24.2	459.6	1,524.4	668.8	89.7	3.9	2,771.2
2018	0.2	0.1	0.3	24.4	462.9	1,535.4	673.6	90.3	3.9	2,791.1

INDUSTRY: WAREHOUSE CLUBS & SUPERCENTERS (NAICS 45291)
PRODUCT LINE: SPORTS APPAREL (Sub Category)

NAICS 45291: Warehouse Clubs and Superstores This industry comprises establishments known as warehouse clubs, superstores or supercenters primarily engaged in retailing a general line of groceries in combination with general lines of new merchandise, such as apparel, furniture, and appliances.

5-YEAR TREND – ESTIMATED INDUSTRY SALES ($MILLIONS)

Year	Employee Size of Establishment									Total Industry Sales
	1-4 Emps.	5-9 Emps.	10-19 Emps.	20-49 Emps.	50-99 Emps.	100-249 Emps.	250-499 Emps.	500-999 Emps.	Unknown Emps.	
2015	0.2	0.0	0.0	1.4	1.8	221.1	977.5	25.8	0.3	1,228.1
2016	0.2	0.0	0.0	1.5	1.9	229.2	1,013.2	26.8	0.3	1,273.0
2017	0.2	0.0	0.0	1.5	1.9	236.8	1,047.0	27.7	0.3	1,315.5
2018	0.2	0.0	0.0	1.7	2.1	257.2	1,137.2	30.0	0.4	1,428.8
2018	0.2	0.0	0.0	1.8	2.2	273.2	1,207.7	31.9	0.4	1,517.3

INDUSTRY: WOMEN'S CLOTHING STORES (NAICS 44812)
PRODUCT LINE: HOSIERY & SOCKS (Sub Category)

NAICS 44812: Women's Clothing Stores . This industry comprises establishments primarily engaged in retailing a general line of new women's, misses' and juniors' clothing, including maternity wear. These establishments may provide basic alterations, such as hemming, taking in or letting out seams, or lengthening or shortening sleeves.

5-YEAR TREND – ESTIMATED INDUSTRY SALES ($MILLIONS)

| Year | Employee Size of Establishment | | | | | | | | | Total |
	1-4 Emps.	5-9 Emps.	10-19 Emps.	20-49 Emps.	50-99 Emps.	100-249 Emps.	250-499 Emps.	500-999 Emps.	Unknown Emps.	Industry Sales
2015	23.8	54.0	132.4	90.6	28.3	27.5	10.3	9.3	5.5	381.8
2016	24.7	56.1	137.5	94.1	29.4	28.6	10.7	9.7	5.7	396.5
2017	25.6	58.1	142.3	97.4	30.4	29.6	11.1	10.0	5.9	410.5
2018	27.2	61.8	151.3	103.6	32.3	31.5	11.8	10.5	6.3	436.3
2018	29.0	65.8	161.2	110.3	34.4	33.5	12.5	11.1	6.7	464.6

INDUSTRY: FAMILY CLOTHING STORES (NAICS 44814)
PRODUCT LINE: HOSIERY & SOCKS (Sub Category)

NAICS 44814: Family Clothing Stores . This industry comprises establishments primarily engaged in retailing a general line of new clothing for men, women, and children, without specializing in sales for an individual gender or age group. These establishments may provide basic alterations, such as hemming, taking in or letting out seams, or lengthening or shortening sleeves.

5-YEAR TREND – ESTIMATED INDUSTRY SALES ($MILLIONS)

| Year | Employee Size of Establishment | | | | | | | | | Total |
	1-4 Emps.	5-9 Emps.	10-19 Emps.	20-49 Emps.	50-99 Emps.	100-249 Emps.	250-499 Emps.	500-999 Emps.	Unknown Emps.	Industry Sales
2015	14.3	25.7	110.6	339.1	355.7	88.7	87.7	34.8	3.9	1,060.4
2016	14.8	26.6	114.6	351.2	368.4	91.9	90.8	36.0	4.0	1,098.4
2017	15.3	27.5	118.3	362.7	380.4	94.9	93.8	37.2	4.1	1,134.3
2018	16.3	29.2	125.5	384.8	403.6	100.7	99.5	39.3	4.4	1,203.2
2018	17.3	31.0	133.4	409.0	428.9	107.0	105.8	41.7	4.7	1,278.8

INDUSTRY: DEPARTMENT STORES (NAICS 45211)
PRODUCT LINE: HOSIERY & SOCKS (Sub Category)

NAICS 45211: Department Stores Industry . This industry comprises establishments known as department stores primarily engaged in retailing a wide range of the following new products with no one merchandise line predominating: apparel, furniture, appliances and home furnishings; and selected additional items, such as paint, hardware, toiletries, cosmetics, photographic equipment, jewelry, toys, and sporting goods. Merchandise lines are normally arranged in separate departments.

5-YEAR TREND – ESTIMATED INDUSTRY SALES ($MILLIONS)

Year	Employee Size of Establishment									Total Industry Sales
	1-4 Emps.	5-9 Emps.	10-19 Emps.	20-49 Emps.	50-99 Emps.	100-249 Emps.	250-499 Emps.	500-999 Emps.	Unknown Emps.	
2015	0.1	0.0	0.1	6.3	119.7	397.0	174.2	23.3	1.0	721.7
2016	0.1	0.0	0.1	6.4	121.2	402.1	176.4	23.6	1.0	731.0
2017	0.1	0.0	0.1	6.5	122.6	406.5	178.3	23.9	1.0	738.9
2018	0.1	0.0	0.1	6.5	123.1	408.3	179.1	24.0	1.0	742.3
2018	0.1	0.0	0.1	6.5	124.0	411.3	180.4	24.2	1.0	747.7

INDUSTRY: WAREHOUSE CLUBS & SUPERCENTERS (NAICS 45291)
PRODUCT LINE: HOSIERY & SOCKS (Sub Category)

NAICS 45291: Warehouse Clubs and Superstores This industry comprises establishments known as warehouse clubs, superstores or supercenters primarily engaged in retailing a general line of groceries in combination with general lines of new merchandise, such as apparel, furniture, and appliances.

5-YEAR TREND – ESTIMATED INDUSTRY SALES ($MILLIONS)

Year	Employee Size of Establishment									Total Industry Sales
	1-4 Emps.	5-9 Emps.	10-19 Emps.	20-49 Emps.	50-99 Emps.	100-249 Emps.	250-499 Emps.	500-999 Emps.	Unknown Emps.	
2015	0.2	0.0	0.0	1.6	2.0	242.3	1,071.2	28.3	0.3	1,345.9
2016	0.2	0.0	0.0	1.6	2.0	251.2	1,110.4	29.3	0.3	1,395.1
2017	0.2	0.0	0.0	1.7	2.1	259.5	1,147.4	30.3	0.4	1,441.6
2018	0.2	0.0	0.0	1.8	2.3	281.9	1,246.2	32.9	0.4	1,565.8
2018	0.2	0.0	0.0	1.9	2.4	299.4	1,323.5	35.0	0.4	1,662.9

INDUSTRY: WOMEN'S CLOTHING STORES (NAICS 44812)
PRODUCT LINE: BRAS & UNDERWEAR (Sub Category)

NAICS 44812: Women's Clothing Stores . This industry comprises establishments primarily engaged in retailing a general line of new women's, misses' and juniors' clothing, including maternity wear. These establishments may provide basic alterations, such as hemming, taking in or letting out seams, or lengthening or shortening sleeves.

5-YEAR TREND — ESTIMATED INDUSTRY SALES ($MILLIONS)

Year	Employee Size of Establishment									Total
	1-4 Emps.	5-9 Emps.	10-19 Emps.	20-49 Emps.	50-99 Emps.	100-249 Emps.	250-499 Emps.	500-999 Emps.	Unknown Emps.	Industry Sales
2015	40.4	91.5	224.2	153.5	47.9	46.6	17.5	15.8	9.3	646.7
2016	41.9	95.1	232.9	159.4	49.8	48.4	18.1	16.4	9.7	671.7
2017	43.4	98.4	241.1	165.0	51.5	50.1	18.8	17.0	10.0	695.4
2018	46.1	104.6	256.3	175.5	54.8	53.3	20.0	17.9	10.7	739.1
2018	49.1	111.4	273.0	186.9	58.3	56.8	21.3	18.7	11.4	786.9

INDUSTRY: FAMILY CLOTHING STORES (NAICS 44814)
PRODUCT LINE: BRAS & UNDERWEAR (Sub Category)

NAICS 44814: Family Clothing Stores . This industry comprises establishments primarily engaged in retailing a general line of new clothing for men, women, and children, without specializing in sales for an individual gender or age group. These establishments may provide basic alterations, such as hemming, taking in or letting out seams, or lengthening or shortening sleeves.

5-YEAR TREND — ESTIMATED INDUSTRY SALES ($MILLIONS)

Year	Employee Size of Establishment									Total
	1-4 Emps.	5-9 Emps.	10-19 Emps.	20-49 Emps.	50-99 Emps.	100-249 Emps.	250-499 Emps.	500-999 Emps.	Unknown Emps.	Industry Sales
2015	21.9	39.3	169.0	517.9	543.3	135.5	134.0	53.1	5.9	1,619.8
2016	22.7	40.7	175.0	536.5	562.7	140.4	138.8	55.0	6.1	1,677.8
2017	23.4	42.0	180.7	554.0	581.1	145.0	143.3	56.8	6.3	1,732.6
2018	24.8	44.5	191.7	587.7	616.4	153.8	152.0	60.1	6.7	1,837.9
2018	26.4	47.3	203.8	624.7	655.2	163.5	161.6	63.7	7.1	1,953.3

INDUSTRY: DEPARTMENT STORES (NAICS 45211)
PRODUCT LINE: BRAS & UNDERWEAR (Sub Category)

NAICS 45211: Department Stores Industry . This industry comprises establishments known as department stores primarily engaged in retailing a wide range of the following new products with no one merchandise line predominating: apparel, furniture, appliances and home furnishings; and selected additional items, such as paint, hardware, toiletries, cosmetics, photographic equipment, jewelry, toys, and sporting goods. Merchandise lines are normally arranged in separate departments.

5-YEAR TREND – ESTIMATED INDUSTRY SALES ($MILLIONS)

Year	Employee Size of Establishment									Total
	1-4 Emps.	5-9 Emps.	10-19 Emps.	20-49 Emps.	50-99 Emps.	100-249 Emps.	250-499 Emps.	500-999 Emps.	Unknown Emps.	Industry Sales
2015	0	0	0	26	491	1,629	715	96	4	2,961
2016	0	0	0	26	498	1,650	724	97	4	3,000
2017	0	0	0	26	503	1,668	732	98	4	3,032
2018	0	0	0	27	505	1,676	735	99	4	3,046
2018	0	0	0	27	509	1,688	740	99	4	3,068

INDUSTRY: WAREHOUSE CLUBS & SUPERCENTERS (NAICS 45291)
PRODUCT LINE: BRAS & UNDERWEAR (Sub Category)

NAICS 45291: Warehouse Clubs and Superstores This industry comprises establishments known as warehouse clubs, superstores or supercenters primarily engaged in retailing a general line of groceries in combination with general lines of new merchandise, such as apparel, furniture, and appliances.

5-YEAR TREND – ESTIMATED INDUSTRY SALES ($MILLIONS)

Year	Employee Size of Establishment									Total
	1-4 Emps.	5-9 Emps.	10-19 Emps.	20-49 Emps.	50-99 Emps.	100-249 Emps.	250-499 Emps.	500-999 Emps.	Unknown Emps.	Industry Sales
2015	0.3	0.0	0.0	2.7	3.4	416.7	1,842.0	48.7	0.6	2,314.3
2016	0.3	0.0	0.1	2.8	3.5	431.9	1,909.4	50.4	0.6	2,398.9
2017	0.3	0.0	0.1	2.9	3.6	446.3	1,973.0	52.1	0.6	2,478.9
2018	0.3	0.0	0.1	3.1	3.9	484.7	2,143.0	56.6	0.7	2,692.4
2018	0.4	0.0	0.1	3.3	4.2	514.8	2,275.8	60.1	0.7	2,859.4

INDUSTRY: WOMEN'S CLOTHING STORES (NAICS 44812)
PRODUCT LINE: LINGERIE & SLEEPWEAR (Sub Category)

NAICS 44812: Women's Clothing Stores . This industry comprises establishments primarily engaged in retailing a general line of new women's, misses' and juniors' clothing, including maternity wear. These establishments may provide basic alterations, such as hemming, taking in or letting out seams, or lengthening or shortening sleeves.

5-YEAR TREND — ESTIMATED INDUSTRY SALES ($MILLIONS)

Year	Employee Size of Establishment									Total Industry Sales
	1-4 Emps.	5-9 Emps.	10-19 Emps.	20-49 Emps.	50-99 Emps.	100-249 Emps.	250-499 Emps.	500-999 Emps.	Unknown Emps.	
2015	63.8	144.7	354.5	242.7	75.8	73.7	27.6	25.0	14.8	1,022.6
2016	66.3	150.3	368.2	252.1	78.7	76.5	28.7	26.0	15.3	1,062.1
2017	68.6	155.6	381.2	261.0	81.5	79.2	29.7	26.9	15.9	1,099.5
2018	72.9	165.4	405.2	277.5	86.6	84.2	31.6	28.2	16.9	1,168.6
2018	77.7	176.2	431.6	295.5	92.2	89.7	33.6	29.6	18.0	1,244.2

INDUSTRY: FAMILY CLOTHING STORES (NAICS 44814)
PRODUCT LINE: LINGERIE & SLEEPWEAR (Sub Category)

NAICS 44814: Family Clothing Stores . This industry comprises establishments primarily engaged in retailing a general line of new clothing for men, women, and children, without specializing in sales for an individual gender or age group. These establishments may provide basic alterations, such as hemming, taking in or letting out seams, or lengthening or shortening sleeves.

5-YEAR TREND — ESTIMATED INDUSTRY SALES ($MILLIONS)

Year	Employee Size of Establishment									Total Industry Sales
	1-4 Emps.	5-9 Emps.	10-19 Emps.	20-49 Emps.	50-99 Emps.	100-249 Emps.	250-499 Emps.	500-999 Emps.	Unknown Emps.	
2015	18.4	33.0	142.1	435.7	457.0	114.0	112.7	44.7	5.0	1,362.6
2016	19.1	34.2	147.2	451.3	473.4	118.1	116.7	46.3	5.2	1,411.4
2017	19.7	35.3	152.0	466.1	488.8	121.9	120.5	47.8	5.3	1,457.5
2018	20.9	37.5	161.3	494.4	518.6	129.4	127.9	50.6	5.7	1,546.1
2018	22.2	39.8	171.4	525.5	551.2	137.5	135.9	53.6	6.0	1,643.2

INDUSTRY: DEPARTMENT STORES (NAICS 45211)
PRODUCT LINE: LINGERIE & SLEEPWEAR (Sub Category)

NAICS 45211: Department Stores Industry . This industry comprises establishments known as department stores primarily engaged in retailing a wide range of the following new products with no one merchandise line predominating: apparel, furniture, appliances and home furnishings; and selected additional items, such as paint, hardware, toiletries, cosmetics, photographic equipment, jewelry, toys, and sporting goods. Merchandise lines are normally arranged in separate departments.

5-YEAR TREND — ESTIMATED INDUSTRY SALES ($MILLIONS)

Year	Employee Size of Establishment									Total
	1-4 Emps.	5-9 Emps.	10-19 Emps.	20-49 Emps.	50-99 Emps.	100-249 Emps.	250-499 Emps.	500-999 Emps.	Unknown Emps.	Industry Sales
2015	0.1	0.0	0.2	14.1	267.8	888.2	389.7	52.2	2.3	1,614.5
2016	0.1	0.0	0.2	14.3	271.3	899.7	394.7	52.9	2.3	1,635.4
2017	0.1	0.0	0.2	14.4	274.2	909.4	398.9	53.4	2.3	1,653.0
2018	0.1	0.0	0.2	14.5	275.4	913.6	400.8	53.7	2.3	1,660.7
2018	0.1	0.0	0.2	14.6	277.4	920.1	403.7	54.1	2.3	1,672.7

INDUSTRY: WAREHOUSE CLUBS & SUPERCENTERS (NAICS 45291)
PRODUCT LINE: LINGERIE & SLEEPWEAR (Sub Category)

NAICS 45291: Warehouse Clubs and Superstores This industry comprises establishments known as warehouse clubs, superstores or supercenters primarily engaged in retailing a general line of groceries in combination with general lines of new merchandise, such as apparel, furniture, and appliances.

5-YEAR TREND — ESTIMATED INDUSTRY SALES ($MILLIONS)

Year	Employee Size of Establishment									Total
	1-4 Emps.	5-9 Emps.	10-19 Emps.	20-49 Emps.	50-99 Emps.	100-249 Emps.	250-499 Emps.	500-999 Emps.	Unknown Emps.	Industry Sales
2015	0.2	0.0	0.0	2.0	2.5	311.9	1,379.0	36.4	0.4	1,732.6
2016	0.2	0.0	0.0	2.1	2.6	323.3	1,429.4	37.8	0.4	1,796.0
2017	0.2	0.0	0.0	2.1	2.7	334.1	1,477.1	39.0	0.5	1,855.9
2018	0.3	0.0	0.0	2.3	2.9	362.9	1,604.3	42.4	0.5	2,015.7
2018	0.3	0.0	0.0	2.5	3.1	385.4	1,703.8	45.0	0.5	2,140.7

INDUSTRY: WOMEN'S CLOTHING STORES (NAICS 44812)
PRODUCT LINE: HATS & WIGS (Sub Category)

NAICS 44812: Women's Clothing Stores . This industry comprises establishments primarily engaged in retailing a general line of new women's, misses' and juniors' clothing, including maternity wear. These establishments may provide basic alterations, such as hemming, taking in or letting out seams, or lengthening or shortening sleeves.

5-YEAR TREND — ESTIMATED INDUSTRY SALES ($MILLIONS)

Year	Employee Size of Establishment									Total Industry Sales
	1-4 Emps.	5-9 Emps.	10-19 Emps.	20-49 Emps.	50-99 Emps.	100-249 Emps.	250-499 Emps.	500-999 Emps.	Unknown Emps.	
2015	5.2	11.8	28.8	19.7	6.2	6.0	2.2	2.0	1.2	83.2
2016	5.4	12.2	29.9	20.5	6.4	6.2	2.3	2.1	1.2	86.4
2017	5.6	12.7	31.0	21.2	6.6	6.4	2.4	2.2	1.3	89.4
2018	5.9	13.5	33.0	22.6	7.0	6.9	2.6	2.3	1.4	95.1
2018	6.3	14.3	35.1	24.0	7.5	7.3	2.7	2.4	1.5	101.2

INDUSTRY: FAMILY CLOTHING STORES (NAICS 44814)
PRODUCT LINE: HATS & WIGS (Sub Category)

NAICS 44814: Family Clothing Stores . This industry comprises establishments primarily engaged in retailing a general line of new clothing for men, women, and children, without specializing in sales for an individual gender or age group. These establishments may provide basic alterations, such as hemming, taking in or letting out seams, or lengthening or shortening sleeves.

5-YEAR TREND — ESTIMATED INDUSTRY SALES ($MILLIONS)

Year	Employee Size of Establishment									Total Industry Sales
	1-4 Emps.	5-9 Emps.	10-19 Emps.	20-49 Emps.	50-99 Emps.	100-249 Emps.	250-499 Emps.	500-999 Emps.	Unknown Emps.	
2015	10.3	18.5	79.8	244.5	256.4	64.0	63.2	25.1	2.8	764.5
2016	10.7	19.2	82.6	253.2	265.6	66.3	65.5	26.0	2.9	791.9
2017	11.1	19.8	85.3	261.5	274.3	68.4	67.6	26.8	3.0	817.8
2018	11.7	21.0	90.5	277.4	291.0	72.6	71.7	28.4	3.2	867.5
2018	12.5	22.3	96.2	294.9	309.3	77.2	76.3	30.1	3.4	922.0

INDUSTRY: WOMEN'S CLOTHING STORES (NAICS 44812)
PRODUCT LINE: ACCESSORIES & HANDBAGS (Sub Category)

NAICS 44812: Women's Clothing Stores . This industry comprises establishments primarily engaged in retailing a general line of new women's, misses' and juniors' clothing, including maternity wear. These establishments may provide basic alterations, such as hemming, taking in or letting out seams, or lengthening or shortening sleeves.

5-YEAR TREND – ESTIMATED INDUSTRY SALES ($MILLIONS)

Year	Employee Size of Establishment									Total Industry Sales
	1-4 Emps.	5-9 Emps.	10-19 Emps.	20-49 Emps.	50-99 Emps.	100-249 Emps.	250-499 Emps.	500-999 Emps.	Unknown Emps.	
2015	136.8	310.2	760.0	520.3	162.4	158.0	59.2	53.7	31.7	2,192.2
2016	142.1	322.2	789.3	540.4	168.7	164.1	61.5	55.7	32.9	2,276.8
2017	147.1	333.5	817.1	559.4	174.6	169.9	63.6	57.7	34.1	2,357.0
2018	156.4	354.6	868.8	594.8	185.7	180.6	67.6	60.5	36.2	2,505.2
2018	166.6	377.7	925.3	633.5	197.7	192.4	72.0	63.5	38.6	2,667.4

INDUSTRY: FAMILY CLOTHING STORES (NAICS 44814)
PRODUCT LINE: ACCESSORIES & HANDBAGS (Sub Category)

NAICS 44814: Family Clothing Stores . This industry comprises establishments primarily engaged in retailing a general line of new clothing for men, women, and children, without specializing in sales for an individual gender or age group. These establishments may provide basic alterations, such as hemming, taking in or letting out seams, or lengthening or shortening sleeves.

5-YEAR TREND – ESTIMATED INDUSTRY SALES ($MILLIONS)

Year	Employee Size of Establishment									Total Industry Sales
	1-4 Emps.	5-9 Emps.	10-19 Emps.	20-49 Emps.	50-99 Emps.	100-249 Emps.	250-499 Emps.	500-999 Emps.	Unknown Emps.	
2015	57.0	102.2	440.0	1,348.9	1,414.8	352.9	348.8	138.2	15.4	4,218.3
2016	59.1	105.9	455.8	1,397.2	1,465.4	365.6	361.3	143.2	16.0	4,369.4
2017	61.0	109.3	470.7	1,442.8	1,513.2	377.5	373.1	147.9	16.5	4,512.0
2018	64.7	116.0	499.3	1,530.6	1,605.3	400.5	395.8	156.5	17.5	4,786.2
2018	68.8	123.3	530.7	1,626.8	1,706.3	425.7	420.7	165.9	18.6	5,086.9

INDUSTRY: DEPARTMENT STORES (NAICS 45211)
PRODUCT LINE: ACCESSORIES & HANDBAGS (Sub Category)

NAICS 45211: Department Stores Industry . This industry comprises establishments known as department stores primarily engaged in retailing a wide range of the following new products with no one merchandise line predominating: apparel, furniture, appliances and home furnishings; and selected additional items, such as paint, hardware, toiletries, cosmetics, photographic equipment, jewelry, toys, and sporting goods. Merchandise lines are normally arranged in separate departments.

5-YEAR TREND – ESTIMATED INDUSTRY SALES ($MILLIONS)

Year	Employee Size of Establishment									Total
	1-4 Emps.	5-9 Emps.	10-19 Emps.	20-49 Emps.	50-99 Emps.	100-249 Emps.	250-499 Emps.	500-999 Emps.	Unknown Emps.	Industry Sales
2015	0.1	0.0	0.2	16.9	320.3	1,062.5	466.1	62.4	2.7	1,931.4
2016	0.1	0.0	0.2	17.1	324.5	1,076.2	472.1	63.2	2.7	1,956.3
2017	0.1	0.1	0.2	17.3	328.0	1,087.8	477.2	63.9	2.8	1,977.4
2018	0.1	0.1	0.2	17.4	329.5	1,092.8	479.4	64.3	2.8	1,986.6
2018	0.1	0.1	0.2	17.5	331.9	1,100.7	482.9	64.7	2.8	2,000.9

INDUSTRY: WAREHOUSE CLUBS & SUPERCENTERS (NAICS 45291)
PRODUCT LINE: ACCESSORIES & HANDBAGS (Sub Category)

NAICS 45291: Warehouse Clubs and Superstores This industry comprises establishments known as warehouse clubs, superstores or supercenters primarily engaged in retailing a general line of groceries in combination with general lines of new merchandise, such as apparel, furniture, and appliances.

5-YEAR TREND – ESTIMATED INDUSTRY SALES ($MILLIONS)

Year	Employee Size of Establishment									Total
	1-4 Emps.	5-9 Emps.	10-19 Emps.	20-49 Emps.	50-99 Emps.	100-249 Emps.	250-499 Emps.	500-999 Emps.	Unknown Emps.	Industry Sales
2015	0.1	0.0	0.0	1.3	1.7	205.9	910.4	24.1	0.3	1,143.9
2016	0.1	0.0	0.0	1.4	1.7	213.5	943.7	24.9	0.3	1,185.7
2017	0.2	0.0	0.0	1.4	1.8	220.6	975.2	25.8	0.3	1,225.2
2018	0.2	0.0	0.0	1.5	1.9	239.6	1,059.1	28.0	0.3	1,330.7
2018	0.2	0.0	0.0	1.6	2.1	254.4	1,124.8	29.7	0.4	1,413.2

INDUSTRY: WOMEN'S CLOTHING STORES (NAICS 44812)
PRODUCT LINE: WOMEN'S SWEAT TOPS & PANTS (Sub Category)

NAICS 44812: Women's Clothing Stores . This industry comprises establishments primarily engaged in retailing a general line of new women's, misses' and juniors' clothing, including maternity wear. These establishments may provide basic alterations, such as hemming, taking in or letting out seams, or lengthening or shortening sleeves.

5-YEAR TREND – ESTIMATED INDUSTRY SALES ($MILLIONS)

Year	Employee Size of Establishment									Total Industry Sales
	1-4 Emps.	5-9 Emps.	10-19 Emps.	20-49 Emps.	50-99 Emps.	100-249 Emps.	250-499 Emps.	500-999 Emps.	Unknown Emps.	
2015	37.1	84.1	206.1	141.1	44.1	42.9	16.0	14.6	8.6	594.6
2016	38.5	87.4	214.1	146.6	45.8	44.5	16.7	15.1	8.9	617.6
2017	39.9	90.5	221.6	151.8	47.4	46.1	17.3	15.6	9.2	639.4
2018	42.4	96.2	235.7	161.3	50.4	49.0	18.3	16.4	9.8	679.5
2018	45.2	102.5	251.0	171.8	53.6	52.2	19.5	17.2	10.5	723.5

INDUSTRY: FAMILY CLOTHING STORES (NAICS 44814)
PRODUCT LINE: WOMEN'S SWEAT TOPS & PANTS (Sub Category)

NAICS 44814: Family Clothing Stores . This industry comprises establishments primarily engaged in retailing a general line of new clothing for men, women, and children, without specializing in sales for an individual gender or age group. These establishments may provide basic alterations, such as hemming, taking in or letting out seams, or lengthening or shortening sleeves.

5-YEAR TREND – ESTIMATED INDUSTRY SALES ($MILLIONS)

Year	Employee Size of Establishment									Total Industry Sales
	1-4 Emps.	5-9 Emps.	10-19 Emps.	20-49 Emps.	50-99 Emps.	100-249 Emps.	250-499 Emps.	500-999 Emps.	Unknown Emps.	
2015	27.8	49.8	214.2	656.6	688.7	171.8	169.8	67.3	7.5	2,053.4
2016	28.7	51.5	221.9	680.1	713.3	178.0	175.9	69.7	7.8	2,126.9
2017	29.7	53.2	229.1	702.3	736.6	183.8	181.6	72.0	8.0	2,196.3
2018	31.5	56.5	243.1	745.0	781.4	194.9	192.7	76.2	8.5	2,329.8
2018	33.5	60.0	258.3	791.9	830.6	207.2	204.8	80.8	9.1	2,476.1

INDUSTRY: WOMEN'S CLOTHING STORES (NAICS 44812)
PRODUCT LINE: UNIFORMS & OTHER APPAREL (Sub Category)

NAICS 44812: Women's Clothing Stores . This industry comprises establishments primarily engaged in retailing a general line of new women's, misses' and juniors' clothing, including maternity wear. These establishments may provide basic alterations, such as hemming, taking in or letting out seams, or lengthening or shortening sleeves.

5-YEAR TREND – ESTIMATED INDUSTRY SALES ($MILLIONS)

Year	Employee Size of Establishment									Total Industry Sales
	1-4 Emps.	5-9 Emps.	10-19 Emps.	20-49 Emps.	50-99 Emps.	100-249 Emps.	250-499 Emps.	500-999 Emps.	Unknown Emps.	
2015	17.2	39.1	95.7	65.5	20.5	19.9	7.5	6.8	4.0	276.1
2016	17.9	40.6	99.4	68.1	21.2	20.7	7.7	7.0	4.1	286.8
2017	18.5	42.0	102.9	70.5	22.0	21.4	8.0	7.3	4.3	296.9
2018	19.7	44.7	109.4	74.9	23.4	22.7	8.5	7.6	4.6	315.5
2018	21.0	47.6	116.5	79.8	24.9	24.2	9.1	8.0	4.9	335.9

INDUSTRY: FAMILY CLOTHING STORES (NAICS 44814)
PRODUCT LINE: UNIFORMS & OTHER APPAREL (Sub Category)

NAICS 44814: Family Clothing Stores . This industry comprises establishments primarily engaged in retailing a general line of new clothing for men, women, and children, without specializing in sales for an individual gender or age group. These establishments may provide basic alterations, such as hemming, taking in or letting out seams, or lengthening or shortening sleeves.

5-YEAR TREND – ESTIMATED INDUSTRY SALES ($MILLIONS)

Year	Employee Size of Establishment									Total Industry Sales
	1-4 Emps.	5-9 Emps.	10-19 Emps.	20-49 Emps.	50-99 Emps.	100-249 Emps.	250-499 Emps.	500-999 Emps.	Unknown Emps.	
2015	2.2	3.9	16.9	51.8	54.3	13.5	13.4	5.3	0.6	161.9
2016	2.3	4.1	17.5	53.6	56.2	14.0	13.9	5.5	0.6	167.7
2017	2.3	4.2	18.1	55.4	58.1	14.5	14.3	5.7	0.6	173.2
2018	2.5	4.5	19.2	58.7	61.6	15.4	15.2	6.0	0.7	183.7
2018	2.6	4.7	20.4	62.4	65.5	16.3	16.1	6.4	0.7	195.3

INDUSTRY: DEPARTMENT STORES (NAICS 45211)
PRODUCT LINE: UNIFORMS & OTHER APPAREL (Sub Category)

NAICS 45211: Department Stores Industry . This industry comprises establishments known as department stores primarily engaged in retailing a wide range of the following new products with no one merchandise line predominating: apparel, furniture, appliances and home furnishings; and selected additional items, such as paint, hardware, toiletries, cosmetics, photographic equipment, jewelry, toys, and sporting goods. Merchandise lines are normally arranged in separate departments.

5-YEAR TREND – ESTIMATED INDUSTRY SALES ($MILLIONS)

Year	Employee Size of Establishment									Total Industry Sales
	1-4 Emps.	5-9 Emps.	10-19 Emps.	20-49 Emps.	50-99 Emps.	100-249 Emps.	250-499 Emps.	500-999 Emps.	Unknown Emps.	
2015	0.0	0.0	0.0	1.6	30.0	99.4	43.6	5.8	0.3	180.6
2016	0.0	0.0	0.0	1.6	30.3	100.6	44.2	5.9	0.3	182.9
2017	0.0	0.0	0.0	1.6	30.7	101.7	44.6	6.0	0.3	184.9
2018	0.0	0.0	0.0	1.6	30.8	102.2	44.8	6.0	0.3	185.8
2018	0.0	0.0	0.0	1.6	31.0	102.9	45.2	6.1	0.3	187.1

INDUSTRY: SUPERMARKETS & GROCERY STORES (NAICS 44511)
PRODUCT LINE: CHILDREN'S WEAR (Main Category)

NAICS 44511: Grocery Stores Industry. This industry comprises establishments generally known as supermarkets and grocery stores primarily engaged in retailing a general line of food, such as canned and frozen foods; fresh fruits and vegetables; and fresh and prepared meats, fish, and poultry. Included in this industry are delicatessen-type establishments primarily engaged in retailing a general line of food.

5-YEAR TREND – ESTIMATED INDUSTRY SALES ($MILLIONS)

Year	Employee Size of Establishment									Total Industry Sales
	1-4 Emps.	5-9 Emps.	10-19 Emps.	20-49 Emps.	50-99 Emps.	100-249 Emps.	250-499 Emps.	500-999 Emps.	Unknown Emps.	
2015	0.8	0.6	1.5	5.0	12.1	27.6	8.0	1.1	0.2	56.8
2016	0.8	0.6	1.5	4.9	11.9	27.1	7.8	1.1	0.1	55.8
2017	0.8	0.6	1.5	4.8	11.7	26.6	7.7	1.1	0.1	54.7
2018	0.8	0.6	1.5	4.8	11.7	26.6	7.7	1.1	0.1	54.8
2018	0.8	0.6	1.5	4.8	11.7	26.6	7.7	1.1	0.1	54.9

INDUSTRY: PHARMACIES & DRUG STORES (NAICS 44611)
PRODUCT LINE: CHILDREN'S WEAR (Main Category)

NAICS 44611 Pharmacies and Drug Stores – This industry comprises establishments known as pharmacies and drug stores engaged in retailing prescription or nonprescription drugs and medicines.

5-YEAR TREND – ESTIMATED INDUSTRY SALES ($MILLIONS)

Year	Employee Size of Establishment									Total Industry Sales
	1-4 Emps.	5-9 Emps.	10-19 Emps.	20-49 Emps.	50-99 Emps.	100-249 Emps.	250-499 Emps.	500-999 Emps.	Unknown Emps.	
2015	0.6	1.4	5.9	16.7	1.6	0.6	0.2	0.1	0.0	27.0
2016	0.6	1.5	6.2	17.5	1.6	0.6	0.2	0.1	0.0	28.4
2017	0.6	1.5	6.5	18.4	1.7	0.7	0.2	0.1	0.1	29.8
2018	0.7	1.7	7.0	19.8	1.9	0.7	0.2	0.1	0.1	32.0
2018	0.7	1.8	7.5	21.3	2.0	0.8	0.2	0.1	0.1	34.5

INDUSTRY: MEN'S CLOTHING STORES (NAICS 44811)
PRODUCT LINE: CHILDREN'S WEAR (Main Category)

NAICS 44811: Men's Clothing Stores. This industry comprises establishments primarily engaged in retailing a general line of new men's and boys' clothing. These establishments may provide basic alterations, such as hemming, taking in or letting out seams, or lengthening or shortening sleeves.

5-YEAR TREND – ESTIMATED INDUSTRY SALES ($MILLIONS)

Year	Employee Size of Establishment									Total Industry Sales
	1-4 Emps.	5-9 Emps.	10-19 Emps.	20-49 Emps.	50-99 Emps.	100-249 Emps.	250-499 Emps.	500-999 Emps.	Unknown Emps.	
2015	11.0	16.4	38.4	22.4	5.7	2.9	1.2	0.1	1.8	99.8
2016	11.5	17.2	40.1	23.4	6.0	3.0	1.3	0.1	1.9	104.4
2017	12.0	17.9	41.8	24.4	6.2	3.1	1.3	0.1	2.0	108.8
2018	12.4	18.5	43.3	25.2	6.4	3.2	1.4	0.1	2.1	112.7
2018	12.9	19.2	44.9	26.2	6.7	3.4	1.4	0.1	2.1	116.8

INDUSTRY: WOMEN'S CLOTHING STORES (NAICS 44812)
PRODUCT LINE: CHILDREN'S WEAR (Main Category)

NAICS 44812: Women's Clothing Stores . This industry comprises establishments primarily engaged in retailing a general line of new women's, misses' and juniors' clothing, including maternity wear. These establishments may provide basic alterations, such as hemming, taking in or letting out seams, or lengthening or shortening sleeves.

5-YEAR TREND – ESTIMATED INDUSTRY SALES ($MILLIONS)

Year	Employee Size of Establishment									Total
	1-4 Emps.	5-9 Emps.	10-19 Emps.	20-49 Emps.	50-99 Emps.	100-249 Emps.	250-499 Emps.	500-999 Emps.	Unknown Emps.	Industry Sales
2015	16.2	36.7	90.0	61.6	19.2	18.7	7.0	6.4	3.8	259.6
2016	16.8	38.2	93.5	64.0	20.0	19.4	7.3	6.6	3.9	269.6
2017	17.4	39.5	96.8	66.3	20.7	20.1	7.5	6.8	4.0	279.1
2018	18.5	42.0	102.9	70.4	22.0	21.4	8.0	7.2	4.3	296.7
2018	19.7	44.7	109.6	75.0	23.4	22.8	8.5	7.5	4.6	315.9

INDUSTRY: FAMILY CLOTHING STORES (NAICS 44814)
PRODUCT LINE: CHILDREN'S WEAR (Main Category)

NAICS 44814: Family Clothing Stores . This industry comprises establishments primarily engaged in retailing a general line of new clothing for men, women, and children, without specializing in sales for an individual gender or age group. These establishments may provide basic alterations, such as hemming, taking in or letting out seams, or lengthening or shortening sleeves.

5-YEAR TREND – ESTIMATED INDUSTRY SALES ($MILLIONS)

Year	Employee Size of Establishment									Total
	1-4 Emps.	5-9 Emps.	10-19 Emps.	20-49 Emps.	50-99 Emps.	100-249 Emps.	250-499 Emps.	500-999 Emps.	Unknown Emps.	Industry Sales
2015	154.8	277.6	1,194.8	3,662.3	3,841.2	958.3	947.2	375.4	41.9	11,453.3
2016	160.3	287.5	1,237.5	3,793.5	3,978.8	992.6	981.1	388.8	43.4	11,863.5
2017	165.6	296.9	1,277.9	3,917.3	4,108.7	1,025.0	1,013.1	401.5	44.8	12,250.7
2018	175.6	315.0	1,355.7	4,155.7	4,358.7	1,087.4	1,074.8	424.9	47.5	12,995.2
2018	186.7	334.8	1,441.0	4,417.1	4,632.9	1,155.8	1,142.4	450.5	50.5	13,811.5

INDUSTRY: DEPARTMENT STORES (NAICS 45211)
PRODUCT LINE: CHILDREN'S WEAR (Main Category)

NAICS 45211: Department Stores Industry . This industry comprises establishments known as department stores primarily engaged in retailing a wide range of the following new products with no one merchandise line predominating: apparel, furniture, appliances and home furnishings; and selected additional items, such as paint, hardware, toiletries, cosmetics, photographic equipment, jewelry, toys, and sporting goods. Merchandise lines are normally arranged in separate departments.

5-YEAR TREND — ESTIMATED INDUSTRY SALES ($MILLIONS)

Year	Employee Size of Establishment									Total
	1-4 Emps.	5-9 Emps.	10-19 Emps.	20-49 Emps.	50-99 Emps.	100-249 Emps.	250-499 Emps.	500-999 Emps.	Unknown Emps.	Industry Sales
2015	0.6	0.2	0.9	74.0	1,405.7	4,662.3	2,045.4	273.9	11.9	8,475.0
2016	0.6	0.2	0.9	75.0	1,423.8	4,722.5	2,071.8	277.4	12.0	8,584.4
2017	0.6	0.2	1.0	75.8	1,439.2	4,773.4	2,094.1	280.4	12.2	8,676.9
2018	0.6	0.2	1.0	76.2	1,445.8	4,795.4	2,103.8	282.0	12.2	8,717.2
2018	0.6	0.2	1.0	76.7	1,456.2	4,830.0	2,118.9	284.1	12.3	8,780.0

INDUSTRY: WAREHOUSE CLUBS & SUPERCENTERS (NAICS 45291)
PRODUCT LINE: CHILDREN'S WEAR (Main Category)

NAICS 45291: Warehouse Clubs and Superstores This industry comprises establishments known as warehouse clubs, superstores or supercenters primarily engaged in retailing a general line of groceries in combination with general lines of new merchandise, such as apparel, furniture, and appliances.

5-YEAR TREND — ESTIMATED INDUSTRY SALES ($MILLIONS)

Year	Employee Size of Establishment									Total
	1-4 Emps.	5-9 Emps.	10-19 Emps.	20-49 Emps.	50-99 Emps.	100-249 Emps.	250-499 Emps.	500-999 Emps.	Unknown Emps.	Industry Sales
2015	1.6	0.1	0.3	14.8	18.7	2,305.6	10,192.8	269.3	3.2	12,806.3
2016	1.6	0.1	0.3	15.4	19.4	2,389.9	10,565.4	279.2	3.3	13,274.5
2017	1.7	0.1	0.3	15.9	20.0	2,469.6	10,917.7	288.5	3.4	13,717.0
2018	1.9	0.1	0.3	17.2	21.7	2,682.3	11,858.0	313.3	3.7	14,898.4
2018	2.0	0.1	0.3	18.3	23.1	2,848.6	12,593.1	332.7	3.9	15,822.1

INDUSTRY: ELECTRONIC SHOPPING & MAIL ORDER (NAICS 45411)
PRODUCT LINE: CHILDREN'S WEAR (Main Category)

NAICS 45411: Electronic Shopping and Mail-Order Houses This industry comprises establishments primarily engaged in retailing all types of merchandise by means of mail or by electronic media, such as interactive television or computer. Included in this industry are establishments primarily engaged in retailing from catalogue showrooms of mail-order houses.

5-YEAR TREND — ESTIMATED INDUSTRY SALES ($MILLIONS)

Year	Employee Size of Establishment									Total Industry Sales
	1-4 Emps.	5-9 Emps.	10-19 Emps.	20-49 Emps.	50-99 Emps.	100-249 Emps.	250-499 Emps.	500-999 Emps.	Unknown Emps.	
2015	265.8	141.1	209.6	339.0	243.9	475.5	695.7	881.2	40.2	3,292.0
2016	283.6	150.5	223.6	361.7	260.1	507.2	742.1	940.0	42.9	3,511.6
2017	300.8	159.7	237.1	383.6	275.9	537.9	787.1	997.1	45.5	3,724.7
2018	342.2	181.7	269.8	436.5	314.0	612.1	895.6	1,106.8	51.8	4,210.6
2018	380.1	201.8	299.7	484.8	348.7	679.9	994.8	1,208.0	57.5	4,655.4

INDUSTRY: BOOK STORES (NAICS 451211)
PRODUCT LINE: CHILDREN'S WEAR (Main Category)

NAICS 451211: Book Stores. This industry comprises establishments primarily engaged in the retail sale of new books and magazines. Establishments primarily engaged in the retail sale of used books are classified in 5932.

5-YEAR TREND — ESTIMATED INDUSTRY SALES ($MILLIONS)

Year	Employee Size of Establishment									Total Industry Sales
	1-4 Emps.	5-9 Emps.	10-19 Emps.	20-49 Emps.	50-99 Emps.	100-249 Emps.	250-499 Emps.	500-999 Emps.	Unknown Emps.	
2015	0.4	0.6	1.2	3.1	1.4	0.5	0.1	0.4	0.2	7.8
2016	0.4	0.6	1.2	3.2	1.5	0.6	0.1	0.4	0.2	8.2
2017	0.4	0.6	1.3	3.4	1.5	0.6	0.1	0.4	0.2	8.6
2018	0.4	0.6	1.3	3.4	1.6	0.6	0.1	0.4	0.2	8.7
2018	0.4	0.6	1.3	3.5	1.6	0.6	0.1	0.4	0.2	8.8

INDUSTRY: MEN'S CLOTHING STORES (NAICS 44811)
PRODUCT LINE: BOYS' WEAR & ACCESSORIES (Sub Category)

NAICS 44811: Men's Clothing Stores. This industry comprises establishments primarily engaged in retailing a general line of new men's and boys' clothing. These establishments may provide basic alterations, such as hemming, taking in or letting out seams, or lengthening or shortening sleeves.

5-YEAR TREND — ESTIMATED INDUSTRY SALES ($MILLIONS)

Year	Employee Size of Establishment									Total Industry Sales
	1-4 Emps.	5-9 Emps.	10-19 Emps.	20-49 Emps.	50-99 Emps.	100-249 Emps.	250-499 Emps.	500-999 Emps.	Unknown Emps.	
2015	8.0	11.9	27.8	16.2	4.1	2.1	0.9	0.0	1.3	72.3
2016	8.3	12.4	29.0	16.9	4.3	2.2	0.9	0.0	1.4	75.6
2017	8.7	13.0	30.3	17.6	4.5	2.3	1.0	0.1	1.4	78.8
2018	9.0	13.4	31.3	18.3	4.7	2.3	1.0	0.1	1.5	81.6
2018	9.3	13.9	32.5	18.9	4.8	2.4	1.0	0.1	1.6	84.6

INDUSTRY: WOMEN'S CLOTHING STORES (NAICS 44812)
PRODUCT LINE: BOYS' WEAR & ACCESSORIES (Sub Category)

NAICS 44812: Women's Clothing Stores . This industry comprises establishments primarily engaged in retailing a general line of new women's, misses' and juniors' clothing, including maternity wear. These establishments may provide basic alterations, such as hemming, taking in or letting out seams, or lengthening or shortening sleeves.

5-YEAR TREND — ESTIMATED INDUSTRY SALES ($MILLIONS)

Year	Employee Size of Establishment									Total Industry Sales
	1-4 Emps.	5-9 Emps.	10-19 Emps.	20-49 Emps.	50-99 Emps.	100-249 Emps.	250-499 Emps.	500-999 Emps.	Unknown Emps.	
2015	3.3	7.6	18.5	12.7	4.0	3.9	1.4	1.3	0.8	53.5
2016	3.5	7.9	19.3	13.2	4.1	4.0	1.5	1.4	0.8	55.5
2017	3.6	8.1	19.9	13.6	4.3	4.1	1.6	1.4	0.8	57.5
2018	3.8	8.7	21.2	14.5	4.5	4.4	1.6	1.5	0.9	61.1
2018	4.1	9.2	22.6	15.5	4.8	4.7	1.8	1.5	0.9	65.1

INDUSTRY: FAMILY CLOTHING STORES (NAICS 44814)
PRODUCT LINE: BOYS' WEAR & ACCESSORIES (Sub Category)

NAICS 44814: Family Clothing Stores . This industry comprises establishments primarily engaged in retailing a general line of new clothing for men, women, and children, without specializing in sales for an individual gender or age group. These establishments may provide basic alterations, such as hemming, taking in or letting out seams, or lengthening or shortening sleeves.

5-YEAR TREND — ESTIMATED INDUSTRY SALES ($MILLIONS)

Year	Employee Size of Establishment									Total Industry Sales
	1-4 Emps.	5-9 Emps.	10-19 Emps.	20-49 Emps.	50-99 Emps.	100-249 Emps.	250-499 Emps.	500-999 Emps.	Unknown Emps.	
2015	56.1	100.6	432.9	1,327.0	1,391.9	347.2	343.2	136.0	15.2	4,150.1
2016	58.1	104.2	448.4	1,374.5	1,441.7	359.7	355.5	140.9	15.7	4,298.7
2017	60.0	107.6	463.1	1,419.4	1,488.8	371.4	367.1	145.5	16.2	4,439.0
2018	63.6	114.1	491.2	1,505.8	1,579.3	394.0	389.4	154.0	17.2	4,708.7
2018	67.6	121.3	522.1	1,600.5	1,678.7	418.8	413.9	163.2	18.3	5,004.5

INDUSTRY: DEPARTMENT STORES (NAICS 45211)
PRODUCT LINE: BOYS' WEAR & ACCESSORIES (Sub Category)

NAICS 45211: Department Stores Industry . **This industry comprises** establishments known as department stores primarily engaged in retailing a wide range of the following new products with no one merchandise line predominating: apparel, furniture, appliances and home furnishings; and selected additional items, such as paint, hardware, toiletries, cosmetics, photographic equipment, jewelry, toys, and sporting goods. Merchandise lines are normally arranged in separate departments.

5-YEAR TREND — ESTIMATED INDUSTRY SALES ($MILLIONS)

Year	Employee Size of Establishment									Total Industry Sales
	1-4 Emps.	5-9 Emps.	10-19 Emps.	20-49 Emps.	50-99 Emps.	100-249 Emps.	250-499 Emps.	500-999 Emps.	Unknown Emps.	
2015	0.2	0.1	0.3	23.0	435.9	1,445.6	634.2	84.9	3.7	2,627.8
2016	0.2	0.1	0.3	23.3	441.5	1,464.3	642.4	86.0	3.7	2,661.7
2017	0.2	0.1	0.3	23.5	446.2	1,480.1	649.3	87.0	3.8	2,690.4
2018	0.2	0.1	0.3	23.6	448.3	1,486.9	652.3	87.4	3.8	2,702.9
2018	0.2	0.1	0.3	23.8	451.5	1,497.6	657.0	88.1	3.8	2,722.4

INDUSTRY: WAREHOUSE CLUBS & SUPERCENTERS (NAICS 45291)
PRODUCT LINE: BOYS' WEAR & ACCESSORIES (Sub Category)

NAICS 45291: Warehouse Clubs and Superstores This industry comprises establishments known as warehouse clubs, superstores or supercenters primarily engaged in retailing a general line of groceries in combination with general lines of new merchandise, such as apparel, furniture, and appliances.

5-YEAR TREND – ESTIMATED INDUSTRY SALES ($MILLIONS)

Year	Employee Size of Establishment									Total
	1-4 Emps.	5-9 Emps.	10-19 Emps.	20-49 Emps.	50-99 Emps.	100-249 Emps.	250-499 Emps.	500-999 Emps.	Unknown Emps.	Industry Sales
2015	0.4	0.0	0.1	3.6	4.6	563.7	2,492.0	65.8	0.8	3,131.0
2016	0.4	0.0	0.1	3.8	4.7	584.3	2,583.1	68.2	0.8	3,245.5
2017	0.4	0.0	0.1	3.9	4.9	603.8	2,669.3	70.5	0.8	3,353.7
2018	0.5	0.0	0.1	4.2	5.3	655.8	2,899.2	76.6	0.9	3,642.5
2018	0.5	0.0	0.1	4.5	5.6	696.4	3,078.9	81.3	1.0	3,868.4

INDUSTRY: MEN'S CLOTHING STORES (NAICS 44811)
PRODUCT LINE: GIRLS' WEAR & ACCESSORIES (Sub Category)

NAICS 44811: Men's Clothing Stores. This industry comprises establishments primarily engaged in retailing a general line of new men's and boys' clothing. These establishments may provide basic alterations, such as hemming, taking in or letting out seams, or lengthening or shortening sleeves.

5-YEAR TREND – ESTIMATED INDUSTRY SALES ($MILLIONS)

Year	Employee Size of Establishment									Total
	1-4 Emps.	5-9 Emps.	10-19 Emps.	20-49 Emps.	50-99 Emps.	100-249 Emps.	250-499 Emps.	500-999 Emps.	Unknown Emps.	Industry Sales
2015	2.6	3.9	9.0	5.3	1.3	0.7	0.3	0.0	0.4	23.6
2016	2.7	4.1	9.5	5.5	1.4	0.7	0.3	0.0	0.5	24.6
2017	2.8	4.2	9.9	5.7	1.5	0.7	0.3	0.0	0.5	25.7
2018	2.9	4.4	10.2	6.0	1.5	0.8	0.3	0.0	0.5	26.6
2018	3.0	4.5	10.6	6.2	1.6	0.8	0.3	0.0	0.5	27.6

INDUSTRY: WOMEN'S CLOTHING STORES (NAICS 44812)
PRODUCT LINE: GIRLS' WEAR & ACCESSORIES (Sub Category)

NAICS 44812: Women's Clothing Stores . This industry comprises establishments primarily engaged in retailing a general line of new women's, misses' and juniors' clothing, including maternity wear. These establishments may provide basic alterations, such as hemming, taking in or letting out seams, or lengthening or shortening sleeves.

5-YEAR TREND — ESTIMATED INDUSTRY SALES ($MILLIONS)

Year	Employee Size of Establishment									Total Industry Sales
	1-4 Emps.	5-9 Emps.	10-19 Emps.	20-49 Emps.	50-99 Emps.	100-249 Emps.	250-499 Emps.	500-999 Emps.	Unknown Emps.	
2015	0.7	1.5	3.8	7.7	5.6	368.7	32.6	0.6	0.3	421.5
2016	0.8	1.5	4.0	7.9	5.8	380.8	33.7	0.6	0.3	435.4
2017	0.8	1.6	4.1	8.2	6.0	392.3	34.7	0.6	0.3	448.5
2018	0.8	1.7	4.3	8.6	6.3	412.3	36.5	0.7	0.3	471.3
2018	0.9	1.7	4.5	9.0	6.6	434.2	38.4	0.7	0.3	496.4

INDUSTRY: FAMILY CLOTHING STORES (NAICS 44814)
PRODUCT LINE: GIRLS' WEAR & ACCESSORIES (Sub Category)

NAICS 44814: Family Clothing Stores . This industry comprises establishments primarily engaged in retailing a general line of new clothing for men, women, and children, without specializing in sales for an individual gender or age group. These establishments may provide basic alterations, such as hemming, taking in or letting out seams, or lengthening or shortening sleeves.

5-YEAR TREND — ESTIMATED INDUSTRY SALES ($MILLIONS)

Year	Employee Size of Establishment									Total Industry Sales
	1-4 Emps.	5-9 Emps.	10-19 Emps.	20-49 Emps.	50-99 Emps.	100-249 Emps.	250-499 Emps.	500-999 Emps.	Unknown Emps.	
2015	60.2	107.9	464.5	1,423.8	1,493.3	372.5	368.2	145.9	16.3	4,452.6
2016	62.3	111.8	481.1	1,474.7	1,546.8	385.9	381.4	151.2	16.9	4,612.0
2017	64.4	115.4	496.8	1,522.9	1,597.3	398.5	393.9	156.1	17.4	4,762.6
2018	68.3	122.4	527.0	1,615.5	1,694.5	422.7	417.8	165.2	18.5	5,052.0
2018	72.6	130.1	560.2	1,717.2	1,801.1	449.3	444.1	175.1	19.6	5,369.3

INDUSTRY: DEPARTMENT STORES (NAICS 45211)
PRODUCT LINE: GIRLS' WEAR & ACCESSORIES (Sub Category)

NAICS 45211: Department Stores Industry . This industry comprises establishments known as department stores primarily engaged in retailing a wide range of the following new products with no one merchandise line predominating: apparel, furniture, appliances and home furnishings; and selected additional items, such as paint, hardware, toiletries, cosmetics, photographic equipment, jewelry, toys, and sporting goods. Merchandise lines are normally arranged in separate departments.

5-YEAR TREND — ESTIMATED INDUSTRY SALES ($MILLIONS)

Year	Employee Size of Establishment									Total
	1-4 Emps.	5-9 Emps.	10-19 Emps.	20-49 Emps.	50-99 Emps.	100-249 Emps.	250-499 Emps.	500-999 Emps.	Unknown Emps.	Industry Sales
2015	0.2	0.1	0.3	22.0	418.5	1,388.2	609.0	81.6	3.5	2,523.4
2016	0.2	0.1	0.3	22.3	423.9	1,406.1	616.9	82.6	3.6	2,556.0
2017	0.2	0.1	0.3	22.6	428.5	1,421.3	623.5	83.5	3.6	2,583.5
2018	0.2	0.1	0.3	22.7	430.5	1,427.8	626.4	84.0	3.6	2,595.5
2018	0.2	0.1	0.3	22.8	433.6	1,438.1	630.9	84.6	3.7	2,614.2

INDUSTRY: WAREHOUSE CLUBS & SUPERCENTERS (NAICS 45291)
PRODUCT LINE: GIRLS' WEAR & ACCESSORIES (Sub Category)

NAICS 45291: Warehouse Clubs and Superstores This industry comprises establishments known as warehouse clubs, superstores or supercenters primarily engaged in retailing a general line of groceries in combination with general lines of new merchandise, such as apparel, furniture, and appliances.

5-YEAR TREND — ESTIMATED INDUSTRY SALES ($MILLIONS)

Year	Employee Size of Establishment									Total
	1-4 Emps.	5-9 Emps.	10-19 Emps.	20-49 Emps.	50-99 Emps.	100-249 Emps.	250-499 Emps.	500-999 Emps.	Unknown Emps.	Industry Sales
2015	0.0	0.0	0.0	0.0	0.1	6.7	29.5	0.8	0.0	37.0
2016	0.0	0.0	0.0	0.0	0.1	6.9	30.6	0.8	0.0	38.4
2017	0.0	0.0	0.0	0.0	0.1	7.1	31.6	0.8	0.0	39.7
2018	0.0	0.0	0.0	0.0	0.1	7.8	34.3	0.9	0.0	43.1
2018	0.0	0.0	0.0	0.1	0.1	8.2	36.4	1.0	0.0	45.8

INDUSTRY: MEN'S CLOTHING STORES (NAICS 44811)
PRODUCT LINE: INFANTS' & TODDLERS' WEAR (Sub Category)

NAICS 44811: Men's Clothing Stores. This industry comprises establishments primarily engaged in retailing a general line of new men's and boys' clothing. These establishments may provide basic alterations, such as hemming, taking in or letting out seams, or lengthening or shortening sleeves.

5-Year Trend – Estimated Industry Sales ($Millions)

Year	Employee Size of Establishment									Total Industry Sales
	1-4 Emps.	5-9 Emps.	10-19 Emps.	20-49 Emps.	50-99 Emps.	100-249 Emps.	250-499 Emps.	500-999 Emps.	Unknown Emps.	
2015	0.4	0.7	1.5	0.9	0.2	0.1	0.0	0.0	0.1	4.0
2016	0.5	0.7	1.6	0.9	0.2	0.1	0.1	0.0	0.1	4.2
2017	0.5	0.7	1.7	1.0	0.2	0.1	0.1	0.0	0.1	4.4
2018	0.5	0.7	1.7	1.0	0.3	0.1	0.1	0.0	0.1	4.5
2018	0.5	0.8	1.8	1.0	0.3	0.1	0.1	0.0	0.1	4.7

INDUSTRY: WOMEN'S CLOTHING STORES (NAICS 44812)
PRODUCT LINE: INFANTS' & TODDLERS' WEAR (Sub Category)

NAICS 44812: Women's Clothing Stores . This industry comprises establishments primarily engaged in retailing a general line of new women's, misses' and juniors' clothing, including maternity wear. These establishments may provide basic alterations, such as hemming, taking in or letting out seams, or lengthening or shortening sleeves.

5-Year Trend – Estimated Industry Sales ($Millions)

Year	Employee Size of Establishment									Total Industry Sales
	1-4 Emps.	5-9 Emps.	10-19 Emps.	20-49 Emps.	50-99 Emps.	100-249 Emps.	250-499 Emps.	500-999 Emps.	Unknown Emps.	
2015	5.3	12.1	29.5	20.2	6.3	6.1	2.3	2.1	1.2	85.2
2016	5.5	12.5	30.7	21.0	6.6	6.4	2.4	2.2	1.3	88.5
2017	5.7	13.0	31.8	21.7	6.8	6.6	2.5	2.2	1.3	91.6
2018	6.1	13.8	33.8	23.1	7.2	7.0	2.6	2.4	1.4	97.4
2018	6.5	14.7	36.0	24.6	7.7	7.5	2.8	2.5	1.5	103.7

INDUSTRY: FAMILY CLOTHING STORES (NAICS 44814)
PRODUCT LINE: INFANTS' & TODDLERS' WEAR (Sub Category)

NAICS 44814: Family Clothing Stores . This industry comprises establishments primarily engaged in retailing a general line of new clothing for men, women, and children, without specializing in sales for an individual gender or age group. These establishments may provide basic alterations, such as hemming, taking in or letting out seams, or lengthening or shortening sleeves.

5-YEAR TREND — ESTIMATED INDUSTRY SALES ($MILLIONS)

Year	Employee Size of Establishment									Total
	1-4 Emps.	5-9 Emps.	10-19 Emps.	20-49 Emps.	50-99 Emps.	100-249 Emps.	250-499 Emps.	500-999 Emps.	Unknown Emps.	Industry Sales
2015	38.5	69.1	297.4	911.5	956.1	238.5	235.7	93.4	10.4	2,850.7
2016	39.9	71.6	308.0	944.2	990.3	247.1	244.2	96.8	10.8	2,952.8
2017	41.2	73.9	318.1	975.0	1,022.6	255.1	252.2	99.9	11.1	3,049.2
2018	43.7	78.4	337.4	1,034.3	1,084.9	270.6	267.5	105.8	11.8	3,234.4
2018	46.5	83.3	358.7	1,099.4	1,153.1	287.7	284.3	112.1	12.6	3,437.6

INDUSTRY: DEPARTMENT STORES (NAICS 45211)
PRODUCT LINE: INFANTS' & TODDLERS' WEAR (Sub Category)

NAICS 45211: Department Stores Industry . This industry comprises establishments known as department stores primarily engaged in retailing a wide range of the following new products with no one merchandise line predominating: apparel, furniture, appliances and home furnishings; and selected additional items, such as paint, hardware, toiletries, cosmetics, photographic equipment, jewelry, toys, and sporting goods. Merchandise lines are normally arranged in separate departments.

5-YEAR TREND — ESTIMATED INDUSTRY SALES ($MILLIONS)

Year	Employee Size of Establishment									Total
	1-4 Emps.	5-9 Emps.	10-19 Emps.	20-49 Emps.	50-99 Emps.	100-249 Emps.	250-499 Emps.	500-999 Emps.	Unknown Emps.	Industry Sales
2015	0.2	0.1	0.4	29.0	551.3	1,828.5	802.2	107.4	4.7	3,323.8
2016	0.2	0.1	0.4	29.4	558.4	1,852.1	812.5	108.8	4.7	3,366.7
2017	0.3	0.1	0.4	29.7	564.4	1,872.1	821.3	110.0	4.8	3,403.0
2018	0.3	0.1	0.4	29.9	567.0	1,880.7	825.1	110.6	4.8	3,418.8
2018	0.3	0.1	0.4	30.1	571.1	1,894.3	831.0	111.4	4.8	3,443.4

INDUSTRY: WAREHOUSE CLUBS & SUPERCENTERS (NAICS 45291)
PRODUCT LINE: INFANTS' & TODDLERS' WEAR (Sub Category)

NAICS 45291: Warehouse Clubs and Superstores This industry comprises establishments known as warehouse clubs, superstores or supercenters primarily engaged in retailing a general line of groceries in combination with general lines of new merchandise, such as apparel, furniture, and appliances.

5-YEAR TREND — ESTIMATED INDUSTRY SALES ($MILLIONS)

Year	Employee Size of Establishment									Total
	1-4 Emps.	5-9 Emps.	10-19 Emps.	20-49 Emps.	50-99 Emps.	100-249 Emps.	250-499 Emps.	500-999 Emps.	Unknown Emps.	Industry Sales
2015	0.8	0.0	0.1	7.8	9.8	1,214.1	5,367.5	141.8	1.7	6,743.8
2016	0.9	0.0	0.1	8.1	10.2	1,258.5	5,563.8	147.0	1.7	6,990.3
2017	0.9	0.0	0.2	8.4	10.5	1,300.5	5,749.3	151.9	1.8	7,223.4
2018	1.0	0.0	0.2	9.1	11.4	1,412.5	6,244.4	165.0	1.9	7,845.5
2018	1.0	0.0	0.2	9.6	12.1	1,500.1	6,631.6	175.2	2.1	8,331.9

INDUSTRY: HARDWARE STORES (NAICS 44413)
PRODUCT LINE: FOOTWEAR (Main Category)

NAICS 44413: Hardware Stores. Establishments primarily engaged in the retail sale of a number of basic hardware lines, such as tools, builders' hardware, paint and glass, housewares and household appliances, and cutlery.

5-YEAR TREND — ESTIMATED INDUSTRY SALES ($MILLIONS)

Year	Employee Size of Establishment									Total
	1-4 Emps.	5-9 Emps.	10-19 Emps.	20-49 Emps.	50-99 Emps.	100-249 Emps.	250-499 Emps.	500-999 Emps.	Unknown Emps.	Industry Sales
2015	2.6	4.1	8.2	11.5	2.1	0.5	0.1	0.0	0.2	29.4
2016	2.6	4.2	8.4	11.8	2.2	0.5	0.1	0.0	0.2	30.0
2017	2.7	4.3	8.5	12.0	2.2	0.5	0.1	0.0	0.2	30.5
2018	2.8	4.5	8.9	12.5	2.3	0.5	0.2	0.0	0.2	31.9
2018	2.9	4.7	9.4	13.1	2.4	0.6	0.2	0.0	0.2	33.5

INDUSTRY: SUPERMARKETS & GROCERY STORES (NAICS 44511)
PRODUCT LINE: FOOTWEAR (Main Category)

NAICS 44511: Grocery Stores Industry. This industry comprises establishments generally known as supermarkets and grocery stores primarily engaged in retailing a general line of food, such as canned and frozen foods; fresh fruits and vegetables; and fresh and prepared meats, fish, and poultry. Included in this industry are delicatessen-type establishments primarily engaged in retailing a general line of food.

5-YEAR TREND — ESTIMATED INDUSTRY SALES ($MILLIONS)

Year	Employee Size of Establishment									Total Industry Sales
	1-4 Emps.	5-9 Emps.	10-19 Emps.	20-49 Emps.	50-99 Emps.	100-249 Emps.	250-499 Emps.	500-999 Emps.	Unknown Emps.	
2015	0.5	0.4	1.0	3.3	7.9	18.0	5.2	0.7	0.1	37.1
2016	0.5	0.4	1.0	3.2	7.8	17.7	5.1	0.7	0.1	36.5
2017	0.5	0.4	1.0	3.1	7.6	17.4	5.0	0.7	0.1	35.7
2018	0.5	0.4	1.0	3.1	7.6	17.4	5.0	0.7	0.1	35.7
2018	0.5	0.4	1.0	3.1	7.6	17.4	5.0	0.7	0.1	35.8

INDUSTRY: PHARMACIES & DRUG STORES (NAICS 44611)
PRODUCT LINE: FOOTWEAR (Main Category)

NAICS 44611 Pharmacies and Drug Stores – This industry comprises establishments known as pharmacies and drug stores engaged in retailing prescription or nonprescription drugs and medicines.

5-YEAR TREND — ESTIMATED INDUSTRY SALES ($MILLIONS)

Year	Employee Size of Establishment									Total Industry Sales
	1-4 Emps.	5-9 Emps.	10-19 Emps.	20-49 Emps.	50-99 Emps.	100-249 Emps.	250-499 Emps.	500-999 Emps.	Unknown Emps.	
2015	4.1	10.2	43.1	121.9	11.5	4.5	1.4	0.6	0.3	197.6
2016	4.3	10.8	45.4	128.3	12.1	4.7	1.5	0.6	0.4	208.0
2017	4.5	11.3	47.6	134.5	12.6	5.0	1.5	0.6	0.4	217.9
2018	4.9	12.1	51.2	144.6	13.6	5.3	1.7	0.6	0.4	234.3
2018	5.2	13.0	55.1	155.6	14.6	5.7	1.8	0.7	0.4	252.2

INDUSTRY: MEN'S CLOTHING STORES (NAICS 44811)
PRODUCT LINE: FOOTWEAR (Main Category)

NAICS 44811: Men's Clothing Stores. This industry comprises establishments primarily engaged in retailing a general line of new men's and boys' clothing. These establishments may provide basic alterations, such as hemming, taking in or letting out seams, or lengthening or shortening sleeves.

5-YEAR TREND — ESTIMATED INDUSTRY SALES ($MILLIONS)

Year	Employee Size of Establishment									Total
	1-4 Emps.	5-9 Emps.	10-19 Emps.	20-49 Emps.	50-99 Emps.	100-249 Emps.	250-499 Emps.	500-999 Emps.	Unknown Emps.	Industry Sales
2015	37.8	56.4	131.6	76.7	19.6	9.8	4.1	0.2	6.3	342.5
2016	39.5	59.0	137.7	80.2	20.5	10.3	4.3	0.2	6.6	358.3
2017	41.2	61.5	143.4	83.6	21.4	10.7	4.5	0.2	6.8	373.4
2018	42.6	63.6	148.5	86.6	22.1	11.1	4.7	0.2	7.1	386.5
2018	44.2	66.0	153.9	89.7	22.9	11.5	4.8	0.3	7.4	400.7

INDUSTRY: WOMEN'S CLOTHING STORES (NAICS 44812)
PRODUCT LINE: FOOTWEAR (Main Category)

NAICS 44812: Women's Clothing Stores . This industry comprises establishments primarily engaged in retailing a general line of new women's, misses' and juniors' clothing, including maternity wear. These establishments may provide basic alterations, such as hemming, taking in or letting out seams, or lengthening or shortening sleeves.

5-YEAR TREND — ESTIMATED INDUSTRY SALES ($MILLIONS)

Year	Employee Size of Establishment									Total
	1-4 Emps.	5-9 Emps.	10-19 Emps.	20-49 Emps.	50-99 Emps.	100-249 Emps.	250-499 Emps.	500-999 Emps.	Unknown Emps.	Industry Sales
2015	89.6	203.2	497.8	340.9	106.4	103.5	38.8	35.1	20.8	1,436.1
2016	93.1	211.1	517.1	354.0	110.5	107.5	40.3	36.5	21.6	1,491.5
2017	96.4	218.5	535.3	366.5	114.4	111.3	41.7	37.8	22.3	1,544.1
2018	102.4	232.3	569.1	389.6	121.6	118.3	44.3	39.6	23.7	1,641.1
2018	109.1	247.4	606.2	415.0	129.5	126.0	47.2	41.6	25.3	1,747.4

INDUSTRY: FAMILY CLOTHING STORES (NAICS 44814)
PRODUCT LINE: FOOTWEAR (Main Category)

NAICS 44814: Family Clothing Stores . This industry comprises establishments primarily engaged in retailing a general line of new clothing for men, women, and children, without specializing in sales for an individual gender or age group. These establishments may provide basic alterations, such as hemming, taking in or letting out seams, or lengthening or shortening sleeves.

5-YEAR TREND — ESTIMATED INDUSTRY SALES ($MILLIONS)

Year	Employee Size of Establishment									Total
	1-4 Emps.	5-9 Emps.	10-19 Emps.	20-49 Emps.	50-99 Emps.	100-249 Emps.	250-499 Emps.	500-999 Emps.	Unknown Emps.	Industry Sales
2015	77.8	139.5	600.3	1,840.2	1,930.1	481.5	475.9	188.6	21.0	5,754.9
2016	80.6	144.5	621.8	1,906.1	1,999.2	498.7	493.0	195.4	21.8	5,960.9
2017	83.2	149.2	642.1	1,968.3	2,064.4	515.0	509.0	201.7	22.5	6,155.5
2018	88.3	158.3	681.2	2,088.1	2,190.1	546.4	540.0	213.5	23.9	6,529.6
2018	93.8	168.2	724.0	2,219.4	2,327.8	580.7	574.0	226.3	25.4	6,939.8

INDUSTRY: DEPARTMENT STORES (NAICS 45211)
PRODUCT LINE: FOOTWEAR (Main Category)

NAICS 45211: Department Stores Industry . This industry comprises establishments known as department stores primarily engaged in retailing a wide range of the following new products with no one merchandise line predominating: apparel, furniture, appliances and home furnishings; and selected additional items, such as paint, hardware, toiletries, cosmetics, photographic equipment, jewelry, toys, and sporting goods. Merchandise lines are normally arranged in separate departments.

5-YEAR TREND — ESTIMATED INDUSTRY SALES ($MILLIONS)

Year	Employee Size of Establishment									Total
	1-4 Emps.	5-9 Emps.	10-19 Emps.	20-49 Emps.	50-99 Emps.	100-249 Emps.	250-499 Emps.	500-999 Emps.	Unknown Emps.	Industry Sales
2015	0.4	0.1	0.5	43.1	817.3	2,710.7	1,189.2	159.2	6.9	4,927.4
2016	0.4	0.1	0.5	43.6	827.8	2,745.7	1,204.5	161.3	7.0	4,991.0
2017	0.4	0.1	0.6	44.1	836.7	2,775.2	1,217.5	163.0	7.1	5,044.7
2018	0.4	0.1	0.6	44.3	840.6	2,788.0	1,223.1	164.0	7.1	5,068.2
2018	0.4	0.1	0.6	44.6	846.7	2,808.1	1,231.9	165.2	7.2	5,104.7

INDUSTRY: WAREHOUSE CLUBS & SUPERCENTERS (NAICS 45291)
PRODUCT LINE: FOOTWEAR (Main Category)

NAICS 45291: Warehouse Clubs and Superstores This industry comprises establishments known as warehouse clubs, superstores or supercenters primarily engaged in retailing a general line of groceries in combination with general lines of new merchandise, such as apparel, furniture, and appliances.

5-YEAR TREND – ESTIMATED INDUSTRY SALES ($MILLIONS)

Year	Employee Size of Establishment									Total
	1-4 Emps.	5-9 Emps.	10-19 Emps.	20-49 Emps.	50-99 Emps.	100-249 Emps.	250-499 Emps.	500-999 Emps.	Unknown Emps.	Industry Sales
2015	0.6	0.0	0.1	5.3	6.7	825.4	3,649.1	96.4	1.1	4,584.7
2016	0.6	0.0	0.1	5.5	6.9	855.6	3,782.5	99.9	1.2	4,752.3
2017	0.6	0.0	0.1	5.7	7.2	884.1	3,908.6	103.3	1.2	4,910.8
2018	0.7	0.0	0.1	6.2	7.8	960.3	4,245.2	112.2	1.3	5,333.7
2018	0.7	0.0	0.1	6.6	8.3	1,019.8	4,508.4	119.1	1.4	5,664.4

INDUSTRY: ELECTRONIC SHOPPING & MAIL ORDER (NAICS 45411)
PRODUCT LINE: FOOTWEAR (Main Category)

NAICS 45411: Electronic Shopping and Mail-Order Houses This industry comprises establishments primarily engaged in retailing all types of merchandise by means of mail or by electronic media, such as interactive television or computer. Included in this industry are establishments primarily engaged in retailing from catalogue showrooms of mail-order houses.

5-YEAR TREND – ESTIMATED INDUSTRY SALES ($MILLIONS)

Year	Employee Size of Establishment									Total
	1-4 Emps.	5-9 Emps.	10-19 Emps.	20-49 Emps.	50-99 Emps.	100-249 Emps.	250-499 Emps.	500-999 Emps.	Unknown Emps.	Industry Sales
2015	459.3	243.8	362.1	585.8	421.3	821.4	1,201.9	1,522.5	69.5	5,687.6
2016	489.9	260.1	386.2	624.9	449.5	876.3	1,282.1	1,624.1	74.1	6,067.0
2017	519.6	275.9	409.7	662.8	476.7	929.4	1,359.9	1,722.6	78.6	6,435.1
2018	591.3	313.9	466.2	754.2	542.5	1,057.6	1,547.4	1,912.1	89.4	7,274.6
2018	656.7	348.7	517.8	837.7	602.5	1,174.7	1,718.7	2,087.1	99.3	8,043.1

INDUSTRY: MEN'S CLOTHING STORES (NAICS 44811)
PRODUCT LINE: MEN'S FOOTWEAR (Sub Category)

NAICS 44811: Men's Clothing Stores. This industry comprises establishments primarily engaged in retailing a general line of new men's and boys' clothing. These establishments may provide basic alterations, such as hemming, taking in or letting out seams, or lengthening or shortening sleeves.

5-YEAR TREND – ESTIMATED INDUSTRY SALES ($MILLIONS)

Year	Employee Size of Establishment									Total Industry Sales
	1-4 Emps.	5-9 Emps.	10-19 Emps.	20-49 Emps.	50-99 Emps.	100-249 Emps.	250-499 Emps.	500-999 Emps.	Unknown Emps.	
2015	29.5	44.0	102.8	59.9	15.3	7.7	3.2	0.2	4.9	267.5
2016	30.9	46.0	107.5	62.7	16.0	8.0	3.4	0.2	5.1	279.8
2017	32.2	48.0	112.0	65.3	16.7	8.4	3.5	0.2	5.3	291.5
2018	33.3	49.7	115.9	67.6	17.3	8.7	3.6	0.2	5.5	301.8
2018	34.5	51.5	120.2	70.1	17.9	9.0	3.8	0.2	5.7	312.9

INDUSTRY: WOMEN'S CLOTHING STORES (NAICS 44812)
PRODUCT LINE: MEN'S FOOTWEAR (Sub Category)

NAICS 44812: Women's Clothing Stores . This industry comprises establishments primarily engaged in retailing a general line of new women's, misses' and juniors' clothing, including maternity wear. These establishments may provide basic alterations, such as hemming, taking in or letting out seams, or lengthening or shortening sleeves.

5-YEAR TREND – ESTIMATED INDUSTRY SALES ($MILLIONS)

Year	Employee Size of Establishment									Total Industry Sales
	1-4 Emps.	5-9 Emps.	10-19 Emps.	20-49 Emps.	50-99 Emps.	100-249 Emps.	250-499 Emps.	500-999 Emps.	Unknown Emps.	
2015	1.8	4.1	10.1	6.9	2.2	2.1	0.8	0.7	0.4	29.0
2016	1.9	4.3	10.5	7.2	2.2	2.2	0.8	0.7	0.4	30.2
2017	1.9	4.4	10.8	7.4	2.3	2.3	0.8	0.8	0.5	31.2
2018	2.1	4.7	11.5	7.9	2.5	2.4	0.9	0.8	0.5	33.2
2018	2.2	5.0	12.3	8.4	2.6	2.5	1.0	0.8	0.5	35.3

INDUSTRY: FAMILY CLOTHING STORES (NAICS 44814)
PRODUCT LINE: MEN'S FOOTWEAR (Sub Category)

NAICS 44814: Family Clothing Stores . This industry comprises establishments primarily engaged in retailing a general line of new clothing for men, women, and children, without specializing in sales for an individual gender or age group. These establishments may provide basic alterations, such as hemming, taking in or letting out seams, or lengthening or shortening sleeves.

5-YEAR TREND — ESTIMATED INDUSTRY SALES ($MILLIONS)

Year	Employee Size of Establishment									Total Industry Sales
	1-4 Emps.	5-9 Emps.	10-19 Emps.	20-49 Emps.	50-99 Emps.	100-249 Emps.	250-499 Emps.	500-999 Emps.	Unknown Emps.	
2015	15.1	27.1	116.7	357.9	375.3	93.6	92.6	36.7	4.1	1,119.2
2016	15.7	28.1	120.9	370.7	388.8	97.0	95.9	38.0	4.2	1,159.2
2017	16.2	29.0	124.9	382.8	401.5	100.2	99.0	39.2	4.4	1,197.1
2018	17.2	30.8	132.5	406.1	425.9	106.3	105.0	41.5	4.6	1,269.8
2018	18.2	32.7	140.8	431.6	452.7	112.9	111.6	44.0	4.9	1,349.6

INDUSTRY: DEPARTMENT STORES (NAICS 45211)
PRODUCT LINE: MEN'S FOOTWEAR (Sub Category)

NAICS 45211: Department Stores Industry . This industry comprises establishments known as department stores primarily engaged in retailing a wide range of the following new products with no one merchandise line predominating: apparel, furniture, appliances and home furnishings; and selected additional items, such as paint, hardware, toiletries, cosmetics, photographic equipment, jewelry, toys, and sporting goods. Merchandise lines are normally arranged in separate departments.

5-YEAR TREND — ESTIMATED INDUSTRY SALES ($MILLIONS)

Year	Employee Size of Establishment									Total Industry Sales
	1-4 Emps.	5-9 Emps.	10-19 Emps.	20-49 Emps.	50-99 Emps.	100-249 Emps.	250-499 Emps.	500-999 Emps.	Unknown Emps.	
2015	0.1	0.0	0.1	7.8	148.1	491.2	215.5	28.9	1.3	892.8
2016	0.1	0.0	0.1	7.9	150.0	497.5	218.3	29.2	1.3	904.4
2017	0.1	0.0	0.1	8.0	151.6	502.9	220.6	29.5	1.3	914.1
2018	0.1	0.0	0.1	8.0	152.3	505.2	221.6	29.7	1.3	918.3
2018	0.1	0.0	0.1	8.1	153.4	508.8	223.2	29.9	1.3	925.0

INDUSTRY: MEN'S CLOTHING STORES (NAICS 44811)
PRODUCT LINE: WOMEN'S FOOTWEAR (Sub Category)

NAICS 44811: Men's Clothing Stores. This industry comprises establishments primarily engaged in retailing a general line of new men's and boys' clothing. These establishments may provide basic alterations, such as hemming, taking in or letting out seams, or lengthening or shortening sleeves.

5-YEAR TREND — ESTIMATED INDUSTRY SALES ($MILLIONS)

Year	Employee Size of Establishment									Total
	1-4 Emps.	5-9 Emps.	10-19 Emps.	20-49 Emps.	50-99 Emps.	100-249 Emps.	250-499 Emps.	500-999 Emps.	Unknown Emps.	Industry Sales
2015	1.4	2.1	4.8	2.8	0.7	0.4	0.2	0.0	0.2	12.5
2016	1.4	2.2	5.0	2.9	0.7	0.4	0.2	0.0	0.2	13.1
2017	1.5	2.2	5.2	3.0	0.8	0.4	0.2	0.0	0.2	13.6
2018	1.6	2.3	5.4	3.2	0.8	0.4	0.2	0.0	0.3	14.1
2018	1.6	2.4	5.6	3.3	0.8	0.4	0.2	0.0	0.3	14.6

INDUSTRY: WOMEN'S CLOTHING STORES (NAICS 44812)
PRODUCT LINE: WOMEN'S FOOTWEAR (Sub Category)

NAICS 44812: Women's Clothing Stores . This industry comprises establishments primarily engaged in retailing a general line of new women's, misses' and juniors' clothing, including maternity wear. These establishments may provide basic alterations, such as hemming, taking in or letting out seams, or lengthening or shortening sleeves.

5-YEAR TREND — ESTIMATED INDUSTRY SALES ($MILLIONS)

Year	Employee Size of Establishment									Total
	1-4 Emps.	5-9 Emps.	10-19 Emps.	20-49 Emps.	50-99 Emps.	100-249 Emps.	250-499 Emps.	500-999 Emps.	Unknown Emps.	Industry Sales
2015	85.6	194.2	475.8	325.7	101.7	98.9	37.0	33.6	19.8	1,372.4
2016	88.9	201.7	494.1	338.3	105.6	102.7	38.5	34.9	20.6	1,425.3
2017	92.1	208.8	511.5	350.2	109.3	106.3	39.8	36.1	21.3	1,475.6
2018	97.9	222.0	543.9	372.4	116.2	113.1	42.3	37.9	22.7	1,568.3
2018	104.3	236.5	579.3	396.6	123.8	120.4	45.1	39.8	24.1	1,669.8

INDUSTRY: FAMILY CLOTHING STORES (NAICS 44814)
PRODUCT LINE: WOMEN'S FOOTWEAR (Sub Category)

NAICS 44814: Family Clothing Stores . This industry comprises establishments primarily engaged in retailing a general line of new clothing for men, women, and children, without specializing in sales for an individual gender or age group. These establishments may provide basic alterations, such as hemming, taking in or letting out seams, or lengthening or shortening sleeves.

5-YEAR TREND — ESTIMATED INDUSTRY SALES ($MILLIONS)

Year	Employee Size of Establishment									Total Industry Sales
	1-4 Emps.	5-9 Emps.	10-19 Emps.	20-49 Emps.	50-99 Emps.	100-249 Emps.	250-499 Emps.	500-999 Emps.	Unknown Emps.	
2015	34.0	61.0	262.4	804.2	843.5	210.4	208.0	82.4	9.2	2,515.1
2016	35.2	63.1	271.8	833.0	873.7	218.0	215.4	85.4	9.5	2,605.2
2017	36.4	65.2	280.6	860.2	902.2	225.1	222.5	88.2	9.8	2,690.2
2018	38.6	69.2	297.7	912.6	957.1	238.8	236.0	93.3	10.4	2,853.7
2018	41.0	73.5	316.4	970.0	1,017.4	253.8	250.9	98.9	11.1	3,032.9

INDUSTRY: DEPARTMENT STORES (NAICS 45211)
PRODUCT LINE: WOMEN'S FOOTWEAR (Sub Category)

NAICS 45211: Department Stores Industry . This industry comprises establishments known as department stores primarily engaged in retailing a wide range of the following new products with no one merchandise line predominating: apparel, furniture, appliances and home furnishings; and selected additional items, such as paint, hardware, toiletries, cosmetics, photographic equipment, jewelry, toys, and sporting goods. Merchandise lines are normally arranged in separate departments.

5-YEAR TREND — ESTIMATED INDUSTRY SALES ($MILLIONS)

Year	Employee Size of Establishment									Total Industry Sales
	1-4 Emps.	5-9 Emps.	10-19 Emps.	20-49 Emps.	50-99 Emps.	100-249 Emps.	250-499 Emps.	500-999 Emps.	Unknown Emps.	
2015	5.5	10.9	28.5	56.9	41.8	2,731.8	241.6	4.5	1.9	3,123.3
2016	5.7	11.3	29.4	58.7	43.1	2,821.9	249.6	4.6	2.0	3,226.4
2017	5.9	11.6	30.3	60.5	44.4	2,906.5	257.1	4.8	2.0	3,323.1
2018	6.2	12.2	31.8	63.6	46.7	3,054.6	270.2	5.0	2.1	3,492.4
2018	6.5	12.9	33.5	67.0	49.2	3,216.9	284.5	5.3	2.2	3,677.9

INDUSTRY: FAMILY CLOTHING STORES (NAICS 44814)
PRODUCT LINE: CHILDREN'S FOOTWEAR (Sub Category)

NAICS 44814: Family Clothing Stores . This industry comprises establishments primarily engaged in retailing a general line of new clothing for men, women, and children, without specializing in sales for an individual gender or age group. These establishments may provide basic alterations, such as hemming, taking in or letting out seams, or lengthening or shortening sleeves.

5-YEAR TREND — ESTIMATED INDUSTRY SALES ($MILLIONS)

Year	Employee Size of Establishment									Total Industry Sales
	1-4 Emps.	5-9 Emps.	10-19 Emps.	20-49 Emps.	50-99 Emps.	100-249 Emps.	250-499 Emps.	500-999 Emps.	Unknown Emps.	
2015	6.1	11.0	47.2	144.6	151.7	37.8	37.4	14.8	1.7	452.4
2016	6.3	11.4	48.9	149.8	157.1	39.2	38.7	15.4	1.7	468.5
2017	6.5	11.7	50.5	154.7	162.3	40.5	40.0	15.9	1.8	483.8
2018	6.9	12.4	53.5	164.1	172.1	42.9	42.4	16.8	1.9	513.2
2018	7.4	13.2	56.9	174.5	183.0	45.6	45.1	17.8	2.0	545.5

INDUSTRY: DEPARTMENT STORES (NAICS 45211)
PRODUCT LINE: CHILDREN'S FOOTWEAR (Sub Category)

NAICS 45211: Department Stores Industry . This industry comprises establishments known as department stores primarily engaged in retailing a wide range of the following new products with no one merchandise line predominating: apparel, furniture, appliances and home furnishings; and selected additional items, such as paint, hardware, toiletries, cosmetics, photographic equipment, jewelry, toys, and sporting goods. Merchandise lines are normally arranged in separate departments.

5-YEAR TREND — ESTIMATED INDUSTRY SALES ($MILLIONS)

Year	Employee Size of Establishment									Total Industry Sales
	1-4 Emps.	5-9 Emps.	10-19 Emps.	20-49 Emps.	50-99 Emps.	100-249 Emps.	250-499 Emps.	500-999 Emps.	Unknown Emps.	
2015	0.0	0.0	0.0	4.0	75.0	248.8	109.2	14.6	0.6	452.3
2016	0.0	0.0	0.1	4.0	76.0	252.0	110.6	14.8	0.6	458.1
2017	0.0	0.0	0.1	4.0	76.8	254.7	111.8	15.0	0.6	463.0
2018	0.0	0.0	0.1	4.1	77.2	255.9	112.3	15.1	0.7	465.2
2018	0.0	0.0	0.1	4.1	77.7	257.8	113.1	15.2	0.7	468.5

INDUSTRY: MEN'S CLOTHING STORES (NAICS 44811)
PRODUCT LINE: MEN'S ATHLETIC FOOTWEAR (Sub Category)

NAICS 44811: Men's Clothing Stores. This industry comprises establishments primarily engaged in retailing a general line of new men's and boys' clothing. These establishments may provide basic alterations, such as hemming, taking in or letting out seams, or lengthening or shortening sleeves.

5-YEAR TREND – ESTIMATED INDUSTRY SALES ($MILLIONS)

Year	Employee Size of Establishment									Total Industry Sales
	1-4 Emps.	5-9 Emps.	10-19 Emps.	20-49 Emps.	50-99 Emps.	100-249 Emps.	250-499 Emps.	500-999 Emps.	Unknown Emps.	
2015	6.2	9.2	21.5	12.5	3.2	1.6	0.7	0.0	1.0	55.9
2016	6.5	9.6	22.5	13.1	3.3	1.7	0.7	0.0	1.1	58.5
2017	6.7	10.0	23.4	13.7	3.5	1.7	0.7	0.0	1.1	61.0
2018	7.0	10.4	24.2	14.1	3.6	1.8	0.8	0.0	1.2	63.1
2018	7.2	10.8	25.1	14.7	3.7	1.9	0.8	0.0	1.2	65.4

INDUSTRY: FAMILY CLOTHING STORES (NAICS 44814)
PRODUCT LINE: MEN'S ATHLETIC FOOTWEAR (Sub Category)

NAICS 44814: Family Clothing Stores . This industry comprises establishments primarily engaged in retailing a general line of new clothing for men, women, and children, without specializing in sales for an individual gender or age group. These establishments may provide basic alterations, such as hemming, taking in or letting out seams, or lengthening or shortening sleeves.

5-YEAR TREND – ESTIMATED INDUSTRY SALES ($MILLIONS)

Year	Employee Size of Establishment									Total Industry Sales
	1-4 Emps.	5-9 Emps.	10-19 Emps.	20-49 Emps.	50-99 Emps.	100-249 Emps.	250-499 Emps.	500-999 Emps.	Unknown Emps.	
2015	11.3	20.2	86.8	266.2	279.2	69.7	68.8	27.3	3.0	832.5
2016	11.7	20.9	90.0	275.7	289.2	72.1	71.3	28.3	3.2	862.3
2017	12.0	21.6	92.9	284.7	298.6	74.5	73.6	29.2	3.3	890.5
2018	12.8	22.9	98.5	302.1	316.8	79.0	78.1	30.9	3.5	944.6
2018	13.6	24.3	104.7	321.1	336.8	84.0	83.0	32.7	3.7	1,003.9

INDUSTRY: DEPARTMENT STORES (NAICS 45211)
PRODUCT LINE: MEN'S ATHLETIC FOOTWEAR (Sub Category)

NAICS 45211: Department Stores Industry . This industry comprises establishments known as department stores primarily engaged in retailing a wide range of the following new products with no one merchandise line predominating: apparel, furniture, appliances and home furnishings; and selected additional items, such as paint, hardware, toiletries, cosmetics, photographic equipment, jewelry, toys, and sporting goods. Merchandise lines are normally arranged in separate departments.

5-YEAR TREND — ESTIMATED INDUSTRY SALES ($MILLIONS)

Year	Employee Size of Establishment									Total Industry Sales
	1-4 Emps.	5-9 Emps.	10-19 Emps.	20-49 Emps.	50-99 Emps.	100-249 Emps.	250-499 Emps.	500-999 Emps.	Unknown Emps.	
2015	0.0	0.0	0.1	4.3	81.7	270.8	118.8	15.9	0.7	492.3
2016	0.0	0.0	0.1	4.4	82.7	274.3	120.3	16.1	0.7	498.6
2017	0.0	0.0	0.1	4.4	83.6	277.3	121.6	16.3	0.7	504.0
2018	0.0	0.0	0.1	4.4	84.0	278.6	122.2	16.4	0.7	506.4
2018	0.0	0.0	0.1	4.5	84.6	280.6	123.1	16.5	0.7	510.0

INDUSTRY: WOMEN'S CLOTHING STORES (NAICS 44812)
PRODUCT LINE: WOMEN'S ATHLETIC FOOTWEAR (Sub Category)

NAICS 44812: Women's Clothing Stores . This industry comprises establishments primarily engaged in retailing a general line of new women's, misses' and juniors' clothing, including maternity wear. These establishments may provide basic alterations, such as hemming, taking in or letting out seams, or lengthening or shortening sleeves.

5-YEAR TREND — ESTIMATED INDUSTRY SALES ($MILLIONS)

Year	Employee Size of Establishment									Total Industry Sales
	1-4 Emps.	5-9 Emps.	10-19 Emps.	20-49 Emps.	50-99 Emps.	100-249 Emps.	250-499 Emps.	500-999 Emps.	Unknown Emps.	
2015	1.3	3.1	7.5	5.1	1.6	1.6	0.6	0.5	0.3	21.6
2016	1.4	3.2	7.8	5.3	1.7	1.6	0.6	0.5	0.3	22.4
2017	1.4	3.3	8.1	5.5	1.7	1.7	0.6	0.6	0.3	23.2
2018	1.5	3.5	8.6	5.9	1.8	1.8	0.7	0.6	0.4	24.7
2018	1.6	3.7	9.1	6.2	1.9	1.9	0.7	0.6	0.4	26.3

INDUSTRY: FAMILY CLOTHING STORES (NAICS 44814)
PRODUCT LINE: WOMEN'S ATHLETIC FOOTWEAR (Sub Category)

NAICS 44814: Family Clothing Stores . This industry comprises establishments primarily engaged in retailing a general line of new clothing for men, women, and children, without specializing in sales for an individual gender or age group. These establishments may provide basic alterations, such as hemming, taking in or letting out seams, or lengthening or shortening sleeves.

5-YEAR TREND — ESTIMATED INDUSTRY SALES ($MILLIONS)

Year	Employee Size of Establishment									Total Industry Sales
	1-4 Emps.	5-9 Emps.	10-19 Emps.	20-49 Emps.	50-99 Emps.	100-249 Emps.	250-499 Emps.	500-999 Emps.	Unknown Emps.	
2015	8.6	15.5	66.8	204.6	214.6	53.5	52.9	21.0	2.3	640.0
2016	9.0	16.1	69.1	212.0	222.3	55.5	54.8	21.7	2.4	662.9
2017	9.3	16.6	71.4	218.9	229.6	57.3	56.6	22.4	2.5	684.5
2018	9.8	17.6	75.8	232.2	243.5	60.8	60.1	23.7	2.7	726.1
2018	10.4	18.7	80.5	246.8	258.9	64.6	63.8	25.2	2.8	771.7

INDUSTRY: DEPARTMENT STORES (NAICS 45211)
PRODUCT LINE: WOMEN'S ATHLETIC FOOTWEAR (Sub Category)

NAICS 45211: Department Stores Industry . This industry comprises establishments known as department stores primarily engaged in retailing a wide range of the following new products with no one merchandise line predominating: apparel, furniture, appliances and home furnishings; and selected additional items, such as paint, hardware, toiletries, cosmetics, photographic equipment, jewelry, toys, and sporting goods. Merchandise lines are normally arranged in separate departments.

5-YEAR TREND — ESTIMATED INDUSTRY SALES ($MILLIONS)

Year	Employee Size of Establishment									Total Industry Sales
	1-4 Emps.	5-9 Emps.	10-19 Emps.	20-49 Emps.	50-99 Emps.	100-249 Emps.	250-499 Emps.	500-999 Emps.	Unknown Emps.	
2015	0.0	0.0	0.1	4.3	81.1	269.1	118.1	15.8	0.7	489.2
2016	0.0	0.0	0.1	4.3	82.2	272.6	119.6	16.0	0.7	495.5
2017	0.0	0.0	0.1	4.4	83.1	275.5	120.9	16.2	0.7	500.9
2018	0.0	0.0	0.1	4.4	83.5	276.8	121.4	16.3	0.7	503.2
2018	0.0	0.0	0.1	4.4	84.1	278.8	122.3	16.4	0.7	506.8

INDUSTRY: FAMILY CLOTHING STORES (NAICS 44814)
PRODUCT LINE: CHILDREN'S ATHLETIC FOOTWEAR (Sub Category)

NAICS 44814: Family Clothing Stores . This industry comprises establishments primarily engaged in retailing a general line of new clothing for men, women, and children, without specializing in sales for an individual gender or age group. These establishments may provide basic alterations, such as hemming, taking in or letting out seams, or lengthening or shortening sleeves.

5-Year Trend – Estimated Industry Sales ($Millions)

Year	Employee Size of Establishment									Total Industry Sales
	1-4 Emps.	5-9 Emps.	10-19 Emps.	20-49 Emps.	50-99 Emps.	100-249 Emps.	250-499 Emps.	500-999 Emps.	Unknown Emps.	
2015	2.4	4.3	18.6	57.0	59.7	14.9	14.7	5.8	0.7	178.1
2016	2.5	4.5	19.2	59.0	61.9	15.4	15.3	6.0	0.7	184.5
2017	2.6	4.6	19.9	60.9	63.9	15.9	15.8	6.2	0.7	190.5
2018	2.7	4.9	21.1	64.6	67.8	16.9	16.7	6.6	0.7	202.1
2018	2.9	5.2	22.4	68.7	72.0	18.0	17.8	7.0	0.8	214.8

INDUSTRY: DEPARTMENT STORES (NAICS 45211)
PRODUCT LINE: CHILDREN'S ATHLETIC FOOTWEAR (Sub Category)

NAICS 45211: Department Stores Industry . This industry comprises establishments known as department stores primarily engaged in retailing a wide range of the following new products with no one merchandise line predominating: apparel, furniture, appliances and home furnishings; and selected additional items, such as paint, hardware, toiletries, cosmetics, photographic equipment, jewelry, toys, and sporting goods. Merchandise lines are normally arranged in separate departments.

5-Year Trend – Estimated Industry Sales ($Millions)

Year	Employee Size of Establishment									Total Industry Sales
	1-4 Emps.	5-9 Emps.	10-19 Emps.	20-49 Emps.	50-99 Emps.	100-249 Emps.	250-499 Emps.	500-999 Emps.	Unknown Emps.	
2015	0.0	0.0	0.0	0.8	15.6	51.8	22.7	3.0	0.1	94.1
2016	0.0	0.0	0.0	0.8	15.8	52.5	23.0	3.1	0.1	95.4
2017	0.0	0.0	0.0	0.8	16.0	53.0	23.3	3.1	0.1	96.4
2018	0.0	0.0	0.0	0.8	16.1	53.3	23.4	3.1	0.1	96.8
2018	0.0	0.0	0.0	0.9	16.2	53.7	23.5	3.2	0.1	97.5

INDUSTRY: FAMILY CLOTHING STORES (NAICS 44814)
PRODUCT LINE: FOOTWEAR ACCESSORIES (Sub Category)

NAICS 44814: Family Clothing Stores . This industry comprises establishments primarily engaged in retailing a general line of new clothing for men, women, and children, without specializing in sales for an individual gender or age group. These establishments may provide basic alterations, such as hemming, taking in or letting out seams, or lengthening or shortening sleeves.

5-YEAR TREND — ESTIMATED INDUSTRY SALES ($MILLIONS)

Year	Employee Size of Establishment									Total Industry Sales
	1-4 Emps.	5-9 Emps.	10-19 Emps.	20-49 Emps.	50-99 Emps.	100-249 Emps.	250-499 Emps.	500-999 Emps.	Unknown Emps.	
2015	0.2	0.4	1.8	5.6	5.9	1.5	1.5	0.6	0.1	17.7
2016	0.2	0.4	1.9	5.9	6.1	1.5	1.5	0.6	0.1	18.3
2017	0.3	0.5	2.0	6.0	6.3	1.6	1.6	0.6	0.1	18.9
2018	0.3	0.5	2.1	6.4	6.7	1.7	1.7	0.7	0.1	20.0
2018	0.3	0.5	2.2	6.8	7.1	1.8	1.8	0.7	0.1	21.3

INDUSTRY: DEPARTMENT STORES (NAICS 45211)
PRODUCT LINE: FOOTWEAR ACCESSORIES (Sub Category)

NAICS 45211: Department Stores Industry . This industry comprises establishments known as department stores primarily engaged in retailing a wide range of the following new products with no one merchandise line predominating: apparel, furniture, appliances and home furnishings; and selected additional items, such as paint, hardware, toiletries, cosmetics, photographic equipment, jewelry, toys, and sporting goods. Merchandise lines are normally arranged in separate departments.

5-YEAR TREND — ESTIMATED INDUSTRY SALES ($MILLIONS)

Year	Employee Size of Establishment									Total Industry Sales
	1-4 Emps.	5-9 Emps.	10-19 Emps.	20-49 Emps.	50-99 Emps.	100-249 Emps.	250-499 Emps.	500-999 Emps.	Unknown Emps.	
2015	0.0	0.0	0.0	0.1	2.0	6.5	2.9	0.4	0.0	11.9
2016	0.0	0.0	0.0	0.1	2.0	6.6	2.9	0.4	0.0	12.0
2017	0.0	0.0	0.0	0.1	2.0	6.7	2.9	0.4	0.0	12.2
2018	0.0	0.0	0.0	0.1	2.0	6.7	3.0	0.4	0.0	12.2
2018	0.0	0.0	0.0	0.1	2.0	6.8	3.0	0.4	0.0	12.3

INDUSTRY: HOME CENTERS INDUSTRY (NAICS 44411)
PRODUCT LINE: HOUSEHOLD APPLIANCES (Main Category)

NAICS 44411: Home Centers. This industry comprises establishments known as home centers primarily engaged in retailing a general line of new home repair and improvement materials and supplies, such as lumber, plumbing goods, electrical goods, tools, housewares, hardware, and lawn and garden supplies, with no one merchandise line predominating. The merchandise lines are normally arranged in separate departments.

5-YEAR TREND — ESTIMATED INDUSTRY SALES ($MILLIONS)

Year	Employee Size of Establishment									Total Industry Sales
	1-4 Emps.	5-9 Emps.	10-19 Emps.	20-49 Emps.	50-99 Emps.	100-249 Emps.	250-499 Emps.	500-999 Emps.	Unknown Emps.	
2015	13	25	65	131	96	6,276	555	10	4	7,176
2016	13	26	68	135	99	6,483	573	11	5	7,412
2017	13	27	70	139	102	6,678	591	11	5	7,635
2018	14	28	73	146	107	7,018	621	11	5	8,024
2018	15	30	77	154	113	7,391	654	12	5	8,450

INDUSTRY: HARDWARE STORES (NAICS 44413)
PRODUCT LINE: HOUSEHOLD APPLIANCES (Main Category)

NAICS 44413: Hardware Stores. Establishments primarily engaged in the retail sale of a number of basic hardware lines, such as tools, builders' hardware, paint and glass, housewares and household appliances, and cutlery.

5-YEAR TREND — ESTIMATED INDUSTRY SALES ($MILLIONS)

Year	Employee Size of Establishment									Total Industry Sales
	1-4 Emps.	5-9 Emps.	10-19 Emps.	20-49 Emps.	50-99 Emps.	100-249 Emps.	250-499 Emps.	500-999 Emps.	Unknown Emps.	
2015	35.7	57.2	114.4	160.2	29.3	6.9	1.9	0.1	3.0	408.8
2016	36.3	58.3	116.6	163.2	29.9	7.0	2.0	0.1	3.1	416.5
2017	36.9	59.3	118.5	165.9	30.4	7.1	2.0	0.1	3.1	423.4
2018	38.7	62.0	124.0	173.7	31.8	7.5	2.1	0.1	3.3	443.1
2018	40.6	65.1	130.1	182.2	33.4	7.8	2.2	0.1	3.4	464.9

INDUSTRY: DEPARTMENT STORES (NAICS 45211)
PRODUCT LINE: HOUSEHOLD APPLIANCES (Main Category)

NAICS 45211: Department Stores Industry . This industry comprises establishments known as department stores primarily engaged in retailing a wide range of the following new products with no one merchandise line predominating: apparel, furniture, appliances and home furnishings; and selected additional items, such as paint, hardware, toiletries, cosmetics, photographic equipment, jewelry, toys, and sporting goods. Merchandise lines are normally arranged in separate departments.

5-YEAR TREND – ESTIMATED INDUSTRY SALES ($MILLIONS)

Year	Employee Size of Establishment									Total
	1-4 Emps.	5-9 Emps.	10-19 Emps.	20-49 Emps.	50-99 Emps.	100-249 Emps.	250-499 Emps.	500-999 Emps.	Unknown Emps.	Industry Sales
2015	0	0	1	43	823	2,730	1,198	160	7	4,963
2016	0	0	1	44	834	2,765	1,213	162	7	5,027
2017	0	0	1	44	843	2,795	1,226	164	7	5,081
2018	0	0	1	45	847	2,808	1,232	165	7	5,105
2018	0	0	1	45	853	2,828	1,241	166	7	5,141

INDUSTRY: WAREHOUSE CLUBS & SUPERCENTERS (NAICS 45211)
PRODUCT LINE: HOUSEHOLD APPLIANCES (Main Category)

NAICS 45291: Warehouse Clubs and Superstores This industry comprises establishments known as warehouse clubs, superstores or supercenters primarily engaged in retailing a general line of groceries in combination with general lines of new merchandise, such as apparel, furniture, and appliances.

5-YEAR TREND – ESTIMATED INDUSTRY SALES ($MILLIONS)

Year	Employee Size of Establishment									Total
	1-4 Emps.	5-9 Emps.	10-19 Emps.	20-49 Emps.	50-99 Emps.	100-249 Emps.	250-499 Emps.	500-999 Emps.	Unknown Emps.	Industry Sales
2015	0.1	0.0	0.1	11.9	225.2	746.8	327.6	43.9	1.9	1,357.6
2016	0.1	0.0	0.2	12.0	228.1	756.5	331.9	44.4	1.9	1,375.1
2017	0.1	0.0	0.2	12.1	230.5	764.6	335.4	44.9	1.9	1,389.9
2018	0.1	0.0	0.2	12.2	231.6	768.1	337.0	45.2	2.0	1,396.4
2018	0.1	0.0	0.2	12.3	233.3	773.7	339.4	45.5	2.0	1,406.4

INDUSTRY: ELECTRONIC SHOPPING & MAIL ORDER (NAICS 45291)
PRODUCT LINE: HOUSEHOLD APPLIANCES (Main Category)

NAICS 45411: Electronic Shopping and Mail-Order Houses This industry comprises establishments primarily engaged in retailing all types of merchandise by means of mail or by electronic media, such as interactive television or computer. Included in this industry are establishments primarily engaged in retailing from catalogue showrooms of mail-order houses.

5-YEAR TREND — ESTIMATED INDUSTRY SALES ($MILLIONS)

Year	Employee Size of Establishment									Total Industry Sales
	1-4 Emps.	5-9 Emps.	10-19 Emps.	20-49 Emps.	50-99 Emps.	100-249 Emps.	250-499 Emps.	500-999 Emps.	Unknown Emps.	
2015	0.4	0.0	0.1	3.6	4.6	564.6	2,496.1	65.9	0.8	3,136.1
2016	0.4	0.0	0.1	3.8	4.7	585.3	2,587.3	68.4	0.8	3,250.7
2017	0.4	0.0	0.1	3.9	4.9	604.8	2,673.6	70.6	0.8	3,359.1
2018	0.5	0.0	0.1	4.2	5.3	656.8	2,903.8	76.7	0.9	3,648.4
2018	0.5	0.0	0.1	4.5	5.7	697.6	3,083.9	81.5	1.0	3,874.6

INDUSTRY: DEPARTMENT STORES (NAICS 45211)
PRODUCT LINE: KITCHEN APPLIANCES (Sub Category)

NAICS 45211: Department Stores Industry . This industry comprises establishments known as department stores primarily engaged in retailing a wide range of the following new products with no one merchandise line predominating: apparel, furniture, appliances and home furnishings; and selected additional items, such as paint, hardware, toiletries, cosmetics, photographic equipment, jewelry, toys, and sporting goods. Merchandise lines are normally arranged in separate departments.

5-YEAR TREND — ESTIMATED INDUSTRY SALES ($MILLIONS)

Year	Employee Size of Establishment									Total Industry Sales
	1-4 Emps.	5-9 Emps.	10-19 Emps.	20-49 Emps.	50-99 Emps.	100-249 Emps.	250-499 Emps.	500-999 Emps.	Unknown Emps.	
2015	0	0	0	29	558	1,850	812	109	5	3,364
2016	0	0	0	30	565	1,874	822	110	5	3,407
2017	0	0	0	30	571	1,894	831	111	5	3,444
2018	0	0	0	30	574	1,903	835	112	5	3,460
2018	0	0	0	30	578	1,917	841	113	5	3,485

INDUSTRY: WAREHOUSE CLUBS & SUPERCENTERS (NAICS 45291)
PRODUCT LINE: KITCHEN APPLIANCES (Sub Category)

NAICS 45291: Warehouse Clubs and Superstores This industry comprises establishments known as warehouse clubs, superstores or supercenters primarily engaged in retailing a general line of groceries in combination with general lines of new merchandise, such as apparel, furniture, and appliances.

5-YEAR TREND – ESTIMATED INDUSTRY SALES ($MILLIONS)

Year	Employee Size of Establishment									Total Industry Sales
	1-4 Emps.	5-9 Emps.	10-19 Emps.	20-49 Emps.	50-99 Emps.	100-249 Emps.	250-499 Emps.	500-999 Emps.	Unknown Emps.	
2015	0.2	0.0	0.0	2.3	2.9	361.2	1,596.8	42.2	0.5	2,006.2
2016	0.3	0.0	0.0	2.4	3.0	374.4	1,655.2	43.7	0.5	2,079.6
2017	0.3	0.0	0.0	2.5	3.1	386.9	1,710.4	45.2	0.5	2,148.9
2018	0.3	0.0	0.0	2.7	3.4	420.2	1,857.7	49.1	0.6	2,334.0
2018	0.3	0.0	0.1	2.9	3.6	446.3	1,972.8	52.1	0.6	2,478.7

INDUSTRY: DEPARTMENT STORES (NAICS 45211)
PRODUCT LINE: LAUNDRY APPLIANCES (Sub Category)

NAICS 45211: Department Stores Industry . This industry comprises establishments known as department stores primarily engaged in retailing a wide range of the following new products with no one merchandise line predominating: apparel, furniture, appliances and home furnishings; and selected additional items, such as paint, hardware, toiletries, cosmetics, photographic equipment, jewelry, toys, and sporting goods. Merchandise lines are normally arranged in separate departments.

5-YEAR TREND – ESTIMATED INDUSTRY SALES ($MILLIONS)

Year	Employee Size of Establishment									Total Industry Sales
	1-4 Emps.	5-9 Emps.	10-19 Emps.	20-49 Emps.	50-99 Emps.	100-249 Emps.	250-499 Emps.	500-999 Emps.	Unknown Emps.	
2015	0.0	0.0	0.0	0.3	5.1	16.8	7.4	1.0	0.0	30.6
2016	0.0	0.0	0.0	0.3	5.1	17.1	7.5	1.0	0.0	31.0
2017	0.0	0.0	0.0	0.3	5.2	17.2	7.6	1.0	0.0	31.4
2018	0.0	0.0	0.0	0.3	5.2	17.3	7.6	1.0	0.0	31.5
2018	0.0	0.0	0.0	0.3	5.3	17.5	7.7	1.0	0.0	31.7

INDUSTRY: DEPARTMENT STORES (NAICS 45211)
PRODUCT LINE: OTHER APPLIANCES (Sub Category)

NAICS 45211: Department Stores Industry . This industry comprises establishments known as department stores primarily engaged in retailing a wide range of the following new products with no one merchandise line predominating: apparel, furniture, appliances and home furnishings; and selected additional items, such as paint, hardware, toiletries, cosmetics, photographic equipment, jewelry, toys, and sporting goods. Merchandise lines are normally arranged in separate departments.

5-YEAR TREND – ESTIMATED INDUSTRY SALES ($MILLIONS)

Year	Employee Size of Establishment									Total Industry Sales
	1-4 Emps.	5-9 Emps.	10-19 Emps.	20-49 Emps.	50-99 Emps.	100-249 Emps.	250-499 Emps.	500-999 Emps.	Unknown Emps.	
2015	0.1	0.0	0.2	14.0	265.3	879.8	386.0	51.7	2.2	1,599.2
2016	0.1	0.0	0.2	14.2	268.7	891.1	390.9	52.4	2.3	1,619.9
2017	0.1	0.0	0.2	14.3	271.6	900.7	395.2	52.9	2.3	1,637.3
2018	0.1	0.0	0.2	14.4	272.8	904.9	397.0	53.2	2.3	1,644.9
2018	0.1	0.0	0.2	14.5	274.8	911.4	399.8	53.6	2.3	1,656.8

INDUSTRY: WAREHOUSE CLUBS & SUPERCENTERS (NAICS 45291)
PRODUCT LINE: OTHER APPLIANCES (Sub Category)

NAICS 45291: Warehouse Clubs and Superstores This industry comprises establishments known as warehouse clubs, superstores or supercenters primarily engaged in retailing a general line of groceries in combination with general lines of new merchandise, such as apparel, furniture, and appliances.

5-YEAR TREND – ESTIMATED INDUSTRY SALES ($MILLIONS)

Year	Employee Size of Establishment									Total Industry Sales
	1-4 Emps.	5-9 Emps.	10-19 Emps.	20-49 Emps.	50-99 Emps.	100-249 Emps.	250-499 Emps.	500-999 Emps.	Unknown Emps.	
2015	0.5	0.0	0.1	4.6	5.8	721.7	3,190.7	84.3	1.0	4,008.9
2016	0.5	0.0	0.1	4.8	6.1	748.1	3,307.4	87.4	1.0	4,155.4
2017	0.5	0.0	0.1	5.0	6.3	773.1	3,417.7	90.3	1.1	4,294.0
2018	0.6	0.0	0.1	5.4	6.8	839.7	3,712.0	98.1	1.2	4,663.8
2018	0.6	0.0	0.1	5.7	7.2	891.7	3,942.2	104.2	1.2	4,953.0

INDUSTRY: HOME CENTERS INDUSTRY (NAICS 44411)
PRODUCT LINE: SMALL ELECTRICAL APPLIANCES (Main Category)

NAICS 44411: Home Centers. This industry comprises establishments known as home centers primarily engaged in retailing a general line of new home repair and improvement materials and supplies, such as lumber, plumbing goods, electrical goods, tools, housewares, hardware, and lawn and garden supplies, with no one merchandise line predominating. The merchandise lines are normally arranged in separate departments.

5-YEAR TREND — ESTIMATED INDUSTRY SALES ($MILLIONS)

Year	Employee Size of Establishment									Total Industry Sales
	1-4 Emps.	5-9 Emps.	10-19 Emps.	20-49 Emps.	50-99 Emps.	100-249 Emps.	250-499 Emps.	500-999 Emps.	Unknown Emps.	
2015	1.0	2.0	5.2	10.5	7.7	502.9	44.5	0.8	0.4	574.9
2016	1.0	2.1	5.4	10.8	7.9	519.5	45.9	0.9	0.4	593.9
2017	1.1	2.1	5.6	11.1	8.2	535.0	47.3	0.9	0.4	611.7
2018	1.1	2.3	5.9	11.7	8.6	562.3	49.7	0.9	0.4	642.9
2018	1.2	2.4	6.2	12.3	9.1	592.2	52.4	1.0	0.4	677.0

INDUSTRY: HARDWARE STORES (NAICS 44413)
PRODUCT LINE: SMALL ELECTRICAL APPLIANCES (Main Category)

NAICS 44413: Hardware Stores. Establishments primarily engaged in the retail sale of a number of basic hardware lines, such as tools, builders' hardware, paint and glass, housewares and household appliances, and cutlery.

5-YEAR TREND — ESTIMATED INDUSTRY SALES ($MILLIONS)

Year	Employee Size of Establishment									Total Industry Sales
	1-4 Emps.	5-9 Emps.	10-19 Emps.	20-49 Emps.	50-99 Emps.	100-249 Emps.	250-499 Emps.	500-999 Emps.	Unknown Emps.	
2015	27.5	44.1	88.1	123.4	22.6	5.3	1.5	0.1	2.3	314.8
2016	28.0	44.9	89.8	125.7	23.0	5.4	1.5	0.1	2.4	320.8
2017	28.4	45.6	91.3	127.8	23.4	5.5	1.5	0.1	2.4	326.0
2018	29.8	47.8	95.5	133.8	24.5	5.7	1.6	0.1	2.5	341.3
2018	31.2	50.1	100.2	140.3	25.7	6.0	1.7	0.1	2.6	358.1

INDUSTRY: SUPERMARKETS INDUSTRY (NAICS 44511)
PRODUCT LINE: SMALL ELECTRICAL APPLIANCES (Main Category)

NAICS 44511: Grocery Stores Industry. This industry comprises establishments generally known as supermarkets and grocery stores primarily engaged in retailing a general line of food, such as canned and frozen foods; fresh fruits and vegetables; and fresh and prepared meats, fish, and poultry. Included in this industry are delicatessen-type establishments primarily engaged in retailing a general line of food.

5-YEAR TREND — ESTIMATED INDUSTRY SALES ($MILLIONS)

Year	Employee Size of Establishment									Total Industry Sales
	1-4 Emps.	5-9 Emps.	10-19 Emps.	20-49 Emps.	50-99 Emps.	100-249 Emps.	250-499 Emps.	500-999 Emps.	Unknown Emps.	
2015	2.8	2.1	5.3	17.5	42.4	96.6	27.9	3.8	0.5	198.9
2016	2.8	2.1	5.3	17.2	41.6	94.9	27.4	3.8	0.5	195.5
2017	2.7	2.0	5.2	16.8	40.8	93.1	26.8	3.7	0.5	191.6
2018	2.7	2.0	5.2	16.8	40.8	93.1	26.8	3.7	0.5	191.7
2018	2.7	2.0	5.2	16.9	40.9	93.3	26.9	3.7	0.5	192.1

INDUSTRY: PHARMACIES & DRUG STORES INDUSTRY (NAICS 44611)
PRODUCT LINE: SMALL ELECTRICAL APPLIANCES (Main Category)

NAICS 44611 Pharmacies and Drug Stores – This industry comprises establishments known as pharmacies and drug stores engaged in retailing prescription or nonprescription drugs and medicines.

5-YEAR TREND — ESTIMATED INDUSTRY SALES ($MILLIONS)

Year	Employee Size of Establishment									Total Industry Sales
	1-4 Emps.	5-9 Emps.	10-19 Emps.	20-49 Emps.	50-99 Emps.	100-249 Emps.	250-499 Emps.	500-999 Emps.	Unknown Emps.	
2015	18.3	45.7	193.1	545.6	51.3	20.1	6.2	2.5	1.5	884.4
2016	19.3	48.1	203.2	574.2	53.9	21.2	6.6	2.6	1.6	930.6
2017	20.2	50.4	212.9	601.6	56.5	22.2	6.9	2.8	1.7	975.1
2018	21.7	54.2	228.9	646.9	60.8	23.9	7.4	2.9	1.8	1,048.5
2018	23.4	58.3	246.4	696.4	65.4	25.7	8.0	3.0	2.0	1,128.6

INDUSTRY: DEPARTMENT STORES INDUSTRY (NAICS 45211)
PRODUCT LINE: SMALL ELECTRICAL APPLIANCES (Main Category)

NAICS 45211: Department Stores Industry . This industry comprises establishments known as department stores primarily engaged in retailing a wide range of the following new products with no one merchandise line predominating: apparel, furniture, appliances and home furnishings; and selected additional items, such as paint, hardware, toiletries, cosmetics, photographic equipment, jewelry, toys, and sporting goods. Merchandise lines are normally arranged in separate departments.

5-YEAR TREND — ESTIMATED INDUSTRY SALES ($MILLIONS)

Year	1-4 Emps.	5-9 Emps.	10-19 Emps.	20-49 Emps.	50-99 Emps.	100-249 Emps.	250-499 Emps.	500-999 Emps.	Unknown Emps.	Total Industry Sales
2015	0.1	0.0	0.2	16.3	309.2	1,025.5	449.9	60.2	2.6	1,864.1
2016	0.1	0.0	0.2	16.5	313.2	1,038.7	455.7	61.0	2.6	1,888.1
2017	0.1	0.0	0.2	16.7	316.5	1,049.9	460.6	61.7	2.7	1,908.5
2018	0.1	0.0	0.2	16.8	318.0	1,054.7	462.7	62.0	2.7	1,917.3
2018	0.1	0.0	0.2	16.9	320.3	1,062.4	466.1	62.5	2.7	1,931.2

INDUSTRY: WAREHOUSE CLUBS & SUPERCENTERS (NAICS 45291)
PRODUCT LINE: SMALL ELECTRICAL APPLIANCES (Main Category)

NAICS 45291: Warehouse Clubs and Superstores This industry comprises establishments known as warehouse clubs, superstores or supercenters primarily engaged in retailing a general line of groceries in combination with general lines of new merchandise, such as apparel, furniture, and appliances.

5-YEAR TREND — ESTIMATED INDUSTRY SALES ($MILLIONS)

Year	1-4 Emps.	5-9 Emps.	10-19 Emps.	20-49 Emps.	50-99 Emps.	100-249 Emps.	250-499 Emps.	500-999 Emps.	Unknown Emps.	Total Industry Sales
2015	0.8	0.0	0.1	7.4	9.3	1,145.5	5,064.0	133.8	1.6	6,362.5
2016	0.8	0.0	0.1	7.6	9.6	1,187.4	5,249.2	138.7	1.6	6,595.1
2017	0.8	0.0	0.1	7.9	9.9	1,227.0	5,424.2	143.3	1.7	6,815.0
2018	0.9	0.0	0.2	8.6	10.8	1,332.6	5,891.3	155.7	1.8	7,401.9
2018	1.0	0.0	0.2	9.1	11.5	1,415.2	6,256.6	165.3	1.9	7,860.8

INDUSTRY: ELECTRONIC SHOPPING & MAIL-ORDER (NAICS 45411)
PRODUCT LINE: SMALL ELECTRICAL APPLIANCES (Main Category)

NAICS 45411: Electronic Shopping and Mail-Order Houses This industry comprises establishments primarily engaged in retailing all types of merchandise by means of mail or by electronic media, such as interactive television or computer. Included in this industry are establishments primarily engaged in retailing from catalogue showrooms of mail-order houses.

5-YEAR TREND — ESTIMATED INDUSTRY SALES ($MILLIONS)

Year	Employee Size of Establishment									Total
	1-4 Emps.	5-9 Emps.	10-19 Emps.	20-49 Emps.	50-99 Emps.	100-249 Emps.	250-499 Emps.	500-999 Emps.	Unknown Emps.	Industry Sales
2015	102.7	54.6	81.0	131.1	94.3	183.8	268.9	340.6	15.5	1,272.5
2016	109.6	58.2	86.4	139.8	100.6	196.0	286.8	363.4	16.6	1,357.4
2017	116.3	61.7	91.7	148.3	106.7	207.9	304.2	385.4	17.6	1,439.7
2018	132.3	70.2	104.3	168.7	121.4	236.6	346.2	427.8	20.0	1,627.5
2018	146.9	78.0	115.8	187.4	134.8	262.8	384.5	466.9	22.2	1,799.5

INDUSTRY: HARDWARE CENTERS INDUSTRY (NAICS 44413)
PRODUCT LINE: TVs & VIDEO EQUIPMENT (Main Category)

NAICS 44413: Hardware Stores. Establishments primarily engaged in the retail sale of a number of basic hardware lines, such as tools, builders' hardware, paint and glass, housewares and household appliances, and cutlery.

5-YEAR TREND — ESTIMATED INDUSTRY SALES ($MILLIONS)

Year	Employee Size of Establishment									Total
	1-4 Emps.	5-9 Emps.	10-19 Emps.	20-49 Emps.	50-99 Emps.	100-249 Emps.	250-499 Emps.	500-999 Emps.	Unknown Emps.	Industry Sales
2015	2.7	4.4	8.7	12.2	2.2	0.5	0.1	0.0	0.2	31.2
2016	2.8	4.4	8.9	12.4	2.3	0.5	0.1	0.0	0.2	31.7
2017	2.8	4.5	9.0	12.7	2.3	0.5	0.2	0.0	0.2	32.3
2018	2.9	4.7	9.5	13.2	2.4	0.6	0.2	0.0	0.2	33.8
2018	3.1	5.0	9.9	13.9	2.5	0.6	0.2	0.0	0.3	35.4

INDUSTRY: PHARMACIES & DRUG STORES (NAICS 44611)
PRODUCT LINE: TVs & VIDEO EQUIPMENT (Main Category)

NAICS 44611 Pharmacies and Drug Stores – this industry comprises establishments known as pharmacies and drug stores engaged in retailing prescription or nonprescription drugs and medicines.

5-YEAR TREND – ESTIMATED INDUSTRY SALES ($MILLIONS)

Year	Employee Size of Establishment									Total Industry Sales
	1-4 Emps.	5-9 Emps.	10-19 Emps.	20-49 Emps.	50-99 Emps.	100-249 Emps.	250-499 Emps.	500-999 Emps.	Unknown Emps.	
2015	4.1	10.2	42.9	121.2	11.4	4.5	1.4	0.6	0.3	196.5
2016	4.3	10.7	45.1	127.6	12.0	4.7	1.5	0.6	0.4	206.7
2017	4.5	11.2	47.3	133.7	12.6	4.9	1.5	0.6	0.4	216.6
2018	4.8	12.0	50.9	143.7	13.5	5.3	1.6	0.6	0.4	232.9
2018	5.2	13.0	54.7	154.7	14.5	5.7	1.8	0.7	0.4	250.7

INDUSTRY: PRERECORDED TAPE/CDs STORES (NAICS 45122)
PRODUCT LINE: TVs & VIDEO EQUIPMENT (Main Category)

NAICS 45122: Prerecorded Tape, Compact Disc, and Record Stores .
This industry comprises establishments primarily engaged in retailing new prerecorded audio and video tapes, compact discs (CDs), and phonograph records.

5-YEAR TREND – ESTIMATED INDUSTRY SALES ($MILLIONS)

Year	Employee Size of Establishment									Total Industry Sales
	1-4 Emps.	5-9 Emps.	10-19 Emps.	20-49 Emps.	50-99 Emps.	100-249 Emps.	250-499 Emps.	500-999 Emps.	Unknown Emps.	
2015	62.9	124.9	325.1	649.2	476.7	31,186.7	2,758.1	51.1	21.8	35,656.5
2016	65.0	129.0	335.8	670.6	492.4	32,215.3	2,849.1	52.7	22.5	36,832.5
2017	66.9	132.9	345.9	690.7	507.2	33,181.6	2,934.6	54.3	23.2	37,937.3
2018	70.4	139.7	363.5	725.9	533.0	34,872.1	3,084.1	57.1	24.3	39,870.1
2018	74.1	147.1	382.8	764.5	561.3	36,724.1	3,247.9	60.1	25.6	41,987.5

INDUSTRY: WAREHOUSE CLUBS & SUPERCENTERS (NAICS 45291)
PRODUCT LINE: TVs & VIDEO EQUIPMENT (Main Category)

NAICS 45291: Warehouse Clubs and Superstores This industry comprises establishments known as warehouse clubs, superstores or supercenters primarily engaged in retailing a general line of groceries in combination with general lines of new merchandise, such as apparel, furniture, and appliances.

5-YEAR TREND — ESTIMATED INDUSTRY SALES ($MILLIONS)

Year	Employee Size of Establishment									Total Industry Sales
	1-4 Emps.	5-9 Emps.	10-19 Emps.	20-49 Emps.	50-99 Emps.	100-249 Emps.	250-499 Emps.	500-999 Emps.	Unknown Emps.	
2015	1.8	0.1	0.3	16.5	20.8	2,570.0	11,361.7	300.2	3.5	14,274.9
2016	1.8	0.1	0.3	17.1	21.6	2,664.0	11,777.1	311.2	3.7	14,796.8
2017	1.9	0.1	0.3	17.7	22.3	2,752.8	12,169.8	321.5	3.8	15,290.2
2018	2.1	0.1	0.4	19.2	24.2	2,989.9	13,217.9	349.2	4.1	16,607.0
2018	2.2	0.1	0.4	20.4	25.7	3,175.3	14,037.4	370.9	4.4	17,636.7

INDUSTRY: ELECTRONIC SHOPPING & MAIL-ORDER (NAICS 45411)
PRODUCT LINE: TVs & VIDEO EQUIPMENT (Main Category)

NAICS 45411: Electronic Shopping and Mail-Order Houses This industry comprises establishments primarily engaged in retailing all types of merchandise by means of mail or by electronic media, such as interactive television or computer. Included in this industry are establishments primarily engaged in retailing from catalogue showrooms of mail-order houses.

5-YEAR TREND — ESTIMATED INDUSTRY SALES ($MILLIONS)

Year	Employee Size of Establishment									Total Industry Sales
	1-4 Emps.	5-9 Emps.	10-19 Emps.	20-49 Emps.	50-99 Emps.	100-249 Emps.	250-499 Emps.	500-999 Emps.	Unknown Emps.	
2015	674.7	358.2	531.9	860.6	619.0	1,206.8	1,765.7	2,236.7	102.0	8,355.6
2016	719.7	382.1	567.4	918.0	660.3	1,287.3	1,883.5	2,386.0	108.8	8,913.1
2017	763.4	405.3	601.8	973.7	700.4	1,365.4	1,997.8	2,530.7	115.4	9,453.9
2018	868.7	461.2	684.9	1,108.0	796.9	1,553.7	2,273.3	2,809.2	131.4	10,687.2
2018	964.8	512.2	760.7	1,230.6	885.2	1,725.7	2,525.0	3,066.1	145.9	11,816.2

INDUSTRY: BOOK STORES INDUSTRY (NAICS 451211)
PRODUCT LINE: TVs & VIDEO EQUIPMENT (Main Category)

NAICS 451211: Book Stores. this industry comprises establishments primarily engaged in the retail sale of new books and magazines. Establishments primarily engaged in the retail sale of used books are classified in 5932.

5-YEAR TREND — ESTIMATED INDUSTRY SALES ($MILLIONS)

Year	Employee Size of Establishment									Total
	1-4 Emps.	5-9 Emps.	10-19 Emps.	20-49 Emps.	50-99 Emps.	100-249 Emps.	250-499 Emps.	500-999 Emps.	Unknown Emps.	Industry Sales
2015	15.5	23.8	49.1	128.7	58.1	22.9	4.2	15.4	8.0	325.7
2016	16.4	25.0	51.8	135.7	61.3	24.2	4.4	16.2	8.4	343.5
2017	17.2	26.3	54.4	142.5	64.3	25.4	4.6	17.0	8.8	360.6
2018	17.3	26.5	54.8	143.5	64.8	25.5	4.7	17.5	8.9	363.5
2018	17.5	26.7	55.2	144.7	65.3	25.7	4.7	18.0	9.0	366.7

INDUSTRY: DEPARTMENT STORES INDUSTRY (NAICS 45211)
PRODUCT LINE: TELEVISIONS (Sub Category)

NAICS 45211: Department Stores Industry . this industry comprises establishments known as department stores primarily engaged in retailing a wide range of the following new products with no one merchandise line predominating: apparel, furniture, appliances and home furnishings; and selected additional items, such as paint, hardware, toiletries, cosmetics, photographic equipment, jewelry, toys, and sporting goods. merchandise lines are normally arranged in separate departments.

5-YEAR TREND — ESTIMATED INDUSTRY SALES ($MILLIONS)

Year	Employee Size of Establishment									Total
	1-4 Emps.	5-9 Emps.	10-19 Emps.	20-49 Emps.	50-99 Emps.	100-249 Emps.	250-499 Emps.	500-999 Emps.	Unknown Emps.	Industry Sales
2015	0.1	0.0	0.2	12.7	241.5	801.1	351.5	47.1	2.0	1,456.3
2016	0.1	0.0	0.2	12.9	244.7	811.5	356.0	47.7	2.1	1,475.1
2017	0.1	0.0	0.2	13.0	247.3	820.2	359.8	48.2	2.1	1,491.0
2018	0.1	0.0	0.2	13.1	248.4	824.0	361.5	48.5	2.1	1,497.9
2018	0.1	0.0	0.2	13.2	250.2	829.9	364.1	48.8	2.1	1,508.7

INDUSTRY: WAREHOUSE CLUBS & SUPERCENTERS (NAICS 45291)
PRODUCT LINE: TELEVISIONS (Sub Category)

NAICS 45291: Warehouse Clubs and Superstores This industry comprises establishments known as warehouse clubs, superstores or supercenters primarily engaged in retailing a general line of groceries in combination with general lines of new merchandise, such as apparel, furniture, and appliances.

5-YEAR TREND — ESTIMATED INDUSTRY SALES ($MILLIONS)

Year	Employee Size of Establishment									Total Industry Sales
	1-4 Emps.	5-9 Emps.	10-19 Emps.	20-49 Emps.	50-99 Emps.	100-249 Emps.	250-499 Emps.	500-999 Emps.	Unknown Emps.	
2015	0.8	0.0	0.1	7.4	9.4	1,157.1	5,115.6	135.2	1.6	6,427.3
2016	0.8	0.0	0.1	7.7	9.7	1,199.5	5,302.6	140.1	1.7	6,662.3
2017	0.9	0.0	0.1	8.0	10.0	1,239.4	5,479.4	144.8	1.7	6,884.4
2018	0.9	0.0	0.2	8.7	10.9	1,346.2	5,951.3	157.2	1.9	7,477.3
2018	1.0	0.0	0.2	9.2	11.6	1,429.7	6,320.3	167.0	2.0	7,940.9

INDUSTRY: ELECTRONIC SHOPPING & MAIL-ORDER (NAICS 45411)
PRODUCT LINE: TELEVISIONS (Sub Category)

NAICS 45411: Electronic Shopping and Mail-Order Houses This industry comprises establishments primarily engaged in retailing all types of merchandise by means of mail or by electronic media, such as interactive television or computer. Included in this industry are establishments primarily engaged in retailing from catalogue showrooms of mail-order houses.

5-YEAR TREND — ESTIMATED INDUSTRY SALES ($MILLIONS)

Year	Employee Size of Establishment									Total Industry Sales
	1-4 Emps.	5-9 Emps.	10-19 Emps.	20-49 Emps.	50-99 Emps.	100-249 Emps.	250-499 Emps.	500-999 Emps.	Unknown Emps.	
2015	77.8	41.3	61.3	99.2	71.3	139.1	203.5	257.8	11.8	962.9
2016	82.9	44.0	65.4	105.8	76.1	148.4	217.1	275.0	12.5	1,027.2
2017	88.0	46.7	69.4	112.2	80.7	157.4	230.2	291.7	13.3	1,089.5
2018	100.1	53.1	78.9	127.7	91.8	179.1	262.0	323.7	15.1	1,231.6
2018	111.2	59.0	87.7	141.8	102.0	198.9	291.0	353.4	16.8	1,361.8

INDUSTRY: PRERECORDED TAPE/CDs STORES (NAICS 45122)
PRODUCT LINE: VIDEO RECORDERS & CAMERAS (Sub Category)

NAICS 45122: Prerecorded Tape, Compact Disc, and Record Stores .
This industry comprises establishments primarily engaged in retailing new
prerecorded audio and video tapes, compact discs (CDs), and phonograph
records.

5-YEAR TREND – ESTIMATED INDUSTRY SALES ($MILLIONS)

Year	Employee Size of Establishment									Total Industry Sales
	1-4 Emps.	5-9 Emps.	10-19 Emps.	20-49 Emps.	50-99 Emps.	100-249 Emps.	250-499 Emps.	500-999 Emps.	Unknown Emps.	
2015	3.6	7.1	18.4	36.8	27.1	1,769.9	156.5	2.9	1.2	2,023.5
2016	3.7	7.3	19.1	38.1	27.9	1,828.2	161.7	3.0	1.3	2,090.3
2017	3.8	7.5	19.6	39.2	28.8	1,883.1	166.5	3.1	1.3	2,152.9
2018	4.0	7.9	20.6	41.2	30.2	1,979.0	175.0	3.2	1.4	2,262.6
2018	4.2	8.3	21.7	43.4	31.9	2,084.1	184.3	3.4	1.5	2,382.8

INDUSTRY: PRERECORDED TAPE/CDs STORES (NAICS 45122)
PRODUCT LINE: VIDEO TAPES & DISCS (Sub Category)

NAICS 45122: Prerecorded Tape, Compact Disc, and Record Stores .
This industry comprises establishments primarily engaged in retailing new
prerecorded audio and video tapes, compact discs (CDs), and phonograph
records.

5-YEAR TREND – ESTIMATED INDUSTRY SALES ($MILLIONS)

Year	Employee Size of Establishment									Total Industry Sales
	1-4 Emps.	5-9 Emps.	10-19 Emps.	20-49 Emps.	50-99 Emps.	100-249 Emps.	250-499 Emps.	500-999 Emps.	Unknown Emps.	
2015	59.3	117.8	306.5	611.9	449.3	29,397.5	2,599.9	48.1	20.5	33,610.9
2016	61.3	121.6	316.6	632.1	464.2	30,367.1	2,685.7	49.7	21.2	34,719.4
2017	63.1	125.3	326.1	651.1	478.1	31,277.9	2,766.2	51.2	21.8	35,760.8
2018	66.3	131.7	342.7	684.3	502.4	32,871.4	2,907.1	53.8	22.9	37,582.7
2018	69.8	138.7	360.9	720.6	529.1	34,617.2	3,061.5	56.6	24.2	39,578.7

INDUSTRY: DEPARTMENT STORES INDUSTRY (NAICS 45211)
PRODUCT LINE: OTHER VIDEO EQUIPMENT (Sub Category)

NAICS 45211: Department Stores Industry . this industry comprises establishments known as department stores primarily engaged in retailing a wide range of the following new products with no one merchandise line predominating: apparel, furniture, appliances and home furnishings; and selected additional items, such as paint, hardware, toiletries, cosmetics, photographic equipment, jewelry, toys, and sporting goods. merchandise lines are normally arranged in separate departments.

5-YEAR TREND – ESTIMATED INDUSTRY SALES ($MILLIONS)

Year	1-4 Emps.	5-9 Emps.	10-19 Emps.	20-49 Emps.	50-99 Emps.	100-249 Emps.	250-499 Emps.	500-999 Emps.	Unknown Emps.	Total Industry Sales
2015	0.2	0.1	0.3	20.5	388.7	1,289.1	565.5	75.7	3.3	2,343.2
2016	0.2	0.1	0.3	20.7	393.7	1,305.7	572.8	76.7	3.3	2,373.5
2017	0.2	0.1	0.3	21.0	397.9	1,319.8	579.0	77.5	3.4	2,399.0
2018	0.2	0.1	0.3	21.1	399.7	1,325.9	581.7	78.0	3.4	2,410.2
2018	0.2	0.1	0.3	21.2	402.6	1,335.4	585.8	78.5	3.4	2,427.5

INDUSTRY: WAREHOUSE CLUBS & SUPERCENTERS (NAICS 45291)
PRODUCT LINE: OTHER VIDEO EQUIPMENT (Sub Category)

NAICS 45291: **Warehouse Clubs and Superstores** This industry comprises establishments known as warehouse clubs, superstores or supercenters primarily engaged in retailing a general line of groceries in combination with general lines of new merchandise, such as apparel, furniture, and appliances.

5-YEAR TREND – ESTIMATED INDUSTRY SALES ($MILLIONS)

Year	1-4 Emps.	5-9 Emps.	10-19 Emps.	20-49 Emps.	50-99 Emps.	100-249 Emps.	250-499 Emps.	500-999 Emps.	Unknown Emps.	Total Industry Sales
2015	1.0	0.0	0.2	9.1	11.4	1,412.9	6,246.1	165.0	1.9	7,847.7
2016	1.0	0.0	0.2	9.4	11.9	1,464.5	6,474.5	171.1	2.0	8,134.6
2017	1.0	0.0	0.2	9.7	12.3	1,513.4	6,690.4	176.8	2.1	8,405.8
2018	1.1	0.0	0.2	10.6	13.3	1,643.7	7,266.6	192.0	2.3	9,129.7
2018	1.2	0.0	0.2	11.2	14.1	1,745.6	7,717.1	203.9	2.4	9,695.8

INDUSTRY: ELECTRONIC SHOPPING & MAIL-ORDER (NAICS 45411)
PRODUCT LINE: OTHER VIDEO EQUIPMENT (Sub Category)

NAICS 45411: Electronic Shopping and Mail-Order Houses This industry comprises establishments primarily engaged in retailing all types of merchandise by means of mail or by electronic media, such as interactive television or computer. Included in this industry are establishments primarily engaged in retailing from catalogue showrooms of mail-order houses.

5-YEAR TREND – ESTIMATED INDUSTRY SALES ($MILLIONS)

Year	Employee Size of Establishment									Total Industry Sales
	1-4 Emps.	5-9 Emps.	10-19 Emps.	20-49 Emps.	50-99 Emps.	100-249 Emps.	250-499 Emps.	500-999 Emps.	Unknown Emps.	
2015	596.9	316.9	470.6	761.4	547.7	1,067.7	1,562.2	1,979.0	90.3	7,392.7
2016	636.8	338.1	502.0	812.2	584.2	1,139.0	1,666.4	2,111.0	96.3	7,885.9
2017	675.4	358.6	532.5	861.5	619.6	1,208.1	1,767.5	2,239.1	102.1	8,364.4
2018	768.5	408.0	605.9	980.3	705.1	1,374.7	2,011.3	2,485.4	116.2	9,455.5
2018	853.6	453.2	673.0	1,088.8	783.2	1,526.8	2,234.0	2,712.8	129.1	10,454.4

INDUSTRY: HARDWARE STORES (NAICS 44413)
PRODUCT LINE: AUDIO EQUIPMENT (Main Category)

NAICS 44413: Hardware Stores. Establishments primarily engaged in the retail sale of a number of basic hardware lines, such as tools, builders' hardware, paint and glass, housewares and household appliances, and cutlery.

5-YEAR TREND – ESTIMATED INDUSTRY SALES ($MILLIONS)

Year	Employee Size of Establishment									Total Industry Sales
	1-4 Emps.	5-9 Emps.	10-19 Emps.	20-49 Emps.	50-99 Emps.	100-249 Emps.	250-499 Emps.	500-999 Emps.	Unknown Emps.	
2015	1.8	2.8	5.7	8.0	1.5	0.3	0.1	0.0	0.1	20.4
2016	1.8	2.9	5.8	8.1	1.5	0.3	0.1	0.0	0.2	20.7
2017	1.8	3.0	5.9	8.3	1.5	0.4	0.1	0.0	0.2	21.1
2018	1.9	3.1	6.2	8.6	1.6	0.4	0.1	0.0	0.2	22.1
2018	2.0	3.2	6.5	9.1	1.7	0.4	0.1	0.0	0.2	23.1

INDUSTRY: SUPERMARKETS INDUSTRY (NAICS 44511)
PRODUCT LINE: AUDIO EQUIPMENT (Main Category)

NAICS 44511: Grocery Stores Industry. this industry comprises establishments generally known as supermarkets and grocery stores primarily engaged in retailing a general line of food, such as canned and frozen foods; fresh fruits and vegetables; and fresh and prepared meats, fish, and poultry. Included in this industry are delicatessen-type establishments primarily engaged in retailing a general line of food.

5-YEAR TREND — ESTIMATED INDUSTRY SALES ($MILLIONS)

Year	Employee Size of Establishment									Total
	1-4 Emps.	5-9 Emps.	10-19 Emps.	20-49 Emps.	50-99 Emps.	100-249 Emps.	250-499 Emps.	500-999 Emps.	Unknown Emps.	Industry Sales
2015	5.3	4.0	10.1	32.9	79.9	182.2	52.5	7.2	1.0	375.2
2016	5.2	3.9	9.9	32.4	78.5	179.1	51.6	7.1	1.0	368.7
2017	5.1	3.8	9.7	31.7	77.0	175.5	50.6	7.0	1.0	361.5
2018	5.1	3.8	9.7	31.7	77.0	175.6	50.6	7.0	1.0	361.5
2018	5.1	3.8	9.7	31.8	77.1	175.9	50.7	7.0	1.0	362.3

INDUSTRY: PHARMACIES & DRUG STORES INDUSTRY (NAICS 44611)
PRODUCT LINE: AUDIO EQUIPMENT (Main Category)

NAICS 44611 Pharmacies and Drug Stores – this industry comprises establishments known as pharmacies and drug stores engaged in retailing prescription or nonprescription drugs and medicines.

5-YEAR TREND — ESTIMATED INDUSTRY SALES ($MILLIONS)

Year	Employee Size of Establishment									Total
	1-4 Emps.	5-9 Emps.	10-19 Emps.	20-49 Emps.	50-99 Emps.	100-249 Emps.	250-499 Emps.	500-999 Emps.	Unknown Emps.	Industry Sales
2015	13.5	33.7	142.5	402.8	37.8	14.9	4.6	1.9	1.1	652.9
2016	14.2	35.5	150.0	423.9	39.8	15.6	4.8	2.0	1.2	687.0
2017	14.9	37.2	157.2	444.2	41.7	16.4	5.1	2.0	1.2	719.9
2018	16.0	40.0	169.0	477.6	44.9	17.6	5.5	2.1	1.3	774.1
2018	17.3	43.1	181.9	514.1	48.3	19.0	5.9	2.2	1.4	833.2

INDUSTRY: PRERECORDED TAPES & CDs STORES (NAICS 45122)
PRODUCT LINE: AUDIO EQUIPMENT (Main Category)

NAICS 45122: Prerecorded Tape, Compact Disc, and Record Stores .
This industry comprises establishments primarily engaged in retailing new
prerecorded audio and video tapes, compact discs (CDs), and phonograph
records.

5-YEAR TREND – ESTIMATED INDUSTRY SALES ($MILLIONS)

| Year | Employee Size of Establishment | | | | | | | | | Total |
	1-4 Emps.	5-9 Emps.	10-19 Emps.	20-49 Emps.	50-99 Emps.	100-249 Emps.	250-499 Emps.	500-999 Emps.	Unknown Emps.	Industry Sales
2015	181.6	360.5	938.2	1,873.5	1,375.7	90,001.4	7,959.7	147.4	62.8	102,900.7
2016	187.6	372.4	969.2	1,935.3	1,421.1	92,969.9	8,222.2	152.2	64.9	106,294.7
2017	193.2	383.6	998.2	1,993.3	1,463.7	95,758.4	8,468.9	156.8	66.8	109,482.9
2018	203.1	403.1	1,049.1	2,094.9	1,538.3	100,637.0	8,900.3	164.7	70.2	115,060.7
2018	213.8	424.5	1,104.8	2,206.1	1,620.0	105,981.8	9,373.0	173.4	74.0	121,171.4

INDUSTRY: DEPARTMENT STORES INDUSTRY (NAICS 45211)
PRODUCT LINE: AUDIO EQUIPMENT (Main Category)

NAICS 45211: Department Stores Industry . this industry comprises
establishments known as department stores primarily engaged in retailing
a wide range of the following new products with no one merchandise line
predominating: apparel, furniture, appliances and home furnishings; and
selected additional items, such as paint, hardware, toiletries, cosmetics,
photographic equipment, jewelry, toys, and sporting goods. merchandise lines
are normally arranged in separate departments.

5-YEAR TREND – ESTIMATED INDUSTRY SALES ($MILLIONS)

| Year | Employee Size of Establishment | | | | | | | | | Total |
	1-4 Emps.	5-9 Emps.	10-19 Emps.	20-49 Emps.	50-99 Emps.	100-249 Emps.	250-499 Emps.	500-999 Emps.	Unknown Emps.	Industry Sales
2015	0.2	0.1	0.3	27.7	525.8	1,744.0	765.1	102.5	4.4	3,170.2
2016	0.2	0.1	0.4	28.1	532.6	1,766.5	775.0	103.8	4.5	3,211.1
2017	0.2	0.1	0.4	28.4	538.3	1,785.5	783.3	104.9	4.5	3,245.7
2018	0.2	0.1	0.4	28.5	540.8	1,793.8	786.9	105.5	4.6	3,260.8
2018	0.2	0.1	0.4	28.7	544.7	1,806.7	792.6	106.3	4.6	3,284.3

INDUSTRY: WAREHOUSE CLUBS & SUPERCENTERS (NAICS 45291)
PRODUCT LINE: AUDIO EQUIPMENT (Main Category)

NAICS 45291: Warehouse Clubs and Superstores This industry comprises establishments known as warehouse clubs, superstores or supercenters primarily engaged in retailing a general line of groceries in combination with general lines of new merchandise, such as apparel, furniture, and appliances.

5-YEAR TREND — ESTIMATED INDUSTRY SALES ($MILLIONS)

Year	Employee Size of Establishment									Total Industry Sales
	1-4 Emps.	5-9 Emps.	10-19 Emps.	20-49 Emps.	50-99 Emps.	100-249 Emps.	250-499 Emps.	500-999 Emps.	Unknown Emps.	
2015	1.6	0.1	0.3	14.6	18.4	2,273.1	10,049.0	265.5	3.1	12,625.7
2016	1.6	0.1	0.3	15.1	19.1	2,356.2	10,416.4	275.2	3.2	13,087.3
2017	1.7	0.1	0.3	15.7	19.7	2,434.8	10,763.7	284.4	3.3	13,523.6
2018	1.8	0.1	0.3	17.0	21.4	2,644.4	11,690.7	308.9	3.6	14,688.3
2018	1.9	0.1	0.3	18.1	22.7	2,808.4	12,415.6	328.0	3.9	15,599.0

INDUSTRY: OFFICE SUPPLIES & STATIONERY STORES (NAICS 45321)
PRODUCT LINE: AUDIO EQUIPMENT (Main Category)

NAICS 45321: Office Supplies and Stationery Stores . this industry comprises establishments primarily engaged in one or more of the following: (1) retailing new stationery, school supplies, and office supplies; (2) selling a combination of new office equipment, furniture, and supplies; and (3) selling new office equipment, furniture, and supplies in combination with selling new computers.

5-YEAR TREND — ESTIMATED INDUSTRY SALES ($MILLIONS)

Year	Employee Size of Establishment									Total Industry Sales
	1-4 Emps.	5-9 Emps.	10-19 Emps.	20-49 Emps.	50-99 Emps.	100-249 Emps.	250-499 Emps.	500-999 Emps.	Unknown Emps.	
2015	0.2	0.2	1.0	2.8	0.1	0.1	0.0	0.0	0.1	4.4
2016	0.2	0.2	1.0	2.8	0.1	0.1	0.0	0.0	0.1	4.4
2017	0.2	0.2	1.0	2.8	0.1	0.1	0.0	0.0	0.1	4.4
2018	0.2	0.2	1.0	2.7	0.1	0.1	0.0	0.0	0.1	4.3
2018	0.2	0.2	0.9	2.7	0.1	0.1	0.0	0.0	0.0	4.2

INDUSTRY: ELECTRONIC SHOPPING & MAIL-ORDER (NAICS 45411)
PRODUCT LINE: AUDIO EQUIPMENT (Main Category)

NAICS 45411: Electronic Shopping and Mail-Order Houses This industry comprises establishments primarily engaged in retailing all types of merchandise by means of mail or by electronic media, such as interactive television or computer. Included in this industry are establishments primarily engaged in retailing from catalogue showrooms of mail-order houses.

5-YEAR TREND – ESTIMATED INDUSTRY SALES ($MILLIONS)

Year	Employee Size of Establishment									Total Industry Sales
	1-4 Emps.	5-9 Emps.	10-19 Emps.	20-49 Emps.	50-99 Emps.	100-249 Emps.	250-499 Emps.	500-999 Emps.	Unknown Emps.	
2015	975.6	518.0	769.2	1,244.4	895.1	1,745.0	2,553.2	3,234.2	147.5	12,082.0
2016	1,040.7	552.5	820.5	1,327.4	954.8	1,861.4	2,723.5	3,450.0	157.4	12,888.1
2017	1,103.8	586.0	870.3	1,407.9	1,012.7	1,974.3	2,888.7	3,659.3	166.9	13,670.0
2018	1,256.1	666.9	990.3	1,602.1	1,152.4	2,246.6	3,287.1	4,062.0	190.0	15,453.3
2018	1,395.1	740.7	1,099.9	1,779.4	1,279.9	2,495.3	3,651.0	4,433.6	211.0	17,085.8

INDUSTRY: BOOK STORES INDUSTRY (NAICS 451211)
PRODUCT LINE: AUDIO EQUIPMENT (Main Category)

NAICS 451211: Book Stores. this industry comprises establishments primarily engaged in the retail sale of new books and magazines. Establishments primarily engaged in the retail sale of used books are classified in 5932.

5-YEAR TREND – ESTIMATED INDUSTRY SALES ($MILLIONS)

Year	Employee Size of Establishment									Total Industry Sales
	1-4 Emps.	5-9 Emps.	10-19 Emps.	20-49 Emps.	50-99 Emps.	100-249 Emps.	250-499 Emps.	500-999 Emps.	Unknown Emps.	
2015	28.2	43.1	89.2	233.7	105.5	41.6	7.6	28.0	14.5	591.4
2016	29.8	45.5	94.1	246.5	111.3	43.9	8.0	29.5	15.3	623.6
2017	31.2	47.7	98.8	258.7	116.8	46.0	8.4	30.9	16.0	654.7
2018	31.5	48.1	99.5	260.6	117.6	46.4	8.4	31.8	16.1	660.0
2018	31.7	48.5	100.3	262.7	118.6	46.7	8.5	32.6	16.3	665.9

INDUSTRY: PRERECORDED TAPES & CDs STORES (NAICS 45122)
PRODUCT LINE: STEREO & COMPONENT EQUIPMENT (Sub Category)

NAICS 45122: Prerecorded Tape, Compact Disc, and Record Stores .
This industry comprises establishments primarily engaged in retailing new
prerecorded audio and video tapes, compact discs (CDs), and phonograph
records.

5-YEAR TREND – ESTIMATED INDUSTRY SALES ($MILLIONS)

Year	Employee Size of Establishment									Total Industry Sales
	1-4 Emps.	5-9 Emps.	10-19 Emps.	20-49 Emps.	50-99 Emps.	100-249 Emps.	250-499 Emps.	500-999 Emps.	Unknown Emps.	
2015	1.3	2.7	6.9	13.9	10.2	665.4	58.8	1.1	0.5	760.8
2016	1.4	2.8	7.2	14.3	10.5	687.4	60.8	1.1	0.5	785.9
2017	1.4	2.8	7.4	14.7	10.8	708.0	62.6	1.2	0.5	809.5
2018	1.5	3.0	7.8	15.5	11.4	744.1	65.8	1.2	0.5	850.7
2018	1.6	3.1	8.2	16.3	12.0	783.6	69.3	1.3	0.5	895.9

INDUSTRY: DEPARTMENT STORES INDUSTRY (NAICS 45211)
PRODUCT LINE: STEREO & COMPONENT EQUIPMENT (Sub Category)

NAICS 45211: Department Stores Industry . this industry comprises
establishments known as department stores primarily engaged in retailing
a wide range of the following new products with no one merchandise line
predominating: apparel, furniture, appliances and home furnishings; and
selected additional items, such as paint, hardware, toiletries, cosmetics,
photographic equipment, jewelry, toys, and sporting goods. merchandise lines
are normally arranged in separate departments.

5-YEAR TREND – ESTIMATED INDUSTRY SALES ($MILLIONS)

Year	Employee Size of Establishment									Total Industry Sales
	1-4 Emps.	5-9 Emps.	10-19 Emps.	20-49 Emps.	50-99 Emps.	100-249 Emps.	250-499 Emps.	500-999 Emps.	Unknown Emps.	
2015	0.1	0.0	0.2	13.9	264.8	878.3	385.3	51.6	2.2	1,596.6
2016	0.1	0.0	0.2	14.1	268.2	889.7	390.3	52.3	2.3	1,617.2
2017	0.1	0.0	0.2	14.3	271.1	899.3	394.5	52.8	2.3	1,634.6
2018	0.1	0.0	0.2	14.3	272.4	903.4	396.3	53.1	2.3	1,642.2
2018	0.1	0.0	0.2	14.5	274.3	909.9	399.2	53.5	2.3	1,654.1

INDUSTRY: WAREHOUSE CLUBS & SUPERCENTERS (NAICS 45291)
PRODUCT LINE: STEREO & COMPONENT EQUIPMENT (Sub Category)

NAICS 45291: Warehouse Clubs and Superstores This industry comprises establishments known as warehouse clubs, superstores or supercenters primarily engaged in retailing a general line of groceries in combination with general lines of new merchandise, such as apparel, furniture, and appliances.

5-Year Trend – Estimated Industry Sales ($Millions)

Year	Employee Size of Establishment									Total
	1-4 Emps.	5-9 Emps.	10-19 Emps.	20-49 Emps.	50-99 Emps.	100-249 Emps.	250-499 Emps.	500-999 Emps.	Unknown Emps.	Industry Sales
2015	0.7	0.0	0.1	6.5	8.2	1,007.5	4,453.9	117.7	1.4	5,595.9
2016	0.7	0.0	0.1	6.7	8.5	1,044.3	4,616.7	122.0	1.4	5,800.5
2017	0.7	0.0	0.1	6.9	8.7	1,079.1	4,770.7	126.0	1.5	5,993.9
2018	0.8	0.0	0.1	7.5	9.5	1,172.1	5,181.5	136.9	1.6	6,510.1
2018	0.9	0.0	0.1	8.0	10.1	1,244.7	5,502.8	145.4	1.7	6,913.7

INDUSTRY: ELECTRONIC SHOPPING & MAIL-ORDER (NAICS 45411)
PRODUCT LINE: STEREO & COMPONENT EQUIPMENT (Sub Category)

NAICS 45411: Electronic Shopping and Mail-Order Houses This industry comprises establishments primarily engaged in retailing all types of merchandise by means of mail or by electronic media, such as interactive television or computer. Included in this industry are establishments primarily engaged in retailing from catalogue showrooms of mail-order houses.

5-Year Trend – Estimated Industry Sales ($Millions)

Year	Employee Size of Establishment									Total
	1-4 Emps.	5-9 Emps.	10-19 Emps.	20-49 Emps.	50-99 Emps.	100-249 Emps.	250-499 Emps.	500-999 Emps.	Unknown Emps.	Industry Sales
2015	268.7	142.6	211.8	342.7	246.5	480.6	703.1	890.7	40.6	3,327.3
2016	286.6	152.2	225.9	365.5	262.9	512.6	750.0	950.1	43.3	3,549.2
2017	304.0	161.4	239.7	387.7	278.9	543.7	795.5	1,007.7	46.0	3,764.6
2018	345.9	183.6	272.7	441.2	317.3	618.7	905.2	1,118.6	52.3	4,255.7
2018	384.2	204.0	302.9	490.0	352.5	687.2	1,005.4	1,221.0	58.1	4,705.3

INDUSTRY: PRERECORDED TAPES & CDs STORES (NAICS 45122)
PRODUCT LINE: TAPES & CDs (Sub Category)

NAICS 45122: Prerecorded Tape, Compact Disc, and Record Stores .
This industry comprises establishments primarily engaged in retailing new
prerecorded audio and video tapes, compact discs (CDs), and phonograph
records.

5-YEAR TREND — ESTIMATED INDUSTRY SALES ($MILLIONS)

Year	Employee Size of Establishment									Total
	1-4 Emps.	5-9 Emps.	10-19 Emps.	20-49 Emps.	50-99 Emps.	100-249 Emps.	250-499 Emps.	500-999 Emps.	Unknown Emps.	Industry Sales
2015	179.4	356.1	926.9	1,850.8	1,359.0	88,910.9	7,863.3	145.6	62.0	101,653.9
2016	185.3	367.9	957.4	1,911.8	1,403.8	91,843.4	8,122.6	150.4	64.1	105,006.8
2017	190.9	378.9	986.1	1,969.2	1,446.0	94,598.1	8,366.2	154.9	66.0	108,156.3
2018	200.6	398.2	1,036.4	2,069.5	1,519.6	99,417.6	8,792.5	162.7	69.4	113,666.5
2018	211.2	419.4	1,091.4	2,179.4	1,600.3	104,697.7	9,259.4	171.3	73.1	119,703.2

INDUSTRY: DEPARTMENT STORES INDUSTRY (NAICS 45211)
PRODUCT LINE: TAPES & CDs (Sub Category)

NAICS 45211: Department Stores Industry . this industry comprises
establishments known as department stores primarily engaged in retailing
a wide range of the following new products with no one merchandise line
predominating: apparel, furniture, appliances and home furnishings; and
selected additional items, such as paint, hardware, toiletries, cosmetics,
photographic equipment, jewelry, toys, and sporting goods. merchandise lines
are normally arranged in separate departments.

5-YEAR TREND — ESTIMATED INDUSTRY SALES ($MILLIONS)

Year	Employee Size of Establishment									Total
	1-4 Emps.	5-9 Emps.	10-19 Emps.	20-49 Emps.	50-99 Emps.	100-249 Emps.	250-499 Emps.	500-999 Emps.	Unknown Emps.	Industry Sales
2015	0.1	0.0	0.2	13.7	261.0	865.5	379.7	50.8	2.2	1,573.3
2016	0.1	0.0	0.2	13.9	264.3	876.7	384.6	51.5	2.2	1,593.7
2017	0.1	0.0	0.2	14.1	267.2	886.2	388.8	52.1	2.3	1,610.8
2018	0.1	0.0	0.2	14.1	268.4	890.2	390.6	52.4	2.3	1,618.3
2018	0.1	0.0	0.2	14.2	270.3	896.7	393.4	52.7	2.3	1,630.0

INDUSTRY: WAREHOUSE CLUBS & SUPERCENTERS (NAICS 45291)
PRODUCT LINE: TAPES & CDs (Sub Category)

NAICS 45291: Warehouse Clubs and Superstores This industry comprises establishments known as warehouse clubs, superstores or supercenters primarily engaged in retailing a general line of groceries in combination with general lines of new merchandise, such as apparel, furniture, and appliances.

5-YEAR TREND – ESTIMATED INDUSTRY SALES ($MILLIONS)

Year	Employee Size of Establishment									Total
	1-4 Emps.	5-9 Emps.	10-19 Emps.	20-49 Emps.	50-99 Emps.	100-249 Emps.	250-499 Emps.	500-999 Emps.	Unknown Emps.	Industry Sales
2015	0.9	0.0	0.1	8.0	10.1	1,247.0	5,513.0	145.7	1.7	6,926.5
2016	0.9	0.0	0.2	8.3	10.5	1,292.6	5,714.5	151.0	1.8	7,179.8
2017	0.9	0.0	0.2	8.6	10.8	1,335.7	5,905.1	156.0	1.8	7,419.2
2018	1.0	0.0	0.2	9.3	11.8	1,450.8	6,413.6	169.5	2.0	8,058.1
2018	1.1	0.0	0.2	9.9	12.5	1,540.7	6,811.3	180.0	2.1	8,557.7

INDUSTRY: ELECTRONIC SHOPPING & MAIL-ORDER (NAICS 45411)
PRODUCT LINE: TAPES & CDs (Sub Category)

NAICS 45411: Electronic Shopping and Mail-Order Houses This industry comprises establishments primarily engaged in retailing all types of merchandise by means of mail or by electronic media, such as interactive television or computer. Included in this industry are establishments primarily engaged in retailing from catalogue showrooms of mail-order houses.

5-YEAR TREND – ESTIMATED INDUSTRY SALES ($MILLIONS)

Year	Employee Size of Establishment									Total
	1-4 Emps.	5-9 Emps.	10-19 Emps.	20-49 Emps.	50-99 Emps.	100-249 Emps.	250-499 Emps.	500-999 Emps.	Unknown Emps.	Industry Sales
2015	347.2	184.3	273.8	442.9	318.6	621.1	908.7	1,151.1	52.5	4,300.2
2016	370.4	196.6	292.0	472.4	339.8	662.5	969.3	1,227.9	56.0	4,587.1
2017	392.9	208.6	309.7	501.1	360.4	702.7	1,028.1	1,302.4	59.4	4,865.4
2018	447.0	237.3	352.5	570.2	410.1	799.6	1,169.9	1,445.7	67.6	5,500.1
2018	496.5	263.6	391.5	633.3	455.5	888.1	1,299.4	1,578.0	75.1	6,081.1

INDUSTRY: PRERECORDED TAPES & CDs STORES (NAICS 45122)
PRODUCT LINE: SHEET MUSIC & RELATED ITEMS (Sub Category)

NAICS 45122: Prerecorded Tape, Compact Disc, and Record Stores .
This industry comprises establishments primarily engaged in retailing new
prerecorded audio and video tapes, compact discs (CDs), and phonograph
records.

5-YEAR TREND — ESTIMATED INDUSTRY SALES ($MILLIONS)

Year	Employee Size of Establishment									Total Industry Sales
	1-4 Emps.	5-9 Emps.	10-19 Emps.	20-49 Emps.	50-99 Emps.	100-249 Emps.	250-499 Emps.	500-999 Emps.	Unknown Emps.	
2015	0.8	1.5	4.0	7.9	5.8	380.2	33.6	0.6	0.3	434.6
2016	0.8	1.6	4.1	8.2	6.0	392.7	34.7	0.6	0.3	449.0
2017	0.8	1.6	4.2	8.4	6.2	404.5	35.8	0.7	0.3	462.4
2018	0.9	1.7	4.4	8.8	6.5	425.1	37.6	0.7	0.3	486.0
2018	0.9	1.8	4.7	9.3	6.8	447.7	39.6	0.7	0.3	511.8

INDUSTRY: WAREHOUSE CLUBS & SUPERCENTERS (NAICS 45291)
PRODUCT LINE: OTHER AUDIO & MUSIC ITEMS (Sub Category)

NAICS 45291: Warehouse Clubs and Superstores This industry
comprises establishments known as warehouse clubs, superstores or
supercenters primarily engaged in retailing a general line of groceries
in combination with general lines of new merchandise, such as apparel,
furniture, and appliances.

5-YEAR TREND — ESTIMATED INDUSTRY SALES ($MILLIONS)

Year	Employee Size of Establishment									Total Industry Sales
	1-4 Emps.	5-9 Emps.	10-19 Emps.	20-49 Emps.	50-99 Emps.	100-249 Emps.	250-499 Emps.	500-999 Emps.	Unknown Emps.	
2015	0.0	0.0	0.0	0.1	0.2	18.6	82.2	2.2	0.0	103.2
2016	0.0	0.0	0.0	0.1	0.2	19.3	85.2	2.3	0.0	107.0
2017	0.0	0.0	0.0	0.1	0.2	19.9	88.0	2.3	0.0	110.6
2018	0.0	0.0	0.0	0.1	0.2	21.6	95.6	2.5	0.0	120.1
2018	0.0	0.0	0.0	0.1	0.2	23.0	101.5	2.7	0.0	127.5

INDUSTRY: ELECTRONIC SHOPPING & MAIL-ORDER (NAICS 45411)
PRODUCT LINE: OTHER AUDIO & MUSIC ITEMS (Sub Category)

NAICS 45411: Electronic Shopping and Mail-Order Houses This industry comprises establishments primarily engaged in retailing all types of merchandise by means of mail or by electronic media, such as interactive television or computer. Included in this industry are establishments primarily engaged in retailing from catalogue showrooms of mail-order houses.

5-YEAR TREND – ESTIMATED INDUSTRY SALES ($MILLIONS)

Year	Employee Size of Establishment									Total
	1-4 Emps.	5-9 Emps.	10-19 Emps.	20-49 Emps.	50-99 Emps.	100-249 Emps.	250-499 Emps.	500-999 Emps.	Unknown Emps.	Industry Sales
2015	359.7	191.0	283.6	458.8	330.0	643.4	941.3	1,192.4	54.4	4,454.6
2016	383.7	203.7	302.5	489.4	352.0	686.3	1,004.1	1,272.0	58.0	4,751.8
2017	407.0	216.1	320.9	519.1	373.4	727.9	1,065.1	1,349.2	61.5	5,040.1
2018	463.1	245.9	365.1	590.7	424.9	828.3	1,212.0	1,497.6	70.0	5,697.6
2018	514.4	273.1	405.5	656.1	471.9	920.0	1,346.1	1,634.6	77.8	6,299.5

INDUSTRY: HOME CENTERS INDUSTRY (NAICS 44411)
PRODUCT LINE: FURNITURE (Main Category)

NAICS 44411: Home Centers. This industry comprises establishments known as home centers primarily engaged in retailing a general line of new home repair and improvement materials and supplies, such as lumber, plumbing goods, electrical goods, tools, housewares, hardware, and lawn and garden supplies, with no one merchandise line predominating. The merchandise lines are normally arranged in separate departments.

5-YEAR TREND – ESTIMATED INDUSTRY SALES ($MILLIONS)

Year	Employee Size of Establishment									Total
	1-4 Emps.	5-9 Emps.	10-19 Emps.	20-49 Emps.	50-99 Emps.	100-249 Emps.	250-499 Emps.	500-999 Emps.	Unknown Emps.	Industry Sales
2015	5.1	10.0	26.1	52.2	38.3	2,507.3	221.7	4.1	1.7	2,866.7
2016	5.2	10.4	27.0	53.9	39.6	2,590.0	229.1	4.2	1.8	2,961.3
2017	5.4	10.7	27.8	55.5	40.8	2,667.7	235.9	4.4	1.9	3,050.1
2018	5.7	11.2	29.2	58.4	42.9	2,803.6	248.0	4.6	2.0	3,205.5
2018	6.0	11.8	30.8	61.5	45.1	2,952.5	261.1	4.8	2.1	3,375.7

INDUSTRY: HARDWARE STORES (NAICS 44413)
PRODUCT LINE: FURNITURE (Main Category)

NAICS 44413: Hardware Stores. Establishments primarily engaged
in the retail sale of a number of basic hardware lines, such as tools,
builders' hardware, paint and glass, housewares and household appliances,
and cutlery.

5-YEAR TREND — ESTIMATED INDUSTRY SALES ($MILLIONS)

Year	Employee Size of Establishment									Total Industry Sales
	1-4 Emps.	5-9 Emps.	10-19 Emps.	20-49 Emps.	50-99 Emps.	100-249 Emps.	250-499 Emps.	500-999 Emps.	Unknown Emps.	
2015	29.4	47.2	94.4	132.1	24.2	5.7	1.6	0.1	2.5	337.1
2016	30.0	48.1	96.1	134.6	24.6	5.8	1.6	0.1	2.5	343.4
2017	30.5	48.9	97.7	136.8	25.1	5.9	1.6	0.1	2.6	349.1
2018	31.9	51.1	102.3	143.2	26.2	6.1	1.7	0.1	2.7	365.4
2018	33.4	53.7	107.3	150.3	27.5	6.4	1.8	0.1	2.8	383.4

INDUSTRY: WOMEN'S CLOTHING STORES INDUSTRY (NAICS 44812)
PRODUCT LINE: FURNITURE (Main Category)

NAICS 44812: Women's Clothing Stores . this industry comprises
establishments primarily engaged in retailing a general line of new
women's, misses' and juniors' clothing, including maternity wear.
These establishments may provide basic alterations, such as hemming,
taking in or letting out seams, or lengthening or shortening sleeves.

5-YEAR TREND — ESTIMATED INDUSTRY SALES ($MILLIONS)

Year	Employee Size of Establishment									Total Industry Sales
	1-4 Emps.	5-9 Emps.	10-19 Emps.	20-49 Emps.	50-99 Emps.	100-249 Emps.	250-499 Emps.	500-999 Emps.	Unknown Emps.	
2015	2.0	4.5	10.9	7.5	2.3	2.3	0.9	0.8	0.5	31.6
2016	2.0	4.6	11.4	7.8	2.4	2.4	0.9	0.8	0.5	32.8
2017	2.1	4.8	11.8	8.1	2.5	2.4	0.9	0.8	0.5	33.9
2018	2.3	5.1	12.5	8.6	2.7	2.6	1.0	0.9	0.5	36.1
2018	2.4	5.4	13.3	9.1	2.8	2.8	1.0	0.9	0.6	38.4

INDUSTRY: FAMILY CLOTHING STORES INDUSTRY (NAICS 44814)
PRODUCT LINE: FURNITURE (Main Category)

NAICS 44814: Family Clothing Stores . this industry comprises
establishments primarily engaged in retailing a general line of new clothing
for men, women, and children, without specializing in sales for an individual
gender or age group. These establishments may provide basic alterations,
such as hemming, taking in or letting out seams, or lengthening or shortening sleeves.

5-YEAR TREND – ESTIMATED INDUSTRY SALES ($MILLIONS)

| Year | Employee Size of Establishment | | | | | | | | | Total |
	1-4 Emps.	5-9 Emps.	10-19 Emps.	20-49 Emps.	50-99 Emps.	100-249 Emps.	250-499 Emps.	500-999 Emps.	Unknown Emps.	Industry Sales
2015	0.3	0.6	2.7	8.1	8.5	2.1	2.1	0.8	0.1	25.4
2016	0.4	0.6	2.7	8.4	8.8	2.2	2.2	0.9	0.1	26.3
2017	0.4	0.7	2.8	8.7	9.1	2.3	2.2	0.9	0.1	27.2
2018	0.4	0.7	3.0	9.2	9.7	2.4	2.4	0.9	0.1	28.8
2018	0.4	0.7	3.2	9.8	10.3	2.6	2.5	1.0	0.1	30.7

INDUSTRY: DEPARTMENT STORES INDUSTRY (NAICS 45211)
PRODUCT LINE: FURNITURE (Main Category)

NAICS 45211: Department Stores Industry . this industry comprises
establishments known as department stores primarily engaged in retailing
a wide range of the following new products with no one merchandise line
predominating: apparel, furniture, appliances and home furnishings; and
selected additional items, such as paint, hardware, toiletries, cosmetics,
photographic equipment, jewelry, toys, and sporting goods. merchandise lines
are normally arranged in separate departments.

5-YEAR TREND – ESTIMATED INDUSTRY SALES ($MILLIONS)

| Year | Employee Size of Establishment | | | | | | | | | Total |
	1-4 Emps.	5-9 Emps.	10-19 Emps.	20-49 Emps.	50-99 Emps.	100-249 Emps.	250-499 Emps.	500-999 Emps.	Unknown Emps.	Industry Sales
2015	0.2	0.1	0.3	22.8	433.0	1,436.2	630.1	84.4	3.7	2,610.7
2016	0.2	0.1	0.3	23.1	438.6	1,454.8	638.2	85.5	3.7	2,644.4
2017	0.2	0.1	0.3	23.4	443.3	1,470.4	645.1	86.4	3.7	2,672.9
2018	0.2	0.1	0.3	23.5	445.4	1,477.2	648.1	86.9	3.8	2,685.4
2018	0.2	0.1	0.3	23.6	448.6	1,487.9	652.7	87.5	3.8	2,704.7

INDUSTRY: WAREHOUSE CLUBS & SUPERCENTERS (NAICS 45291)
PRODUCT LINE: FURNITURE (Main Category)

NAICS 45291: Warehouse Clubs and Superstores This industry comprises establishments known as warehouse clubs, superstores or supercenters primarily engaged in retailing a general line of groceries in combination with general lines of new merchandise, such as apparel, furniture, and appliances.

5-YEAR TREND — ESTIMATED INDUSTRY SALES ($MILLIONS)

Year	Employee Size of Establishment									Total Industry Sales
	1-4 Emps.	5-9 Emps.	10-19 Emps.	20-49 Emps.	50-99 Emps.	100-249 Emps.	250-499 Emps.	500-999 Emps.	Unknown Emps.	
2015	0.9	0.0	0.2	8.3	10.5	1,297.3	5,735.0	151.5	1.8	7,205.5
2016	0.9	0.0	0.2	8.6	10.9	1,344.7	5,944.7	157.1	1.9	7,468.9
2017	1.0	0.0	0.2	8.9	11.3	1,389.5	6,142.9	162.3	1.9	7,718.0
2018	1.0	0.0	0.2	9.7	12.2	1,509.2	6,671.9	176.3	2.1	8,382.7
2018	1.1	0.0	0.2	10.3	13.0	1,602.8	7,085.6	187.2	2.2	8,902.4

INDUSTRY: OFFICE SUPPLIES & STATIONERY STORES (NAICS 45321)
PRODUCT LINE: FURNITURE (Main Category)

NAICS 45321: Office Supplies and Stationery Stores . this industry comprises establishments primarily engaged in one or more of the following: (1) retailing new stationery, school supplies, and office supplies; (2) selling a combination of new office equipment, furniture, and supplies; and (3) selling new office equipment, furniture, and supplies in combination with selling new computers.

5-YEAR TREND — ESTIMATED INDUSTRY SALES ($MILLIONS)

Year	Employee Size of Establishment									Total Industry Sales
	1-4 Emps.	5-9 Emps.	10-19 Emps.	20-49 Emps.	50-99 Emps.	100-249 Emps.	250-499 Emps.	500-999 Emps.	Unknown Emps.	
2015	75.0	56.1	296.9	837.0	20.3	20.2	0.1	0.5	15.7	1,321.8
2016	75.0	56.1	297.1	837.6	20.3	20.2	0.1	0.5	15.7	1,322.7
2017	74.9	56.0	296.8	836.5	20.3	20.2	0.1	0.5	15.7	1,321.0
2018	73.2	54.8	290.0	817.5	19.9	19.7	0.1	0.5	15.3	1,291.0
2018	71.7	53.7	284.2	801.0	19.5	19.3	0.1	0.5	15.0	1,265.0

INDUSTRY: ELECTRONIC SHOPPING & MAIL-ORDER (NAICS 45411)
PRODUCT LINE: FURNITURE (Main Category)

NAICS 45411: Electronic Shopping and Mail-Order Houses This industry comprises establishments primarily engaged in retailing all types of merchandise by means of mail or by electronic media, such as interactive television or computer. Included in this industry are establishments primarily engaged in retailing from catalogue showrooms of mail-order houses.

5-YEAR TREND — ESTIMATED INDUSTRY SALES ($MILLIONS)

Year	Employee Size of Establishment									Total Industry Sales
	1-4 Emps.	5-9 Emps.	10-19 Emps.	20-49 Emps.	50-99 Emps.	100-249 Emps.	250-499 Emps.	500-999 Emps.	Unknown Emps.	
2015	475.2	252.3	374.7	606.1	436.0	850.0	1,243.6	1,575.4	71.9	5,885.1
2016	506.9	269.1	399.6	646.6	465.1	906.7	1,326.6	1,680.5	76.7	6,277.8
2017	537.7	285.5	423.9	685.8	493.3	961.7	1,407.1	1,782.4	81.3	6,658.6
2018	611.8	324.8	482.4	780.4	561.3	1,094.3	1,601.2	1,978.6	92.5	7,527.3
2018	679.5	360.8	535.8	866.7	623.4	1,215.5	1,778.4	2,159.6	102.8	8,322.5

INDUSTRY: DEPARTMENT STORES INDUSTRY (NAICS 45211)
PRODUCT LINE: UPHOLSTERED FURNITURE (Sub Category)

NAICS 45211: Department Stores Industry . this industry comprises establishments known as department stores primarily engaged in retailing a wide range of the following new products with no one merchandise line predominating: apparel, furniture, appliances and home furnishings; and selected additional items, such as paint, hardware, toiletries, cosmetics, photographic equipment, jewelry, toys, and sporting goods. merchandise lines are normally arranged in separate departments.

5-YEAR TREND — ESTIMATED INDUSTRY SALES ($MILLIONS)

Year	Employee Size of Establishment									Total Industry Sales
	1-4 Emps.	5-9 Emps.	10-19 Emps.	20-49 Emps.	50-99 Emps.	100-249 Emps.	250-499 Emps.	500-999 Emps.	Unknown Emps.	
2015	0.0	0.0	0.0	3.2	60.0	198.9	87.3	11.7	0.5	361.6
2016	0.0	0.0	0.0	3.2	60.8	201.5	88.4	11.8	0.5	366.3
2017	0.0	0.0	0.0	3.2	61.4	203.7	89.4	12.0	0.5	370.3
2018	0.0	0.0	0.0	3.2	61.7	204.6	89.8	12.0	0.5	372.0
2018	0.0	0.0	0.0	3.3	62.1	206.1	90.4	12.1	0.5	374.7

INDUSTRY: WAREHOUSE CLUBS & SUPERCENTERS (NAICS 45291)
PRODUCT LINE: UPHOLSTERED FURNITURE (Sub Category)

NAICS 45291: Warehouse Clubs and Superstores This industry comprises establishments known as warehouse clubs, superstores or supercenters primarily engaged in retailing a general line of groceries in combination with general lines of new merchandise, such as apparel, furniture, and appliances.

5-YEAR TREND — ESTIMATED INDUSTRY SALES ($MILLIONS)

Year	Employee Size of Establishment									Total Industry Sales
	1-4 Emps.	5-9 Emps.	10-19 Emps.	20-49 Emps.	50-99 Emps.	100-249 Emps.	250-499 Emps.	500-999 Emps.	Unknown Emps.	
2015	0.0	0.0	0.0	0.3	0.4	46.3	204.5	5.4	0.1	256.9
2016	0.0	0.0	0.0	0.3	0.4	47.9	211.9	5.6	0.1	266.3
2017	0.0	0.0	0.0	0.3	0.4	49.5	219.0	5.8	0.1	275.2
2018	0.0	0.0	0.0	0.3	0.4	53.8	237.9	6.3	0.1	298.9
2018	0.0	0.0	0.0	0.4	0.5	57.1	252.6	6.7	0.1	317.4

INDUSTRY: DEPARTMENT STORES INDUSTRY (NAICS 45211)
PRODUCT LINE: SLEEP SOFAS & FUTONS (Sub Category)

NAICS 45211: Department Stores Industry . this industry comprises establishments known as department stores primarily engaged in retailing a wide range of the following new products with no one merchandise line predominating: apparel, furniture, appliances and home furnishings; and selected additional items, such as paint, hardware, toiletries, cosmetics, photographic equipment, jewelry, toys, and sporting goods. merchandise lines are normally arranged in separate departments.

5-YEAR TREND — ESTIMATED INDUSTRY SALES ($MILLIONS)

Year	Employee Size of Establishment									Total Industry Sales
	1-4 Emps.	5-9 Emps.	10-19 Emps.	20-49 Emps.	50-99 Emps.	100-249 Emps.	250-499 Emps.	500-999 Emps.	Unknown Emps.	
2015	0.0	0.0	0.0	0.3	6.5	21.5	9.4	1.3	0.1	39.1
2016	0.0	0.0	0.0	0.3	6.6	21.8	9.6	1.3	0.1	39.6
2017	0.0	0.0	0.0	0.3	6.6	22.0	9.7	1.3	0.1	40.0
2018	0.0	0.0	0.0	0.4	6.7	22.1	9.7	1.3	0.1	40.2
2018	0.0	0.0	0.0	0.4	6.7	22.3	9.8	1.3	0.1	40.5

INDUSTRY: WAREHOUSE CLUBS & SUPERCENTERS (NAICS 45291)
PRODUCT LINE: SLEEP SOFAS & FUTONS (Sub Category)

NAICS 45291: Warehouse Clubs and Superstores This industry comprises establishments known as warehouse clubs, superstores or supercenters primarily engaged in retailing a general line of groceries in combination with general lines of new merchandise, such as apparel, furniture, and appliances.

5-Year Trend – Estimated Industry Sales ($Millions)

Year	Employee Size of Establishment									Total Industry Sales
	1-4 Emps.	5-9 Emps.	10-19 Emps.	20-49 Emps.	50-99 Emps.	100-249 Emps.	250-499 Emps.	500-999 Emps.	Unknown Emps.	
2015	0.0	0.0	0.0	0.2	0.3	36.5	161.3	4.3	0.1	202.6
2016	0.0	0.0	0.0	0.2	0.3	37.8	167.2	4.4	0.1	210.0
2017	0.0	0.0	0.0	0.3	0.3	39.1	172.7	4.6	0.1	217.0
2018	0.0	0.0	0.0	0.3	0.3	42.4	187.6	5.0	0.1	235.7
2018	0.0	0.0	0.0	0.3	0.4	45.1	199.3	5.3	0.1	250.3

INDUSTRY: DEPARTMENT STORES INDUSTRY (NAICS 45211)
PRODUCT LINE: MATTRESSES & SLEEP FURNITURE (Sub Category)

NAICS 45211: Department Stores Industry . this industry comprises establishments known as department stores primarily engaged in retailing a wide range of the following new products with no one merchandise line predominating: apparel, furniture, appliances and home furnishings; and selected additional items, such as paint, hardware, toiletries, cosmetics, photographic equipment, jewelry, toys, and sporting goods. merchandise lines are normally arranged in separate departments.

5-Year Trend – Estimated Industry Sales ($Millions)

Year	Employee Size of Establishment									Total Industry Sales
	1-4 Emps.	5-9 Emps.	10-19 Emps.	20-49 Emps.	50-99 Emps.	100-249 Emps.	250-499 Emps.	500-999 Emps.	Unknown Emps.	
2015	0.0	0.0	0.0	2.8	52.8	175.0	76.8	10.3	0.4	318.0
2016	0.0	0.0	0.0	2.8	53.4	177.2	77.7	10.4	0.5	322.2
2017	0.0	0.0	0.0	2.8	54.0	179.1	78.6	10.5	0.5	325.6
2018	0.0	0.0	0.0	2.9	54.3	180.0	78.9	10.6	0.5	327.1
2018	0.0	0.0	0.0	2.9	54.6	181.3	79.5	10.7	0.5	329.5

INDUSTRY: WAREHOUSE CLUBS & SUPERCENTERS (NAICS 45291)
PRODUCT LINE: MATTRESSES & SLEEP FURNITURE (Sub Category)

NAICS 45291: Warehouse Clubs and Superstores This industry comprises establishments known as warehouse clubs, superstores or supercenters primarily engaged in retailing a general line of groceries in combination with general lines of new merchandise, such as apparel, furniture, and appliances.

5-YEAR TREND – ESTIMATED INDUSTRY SALES ($MILLIONS)

Year	Employee Size of Establishment									Total Industry Sales
	1-4 Emps.	5-9 Emps.	10-19 Emps.	20-49 Emps.	50-99 Emps.	100-249 Emps.	250-499 Emps.	500-999 Emps.	Unknown Emps.	
2015	0.2	0.0	0.0	2.0	2.5	312.2	1,380.3	36.5	0.4	1,734.2
2016	0.2	0.0	0.0	2.1	2.6	323.6	1,430.7	37.8	0.4	1,797.6
2017	0.2	0.0	0.0	2.1	2.7	334.4	1,478.5	39.1	0.5	1,857.5
2018	0.3	0.0	0.0	2.3	2.9	363.2	1,605.8	42.4	0.5	2,017.5
2018	0.3	0.0	0.0	2.5	3.1	385.7	1,705.3	45.1	0.5	2,142.6

INDUSTRY: DEPARTMENT STORES INDUSTRY (NAICS 45211)
PRODUCT LINE: OTHER HOME FURNITURE (Sub Category)

NAICS 45211: Department Stores Industry . this industry comprises establishments known as department stores primarily engaged in retailing a wide range of the following new products with no one merchandise line predominating: apparel, furniture, appliances and home furnishings; and selected additional items, such as paint, hardware, toiletries, cosmetics, photographic equipment, jewelry, toys, and sporting goods. merchandise lines are normally arranged in separate departments.

5-YEAR TREND – ESTIMATED INDUSTRY SALES ($MILLIONS)

Year	Employee Size of Establishment									Total Industry Sales
	1-4 Emps.	5-9 Emps.	10-19 Emps.	20-49 Emps.	50-99 Emps.	100-249 Emps.	250-499 Emps.	500-999 Emps.	Unknown Emps.	
2015	0.0	0.0	0.1	5.3	100.3	332.6	145.9	19.5	0.8	604.7
2016	0.0	0.0	0.1	5.4	101.6	336.9	147.8	19.8	0.9	612.5
2017	0.0	0.0	0.1	5.4	102.7	340.6	149.4	20.0	0.9	619.1
2018	0.0	0.0	0.1	5.4	103.2	342.1	150.1	20.1	0.9	622.0
2018	0.0	0.0	0.1	5.5	103.9	344.6	151.2	20.3	0.9	626.4

INDUSTRY: WAREHOUSE CLUBS & SUPERCENTERS (NAICS 45291)
PRODUCT LINE: OTHER HOME FURNITURE (Sub Category)

NAICS 45291: Warehouse Clubs and Superstores This industry comprises establishments known as warehouse clubs, superstores or supercenters primarily engaged in retailing a general line of groceries in combination with general lines of new merchandise, such as apparel, furniture, and appliances.

5-YEAR TREND – ESTIMATED INDUSTRY SALES ($MILLIONS)

Year	Employee Size of Establishment									Total
	1-4 Emps.	5-9 Emps.	10-19 Emps.	20-49 Emps.	50-99 Emps.	100-249 Emps.	250-499 Emps.	500-999 Emps.	Unknown Emps.	Industry Sales
2015	0.1	0.0	0.0	0.7	0.9	106.6	471.1	12.4	0.1	591.9
2016	0.1	0.0	0.0	0.7	0.9	110.5	488.3	12.9	0.2	613.6
2017	0.1	0.0	0.0	0.7	0.9	114.1	504.6	13.3	0.2	634.0
2018	0.1	0.0	0.0	0.8	1.0	124.0	548.1	14.5	0.2	688.6
2018	0.1	0.0	0.0	0.8	1.1	131.7	582.1	15.4	0.2	731.3

INDUSTRY: DEPARTMENT STORES INDUSTRY (NAICS 45211)
PRODUCT LINE: OTHER OFFICE FURNITURE (Sub Category)

NAICS 45211: Department Stores Industry . this industry comprises establishments known as department stores primarily engaged in retailing a wide range of the following new products with no one merchandise line predominating: apparel, furniture, appliances and home furnishings; and selected additional items, such as paint, hardware, toiletries, cosmetics, photographic equipment, jewelry, toys, and sporting goods. merchandise lines are normally arranged in separate departments.

5-YEAR TREND – ESTIMATED INDUSTRY SALES ($MILLIONS)

Year	Employee Size of Establishment									Total
	1-4 Emps.	5-9 Emps.	10-19 Emps.	20-49 Emps.	50-99 Emps.	100-249 Emps.	250-499 Emps.	500-999 Emps.	Unknown Emps.	Industry Sales
2015	0.1	0.0	0.1	11.2	213.5	708.2	310.7	41.6	1.8	1,287.3
2016	0.1	0.0	0.1	11.4	216.3	717.3	314.7	42.1	1.8	1,303.9
2017	0.1	0.0	0.1	11.5	218.6	725.1	318.1	42.6	1.8	1,318.0
2018	0.1	0.0	0.1	11.6	219.6	728.4	319.6	42.8	1.9	1,324.1
2018	0.1	0.0	0.1	11.7	221.2	733.7	321.9	43.2	1.9	1,333.7

INDUSTRY: WAREHOUSE CLUBS & SUPERCENTERS (NAICS 45291)
PRODUCT LINE: OTHER OFFICE FURNITURE (Sub Category)

NAICS 45291: Warehouse Clubs and Superstores This industry comprises establishments known as warehouse clubs, superstores or supercenters primarily engaged in retailing a general line of groceries in combination with general lines of new merchandise, such as apparel, furniture, and appliances.

5-YEAR TREND – ESTIMATED INDUSTRY SALES ($MILLIONS)

Year	1-4 Emps.	5-9 Emps.	10-19 Emps.	20-49 Emps.	50-99 Emps.	100-249 Emps.	250-499 Emps.	500-999 Emps.	Unknown Emps.	Total Industry Sales
2015	0.5	0.0	0.1	5.1	6.4	795.7	3,517.9	92.9	1.1	4,419.9
2016	0.6	0.0	0.1	5.3	6.7	824.8	3,646.5	96.3	1.1	4,581.5
2017	0.6	0.0	0.1	5.5	6.9	852.3	3,768.0	99.6	1.2	4,734.2
2018	0.6	0.0	0.1	6.0	7.5	925.7	4,092.6	108.1	1.3	5,141.9
2018	0.7	0.0	0.1	6.3	8.0	983.1	4,346.3	114.8	1.4	5,460.7

INDUSTRY: HOME CENTERS INDUSTRY (NAICS 44411)
PRODUCT LINE: FLOORING & COVERINGS (Main Category)

NAICS 44411: Home Centers. This industry comprises establishments known as home centers primarily engaged in retailing a general line of new home repair and improvement materials and supplies, such as lumber, plumbing goods, electrical goods, tools, housewares, hardware, and lawn and garden supplies, with no one merchandise line predominating. The merchandise lines are normally arranged in separate departments.

5-YEAR TREND – ESTIMATED INDUSTRY SALES ($MILLIONS)

Year	1-4 Emps.	5-9 Emps.	10-19 Emps.	20-49 Emps.	50-99 Emps.	100-249 Emps.	250-499 Emps.	500-999 Emps.	Unknown Emps.	Total Industry Sales
2015	16.4	32.6	84.7	169.2	124.2	8,127.9	718.8	13.3	5.7	9,292.9
2016	16.9	33.6	87.5	174.8	128.3	8,396.0	742.5	13.7	5.9	9,599.4
2017	17.4	34.6	90.1	180.0	132.2	8,647.8	764.8	14.2	6.0	9,887.3
2018	18.3	36.4	94.7	189.2	138.9	9,088.4	803.8	14.9	6.3	10,391.0
2018	19.3	38.3	99.8	199.2	146.3	9,571.1	846.5	15.7	6.7	10,942.9

INDUSTRY: HARDWARE STORES (NAICS 44413)
PRODUCT LINE: FLOORING & COVERINGS (Main Category)

NAICS 44413: Hardware Stores. Establishments primarily engaged
in the retail sale of a number of basic hardware lines, such as tools,
builders' hardware, paint and glass, housewares and household appliances,
and cutlery.

5-YEAR TREND – ESTIMATED INDUSTRY SALES ($MILLIONS)

Year	Employee Size of Establishment									Total Industry Sales
	1-4 Emps.	5-9 Emps.	10-19 Emps.	20-49 Emps.	50-99 Emps.	100-249 Emps.	250-499 Emps.	500-999 Emps.	Unknown Emps.	
2015	6.7	10.7	21.4	30.0	5.5	1.3	0.4	0.0	0.6	76.4
2016	6.8	10.9	21.8	30.5	5.6	1.3	0.4	0.0	0.6	77.9
2017	6.9	11.1	22.2	31.0	5.7	1.3	0.4	0.0	0.6	79.2
2018	7.2	11.6	23.2	32.5	5.9	1.4	0.4	0.0	0.6	82.9
2018	7.6	12.2	24.3	34.1	6.2	1.5	0.4	0.0	0.6	86.9

INDUSTRY: DEPARTMENT STORES INDUSTRY (NAICS 45211)
PRODUCT LINE: FLOORING & COVERINGS (Main Category)

NAICS 45211: Department Stores Industry . this industry comprises
establishments known as department stores primarily engaged in retailing
a wide range of the following new products with no one merchandise line
predominating: apparel, furniture, appliances and home furnishings; and
selected additional items, such as paint, hardware, toiletries, cosmetics,
photographic equipment, jewelry, toys, and sporting goods. merchandise lines
are normally arranged in separate departments.

5-YEAR TREND – ESTIMATED INDUSTRY SALES ($MILLIONS)

Year	Employee Size of Establishment									Total Industry Sales
	1-4 Emps.	5-9 Emps.	10-19 Emps.	20-49 Emps.	50-99 Emps.	100-249 Emps.	250-499 Emps.	500-999 Emps.	Unknown Emps.	
2015	0.0	0.0	0.0	3.6	68.4	227.0	99.6	13.3	0.6	412.6
2016	0.0	0.0	0.0	3.7	69.3	229.9	100.9	13.5	0.6	417.9
2017	0.0	0.0	0.0	3.7	70.1	232.4	101.9	13.7	0.6	422.4
2018	0.0	0.0	0.0	3.7	70.4	233.5	102.4	13.7	0.6	424.4
2018	0.0	0.0	0.0	3.7	70.9	235.1	103.2	13.8	0.6	427.4

INDUSTRY: WAREHOUSE CLUBS & SUPERCENTERS (NAICS 45291)
PRODUCT LINE: FLOORING & COVERINGS (Main Category)

NAICS 45291: Warehouse Clubs and Superstores This industry comprises establishments known as warehouse clubs, superstores or supercenters primarily engaged in retailing a general line of groceries in combination with general lines of new merchandise, such as apparel, furniture, and appliances.

5-YEAR TREND — ESTIMATED INDUSTRY SALES ($MILLIONS)

Year	Employee Size of Establishment									Total
	1-4 Emps.	5-9 Emps.	10-19 Emps.	20-49 Emps.	50-99 Emps.	100-249 Emps.	250-499 Emps.	500-999 Emps.	Unknown Emps.	Industry Sales
2015	0.0	0.0	0.0	0.1	0.1	15.9	70.3	1.9	0.0	88.3
2016	0.0	0.0	0.0	0.1	0.1	16.5	72.9	1.9	0.0	91.6
2017	0.0	0.0	0.0	0.1	0.1	17.0	75.3	2.0	0.0	94.6
2018	0.0	0.0	0.0	0.1	0.1	18.5	81.8	2.2	0.0	102.8
2018	0.0	0.0	0.0	0.1	0.2	19.7	86.9	2.3	0.0	109.1

INDUSTRY: ELECTRONIC SHOPPING & MAIL-ORDER (NAICS 45411)
PRODUCT LINE: FLOORING & COVERINGS (Main Category)

NAICS 45411: Electronic Shopping and Mail-Order Houses This industry comprises establishments primarily engaged in retailing all types of merchandise by means of mail or by electronic media, such as interactive television or computer. Included in this industry are establishments primarily engaged in retailing from catalogue showrooms of mail-order houses.

5-YEAR TREND — ESTIMATED INDUSTRY SALES ($MILLIONS)

Year	Employee Size of Establishment									Total
	1-4 Emps.	5-9 Emps.	10-19 Emps.	20-49 Emps.	50-99 Emps.	100-249 Emps.	250-499 Emps.	500-999 Emps.	Unknown Emps.	Industry Sales
2015	82.1	43.6	64.7	104.7	75.3	146.8	214.9	272.2	12.4	1,016.7
2016	87.6	46.5	69.0	111.7	80.3	156.6	229.2	290.3	13.2	1,084.6
2017	92.9	49.3	73.2	118.5	85.2	166.1	243.1	307.9	14.0	1,150.4
2018	105.7	56.1	83.3	134.8	97.0	189.1	276.6	341.8	16.0	1,300.5
2018	117.4	62.3	92.6	149.7	107.7	210.0	307.2	373.1	17.8	1,437.8

INDUSTRY: HOME CENTERS INDUSTRY (NAICS 44411)
PRODUCT LINE: SOFT FLOOR COVERINGS (Sub Category)

NAICS 44411: Home Centers. This industry comprises establishments
known as home centers primarily engaged in retailing a general line of
new home repair and improvement materials and supplies, such as
lumber, plumbing goods, electrical goods, tools, housewares, hardware,
and lawn and garden supplies, with no one merchandise line predominating.
The merchandise lines are normally arranged in separate departments.

5-YEAR TREND – ESTIMATED INDUSTRY SALES ($MILLIONS)

Year	1-4 Emps.	5-9 Emps.	10-19 Emps.	20-49 Emps.	50-99 Emps.	100-249 Emps.	250-499 Emps.	500-999 Emps.	Unknown Emps.	Total Industry Sales
2015	5.8	11.6	30.1	60.1	44.1	2,888.2	255.4	4.7	2.0	3,302.2
2016	6.0	12.0	31.1	62.1	45.6	2,983.5	263.9	4.9	2.1	3,411.1
2017	6.2	12.3	32.0	64.0	47.0	3,073.0	271.8	5.0	2.1	3,513.4
2018	6.5	12.9	33.7	67.2	49.4	3,229.5	285.6	5.3	2.3	3,692.4
2018	6.9	13.6	35.5	70.8	52.0	3,401.0	300.8	5.6	2.4	3,888.5

INDUSTRY: HOME CENTERS INDUSTRY (NAICS 44413)
PRODUCT LINE: SOFT FLOOR COVERINGS (Sub Category)

NAICS 44411: Home Centers. This industry comprises establishments
known as home centers primarily engaged in retailing a general line of
new home repair and improvement materials and supplies, such as
lumber, plumbing goods, electrical goods, tools, housewares, hardware,
and lawn and garden supplies, with no one merchandise line predominating.
The merchandise lines are normally arranged in separate departments.

5-YEAR TREND – ESTIMATED INDUSTRY SALES ($MILLIONS)

Year	1-4 Emps.	5-9 Emps.	10-19 Emps.	20-49 Emps.	50-99 Emps.	100-249 Emps.	250-499 Emps.	500-999 Emps.	Unknown Emps.	Total Industry Sales
2015	2.5	4.0	8.0	11.2	2.0	0.5	0.1	0.0	0.2	28.5
2016	2.5	4.1	8.1	11.4	2.1	0.5	0.1	0.0	0.2	29.0
2017	2.6	4.1	8.3	11.6	2.1	0.5	0.1	0.0	0.2	29.5
2018	2.7	4.3	8.6	12.1	2.2	0.5	0.1	0.0	0.2	30.9
2018	2.8	4.5	9.1	12.7	2.3	0.5	0.2	0.0	0.2	32.4

INDUSTRY: DEPARTMENT STORES INDUSTRY (NAICS 45211)
PRODUCT LINE: SOFT FLOOR COVERINGS (Sub Category)

NAICS 45211: Department Stores Industry . this industry comprises establishments known as department stores primarily engaged in retailing a wide range of the following new products with no one merchandise line predominating: apparel, furniture, appliances and home furnishings; and selected additional items, such as paint, hardware, toiletries, cosmetics, photographic equipment, jewelry, toys, and sporting goods. merchandise lines are normally arranged in separate departments.

5-YEAR TREND – ESTIMATED INDUSTRY SALES ($MILLIONS)

| Year | \multicolumn{9}{c}{Employee Size of Establishment} | Total |
	1-4 Emps.	5-9 Emps.	10-19 Emps.	20-49 Emps.	50-99 Emps.	100-249 Emps.	250-499 Emps.	500-999 Emps.	Unknown Emps.	Industry Sales
2015	0.0	0.0	0.0	3.5	66.6	220.8	96.9	13.0	0.6	401.4
2016	0.0	0.0	0.0	3.6	67.4	223.7	98.1	13.1	0.6	406.6
2017	0.0	0.0	0.0	3.6	68.2	226.1	99.2	13.3	0.6	411.0
2018	0.0	0.0	0.0	3.6	68.5	227.1	99.6	13.4	0.6	412.9
2018	0.0	0.0	0.0	3.6	69.0	228.8	100.4	13.5	0.6	415.9

INDUSTRY: WAREHOUSE CLUBS & SUPERCENTERS (NAICS 45291)
PRODUCT LINE: SOFT FLOOR COVERINGS (Sub Category)

NAICS 45291: Warehouse Clubs and Superstores This industry comprises establishments known as warehouse clubs, superstores or supercenters primarily engaged in retailing a general line of groceries in combination with general lines of new merchandise, such as apparel, furniture, and appliances.

5-YEAR TREND – ESTIMATED INDUSTRY SALES ($MILLIONS)

| Year | \multicolumn{9}{c}{Employee Size of Establishment} | Total |
	1-4 Emps.	5-9 Emps.	10-19 Emps.	20-49 Emps.	50-99 Emps.	100-249 Emps.	250-499 Emps.	500-999 Emps.	Unknown Emps.	Industry Sales
2015	0.0	0.0	0.0	0.1	0.1	14.8	65.2	1.7	0.0	82.0
2016	0.0	0.0	0.0	0.1	0.1	15.3	67.6	1.8	0.0	85.0
2017	0.0	0.0	0.0	0.1	0.1	15.8	69.9	1.8	0.0	87.8
2018	0.0	0.0	0.0	0.1	0.1	17.2	75.9	2.0	0.0	95.3
2018	0.0	0.0	0.0	0.1	0.1	18.2	80.6	2.1	0.0	101.3

INDUSTRY: HOME CENTERS INDUSTRY (NAICS 44411)
PRODUCT LINE: HARDWOOD FLOORING (Sub Category)

NAICS 44411: Home Centers. This industry comprises establishments
known as home centers primarily engaged in retailing a general line of
new home repair and improvement materials and supplies, such as
lumber, plumbing goods, electrical goods, tools, housewares, hardware,
and lawn and garden supplies, with no one merchandise line predominating.
The merchandise lines are normally arranged in separate departments.

5-YEAR TREND — ESTIMATED INDUSTRY SALES ($MILLIONS)

| Year | Employee Size of Establishment | | | | | | | | | Total |
	1-4 Emps.	5-9 Emps.	10-19 Emps.	20-49 Emps.	50-99 Emps.	100-249 Emps.	250-499 Emps.	500-999 Emps.	Unknown Emps.	Industry Sales
2015	0.9	1.8	4.7	9.5	7.0	455.5	40.3	0.7	0.3	520.8
2016	0.9	1.9	4.9	9.8	7.2	470.5	41.6	0.8	0.3	538.0
2017	1.0	1.9	5.1	10.1	7.4	484.7	42.9	0.8	0.3	554.1
2018	1.0	2.0	5.3	10.6	7.8	509.4	45.0	0.8	0.4	582.4
2018	1.1	2.1	5.6	11.2	8.2	536.4	47.4	0.9	0.4	613.3

INDUSTRY: HARDWARE STORES INDUSTRY (NAICS 44413)
PRODUCT LINE: HARDWOOD FLOORING (Sub Category)

NAICS 44413: Hardware Stores. Establishments primarily engaged
in the retail sale of a number of basic hardware lines, such as tools,
builders' hardware, paint and glass, housewares and household appliances,
and cutlery.

5-YEAR TREND — ESTIMATED INDUSTRY SALES ($MILLIONS)

| Year | Employee Size of Establishment | | | | | | | | | Total |
	1-4 Emps.	5-9 Emps.	10-19 Emps.	20-49 Emps.	50-99 Emps.	100-249 Emps.	250-499 Emps.	500-999 Emps.	Unknown Emps.	Industry Sales
2015	0.7	1.2	2.4	3.3	0.6	0.1	0.0	0.0	0.1	8.5
2016	0.8	1.2	2.4	3.4	0.6	0.1	0.0	0.0	0.1	8.7
2017	0.8	1.2	2.5	3.5	0.6	0.1	0.0	0.0	0.1	8.8
2018	0.8	1.3	2.6	3.6	0.7	0.2	0.0	0.0	0.1	9.3
2018	0.8	1.4	2.7	3.8	0.7	0.2	0.0	0.0	0.1	9.7

INDUSTRY: HOME CENTERS INDUSTRY (NAICS 44411)
PRODUCT LINE: OTHER HARD FLOORING (Sub Category)

NAICS 44411: Home Centers. This industry comprises establishments known as home centers primarily engaged in retailing a general line of new home repair and improvement materials and supplies, such as lumber, plumbing goods, electrical goods, tools, housewares, hardware, and lawn and garden supplies, with no one merchandise line predominating. The merchandise lines are normally arranged in separate departments.

5-YEAR TREND — ESTIMATED INDUSTRY SALES ($MILLIONS)

Year	Employee Size of Establishment									Total Industry Sales
	1-4 Emps.	5-9 Emps.	10-19 Emps.	20-49 Emps.	50-99 Emps.	100-249 Emps.	250-499 Emps.	500-999 Emps.	Unknown Emps.	
2015	9.7	19.2	49.9	99.6	73.1	4,784.2	423.1	7.8	3.3	5,469.9
2016	10.0	19.8	51.5	102.9	75.5	4,942.0	437.1	8.1	3.4	5,650.3
2017	10.3	20.4	53.1	106.0	77.8	5,090.2	450.2	8.3	3.6	5,819.8
2018	10.8	21.4	55.8	111.4	81.8	5,349.5	473.1	8.8	3.7	6,116.3
2018	11.4	22.6	58.7	117.3	86.1	5,633.7	498.2	9.2	3.9	6,441.1

INDUSTRY: HARDWARE STORES INDUSTRY (NAICS 44413)
PRODUCT LINE: OTHER HARD FLOORING (Sub Category)

NAICS 44413: Hardware Stores. Establishments primarily engaged in the retail sale of a number of basic hardware lines, such as tools, builders' hardware, paint and glass, housewares and household appliances, and cutlery.

5-YEAR TREND — ESTIMATED INDUSTRY SALES ($MILLIONS)

Year	Employee Size of Establishment									Total Industry Sales
	1-4 Emps.	5-9 Emps.	10-19 Emps.	20-49 Emps.	50-99 Emps.	100-249 Emps.	250-499 Emps.	500-999 Emps.	Unknown Emps.	
2015	3.4	5.5	11.0	15.4	2.8	0.7	0.2	0.0	0.3	39.4
2016	3.5	5.6	11.2	15.7	2.9	0.7	0.2	0.0	0.3	40.1
2017	3.6	5.7	11.4	16.0	2.9	0.7	0.2	0.0	0.3	40.8
2018	3.7	6.0	11.9	16.7	3.1	0.7	0.2	0.0	0.3	42.7
2018	3.9	6.3	12.5	17.5	3.2	0.8	0.2	0.0	0.3	44.8

INDUSTRY: DEPARTMENT STORES INDUSTRY (NAICS 45211)
PRODUCT LINE: OTHER HARD FLOORING (Sub Category)

NAICS 45211: Department Stores Industry . this industry comprises
establishments known as department stores primarily engaged in retailing
a wide range of the following new products with no one merchandise line
predominating: apparel, furniture, appliances and home furnishings; and
selected additional items, such as paint, hardware, toiletries, cosmetics,
photographic equipment, jewelry, toys, and sporting goods. merchandise lines
are normally arranged in separate departments.

5-YEAR TREND – ESTIMATED INDUSTRY SALES ($MILLIONS)

Year	Employee Size of Establishment									Total
	1-4 Emps.	5-9 Emps.	10-19 Emps.	20-49 Emps.	50-99 Emps.	100-249 Emps.	250-499 Emps.	500-999 Emps.	Unknown Emps.	Industry Sales
2015	0.0	0.0	0.0	0.0	0.7	2.4	1.0	0.1	0.0	4.3
2016	0.0	0.0	0.0	0.0	0.7	2.4	1.1	0.1	0.0	4.4
2017	0.0	0.0	0.0	0.0	0.7	2.4	1.1	0.1	0.0	4.4
2018	0.0	0.0	0.0	0.0	0.7	2.4	1.1	0.1	0.0	4.4
2018	0.0	0.0	0.0	0.0	0.7	2.5	1.1	0.1	0.0	4.5

INDUSTRY: HOME CENTERS INDUSTRY (NAICS 44411)
PRODUCT LINE: COMPUTER HARDWARE & SOFTWARE (Main Category)

NAICS 44411: Home Centers. This industry comprises establishments
known as home centers primarily engaged in retailing a general line of
new home repair and improvement materials and supplies, such as
lumber, plumbing goods, electrical goods, tools, housewares, hardware,
and lawn and garden supplies, with no one merchandise line predominating.
The merchandise lines are normally arranged in separate departments.

5-YEAR TREND – ESTIMATED INDUSTRY SALES ($MILLIONS)

Year	Employee Size of Establishment									Total
	1-4 Emps.	5-9 Emps.	10-19 Emps.	20-49 Emps.	50-99 Emps.	100-249 Emps.	250-499 Emps.	500-999 Emps.	Unknown Emps.	Industry Sales
2015	1.1	2.1	5.6	11.1	8.2	535.5	47.4	0.9	0.4	612.2
2016	1.1	2.2	5.8	11.5	8.5	553.1	48.9	0.9	0.4	632.4
2017	1.1	2.3	5.9	11.9	8.7	569.7	50.4	0.9	0.4	651.4
2018	1.2	2.4	6.2	12.5	9.2	598.7	53.0	1.0	0.4	684.5
2018	1.3	2.5	6.6	13.1	9.6	630.5	55.8	1.0	0.4	720.9

INDUSTRY: PRERECORDED TAPES/CDs STORES (NAICS 45122)
PRODUCT LINE: COMPUTER HARDWARE & SOFTWARE (Main Category)

NAICS 45122: Prerecorded Tape, Compact Disc, and Record Stores .
This industry comprises establishments primarily engaged in retailing new
prerecorded audio and video tapes, compact discs (CDs), and phonograph
records.

5-YEAR TREND – ESTIMATED INDUSTRY SALES ($MILLIONS)

Year	Employee Size of Establishment									Total Industry Sales
	1-4 Emps.	5-9 Emps.	10-19 Emps.	20-49 Emps.	50-99 Emps.	100-249 Emps.	250-499 Emps.	500-999 Emps.	Unknown Emps.	
2015	2.8	5.6	14.7	29.3	21.5	1,407.8	124.5	2.3	1.0	1,609.6
2016	2.9	5.8	15.2	30.3	22.2	1,454.2	128.6	2.4	1.0	1,662.7
2017	3.0	6.0	15.6	31.2	22.9	1,497.9	132.5	2.5	1.0	1,712.5
2018	3.2	6.3	16.4	32.8	24.1	1,574.2	139.2	2.6	1.1	1,799.8
2018	3.3	6.6	17.3	34.5	25.3	1,657.8	146.6	2.7	1.2	1,895.4

INDUSTRY: DEPARTMENT STORES INDUSTRY (NAICS 45211)
PRODUCT LINE: COMPUTER HARDWARE & SOFTWARE (Main Category)

NAICS 45211: Department Stores Industry . this industry comprises
establishments known as department stores primarily engaged in retailing
a wide range of the following new products with no one merchandise line
predominating: apparel, furniture, appliances and home furnishings; and
selected additional items, such as paint, hardware, toiletries, cosmetics,
photographic equipment, jewelry, toys, and sporting goods. merchandise lines
are normally arranged in separate departments.

5-YEAR TREND – ESTIMATED INDUSTRY SALES ($MILLIONS)

Year	Employee Size of Establishment									Total Industry Sales
	1-4 Emps.	5-9 Emps.	10-19 Emps.	20-49 Emps.	50-99 Emps.	100-249 Emps.	250-499 Emps.	500-999 Emps.	Unknown Emps.	
2015	0.0	0.0	0.1	4.9	93.4	309.9	136.0	18.2	0.8	563.3
2016	0.0	0.0	0.1	5.0	94.6	313.9	137.7	18.4	0.8	570.6
2017	0.0	0.0	0.1	5.0	95.7	317.3	139.2	18.6	0.8	576.7
2018	0.0	0.0	0.1	5.1	96.1	318.7	139.8	18.7	0.8	579.4
2018	0.0	0.0	0.1	5.1	96.8	321.0	140.8	18.9	0.8	583.6

INDUSTRY: WAREHOUSE CLUBS & SUPERCENTERS (NAICS 45291)
PRODUCT LINE: COMPUTER HARDWARE & SOFTWARE (Main Category)

NAICS 45291: Warehouse Clubs and Superstores This industry comprises establishments known as warehouse clubs, superstores or supercenters primarily engaged in retailing a general line of groceries in combination with general lines of new merchandise, such as apparel, furniture, and appliances.

5-YEAR TREND — ESTIMATED INDUSTRY SALES ($MILLIONS)

Year	Employee Size of Establishment									Total Industry Sales
	1-4 Emps.	5-9 Emps.	10-19 Emps.	20-49 Emps.	50-99 Emps.	100-249 Emps.	250-499 Emps.	500-999 Emps.	Unknown Emps.	
2015	1.1	0.0	0.2	10.3	13.0	1,608.4	7,110.5	187.9	2.2	8,933.7
2016	1.2	0.0	0.2	10.7	13.5	1,667.2	7,370.4	194.7	2.3	9,260.3
2017	1.2	0.0	0.2	11.1	14.0	1,722.8	7,616.2	201.2	2.4	9,569.0
2018	1.3	0.0	0.2	12.0	15.2	1,871.2	8,272.1	218.6	2.6	10,393.1
2018	1.4	0.0	0.2	12.8	16.1	1,987.2	8,785.0	232.1	2.7	11,037.5

INDUSTRY: OFFICE SUPPLY & STATIONERY STORES (NAICS 45321)
PRODUCT LINE: COMPUTER HARDWARE & SOFTWARE (Main Category)

NAICS 45321: Office Supplies and Stationery Stores . this industry comprises establishments primarily engaged in one or more of the following: (1) retailing new stationery, school supplies, and office supplies; (2) selling a combination of new office equipment, furniture, and supplies; and (3) selling new office equipment, furniture, and supplies in combination with selling new computers.

5-YEAR TREND — ESTIMATED INDUSTRY SALES ($MILLIONS)

Year	Employee Size of Establishment									Total Industry Sales
	1-4 Emps.	5-9 Emps.	10-19 Emps.	20-49 Emps.	50-99 Emps.	100-249 Emps.	250-499 Emps.	500-999 Emps.	Unknown Emps.	
2015	107.1	80.1	424.4	1,196.3	29.0	28.8	0.1	0.7	22.4	1,889.1
2016	107.2	80.2	424.7	1,197.1	29.1	28.9	0.1	0.7	22.4	1,890.4
2017	107.1	80.1	424.1	1,195.6	29.0	28.8	0.1	0.7	22.4	1,888.0
2018	104.6	78.3	414.5	1,168.4	28.4	28.2	0.1	0.7	21.9	1,845.2
2018	102.5	76.7	406.1	1,144.9	27.8	27.6	0.1	0.7	21.4	1,807.9

INDUSTRY: ELECTRONIC SHOPPING & MAIL-ORDER (NAICS 45411)
PRODUCT LINE: COMPUTER HARDWARE & SOFTWARE (Main Category)

NAICS 45411: Electronic Shopping and Mail-Order Houses This industry comprises establishments primarily engaged in retailing all types of merchandise by means of mail or by electronic media, such as interactive television or computer. Included in this industry are establishments primarily engaged in retailing from catalogue showrooms of mail-order houses.

5-YEAR TREND — ESTIMATED INDUSTRY SALES ($MILLIONS)

Year	Employee Size of Establishment									Total Industry Sales
	1-4 Emps.	5-9 Emps.	10-19 Emps.	20-49 Emps.	50-99 Emps.	100-249 Emps.	250-499 Emps.	500-999 Emps.	Unknown Emps.	
2015	5,185.9	2,753.3	4,088.6	6,614.5	4,757.8	9,275.8	13,571.7	17,192.1	784.3	64,223.9
2016	5,531.9	2,937.0	4,361.4	7,055.9	5,075.2	9,894.6	14,477.2	18,339.1	836.6	68,508.8
2017	5,867.5	3,115.2	4,626.0	7,483.9	5,383.1	10,494.9	15,355.5	19,451.8	887.3	72,665.3
2018	6,676.7	3,544.8	5,264.0	8,516.1	6,125.6	11,942.4	17,473.3	21,591.9	1,009.7	82,144.5
2018	7,415.8	3,937.2	5,846.6	9,458.8	6,803.6	13,264.3	19,407.5	23,567.3	1,121.5	90,822.5

INDUSTRY: BOOK STORES INDUSTRY (NAICS 451211)
PRODUCT LINE: COMPUTER HARDWARE & SOFTWARE (Main Category)

NAICS 451211: Book Stores. this industry comprises establishments primarily engaged in the retail sale of new books and magazines. Establishments primarily engaged in the retail sale of used books are classified in 5932.

5-YEAR TREND — ESTIMATED INDUSTRY SALES ($MILLIONS)

Year	Employee Size of Establishment									Total Industry Sales
	1-4 Emps.	5-9 Emps.	10-19 Emps.	20-49 Emps.	50-99 Emps.	100-249 Emps.	250-499 Emps.	500-999 Emps.	Unknown Emps.	
2015	3.9	5.9	12.2	32.0	14.4	5.7	1.0	3.8	2.0	80.9
2016	4.1	6.2	12.9	33.7	15.2	6.0	1.1	4.0	2.1	85.4
2017	4.3	6.5	13.5	35.4	16.0	6.3	1.1	4.2	2.2	89.6
2018	4.3	6.6	13.6	35.7	16.1	6.3	1.2	4.3	2.2	90.3
2018	4.3	6.6	13.7	36.0	16.2	6.4	1.2	4.5	2.2	91.1

INDUSTRY: DEPARTMENT STORES INDUSTRY (NAICS 45211)
PRODUCT LINE: COMPUTER HARDWARE & PERIPHERALS (Sub Category)

NAICS 45211: Department Stores Industry . this industry comprises establishments known as department stores primarily engaged in retailing a wide range of the following new products with no one merchandise line predominating: apparel, furniture, appliances and home furnishings; and selected additional items, such as paint, hardware, toiletries, cosmetics, photographic equipment, jewelry, toys, and sporting goods. merchandise lines are normally arranged in separate departments.

5-YEAR TREND – ESTIMATED INDUSTRY SALES ($MILLIONS)

Year	Employee Size of Establishment									Total
	1-4 Emps.	5-9 Emps.	10-19 Emps.	20-49 Emps.	50-99 Emps.	100-249 Emps.	250-499 Emps.	500-999 Emps.	Unknown Emps.	Industry Sales
2015	0.0	0.0	0.0	3.6	68.9	228.4	100.2	13.4	0.6	415.1
2016	0.0	0.0	0.0	3.7	69.7	231.3	101.5	13.6	0.6	420.5
2017	0.0	0.0	0.0	3.7	70.5	233.8	102.6	13.7	0.6	425.0
2018	0.0	0.0	0.0	3.7	70.8	234.9	103.1	13.8	0.6	427.0
2018	0.0	0.0	0.0	3.8	71.3	236.6	103.8	13.9	0.6	430.1

INDUSTRY: WAREHOUSE CLUBS & SUPERCENTERS (NAICS 45291)
PRODUCT LINE: COMPUTER HARDWARE & PERIPHERALS (Sub Category)

NAICS 45291: Warehouse Clubs and Superstores This industry comprises establishments known as warehouse clubs, superstores or supercenters primarily engaged in retailing a general line of groceries in combination with general lines of new merchandise, such as apparel, furniture, and appliances.

5-YEAR TREND – ESTIMATED INDUSTRY SALES ($MILLIONS)

Year	Employee Size of Establishment									Total
	1-4 Emps.	5-9 Emps.	10-19 Emps.	20-49 Emps.	50-99 Emps.	100-249 Emps.	250-499 Emps.	500-999 Emps.	Unknown Emps.	Industry Sales
2015	0.8	0.0	0.1	7.0	8.9	1,093.5	4,834.2	127.7	1.5	6,073.7
2016	0.8	0.0	0.1	7.3	9.2	1,133.5	5,010.9	132.4	1.6	6,295.8
2017	0.8	0.0	0.1	7.5	9.5	1,171.3	5,178.0	136.8	1.6	6,505.7
2018	0.9	0.0	0.2	8.2	10.3	1,272.1	5,623.9	148.6	1.8	7,066.0
2018	0.9	0.0	0.2	8.7	10.9	1,351.0	5,972.6	157.8	1.9	7,504.0

INDUSTRY: ELECTRONIC SHOPPING & MAIL-ORDER (NAICS 45411)
PRODUCT LINE: COMPUTER HARDWARE & PERIPHERALS (Sub Category)

NAICS 45411: Electronic Shopping and Mail-Order Houses This industry comprises establishments primarily engaged in retailing all types of merchandise by means of mail or by electronic media, such as interactive television or computer. Included in this industry are establishments primarily engaged in retailing from catalogue showrooms of mail-order houses.

5-YEAR TREND — ESTIMATED INDUSTRY SALES ($MILLIONS)

Year	Employee Size of Establishment									Total
	1-4 Emps.	5-9 Emps.	10-19 Emps.	20-49 Emps.	50-99 Emps.	100-249 Emps.	250-499 Emps.	500-999 Emps.	Unknown Emps.	Industry Sales
2015	4,785.1	2,540.5	3,772.6	6,103.4	4,390.1	8,558.9	12,522.9	15,863.5	723.7	59,260.7
2016	5,104.4	2,710.0	4,024.3	6,510.6	4,683.0	9,130.0	13,358.4	16,921.9	771.9	63,214.5
2017	5,414.1	2,874.4	4,268.5	6,905.6	4,967.1	9,683.9	14,168.9	17,948.5	818.8	67,049.7
2018	6,160.8	3,270.9	4,857.2	7,858.0	5,652.2	11,019.5	16,123.0	19,923.3	931.7	75,796.4
2018	6,842.7	3,632.9	5,394.8	8,727.8	6,277.8	12,239.2	17,907.7	21,746.0	1,034.8	83,803.8

INDUSTRY: BOOK STORES INDUSTRY (NAICS 451211)
PRODUCT LINE: COMPUTER HARDWARE & PERIPHERALS (Sub Category)

NAICS 451211: Book Stores. this industry comprises establishments primarily engaged in the retail sale of new books and magazines. Establishments primarily engaged in the retail sale of used books are classified in 5932.

5-YEAR TREND — ESTIMATED INDUSTRY SALES ($MILLIONS)

Year	Employee Size of Establishment									Total
	1-4 Emps.	5-9 Emps.	10-19 Emps.	20-49 Emps.	50-99 Emps.	100-249 Emps.	250-499 Emps.	500-999 Emps.	Unknown Emps.	Industry Sales
2015	1.9	2.9	5.9	15.6	7.0	2.8	0.5	1.9	1.0	39.4
2016	2.0	3.0	6.3	16.4	7.4	2.9	0.5	2.0	1.0	41.5
2017	2.1	3.2	6.6	17.2	7.8	3.1	0.6	2.1	1.1	43.6
2018	2.1	3.2	6.6	17.3	7.8	3.1	0.6	2.1	1.1	43.9
2018	2.1	3.2	6.7	17.5	7.9	3.1	0.6	2.2	1.1	44.3

INDUSTRY: DEPARTMENT STORES INDUSTRY (NAICS 45211)
PRODUCT LINE: COMPUTER PREPACKAGED SOFTWARE (Sub Category)

NAICS 45211: Department Stores Industry . this industry comprises establishments known as department stores primarily engaged in retailing a wide range of the following new products with no one merchandise line predominating: apparel, furniture, appliances and home furnishings; and selected additional items, such as paint, hardware, toiletries, cosmetics, photographic equipment, jewelry, toys, and sporting goods. merchandise lines are normally arranged in separate departments.

5-YEAR TREND – ESTIMATED INDUSTRY SALES ($MILLIONS)

Year	Employee Size of Establishment									Total
	1-4 Emps.	5-9 Emps.	10-19 Emps.	20-49 Emps.	50-99 Emps.	100-249 Emps.	250-499 Emps.	500-999 Emps.	Unknown Emps.	Industry Sales
2015	0.0	0.0	0.0	1.3	24.6	81.5	35.8	4.8	0.2	148.2
2016	0.0	0.0	0.0	1.3	24.9	82.6	36.2	4.9	0.2	150.1
2017	0.0	0.0	0.0	1.3	25.2	83.5	36.6	4.9	0.2	151.7
2018	0.0	0.0	0.0	1.3	25.3	83.8	36.8	4.9	0.2	152.4
2018	0.0	0.0	0.0	1.3	25.5	84.4	37.0	5.0	0.2	153.5

INDUSTRY: WAREHOUSE CLUBS & SUPERCENTERS (NAICS 45291)
PRODUCT LINE: COMPUTER PREPACKAGED SOFTWARE (Sub Category)

NAICS 45291: Warehouse Clubs and Superstores This industry comprises establishments known as warehouse clubs, superstores or supercenters primarily engaged in retailing a general line of groceries in combination with general lines of new merchandise, such as apparel, furniture, and appliances.

5-YEAR TREND – ESTIMATED INDUSTRY SALES ($MILLIONS)

Year	Employee Size of Establishment									Total
	1-4 Emps.	5-9 Emps.	10-19 Emps.	20-49 Emps.	50-99 Emps.	100-249 Emps.	250-499 Emps.	500-999 Emps.	Unknown Emps.	Industry Sales
2015	0.4	0.0	0.1	3.3	4.2	514.9	2,276.3	60.1	0.7	2,860.0
2016	0.4	0.0	0.1	3.4	4.3	533.7	2,359.5	62.3	0.7	2,964.5
2017	0.4	0.0	0.1	3.5	4.5	551.5	2,438.2	64.4	0.8	3,063.4
2018	0.4	0.0	0.1	3.9	4.9	599.0	2,648.2	70.0	0.8	3,327.2
2018	0.4	0.0	0.1	4.1	5.2	636.2	2,812.4	74.3	0.9	3,533.5

INDUSTRY: ELECTRONIC SHOPPING & MAIL-ORDER (NAICS 45411)
PRODUCT LINE: COMPUTER PREPACKAGED SOFTWARE (Sub Category)

NAICS 45411: Electronic Shopping and Mail-Order Houses This industry comprises establishments primarily engaged in retailing all types of merchandise by means of mail or by electronic media, such as interactive television or computer. Included in this industry are establishments primarily engaged in retailing from catalogue showrooms of mail-order houses.

5-YEAR TREND — ESTIMATED INDUSTRY SALES ($MILLIONS)

Year	Employee Size of Establishment									Total Industry Sales
	1-4 Emps.	5-9 Emps.	10-19 Emps.	20-49 Emps.	50-99 Emps.	100-249 Emps.	250-499 Emps.	500-999 Emps.	Unknown Emps.	
2015	400.8	212.8	316.0	511.2	367.7	716.8	1,048.8	1,328.6	60.6	4,963.2
2016	427.5	227.0	337.0	545.3	392.2	764.7	1,118.8	1,417.2	64.7	5,294.4
2017	453.4	240.7	357.5	578.4	416.0	811.0	1,186.7	1,503.2	68.6	5,615.6
2018	516.0	273.9	406.8	658.1	473.4	922.9	1,350.3	1,668.6	78.0	6,348.1
2018	573.1	304.3	451.8	731.0	525.8	1,025.1	1,499.8	1,821.3	86.7	7,018.8

INDUSTRY: BOOK STORES INDUSTRY (NAICS 451211)
PRODUCT LINE: COMPUTER PREPACKAGED SOFTWARE (Sub Category)

NAICS 451211: Book Stores. this industry comprises establishments primarily engaged in the retail sale of new books and magazines. Establishments primarily engaged in the retail sale of used books are classified in 5932.

5-YEAR TREND — ESTIMATED INDUSTRY SALES ($MILLIONS)

Year	Employee Size of Establishment									Total Industry Sales
	1-4 Emps.	5-9 Emps.	10-19 Emps.	20-49 Emps.	50-99 Emps.	100-249 Emps.	250-499 Emps.	500-999 Emps.	Unknown Emps.	
2015	2.0	3.0	6.3	16.4	7.4	2.9	0.5	2.0	1.0	41.6
2016	2.1	3.2	6.6	17.3	7.8	3.1	0.6	2.1	1.1	43.9
2017	2.2	3.4	6.9	18.2	8.2	3.2	0.6	2.2	1.1	46.0
2018	2.2	3.4	7.0	18.3	8.3	3.3	0.6	2.2	1.1	46.4
2018	2.2	3.4	7.1	18.5	8.3	3.3	0.6	2.3	1.1	46.8

INDUSTRY: HOME CENTERS INDUSTRY (NAICS 44411)
PRODUCT LINE: KITCHENWARE & HOME FURNISHINGS (Main Category)

NAICS 44411: Home Centers. This industry comprises establishments known as home centers primarily engaged in retailing a general line of new home repair and improvement materials and supplies, such as lumber, plumbing goods, electrical goods, tools, housewares, hardware, and lawn and garden supplies, with no one merchandise line predominating. The merchandise lines are normally arranged in separate departments.

5-YEAR TREND — ESTIMATED INDUSTRY SALES ($MILLIONS)

Year	Employee Size of Establishment									Total
	1-4 Emps.	5-9 Emps.	10-19 Emps.	20-49 Emps.	50-99 Emps.	100-249 Emps.	250-499 Emps.	500-999 Emps.	Unknown Emps.	Industry Sales
2015	7.0	14.0	36.3	72.5	53.3	3,484.3	308.1	5.7	2.4	3,983.6
2016	7.3	14.4	37.5	74.9	55.0	3,599.2	318.3	5.9	2.5	4,115.0
2017	7.5	14.8	38.6	77.2	56.7	3,707.1	327.9	6.1	2.6	4,238.5
2018	7.9	15.6	40.6	81.1	59.6	3,896.0	344.6	6.4	2.7	4,454.4
2018	8.3	16.4	42.8	85.4	62.7	4,102.9	362.9	6.7	2.9	4,691.0

INDUSTRY: HARDWARE STORES (NAICS 44413)
PRODUCT LINE: KITCHENWARE & HOME FURNISHINGS (Main Category)

NAICS 44413: Hardware Stores. Establishments primarily engaged in the retail sale of a number of basic hardware lines, such as tools, builders' hardware, paint and glass, housewares and household appliances, and cutlery.

5-YEAR TREND — ESTIMATED INDUSTRY SALES ($MILLIONS)

Year	Employee Size of Establishment									Total
	1-4 Emps.	5-9 Emps.	10-19 Emps.	20-49 Emps.	50-99 Emps.	100-249 Emps.	250-499 Emps.	500-999 Emps.	Unknown Emps.	Industry Sales
2015	38.9	62.4	124.7	174.7	32.0	7.5	2.1	0.1	3.3	445.7
2016	39.6	63.6	127.1	178.0	32.6	7.6	2.1	0.1	3.3	454.1
2017	40.3	64.6	129.2	180.9	33.1	7.8	2.2	0.1	3.4	461.6
2018	42.1	67.6	135.2	189.4	34.7	8.1	2.3	0.1	3.6	483.1
2018	44.2	71.0	141.9	198.7	36.4	8.5	2.4	0.1	3.7	506.9

INDUSTRY: SUPERMARKETS INDUSTRY (NAICS 44511)
PRODUCT LINE: KITCHENWARE & HOME FURNISHINGS (Main Category)

NAICS 44511: Grocery Stores Industry. this industry comprises establishments generally known as supermarkets and grocery stores primarily engaged in retailing a general line of food, such as canned and frozen foods; fresh fruits and vegetables; and fresh and prepared meats, fish, and poultry. Included in this industry are delicatessen-type establishments primarily engaged in retailing a general line of food.

5-YEAR TREND – ESTIMATED INDUSTRY SALES ($MILLIONS)

Year	Employee Size of Establishment									Total Industry Sales
	1-4 Emps.	5-9 Emps.	10-19 Emps.	20-49 Emps.	50-99 Emps.	100-249 Emps.	250-499 Emps.	500-999 Emps.	Unknown Emps.	
2015	26.7	20.0	50.7	165.5	401.4	915.3	263.9	36.4	5.1	1,884.8
2016	26.2	19.6	49.8	162.6	394.4	899.4	259.3	35.7	5.0	1,852.1
2017	25.7	19.2	48.8	159.4	386.6	881.7	254.2	35.0	4.9	1,815.6
2018	25.7	19.2	48.8	159.4	386.7	881.8	254.2	35.0	4.9	1,815.8
2018	25.8	19.3	48.9	159.8	387.5	883.7	254.8	35.1	4.9	1,819.6

INDUSTRY: BEER, WINE & LIQUOR STORES (NAICS 44531)
PRODUCT LINE: KITCHENWARE & HOME FURNISHINGS (Main Category)

NAICS 44531: Beer & Wine & Liquor Stores. Establishments primarily engaged in the retail sale of packaged alcoholic beverages, such as ale, beer, wine, and liquor, for consumption off the premises. Stores selling prepared drinks for consumption on the premises are classified in SIC 5813.

5-YEAR TREND – ESTIMATED INDUSTRY SALES ($MILLIONS)

Year	Employee Size of Establishment									Total Industry Sales
	1-4 Emps.	5-9 Emps.	10-19 Emps.	20-49 Emps.	50-99 Emps.	100-249 Emps.	250-499 Emps.	500-999 Emps.	Unknown Emps.	
2015	9.8	9.5	8.0	5.8	0.8	0.6	0.0	0.3	0.5	35.2
2016	10.2	9.9	8.3	6.0	0.8	0.6	0.0	0.3	0.6	36.7
2017	10.6	10.3	8.6	6.3	0.8	0.6	0.0	0.3	0.6	38.1
2018	11.3	11.0	9.2	6.7	0.9	0.6	0.0	0.3	0.6	40.8
2018	12.1	11.8	9.9	7.2	0.9	0.7	0.0	0.4	0.7	43.7

INDUSTRY: PHARMACIES & DRUG STORES INDUSTRY (NAICS 44611)
PRODUCT LINE: KITCHENWARE & HOME FURNISHINGS (Main Category)

NAICS 44611 Pharmacies and Drug Stores – this industry comprises establishments known as pharmacies and drug stores engaged in retailing prescription or nonprescription drugs and medicines.

5-YEAR TREND – ESTIMATED INDUSTRY SALES ($MILLIONS)

Year	Employee Size of Establishment									Total Industry Sales
	1-4 Emps.	5-9 Emps.	10-19 Emps.	20-49 Emps.	50-99 Emps.	100-249 Emps.	250-499 Emps.	500-999 Emps.	Unknown Emps.	
2015	11.4	28.5	120.3	340.0	31.9	12.5	3.9	1.6	1.0	551.1
2016	12.0	30.0	126.6	357.8	33.6	13.2	4.1	1.6	1.0	579.9
2017	12.6	31.4	132.7	374.9	35.2	13.8	4.3	1.7	1.1	607.7
2018	13.5	33.8	142.6	403.1	37.9	14.9	4.6	1.8	1.1	653.4
2018	14.6	36.4	153.6	434.0	40.8	16.0	5.0	1.9	1.2	703.3

INDUSTRY: MEN'S CLOTHING STORES INDUSTRY (NAICS 44811)
PRODUCT LINE: KITCHENWARE & HOME FURNISHINGS (Main Category)

NAICS 44811: Men's Clothing Stores. this industry comprises establishments primarily engaged in retailing a general line of new men's and boys' clothing. These establishments may provide basic alterations, such as hemming, taking in or letting out seams, or lengthening or shortening sleeves.

5-YEAR TREND – ESTIMATED INDUSTRY SALES ($MILLIONS)

Year	Employee Size of Establishment									Total Industry Sales
	1-4 Emps.	5-9 Emps.	10-19 Emps.	20-49 Emps.	50-99 Emps.	100-249 Emps.	250-499 Emps.	500-999 Emps.	Unknown Emps.	
2015	1.5	2.3	5.3	3.1	0.8	0.4	0.2	0.0	0.3	13.7
2016	1.6	2.4	5.5	3.2	0.8	0.4	0.2	0.0	0.3	14.3
2017	1.6	2.5	5.7	3.3	0.9	0.4	0.2	0.0	0.3	14.9
2018	1.7	2.5	5.9	3.5	0.9	0.4	0.2	0.0	0.3	15.5
2018	1.8	2.6	6.2	3.6	0.9	0.5	0.2	0.0	0.3	16.0

INDUSTRY: WOMEN'S CLOTHING STORES INDUSTRY (NAICS 44812)
PRODUCT LINE: KITCHENWARE & HOME FURNISHINGS (Main Category)

NAICS 44812: Women's Clothing Stores . this industry comprises establishments primarily engaged in retailing a general line of new women's, misses' and juniors' clothing, including maternity wear. These establishments may provide basic alterations, such as hemming, taking in or letting out seams, or lengthening or shortening sleeves.

5-YEAR TREND – ESTIMATED INDUSTRY SALES ($MILLIONS)

Year	Employee Size of Establishment									Total Industry Sales
	1-4 Emps.	5-9 Emps.	10-19 Emps.	20-49 Emps.	50-99 Emps.	100-249 Emps.	250-499 Emps.	500-999 Emps.	Unknown Emps.	
2015	8.1	18.3	44.9	30.8	9.6	9.3	3.5	3.2	1.9	129.7
2016	8.4	19.1	46.7	32.0	10.0	9.7	3.6	3.3	1.9	134.7
2017	8.7	19.7	48.3	33.1	10.3	10.0	3.8	3.4	2.0	139.4
2018	9.2	21.0	51.4	35.2	11.0	10.7	4.0	3.6	2.1	148.2
2018	9.9	22.3	54.7	37.5	11.7	11.4	4.3	3.8	2.3	157.8

INDUSTRY: FAMILY CLOTHING STORES INDUSTRY (NAICS 44814)
PRODUCT LINE: KITCHENWARE & HOME FURNISHINGS (Main Category)

NAICS 44814: Family Clothing Stores . this industry comprises establishments primarily engaged in retailing a general line of new clothing for men, women, and children, without specializing in sales for an individual gender or age group. These establishments may provide basic alterations, such as hemming, taking in or letting out seams, or lengthening or shortening sleeves.

5-YEAR TREND – ESTIMATED INDUSTRY SALES ($MILLIONS)

Year	Employee Size of Establishment									Total Industry Sales
	1-4 Emps.	5-9 Emps.	10-19 Emps.	20-49 Emps.	50-99 Emps.	100-249 Emps.	250-499 Emps.	500-999 Emps.	Unknown Emps.	
2015	56.3	101.0	434.9	1,333.1	1,398.2	348.8	344.8	136.6	15.2	4,169.1
2016	58.4	104.7	450.5	1,380.9	1,448.3	361.3	357.1	141.5	15.8	4,318.4
2017	60.3	108.1	465.2	1,425.9	1,495.6	373.1	368.8	146.1	16.3	4,459.4
2018	63.9	114.6	493.5	1,512.7	1,586.6	395.8	391.2	154.7	17.3	4,730.4
2018	68.0	121.9	524.5	1,607.9	1,686.4	420.7	415.8	164.0	18.4	5,027.5

INDUSTRY: PRERECORDED TAPES & CDs STORES (NAICS 45122)
PRODUCT LINE: KITCHENWARE & HOME FURNISHINGS (Main Category)

NAICS 45122: Prerecorded Tape, Compact Disc, and Record Stores .
This industry comprises establishments primarily engaged in retailing new
prerecorded audio and video tapes, compact discs (CDs), and phonograph
records.

5-YEAR TREND – ESTIMATED INDUSTRY SALES ($MILLIONS)

Year	Employee Size of Establishment									Total
	1-4 Emps.	5-9 Emps.	10-19 Emps.	20-49 Emps.	50-99 Emps.	100-249 Emps.	250-499 Emps.	500-999 Emps.	Unknown Emps.	Industry Sales
2015	0.1	0.3	0.7	1.5	1.1	70.8	6.3	0.1	0.0	80.9
2016	0.1	0.3	0.8	1.5	1.1	73.1	6.5	0.1	0.1	83.6
2017	0.2	0.3	0.8	1.6	1.2	75.3	6.7	0.1	0.1	86.1
2018	0.2	0.3	0.8	1.6	1.2	79.1	7.0	0.1	0.1	90.5
2018	0.2	0.3	0.9	1.7	1.3	83.3	7.4	0.1	0.1	95.3

INDUSTRY: DEPARTMENT STORES INDUSTRY (NAICS 45211)
PRODUCT LINE: KITCHENWARE & HOME FURNISHINGS (Main Category)

NAICS 45211: Department Stores Industry . this industry comprises
establishments known as department stores primarily engaged in retailing
a wide range of the following new products with no one merchandise line
predominating: apparel, furniture, appliances and home furnishings; and
selected additional items, such as paint, hardware, toiletries, cosmetics,
photographic equipment, jewelry, toys, and sporting goods. merchandise lines
are normally arranged in separate departments.

5-YEAR TREND – ESTIMATED INDUSTRY SALES ($MILLIONS)

Year	Employee Size of Establishment									Total
	1-4 Emps.	5-9 Emps.	10-19 Emps.	20-49 Emps.	50-99 Emps.	100-249 Emps.	250-499 Emps.	500-999 Emps.	Unknown Emps.	Industry Sales
2015	0.4	0.1	0.6	45.3	860.9	2,855.2	1,252.6	167.7	7.3	5,190.2
2016	0.4	0.1	0.6	45.9	872.0	2,892.1	1,268.8	169.9	7.4	5,257.2
2017	0.4	0.1	0.6	46.4	881.4	2,923.3	1,282.4	171.7	7.4	5,313.8
2018	0.4	0.1	0.6	46.6	885.4	2,936.7	1,288.4	172.7	7.5	5,338.5
2018	0.4	0.1	0.6	47.0	891.8	2,957.9	1,297.6	174.0	7.5	5,377.0

INDUSTRY: WAREHOUSE CLUBS & SUPERCENTERS (NAICS 45291)
PRODUCT LINE: KITCHENWARE & HOME FURNISHINGS (Main Category)

NAICS 45291: Warehouse Clubs and Superstores This industry comprises establishments known as warehouse clubs, superstores or supercenters primarily engaged in retailing a general line of groceries in combination with general lines of new merchandise, such as apparel, furniture, and appliances.

5-YEAR TREND – ESTIMATED INDUSTRY SALES ($MILLIONS)

Year	Employee Size of Establishment									Total Industry Sales
	1-4 Emps.	5-9 Emps.	10-19 Emps.	20-49 Emps.	50-99 Emps.	100-249 Emps.	250-499 Emps.	500-999 Emps.	Unknown Emps.	
2015	1.3	0.0	0.2	12.1	15.2	1,882.2	8,321.0	219.9	2.6	10,454.6
2016	1.3	0.0	0.2	12.5	15.8	1,951.0	8,625.2	227.9	2.7	10,836.8
2017	1.4	0.0	0.2	13.0	16.3	2,016.1	8,912.8	235.5	2.8	11,198.1
2018	1.5	0.1	0.3	14.1	17.7	2,189.7	9,680.4	255.8	3.0	12,162.5
2018	1.6	0.1	0.3	14.9	18.8	2,325.5	10,280.6	271.6	3.2	12,916.6

INDUSTRY: OFFICE SUPPLY & STATIONERY STORES (NAICS 45321)
PRODUCT LINE: KITCHENWARE & HOME FURNISHINGS (Main Category)

NAICS 45321: Office Supplies and Stationery Stores . this industry comprises establishments primarily engaged in one or more of the following: (1) retailing new stationery, school supplies, and office supplies; (2) selling a combination of new office equipment, furniture, and supplies; and (3) selling new office equipment, furniture, and supplies in combination with selling new computers.

5-YEAR TREND – ESTIMATED INDUSTRY SALES ($MILLIONS)

Year	Employee Size of Establishment									Total Industry Sales
	1-4 Emps.	5-9 Emps.	10-19 Emps.	20-49 Emps.	50-99 Emps.	100-249 Emps.	250-499 Emps.	500-999 Emps.	Unknown Emps.	
2015	0.5	0.4	2.2	6.1	0.1	0.1	0.0	0.0	0.1	9.7
2016	0.5	0.4	2.2	6.1	0.1	0.1	0.0	0.0	0.1	9.7
2017	0.5	0.4	2.2	6.1	0.1	0.1	0.0	0.0	0.1	9.6
2018	0.5	0.4	2.1	6.0	0.1	0.1	0.0	0.0	0.1	9.4
2018	0.5	0.4	2.1	5.9	0.1	0.1	0.0	0.0	0.1	9.2

INDUSTRY: ELECTRONIC SHOPPING & MAIL-ORDER (NAICS 45411)

PRODUCT LINE: KITCHENWARE & HOME FURNISHINGS (Main Category)

NAICS 45411: Electronic Shopping and Mail-Order Houses This industry comprises establishments primarily engaged in retailing all types of merchandise by means of mail or by electronic media, such as interactive television or computer. Included in this industry are establishments primarily engaged in retailing from catalogue showrooms of mail-order houses.

5-YEAR TREND — ESTIMATED INDUSTRY SALES ($MILLIONS)

Year	Employee Size of Establishment									Total
	1-4 Emps.	5-9 Emps.	10-19 Emps.	20-49 Emps.	50-99 Emps.	100-249 Emps.	250-499 Emps.	500-999 Emps.	Unknown Emps.	Industry Sales
2015	1,422.6	755.3	1,121.6	1,814.6	1,305.2	2,544.6	3,723.1	4,716.3	215.1	17,618.5
2016	1,517.6	805.7	1,196.4	1,935.6	1,392.3	2,714.4	3,971.5	5,031.0	229.5	18,794.0
2017	1,609.6	854.6	1,269.0	2,053.1	1,476.8	2,879.1	4,212.5	5,336.2	243.4	19,934.2
2018	1,831.6	972.4	1,444.1	2,336.2	1,680.4	3,276.1	4,793.5	5,923.3	277.0	22,534.7
2018	2,034.4	1,080.1	1,603.9	2,594.8	1,866.4	3,638.8	5,324.1	6,465.2	307.7	24,915.3

INDUSTRY: BOOK STORES INDUSTRY (NAICS 451211)

PRODUCT LINE: KITCHENWARE & HOME FURNISHINGS (Main Category)

NAICS 451211: Book Stores. this industry comprises establishments primarily engaged in the retail sale of new books and magazines. Establishments primarily engaged in the retail sale of used books are classified in 5932.

5-YEAR TREND — ESTIMATED INDUSTRY SALES ($MILLIONS)

Year	Employee Size of Establishment									Total
	1-4 Emps.	5-9 Emps.	10-19 Emps.	20-49 Emps.	50-99 Emps.	100-249 Emps.	250-499 Emps.	500-999 Emps.	Unknown Emps.	Industry Sales
2015	2.7	4.2	8.7	22.7	10.3	4.0	0.7	2.7	1.4	57.5
2016	2.9	4.4	9.2	24.0	10.8	4.3	0.8	2.9	1.5	60.7
2017	3.0	4.6	9.6	25.2	11.4	4.5	0.8	3.0	1.6	63.7
2018	3.1	4.7	9.7	25.3	11.4	4.5	0.8	3.1	1.6	64.2
2018	3.1	4.7	9.8	25.6	11.5	4.5	0.8	3.2	1.6	64.8

INDUSTRY: DEPARTMENT STORES INDUSTRY (NAICS 45211)
PRODUCT LINE: COOKWARE & COOKING ACCESSORIES (Sub Category)

NAICS 45211: Department Stores Industry . this industry comprises establishments known as department stores primarily engaged in retailing a wide range of the following new products with no one merchandise line predominating: apparel, furniture, appliances and home furnishings; and selected additional items, such as paint, hardware, toiletries, cosmetics, photographic equipment, jewelry, toys, and sporting goods. merchandise lines are normally arranged in separate departments.

5-YEAR TREND — ESTIMATED INDUSTRY SALES ($MILLIONS)

Year	Employee Size of Establishment									Total Industry Sales
	1-4 Emps.	5-9 Emps.	10-19 Emps.	20-49 Emps.	50-99 Emps.	100-249 Emps.	250-499 Emps.	500-999 Emps.	Unknown Emps.	
2015	0.1	0.0	0.2	12.4	235.3	780.4	342.4	45.8	2.0	1,418.6
2016	0.1	0.0	0.2	12.6	238.3	790.5	346.8	46.4	2.0	1,436.9
2017	0.1	0.0	0.2	12.7	240.9	799.0	350.5	46.9	2.0	1,452.4
2018	0.1	0.0	0.2	12.7	242.0	802.7	352.1	47.2	2.0	1,459.1
2018	0.1	0.0	0.2	12.8	243.7	808.5	354.7	47.6	2.1	1,469.6

INDUSTRY: WAREHOUSE CLUBS & SUPERCENTERS (NAICS 45291)
PRODUCT LINE: COOKWARE & COOKING ACCESSORIES (Sub Category)

NAICS 45291: Warehouse Clubs and Superstores This industry comprises establishments known as warehouse clubs, superstores or supercenters primarily engaged in retailing a general line of groceries in combination with general lines of new merchandise, such as apparel, furniture, and appliances.

5-YEAR TREND — ESTIMATED INDUSTRY SALES ($MILLIONS)

Year	Employee Size of Establishment									Total Industry Sales
	1-4 Emps.	5-9 Emps.	10-19 Emps.	20-49 Emps.	50-99 Emps.	100-249 Emps.	250-499 Emps.	500-999 Emps.	Unknown Emps.	
2015	0.5	0.0	0.1	5.1	6.4	790.2	3,493.6	92.3	1.1	4,389.3
2016	0.6	0.0	0.1	5.3	6.6	819.1	3,621.3	95.7	1.1	4,549.8
2017	0.6	0.0	0.1	5.4	6.9	846.4	3,742.0	98.9	1.2	4,701.5
2018	0.6	0.0	0.1	5.9	7.4	919.3	4,064.3	107.4	1.3	5,106.4
2018	0.7	0.0	0.1	6.3	7.9	976.3	4,316.3	114.0	1.3	5,423.0

INDUSTRY: DEPARTMENT STORES INDUSTRY (NAICS 45211)
PRODUCT LINE: DINNERWARE & GLASSWARE (Sub Category)

NAICS 45211: Department Stores Industry . this industry comprises establishments known as department stores primarily engaged in retailing a wide range of the following new products with no one merchandise line predominating: apparel, furniture, appliances and home furnishings; and selected additional items, such as paint, hardware, toiletries, cosmetics, photographic equipment, jewelry, toys, and sporting goods. merchandise lines are normally arranged in separate departments.

5-YEAR TREND – ESTIMATED INDUSTRY SALES ($MILLIONS)

Year	Employee Size of Establishment									Total
	1-4 Emps.	5-9 Emps.	10-19 Emps.	20-49 Emps.	50-99 Emps.	100-249 Emps.	250-499 Emps.	500-999 Emps.	Unknown Emps.	Industry Sales
2015	0.1	0.0	0.1	11.4	216.2	716.9	314.5	42.1	1.8	1,303.2
2016	0.1	0.0	0.1	11.5	218.9	726.2	318.6	42.7	1.8	1,320.0
2017	0.1	0.0	0.1	11.7	221.3	734.0	322.0	43.1	1.9	1,334.2
2018	0.1	0.0	0.1	11.7	222.3	737.4	323.5	43.4	1.9	1,340.4
2018	0.1	0.0	0.1	11.8	223.9	742.7	325.8	43.7	1.9	1,350.1

INDUSTRY: WAREHOUSE CLUBS & SUPERCENTERS (NAICS 45291)
PRODUCT LINE: DINNERWARE & GLASSWARE (Sub Category)

NAICS 45291: Warehouse Clubs and Superstores This industry comprises establishments known as warehouse clubs, superstores or supercenters primarily engaged in retailing a general line of groceries in combination with general lines of new merchandise, such as apparel, furniture, and appliances.

5-YEAR TREND – ESTIMATED INDUSTRY SALES ($MILLIONS)

Year	Employee Size of Establishment									Total
	1-4 Emps.	5-9 Emps.	10-19 Emps.	20-49 Emps.	50-99 Emps.	100-249 Emps.	250-499 Emps.	500-999 Emps.	Unknown Emps.	Industry Sales
2015	0.1	0.0	0.0	1.2	1.6	191.5	846.4	22.4	0.3	1,063.4
2016	0.1	0.0	0.0	1.3	1.6	198.5	877.3	23.2	0.3	1,102.3
2017	0.1	0.0	0.0	1.3	1.7	205.1	906.6	24.0	0.3	1,139.1
2018	0.2	0.0	0.0	1.4	1.8	222.7	984.7	26.0	0.3	1,237.2
2018	0.2	0.0	0.0	1.5	1.9	236.5	1,045.7	27.6	0.3	1,313.9

INDUSTRY: DEPARTMENT STORES INDUSTRY (NAICS 45211)
PRODUCT LINE: DECORATIVE ACCESSORIES (Sub Category)

NAICS 45211: Department Stores Industry . this industry comprises establishments known as department stores primarily engaged in retailing a wide range of the following new products with no one merchandise line predominating: apparel, furniture, appliances and home furnishings; and selected additional items, such as paint, hardware, toiletries, cosmetics, photographic equipment, jewelry, toys, and sporting goods. merchandise lines are normally arranged in separate departments.

5-YEAR TREND – ESTIMATED INDUSTRY SALES ($MILLIONS)

Year	Employee Size of Establishment									Total
	1-4 Emps.	5-9 Emps.	10-19 Emps.	20-49 Emps.	50-99 Emps.	100-249 Emps.	250-499 Emps.	500-999 Emps.	Unknown Emps.	Industry Sales
2015	0.1	0.0	0.1	11.7	221.4	734.4	322.2	43.1	1.9	1,335.0
2016	0.1	0.0	0.1	11.8	224.3	743.9	326.4	43.7	1.9	1,352.3
2017	0.1	0.0	0.2	11.9	226.7	751.9	329.9	44.2	1.9	1,366.8
2018	0.1	0.0	0.2	12.0	227.8	755.4	331.4	44.4	1.9	1,373.2
2018	0.1	0.0	0.2	12.1	229.4	760.8	333.8	44.8	1.9	1,383.1

INDUSTRY: WAREHOUSE CLUBS & SUPERCENTERS (NAICS 45291)
PRODUCT LINE: DECORATIVE ACCESSORIES (Sub Category)

NAICS 45291: Warehouse Clubs and Superstores This industry comprises establishments known as warehouse clubs, superstores or supercenters primarily engaged in retailing a general line of groceries in combination with general lines of new merchandise, such as apparel, furniture, and appliances.

5-YEAR TREND – ESTIMATED INDUSTRY SALES ($MILLIONS)

Year	Employee Size of Establishment									Total
	1-4 Emps.	5-9 Emps.	10-19 Emps.	20-49 Emps.	50-99 Emps.	100-249 Emps.	250-499 Emps.	500-999 Emps.	Unknown Emps.	Industry Sales
2015	0.4	0.0	0.1	3.6	4.5	558.2	2,467.8	65.2	0.8	3,100.5
2016	0.4	0.0	0.1	3.7	4.7	578.6	2,558.0	67.6	0.8	3,213.9
2017	0.4	0.0	0.1	3.8	4.8	597.9	2,643.3	69.8	0.8	3,321.1
2018	0.4	0.0	0.1	4.2	5.3	649.4	2,871.0	75.9	0.9	3,607.1
2018	0.5	0.0	0.1	4.4	5.6	689.7	3,049.0	80.6	0.9	3,830.7

INDUSTRY: DEPARTMENT STORES INDUSTRY (NAICS 45211)
PRODUCT LINE: OTHER KITCHENWARE (Sub Category)

NAICS 45211: Department Stores Industry . this industry comprises establishments known as department stores primarily engaged in retailing a wide range of the following new products with no one merchandise line predominating: apparel, furniture, appliances and home furnishings; and selected additional items, such as paint, hardware, toiletries, cosmetics, photographic equipment, jewelry, toys, and sporting goods. merchandise lines are normally arranged in separate departments.

5-YEAR TREND – ESTIMATED INDUSTRY SALES ($MILLIONS)

Year	Employee Size of Establishment									Total Industry Sales
	1-4 Emps.	5-9 Emps.	10-19 Emps.	20-49 Emps.	50-99 Emps.	100-249 Emps.	250-499 Emps.	500-999 Emps.	Unknown Emps.	
2015	0.1	0.0	0.1	9.9	188.0	623.5	273.5	36.6	1.6	1,133.4
2016	0.1	0.0	0.1	10.0	190.4	631.5	277.1	37.1	1.6	1,148.0
2017	0.1	0.0	0.1	10.1	192.5	638.3	280.0	37.5	1.6	1,160.4
2018	0.1	0.0	0.1	10.2	193.3	641.3	281.3	37.7	1.6	1,165.7
2018	0.1	0.0	0.1	10.3	194.7	645.9	283.4	38.0	1.6	1,174.2

INDUSTRY: WAREHOUSE CLUBS & SUPERCENTERS (NAICS 45291)
PRODUCT LINE: OTHER KITCHENWARE (Sub Category)

NAICS 45291: Warehouse Clubs and Superstores This industry comprises establishments known as warehouse clubs, superstores or supercenters primarily engaged in retailing a general line of groceries in combination with general lines of new merchandise, such as apparel, furniture, and appliances.

5-YEAR TREND – ESTIMATED INDUSTRY SALES ($MILLIONS)

Year	Employee Size of Establishment									Total Industry Sales
	1-4 Emps.	5-9 Emps.	10-19 Emps.	20-49 Emps.	50-99 Emps.	100-249 Emps.	250-499 Emps.	500-999 Emps.	Unknown Emps.	
2015	0.2	0.0	0.0	2.2	2.8	342.3	1,513.3	40.0	0.5	1,901.3
2016	0.2	0.0	0.0	2.3	2.9	354.8	1,568.6	41.4	0.5	1,970.8
2017	0.3	0.0	0.0	2.4	3.0	366.6	1,620.9	42.8	0.5	2,036.5
2018	0.3	0.0	0.0	2.6	3.2	398.2	1,760.5	46.5	0.5	2,211.9
2018	0.3	0.0	0.1	2.7	3.4	422.9	1,869.6	49.4	0.6	2,349.0

INDUSTRY: OFFICE SUPPLY & STATIONERY STORES (NAICS 45321)
PRODUCT LINE: GIFTWARE (Sub Category)

NAICS 45321: Office Supplies and Stationery Stores . this industry comprises establishments primarily engaged in one or more of the following: (1) retailing new stationery, school supplies, and office supplies; (2) selling a combination of new office equipment, furniture, and supplies; and (3) selling new office equipment, furniture, and supplies in combination with selling new computers.

5-YEAR TREND — ESTIMATED INDUSTRY SALES ($MILLIONS)

Year	Employee Size of Establishment									Total Industry Sales
	1-4 Emps.	5-9 Emps.	10-19 Emps.	20-49 Emps.	50-99 Emps.	100-249 Emps.	250-499 Emps.	500-999 Emps.	Unknown Emps.	
2015	0.4	0.3	1.7	4.7	0.1	0.1	0.0	0.0	0.1	7.5
2016	0.4	0.3	1.7	4.7	0.1	0.1	0.0	0.0	0.1	7.5
2017	0.4	0.3	1.7	4.7	0.1	0.1	0.0	0.0	0.1	7.5
2018	0.4	0.3	1.6	4.6	0.1	0.1	0.0	0.0	0.1	7.3
2018	0.4	0.3	1.6	4.5	0.1	0.1	0.0	0.0	0.1	7.2

INDUSTRY: BOOK STORES INDUSTRY (NAICS 451211)
PRODUCT LINE: GIFTWARE (Sub Category)

NAICS 451211: Book Stores. this industry comprises establishments primarily engaged in the retail sale of new books and magazines. Establishments primarily engaged in the retail sale of used books are classified in 5932.

5-YEAR TREND — ESTIMATED INDUSTRY SALES ($MILLIONS)

Year	Employee Size of Establishment									Total Industry Sales
	1-4 Emps.	5-9 Emps.	10-19 Emps.	20-49 Emps.	50-99 Emps.	100-249 Emps.	250-499 Emps.	500-999 Emps.	Unknown Emps.	
2015	1.9	2.9	6.1	15.9	7.2	2.8	0.5	1.9	1.0	40.3
2016	2.0	3.1	6.4	16.8	7.6	3.0	0.5	2.0	1.0	42.4
2017	2.1	3.2	6.7	17.6	7.9	3.1	0.6	2.1	1.1	44.6
2018	2.1	3.3	6.8	17.7	8.0	3.2	0.6	2.2	1.1	44.9
2018	2.2	3.3	6.8	17.9	8.1	3.2	0.6	2.2	1.1	45.3

INDUSTRY: BOOK STORES INDUSTRY (NAICS 451211)
PRODUCT LINE: OTHER HOME FURNISHINGS (Sub Category)

NAICS 451211: Book Stores. this industry comprises establishments primarily engaged in the retail sale of new books and magazines. Establishments primarily engaged in the retail sale of used books are classified in 5932.

5-YEAR TREND – ESTIMATED INDUSTRY SALES ($MILLIONS)

Year	Employee Size of Establishment									Total
	1-4 Emps.	5-9 Emps.	10-19 Emps.	20-49 Emps.	50-99 Emps.	100-249 Emps.	250-499 Emps.	500-999 Emps.	Unknown Emps.	Industry Sales
2015	0.8	1.3	2.6	6.8	3.1	1.2	0.2	0.8	0.4	17.3
2016	0.9	1.3	2.7	7.2	3.2	1.3	0.2	0.9	0.4	18.2
2017	0.9	1.4	2.9	7.6	3.4	1.3	0.2	0.9	0.5	19.1
2018	0.9	1.4	2.9	7.6	3.4	1.4	0.2	0.9	0.5	19.3
2018	0.9	1.4	2.9	7.7	3.5	1.4	0.2	1.0	0.5	19.5

INDUSTRY: SUPERMARKETS INDUSTRY (NAICS 44511)
PRODUCT LINE: JEWELRY & WATCHES (Main Category)

NAICS 44511: Grocery Stores Industry. this industry comprises establishments generally known as supermarkets and grocery stores primarily engaged in retailing a general line of food, such as canned and frozen foods; fresh fruits and vegetables; and fresh and prepared meats, fish, and poultry. Included in this industry are delicatessen-type establishments primarily engaged in retailing a general line of food.

5-YEAR TREND – ESTIMATED INDUSTRY SALES ($MILLIONS)

Year	Employee Size of Establishment									Total
	1-4 Emps.	5-9 Emps.	10-19 Emps.	20-49 Emps.	50-99 Emps.	100-249 Emps.	250-499 Emps.	500-999 Emps.	Unknown Emps.	Industry Sales
2015	2.8	2.1	5.3	17.2	41.8	95.2	27.4	3.8	0.5	196.1
2016	2.7	2.0	5.2	16.9	41.0	93.6	27.0	3.7	0.5	192.7
2017	2.7	2.0	5.1	16.6	40.2	91.7	26.4	3.6	0.5	188.9
2018	2.7	2.0	5.1	16.6	40.2	91.7	26.4	3.6	0.5	188.9
2018	2.7	2.0	5.1	16.6	40.3	91.9	26.5	3.6	0.5	189.3

INDUSTRY: BEER, WINE & LIQUOR STORES (NAICS 44531)
PRODUCT LINE: JEWELRY & WATCHES (Main Category)

NAICS 44531: Beer & Wine & Liquor Stores. Establishments primarily engaged in the retail sale of packaged alcoholic beverages, such as ale, beer, wine, and liquor, for consumption off the premises. Stores selling prepared drinks for consumption on the premises are classified in SIC 5813.

5-YEAR TREND – ESTIMATED INDUSTRY SALES ($MILLIONS)

| Year | Employee Size of Establishment | | | | | | | | | Total |
	1-4 Emps.	5-9 Emps.	10-19 Emps.	20-49 Emps.	50-99 Emps.	100-249 Emps.	250-499 Emps.	500-999 Emps.	Unknown Emps.	Industry Sales
2015	2.8	2.7	2.3	1.7	0.2	0.2	0.0	0.1	0.2	10.0
2016	2.9	2.8	2.4	1.7	0.2	0.2	0.0	0.1	0.2	10.4
2017	3.0	2.9	2.4	1.8	0.2	0.2	0.0	0.1	0.2	10.8
2018	3.2	3.1	2.6	1.9	0.3	0.2	0.0	0.1	0.2	11.6
2018	3.5	3.4	2.8	2.1	0.3	0.2	0.0	0.1	0.2	12.4

INDUSTRY: PHARMACIES & DRUG STORES (NAICS 44611)
PRODUCT LINE: JEWELRY & WATCHES (Main Category)

NAICS 44611 Pharmacies and Drug Stores – this industry comprises establishments known as pharmacies and drug stores engaged in retailing prescription or nonprescription drugs and medicines.

5-YEAR TREND – ESTIMATED INDUSTRY SALES ($MILLIONS)

| Year | Employee Size of Establishment | | | | | | | | | Total |
	1-4 Emps.	5-9 Emps.	10-19 Emps.	20-49 Emps.	50-99 Emps.	100-249 Emps.	250-499 Emps.	500-999 Emps.	Unknown Emps.	Industry Sales
2015	4.9	12.2	51.6	145.7	13.7	5.4	1.7	0.7	0.4	236.2
2016	5.1	12.8	54.3	153.4	14.4	5.7	1.8	0.7	0.4	248.6
2017	5.4	13.5	56.9	160.7	15.1	5.9	1.8	0.7	0.5	260.5
2018	5.8	14.5	61.1	172.8	16.2	6.4	2.0	0.8	0.5	280.1
2018	6.2	15.6	65.8	186.0	17.5	6.9	2.1	0.8	0.5	301.5

INDUSTRY: MEN'S CLOTHING STORES INDUSTRY (NAICS 44811)
PRODUCT LINE: JEWELRY & WATCHES (Main Category)

NAICS 44811: Men's Clothing Stores. this industry comprises establishments primarily engaged in retailing a general line of new men's and boys' clothing. These establishments may provide basic alterations, such as hemming, taking in or letting out seams, or lengthening or shortening sleeves.

5-YEAR TREND – ESTIMATED INDUSTRY SALES ($MILLIONS)

Year	Employee Size of Establishment									Total Industry Sales
	1-4 Emps.	5-9 Emps.	10-19 Emps.	20-49 Emps.	50-99 Emps.	100-249 Emps.	250-499 Emps.	500-999 Emps.	Unknown Emps.	
2015	1.0	1.5	3.6	2.1	0.5	0.3	0.1	0.0	0.2	9.4
2016	1.1	1.6	3.8	2.2	0.6	0.3	0.1	0.0	0.2	9.8
2017	1.1	1.7	3.9	2.3	0.6	0.3	0.1	0.0	0.2	10.2
2018	1.2	1.7	4.1	2.4	0.6	0.3	0.1	0.0	0.2	10.6
2018	1.2	1.8	4.2	2.5	0.6	0.3	0.1	0.0	0.2	11.0

INDUSTRY: WOMEN'S CLOTHING STORES INDUSTRY (NAICS 44812)
PRODUCT LINE: JEWELRY & WATCHES (Main Category)

NAICS 44812: Women's Clothing Stores . this industry comprises establishments primarily engaged in retailing a general line of new women's, misses' and juniors' clothing, including maternity wear. These establishments may provide basic alterations, such as hemming, taking in or letting out seams, or lengthening or shortening sleeves.

5-YEAR TREND – ESTIMATED INDUSTRY SALES ($MILLIONS)

Year	Employee Size of Establishment									Total Industry Sales
	1-4 Emps.	5-9 Emps.	10-19 Emps.	20-49 Emps.	50-99 Emps.	100-249 Emps.	250-499 Emps.	500-999 Emps.	Unknown Emps.	
2015	76.0	172.3	422.0	288.9	90.2	87.7	32.9	29.8	17.6	1,217.2
2016	78.9	178.9	438.3	300.1	93.7	91.1	34.1	30.9	18.3	1,264.2
2017	81.7	185.2	453.7	310.6	97.0	94.3	35.3	32.0	18.9	1,308.8
2018	86.8	196.9	482.4	330.3	103.1	100.3	37.6	33.6	20.1	1,391.0
2018	92.5	209.7	513.8	351.8	109.8	106.8	40.0	35.3	21.4	1,481.1

INDUSTRY: FAMILY CLOTHING STORES INDUSTRY (NAICS 44814)
PRODUCT LINE: JEWELRY & WATCHES (Main Category)

NAICS 44814: Family Clothing Stores . this industry comprises establishments primarily engaged in retailing a general line of new clothing for men, women, and children, without specializing in sales for an individual gender or age group. These establishments may provide basic alterations, such as hemming, taking in or letting out seams, or lengthening or shortening sleeves.

5-YEAR TREND — ESTIMATED INDUSTRY SALES ($MILLIONS)

Year	Employee Size of Establishment									Total Industry Sales
	1-4 Emps.	5-9 Emps.	10-19 Emps.	20-49 Emps.	50-99 Emps.	100-249 Emps.	250-499 Emps.	500-999 Emps.	Unknown Emps.	
2015	18.7	33.6	144.6	443.1	464.8	115.9	114.6	45.4	5.1	1,385.8
2016	19.4	34.8	149.7	459.0	481.4	120.1	118.7	47.0	5.2	1,435.4
2017	20.0	35.9	154.6	474.0	497.1	124.0	122.6	48.6	5.4	1,482.3
2018	21.3	38.1	164.0	502.8	527.4	131.6	130.0	51.4	5.7	1,572.4
2018	22.6	40.5	174.4	534.4	560.6	139.8	138.2	54.5	6.1	1,671.1

INDUSTRY: PRERECORDED TAPES & CDs STORES (NAICS 45122)
PRODUCT LINE: JEWELRY & WATCHES (Main Category)

NAICS 45122: Prerecorded Tape, Compact Disc, and Record Stores . This industry comprises establishments primarily engaged in retailing new prerecorded audio and video tapes, compact discs (CDs), and phonograph records.

5-YEAR TREND — ESTIMATED INDUSTRY SALES ($MILLIONS)

Year	Employee Size of Establishment									Total Industry Sales
	1-4 Emps.	5-9 Emps.	10-19 Emps.	20-49 Emps.	50-99 Emps.	100-249 Emps.	250-499 Emps.	500-999 Emps.	Unknown Emps.	
2015	0.6	1.1	3.0	5.9	4.3	283.1	25.0	0.5	0.2	323.7
2016	0.6	1.2	3.0	6.1	4.5	292.5	25.9	0.5	0.2	334.4
2017	0.6	1.2	3.1	6.3	4.6	301.3	26.6	0.5	0.2	344.4
2018	0.6	1.3	3.3	6.6	4.8	316.6	28.0	0.5	0.2	362.0
2018	0.7	1.3	3.5	6.9	5.1	333.4	29.5	0.5	0.2	381.2

INDUSTRY: DEPARTMENT STORES INDUSTRY (NAICS 45211)
PRODUCT LINE: JEWELRY & WATCHES (Main Category)

NAICS 45211: Department Stores Industry . this industry comprises establishments known as department stores primarily engaged in retailing a wide range of the following new products with no one merchandise line predominating: apparel, furniture, appliances and home furnishings; and selected additional items, such as paint, hardware, toiletries, cosmetics, photographic equipment, jewelry, toys, and sporting goods. merchandise lines are normally arranged in separate departments.

5-YEAR TREND – ESTIMATED INDUSTRY SALES ($MILLIONS)

Year	Employee Size of Establishment									Total
	1-4 Emps.	5-9 Emps.	10-19 Emps.	20-49 Emps.	50-99 Emps.	100-249 Emps.	250-499 Emps.	500-999 Emps.	Unknown Emps.	Industry Sales
2015	0.2	0.1	0.4	28.7	544.6	1,806.4	792.5	106.1	4.6	3,283.5
2016	0.2	0.1	0.4	29.1	551.6	1,829.7	802.7	107.5	4.7	3,325.9
2017	0.2	0.1	0.4	29.4	557.6	1,849.4	811.3	108.6	4.7	3,361.7
2018	0.2	0.1	0.4	29.5	560.2	1,857.9	815.1	109.3	4.7	3,377.4
2018	0.3	0.1	0.4	29.7	564.2	1,871.3	820.9	110.1	4.8	3,401.7

INDUSTRY: WAREHOUSE CLUBS & SUPERCENTERS (NAICS 45291)
PRODUCT LINE: JEWELRY & WATCHES (Main Category)

NAICS 45291: Warehouse Clubs and Superstores This industry comprises establishments known as warehouse clubs, superstores or supercenters primarily engaged in retailing a general line of groceries in combination with general lines of new merchandise, such as apparel, furniture, and appliances.

5-YEAR TREND – ESTIMATED INDUSTRY SALES ($MILLIONS)

Year	Employee Size of Establishment									Total
	1-4 Emps.	5-9 Emps.	10-19 Emps.	20-49 Emps.	50-99 Emps.	100-249 Emps.	250-499 Emps.	500-999 Emps.	Unknown Emps.	Industry Sales
2015	0.7	0.0	0.1	6.9	8.6	1,066.6	4,715.3	124.6	1.5	5,924.3
2016	0.8	0.0	0.1	7.1	9.0	1,105.6	4,887.7	129.1	1.5	6,140.9
2017	0.8	0.0	0.1	7.3	9.3	1,142.5	5,050.7	133.4	1.6	6,345.7
2018	0.9	0.0	0.1	8.0	10.1	1,240.9	5,485.6	144.9	1.7	6,892.2
2018	0.9	0.0	0.2	8.5	10.7	1,317.8	5,825.7	153.9	1.8	7,319.5

INDUSTRY: ELECTRONIC SHOPPING & MAIL-ORDER (NAICS 45411)
PRODUCT LINE: JEWELRY & WATCHES (Main Category)

NAICS 45411: Electronic Shopping and Mail-Order Houses This industry comprises establishments primarily engaged in retailing all types of merchandise by means of mail or by electronic media, such as interactive television or computer. Included in this industry are establishments primarily engaged in retailing from catalogue showrooms of mail-order houses.

5-YEAR TREND — ESTIMATED INDUSTRY SALES ($MILLIONS)

Year	Employee Size of Establishment									Total Industry Sales
	1-4 Emps.	5-9 Emps.	10-19 Emps.	20-49 Emps.	50-99 Emps.	100-249 Emps.	250-499 Emps.	500-999 Emps.	Unknown Emps.	
2015	1,196.6	635.3	943.4	1,526.3	1,097.9	2,140.4	3,131.7	3,967.1	181.0	14,819.6
2016	1,276.5	677.7	1,006.4	1,628.1	1,171.1	2,283.2	3,340.6	4,231.7	193.0	15,808.3
2017	1,353.9	718.8	1,067.4	1,726.9	1,242.2	2,421.7	3,543.3	4,488.5	204.8	16,767.4
2018	1,540.7	818.0	1,214.7	1,965.1	1,413.5	2,755.7	4,032.0	4,982.3	233.0	18,954.8
2018	1,711.2	908.5	1,349.1	2,182.6	1,569.9	3,060.7	4,478.3	5,438.1	258.8	20,957.2

INDUSTRY: BOOK STORES INDUSTRY (NAICS 451211)
PRODUCT LINE: JEWELRY & WATCHES (Main Category)

NAICS 451211: Book Stores. this industry comprises establishments primarily engaged in the retail sale of new books and magazines. Establishments primarily engaged in the retail sale of used books are classified in 5932.

5-YEAR TREND — ESTIMATED INDUSTRY SALES ($MILLIONS)

Year	Employee Size of Establishment									Total Industry Sales
	1-4 Emps.	5-9 Emps.	10-19 Emps.	20-49 Emps.	50-99 Emps.	100-249 Emps.	250-499 Emps.	500-999 Emps.	Unknown Emps.	
2015	0.8	1.3	2.6	6.9	3.1	1.2	0.2	0.8	0.4	17.3
2016	0.9	1.3	2.8	7.2	3.3	1.3	0.2	0.9	0.4	18.3
2017	0.9	1.4	2.9	7.6	3.4	1.3	0.2	0.9	0.5	19.2
2018	0.9	1.4	2.9	7.6	3.4	1.4	0.2	0.9	0.5	19.3
2018	0.9	1.4	2.9	7.7	3.5	1.4	0.2	1.0	0.5	19.5

INDUSTRY: DEPARTMENT STORES INDUSTRY (NAICS 45211)
PRODUCT LINE: GOLD JEWELRY (Sub Category)

NAICS 45211: Department Stores Industry . this industry comprises establishments known as department stores primarily engaged in retailing a wide range of the following new products with no one merchandise line predominating: apparel, furniture, appliances and home furnishings; and selected additional items, such as paint, hardware, toiletries, cosmetics, photographic equipment, jewelry, toys, and sporting goods. merchandise lines are normally arranged in separate departments.

5-YEAR TREND – ESTIMATED INDUSTRY SALES ($MILLIONS)

Year	Employee Size of Establishment									Total
	1-4 Emps.	5-9 Emps.	10-19 Emps.	20-49 Emps.	50-99 Emps.	100-249 Emps.	250-499 Emps.	500-999 Emps.	Unknown Emps.	Industry Sales
2015	0.0	0.0	0.1	4.6	87.0	288.7	126.7	17.0	0.7	524.8
2016	0.0	0.0	0.1	4.6	88.2	292.4	128.3	17.2	0.7	531.6
2017	0.0	0.0	0.1	4.7	89.1	295.6	129.7	17.4	0.8	537.3
2018	0.0	0.0	0.1	4.7	89.5	296.9	130.3	17.5	0.8	539.8
2018	0.0	0.0	0.1	4.7	90.2	299.1	131.2	17.6	0.8	543.7

INDUSTRY: WAREHOUSE CLUBS & SUPERCENTERS (NAICS 45291)
PRODUCT LINE: GOLD JEWELRY (Sub Category)

NAICS 45291: Warehouse Clubs and Superstores This industry comprises establishments known as warehouse clubs, superstores or supercenters primarily engaged in retailing a general line of groceries in combination with general lines of new merchandise, such as apparel, furniture, and appliances.

5-YEAR TREND – ESTIMATED INDUSTRY SALES ($MILLIONS)

Year	Employee Size of Establishment									Total
	1-4 Emps.	5-9 Emps.	10-19 Emps.	20-49 Emps.	50-99 Emps.	100-249 Emps.	250-499 Emps.	500-999 Emps.	Unknown Emps.	Industry Sales
2015	0.2	0.0	0.0	1.9	2.4	293.6	1,297.7	34.3	0.4	1,630.5
2016	0.2	0.0	0.0	2.0	2.5	304.3	1,345.2	35.5	0.4	1,690.1
2017	0.2	0.0	0.0	2.0	2.5	314.4	1,390.0	36.7	0.4	1,746.5
2018	0.2	0.0	0.0	2.2	2.8	341.5	1,509.8	39.9	0.5	1,896.9
2018	0.3	0.0	0.0	2.3	2.9	362.7	1,603.4	42.4	0.5	2,014.5

INDUSTRY: DEPARTMENT STORES INDUSTRY (NAICS 45211)

PRODUCT LINE: DIAMOND & GEMSTONE JEWELRY (Sub Category)

NAICS 45211: Department Stores Industry . this industry comprises establishments known as department stores primarily engaged in retailing a wide range of the following new products with no one merchandise line predominating: apparel, furniture, appliances and home furnishings; and selected additional items, such as paint, hardware, toiletries, cosmetics, photographic equipment, jewelry, toys, and sporting goods. merchandise lines are normally arranged in separate departments.

5-YEAR TREND – ESTIMATED INDUSTRY SALES ($MILLIONS)

Year	Employee Size of Establishment									Total Industry Sales
	1-4 Emps.	5-9 Emps.	10-19 Emps.	20-49 Emps.	50-99 Emps.	100-249 Emps.	250-499 Emps.	500-999 Emps.	Unknown Emps.	
2015	0.1	0.0	0.1	8.3	157.5	522.4	229.2	30.7	1.3	949.5
2016	0.1	0.0	0.1	8.4	159.5	529.1	232.1	31.1	1.3	961.8
2017	0.1	0.0	0.1	8.5	161.2	534.8	234.6	31.4	1.4	972.2
2018	0.1	0.0	0.1	8.5	162.0	537.3	235.7	31.6	1.4	976.7
2018	0.1	0.0	0.1	8.6	163.2	541.1	237.4	31.8	1.4	983.7

INDUSTRY: WAREHOUSE CLUBS & SUPERCENTERS (NAICS 45291)

PRODUCT LINE: DIAMOND & GEMSTONE JEWELRY (Sub Category)

NAICS 45291: Warehouse Clubs and Superstores This industry comprises establishments known as warehouse clubs, superstores or supercenters primarily engaged in retailing a general line of groceries in combination with general lines of new merchandise, such as apparel, furniture, and appliances.

5-YEAR TREND – ESTIMATED INDUSTRY SALES ($MILLIONS)

Year	Employee Size of Establishment									Total Industry Sales
	1-4 Emps.	5-9 Emps.	10-19 Emps.	20-49 Emps.	50-99 Emps.	100-249 Emps.	250-499 Emps.	500-999 Emps.	Unknown Emps.	
2015	0.2	0.0	0.0	1.7	2.2	265.7	1,174.8	31.0	0.4	1,476.1
2016	0.2	0.0	0.0	1.8	2.2	275.5	1,217.8	32.2	0.4	1,530.0
2017	0.2	0.0	0.0	1.8	2.3	284.6	1,258.4	33.2	0.4	1,581.1
2018	0.2	0.0	0.0	2.0	2.5	309.2	1,366.8	36.1	0.4	1,717.2
2018	0.2	0.0	0.0	2.1	2.7	328.3	1,451.5	38.3	0.5	1,823.7

INDUSTRY: DEPARTMENT STORES INDUSTRY (NAICS 45211)
PRODUCT LINE: OTHER FINE JEWELRY (Sub Category)

NAICS 45211: Department Stores Industry . this industry comprises establishments known as department stores primarily engaged in retailing a wide range of the following new products with no one merchandise line predominating: apparel, furniture, appliances and home furnishings; and selected additional items, such as paint, hardware, toiletries, cosmetics, photographic equipment, jewelry, toys, and sporting goods. merchandise lines are normally arranged in separate departments.

5-YEAR TREND – ESTIMATED INDUSTRY SALES ($MILLIONS)

Year	Employee Size of Establishment									Total Industry Sales
	1-4 Emps.	5-9 Emps.	10-19 Emps.	20-49 Emps.	50-99 Emps.	100-249 Emps.	250-499 Emps.	500-999 Emps.	Unknown Emps.	
2015	0.1	0.0	0.2	15.8	300.1	995.3	436.6	58.5	2.5	1,809.2
2016	0.1	0.0	0.2	16.0	304.0	1,008.1	442.3	59.2	2.6	1,832.6
2017	0.1	0.0	0.2	16.2	307.2	1,019.0	447.0	59.9	2.6	1,852.3
2018	0.1	0.0	0.2	16.3	308.6	1,023.7	449.1	60.2	2.6	1,860.9
2018	0.1	0.0	0.2	16.4	310.9	1,031.1	452.3	60.6	2.6	1,874.3

INDUSTRY: WAREHOUSE CLUBS & SUPERCENTERS (NAICS 45291)
PRODUCT LINE: OTHER FINE JEWELRY (Sub Category)

NAICS 45291: Warehouse Clubs and Superstores This industry comprises establishments known as warehouse clubs, superstores or supercenters primarily engaged in retailing a general line of groceries in combination with general lines of new merchandise, such as apparel, furniture, and appliances.

5-YEAR TREND – ESTIMATED INDUSTRY SALES ($MILLIONS)

Year	Employee Size of Establishment									Total Industry Sales
	1-4 Emps.	5-9 Emps.	10-19 Emps.	20-49 Emps.	50-99 Emps.	100-249 Emps.	250-499 Emps.	500-999 Emps.	Unknown Emps.	
2015	0.4	0.0	0.1	3.3	4.1	507.3	2,242.7	59.3	0.7	2,817.8
2016	0.4	0.0	0.1	3.4	4.3	525.8	2,324.7	61.4	0.7	2,920.8
2017	0.4	0.0	0.1	3.5	4.4	543.4	2,402.2	63.5	0.7	3,018.2
2018	0.4	0.0	0.1	3.8	4.8	590.2	2,609.1	68.9	0.8	3,278.1
2018	0.4	0.0	0.1	4.0	5.1	626.8	2,770.9	73.2	0.9	3,481.3

INDUSTRY: MEN'S CLOTHING STORES INDUSTRY (NAICS 44811)
PRODUCT LINE: COSTUME & NOVELTY JEWELRY (Sub Category)

NAICS 44811: Men's Clothing Stores. this industry comprises establishments primarily engaged in retailing a general line of new men's and boys' clothing. These establishments may provide basic alterations, such as hemming, taking in or letting out seams, or lengthening or shortening sleeves.

5-YEAR TREND – ESTIMATED INDUSTRY SALES ($MILLIONS)

Year	Employee Size of Establishment									Total
	1-4 Emps.	5-9 Emps.	10-19 Emps.	20-49 Emps.	50-99 Emps.	100-249 Emps.	250-499 Emps.	500-999 Emps.	Unknown Emps.	Industry Sales
2015	0.5	0.8	1.9	1.1	0.3	0.1	0.1	0.0	0.1	4.8
2016	0.6	0.8	1.9	1.1	0.3	0.1	0.1	0.0	0.1	5.1
2017	0.6	0.9	2.0	1.2	0.3	0.2	0.1	0.0	0.1	5.3
2018	0.6	0.9	2.1	1.2	0.3	0.2	0.1	0.0	0.1	5.5
2018	0.6	0.9	2.2	1.3	0.3	0.2	0.1	0.0	0.1	5.7

INDUSTRY: WOMEN'S CLOTHING STORES INDUSTRY (NAICS 44812)
PRODUCT LINE: COSTUME & NOVELTY JEWELRY (Sub Category)

NAICS 44812: Women's Clothing Stores . this industry comprises establishments primarily engaged in retailing a general line of new women's, misses' and juniors' clothing, including maternity wear. These establishments may provide basic alterations, such as hemming, taking in or letting out seams, or lengthening or shortening sleeves.

5-YEAR TREND – ESTIMATED INDUSTRY SALES ($MILLIONS)

Year	Employee Size of Establishment									Total
	1-4 Emps.	5-9 Emps.	10-19 Emps.	20-49 Emps.	50-99 Emps.	100-249 Emps.	250-499 Emps.	500-999 Emps.	Unknown Emps.	Industry Sales
2015	65.5	148.5	363.7	249.0	77.7	75.6	28.3	25.7	15.2	1,049.2
2016	68.0	154.2	377.8	258.6	80.7	78.5	29.4	26.7	15.7	1,089.7
2017	70.4	159.6	391.1	267.8	83.6	81.3	30.4	27.6	16.3	1,128.1
2018	74.8	169.7	415.8	284.7	88.9	86.4	32.4	29.0	17.3	1,199.0
2018	79.7	180.8	442.9	303.2	94.6	92.1	34.5	30.4	18.5	1,276.7

INDUSTRY: FAMILY CLOTHING STORES INDUSTRY (NAICS 44814)
PRODUCT LINE: COSTUME & NOVELTY JEWELRY (Sub Category)

NAICS 44814: Family Clothing Stores . this industry comprises establishments primarily engaged in retailing a general line of new clothing for men, women, and children, without specializing in sales for an individual gender or age group. These establishments may provide basic alterations, such as hemming, taking in or letting out seams, or lengthening or shortening sleeves.

5-YEAR TREND – ESTIMATED INDUSTRY SALES ($MILLIONS)

Year	Employee Size of Establishment									Total
	1-4 Emps.	5-9 Emps.	10-19 Emps.	20-49 Emps.	50-99 Emps.	100-249 Emps.	250-499 Emps.	500-999 Emps.	Unknown Emps.	Industry Sales
2015	7.0	12.5	54.0	165.6	173.6	43.3	42.8	17.0	1.9	517.8
2016	7.2	13.0	55.9	171.5	179.9	44.9	44.4	17.6	2.0	536.3
2017	7.5	13.4	57.8	177.1	185.7	46.3	45.8	18.1	2.0	553.8
2018	7.9	14.2	61.3	187.9	197.0	49.2	48.6	19.2	2.1	587.5
2018	8.4	15.1	65.1	199.7	209.4	52.2	51.6	20.4	2.3	624.4

INDUSTRY: MEN'S CLOTHING STORES INDUSTRY (NAICS 44811)
PRODUCT LINE: OTHER JEWELRY (Sub Category)

NAICS 44811: Men's Clothing Stores. this industry comprises establishments primarily engaged in retailing a general line of new men's and boys' clothing. These establishments may provide basic alterations, such as hemming, taking in or letting out seams, or lengthening or shortening sleeves.

5-YEAR TREND – ESTIMATED INDUSTRY SALES ($MILLIONS)

Year	Employee Size of Establishment									Total
	1-4 Emps.	5-9 Emps.	10-19 Emps.	20-49 Emps.	50-99 Emps.	100-249 Emps.	250-499 Emps.	500-999 Emps.	Unknown Emps.	Industry Sales
2015	0.5	0.8	1.8	1.0	0.3	0.1	0.1	0.0	0.1	4.6
2016	0.5	0.8	1.8	1.1	0.3	0.1	0.1	0.0	0.1	4.8
2017	0.5	0.8	1.9	1.1	0.3	0.1	0.1	0.0	0.1	5.0
2018	0.6	0.8	2.0	1.2	0.3	0.1	0.1	0.0	0.1	5.1
2018	0.6	0.9	2.0	1.2	0.3	0.2	0.1	0.0	0.1	5.3

INDUSTRY: WOMEN'S CLOTHING STORES INDUSTRY (NAICS 44812)

PRODUCT LINE: OTHER JEWELRY (Sub Category)

NAICS 44812: Women's Clothing Stores . this industry comprises establishments primarily engaged in retailing a general line of new women's, misses' and juniors' clothing, including maternity wear. These establishments may provide basic alterations, such as hemming, taking in or letting out seams, or lengthening or shortening sleeves.

5-YEAR TREND – ESTIMATED INDUSTRY SALES ($MILLIONS)

Year	Employee Size of Establishment									Total Industry Sales
	1-4 Emps.	5-9 Emps.	10-19 Emps.	20-49 Emps.	50-99 Emps.	100-249 Emps.	250-499 Emps.	500-999 Emps.	Unknown Emps.	
2015	10.5	23.8	58.2	39.9	12.4	12.1	4.5	4.1	2.4	168.0
2016	10.9	24.7	60.5	41.4	12.9	12.6	4.7	4.3	2.5	174.5
2017	11.3	25.6	62.6	42.9	13.4	13.0	4.9	4.4	2.6	180.6
2018	12.0	27.2	66.6	45.6	14.2	13.8	5.2	4.6	2.8	192.0
2018	12.8	28.9	70.9	48.6	15.2	14.7	5.5	4.9	3.0	204.4

INDUSTRY: FAMILY CLOTHING STORES INDUSTRY (NAICS 44814)

PRODUCT LINE: OTHER JEWELRY (Sub Category)

NAICS 44814: Family Clothing Stores . this industry comprises establishments primarily engaged in retailing a general line of new clothing for men, women, and children, without specializing in sales for an individual gender or age group. These establishments may provide basic alterations, such as hemming, taking in or letting out seams, or lengthening or shortening sleeves.

5-YEAR TREND – ESTIMATED INDUSTRY SALES ($MILLIONS)

Year	Employee Size of Establishment									Total Industry Sales
	1-4 Emps.	5-9 Emps.	10-19 Emps.	20-49 Emps.	50-99 Emps.	100-249 Emps.	250-499 Emps.	500-999 Emps.	Unknown Emps.	
2015	11.7	21.0	90.6	277.6	291.1	72.6	71.8	28.4	3.2	868.0
2016	12.2	21.8	93.8	287.5	301.6	75.2	74.4	29.5	3.3	899.1
2017	12.5	22.5	96.9	296.9	311.4	77.7	76.8	30.4	3.4	928.5
2018	13.3	23.9	102.7	315.0	330.3	82.4	81.5	32.2	3.6	984.9
2018	14.1	25.4	109.2	334.8	351.1	87.6	86.6	34.1	3.8	1,046.8

INDUSTRY: SUPERMARKETS INDUSTRY (NAICS 44511)
PRODUCT LINE: BOOKS (Main Category)

NAICS 44511: Grocery Stores Industry. this industry comprises establishments generally known as supermarkets and grocery stores primarily engaged in retailing a general line of food, such as canned and frozen foods; fresh fruits and vegetables; and fresh and prepared meats, fish, and poultry. Included in this industry are delicatessen-type establishments primarily engaged in retailing a general line of food.

5-Year Trend – Estimated Industry Sales ($Millions)

Year	Employee Size of Establishment									Total
	1-4 Emps.	5-9 Emps.	10-19 Emps.	20-49 Emps.	50-99 Emps.	100-249 Emps.	250-499 Emps.	500-999 Emps.	Unknown Emps.	Industry Sales
2015	13.2	9.9	25.1	81.8	198.5	452.8	130.5	18.0	2.5	932.3
2016	13.0	9.7	24.6	80.4	195.1	444.9	128.3	17.7	2.5	916.1
2017	12.7	9.5	24.1	78.8	191.3	436.1	125.7	17.3	2.4	898.1
2018	12.7	9.5	24.1	78.9	191.3	436.2	125.7	17.3	2.4	898.2
2018	12.7	9.5	24.2	79.0	191.7	437.1	126.0	17.3	2.4	900.1

INDUSTRY: PHARMACIES & DRUG STORES (NAICS 44611)
PRODUCT LINE: BOOKS (Main Category)

NAICS 44611 Pharmacies and Drug Stores – this industry comprises establishments known as pharmacies and drug stores engaged in retailing prescription or nonprescription drugs and medicines.

5-Year Trend – Estimated Industry Sales ($Millions)

Year	Employee Size of Establishment									Total
	1-4 Emps.	5-9 Emps.	10-19 Emps.	20-49 Emps.	50-99 Emps.	100-249 Emps.	250-499 Emps.	500-999 Emps.	Unknown Emps.	Industry Sales
2015	4.3	10.8	45.7	129.2	12.1	4.8	1.5	0.6	0.4	209.4
2016	4.6	11.4	48.1	136.0	12.8	5.0	1.6	0.6	0.4	220.4
2017	4.8	11.9	50.4	142.5	13.4	5.3	1.6	0.7	0.4	230.9
2018	5.1	12.8	54.2	153.2	14.4	5.7	1.8	0.7	0.4	248.3
2018	5.5	13.8	58.4	164.9	15.5	6.1	1.9	0.7	0.5	267.3

INDUSTRY: GAS STATIONS W/CONVENIENCE STORES (NAICS 44711)
PRODUCT LINE: BOOKS (Main Category)

NAICS 44711: Gas Stations with Convenience Stores. this industry comprises establishments primarily engaged in selling gasoline and lubricating oils. These establishments frequently sell other merchandise, such as tires, batteries, and other automobile parts, or perform minor repair work. Gasoline stations combined with other activities, such as grocery stores, convenience stores, or carwashes, are classified according to the primary activity.

5-YEAR TREND — ESTIMATED INDUSTRY SALES ($MILLIONS)

Year	Employee Size of Establishment									Total Industry Sales
	1-4 Emps.	5-9 Emps.	10-19 Emps.	20-49 Emps.	50-99 Emps.	100-249 Emps.	250-499 Emps.	500-999 Emps.	Unknown Emps.	
2015	7.9	21.2	34.4	21.2	1.9	1.2	0.2	0.0	0.1	87.9
2016	8.5	22.9	37.0	22.8	2.0	1.2	0.2	0.0	0.1	94.6
2017	9.1	24.4	39.5	24.3	2.1	1.3	0.2	0.0	0.1	101.1
2018	9.9	26.6	43.1	26.5	2.3	1.5	0.2	0.0	0.1	110.3
2018	10.8	29.0	47.0	28.9	2.5	1.6	0.2	0.0	0.1	120.2

INDUSTRY: PRERECORDED TAPES & CDs STORES (NAICS 45122)
PRODUCT LINE: BOOKS (Main Category)

NAICS 45122: Prerecorded Tape, Compact Disc, and Record Stores . This industry comprises establishments primarily engaged in retailing new prerecorded audio and video tapes, compact discs (CDs), and phonograph records.

5-YEAR TREND — ESTIMATED INDUSTRY SALES ($MILLIONS)

Year	Employee Size of Establishment									Total Industry Sales
	1-4 Emps.	5-9 Emps.	10-19 Emps.	20-49 Emps.	50-99 Emps.	100-249 Emps.	250-499 Emps.	500-999 Emps.	Unknown Emps.	
2015	6.9	13.8	35.9	71.7	52.6	3,442.4	304.4	5.6	2.4	3,935.8
2016	7.2	14.2	37.1	74.0	54.4	3,556.0	314.5	5.8	2.5	4,065.6
2017	7.4	14.7	38.2	76.2	56.0	3,662.6	323.9	6.0	2.6	4,187.6
2018	7.8	15.4	40.1	80.1	58.8	3,849.2	340.4	6.3	2.7	4,400.9
2018	8.2	16.2	42.3	84.4	62.0	4,053.6	358.5	6.6	2.8	4,634.6

INDUSTRY: DEPARTMENT STORES INDUSTRY (NAICS 45211)
PRODUCT LINE: BOOKS (Main Category)

NAICS 45211: Department Stores Industry . this industry comprises establishments known as department stores primarily engaged in retailing a wide range of the following new products with no one merchandise line predominating: apparel, furniture, appliances and home furnishings; and selected additional items, such as paint, hardware, toiletries, cosmetics, photographic equipment, jewelry, toys, and sporting goods. merchandise lines are normally arranged in separate departments.

5-YEAR TREND – ESTIMATED INDUSTRY SALES ($MILLIONS)

Year	Employee Size of Establishment									Total Industry Sales
	1-4 Emps.	5-9 Emps.	10-19 Emps.	20-49 Emps.	50-99 Emps.	100-249 Emps.	250-499 Emps.	500-999 Emps.	Unknown Emps.	
2015	0.0	0.0	0.0	3.3	62.3	206.7	90.7	12.1	0.5	375.7
2016	0.0	0.0	0.0	3.3	63.1	209.3	91.8	12.3	0.5	380.5
2017	0.0	0.0	0.0	3.4	63.8	211.6	92.8	12.4	0.5	384.6
2018	0.0	0.0	0.0	3.4	64.1	212.6	93.3	12.5	0.5	386.4
2018	0.0	0.0	0.0	3.4	64.6	214.1	93.9	12.6	0.5	389.2

INDUSTRY: WAREHOUSE CLUBS & SUPERCENTERS (NAICS 45291)
PRODUCT LINE: BOOKS (Main Category)

NAICS 45291: Warehouse Clubs and Superstores This industry comprises establishments known as warehouse clubs, superstores or supercenters primarily engaged in retailing a general line of groceries in combination with general lines of new merchandise, such as apparel, furniture, and appliances.

5-YEAR TREND – ESTIMATED INDUSTRY SALES ($MILLIONS)

Year	Employee Size of Establishment									Total Industry Sales
	1-4 Emps.	5-9 Emps.	10-19 Emps.	20-49 Emps.	50-99 Emps.	100-249 Emps.	250-499 Emps.	500-999 Emps.	Unknown Emps.	
2015	0.7	0.0	0.1	6.7	8.4	1,038.4	4,590.8	121.3	1.4	5,768.0
2016	0.7	0.0	0.1	6.9	8.7	1,076.4	4,758.7	125.7	1.5	5,978.8
2017	0.8	0.0	0.1	7.2	9.0	1,112.3	4,917.3	129.9	1.5	6,178.2
2018	0.8	0.0	0.1	7.8	9.8	1,208.1	5,340.9	141.1	1.7	6,710.3
2018	0.9	0.0	0.2	8.2	10.4	1,283.0	5,672.0	149.9	1.8	7,126.3

INDUSTRY: OFFICE SUPPLY & STATIONERY STORES (NAICS 45321)
PRODUCT LINE: BOOKS (Main Category)

NAICS 45321: Office Supplies and Stationery Stores . this industry comprises establishments primarily engaged in one or more of the following: (1) retailing new stationery, school supplies, and office supplies; (2) selling a combination of new office equipment, furniture, and supplies; and (3) selling new office equipment, furniture, and supplies in combination with selling new computers.

5-YEAR TREND – ESTIMATED INDUSTRY SALES ($MILLIONS)

Year	Employee Size of Establishment									Total
	1-4 Emps.	5-9 Emps.	10-19 Emps.	20-49 Emps.	50-99 Emps.	100-249 Emps.	250-499 Emps.	500-999 Emps.	Unknown Emps.	Industry Sales
2015	1.8	1.3	7.0	19.6	0.5	0.5	0.0	0.0	0.4	31.0
2016	1.8	1.3	7.0	19.6	0.5	0.5	0.0	0.0	0.4	31.0
2017	1.8	1.3	7.0	19.6	0.5	0.5	0.0	0.0	0.4	31.0
2018	1.7	1.3	6.8	19.2	0.5	0.5	0.0	0.0	0.4	30.3
2018	1.7	1.3	6.7	18.8	0.5	0.5	0.0	0.0	0.4	29.7

INDUSTRY: ELECTRONIC SHOPPING & MAIL-ORDER (NAICS 45411)
PRODUCT LINE: BOOKS (Main Category)

NAICS 45411: Electronic Shopping and Mail-Order Houses This industry comprises establishments primarily engaged in retailing all types of merchandise by means of mail or by electronic media, such as interactive television or computer. Included in this industry are establishments primarily engaged in retailing from catalogue showrooms of mail-order houses.

5-YEAR TREND – ESTIMATED INDUSTRY SALES ($MILLIONS)

Year	Employee Size of Establishment									Total
	1-4 Emps.	5-9 Emps.	10-19 Emps.	20-49 Emps.	50-99 Emps.	100-249 Emps.	250-499 Emps.	500-999 Emps.	Unknown Emps.	Industry Sales
2015	1,076.8	571.7	849.0	1,373.5	987.9	1,926.0	2,818.1	3,569.8	162.8	13,335.7
2016	1,148.7	609.8	905.6	1,465.1	1,053.8	2,054.6	3,006.1	3,808.0	173.7	14,225.4
2017	1,218.3	646.8	960.5	1,554.0	1,117.8	2,179.2	3,188.5	4,039.0	184.2	15,088.4
2018	1,386.4	736.1	1,093.0	1,768.3	1,271.9	2,479.8	3,628.2	4,483.4	209.7	17,056.7
2018	1,539.8	817.5	1,214.0	1,964.0	1,412.7	2,754.2	4,029.8	4,893.6	232.9	18,858.7

INDUSTRY: BOOK STORES INDUSTRY (NAICS 451211)
PRODUCT LINE: BOOKS (Main Category)

NAICS 451211: Book Stores. this industry comprises establishments primarily engaged in the retail sale of new books and magazines. Establishments primarily engaged in the retail sale of used books are classified in 5932.

5-YEAR TREND – ESTIMATED INDUSTRY SALES ($MILLIONS)

Year	Employee Size of Establishment									Total Industry Sales
	1-4 Emps.	5-9 Emps.	10-19 Emps.	20-49 Emps.	50-99 Emps.	100-249 Emps.	250-499 Emps.	500-999 Emps.	Unknown Emps.	
2015	354.8	542.1	1,121.8	2,938.2	1,326.4	522.8	95.2	351.4	182.0	7,434.8
2016	374.2	571.6	1,182.9	3,098.3	1,398.6	551.3	100.4	370.5	191.9	7,839.7
2017	392.8	600.1	1,241.7	3,252.4	1,468.2	578.7	105.4	389.0	201.4	8,229.8
2018	395.6	604.4	1,250.7	3,275.8	1,478.7	582.9	106.2	399.5	202.9	8,296.6
2018	398.8	609.3	1,260.8	3,302.3	1,490.7	587.6	107.0	409.9	204.5	8,371.0

INDUSTRY: BOOK STORES INDUSTRY (NAICS 451211)
PRODUCT LINE: TRADE BOOKS (Sub Category)

NAICS 451211: Book Stores. this industry comprises establishments primarily engaged in the retail sale of new books and magazines. Establishments primarily engaged in the retail sale of used books are classified in 5932.

5-YEAR TREND – ESTIMATED INDUSTRY SALES ($MILLIONS)

Year	Employee Size of Establishment									Total Industry Sales
	1-4 Emps.	5-9 Emps.	10-19 Emps.	20-49 Emps.	50-99 Emps.	100-249 Emps.	250-499 Emps.	500-999 Emps.	Unknown Emps.	
2015	188.8	288.4	596.8	1,563.2	705.7	278.1	50.7	187.0	96.8	3,955.5
2016	199.1	304.1	629.3	1,648.4	744.1	293.3	53.4	197.1	102.1	4,171.0
2017	209.0	319.3	660.6	1,730.4	781.1	307.9	56.1	206.9	107.2	4,378.5
2018	210.5	321.6	665.4	1,742.8	786.7	310.1	56.5	212.6	107.9	4,414.0
2018	212.2	324.2	670.8	1,756.9	793.1	312.6	57.0	218.1	108.8	4,453.6

INDUSTRY: BOOK STORES INDUSTRY (NAICS 451211)
PRODUCT LINE: MASS MARKET PAPERBACK BOOKS (Sub Category)

NAICS 451211: Book Stores. this industry comprises establishments primarily engaged in the retail sale of new books and magazines. Establishments primarily engaged in the retail sale of used books are classified in 5932.

5-YEAR TREND — ESTIMATED INDUSTRY SALES ($MILLIONS)

Year	Employee Size of Establishment									Total Industry Sales
	1-4 Emps.	5-9 Emps.	10-19 Emps.	20-49 Emps.	50-99 Emps.	100-249 Emps.	250-499 Emps.	500-999 Emps.	Unknown Emps.	
2015	11.5	17.5	36.3	95.0	42.9	16.9	3.1	11.4	5.9	240.3
2016	12.1	18.5	38.2	100.1	45.2	17.8	3.2	12.0	6.2	253.4
2017	12.7	19.4	40.1	105.1	47.5	18.7	3.4	12.6	6.5	266.0
2018	12.8	19.5	40.4	105.9	47.8	18.8	3.4	12.9	6.6	268.2
2018	12.9	19.7	40.8	106.7	48.2	19.0	3.5	13.2	6.6	270.6

INDUSTRY: BOOK STORES INDUSTRY (NAICS 451211)
PRODUCT LINE: RELIGIOUS BOOKS (Sub Category)

NAICS 451211: Book Stores. this industry comprises establishments primarily engaged in the retail sale of new books and magazines. Establishments primarily engaged in the retail sale of used books are classified in 5932.

5-YEAR TREND — ESTIMATED INDUSTRY SALES ($MILLIONS)

Year	Employee Size of Establishment									Total Industry Sales
	1-4 Emps.	5-9 Emps.	10-19 Emps.	20-49 Emps.	50-99 Emps.	100-249 Emps.	250-499 Emps.	500-999 Emps.	Unknown Emps.	
2015	21.9	33.5	69.4	181.7	82.0	32.3	5.9	21.7	11.3	459.7
2016	23.1	35.3	73.1	191.6	86.5	34.1	6.2	22.9	11.9	484.7
2017	24.3	37.1	76.8	201.1	90.8	35.8	6.5	24.1	12.5	508.9
2018	24.5	37.4	77.3	202.5	91.4	36.0	6.6	24.7	12.5	513.0
2018	24.7	37.7	78.0	204.2	92.2	36.3	6.6	25.3	12.6	517.6

INDUSTRY: BOOK STORES INDUSTRY (NAICS 451211)
PRODUCT LINE: GENERAL REFERENCE BOOKS (Sub Category)

NAICS 451211: Book Stores. this industry comprises establishments primarily engaged in the retail sale of new books and magazines. Establishments primarily engaged in the retail sale of used books are classified in 5932.

5-YEAR TREND — ESTIMATED INDUSTRY SALES ($MILLIONS)

Year	Employee Size of Establishment									Total Industry Sales
	1-4 Emps.	5-9 Emps.	10-19 Emps.	20-49 Emps.	50-99 Emps.	100-249 Emps.	250-499 Emps.	500-999 Emps.	Unknown Emps.	
2015	2.9	4.5	9.3	24.3	11.0	4.3	0.8	2.9	1.5	61.5
2016	3.1	4.7	9.8	25.6	11.6	4.6	0.8	3.1	1.6	64.8
2017	3.2	5.0	10.3	26.9	12.1	4.8	0.9	3.2	1.7	68.1
2018	3.3	5.0	10.3	27.1	12.2	4.8	0.9	3.3	1.7	68.6
2018	3.3	5.0	10.4	27.3	12.3	4.9	0.9	3.4	1.7	69.2

INDUSTRY: BOOK STORES INDUSTRY (NAICS 451211)
PRODUCT LINE: TEXTBOOKS (Sub Category)

NAICS 451211: Book Stores. this industry comprises establishments primarily engaged in the retail sale of new books and magazines. Establishments primarily engaged in the retail sale of used books are classified in 5932.

5-YEAR TREND — ESTIMATED INDUSTRY SALES ($MILLIONS)

Year	Employee Size of Establishment									Total Industry Sales
	1-4 Emps.	5-9 Emps.	10-19 Emps.	20-49 Emps.	50-99 Emps.	100-249 Emps.	250-499 Emps.	500-999 Emps.	Unknown Emps.	
2015	117.3	179.2	370.9	971.4	438.5	172.8	31.5	116.2	60.2	2,457.9
2016	123.7	189.0	391.1	1,024.3	462.4	182.2	33.2	122.5	63.4	2,591.7
2017	129.9	198.4	410.5	1,075.2	485.4	191.3	34.9	128.6	66.6	2,720.7
2018	130.8	199.8	413.5	1,082.9	488.9	192.7	35.1	132.1	67.1	2,742.8
2018	131.8	201.4	416.8	1,091.7	492.8	194.2	35.4	135.5	67.6	2,767.4

INDUSTRY: BOOK STORES INDUSTRY (NAICS 451211)
PRODUCT LINE: PROFESSIONAL BOOKS (Sub Category)

NAICS 451211: Book Stores. this industry comprises establishments primarily engaged in the retail sale of new books and magazines. Establishments primarily engaged in the retail sale of used books are classified in 5932.

5-Year Trend – Estimated Industry Sales ($Millions)

Year	Employee Size of Establishment									Total Industry Sales
	1-4 Emps.	5-9 Emps.	10-19 Emps.	20-49 Emps.	50-99 Emps.	100-249 Emps.	250-499 Emps.	500-999 Emps.	Unknown Emps.	
2015	3.5	5.4	11.1	29.2	13.2	5.2	0.9	3.5	1.8	73.9
2016	3.7	5.7	11.8	30.8	13.9	5.5	1.0	3.7	1.9	77.9
2017	3.9	6.0	12.3	32.3	14.6	5.8	1.0	3.9	2.0	81.8
2018	3.9	6.0	12.4	32.5	14.7	5.8	1.1	4.0	2.0	82.4
2018	4.0	6.1	12.5	32.8	14.8	5.8	1.1	4.1	2.0	83.2

INDUSTRY: BOOK STORES INDUSTRY (NAICS 451211)
PRODUCT LINE: OTHER BOOKS (Sub Category)

NAICS 451211: Book Stores. this industry comprises establishments primarily engaged in the retail sale of new books and magazines. Establishments primarily engaged in the retail sale of used books are classified in 5932.

5-Year Trend – Estimated Industry Sales ($Millions)

Year	Employee Size of Establishment									Total Industry Sales
	1-4 Emps.	5-9 Emps.	10-19 Emps.	20-49 Emps.	50-99 Emps.	100-249 Emps.	250-499 Emps.	500-999 Emps.	Unknown Emps.	
2015	8.9	13.6	28.1	73.5	33.2	13.1	2.4	8.8	4.6	186.0
2016	9.4	14.3	29.6	77.5	35.0	13.8	2.5	9.3	4.8	196.1
2017	9.8	15.0	31.1	81.4	36.7	14.5	2.6	9.7	5.0	205.9
2018	9.9	15.1	31.3	81.9	37.0	14.6	2.7	10.0	5.1	207.5
2018	10.0	15.2	31.5	82.6	37.3	14.7	2.7	10.3	5.1	209.4

INDUSTRY: HOME CENTERS INDUSTRY (NAICS 44411)
PRODUCT LINE: TOYS & GAMES (Main Category)

NAICS 44411: Home Centers. This industry comprises establishments
known as home centers primarily engaged in retailing a general line of
new home repair and improvement materials and supplies, such as
lumber, plumbing goods, electrical goods, tools, housewares, hardware,
and lawn and garden supplies, with no one merchandise line predominating.
The merchandise lines are normally arranged in separate departments.

5-YEAR TREND — ESTIMATED INDUSTRY SALES ($MILLIONS)

Year	Employee Size of Establishment									Total Industry Sales
	1-4 Emps.	5-9 Emps.	10-19 Emps.	20-49 Emps.	50-99 Emps.	100-249 Emps.	250-499 Emps.	500-999 Emps.	Unknown Emps.	
2015	0.0	0.0	0.1	0.1	0.1	5.8	0.5	0.0	0.0	6.6
2016	0.0	0.0	0.1	0.1	0.1	6.0	0.5	0.0	0.0	6.8
2017	0.0	0.0	0.1	0.1	0.1	6.1	0.5	0.0	0.0	7.0
2018	0.0	0.0	0.1	0.1	0.1	6.4	0.6	0.0	0.0	7.4
2018	0.0	0.0	0.1	0.1	0.1	6.8	0.6	0.0	0.0	7.8

INDUSTRY: HARDWARE STORES (NAICS 44413)
PRODUCT LINE: TOYS & GAMES (Main Category)

NAICS 44413: Hardware Stores. Establishments primarily engaged
in the retail sale of a number of basic hardware lines, such as tools,
builders' hardware, paint and glass, housewares and household appliances,
and cutlery.

5-YEAR TREND — ESTIMATED INDUSTRY SALES ($MILLIONS)

Year	Employee Size of Establishment									Total Industry Sales
	1-4 Emps.	5-9 Emps.	10-19 Emps.	20-49 Emps.	50-99 Emps.	100-249 Emps.	250-499 Emps.	500-999 Emps.	Unknown Emps.	
2015	6.5	10.4	20.8	29.1	5.3	1.3	0.4	0.0	0.5	74.3
2016	6.6	10.6	21.2	29.7	5.4	1.3	0.4	0.0	0.6	75.7
2017	6.7	10.8	21.5	30.2	5.5	1.3	0.4	0.0	0.6	77.0
2018	7.0	11.3	22.6	31.6	5.8	1.4	0.4	0.0	0.6	80.6
2018	7.4	11.8	23.7	33.1	6.1	1.4	0.4	0.0	0.6	84.5

INDUSTRY: SUPERMARKETS INDUSTRY (NAICS 44511)
PRODUCT LINE: TOYS & GAMES (Main Category)

NAICS 44511: Grocery Stores Industry. this industry comprises establishments generally known as supermarkets and grocery stores primarily engaged in retailing a general line of food, such as canned and frozen foods; fresh fruits and vegetables; and fresh and prepared meats, fish, and poultry. Included in this industry are delicatessen-type establishments primarily engaged in retailing a general line of food.

5-YEAR TREND — ESTIMATED INDUSTRY SALES ($MILLIONS)

Year	Employee Size of Establishment									Total Industry Sales
	1-4 Emps.	5-9 Emps.	10-19 Emps.	20-49 Emps.	50-99 Emps.	100-249 Emps.	250-499 Emps.	500-999 Emps.	Unknown Emps.	
2015	6.9	5.2	13.1	42.8	103.8	236.6	68.2	9.4	1.3	487.3
2016	6.8	5.1	12.9	42.0	102.0	232.5	67.0	9.2	1.3	478.8
2017	6.6	5.0	12.6	41.2	100.0	228.0	65.7	9.1	1.3	469.4
2018	6.6	5.0	12.6	41.2	100.0	228.0	65.7	9.1	1.3	469.5
2018	6.7	5.0	12.6	41.3	100.2	228.5	65.9	9.1	1.3	470.4

INDUSTRY: PHARMACIES & DRUG STORES (NAICS 44611)
PRODUCT LINE: TOYS & GAMES (Main Category)

NAICS 44611 Pharmacies and Drug Stores – this industry comprises establishments known as pharmacies and drug stores engaged in retailing prescription or nonprescription drugs and medicines.

5-YEAR TREND — ESTIMATED INDUSTRY SALES ($MILLIONS)

Year	Employee Size of Establishment									Total Industry Sales
	1-4 Emps.	5-9 Emps.	10-19 Emps.	20-49 Emps.	50-99 Emps.	100-249 Emps.	250-499 Emps.	500-999 Emps.	Unknown Emps.	
2015	13.7	34.3	144.9	409.4	38.5	15.1	4.7	1.9	1.1	663.6
2016	14.5	36.1	152.5	430.8	40.5	15.9	4.9	2.0	1.2	698.3
2017	15.1	37.8	159.7	451.5	42.4	16.7	5.2	2.1	1.3	731.7
2018	16.3	40.7	171.8	485.5	45.6	17.9	5.6	2.2	1.4	786.8
2018	17.5	43.8	184.9	522.6	49.1	19.3	6.0	2.3	1.5	846.9

INDUSTRY: GAS STATIONS W/CONVENIENCE STORES (NAICS 44711)
PRODUCT LINE: TOYS & GAMES (Main Category)

NAICS 44711: Gas Stations with Convenience Stores. this industry comprises establishments primarily engaged in selling gasoline and lubricating oils. These establishments frequently sell other merchandise, such as tires, batteries, and other automobile parts, or perform minor repair work. Gasoline stations combined with other activities, such as grocery stores, convenience stores, or carwashes, are classified according to the primary activity.

5-YEAR TREND – ESTIMATED INDUSTRY SALES ($MILLIONS)

Year	Employee Size of Establishment									Total Industry Sales
	1-4 Emps.	5-9 Emps.	10-19 Emps.	20-49 Emps.	50-99 Emps.	100-249 Emps.	250-499 Emps.	500-999 Emps.	Unknown Emps.	
2015	1.1	3.1	5.0	3.1	0.3	0.2	0.0	0.0	0.0	12.8
2016	1.2	3.3	5.4	3.3	0.3	0.2	0.0	0.0	0.0	13.8
2017	1.3	3.6	5.7	3.5	0.3	0.2	0.0	0.0	0.0	14.7
2018	1.4	3.9	6.3	3.9	0.3	0.2	0.0	0.0	0.0	16.0
2018	1.6	4.2	6.8	4.2	0.4	0.2	0.0	0.0	0.0	17.5

INDUSTRY: FAMILY CLOTHING STORES INDUSTRY (NAICS 44814)
PRODUCT LINE: TOYS & GAMES (Main Category)

NAICS 44814: Family Clothing Stores . this industry comprises establishments primarily engaged in retailing a general line of new clothing for men, women, and children, without specializing in sales for an individual gender or age group. These establishments may provide basic alterations, such as hemming, taking in or letting out seams, or lengthening or shortening sleeves.

5-YEAR TREND – ESTIMATED INDUSTRY SALES ($MILLIONS)

Year	Employee Size of Establishment									Total Industry Sales
	1-4 Emps.	5-9 Emps.	10-19 Emps.	20-49 Emps.	50-99 Emps.	100-249 Emps.	250-499 Emps.	500-999 Emps.	Unknown Emps.	
2015	29.9	53.7	231.0	708.2	742.8	185.3	183.2	72.6	8.1	2,214.7
2016	31.0	55.6	239.3	733.5	769.4	191.9	189.7	75.2	8.4	2,294.0
2017	32.0	57.4	247.1	757.5	794.5	198.2	195.9	77.6	8.7	2,368.9
2018	34.0	60.9	262.1	803.6	842.8	210.3	207.8	82.2	9.2	2,512.9
2018	36.1	64.7	278.6	854.1	895.9	223.5	220.9	87.1	9.8	2,670.7

INDUSTRY: PRERECORDED TAPES & CDs STORES (NAICS 45122)
PRODUCT LINE: TOYS & GAMES (Main Category)

NAICS 45122: Prerecorded Tape, Compact Disc, and Record Stores .
This industry comprises establishments primarily engaged in retailing new
prerecorded audio and video tapes, compact discs (CDs), and phonograph
records.

5-YEAR TREND — ESTIMATED INDUSTRY SALES ($MILLIONS)

Year	Employee Size of Establishment									Total Industry Sales
	1-4 Emps.	5-9 Emps.	10-19 Emps.	20-49 Emps.	50-99 Emps.	100-249 Emps.	250-499 Emps.	500-999 Emps.	Unknown Emps.	
2015	8.5	16.9	44.1	88.0	64.6	4,229.4	374.0	6.9	3.0	4,835.6
2016	8.8	17.5	45.5	90.9	66.8	4,368.9	386.4	7.2	3.0	4,995.1
2017	9.1	18.0	46.9	93.7	68.8	4,499.9	398.0	7.4	3.1	5,144.9
2018	9.5	18.9	49.3	98.4	72.3	4,729.2	418.3	7.7	3.3	5,407.0
2018	10.0	19.9	51.9	103.7	76.1	4,980.4	440.5	8.1	3.5	5,694.2

INDUSTRY: DEPARTMENT STORES INDUSTRY (NAICS 45211)
PRODUCT LINE: TOYS & GAMES (Main Category)

NAICS 45211: Department Stores Industry . this industry comprises
establishments known as department stores primarily engaged in retailing
a wide range of the following new products with no one merchandise line
predominating: apparel, furniture, appliances and home furnishings; and
selected additional items, such as paint, hardware, toiletries, cosmetics,
photographic equipment, jewelry, toys, and sporting goods. merchandise lines
are normally arranged in separate departments.

5-YEAR TREND — ESTIMATED INDUSTRY SALES ($MILLIONS)

Year	Employee Size of Establishment									Total Industry Sales
	1-4 Emps.	5-9 Emps.	10-19 Emps.	20-49 Emps.	50-99 Emps.	100-249 Emps.	250-499 Emps.	500-999 Emps.	Unknown Emps.	
2015	0.3	0.1	0.5	38.9	737.8	2,447.2	1,073.6	143.8	6.2	4,448.5
2016	0.3	0.1	0.5	39.4	747.4	2,478.8	1,087.5	145.6	6.3	4,505.9
2017	0.3	0.1	0.5	39.8	755.4	2,505.5	1,099.2	147.2	6.4	4,554.4
2018	0.3	0.1	0.5	40.0	758.9	2,517.1	1,104.3	148.0	6.4	4,575.6
2018	0.3	0.1	0.5	40.3	764.4	2,535.2	1,112.2	149.1	6.5	4,608.6

INDUSTRY: WAREHOUSE CLUBS & SUPERCENTERS (NAICS 45291)
PRODUCT LINE: TOYS & GAMES (Main Category)

NAICS 45291: Warehouse Clubs and Superstores This industry comprises establishments known as warehouse clubs, superstores or supercenters primarily engaged in retailing a general line of groceries in combination with general lines of new merchandise, such as apparel, furniture, and appliances.

5-YEAR TREND – ESTIMATED INDUSTRY SALES ($MILLIONS)

Year	Employee Size of Establishment									Total Industry Sales
	1-4 Emps.	5-9 Emps.	10-19 Emps.	20-49 Emps.	50-99 Emps.	100-249 Emps.	250-499 Emps.	500-999 Emps.	Unknown Emps.	
2015	2.0	0.1	0.3	18.5	23.3	2,880.6	12,734.9	336.5	4.0	16,000.2
2016	2.1	0.1	0.4	19.2	24.2	2,985.9	13,200.5	348.8	4.1	16,585.1
2017	2.1	0.1	0.4	19.8	25.0	3,085.5	13,640.6	360.4	4.2	17,138.1
2018	2.3	0.1	0.4	21.5	27.1	3,351.2	14,815.4	391.4	4.6	18,614.1
2018	2.5	0.1	0.4	22.9	28.8	3,559.0	15,733.9	415.7	4.9	19,768.2

INDUSTRY: OFFICE SUPPLY & STATIONERY STORES (NAICS 45321)
PRODUCT LINE: TOYS & GAMES (Main Category)

NAICS 45321: Office Supplies and Stationery Stores . this industry comprises establishments primarily engaged in one or more of the following: (1) retailing new stationery, school supplies, and office supplies; (2) selling a combination of new office equipment, furniture, and supplies; and (3) selling new office equipment, furniture, and supplies in combination with selling new computers.

5-YEAR TREND – ESTIMATED INDUSTRY SALES ($MILLIONS)

Year	Employee Size of Establishment									Total Industry Sales
	1-4 Emps.	5-9 Emps.	10-19 Emps.	20-49 Emps.	50-99 Emps.	100-249 Emps.	250-499 Emps.	500-999 Emps.	Unknown Emps.	
2015	0.9	0.7	3.5	10.0	0.2	0.2	0.0	0.0	0.2	15.8
2016	0.9	0.7	3.5	10.0	0.2	0.2	0.0	0.0	0.2	15.8
2017	0.9	0.7	3.5	10.0	0.2	0.2	0.0	0.0	0.2	15.8
2018	0.9	0.7	3.5	9.8	0.2	0.2	0.0	0.0	0.2	15.4
2018	0.9	0.6	3.4	9.6	0.2	0.2	0.0	0.0	0.2	15.1

INDUSTRY: ELECTRONIC SHOPPING & MAIL-ORDER (NAICS 45411)
PRODUCT LINE: TOYS & GAMES (Main Category)

NAICS 45411: Electronic Shopping and Mail-Order Houses This industry comprises establishments primarily engaged in retailing all types of merchandise by means of mail or by electronic media, such as interactive television or computer. Included in this industry are establishments primarily engaged in retailing from catalogue showrooms of mail-order houses.

5-YEAR TREND – ESTIMATED INDUSTRY SALES ($MILLIONS)

Year	Employee Size of Establishment									Total Industry Sales
	1-4 Emps.	5-9 Emps.	10-19 Emps.	20-49 Emps.	50-99 Emps.	100-249 Emps.	250-499 Emps.	500-999 Emps.	Unknown Emps.	
2015	673.8	357.7	531.2	859.4	618.2	1,205.2	1,763.4	2,233.8	101.9	8,344.6
2016	718.8	381.6	566.7	916.8	659.4	1,285.6	1,881.0	2,382.8	108.7	8,901.3
2017	762.4	404.8	601.0	972.4	699.4	1,363.6	1,995.1	2,527.4	115.3	9,441.4
2018	867.5	460.6	683.9	1,106.5	795.9	1,551.7	2,270.3	2,805.4	131.2	10,673.0
2018	963.5	511.6	759.6	1,229.0	884.0	1,723.4	2,521.6	3,062.1	145.7	11,800.5

INDUSTRY: BOOK STORES INDUSTRY (NAICS 451211)
PRODUCT LINE: TOYS & GAMES (Main Category)

NAICS 451211: Book Stores. this industry comprises establishments primarily engaged in the retail sale of new books and magazines. Establishments primarily engaged in the retail sale of used books are classified in 5932.

5-YEAR TREND – ESTIMATED INDUSTRY SALES ($MILLIONS)

Year	Employee Size of Establishment									Total Industry Sales
	1-4 Emps.	5-9 Emps.	10-19 Emps.	20-49 Emps.	50-99 Emps.	100-249 Emps.	250-499 Emps.	500-999 Emps.	Unknown Emps.	
2015	1.1	1.7	3.5	9.2	4.1	1.6	0.3	1.1	0.6	23.2
2016	1.2	1.8	3.7	9.7	4.4	1.7	0.3	1.2	0.6	24.5
2017	1.2	1.9	3.9	10.2	4.6	1.8	0.3	1.2	0.6	25.7
2018	1.2	1.9	3.9	10.2	4.6	1.8	0.3	1.2	0.6	25.9
2018	1.2	1.9	3.9	10.3	4.7	1.8	0.3	1.3	0.6	26.1

INDUSTRY: PHARMACIES & DRUG STORES (NAICS 44611)
PRODUCT LINE: TOYS (Sub Category)

NAICS 44611 Pharmacies and Drug Stores – this industry comprises establishments known as pharmacies and drug stores engaged in retailing prescription or nonprescription drugs and medicines.

5-YEAR TREND – ESTIMATED INDUSTRY SALES ($MILLIONS)

Year	Employee Size of Establishment									Total
	1-4 Emps.	5-9 Emps.	10-19 Emps.	20-49 Emps.	50-99 Emps.	100-249 Emps.	250-499 Emps.	500-999 Emps.	Unknown Emps.	Industry Sales
2015	12.1	30.2	127.7	360.9	33.9	13.3	4.1	1.7	1.0	584.9
2016	12.7	31.8	134.4	379.8	35.7	14.0	4.3	1.7	1.1	615.6
2017	13.4	33.3	140.8	397.9	37.4	14.7	4.6	1.8	1.1	645.0
2018	14.4	35.9	151.4	427.9	40.2	15.8	4.9	1.9	1.2	693.5
2018	15.5	38.6	163.0	460.6	43.3	17.0	5.3	2.0	1.3	746.5

INDUSTRY: DEPARTMENT STORES INDUSTRY (NAICS 45211)
PRODUCT LINE: TOYS (Sub Category)

NAICS 45211: Department Stores Industry . this industry comprises establishments known as department stores primarily engaged in retailing a wide range of the following new products with no one merchandise line predominating: apparel, furniture, appliances and home furnishings; and selected additional items, such as paint, hardware, toiletries, cosmetics, photographic equipment, jewelry, toys, and sporting goods. merchandise lines are normally arranged in separate departments.

5-YEAR TREND – ESTIMATED INDUSTRY SALES ($MILLIONS)

Year	Employee Size of Establishment									Total
	1-4 Emps.	5-9 Emps.	10-19 Emps.	20-49 Emps.	50-99 Emps.	100-249 Emps.	250-499 Emps.	500-999 Emps.	Unknown Emps.	Industry Sales
2015	0.2	0.1	0.3	26.1	496.3	1,646.1	722.2	96.7	4.2	2,992.3
2016	0.2	0.1	0.3	26.5	502.7	1,667.4	731.5	98.0	4.2	3,030.9
2017	0.2	0.1	0.3	26.8	508.1	1,685.3	739.4	99.0	4.3	3,063.6
2018	0.2	0.1	0.3	26.9	510.5	1,693.1	742.8	99.6	4.3	3,077.8
2018	0.2	0.1	0.3	27.1	514.2	1,705.3	748.1	100.3	4.3	3,100.0

INDUSTRY: ELECTRONIC SHOPPING & MAIL-ORDER (NAICS 45411)
PRODUCT LINE: TOYS (Sub Category)

NAICS 45411: Electronic Shopping and Mail-Order Houses This industry comprises establishments primarily engaged in retailing all types of merchandise by means of mail or by electronic media, such as interactive television or computer. Included in this industry are establishments primarily engaged in retailing from catalogue showrooms of mail-order houses.

5-YEAR TREND — ESTIMATED INDUSTRY SALES ($MILLIONS)

Year	\multicolumn{9}{c|}{Employee Size of Establishment}	Total Industry Sales
	1-4 Emps.	5-9 Emps.	10-19 Emps.	20-49 Emps.	50-99 Emps.	100-249 Emps.	250-499 Emps.	500-999 Emps.	Unknown Emps.	
2015	349.9	185.8	275.9	446.3	321.0	625.9	915.7	1,160.0	52.9	4,333.3
2016	373.2	198.2	294.3	476.1	342.4	667.6	976.8	1,237.4	56.4	4,622.4
2017	395.9	210.2	312.1	505.0	363.2	708.1	1,036.1	1,312.4	59.9	4,902.9
2018	450.5	239.2	355.2	574.6	413.3	805.8	1,179.0	1,456.9	68.1	5,542.5
2018	500.4	265.7	394.5	638.2	459.1	895.0	1,309.5	1,590.1	75.7	6,128.0

INDUSTRY: PHARMACIES & DRUG STORES (NAICS 44611)
PRODUCT LINE: GAMES (Sub Category)

NAICS 44611 Pharmacies and Drug Stores – this industry comprises establishments known as pharmacies and drug stores engaged in retailing prescription or nonprescription drugs and medicines.

5-YEAR TREND — ESTIMATED INDUSTRY SALES ($MILLIONS)

Year	\multicolumn{9}{c|}{Employee Size of Establishment}	Total Industry Sales
	1-4 Emps.	5-9 Emps.	10-19 Emps.	20-49 Emps.	50-99 Emps.	100-249 Emps.	250-499 Emps.	500-999 Emps.	Unknown Emps.	
2015	0.5	1.3	5.5	15.6	1.5	0.6	0.2	0.1	0.0	25.3
2016	0.6	1.4	5.8	16.4	1.5	0.6	0.2	0.1	0.0	26.6
2017	0.6	1.4	6.1	17.2	1.6	0.6	0.2	0.1	0.0	27.9
2018	0.6	1.6	6.6	18.5	1.7	0.7	0.2	0.1	0.1	30.0
2018	0.7	1.7	7.1	19.9	1.9	0.7	0.2	0.1	0.1	32.3

INDUSTRY: DEPARTMENT STORES INDUSTRY (NAICS 45211)
PRODUCT LINE: GAMES (Sub Category)

NAICS 45211: Department Stores Industry . this industry comprises establishments known as department stores primarily engaged in retailing a wide range of the following new products with no one merchandise line predominating: apparel, furniture, appliances and home furnishings; and selected additional items, such as paint, hardware, toiletries, cosmetics, photographic equipment, jewelry, toys, and sporting goods. merchandise lines are normally arranged in separate departments.

5-YEAR TREND — ESTIMATED INDUSTRY SALES ($MILLIONS)

Year	Employee Size of Establishment									Total Industry Sales
	1-4 Emps.	5-9 Emps.	10-19 Emps.	20-49 Emps.	50-99 Emps.	100-249 Emps.	250-499 Emps.	500-999 Emps.	Unknown Emps.	
2015	0.1	0.0	0.2	12.7	240.9	799.1	350.6	46.9	2.0	1,452.5
2016	0.1	0.0	0.2	12.9	244.0	809.4	355.1	47.6	2.1	1,471.3
2017	0.1	0.0	0.2	13.0	246.7	818.1	358.9	48.1	2.1	1,487.1
2018	0.1	0.0	0.2	13.1	247.8	821.9	360.6	48.3	2.1	1,494.0
2018	0.1	0.0	0.2	13.1	249.6	827.8	363.2	48.7	2.1	1,504.8

INDUSTRY: ELECTRONIC SHOPPING & MAIL-ORDER (NAICS 45411)
PRODUCT LINE: GAMES (Sub Category)

NAICS 45411: Electronic Shopping and Mail-Order Houses This industry comprises establishments primarily engaged in retailing all types of merchandise by means of mail or by electronic media, such as interactive television or computer. Included in this industry are establishments primarily engaged in retailing from catalogue showrooms of mail-order houses.

5-YEAR TREND — ESTIMATED INDUSTRY SALES ($MILLIONS)

Year	Employee Size of Establishment									Total Industry Sales
	1-4 Emps.	5-9 Emps.	10-19 Emps.	20-49 Emps.	50-99 Emps.	100-249 Emps.	250-499 Emps.	500-999 Emps.	Unknown Emps.	
2015	86.9	46.1	68.5	110.8	79.7	155.4	227.4	288.1	13.1	1,076.2
2016	92.7	49.2	73.1	118.2	85.0	165.8	242.6	307.3	14.0	1,148.0
2017	98.3	52.2	77.5	125.4	90.2	175.9	257.3	325.9	14.9	1,217.6
2018	111.9	59.4	88.2	142.7	102.6	200.1	292.8	361.8	16.9	1,376.5
2018	124.3	66.0	98.0	158.5	114.0	222.3	325.2	394.9	18.8	1,521.9

INDUSTRY: PHARMACIES & DRUG STORES (NAICS 44611)
PRODUCT LINE: HOBBY GOODS (Sub Category)

NAICS 44611 Pharmacies and Drug Stores – this industry comprises establishments known as pharmacies and drug stores engaged in retailing prescription or nonprescription drugs and medicines.

5-YEAR TREND – ESTIMATED INDUSTRY SALES ($MILLIONS)

Year	Employee Size of Establishment									Total Industry Sales
	1-4 Emps.	5-9 Emps.	10-19 Emps.	20-49 Emps.	50-99 Emps.	100-249 Emps.	250-499 Emps.	500-999 Emps.	Unknown Emps.	
2015	1.1	2.8	11.6	32.9	3.1	1.2	0.4	0.2	0.1	53.3
2016	1.2	2.9	12.3	34.6	3.3	1.3	0.4	0.2	0.1	56.1
2017	1.2	3.0	12.8	36.3	3.4	1.3	0.4	0.2	0.1	58.8
2018	1.3	3.3	13.8	39.0	3.7	1.4	0.4	0.2	0.1	63.2
2018	1.4	3.5	14.9	42.0	3.9	1.5	0.5	0.2	0.1	68.1

INDUSTRY: ELECTRONIC SHOPPING & MAIL-ORDER (NAICS 45411)
PRODUCT LINE: HOBBY GOODS (Sub Category)

NAICS 45411: Electronic Shopping and Mail-Order Houses This industry comprises establishments primarily engaged in retailing all types of merchandise by means of mail or by electronic media, such as interactive television or computer. Included in this industry are establishments primarily engaged in retailing from catalogue showrooms of mail-order houses.

5-YEAR TREND – ESTIMATED INDUSTRY SALES ($MILLIONS)

Year	Employee Size of Establishment									Total Industry Sales
	1-4 Emps.	5-9 Emps.	10-19 Emps.	20-49 Emps.	50-99 Emps.	100-249 Emps.	250-499 Emps.	500-999 Emps.	Unknown Emps.	
2015	237.0	125.8	186.8	302.3	217.4	423.9	620.2	785.7	35.8	2,935.0
2016	252.8	134.2	199.3	322.5	231.9	452.2	661.6	838.1	38.2	3,130.9
2017	268.1	142.4	211.4	342.0	246.0	479.6	701.7	888.9	40.6	3,320.8
2018	305.1	162.0	240.6	389.2	279.9	545.8	798.5	986.8	46.1	3,754.0
2018	338.9	179.9	267.2	432.3	310.9	606.2	886.9	1,077.0	51.3	4,150.6

INDUSTRY: HOME CENTERS INDUSTRY (NAICS 44411)
PRODUCT LINE: SPORTING & RECREATION GOODS (Main Category)

NAICS 44411: Home Centers. This industry comprises establishments
known as home centers primarily engaged in retailing a general line of
new home repair and improvement materials and supplies, such as
lumber, plumbing goods, electrical goods, tools, housewares, hardware,
and lawn and garden supplies, with no one merchandise line predominating.
The merchandise lines are normally arranged in separate departments.

5-YEAR TREND — ESTIMATED INDUSTRY SALES ($MILLIONS)

Year	Employee Size of Establishment									Total Industry Sales
	1-4 Emps.	5-9 Emps.	10-19 Emps.	20-49 Emps.	50-99 Emps.	100-249 Emps.	250-499 Emps.	500-999 Emps.	Unknown Emps.	
2015	0.3	0.5	1.4	2.7	2.0	129.8	11.5	0.2	0.1	148.4
2016	0.3	0.5	1.4	2.8	2.0	134.1	11.9	0.2	0.1	153.3
2017	0.3	0.6	1.4	2.9	2.1	138.1	12.2	0.2	0.1	157.9
2018	0.3	0.6	1.5	3.0	2.2	145.1	12.8	0.2	0.1	165.9
2018	0.3	0.6	1.6	3.2	2.3	152.8	13.5	0.3	0.1	174.7

INDUSTRY: HARDWARE STORES (NAICS 44413)
PRODUCT LINE: SPORTING & RECREATION GOODS (Main Category)

NAICS 44413: Hardware Stores. Establishments primarily engaged
in the retail sale of a number of basic hardware lines, such as tools,
builders' hardware, paint and glass, housewares and household appliances,
and cutlery.

5-YEAR TREND — ESTIMATED INDUSTRY SALES ($MILLIONS)

Year	Employee Size of Establishment									Total Industry Sales
	1-4 Emps.	5-9 Emps.	10-19 Emps.	20-49 Emps.	50-99 Emps.	100-249 Emps.	250-499 Emps.	500-999 Emps.	Unknown Emps.	
2015	17.6	28.2	56.4	79.0	14.5	3.4	1.0	0.0	1.5	201.5
2016	17.9	28.7	57.5	80.5	14.7	3.5	1.0	0.0	1.5	205.3
2017	18.2	29.2	58.4	81.8	15.0	3.5	1.0	0.0	1.5	208.6
2018	19.1	30.6	61.1	85.6	15.7	3.7	1.0	0.1	1.6	218.4
2018	20.0	32.1	64.1	89.8	16.4	3.9	1.1	0.1	1.7	229.1

| INDUSTRY: SUPERMARKETS INDUSTRY (NAICS 44511) |
| PRODUCT LINE: SPORTING & RECREATION GOODS (Main Category) |

NAICS 44511: Grocery Stores Industry. this industry comprises establishments generally known as supermarkets and grocery stores primarily engaged in retailing a general line of food, such as canned and frozen foods; fresh fruits and vegetables; and fresh and prepared meats, fish, and poultry. Included in this industry are delicatessen-type establishments primarily engaged in retailing a general line of food.

5-YEAR TREND – ESTIMATED INDUSTRY SALES ($MILLIONS)

Year	Employee Size of Establishment									Total Industry Sales
	1-4 Emps.	5-9 Emps.	10-19 Emps.	20-49 Emps.	50-99 Emps.	100-249 Emps.	250-499 Emps.	500-999 Emps.	Unknown Emps.	
2015	86.0	64.4	163.2	533.2	1,293.4	2,949.5	850.3	117.2	16.3	6,073.4
2016	84.5	63.3	160.4	524.0	1,270.9	2,898.3	835.5	115.2	16.0	5,968.1
2017	82.9	62.0	157.2	513.6	1,245.9	2,841.2	819.1	112.9	15.7	5,850.6
2018	82.9	62.0	157.3	513.7	1,246.1	2,841.6	819.2	112.9	15.7	5,851.3
2018	83.0	62.2	157.6	514.8	1,248.7	2,847.6	820.9	113.0	15.7	5,863.5

| INDUSTRY: PHARMACIES & DRUG STORES (NAICS 44611) |
| PRODUCT LINE: SPORTING & RECREATION GOODS (Main Category) |

NAICS 44611 Pharmacies and Drug Stores – this industry comprises establishments known as pharmacies and drug stores engaged in retailing prescription or nonprescription drugs and medicines.

5-YEAR TREND – ESTIMATED INDUSTRY SALES ($MILLIONS)

Year	Employee Size of Establishment									Total Industry Sales
	1-4 Emps.	5-9 Emps.	10-19 Emps.	20-49 Emps.	50-99 Emps.	100-249 Emps.	250-499 Emps.	500-999 Emps.	Unknown Emps.	
2015	0.6	1.5	6.3	17.9	1.7	0.7	0.2	0.1	0.1	29.0
2016	0.6	1.6	6.7	18.8	1.8	0.7	0.2	0.1	0.1	30.5
2017	0.7	1.7	7.0	19.7	1.9	0.7	0.2	0.1	0.1	32.0
2018	0.7	1.8	7.5	21.2	2.0	0.8	0.2	0.1	0.1	34.4
2018	0.8	1.9	8.1	22.8	2.1	0.8	0.3	0.1	0.1	37.0

INDUSTRY: GAS STATIONS W/CONVENIENCE STORES (NAICS 44711)
PRODUCT LINE: SPORTING & RECREATION GOODS (Main Category)

NAICS 44711: Gas Stations with Convenience Stores. this industry comprises establishments primarily engaged in selling gasoline and lubricating oils. These establishments frequently sell other merchandise, such as tires, batteries, and other automobile parts, or perform minor repair work. Gasoline stations combined with other activities, such as grocery stores, convenience stores, or carwashes, are classified according to the primary activity.

5-YEAR TREND – ESTIMATED INDUSTRY SALES ($MILLIONS)

Year	Employee Size of Establishment									Total Industry Sales
	1-4 Emps.	5-9 Emps.	10-19 Emps.	20-49 Emps.	50-99 Emps.	100-249 Emps.	250-499 Emps.	500-999 Emps.	Unknown Emps.	
2015	18.0	48.3	78.2	48.1	4.2	2.6	0.4	0.0	0.2	200.0
2016	19.3	52.0	84.1	51.8	4.5	2.8	0.4	0.0	0.2	215.2
2017	20.6	55.6	89.9	55.3	4.8	3.0	0.4	0.0	0.2	229.9
2018	22.5	60.6	98.1	60.3	5.3	3.3	0.5	0.0	0.3	250.8
2018	24.5	66.1	106.9	65.8	5.8	3.6	0.5	0.0	0.3	273.4

INDUSTRY: MEN'S CLOTHING STORES INDUSTRY (NAICS 44811)
PRODUCT LINE: SPORTING & RECREATION GOODS (Main Category)

NAICS 44811: Men's Clothing Stores. this industry comprises establishments primarily engaged in retailing a general line of new men's and boys' clothing. These establishments may provide basic alterations, such as hemming, taking in or letting out seams, or lengthening or shortening sleeves.

5-YEAR TREND – ESTIMATED INDUSTRY SALES ($MILLIONS)

Year	Employee Size of Establishment									Total Industry Sales
	1-4 Emps.	5-9 Emps.	10-19 Emps.	20-49 Emps.	50-99 Emps.	100-249 Emps.	250-499 Emps.	500-999 Emps.	Unknown Emps.	
2015	1.2	1.9	4.3	2.5	0.6	0.3	0.1	0.0	0.2	11.3
2016	1.3	1.9	4.5	2.7	0.7	0.3	0.1	0.0	0.2	11.8
2017	1.4	2.0	4.7	2.8	0.7	0.4	0.1	0.0	0.2	12.3
2018	1.4	2.1	4.9	2.9	0.7	0.4	0.2	0.0	0.2	12.8
2018	1.5	2.2	5.1	3.0	0.8	0.4	0.2	0.0	0.2	13.2

INDUSTRY: FAMILY CLOTHING STORES INDUSTRY (NAICS 44814)
PRODUCT LINE: SPORTING & RECREATION GOODS (Main Category)

NAICS 44814: Family Clothing Stores . this industry comprises
establishments primarily engaged in retailing a general line of new clothing
for men, women, and children, without specializing in sales for an individual
gender or age group. These establishments may provide basic alterations,
such as hemming, taking in or letting out seams, or lengthening or shortening sleeves.

5-YEAR TREND — ESTIMATED INDUSTRY SALES ($MILLIONS)

Year	Employee Size of Establishment									Total Industry Sales
	1-4 Emps.	5-9 Emps.	10-19 Emps.	20-49 Emps.	50-99 Emps.	100-249 Emps.	250-499 Emps.	500-999 Emps.	Unknown Emps.	
2015	2.1	3.8	16.1	49.5	51.9	12.9	12.8	5.1	0.6	154.7
2016	2.2	3.9	16.7	51.3	53.8	13.4	13.3	5.3	0.6	160.3
2017	2.2	4.0	17.3	52.9	55.5	13.8	13.7	5.4	0.6	165.5
2018	2.4	4.3	18.3	56.1	58.9	14.7	14.5	5.7	0.6	175.6
2018	2.5	4.5	19.5	59.7	62.6	15.6	15.4	6.1	0.7	186.6

INDUSTRY: DEPARTMENT STORES INDUSTRY (NAICS 45211)
PRODUCT LINE: SPORTING & RECREATION GOODS (Main Category)

NAICS 45211: Department Stores Industry . this industry comprises
establishments known as department stores primarily engaged in retailing
a wide range of the following new products with no one merchandise line
predominating: apparel, furniture, appliances and home furnishings; and
selected additional items, such as paint, hardware, toiletries, cosmetics,
photographic equipment, jewelry, toys, and sporting goods. merchandise lines
are normally arranged in separate departments.

5-YEAR TREND — ESTIMATED INDUSTRY SALES ($MILLIONS)

Year	Employee Size of Establishment									Total Industry Sales
	1-4 Emps.	5-9 Emps.	10-19 Emps.	20-49 Emps.	50-99 Emps.	100-249 Emps.	250-499 Emps.	500-999 Emps.	Unknown Emps.	
2015	0.2	0.1	0.3	24.8	471.2	1,562.8	685.6	91.8	4.0	2,840.9
2016	0.2	0.1	0.3	25.1	477.3	1,583.0	694.5	93.0	4.0	2,877.6
2017	0.2	0.1	0.3	25.4	482.4	1,600.1	702.0	94.0	4.1	2,908.6
2018	0.2	0.1	0.3	25.5	484.6	1,607.5	705.2	94.5	4.1	2,922.1
2018	0.2	0.1	0.3	25.7	488.1	1,619.0	710.3	95.2	4.1	2,943.1

INDUSTRY: WAREHOUSE CLUBS & SUPERCENTERS (NAICS 45291)
PRODUCT LINE: SPORTING & RECREATION GOODS (Main Category)

NAICS 45291: Warehouse Clubs and Superstores This industry comprises establishments known as warehouse clubs, superstores or supercenters primarily engaged in retailing a general line of groceries in combination with general lines of new merchandise, such as apparel, furniture, and appliances.

5-YEAR TREND – ESTIMATED INDUSTRY SALES ($MILLIONS)

Year	Employee Size of Establishment									Total Industry Sales
	1-4 Emps.	5-9 Emps.	10-19 Emps.	20-49 Emps.	50-99 Emps.	100-249 Emps.	250-499 Emps.	500-999 Emps.	Unknown Emps.	
2015	1.5	0.1	0.3	13.7	17.3	2,134.9	9,438.2	249.4	2.9	11,858.2
2016	1.5	0.1	0.3	14.2	17.9	2,213.0	9,783.2	258.5	3.0	12,291.7
2017	1.6	0.1	0.3	14.7	18.5	2,286.7	10,109.4	267.1	3.1	12,701.5
2018	1.7	0.1	0.3	16.0	20.1	2,483.7	10,980.1	290.1	3.4	13,795.4
2018	1.8	0.1	0.3	17.0	21.4	2,637.7	11,660.8	308.1	3.6	14,650.7

INDUSTRY: ELECTRONIC SHOPPING & MAIL-ORDER (NAICS 45411)
PRODUCT LINE: SPORTING & RECREATION GOODS (Main Category)

NAICS 45411: Electronic Shopping and Mail-Order Houses This industry comprises establishments primarily engaged in retailing all types of merchandise by means of mail or by electronic media, such as interactive television or computer. Included in this industry are establishments primarily engaged in retailing from catalogue showrooms of mail-order houses.

5-YEAR TREND – ESTIMATED INDUSTRY SALES ($MILLIONS)

Year	Employee Size of Establishment									Total Industry Sales
	1-4 Emps.	5-9 Emps.	10-19 Emps.	20-49 Emps.	50-99 Emps.	100-249 Emps.	250-499 Emps.	500-999 Emps.	Unknown Emps.	
2015	1,161.2	616.5	915.5	1,481.0	1,065.3	2,076.9	3,038.8	3,849.4	175.6	14,380.1
2016	1,238.6	657.6	976.5	1,579.8	1,136.4	2,215.5	3,241.5	4,106.2	187.3	15,339.5
2017	1,313.8	697.5	1,035.8	1,675.7	1,205.3	2,349.9	3,438.2	4,355.4	198.7	16,270.2
2018	1,495.0	793.7	1,178.6	1,906.8	1,371.5	2,674.0	3,912.4	4,834.6	226.1	18,392.6
2018	1,660.4	881.6	1,309.1	2,117.9	1,523.4	2,970.0	4,345.5	5,276.8	251.1	20,335.7

INDUSTRY: DEPARTMENT STORES INDUSTRY (NAICS 45211)
PRODUCT LINE: EXERCISE & FITNESS EQUIPMENT (Sub Category)

NAICS 45211: Department Stores Industry . this industry comprises establishments known as department stores primarily engaged in retailing a wide range of the following new products with no one merchandise line predominating: apparel, furniture, appliances and home furnishings; and selected additional items, such as paint, hardware, toiletries, cosmetics, photographic equipment, jewelry, toys, and sporting goods. merchandise lines are normally arranged in separate departments.

5-YEAR TREND — ESTIMATED INDUSTRY SALES ($MILLIONS)

Year	Employee Size of Establishment									Total Industry Sales
	1-4 Emps.	5-9 Emps.	10-19 Emps.	20-49 Emps.	50-99 Emps.	100-249 Emps.	250-499 Emps.	500-999 Emps.	Unknown Emps.	
2015	0.0	0.0	0.1	5.1	97.1	322.2	141.3	18.9	0.8	585.6
2016	0.0	0.0	0.1	5.2	98.4	326.3	143.2	19.2	0.8	593.2
2017	0.0	0.0	0.1	5.2	99.5	329.9	144.7	19.4	0.8	599.6
2018	0.0	0.0	0.1	5.3	99.9	331.4	145.4	19.5	0.8	602.4
2018	0.0	0.0	0.1	5.3	100.6	333.8	146.4	19.6	0.9	606.7

INDUSTRY: WAREHOUSE CLUBS & SUPERCENTERS (NAICS 45291)
PRODUCT LINE: EXERCISE & FITNESS EQUIPMENT (Sub Category)

NAICS 45291: Warehouse Clubs and Superstores This industry comprises establishments known as warehouse clubs, superstores or supercenters primarily engaged in retailing a general line of groceries in combination with general lines of new merchandise, such as apparel, furniture, and appliances.

5-YEAR TREND — ESTIMATED INDUSTRY SALES ($MILLIONS)

Year	Employee Size of Establishment									Total Industry Sales
	1-4 Emps.	5-9 Emps.	10-19 Emps.	20-49 Emps.	50-99 Emps.	100-249 Emps.	250-499 Emps.	500-999 Emps.	Unknown Emps.	
2015	0.3	0.0	0.0	2.7	3.4	418.6	1,850.5	48.9	0.6	2,325.0
2016	0.3	0.0	0.1	2.8	3.5	433.9	1,918.2	50.7	0.6	2,410.0
2017	0.3	0.0	0.1	2.9	3.6	448.4	1,982.1	52.4	0.6	2,490.4
2018	0.3	0.0	0.1	3.1	3.9	487.0	2,152.8	56.9	0.7	2,704.9
2018	0.4	0.0	0.1	3.3	4.2	517.2	2,286.3	60.4	0.7	2,872.6

INDUSTRY: DEPARTMENT STORES INDUSTRY (NAICS 45211)
PRODUCT LINE: FIREARMS & HUNTING EQUIPMENT (Sub Category)

NAICS 45211: Department Stores Industry . this industry comprises establishments known as department stores primarily engaged in retailing a wide range of the following new products with no one merchandise line predominating: apparel, furniture, appliances and home furnishings; and selected additional items, such as paint, hardware, toiletries, cosmetics, photographic equipment, jewelry, toys, and sporting goods. merchandise lines are normally arranged in separate departments.

5-YEAR TREND – ESTIMATED INDUSTRY SALES ($MILLIONS)

Year	Employee Size of Establishment									Total Industry Sales
	1-4 Emps.	5-9 Emps.	10-19 Emps.	20-49 Emps.	50-99 Emps.	100-249 Emps.	250-499 Emps.	500-999 Emps.	Unknown Emps.	
2015	0.0	0.0	0.0	3.9	73.9	245.2	107.6	14.4	0.6	445.7
2016	0.0	0.0	0.0	3.9	74.9	248.3	108.9	14.6	0.6	451.4
2017	0.0	0.0	0.1	4.0	75.7	251.0	110.1	14.7	0.6	456.3
2018	0.0	0.0	0.1	4.0	76.0	252.2	110.6	14.8	0.6	458.4
2018	0.0	0.0	0.1	4.0	76.6	254.0	111.4	14.9	0.6	461.7

INDUSTRY: WAREHOUSE CLUBS & SUPERCENTERS (NAICS 45291)
PRODUCT LINE: FIREARMS & HUNTING EQUIPMENT (Sub Category)

NAICS 45291: Warehouse Clubs and Superstores This industry comprises establishments known as warehouse clubs, superstores or supercenters primarily engaged in retailing a general line of groceries in combination with general lines of new merchandise, such as apparel, furniture, and appliances.

5-YEAR TREND – ESTIMATED INDUSTRY SALES ($MILLIONS)

Year	Employee Size of Establishment									Total Industry Sales
	1-4 Emps.	5-9 Emps.	10-19 Emps.	20-49 Emps.	50-99 Emps.	100-249 Emps.	250-499 Emps.	500-999 Emps.	Unknown Emps.	
2015	0.3	0.0	0.1	3.1	3.9	479.8	2,121.1	56.0	0.7	2,665.0
2016	0.3	0.0	0.1	3.2	4.0	497.3	2,198.7	58.1	0.7	2,762.4
2017	0.4	0.0	0.1	3.3	4.2	513.9	2,272.0	60.0	0.7	2,854.5
2018	0.4	0.0	0.1	3.6	4.5	558.2	2,467.6	65.2	0.8	3,100.4
2018	0.4	0.0	0.1	3.8	4.8	592.8	2,620.6	69.2	0.8	3,292.6

INDUSTRY: DEPARTMENT STORES INDUSTRY (NAICS 45211)
PRODUCT LINE: FISHING TACKLE EQUIPMENT (Sub Category)

NAICS 45211: Department Stores Industry . this industry comprises establishments known as department stores primarily engaged in retailing a wide range of the following new products with no one merchandise line predominating: apparel, furniture, appliances and home furnishings; and selected additional items, such as paint, hardware, toiletries, cosmetics, photographic equipment, jewelry, toys, and sporting goods. merchandise lines are normally arranged in separate departments.

5-Year Trend – Estimated Industry Sales ($Millions)

Year	Employee Size of Establishment									Total Industry Sales
	1-4 Emps.	5-9 Emps.	10-19 Emps.	20-49 Emps.	50-99 Emps.	100-249 Emps.	250-499 Emps.	500-999 Emps.	Unknown Emps.	
2015	0.0	0.0	0.0	2.1	40.7	135.0	59.2	7.9	0.3	245.4
2016	0.0	0.0	0.0	2.2	41.2	136.7	60.0	8.0	0.3	248.5
2017	0.0	0.0	0.0	2.2	41.7	138.2	60.6	8.1	0.4	251.2
2018	0.0	0.0	0.0	2.2	41.9	138.8	60.9	8.2	0.4	252.4
2018	0.0	0.0	0.0	2.2	42.2	139.8	61.3	8.2	0.4	254.2

INDUSTRY: WAREHOUSE CLUBS & SUPERCENTERS (NAICS 45291)
PRODUCT LINE: FISHING TACKLE EQUIPMENT (Sub Category)

NAICS 45291: Warehouse Clubs and Superstores This industry comprises establishments known as warehouse clubs, superstores or supercenters primarily engaged in retailing a general line of groceries in combination with general lines of new merchandise, such as apparel, furniture, and appliances.

5-Year Trend – Estimated Industry Sales ($Millions)

Year	Employee Size of Establishment									Total Industry Sales
	1-4 Emps.	5-9 Emps.	10-19 Emps.	20-49 Emps.	50-99 Emps.	100-249 Emps.	250-499 Emps.	500-999 Emps.	Unknown Emps.	
2015	0.2	0.0	0.0	1.7	2.2	271.7	1,201.0	31.7	0.4	1,509.0
2016	0.2	0.0	0.0	1.8	2.3	281.6	1,244.9	32.9	0.4	1,564.1
2017	0.2	0.0	0.0	1.9	2.4	291.0	1,286.4	34.0	0.4	1,616.3
2018	0.2	0.0	0.0	2.0	2.6	316.1	1,397.2	36.9	0.4	1,755.5
2018	0.2	0.0	0.0	2.2	2.7	335.6	1,483.8	39.2	0.5	1,864.3

INDUSTRY: DEPARTMENT STORES INDUSTRY (NAICS 45211)
PRODUCT LINE: CAMPING & BACKPACKING EQUIPMENT (Sub Category)

NAICS 45211: Department Stores Industry . this industry comprises establishments known as department stores primarily engaged in retailing a wide range of the following new products with no one merchandise line predominating: apparel, furniture, appliances and home furnishings; and selected additional items, such as paint, hardware, toiletries, cosmetics, photographic equipment, jewelry, toys, and sporting goods. merchandise lines are normally arranged in separate departments.

5-YEAR TREND – ESTIMATED INDUSTRY SALES ($MILLIONS)

Year	Employee Size of Establishment									Total Industry Sales
	1-4 Emps.	5-9 Emps.	10-19 Emps.	20-49 Emps.	50-99 Emps.	100-249 Emps.	250-499 Emps.	500-999 Emps.	Unknown Emps.	
2015	0.0	0.0	0.1	5.3	100.6	333.8	146.4	19.6	0.9	606.7
2016	0.0	0.0	0.1	5.4	101.9	338.1	148.3	19.9	0.9	614.5
2017	0.0	0.0	0.1	5.4	103.0	341.7	149.9	20.1	0.9	621.1
2018	0.0	0.0	0.1	5.5	103.5	343.3	150.6	20.2	0.9	624.0
2018	0.0	0.0	0.1	5.5	104.2	345.8	151.7	20.3	0.9	628.5

INDUSTRY: WAREHOUSE CLUBS & SUPERCENTERS (NAICS 45291)
PRODUCT LINE: CAMPING & BACKPACKING EQUIPMENT (Sub Category)

NAICS 45291: Warehouse Clubs and Superstores This industry comprises establishments known as warehouse clubs, superstores or supercenters primarily engaged in retailing a general line of groceries in combination with general lines of new merchandise, such as apparel, furniture, and appliances.

5-YEAR TREND – ESTIMATED INDUSTRY SALES ($MILLIONS)

Year	Employee Size of Establishment									Total Industry Sales
	1-4 Emps.	5-9 Emps.	10-19 Emps.	20-49 Emps.	50-99 Emps.	100-249 Emps.	250-499 Emps.	500-999 Emps.	Unknown Emps.	
2015	0.2	0.0	0.0	2.0	2.5	313.0	1,383.9	36.6	0.4	1,738.8
2016	0.2	0.0	0.0	2.1	2.6	324.5	1,434.5	37.9	0.4	1,802.4
2017	0.2	0.0	0.0	2.2	2.7	335.3	1,482.4	39.2	0.5	1,862.5
2018	0.3	0.0	0.0	2.3	2.9	364.2	1,610.0	42.5	0.5	2,022.9
2018	0.3	0.0	0.0	2.5	3.1	386.8	1,709.9	45.2	0.5	2,148.3

INDUSTRY: DEPARTMENT STORES INDUSTRY (NAICS 45211)
PRODUCT LINE: BICYCLES & ACCESSORIES EQUIPMENT (Sub Category)

NAICS 45211: Department Stores Industry . this industry comprises establishments known as department stores primarily engaged in retailing a wide range of the following new products with no one merchandise line predominating: apparel, furniture, appliances and home furnishings; and selected additional items, such as paint, hardware, toiletries, cosmetics, photographic equipment, jewelry, toys, and sporting goods. merchandise lines are normally arranged in separate departments.

5-YEAR TREND – ESTIMATED INDUSTRY SALES ($MILLIONS)

Year	Employee Size of Establishment									Total Industry Sales
	1-4 Emps.	5-9 Emps.	10-19 Emps.	20-49 Emps.	50-99 Emps.	100-249 Emps.	250-499 Emps.	500-999 Emps.	Unknown Emps.	
2015	0.0	0.0	0.0	3.4	63.6	211.0	92.5	12.4	0.5	383.5
2016	0.0	0.0	0.0	3.4	64.4	213.7	93.7	12.6	0.5	388.4
2017	0.0	0.0	0.0	3.4	65.1	216.0	94.8	12.7	0.6	392.6
2018	0.0	0.0	0.0	3.4	65.4	217.0	95.2	12.8	0.6	394.4
2018	0.0	0.0	0.0	3.5	65.9	218.5	95.9	12.9	0.6	397.3

INDUSTRY: WAREHOUSE CLUBS & SUPERCENTERS (NAICS 45291)
PRODUCT LINE: BICYCLES & ACCESSORIES EQUIPMENT (Sub Category)

NAICS 45291: Warehouse Clubs and Superstores This industry comprises establishments known as warehouse clubs, superstores or supercenters primarily engaged in retailing a general line of groceries in combination with general lines of new merchandise, such as apparel, furniture, and appliances.

5-YEAR TREND – ESTIMATED INDUSTRY SALES ($MILLIONS)

Year	Employee Size of Establishment									Total Industry Sales
	1-4 Emps.	5-9 Emps.	10-19 Emps.	20-49 Emps.	50-99 Emps.	100-249 Emps.	250-499 Emps.	500-999 Emps.	Unknown Emps.	
2015	0.2	0.0	0.0	1.8	2.3	282.9	1,250.6	33.0	0.4	1,571.3
2016	0.2	0.0	0.0	1.9	2.4	293.2	1,296.3	34.3	0.4	1,628.7
2017	0.2	0.0	0.0	1.9	2.5	303.0	1,339.5	35.4	0.4	1,683.0
2018	0.2	0.0	0.0	2.1	2.7	329.1	1,454.9	38.4	0.5	1,828.0
2018	0.2	0.0	0.0	2.2	2.8	349.5	1,545.1	40.8	0.5	1,941.3

INDUSTRY: DEPARTMENT STORES INDUSTRY (NAICS 45211)
PRODUCT LINE: BOATS & ACCESSORIES EQUIPMENT (Sub Category)

NAICS 45211: Department Stores Industry . this industry comprises establishments known as department stores primarily engaged in retailing a wide range of the following new products with no one merchandise line predominating: apparel, furniture, appliances and home furnishings; and selected additional items, such as paint, hardware, toiletries, cosmetics, photographic equipment, jewelry, toys, and sporting goods. merchandise lines are normally arranged in separate departments.

5-YEAR TREND — ESTIMATED INDUSTRY SALES ($MILLIONS)

Year	Employee Size of Establishment									Total Industry Sales
	1-4 Emps.	5-9 Emps.	10-19 Emps.	20-49 Emps.	50-99 Emps.	100-249 Emps.	250-499 Emps.	500-999 Emps.	Unknown Emps.	
2015	0.0	0.0	0.0	0.6	11.7	38.8	17.0	2.3	0.1	70.6
2016	0.0	0.0	0.0	0.6	11.9	39.3	17.2	2.3	0.1	71.5
2017	0.0	0.0	0.0	0.6	12.0	39.7	17.4	2.3	0.1	72.2
2018	0.0	0.0	0.0	0.6	12.0	39.9	17.5	2.3	0.1	72.6
2018	0.0	0.0	0.0	0.6	12.1	40.2	17.6	2.4	0.1	73.1

INDUSTRY: WAREHOUSE CLUBS & SUPERCENTERS (NAICS 45291)
PRODUCT LINE: BOATS & ACCESSORIES EQUIPMENT (Sub Category)

NAICS 45291: Warehouse Clubs and Superstores This industry comprises establishments known as warehouse clubs, superstores or supercenters primarily engaged in retailing a general line of groceries in combination with general lines of new merchandise, such as apparel, furniture, and appliances.

5-YEAR TREND — ESTIMATED INDUSTRY SALES ($MILLIONS)

Year	Employee Size of Establishment									Total Industry Sales
	1-4 Emps.	5-9 Emps.	10-19 Emps.	20-49 Emps.	50-99 Emps.	100-249 Emps.	250-499 Emps.	500-999 Emps.	Unknown Emps.	
2015	0.1	0.0	0.0	0.7	0.9	108.7	480.6	12.7	0.1	603.9
2016	0.1	0.0	0.0	0.7	0.9	112.7	498.2	13.2	0.2	626.0
2017	0.1	0.0	0.0	0.7	0.9	116.5	514.8	13.6	0.2	646.8
2018	0.1	0.0	0.0	0.8	1.0	126.5	559.2	14.8	0.2	702.5
2018	0.1	0.0	0.0	0.9	1.1	134.3	593.8	15.7	0.2	746.1

INDUSTRY: ELECTRONIC SHOPPING & MAIL-ORDER (NAICS 45411)
PRODUCT LINE: BOATS & ACCESSORIES EQUIPMENT (Sub Category)

NAICS 45411: Electronic Shopping and Mail-Order Houses This industry comprises establishments primarily engaged in retailing all types of merchandise by means of mail or by electronic media, such as interactive television or computer. Included in this industry are establishments primarily engaged in retailing from catalogue showrooms of mail-order houses.

5-YEAR TREND — ESTIMATED INDUSTRY SALES ($MILLIONS)

Year	Employee Size of Establishment									Total Industry Sales
	1-4 Emps.	5-9 Emps.	10-19 Emps.	20-49 Emps.	50-99 Emps.	100-249 Emps.	250-499 Emps.	500-999 Emps.	Unknown Emps.	
2015	91.2	48.4	71.9	116.4	83.7	163.2	238.8	302.5	13.8	1,130.0
2016	97.3	51.7	76.7	124.2	89.3	174.1	254.7	322.7	14.7	1,205.4
2017	103.2	54.8	81.4	131.7	94.7	184.7	270.2	342.3	15.6	1,278.6
2018	117.5	62.4	92.6	149.8	107.8	210.1	307.5	379.9	17.8	1,445.4
2018	130.5	69.3	102.9	166.4	119.7	233.4	341.5	414.7	19.7	1,598.1

INDUSTRY: ELECTRONIC SHOPPING & MAIL-ORDER (NAICS 45411)
PRODUCT LINE: OTHER SPORTING GOODS (Sub Category)

NAICS 45411: Electronic Shopping and Mail-Order Houses This industry comprises establishments primarily engaged in retailing all types of merchandise by means of mail or by electronic media, such as interactive television or computer. Included in this industry are establishments primarily engaged in retailing from catalogue showrooms of mail-order houses.

5-YEAR TREND — ESTIMATED INDUSTRY SALES ($MILLIONS)

Year	Employee Size of Establishment									Total Industry Sales
	1-4 Emps.	5-9 Emps.	10-19 Emps.	20-49 Emps.	50-99 Emps.	100-249 Emps.	250-499 Emps.	500-999 Emps.	Unknown Emps.	
2015	1,069.9	568.0	843.5	1,364.6	981.6	1,913.7	2,800.0	3,546.9	161.8	13,250.1
2016	1,141.3	605.9	899.8	1,455.7	1,047.1	2,041.4	2,986.8	3,783.5	172.6	14,134.1
2017	1,210.5	642.7	954.4	1,544.0	1,110.6	2,165.2	3,168.0	4,013.1	183.1	14,991.6
2018	1,377.5	731.3	1,086.0	1,757.0	1,263.8	2,463.8	3,604.9	4,454.6	208.3	16,947.3
2018	1,530.0	812.3	1,206.2	1,951.4	1,403.7	2,736.6	4,004.0	4,862.2	231.4	18,737.6

INDUSTRY: DEPARTMENT STORES INDUSTRY (NAICS 45211)
PRODUCT LINE: OTHER SPORTING GOODS (Sub Category)

NAICS 45211: Department Stores Industry . this industry comprises establishments known as department stores primarily engaged in retailing a wide range of the following new products with no one merchandise line predominating: apparel, furniture, appliances and home furnishings; and selected additional items, such as paint, hardware, toiletries, cosmetics, photographic equipment, jewelry, toys, and sporting goods. merchandise lines are normally arranged in separate departments.

5-YEAR TREND — ESTIMATED INDUSTRY SALES ($MILLIONS)

Year	Employee Size of Establishment									Total Industry Sales
	1-4 Emps.	5-9 Emps.	10-19 Emps.	20-49 Emps.	50-99 Emps.	100-249 Emps.	250-499 Emps.	500-999 Emps.	Unknown Emps.	
2015	0.0	0.0	0.1	4.4	83.5	277.0	121.5	16.3	0.7	503.5
2016	0.0	0.0	0.1	4.5	84.6	280.6	123.1	16.5	0.7	510.0
2017	0.0	0.0	0.1	4.5	85.5	283.6	124.4	16.7	0.7	515.5
2018	0.0	0.0	0.1	4.5	85.9	284.9	125.0	16.8	0.7	517.9
2018	0.0	0.0	0.1	4.6	86.5	286.9	125.9	16.9	0.7	521.6

INDUSTRY: WAREHOUSE CLUBS & SUPERCENTERS (NAICS 45291)
PRODUCT LINE: OTHER SPORTING GOODS (Sub Category)

NAICS 45291: Warehouse Clubs and Superstores This industry comprises establishments known as warehouse clubs, superstores or supercenters primarily engaged in retailing a general line of groceries in combination with general lines of new merchandise, such as apparel, furniture, and appliances.

5-YEAR TREND — ESTIMATED INDUSTRY SALES ($MILLIONS)

Year	Employee Size of Establishment									Total Industry Sales
	1-4 Emps.	5-9 Emps.	10-19 Emps.	20-49 Emps.	50-99 Emps.	100-249 Emps.	250-499 Emps.	500-999 Emps.	Unknown Emps.	
2015	0.2	0.0	0.0	1.7	2.1	260.2	1,150.3	30.4	0.4	1,445.3
2016	0.2	0.0	0.0	1.7	2.2	269.7	1,192.4	31.5	0.4	1,498.1
2017	0.2	0.0	0.0	1.8	2.3	278.7	1,232.2	32.6	0.4	1,548.1
2018	0.2	0.0	0.0	1.9	2.5	302.7	1,338.3	35.4	0.4	1,681.4
2018	0.2	0.0	0.0	2.1	2.6	321.5	1,421.2	37.5	0.4	1,785.7

INDUSTRY: HOME CENTERS INDUSTRY (NAICS 44411)
PRODUCT LINE: HARDWARE & BUILDING SUPPLIES (Main Category)

NAICS 44411: Home Centers. This industry comprises establishments known as home centers primarily engaged in retailing a general line of new home repair and improvement materials and supplies, such as lumber, plumbing goods, electrical goods, tools, housewares, hardware, and lawn and garden supplies, with no one merchandise line predominating. The merchandise lines are normally arranged in separate departments.

5-Year Trend — Estimated Industry Sales ($Millions)

Year	Employee Size of Establishment									Total
	1-4 Emps.	5-9 Emps.	10-19 Emps.	20-49 Emps.	50-99 Emps.	100-249 Emps.	250-499 Emps.	500-999 Emps.	Unknown Emps.	Industry Sales
2015	78.3	155.5	404.6	807.9	593.3	38,812.4	3,432.6	63.5	27.1	44,375.2
2016	80.9	160.6	417.9	834.6	612.8	40,092.6	3,545.8	65.6	28.0	45,838.8
2017	83.3	165.4	430.5	859.6	631.2	41,295.1	3,652.1	67.6	28.8	47,213.7
2018	87.6	173.8	452.4	903.4	663.4	43,399.0	3,838.2	71.0	30.3	49,619.1
2018	92.2	183.1	476.4	951.4	698.6	45,703.9	4,042.0	74.8	31.9	52,254.3

INDUSTRY: HARDWARE STORES (NAICS 44413)
PRODUCT LINE: HARDWARE & BUILDING SUPPLIES (Main Category)

NAICS 44413: Hardware Stores. Establishments primarily engaged in the retail sale of a number of basic hardware lines, such as tools, builders' hardware, paint and glass, housewares and household appliances, and cutlery.

5-Year Trend — Estimated Industry Sales ($Millions)

Year	Employee Size of Establishment									Total
	1-4 Emps.	5-9 Emps.	10-19 Emps.	20-49 Emps.	50-99 Emps.	100-249 Emps.	250-499 Emps.	500-999 Emps.	Unknown Emps.	Industry Sales
2015	998.9	1,602.8	3,204.9	4,488.0	821.6	192.6	54.1	2.7	84.4	11,449.9
2016	1,017.7	1,633.0	3,265.2	4,572.5	837.1	196.2	55.1	2.7	86.0	11,665.5
2017	1,034.5	1,660.0	3,319.1	4,648.0	850.9	199.4	56.0	2.8	87.4	11,858.1
2018	1,082.7	1,737.4	3,474.0	4,864.7	890.6	208.7	58.6	2.9	91.5	12,411.1
2018	1,136.1	1,822.9	3,645.0	5,104.3	934.5	219.0	61.5	2.9	96.0	13,022.3

INDUSTRY: SUPERMARKETS INDUSTRY (NAICS 44511)
PRODUCT LINE: HARDWARE & BUILDING SUPPLIES (Main Category)

NAICS 44511: Grocery Stores Industry. this industry comprises establishments generally known as supermarkets and grocery stores primarily engaged in retailing a general line of food, such as canned and frozen foods; fresh fruits and vegetables; and fresh and prepared meats, fish, and poultry. Included in this industry are delicatessen-type establishments primarily engaged in retailing a general line of food.

5-YEAR TREND – ESTIMATED INDUSTRY SALES ($MILLIONS)

Year	Employee Size of Establishment									Total Industry Sales
	1-4 Emps.	5-9 Emps.	10-19 Emps.	20-49 Emps.	50-99 Emps.	100-249 Emps.	250-499 Emps.	500-999 Emps.	Unknown Emps.	
2015	8.3	6.2	15.8	51.5	124.9	284.8	82.1	11.3	1.6	586.4
2016	8.2	6.1	15.5	50.6	122.7	279.9	80.7	11.1	1.5	576.3
2017	8.0	6.0	15.2	49.6	120.3	274.3	79.1	10.9	1.5	564.9
2018	8.0	6.0	15.2	49.6	120.3	274.4	79.1	10.9	1.5	565.0
2018	8.0	6.0	15.2	49.7	120.6	275.0	79.3	10.9	1.5	566.2

INDUSTRY: PHARMACIES & DRUG STORES (NAICS 44611)
PRODUCT LINE: HARDWARE & BUILDING SUPPLIES (Main Category)

NAICS 44611 Pharmacies and Drug Stores – this industry comprises establishments known as pharmacies and drug stores engaged in retailing prescription or nonprescription drugs and medicines.

5-YEAR TREND – ESTIMATED INDUSTRY SALES ($MILLIONS)

Year	Employee Size of Establishment									Total Industry Sales
	1-4 Emps.	5-9 Emps.	10-19 Emps.	20-49 Emps.	50-99 Emps.	100-249 Emps.	250-499 Emps.	500-999 Emps.	Unknown Emps.	
2015	5.7	14.2	59.8	169.0	15.9	6.2	1.9	0.8	0.5	273.9
2016	6.0	14.9	62.9	177.8	16.7	6.6	2.0	0.8	0.5	288.2
2017	6.3	15.6	65.9	186.3	17.5	6.9	2.1	0.9	0.5	302.0
2018	6.7	16.8	70.9	200.4	18.8	7.4	2.3	0.9	0.6	324.7
2018	7.2	18.1	76.3	215.7	20.3	8.0	2.5	0.9	0.6	349.5

INDUSTRY: GAS STATIONS W/CONVENIENCE STORES (NAICS 44711)
PRODUCT LINE: HARDWARE & BUILDING SUPPLIES (Main Category)

NAICS 44711: Gas Stations with Convenience Stores. this industry comprises establishments primarily engaged in selling gasoline and lubricating oils. These establishments frequently sell other merchandise, such as tires, batteries, and other automobile parts, or perform minor repair work. Gasoline stations combined with other activities, such as grocery stores, convenience stores, or carwashes, are classified according to the primary activity.

5-YEAR TREND — ESTIMATED INDUSTRY SALES ($MILLIONS)

Year	Employee Size of Establishment									Total Industry Sales
	1-4 Emps.	5-9 Emps.	10-19 Emps.	20-49 Emps.	50-99 Emps.	100-249 Emps.	250-499 Emps.	500-999 Emps.	Unknown Emps.	
2015	35.6	95.8	155.1	95.4	8.4	5.2	0.7	0.0	0.4	396.6
2016	38.3	103.1	166.8	102.6	9.0	5.6	0.8	0.0	0.4	426.6
2017	40.9	110.2	178.3	109.7	9.6	6.0	0.8	0.0	0.5	455.9
2018	44.6	120.1	194.4	119.6	10.5	6.5	0.9	0.0	0.5	497.3
2018	48.7	131.0	212.0	130.4	11.4	7.1	1.0	0.0	0.6	542.2

INDUSTRY: DEPARTMENT STORES INDUSTRY (NAICS 45211)
PRODUCT LINE: HARDWARE & BUILDING SUPPLIES (Main Category)

NAICS 45211: Department Stores Industry . this industry comprises establishments known as department stores primarily engaged in retailing a wide range of the following new products with no one merchandise line predominating: apparel, furniture, appliances and home furnishings; and selected additional items, such as paint, hardware, toiletries, cosmetics, photographic equipment, jewelry, toys, and sporting goods. merchandise lines are normally arranged in separate departments.

5-YEAR TREND — ESTIMATED INDUSTRY SALES ($MILLIONS)

Year	Employee Size of Establishment									Total Industry Sales
	1-4 Emps.	5-9 Emps.	10-19 Emps.	20-49 Emps.	50-99 Emps.	100-249 Emps.	250-499 Emps.	500-999 Emps.	Unknown Emps.	
2015	0.2	0.1	0.3	24.3	462.2	1,533.0	672.5	90.1	3.9	2,786.7
2016	0.2	0.1	0.3	24.7	468.2	1,552.8	681.2	91.2	4.0	2,822.7
2017	0.2	0.1	0.3	24.9	473.2	1,569.5	688.6	92.2	4.0	2,853.1
2018	0.2	0.1	0.3	25.0	475.4	1,576.8	691.7	92.7	4.0	2,866.3
2018	0.2	0.1	0.3	25.2	478.8	1,588.2	696.7	93.4	4.0	2,887.0

INDUSTRY: WAREHOUSE CLUBS & SUPERCENTERS (NAICS 45291)
PRODUCT LINE: HARDWARE & BUILDING SUPPLIES (Main Category)

NAICS 45291: Warehouse Clubs and Superstores This industry comprises establishments known as warehouse clubs, superstores or supercenters primarily engaged in retailing a general line of groceries in combination with general lines of new merchandise, such as apparel, furniture, and appliances.

5-YEAR TREND – ESTIMATED INDUSTRY SALES ($MILLIONS)

Year	Employee Size of Establishment									Total Industry Sales
	1-4 Emps.	5-9 Emps.	10-19 Emps.	20-49 Emps.	50-99 Emps.	100-249 Emps.	250-499 Emps.	500-999 Emps.	Unknown Emps.	
2015	1.1	0.0	0.2	10.7	13.5	1,661.2	7,343.7	194.0	2.3	9,226.7
2016	1.2	0.0	0.2	11.1	13.9	1,721.9	7,612.2	201.1	2.4	9,564.1
2017	1.2	0.0	0.2	11.4	14.4	1,779.3	7,866.0	207.8	2.4	9,882.9
2018	1.3	0.0	0.2	12.4	15.7	1,932.5	8,543.5	225.7	2.7	10,734.1
2018	1.4	0.0	0.2	13.2	16.6	2,052.4	9,073.2	239.7	2.8	11,399.6

INDUSTRY: ELECTRONIC SHOPPING & MAIL-ORDER (NAICS 45411)
PRODUCT LINE: HARDWARE & BUILDING SUPPLIES (Main Category)

NAICS 45411: Electronic Shopping and Mail-Order Houses This industry comprises establishments primarily engaged in retailing all types of merchandise by means of mail or by electronic media, such as interactive television or computer. Included in this industry are establishments primarily engaged in retailing from catalogue showrooms of mail-order houses.

5-YEAR TREND – ESTIMATED INDUSTRY SALES ($MILLIONS)

Year	Employee Size of Establishment									Total Industry Sales
	1-4 Emps.	5-9 Emps.	10-19 Emps.	20-49 Emps.	50-99 Emps.	100-249 Emps.	250-499 Emps.	500-999 Emps.	Unknown Emps.	
2015	258.0	137.0	203.4	329.0	236.7	461.4	675.1	855.2	39.0	3,194.8
2016	275.2	146.1	217.0	351.0	252.5	492.2	720.2	912.3	41.6	3,407.9
2017	291.9	155.0	230.1	372.3	267.8	522.1	763.9	967.6	44.1	3,614.7
2018	332.1	176.3	261.9	423.6	304.7	594.1	869.2	1,074.1	50.2	4,086.2
2018	368.9	195.9	290.8	470.5	338.4	659.8	965.4	1,172.3	55.8	4,517.9

INDUSTRY: HOME CENTERS INDUSTRY (NAICS 44411)
PRODUCT LINE: GENERAL HARDWARE (Sub Category)

NAICS 44411: Home Centers. This industry comprises establishments known as home centers primarily engaged in retailing a general line of new home repair and improvement materials and supplies, such as lumber, plumbing goods, electrical goods, tools, housewares, hardware, and lawn and garden supplies, with no one merchandise line predominating. The merchandise lines are normally arranged in separate departments.

5-YEAR TREND — ESTIMATED INDUSTRY SALES ($MILLIONS)

Year	Employee Size of Establishment									Total Industry Sales
	1-4 Emps.	5-9 Emps.	10-19 Emps.	20-49 Emps.	50-99 Emps.	100-249 Emps.	250-499 Emps.	500-999 Emps.	Unknown Emps.	
2015	12.5	24.8	64.5	128.8	94.5	6,185.4	547.0	10.1	4.3	7,071.9
2016	12.9	25.6	66.6	133.0	97.7	6,389.4	565.1	10.5	4.5	7,305.2
2017	13.3	26.4	68.6	137.0	100.6	6,581.1	582.0	10.8	4.6	7,524.3
2018	14.0	27.7	72.1	144.0	105.7	6,916.4	611.7	11.3	4.8	7,907.6
2018	14.7	29.2	75.9	151.6	111.3	7,283.7	644.2	11.9	5.1	8,327.6

INDUSTRY: HARDWARE STORES INDUSTRY (NAICS 44413)
PRODUCT LINE: GENERAL HARDWARE (Sub Category)

NAICS 44413: Hardware Stores. Establishments primarily engaged in the retail sale of a number of basic hardware lines, such as tools, builders' hardware, paint and glass, housewares and household appliances, and cutlery.

5-YEAR TREND — ESTIMATED INDUSTRY SALES ($MILLIONS)

Year	Employee Size of Establishment									Total Industry Sales
	1-4 Emps.	5-9 Emps.	10-19 Emps.	20-49 Emps.	50-99 Emps.	100-249 Emps.	250-499 Emps.	500-999 Emps.	Unknown Emps.	
2015	314.1	504.0	1,007.8	1,411.2	258.4	60.6	17.0	0.8	26.5	3,600.4
2016	320.0	513.5	1,026.7	1,437.8	263.2	61.7	17.3	0.9	27.0	3,668.2
2017	325.3	522.0	1,043.7	1,461.5	267.6	62.7	17.6	0.9	27.5	3,728.8
2018	340.5	546.3	1,092.4	1,529.7	280.0	65.6	18.4	0.9	28.8	3,902.7
2018	357.2	573.2	1,146.2	1,605.0	293.8	68.9	19.3	0.9	30.2	4,094.8

INDUSTRY: HOME CENTERS INDUSTRY (NAICS 44411)
PRODUCT LINE: TOOLS & EQUIPMENT (Sub Category)

NAICS 44411: Home Centers. This industry comprises establishments known as home centers primarily engaged in retailing a general line of new home repair and improvement materials and supplies, such as lumber, plumbing goods, electrical goods, tools, housewares, hardware, and lawn and garden supplies, with no one merchandise line predominating. The merchandise lines are normally arranged in separate departments.

5-YEAR TREND – ESTIMATED INDUSTRY SALES ($MILLIONS)

Year	Employee Size of Establishment									Total Industry Sales
	1-4 Emps.	5-9 Emps.	10-19 Emps.	20-49 Emps.	50-99 Emps.	100-249 Emps.	250-499 Emps.	500-999 Emps.	Unknown Emps.	
2015	21.0	41.6	108.4	216.4	158.9	10,394.7	919.3	17.0	7.3	11,884.5
2016	21.7	43.0	111.9	223.5	164.1	10,737.5	949.6	17.6	7.5	12,276.5
2017	22.3	44.3	115.3	230.2	169.0	11,059.6	978.1	18.1	7.7	12,644.7
2018	23.5	46.6	121.2	241.9	177.7	11,623.0	1,027.9	19.0	8.1	13,288.9
2018	24.7	49.0	127.6	254.8	187.1	12,240.3	1,082.5	20.0	8.5	13,994.6

INDUSTRY: HARDWARE STORES INDUSTRY (NAICS 44413)
PRODUCT LINE: TOOLS & EQUIPMENT (Sub Category)

NAICS 44413: Hardware Stores. Establishments primarily engaged in the retail sale of a number of basic hardware lines, such as tools, builders' hardware, paint and glass, housewares and household appliances, and cutlery.

5-YEAR TREND – ESTIMATED INDUSTRY SALES ($MILLIONS)

Year	Employee Size of Establishment									Total Industry Sales
	1-4 Emps.	5-9 Emps.	10-19 Emps.	20-49 Emps.	50-99 Emps.	100-249 Emps.	250-499 Emps.	500-999 Emps.	Unknown Emps.	
2015	349.2	560.4	1,120.5	1,569.2	287.3	67.3	18.9	0.9	29.5	4,003.3
2016	355.8	571.0	1,141.6	1,598.7	292.7	68.6	19.3	1.0	30.1	4,078.6
2017	361.7	580.4	1,160.5	1,625.1	297.5	69.7	19.6	1.0	30.6	4,146.0
2018	378.6	607.5	1,214.6	1,700.9	311.4	73.0	20.5	1.0	32.0	4,339.4
2018	397.2	637.4	1,274.4	1,784.6	326.7	76.6	21.5	1.0	33.6	4,553.0

INDUSTRY: HOME CENTERS INDUSTRY (NAICS 44411)
PRODUCT LINE: PLUMBING FIXTURES & SUPPLIES (Sub Category)

NAICS 44411: Home Centers. This industry comprises establishments known as home centers primarily engaged in retailing a general line of new home repair and improvement materials and supplies, such as lumber, plumbing goods, electrical goods, tools, housewares, hardware, and lawn and garden supplies, with no one merchandise line predominating. The merchandise lines are normally arranged in separate departments.

5-YEAR TREND — ESTIMATED INDUSTRY SALES ($MILLIONS)

Year	Employee Size of Establishment									Total
	1-4 Emps.	5-9 Emps.	10-19 Emps.	20-49 Emps.	50-99 Emps.	100-249 Emps.	250-499 Emps.	500-999 Emps.	Unknown Emps.	Industry Sales
2015	21.9	43.4	112.9	225.5	165.6	10,834.9	958.2	17.7	7.6	12,387.8
2016	22.6	44.8	116.7	233.0	171.1	11,192.2	989.8	18.3	7.8	12,796.4
2017	23.3	46.2	120.2	240.0	176.2	11,527.9	1,019.5	18.9	8.0	13,180.2
2018	24.4	48.5	126.3	252.2	185.2	12,115.3	1,071.5	19.8	8.5	13,851.7
2018	25.7	51.1	133.0	265.6	195.0	12,758.7	1,128.4	20.9	8.9	14,587.3

INDUSTRY: HARDWARE STORES INDUSTRY (NAICS 44413)
PRODUCT LINE: PLUMBING FIXTURES & SUPPLIES (Sub Category)

NAICS 44413: Hardware Stores. Establishments primarily engaged in the retail sale of a number of basic hardware lines, such as tools, builders' hardware, paint and glass, housewares and household appliances, and cutlery.

5-YEAR TREND — ESTIMATED INDUSTRY SALES ($MILLIONS)

Year	Employee Size of Establishment									Total
	1-4 Emps.	5-9 Emps.	10-19 Emps.	20-49 Emps.	50-99 Emps.	100-249 Emps.	250-499 Emps.	500-999 Emps.	Unknown Emps.	Industry Sales
2015	172.9	277.5	554.9	777.0	142.3	33.3	9.4	0.5	14.6	1,982.4
2016	176.2	282.7	565.3	791.6	144.9	34.0	9.5	0.5	14.9	2,019.7
2017	179.1	287.4	574.7	804.7	147.3	34.5	9.7	0.5	15.1	2,053.0
2018	187.5	300.8	601.5	842.2	154.2	36.1	10.1	0.5	15.8	2,148.8
2018	196.7	315.6	631.1	883.7	161.8	37.9	10.6	0.5	16.6	2,254.6

INDUSTRY: HOME CENTERS INDUSTRY (NAICS 44411)
PRODUCT LINE: WIRE & WIRING PRODUCTS (Sub Category)

NAICS 44411: Home Centers. This industry comprises establishments known as home centers primarily engaged in retailing a general line of new home repair and improvement materials and supplies, such as lumber, plumbing goods, electrical goods, tools, housewares, hardware, and lawn and garden supplies, with no one merchandise line predominating. The merchandise lines are normally arranged in separate departments.

5-YEAR TREND – ESTIMATED INDUSTRY SALES ($MILLIONS)

Year	Employee Size of Establishment									Total Industry Sales
	1-4 Emps.	5-9 Emps.	10-19 Emps.	20-49 Emps.	50-99 Emps.	100-249 Emps.	250-499 Emps.	500-999 Emps.	Unknown Emps.	
2015	3.8	7.5	19.4	38.7	28.4	1,860.7	164.6	3.0	1.3	2,127.3
2016	3.9	7.7	20.0	40.0	29.4	1,922.0	170.0	3.1	1.3	2,197.5
2017	4.0	7.9	20.6	41.2	30.3	1,979.7	175.1	3.2	1.4	2,263.4
2018	4.2	8.3	21.7	43.3	31.8	2,080.5	184.0	3.4	1.5	2,378.7
2018	4.4	8.8	22.8	45.6	33.5	2,191.0	193.8	3.6	1.5	2,505.1

INDUSTRY: HARDWARE STORES INDUSTRY (NAICS 44413)
PRODUCT LINE: WIRE & WIRING PRODUCTS (Sub Category)

NAICS 44413: Hardware Stores. Establishments primarily engaged in the retail sale of a number of basic hardware lines, such as tools, builders' hardware, paint and glass, housewares and household appliances, and cutlery.

5-YEAR TREND – ESTIMATED INDUSTRY SALES ($MILLIONS)

Year	Employee Size of Establishment									Total Industry Sales
	1-4 Emps.	5-9 Emps.	10-19 Emps.	20-49 Emps.	50-99 Emps.	100-249 Emps.	250-499 Emps.	500-999 Emps.	Unknown Emps.	
2015	44.4	71.3	142.5	199.6	36.5	8.6	2.4	0.1	3.8	509.2
2016	45.3	72.6	145.2	203.3	37.2	8.7	2.5	0.1	3.8	518.8
2017	46.0	73.8	147.6	206.7	37.8	8.9	2.5	0.1	3.9	527.3
2018	48.1	77.3	154.5	216.3	39.6	9.3	2.6	0.1	4.1	551.9
2018	50.5	81.1	162.1	227.0	41.6	9.7	2.7	0.1	4.3	579.1

INDUSTRY: HOME CENTERS INDUSTRY (NAICS 44411)
PRODUCT LINE: WELDING SUPPLIES (Sub Category)

NAICS 44411: Home Centers. This industry comprises establishments known as home centers primarily engaged in retailing a general line of new home repair and improvement materials and supplies, such as lumber, plumbing goods, electrical goods, tools, housewares, hardware, and lawn and garden supplies, with no one merchandise line predominating. The merchandise lines are normally arranged in separate departments.

5-YEAR TREND – ESTIMATED INDUSTRY SALES ($MILLIONS)

Year	Employee Size of Establishment									Total Industry Sales
	1-4 Emps.	5-9 Emps.	10-19 Emps.	20-49 Emps.	50-99 Emps.	100-249 Emps.	250-499 Emps.	500-999 Emps.	Unknown Emps.	
2015	0.0	0.0	0.1	0.2	0.2	11.8	1.0	0.0	0.0	13.5
2016	0.0	0.0	0.1	0.3	0.2	12.2	1.1	0.0	0.0	14.0
2017	0.0	0.1	0.1	0.3	0.2	12.6	1.1	0.0	0.0	14.4
2018	0.0	0.1	0.1	0.3	0.2	13.2	1.2	0.0	0.0	15.1
2018	0.0	0.1	0.1	0.3	0.2	13.9	1.2	0.0	0.0	15.9

INDUSTRY: HARDWARE STORES INDUSTRY (NAICS 44413)
PRODUCT LINE: WELDING SUPPLIES (Sub Category)

NAICS 44413: Hardware Stores. Establishments primarily engaged in the retail sale of a number of basic hardware lines, such as tools, builders' hardware, paint and glass, housewares and household appliances, and cutlery.

5-YEAR TREND – ESTIMATED INDUSTRY SALES ($MILLIONS)

Year	Employee Size of Establishment									Total Industry Sales
	1-4 Emps.	5-9 Emps.	10-19 Emps.	20-49 Emps.	50-99 Emps.	100-249 Emps.	250-499 Emps.	500-999 Emps.	Unknown Emps.	
2015	6.5	10.5	20.9	29.3	5.4	1.3	0.4	0.0	0.6	74.7
2016	6.6	10.6	21.3	29.8	5.5	1.3	0.4	0.0	0.6	76.1
2017	6.7	10.8	21.6	30.3	5.5	1.3	0.4	0.0	0.6	77.3
2018	7.1	11.3	22.7	31.7	5.8	1.4	0.4	0.0	0.6	80.9
2018	7.4	11.9	23.8	33.3	6.1	1.4	0.4	0.0	0.6	84.9

INDUSTRY: HOME CENTERS INDUSTRY (NAICS 44411)
PRODUCT LINE: ELECTRICAL SUPPLIES (Sub Category)

NAICS 44411: Home Centers. This industry comprises establishments
known as home centers primarily engaged in retailing a general line of
new home repair and improvement materials and supplies, such as
lumber, plumbing goods, electrical goods, tools, housewares, hardware,
and lawn and garden supplies, with no one merchandise line predominating.
The merchandise lines are normally arranged in separate departments.

5-YEAR TREND — ESTIMATED INDUSTRY SALES ($MILLIONS)

Year	Employee Size of Establishment									Total
	1-4 Emps.	5-9 Emps.	10-19 Emps.	20-49 Emps.	50-99 Emps.	100-249 Emps.	250-499 Emps.	500-999 Emps.	Unknown Emps.	Industry Sales
2015	19.2	38.2	99.3	198.3	145.6	9,525.0	842.4	15.6	6.6	10,890.1
2016	19.9	39.4	102.6	204.8	150.4	9,839.1	870.2	16.1	6.9	11,249.3
2017	20.4	40.6	105.6	211.0	154.9	10,134.2	896.3	16.6	7.1	11,586.7
2018	21.5	42.7	111.0	221.7	162.8	10,650.5	941.9	17.4	7.4	12,177.0
2018	22.6	44.9	116.9	233.5	171.4	11,216.2	992.0	18.3	7.8	12,823.7

INDUSTRY: HARDWARE STORES INDUSTRY (NAICS 44413)
PRODUCT LINE: ELECTRICAL SUPPLIES (Sub Category)

NAICS 44413: Hardware Stores. Establishments primarily engaged
in the retail sale of a number of basic hardware lines, such as tools,
builders' hardware, paint and glass, housewares and household appliances,
and cutlery.

5-YEAR TREND — ESTIMATED INDUSTRY SALES ($MILLIONS)

Year	Employee Size of Establishment									Total
	1-4 Emps.	5-9 Emps.	10-19 Emps.	20-49 Emps.	50-99 Emps.	100-249 Emps.	250-499 Emps.	500-999 Emps.	Unknown Emps.	Industry Sales
2015	111.7	179.2	358.3	501.7	91.9	21.5	6.0	0.3	9.4	1,280.0
2016	113.8	182.6	365.0	511.2	93.6	21.9	6.2	0.3	9.6	1,304.1
2017	115.6	185.6	371.1	519.6	95.1	22.3	6.3	0.3	9.8	1,325.7
2018	121.0	194.2	388.4	543.8	99.6	23.3	6.6	0.3	10.2	1,387.5
2018	127.0	203.8	407.5	570.6	104.5	24.5	6.9	0.3	10.7	1,455.8

INDUSTRY: HOME CENTERS INDUSTRY (NAICS 44411)
PRODUCT LINE: LAWN & GARDEN SUPPLIES (Main Category)

NAICS 44411: Home Centers. This industry comprises establishments known as home centers primarily engaged in retailing a general line of new home repair and improvement materials and supplies, such as lumber, plumbing goods, electrical goods, tools, housewares, hardware, and lawn and garden supplies, with no one merchandise line predominating. The merchandise lines are normally arranged in separate departments.

5-YEAR TREND – ESTIMATED INDUSTRY SALES ($MILLIONS)

Year	Employee Size of Establishment									Total Industry Sales
	1-4 Emps.	5-9 Emps.	10-19 Emps.	20-49 Emps.	50-99 Emps.	100-249 Emps.	250-499 Emps.	500-999 Emps.	Unknown Emps.	
2015	32.5	64.5	167.8	335.0	246.0	16,092.3	1,423.2	26.3	11.2	18,398.8
2016	33.5	66.6	173.3	346.0	254.1	16,623.1	1,470.1	27.2	11.6	19,005.6
2017	34.5	68.6	178.5	356.4	261.7	17,121.7	1,514.2	28.0	11.9	19,575.6
2018	36.3	72.1	187.6	374.6	275.0	17,994.0	1,591.4	29.4	12.6	20,573.0
2018	38.2	75.9	197.5	394.5	289.7	18,949.6	1,675.9	31.0	13.2	21,665.6

INDUSTRY: HARDWARE STORES (NAICS 44413)
PRODUCT LINE: LAWN & GARDEN SUPPLIES (Main Category)

NAICS 44413: Hardware Stores. Establishments primarily engaged in the retail sale of a number of basic hardware lines, such as tools, builders' hardware, paint and glass, housewares and household appliances, and cutlery.

5-YEAR TREND – ESTIMATED INDUSTRY SALES ($MILLIONS)

Year	Employee Size of Establishment									Total Industry Sales
	1-4 Emps.	5-9 Emps.	10-19 Emps.	20-49 Emps.	50-99 Emps.	100-249 Emps.	250-499 Emps.	500-999 Emps.	Unknown Emps.	
2015	267.5	429.3	858.4	1,202.0	220.1	51.6	14.5	0.7	22.6	3,066.7
2016	272.6	437.4	874.5	1,224.7	224.2	52.5	14.8	0.7	23.0	3,124.4
2017	277.1	444.6	889.0	1,244.9	227.9	53.4	15.0	0.7	23.4	3,176.0
2018	290.0	465.3	930.5	1,303.0	238.5	55.9	15.7	0.8	24.5	3,324.1
2018	304.3	488.3	976.3	1,367.1	250.3	58.7	16.5	0.8	25.7	3,487.8

INDUSTRY: SUPERMARKETS INDUSTRY (NAICS 44511)
PRODUCT LINE: LAWN & GARDEN SUPPLIES (Main Category)

NAICS 44511: Grocery Stores Industry. this industry comprises establishments generally known as supermarkets and grocery stores primarily engaged in retailing a general line of food, such as canned and frozen foods; fresh fruits and vegetables; and fresh and prepared meats, fish, and poultry. Included in this industry are delicatessen-type establishments primarily engaged in retailing a general line of food.

5-YEAR TREND – ESTIMATED INDUSTRY SALES ($MILLIONS)

Year	1-4 Emps.	5-9 Emps.	10-19 Emps.	20-49 Emps.	50-99 Emps.	100-249 Emps.	250-499 Emps.	500-999 Emps.	Unknown Emps.	Total Industry Sales
2015	59.1	44.2	112.2	366.4	888.7	2,026.6	584.2	80.5	11.2	4,173.1
2016	58.1	43.5	110.2	360.0	873.3	1,991.5	574.1	79.2	11.0	4,100.8
2017	56.9	42.6	108.0	352.9	856.1	1,952.3	562.8	77.6	10.8	4,020.0
2018	56.9	42.6	108.1	353.0	856.2	1,952.5	562.9	77.5	10.8	4,020.6
2018	57.1	42.7	108.3	353.7	858.0	1,956.6	564.1	77.6	10.8	4,028.9

INDUSTRY: PHARMACIES & DRUG STORES (NAICS 44611)
PRODUCT LINE: LAWN & GARDEN SUPPLIES (Main Category)

NAICS 44611 Pharmacies and Drug Stores – this industry comprises establishments known as pharmacies and drug stores engaged in retailing prescription or nonprescription drugs and medicines.

5-YEAR TREND – ESTIMATED INDUSTRY SALES ($MILLIONS)

Year	1-4 Emps.	5-9 Emps.	10-19 Emps.	20-49 Emps.	50-99 Emps.	100-249 Emps.	250-499 Emps.	500-999 Emps.	Unknown Emps.	Total Industry Sales
2015	5.0	12.6	53.0	149.9	14.1	5.5	1.7	0.7	0.4	242.9
2016	5.3	13.2	55.8	157.7	14.8	5.8	1.8	0.7	0.4	255.6
2017	5.5	13.8	58.5	165.2	15.5	6.1	1.9	0.8	0.5	267.8
2018	6.0	14.9	62.9	177.7	16.7	6.6	2.0	0.8	0.5	288.0
2018	6.4	16.0	67.7	191.3	18.0	7.1	2.2	0.8	0.5	310.0

INDUSTRY: GAS STATIONS W/CONVENIENCE STORES (NAICS 44711)
PRODUCT LINE: LAWN & GARDEN SUPPLIES (Main Category)

NAICS 44711: Gas Stations with Convenience Stores. this industry comprises establishments primarily engaged in selling gasoline and lubricating oils. These establishments frequently sell other merchandise, such as tires, batteries, and other automobile parts, or perform minor repair work. Gasoline stations combined with other activities, such as grocery stores, convenience stores, or carwashes, are classified according to the primary activity.

5-YEAR TREND — ESTIMATED INDUSTRY SALES ($MILLIONS)

Year	Employee Size of Establishment									Total Industry Sales
	1-4 Emps.	5-9 Emps.	10-19 Emps.	20-49 Emps.	50-99 Emps.	100-249 Emps.	250-499 Emps.	500-999 Emps.	Unknown Emps.	
2015	11.0	29.6	47.9	29.5	2.6	1.6	0.2	0.0	0.1	122.5
2016	11.8	31.9	51.6	31.7	2.8	1.7	0.2	0.0	0.1	131.8
2017	12.6	34.0	55.1	33.9	3.0	1.9	0.3	0.0	0.1	140.9
2018	13.8	37.1	60.1	37.0	3.2	2.0	0.3	0.0	0.2	153.7
2018	15.0	40.5	65.5	40.3	3.5	2.2	0.3	0.0	0.2	167.5

INDUSTRY: DEPARTMENT STORES INDUSTRY (NAICS 45211)
PRODUCT LINE: LAWN & GARDEN SUPPLIES (Main Category)

NAICS 45211: Department Stores Industry . this industry comprises establishments known as department stores primarily engaged in retailing a wide range of the following new products with no one merchandise line predominating: apparel, furniture, appliances and home furnishings; and selected additional items, such as paint, hardware, toiletries, cosmetics, photographic equipment, jewelry, toys, and sporting goods. merchandise lines are normally arranged in separate departments.

5-YEAR TREND — ESTIMATED INDUSTRY SALES ($MILLIONS)

Year	Employee Size of Establishment									Total Industry Sales
	1-4 Emps.	5-9 Emps.	10-19 Emps.	20-49 Emps.	50-99 Emps.	100-249 Emps.	250-499 Emps.	500-999 Emps.	Unknown Emps.	
2015	0.2	0.1	0.3	22.0	416.9	1,382.7	606.6	81.2	3.5	2,513.5
2016	0.2	0.1	0.3	22.2	422.3	1,400.6	614.4	82.3	3.6	2,545.9
2017	0.2	0.1	0.3	22.5	426.8	1,415.7	621.1	83.2	3.6	2,573.3
2018	0.2	0.1	0.3	22.6	428.8	1,422.2	623.9	83.6	3.6	2,585.3
2018	0.2	0.1	0.3	22.7	431.9	1,432.4	628.4	84.3	3.6	2,603.9

INDUSTRY: WAREHOUSE CLUBS & SUPERCENTERS (NAICS 45291)
PRODUCT LINE: LAWN & GARDEN SUPPLIES (Main Category)

NAICS 45291: Warehouse Clubs and Superstores This industry comprises establishments known as warehouse clubs, superstores or supercenters primarily engaged in retailing a general line of groceries in combination with general lines of new merchandise, such as apparel, furniture, and appliances.

5-YEAR TREND — ESTIMATED INDUSTRY SALES ($MILLIONS)

Year	Employee Size of Establishment									Total
	1-4 Emps.	5-9 Emps.	10-19 Emps.	20-49 Emps.	50-99 Emps.	100-249 Emps.	250-499 Emps.	500-999 Emps.	Unknown Emps.	Industry Sales
2015	1.6	0.1	0.3	14.7	18.5	2,281.6	10,086.6	266.5	3.1	12,672.8
2016	1.6	0.1	0.3	15.2	19.2	2,365.0	10,455.3	276.2	3.3	13,136.1
2017	1.7	0.1	0.3	15.7	19.8	2,443.8	10,803.9	285.5	3.4	13,574.1
2018	1.8	0.1	0.3	17.1	21.5	2,654.3	11,734.4	310.0	3.7	14,743.2
2018	1.9	0.1	0.3	18.1	22.8	2,818.9	12,461.9	329.2	3.9	15,657.3

INDUSTRY: ELECTRONIC SHOPPING & MAIL-ORDER (NAICS 45411)
PRODUCT LINE: LAWN & GARDEN SUPPLIES (Main Category)

NAICS 45411: Electronic Shopping and Mail-Order Houses This industry comprises establishments primarily engaged in retailing all types of merchandise by means of mail or by electronic media, such as interactive television or computer. Included in this industry are establishments primarily engaged in retailing from catalogue showrooms of mail-order houses.

5-YEAR TREND — ESTIMATED INDUSTRY SALES ($MILLIONS)

Year	Employee Size of Establishment									Total
	1-4 Emps.	5-9 Emps.	10-19 Emps.	20-49 Emps.	50-99 Emps.	100-249 Emps.	250-499 Emps.	500-999 Emps.	Unknown Emps.	Industry Sales
2015	378.0	200.7	298.1	482.2	346.8	676.2	989.4	1,253.3	57.2	4,681.9
2016	403.3	214.1	317.9	514.4	370.0	721.3	1,055.4	1,336.9	61.0	4,994.2
2017	427.7	227.1	337.2	545.6	392.4	765.1	1,119.4	1,418.0	64.7	5,297.2
2018	486.7	258.4	383.7	620.8	446.5	870.6	1,273.8	1,574.0	73.6	5,988.3
2018	540.6	287.0	426.2	689.5	496.0	967.0	1,414.8	1,718.0	81.8	6,620.9

INDUSTRY: HARDWARE STORES INDUSTRY (NAICS 44413)
PRODUCT LINE: CUT FLOWERS (Sub Category)

NAICS 44413: Hardware Stores. Establishments primarily engaged
in the retail sale of a number of basic hardware lines, such as tools,
builders' hardware, paint and glass, housewares and household appliances,
and cutlery.

5-YEAR TREND — ESTIMATED INDUSTRY SALES ($MILLIONS)

Year	Employee Size of Establishment									Total Industry Sales
	1-4 Emps.	5-9 Emps.	10-19 Emps.	20-49 Emps.	50-99 Emps.	100-249 Emps.	250-499 Emps.	500-999 Emps.	Unknown Emps.	
2015	1.7	2.8	5.6	7.8	1.4	0.3	0.1	0.0	0.1	20.0
2016	1.8	2.8	5.7	8.0	1.5	0.3	0.1	0.0	0.1	20.3
2017	1.8	2.9	5.8	8.1	1.5	0.3	0.1	0.0	0.2	20.7
2018	1.9	3.0	6.1	8.5	1.6	0.4	0.1	0.0	0.2	21.6
2018	2.0	3.2	6.4	8.9	1.6	0.4	0.1	0.0	0.2	22.7

INDUSTRY: DEPARTMENT STORES INDUSTRY (NAICS 45211)
PRODUCT LINE: CUT FLOWERS (Sub Category)

NAICS 45211: Department Stores Industry . this industry comprises
establishments known as department stores primarily engaged in retailing
a wide range of the following new products with no one merchandise line
predominating: apparel, furniture, appliances and home furnishings; and
selected additional items, such as paint, hardware, toiletries, cosmetics,
photographic equipment, jewelry, toys, and sporting goods. merchandise lines
are normally arranged in separate departments.

5-YEAR TREND — ESTIMATED INDUSTRY SALES ($MILLIONS)

Year	Employee Size of Establishment									Total Industry Sales
	1-4 Emps.	5-9 Emps.	10-19 Emps.	20-49 Emps.	50-99 Emps.	100-249 Emps.	250-499 Emps.	500-999 Emps.	Unknown Emps.	
2015	0.0	0.0	0.0	0.1	2.5	8.2	3.6	0.5	0.0	14.9
2016	0.0	0.0	0.0	0.1	2.5	8.3	3.6	0.5	0.0	15.0
2017	0.0	0.0	0.0	0.1	2.5	8.4	3.7	0.5	0.0	15.2
2018	0.0	0.0	0.0	0.1	2.5	8.4	3.7	0.5	0.0	15.3
2018	0.0	0.0	0.0	0.1	2.6	8.5	3.7	0.5	0.0	15.4

INDUSTRY: WAREHOUSE CLUBS & SUPERCENTERS (NAICS 45291)
PRODUCT LINE: CUT FLOWERS (Sub Category)

NAICS 45291: Warehouse Clubs and Superstores This industry comprises establishments known as warehouse clubs, superstores or supercenters primarily engaged in retailing a general line of groceries in combination with general lines of new merchandise, such as apparel, furniture, and appliances.

5-YEAR TREND — ESTIMATED INDUSTRY SALES ($MILLIONS)

| Year | Employee Size of Establishment | | | | | | | | | Total |
	1-4 Emps.	5-9 Emps.	10-19 Emps.	20-49 Emps.	50-99 Emps.	100-249 Emps.	250-499 Emps.	500-999 Emps.	Unknown Emps.	Industry Sales
2015	0.3	0.0	0.0	2.5	3.1	386.5	1,708.8	45.1	0.5	2,147.0
2016	0.3	0.0	0.0	2.6	3.2	400.7	1,771.3	46.8	0.6	2,225.5
2017	0.3	0.0	0.0	2.7	3.4	414.0	1,830.3	48.4	0.6	2,299.7
2018	0.3	0.0	0.1	2.9	3.6	449.7	1,988.0	52.5	0.6	2,497.7
2018	0.3	0.0	0.1	3.1	3.9	477.6	2,111.2	55.8	0.7	2,652.6

INDUSTRY: HOME CENTERS INDUSTRY (NAICS 44411)
PRODUCT LINE: INDOOR POTTED PLANTS (Sub Category)

NAICS 44411: Home Centers. This industry comprises establishments known as home centers primarily engaged in retailing a general line of new home repair and improvement materials and supplies, such as lumber, plumbing goods, electrical goods, tools, housewares, hardware, and lawn and garden supplies, with no one merchandise line predominating. The merchandise lines are normally arranged in separate departments.

5-YEAR TREND — ESTIMATED INDUSTRY SALES ($MILLIONS)

| Year | Employee Size of Establishment | | | | | | | | | Total |
	1-4 Emps.	5-9 Emps.	10-19 Emps.	20-49 Emps.	50-99 Emps.	100-249 Emps.	250-499 Emps.	500-999 Emps.	Unknown Emps.	Industry Sales
2015	1.7	3.4	9.0	17.9	13.2	861.0	76.1	1.4	0.6	984.4
2016	1.8	3.6	9.3	18.5	13.6	889.4	78.7	1.5	0.6	1,016.8
2017	1.8	3.7	9.5	19.1	14.0	916.0	81.0	1.5	0.6	1,047.3
2018	1.9	3.9	10.0	20.0	14.7	962.7	85.1	1.6	0.7	1,100.7
2018	2.0	4.1	10.6	21.1	15.5	1,013.8	89.7	1.7	0.7	1,159.2

INDUSTRY: HARDWARE STORES INDUSTRY (NAICS 44413)
PRODUCT LINE: INDOOR POTTED PLANTS (Sub Category)

NAICS 44413: Hardware Stores. Establishments primarily engaged in the retail sale of a number of basic hardware lines, such as tools, builders' hardware, paint and glass, housewares and household appliances, and cutlery.

5-YEAR TREND – ESTIMATED INDUSTRY SALES ($MILLIONS)

Year	Employee Size of Establishment									Total Industry Sales
	1-4 Emps.	5-9 Emps.	10-19 Emps.	20-49 Emps.	50-99 Emps.	100-249 Emps.	250-499 Emps.	500-999 Emps.	Unknown Emps.	
2015	3.7	6.0	12.0	16.8	3.1	0.7	0.2	0.0	0.3	42.9
2016	3.8	6.1	12.2	17.1	3.1	0.7	0.2	0.0	0.3	43.7
2017	3.9	6.2	12.4	17.4	3.2	0.7	0.2	0.0	0.3	44.4
2018	4.1	6.5	13.0	18.2	3.3	0.8	0.2	0.0	0.3	46.5
2018	4.3	6.8	13.7	19.1	3.5	0.8	0.2	0.0	0.4	48.8

INDUSTRY: DEPARTMENT STORES INDUSTRY (NAICS 45211)
PRODUCT LINE: INDOOR POTTED PLANTS (Sub Category)

NAICS 45211: Department Stores Industry . this industry comprises establishments known as department stores primarily engaged in retailing a wide range of the following new products with no one merchandise line predominating: apparel, furniture, appliances and home furnishings; and selected additional items, such as paint, hardware, toiletries, cosmetics, photographic equipment, jewelry, toys, and sporting goods. merchandise lines are normally arranged in separate departments.

5-YEAR TREND – ESTIMATED INDUSTRY SALES ($MILLIONS)

Year	Employee Size of Establishment									Total Industry Sales
	1-4 Emps.	5-9 Emps.	10-19 Emps.	20-49 Emps.	50-99 Emps.	100-249 Emps.	250-499 Emps.	500-999 Emps.	Unknown Emps.	
2015	0.0	0.0	0.0	0.8	14.6	48.4	21.2	2.8	0.1	88.0
2016	0.0	0.0	0.0	0.8	14.8	49.1	21.5	2.9	0.1	89.2
2017	0.0	0.0	0.0	0.8	14.9	49.6	21.8	2.9	0.1	90.1
2018	0.0	0.0	0.0	0.8	15.0	49.8	21.9	2.9	0.1	90.5
2018	0.0	0.0	0.0	0.8	15.1	50.2	22.0	3.0	0.1	91.2

INDUSTRY: WAREHOUSE CLUBS & SUPERCENTERS (NAICS 45291)
PRODUCT LINE: INDOOR POTTED PLANTS (Sub Category)

NAICS 45291: Warehouse Clubs and Superstores This industry comprises establishments known as warehouse clubs, superstores or supercenters primarily engaged in retailing a general line of groceries in combination with general lines of new merchandise, such as apparel, furniture, and appliances.

5-YEAR TREND – ESTIMATED INDUSTRY SALES ($MILLIONS)

Year	Employee Size of Establishment									Total Industry Sales
	1-4 Emps.	5-9 Emps.	10-19 Emps.	20-49 Emps.	50-99 Emps.	100-249 Emps.	250-499 Emps.	500-999 Emps.	Unknown Emps.	
2015	0.1	0.0	0.0	0.7	0.9	106.2	469.4	12.4	0.1	589.7
2016	0.1	0.0	0.0	0.7	0.9	110.1	486.5	12.9	0.2	611.3
2017	0.1	0.0	0.0	0.7	0.9	113.7	502.7	13.3	0.2	631.7
2018	0.1	0.0	0.0	0.8	1.0	123.5	546.0	14.4	0.2	686.1
2018	0.1	0.0	0.0	0.8	1.1	131.2	579.9	15.3	0.2	728.6

INDUSTRY: HOME CENTERS INDUSTRY (NAICS 44411)
PRODUCT LINE: OUTDOOR NURSERY PLANTS (Sub Category)

NAICS 44411: Home Centers. This industry comprises establishments known as home centers primarily engaged in retailing a general line of new home repair and improvement materials and supplies, such as lumber, plumbing goods, electrical goods, tools, housewares, hardware, and lawn and garden supplies, with no one merchandise line predominating. The merchandise lines are normally arranged in separate departments.

5-YEAR TREND – ESTIMATED INDUSTRY SALES ($MILLIONS)

Year	Employee Size of Establishment									Total Industry Sales
	1-4 Emps.	5-9 Emps.	10-19 Emps.	20-49 Emps.	50-99 Emps.	100-249 Emps.	250-499 Emps.	500-999 Emps.	Unknown Emps.	
2015	8.0	15.9	41.3	82.5	60.6	3,963.1	350.5	6.5	2.8	4,531.1
2016	8.3	16.4	42.7	85.2	62.6	4,093.8	362.1	6.7	2.9	4,680.5
2017	8.5	16.9	44.0	87.8	64.5	4,216.6	372.9	6.9	2.9	4,820.9
2018	8.9	17.8	46.2	92.2	67.7	4,431.4	391.9	7.3	3.1	5,066.5
2018	9.4	18.7	48.6	97.1	71.3	4,666.7	412.7	7.6	3.3	5,335.6

INDUSTRY: HARDWARE STORES INDUSTRY (NAICS 44413)
PRODUCT LINE: OUTDOOR NURSERY PLANTS (Sub Category)

NAICS 44413: Hardware Stores. Establishments primarily engaged
in the retail sale of a number of basic hardware lines, such as tools,
builders' hardware, paint and glass, housewares and household appliances,
and cutlery.

5-YEAR TREND – ESTIMATED INDUSTRY SALES ($MILLIONS)

Year	Employee Size of Establishment									Total Industry Sales
	1-4 Emps.	5-9 Emps.	10-19 Emps.	20-49 Emps.	50-99 Emps.	100-249 Emps.	250-499 Emps.	500-999 Emps.	Unknown Emps.	
2015	17.9	28.7	57.5	80.5	14.7	3.5	1.0	0.0	1.5	205.3
2016	18.2	29.3	58.5	82.0	15.0	3.5	1.0	0.0	1.5	209.1
2017	18.5	29.8	59.5	83.3	15.3	3.6	1.0	0.0	1.6	212.6
2018	19.4	31.1	62.3	87.2	16.0	3.7	1.1	0.1	1.6	222.5
2018	20.4	32.7	65.3	91.5	16.8	3.9	1.1	0.1	1.7	233.5

INDUSTRY: DEPARTMENT STORES INDUSTRY (NAICS 45211)
PRODUCT LINE: OUTDOOR NURSERY PLANTS (Sub Category)

NAICS 45211: Department Stores Industry . this industry comprises
establishments known as department stores primarily engaged in retailing
a wide range of the following new products with no one merchandise line
predominating: apparel, furniture, appliances and home furnishings; and
selected additional Items, such as paint, hardware, toiletries, cosmetics,
photographic equipment, jewelry, toys, and sporting goods. merchandise lines
are normally arranged in separate departments.

5-YEAR TREND – ESTIMATED INDUSTRY SALES ($MILLIONS)

Year	Employee Size of Establishment									Total Industry Sales
	1-4 Emps.	5-9 Emps.	10-19 Emps.	20-49 Emps.	50-99 Emps.	100-249 Emps.	250-499 Emps.	500-999 Emps.	Unknown Emps.	
2015	0.0	0.0	0.1	4.1	77.5	257.2	112.8	15.1	0.7	467.6
2016	0.0	0.0	0.1	4.1	78.6	260.5	114.3	15.3	0.7	473.6
2017	0.0	0.0	0.1	4.2	79.4	263.3	115.5	15.5	0.7	478.7
2018	0.0	0.0	0.1	4.2	79.8	264.6	116.1	15.6	0.7	480.9
2018	0.0	0.0	0.1	4.2	80.3	266.5	116.9	15.7	0.7	484.4

INDUSTRY: WAREHOUSE CLUBS & SUPERCENTERS (NAICS 45291)
PRODUCT LINE: OUTDOOR NURSERY PLANTS (Sub Category)

NAICS 45291: Warehouse Clubs and Superstores This industry comprises establishments known as warehouse clubs, superstores or supercenters primarily engaged in retailing a general line of groceries in combination with general lines of new merchandise, such as apparel, furniture, and appliances.

5-YEAR TREND – ESTIMATED INDUSTRY SALES ($MILLIONS)

Year	Employee Size of Establishment									Total Industry Sales
	1-4 Emps.	5-9 Emps.	10-19 Emps.	20-49 Emps.	50-99 Emps.	100-249 Emps.	250-499 Emps.	500-999 Emps.	Unknown Emps.	
2015	0.2	0.0	0.0	2.2	2.8	339.5	1,501.1	39.7	0.5	1,886.0
2016	0.2	0.0	0.0	2.3	2.9	352.0	1,556.0	41.1	0.5	1,954.9
2017	0.3	0.0	0.0	2.3	2.9	363.7	1,607.9	42.5	0.5	2,020.1
2018	0.3	0.0	0.0	2.5	3.2	395.0	1,746.3	46.1	0.5	2,194.1
2018	0.3	0.0	0.0	2.7	3.4	419.5	1,854.6	49.0	0.6	2,330.1

INDUSTRY: HOME CENTERS INDUSTRY (NAICS 44411)
PRODUCT LINE: FERTILIZER & SOIL TREATMENTS (Sub Category)

NAICS 44411: Home Centers. This industry comprises establishments known as home centers primarily engaged in retailing a general line of new home repair and improvement materials and supplies, such as lumber, plumbing goods, electrical goods, tools, housewares, hardware, and lawn and garden supplies, with no one merchandise line predominating. The merchandise lines are normally arranged in separate departments.

5-YEAR TREND – ESTIMATED INDUSTRY SALES ($MILLIONS)

Year	Employee Size of Establishment									Total Industry Sales
	1-4 Emps.	5-9 Emps.	10-19 Emps.	20-49 Emps.	50-99 Emps.	100-249 Emps.	250-499 Emps.	500-999 Emps.	Unknown Emps.	
2015	6.2	12.4	32.3	64.4	47.3	3,095.9	273.8	5.1	2.2	3,539.6
2016	6.5	12.8	33.3	66.6	48.9	3,198.0	282.8	5.2	2.2	3,656.3
2017	6.6	13.2	34.3	68.6	50.3	3,293.9	291.3	5.4	2.3	3,766.0
2018	7.0	13.9	36.1	72.1	52.9	3,461.7	306.2	5.7	2.4	3,957.8
2018	7.4	14.6	38.0	75.9	55.7	3,645.6	322.4	6.0	2.5	4,168.0

INDUSTRY: HARDWARE STORES INDUSTRY (NAICS 44413)
PRODUCT LINE: FERTILIZER & SOIL TREATMENTS (Sub Category)

NAICS 44413: Hardware Stores. Establishments primarily engaged in the retail sale of a number of basic hardware lines, such as tools, builders' hardware, paint and glass, housewares and household appliances, and cutlery.

5-YEAR TREND — ESTIMATED INDUSTRY SALES ($MILLIONS)

Year	Employee Size of Establishment									Total Industry Sales
	1-4 Emps.	5-9 Emps.	10-19 Emps.	20-49 Emps.	50-99 Emps.	100-249 Emps.	250-499 Emps.	500-999 Emps.	Unknown Emps.	
2015	42.7	68.6	137.2	192.1	35.2	8.2	2.3	0.1	3.6	490.0
2016	43.6	69.9	139.7	195.7	35.8	8.4	2.4	0.1	3.7	499.3
2017	44.3	71.0	142.1	198.9	36.4	8.5	2.4	0.1	3.7	507.5
2018	46.3	74.4	148.7	208.2	38.1	8.9	2.5	0.1	3.9	531.2
2018	48.6	78.0	156.0	218.5	40.0	9.4	2.6	0.1	4.1	557.3

INDUSTRY: DEPARTMENT STORES INDUSTRY (NAICS 45211)
PRODUCT LINE: FERTILIZER & SOIL TREATMENTS (Sub Category)

NAICS 45211: Department Stores Industry . this industry comprises establishments known as department stores primarily engaged in retailing a wide range of the following new products with no one merchandise line predominating: apparel, furniture, appliances and home furnishings; and selected additional items, such as paint, hardware, toiletries, cosmetics, photographic equipment, jewelry, toys, and sporting goods. merchandise lines are normally arranged in separate departments.

5-YEAR TREND — ESTIMATED INDUSTRY SALES ($MILLIONS)

Year	Employee Size of Establishment									Total Industry Sales
	1-4 Emps.	5-9 Emps.	10-19 Emps.	20-49 Emps.	50-99 Emps.	100-249 Emps.	250-499 Emps.	500-999 Emps.	Unknown Emps.	
2015	0.0	0.0	0.0	2.2	41.1	136.3	59.8	8.0	0.3	247.8
2016	0.0	0.0	0.0	2.2	41.6	138.1	60.6	8.1	0.4	251.0
2017	0.0	0.0	0.0	2.2	42.1	139.6	61.2	8.2	0.4	253.7
2018	0.0	0.0	0.0	2.2	42.3	140.2	61.5	8.2	0.4	254.9
2018	0.0	0.0	0.0	2.2	42.6	141.2	61.9	8.3	0.4	256.7

INDUSTRY: WAREHOUSE CLUBS & SUPERCENTERS (NAICS 45291)
PRODUCT LINE: FERTILIZER & SOIL TREATMENTS (Sub Category)

NAICS 45291: Warehouse Clubs and Superstores This industry comprises establishments known as warehouse clubs, superstores or supercenters primarily engaged in retailing a general line of groceries in combination with general lines of new merchandise, such as apparel, furniture, and appliances.

5-YEAR TREND — ESTIMATED INDUSTRY SALES ($MILLIONS)

Year	Employee Size of Establishment									Total
	1-4 Emps.	5-9 Emps.	10-19 Emps.	20-49 Emps.	50-99 Emps.	100-249 Emps.	250-499 Emps.	500-999 Emps.	Unknown Emps.	Industry Sales
2015	0.2	0.0	0.0	2.0	2.5	312.8	1,382.7	36.5	0.4	1,737.2
2016	0.2	0.0	0.0	2.1	2.6	324.2	1,433.2	37.9	0.4	1,800.7
2017	0.2	0.0	0.0	2.2	2.7	335.0	1,481.0	39.1	0.5	1,860.8
2018	0.3	0.0	0.0	2.3	2.9	363.9	1,608.6	42.5	0.5	2,021.0
2018	0.3	0.0	0.0	2.5	3.1	386.4	1,708.3	45.1	0.5	2,146.3

INDUSTRY: HOME CENTERS INDUSTRY (NAICS 44411)
PRODUCT LINE: LAWN & GARDEN TOOLS (Sub Category)

NAICS 44411: Home Centers. This industry comprises establishments known as home centers primarily engaged in retailing a general line of new home repair and improvement materials and supplies, such as lumber, plumbing goods, electrical goods, tools, housewares, hardware, and lawn and garden supplies, with no one merchandise line predominating. The merchandise lines are normally arranged in separate departments.

5-YEAR TREND — ESTIMATED INDUSTRY SALES ($MILLIONS)

Year	Employee Size of Establishment									Total
	1-4 Emps.	5-9 Emps.	10-19 Emps.	20-49 Emps.	50-99 Emps.	100-249 Emps.	250-499 Emps.	500-999 Emps.	Unknown Emps.	Industry Sales
2015	2.8	5.5	14.2	28.4	20.9	1,364.8	120.7	2.2	1.0	1,560.4
2016	2.8	5.6	14.7	29.3	21.5	1,409.8	124.7	2.3	1.0	1,611.9
2017	2.9	5.8	15.1	30.2	22.2	1,452.1	128.4	2.4	1.0	1,660.2
2018	3.1	6.1	15.9	31.8	23.3	1,526.1	135.0	2.5	1.1	1,744.8
2018	3.2	6.4	16.8	33.5	24.6	1,607.1	142.1	2.6	1.1	1,837.5

INDUSTRY: HARDWARE STORES INDUSTRY (NAICS 44413)
PRODUCT LINE: LAWN & GARDEN TOOLS (Sub Category)

NAICS 44413: Hardware Stores. Establishments primarily engaged
in the retail sale of a number of basic hardware lines, such as tools,
builders' hardware, paint and glass, housewares and household appliances,
and cutlery.

5-YEAR TREND — ESTIMATED INDUSTRY SALES ($MILLIONS)

Year	Employee Size of Establishment									Total Industry Sales
	1-4 Emps.	5-9 Emps.	10-19 Emps.	20-49 Emps.	50-99 Emps.	100-249 Emps.	250-499 Emps.	500-999 Emps.	Unknown Emps.	
2015	46.7	74.9	149.7	209.6	38.4	9.0	2.5	0.1	3.9	534.9
2016	47.5	76.3	152.5	213.6	39.1	9.2	2.6	0.1	4.0	544.9
2017	48.3	77.5	155.0	217.1	39.7	9.3	2.6	0.1	4.1	553.9
2018	50.6	81.2	162.3	227.2	41.6	9.8	2.7	0.1	4.3	579.8
2018	53.1	85.2	170.3	238.4	43.7	10.2	2.9	0.1	4.5	608.3

INDUSTRY: DEPARTMENT STORES INDUSTRY (NAICS 45211)
PRODUCT LINE: LAWN & GARDEN TOOLS (Sub Category)

NAICS 45211: Department Stores Industry . this industry comprises
establishments known as department stores primarily engaged in retailing
a wide range of the following new products with no one merchandise line
predominating: apparel, furniture, appliances and home furnishings; and
selected additional items, such as paint, hardware, toiletries, cosmetics,
photographic equipment, jewelry, toys, and sporting goods. merchandise lines
are normally arranged in separate departments.

5-YEAR TREND — ESTIMATED INDUSTRY SALES ($MILLIONS)

Year	Employee Size of Establishment									Total Industry Sales
	1-4 Emps.	5-9 Emps.	10-19 Emps.	20-49 Emps.	50-99 Emps.	100-249 Emps.	250-499 Emps.	500-999 Emps.	Unknown Emps.	
2015	0.0	0.0	0.0	0.5	8.6	28.7	12.6	1.7	0.1	52.1
2016	0.0	0.0	0.0	0.5	8.8	29.0	12.7	1.7	0.1	52.8
2017	0.0	0.0	0.0	0.5	8.8	29.3	12.9	1.7	0.1	53.3
2018	0.0	0.0	0.0	0.5	8.9	29.5	12.9	1.7	0.1	53.6
2018	0.0	0.0	0.0	0.5	9.0	29.7	13.0	1.7	0.1	54.0

INDUSTRY: WAREHOUSE CLUBS & SUPERCENTERS (NAICS 45291)
PRODUCT LINE: LAWN & GARDEN TOOLS (Sub Category)

NAICS 45291: Warehouse Clubs and Superstores This industry comprises establishments known as warehouse clubs, superstores or supercenters primarily engaged in retailing a general line of groceries in combination with general lines of new merchandise, such as apparel, furniture, and appliances.

5-YEAR TREND – ESTIMATED INDUSTRY SALES ($MILLIONS)

Year	Employee Size of Establishment									Total
------	1-4 Emps.	5-9 Emps.	10-19 Emps.	20-49 Emps.	50-99 Emps.	100-249 Emps.	250-499 Emps.	500-999 Emps.	Unknown Emps.	Industry Sales
2015	0.0	0.0	0.0	0.5	0.6	70.8	312.9	8.3	0.1	393.2
2016	0.1	0.0	0.0	0.5	0.6	73.4	324.4	8.6	0.1	407.5
2017	0.1	0.0	0.0	0.5	0.6	75.8	335.2	8.9	0.1	421.1
2018	0.1	0.0	0.0	0.5	0.7	82.3	364.0	9.6	0.1	457.4
2018	0.1	0.0	0.0	0.6	0.7	87.5	386.6	10.2	0.1	485.8

INDUSTRY: HOME CENTERS INDUSTRY (NAICS 44411)
PRODUCT LINE: LAWN & GARDEN MACHINERY (Sub Category)

NAICS 44411: Home Centers. This industry comprises establishments known as home centers primarily engaged in retailing a general line of new home repair and improvement materials and supplies, such as lumber, plumbing goods, electrical goods, tools, housewares, hardware, and lawn and garden supplies, with no one merchandise line predominating. The merchandise lines are normally arranged in separate departments.

5-YEAR TREND – ESTIMATED INDUSTRY SALES ($MILLIONS)

Year	Employee Size of Establishment									Total
------	1-4 Emps.	5-9 Emps.	10-19 Emps.	20-49 Emps.	50-99 Emps.	100-249 Emps.	250-499 Emps.	500-999 Emps.	Unknown Emps.	Industry Sales
2015	7.4	14.6	38.0	75.9	55.7	3,644.8	322.3	6.0	2.5	4,167.2
2016	7.6	15.1	39.2	78.4	57.5	3,765.0	333.0	6.2	2.6	4,304.7
2017	7.8	15.5	40.4	80.7	59.3	3,878.0	343.0	6.3	2.7	4,433.8
2018	8.2	16.3	42.5	84.8	62.3	4,075.5	360.4	6.7	2.8	4,659.7
2018	8.7	17.2	44.7	89.3	65.6	4,292.0	379.6	7.0	3.0	4,907.1

INDUSTRY: HARDWARE STORES INDUSTRY (NAICS 44413)
PRODUCT LINE: LAWN & GARDEN MACHINERY (Sub Category)

NAICS 44413: Hardware Stores. Establishments primarily engaged
in the retail sale of a number of basic hardware lines, such as tools,
builders' hardware, paint and glass, housewares and household appliances,
and cutlery.

5-YEAR TREND — ESTIMATED INDUSTRY SALES ($MILLIONS)

Year	Employee Size of Establishment									Total
	1-4 Emps.	5-9 Emps.	10-19 Emps.	20-49 Emps.	50-99 Emps.	100-249 Emps.	250-499 Emps.	500-999 Emps.	Unknown Emps.	Industry Sales
2015	69.0	110.7	221.4	310.0	56.7	13.3	3.7	0.2	5.8	790.8
2016	70.3	112.8	225.5	315.8	57.8	13.6	3.8	0.2	5.9	805.7
2017	71.5	114.7	229.3	321.0	58.8	13.8	3.9	0.2	6.0	819.0
2018	74.8	120.0	239.9	336.0	61.5	14.4	4.0	0.2	6.3	857.2
2018	78.5	125.9	251.8	352.6	64.5	15.1	4.2	0.2	6.6	899.4

INDUSTRY: DEPARTMENT STORES INDUSTRY (NAICS 45211)
PRODUCT LINE: LAWN & GARDEN MACHINERY (Sub Category)

NAICS 45211: Department Stores Industry . this industry comprises
establishments known as department stores primarily engaged in retailing
a wide range of the following new products with no one merchandise line
predominating: apparel, furniture, appliances and home furnishings; and
selected additional items, such as paint, hardware, toiletries, cosmetics,
photographic equipment, jewelry, toys, and sporting goods. merchandise lines
are normally arranged in separate departments.

5-YEAR TREND — ESTIMATED INDUSTRY SALES ($MILLIONS)

Year	Employee Size of Establishment									Total
	1-4 Emps.	5-9 Emps.	10-19 Emps.	20-49 Emps.	50-99 Emps.	100-249 Emps.	250-499 Emps.	500-999 Emps.	Unknown Emps.	Industry Sales
2015	0.1	0.0	0.1	9.0	170.7	566.1	248.3	33.3	1.4	1,029.0
2016	0.1	0.0	0.1	9.1	172.9	573.4	251.5	33.7	1.5	1,042.3
2017	0.1	0.0	0.1	9.2	174.7	579.5	254.3	34.0	1.5	1,053.5
2018	0.1	0.0	0.1	9.2	175.5	582.2	255.4	34.2	1.5	1,058.4
2018	0.1	0.0	0.1	9.3	176.8	586.4	257.3	34.5	1.5	1,066.0

INDUSTRY: WAREHOUSE CLUBS & SUPERCENTERS (NAICS 45291)
PRODUCT LINE: LAWN & GARDEN MACHINERY (Sub Category)

NAICS 45291: Warehouse Clubs and Superstores This industry comprises establishments known as warehouse clubs, superstores or supercenters primarily engaged in retailing a general line of groceries in combination with general lines of new merchandise, such as apparel, furniture, and appliances.

5-YEAR TREND – ESTIMATED INDUSTRY SALES ($MILLIONS)

Year	Employee Size of Establishment									Total
	1-4 Emps.	5-9 Emps.	10-19 Emps.	20-49 Emps.	50-99 Emps.	100-249 Emps.	250-499 Emps.	500-999 Emps.	Unknown Emps.	Industry Sales
2015	0.5	0.0	0.1	4.8	6.0	745.8	3,296.9	87.1	1.0	4,142.3
2016	0.5	0.0	0.1	5.0	6.3	773.0	3,417.4	90.3	1.1	4,293.7
2017	0.6	0.0	0.1	5.1	6.5	798.8	3,531.4	93.3	1.1	4,436.9
2018	0.6	0.0	0.1	5.6	7.0	867.6	3,835.5	101.3	1.2	4,819.0
2018	0.6	0.0	0.1	5.9	7.5	921.4	4,073.3	107.6	1.3	5,117.7

INDUSTRY: HOME CENTERS INDUSTRY (NAICS 44411)
PRODUCT LINE: FARM MACHINERY (Sub Category)

NAICS 44411: Home Centers. This industry comprises establishments known as home centers primarily engaged in retailing a general line of new home repair and improvement materials and supplies, such as lumber, plumbing goods, electrical goods, tools, housewares, hardware, and lawn and garden supplies, with no one merchandise line predominating. The merchandise lines are normally arranged in separate departments.

5-YEAR TREND – ESTIMATED INDUSTRY SALES ($MILLIONS)

Year	Employee Size of Establishment									Total
	1-4 Emps.	5-9 Emps.	10-19 Emps.	20-49 Emps.	50-99 Emps.	100-249 Emps.	250-499 Emps.	500-999 Emps.	Unknown Emps.	Industry Sales
2015	0.1	0.3	0.7	1.4	1.1	69.5	6.1	0.1	0.0	79.4
2016	0.1	0.3	0.7	1.5	1.1	71.8	6.3	0.1	0.1	82.0
2017	0.1	0.3	0.8	1.5	1.1	73.9	6.5	0.1	0.1	84.5
2018	0.2	0.3	0.8	1.6	1.2	77.7	6.9	0.1	0.1	88.8
2018	0.2	0.3	0.9	1.7	1.3	81.8	7.2	0.1	0.1	93.5

INDUSTRY: HARDWARE STORES INDUSTRY (NAICS 44413)
PRODUCT LINE: FARM MACHINERY (Sub Category)

NAICS 44413: Hardware Stores. Establishments primarily engaged in the retail sale of a number of basic hardware lines, such as tools, builders' hardware, paint and glass, housewares and household appliances, and cutlery.

5-Year Trend – Estimated Industry Sales ($Millions)

Year	Employee Size of Establishment									Total
	1-4 Emps.	5-9 Emps.	10-19 Emps.	20-49 Emps.	50-99 Emps.	100-249 Emps.	250-499 Emps.	500-999 Emps.	Unknown Emps.	Industry Sales
2015	11.1	17.8	35.6	49.8	9.1	2.1	0.6	0.0	0.9	127.1
2016	11.3	18.1	36.2	50.8	9.3	2.2	0.6	0.0	1.0	129.5
2017	11.5	18.4	36.8	51.6	9.4	2.2	0.6	0.0	1.0	131.6
2018	12.0	19.3	38.6	54.0	9.9	2.3	0.7	0.0	1.0	137.8
2018	12.6	20.2	40.5	56.7	10.4	2.4	0.7	0.0	1.1	144.6

INDUSTRY: HOME CENTERS INDUSTRY (NAICS 44411)
PRODUCT LINE: OTHER FARM SUPPLIES (Sub Category)

NAICS 44411: Home Centers. This industry comprises establishments known as home centers primarily engaged in retailing a general line of new home repair and improvement materials and supplies, such as lumber, plumbing goods, electrical goods, tools, housewares, hardware, and lawn and garden supplies, with no one merchandise line predominating. The merchandise lines are normally arranged in separate departments.

5-Year Trend – Estimated Industry Sales ($Millions)

Year	Employee Size of Establishment									Total
	1-4 Emps.	5-9 Emps.	10-19 Emps.	20-49 Emps.	50-99 Emps.	100-249 Emps.	250-499 Emps.	500-999 Emps.	Unknown Emps.	Industry Sales
2015	0.1	0.1	0.3	0.6	0.5	29.7	2.6	0.0	0.0	34.0
2016	0.1	0.1	0.3	0.6	0.5	30.7	2.7	0.1	0.0	35.1
2017	0.1	0.1	0.3	0.7	0.5	31.6	2.8	0.1	0.0	36.2
2018	0.1	0.1	0.3	0.7	0.5	33.3	2.9	0.1	0.0	38.0
2018	0.1	0.1	0.4	0.7	0.5	35.0	3.1	0.1	0.0	40.0

INDUSTRY: HARDWARE STORES INDUSTRY (NAICS 44413)
PRODUCT LINE: OTHER FARM SUPPLIES (Sub Category)

NAICS 44413: Hardware Stores. Establishments primarily engaged
in the retail sale of a number of basic hardware lines, such as tools,
builders' hardware, paint and glass, housewares and household appliances,
and cutlery.

5-YEAR TREND — ESTIMATED INDUSTRY SALES ($MILLIONS)

Year	Employee Size of Establishment									Total
	1-4 Emps.	5-9 Emps.	10-19 Emps.	20-49 Emps.	50-99 Emps.	100-249 Emps.	250-499 Emps.	500-999 Emps.	Unknown Emps.	Industry Sales
2015	33.0	52.9	105.9	148.2	27.1	6.4	1.8	0.1	2.8	378.2
2016	33.6	53.9	107.9	151.0	27.7	6.5	1.8	0.1	2.8	385.3
2017	34.2	54.8	109.6	153.5	28.1	6.6	1.9	0.1	2.9	391.7
2018	35.8	57.4	114.8	160.7	29.4	6.9	1.9	0.1	3.0	410.0
2018	37.5	60.2	120.4	168.6	30.9	7.2	2.0	0.1	3.2	430.1

INDUSTRY: HOME CENTERS INDUSTRY (NAICS 44411)
PRODUCT LINE: OTHER LAWN & GARDEN SUPPLIES (Sub Category)

NAICS 44411: Home Centers. This industry comprises establishments
known as home centers primarily engaged in retailing a general line of
new home repair and improvement materials and supplies, such as
lumber, plumbing goods, electrical goods, tools, housewares, hardware,
and lawn and garden supplies, with no one merchandise line predominating.
The merchandise lines are normally arranged in separate departments.

5-YEAR TREND — ESTIMATED INDUSTRY SALES ($MILLIONS)

Year	Employee Size of Establishment									Total
	1-4 Emps.	5-9 Emps.	10-19 Emps.	20-49 Emps.	50-99 Emps.	100-249 Emps.	250-499 Emps.	500-999 Emps.	Unknown Emps.	Industry Sales
2015	6.2	12.3	31.9	63.7	46.8	3,061.7	270.8	5.0	2.1	3,500.6
2016	6.4	12.7	33.0	65.8	48.3	3,162.7	279.7	5.2	2.2	3,616.0
2017	6.6	13.0	34.0	67.8	49.8	3,257.6	288.1	5.3	2.3	3,724.5
2018	6.9	13.7	35.7	71.3	52.3	3,423.6	302.8	5.6	2.4	3,914.2
2018	7.3	14.4	37.6	75.1	55.1	3,605.4	318.9	5.9	2.5	4,122.1

INDUSTRY: HARDWARE STORES INDUSTRY (NAICS 44413)
PRODUCT LINE: OTHER LAWN & GARDEN SUPPLIES (Sub Category)

NAICS 44413: Hardware Stores. Establishments primarily engaged
in the retail sale of a number of basic hardware lines, such as tools,
builders' hardware, paint and glass, housewares and household appliances,
and cutlery.

5-YEAR TREND – ESTIMATED INDUSTRY SALES ($MILLIONS)

Year	Employee Size of Establishment									Total Industry Sales
	1-4 Emps.	5-9 Emps.	10-19 Emps.	20-49 Emps.	50-99 Emps.	100-249 Emps.	250-499 Emps.	500-999 Emps.	Unknown Emps.	
2015	41.7	66.8	133.7	187.2	34.3	8.0	2.3	0.1	3.5	477.5
2016	42.4	68.1	136.2	190.7	34.9	8.2	2.3	0.1	3.6	486.5
2017	43.1	69.2	138.4	193.8	35.5	8.3	2.3	0.1	3.6	494.5
2018	45.2	72.5	144.9	202.9	37.1	8.7	2.4	0.1	3.8	517.6
2018	47.4	76.0	152.0	212.9	39.0	9.1	2.6	0.1	4.0	543.1

INDUSTRY: DEPARTMENT STORES INDUSTRY (NAICS 45211)
PRODUCT LINE: OTHER LAWN & GARDEN SUPPLIES (Sub Category)

NAICS 45211: Department Stores Industry . this industry comprises
establishments known as department stores primarily engaged in retailing
a wide range of the following new products with no one merchandise line
predominating: apparel, furniture, appliances and home furnishings; and
selected additional items, such as paint, hardware, toiletries, cosmetics,
photographic equipment, jewelry, toys, and sporting goods. merchandise lines
are normally arranged in separate departments.

5-YEAR TREND – ESTIMATED INDUSTRY SALES ($MILLIONS)

Year	Employee Size of Establishment									Total Industry Sales
	1-4 Emps.	5-9 Emps.	10-19 Emps.	20-49 Emps.	50-99 Emps.	100-249 Emps.	250-499 Emps.	500-999 Emps.	Unknown Emps.	
2015	0.0	0.0	0.1	5.3	100.4	332.8	146.0	19.6	0.8	605.0
2016	0.0	0.0	0.1	5.4	101.6	337.1	147.9	19.8	0.9	612.8
2017	0.0	0.0	0.1	5.4	102.7	340.8	149.5	20.0	0.9	619.4
2018	0.0	0.0	0.1	5.4	103.2	342.3	150.2	20.1	0.9	622.3
2018	0.0	0.0	0.1	5.5	104.0	344.8	151.3	20.3	0.9	626.8

INDUSTRY: WAREHOUSE CLUBS & SUPERCENTERS (NAICS 45291)
PRODUCT LINE: OTHER LAWN & GARDEN SUPPLIES (Sub Category)

NAICS 45291: Warehouse Clubs and Superstores This industry comprises establishments known as warehouse clubs, superstores or supercenters primarily engaged in retailing a general line of groceries in combination with general lines of new merchandise, such as apparel, furniture, and appliances.

5-YEAR TREND — ESTIMATED INDUSTRY SALES ($MILLIONS)

Year	Employee Size of Establishment									Total
	1-4 Emps.	5-9 Emps.	10-19 Emps.	20-49 Emps.	50-99 Emps.	100-249 Emps.	250-499 Emps.	500-999 Emps.	Unknown Emps.	Industry Sales
2015	0.2	0.0	0.0	2.0	2.6	316.7	1,400.1	37.0	0.4	1,759.1
2016	0.2	0.0	0.0	2.1	2.7	328.3	1,451.3	38.3	0.5	1,823.4
2017	0.2	0.0	0.0	2.2	2.7	339.2	1,499.7	39.6	0.5	1,884.2
2018	0.3	0.0	0.0	2.4	3.0	368.4	1,628.8	43.0	0.5	2,046.5
2018	0.3	0.0	0.0	2.5	3.2	391.3	1,729.8	45.7	0.5	2,173.3

INDUSTRY: HOME CENTERS INDUSTRY (NAICS 44411)
PRODUCT LINE: LUMBER & BUILDING MATERIALS (Main Category)

NAICS 44411: Home Centers. This industry comprises establishments known as home centers primarily engaged in retailing a general line of new home repair and improvement materials and supplies, such as lumber, plumbing goods, electrical goods, tools, housewares, hardware, and lawn and garden supplies, with no one merchandise line predominating. The merchandise lines are normally arranged in separate departments.

5-YEAR TREND — ESTIMATED INDUSTRY SALES ($MILLIONS)

Year	Employee Size of Establishment									Total
	1-4 Emps.	5-9 Emps.	10-19 Emps.	20-49 Emps.	50-99 Emps.	100-249 Emps.	250-499 Emps.	500-999 Emps.	Unknown Emps.	Industry Sales
2015	92.9	184.4	480.0	958.4	703.8	46,042.0	4,071.9	75.4	32.1	52,640.9
2016	96.0	190.5	495.8	990.0	727.0	47,560.6	4,206.3	77.9	33.2	54,377.2
2017	98.8	196.2	510.7	1,019.7	748.8	48,987.1	4,332.4	80.2	34.2	56,008.2
2018	103.9	206.2	536.7	1,071.7	786.9	51,482.9	4,553.1	84.3	35.9	58,861.6
2018	109.4	217.2	565.2	1,128.6	828.7	54,217.1	4,795.0	88.7	37.8	61,987.7

INDUSTRY: HARDWARE STORES (NAICS 44413)
PRODUCT LINE: LUMBER & BUILDING MATERIALS (Main Category)

NAICS 44413: Hardware Stores. Establishments primarily engaged
in the retail sale of a number of basic hardware lines, such as tools,
builders' hardware, paint and glass, housewares and household appliances,
and cutlery.

5-YEAR TREND – ESTIMATED INDUSTRY SALES ($MILLIONS)

Year	Employee Size of Establishment									Total Industry Sales
	1-4 Emps.	5-9 Emps.	10-19 Emps.	20-49 Emps.	50-99 Emps.	100-249 Emps.	250-499 Emps.	500-999 Emps.	Unknown Emps.	
2015	120.3	193.0	386.0	540.5	98.9	23.2	6.5	0.3	10.2	1,378.9
2016	122.6	196.7	393.2	550.7	100.8	23.6	6.6	0.3	10.4	1,404.9
2017	124.6	199.9	399.7	559.8	102.5	24.0	6.7	0.3	10.5	1,428.1
2018	130.4	209.2	418.4	585.9	107.3	25.1	7.1	0.3	11.0	1,494.7
2018	136.8	219.5	439.0	614.7	112.5	26.4	7.4	0.4	11.6	1,568.3

INDUSTRY: WAREHOUSE CLUBS & SUPERCENTERS (NAICS 45291)
PRODUCT LINE: LUMBER & BUILDING MATERIALS (Main Category)

NAICS 45291: Warehouse Clubs and Superstores This industry
comprises establishments known as warehouse clubs, superstores or
supercenters primarily engaged in retailing a general line of groceries
in combination with general lines of new merchandise, such as apparel,
furniture, and appliances.

5-YEAR TREND – ESTIMATED INDUSTRY SALES ($MILLIONS)

Year	Employee Size of Establishment									Total Industry Sales
	1-4 Emps.	5-9 Emps.	10-19 Emps.	20-49 Emps.	50-99 Emps.	100-249 Emps.	250-499 Emps.	500-999 Emps.	Unknown Emps.	
2015	0.0	0.0	0.0	0.0	0.1	7.6	33.7	0.9	0.0	42.3
2016	0.0	0.0	0.0	0.1	0.1	7.9	34.9	0.9	0.0	43.9
2017	0.0	0.0	0.0	0.1	0.1	8.2	36.1	1.0	0.0	45.3
2018	0.0	0.0	0.0	0.1	0.1	8.9	39.2	1.0	0.0	49.2
2018	0.0	0.0	0.0	0.1	0.1	9.4	41.6	1.1	0.0	52.3

INDUSTRY: ELECTRONIC SHOPPING & MAIL-ORDER (NAICS 45411)
PRODUCT LINE: LUMBER & BUILDING MATERIALS (Main Category)

NAICS 45411: Electronic Shopping and Mail-Order Houses This industry comprises establishments primarily engaged in retailing all types of merchandise by means of mail or by electronic media, such as interactive television or computer. Included in this industry are establishments primarily engaged in retailing from catalogue showrooms of mail-order houses.

5-Year Trend — Estimated Industry Sales ($Millions)

Year	Employee Size of Establishment									Total
	1-4 Emps.	5-9 Emps.	10-19 Emps.	20-49 Emps.	50-99 Emps.	100-249 Emps.	250-499 Emps.	500-999 Emps.	Unknown Emps.	Industry Sales
2015	46.0	24.4	36.3	58.7	42.2	82.3	120.4	152.6	7.0	570.0
2016	49.1	26.1	38.7	62.6	45.0	87.8	128.5	162.8	7.4	608.0
2017	52.1	27.6	41.1	66.4	47.8	93.1	136.3	172.6	7.9	644.9
2018	59.3	31.5	46.7	75.6	54.4	106.0	155.1	191.6	9.0	729.0
2018	65.8	34.9	51.9	83.9	60.4	117.7	172.2	209.2	10.0	806.0

INDUSTRY: HOME CENTERS INDUSTRY (NAICS 44411)
PRODUCT LINE: NONTREATED LUMBER (Sub Category)

NAICS 44411: Home Centers. This industry comprises establishments known as home centers primarily engaged in retailing a general line of new home repair and improvement materials and supplies, such as lumber, plumbing goods, electrical goods, tools, housewares, hardware, and lawn and garden supplies, with no one merchandise line predominating. The merchandise lines are normally arranged in separate departments.

5-Year Trend — Estimated Industry Sales ($Millions)

Year	Employee Size of Establishment									Total
	1-4 Emps.	5-9 Emps.	10-19 Emps.	20-49 Emps.	50-99 Emps.	100-249 Emps.	250-499 Emps.	500-999 Emps.	Unknown Emps.	Industry Sales
2015	7.2	14.3	37.3	74.5	54.7	3,580.7	316.7	5.9	2.5	4,093.9
2016	7.5	14.8	38.6	77.0	56.5	3,698.8	327.1	6.1	2.6	4,229.0
2017	7.7	15.3	39.7	79.3	58.2	3,809.8	336.9	6.2	2.7	4,355.8
2018	8.1	16.0	41.7	83.3	61.2	4,003.9	354.1	6.6	2.8	4,577.7
2018	8.5	16.9	44.0	87.8	64.5	4,216.5	372.9	6.9	2.9	4,820.9

INDUSTRY: HARDWARE STORES INDUSTRY (NAICS 44413)
PRODUCT LINE: NONTREATED LUMBER (Sub Category)

NAICS 44413: Hardware Stores. Establishments primarily engaged
in the retail sale of a number of basic hardware lines, such as tools,
builders' hardware, paint and glass, housewares and household appliances,
and cutlery.

5-YEAR TREND – ESTIMATED INDUSTRY SALES ($MILLIONS)

Year	Employee Size of Establishment									Total Industry Sales
	1-4 Emps.	5-9 Emps.	10-19 Emps.	20-49 Emps.	50-99 Emps.	100-249 Emps.	250-499 Emps.	500-999 Emps.	Unknown Emps.	
2015	11.2	18.0	36.0	50.4	9.2	2.2	0.6	0.0	0.9	128.7
2016	11.4	18.4	36.7	51.4	9.4	2.2	0.6	0.0	1.0	131.1
2017	11.6	18.7	37.3	52.2	9.6	2.2	0.6	0.0	1.0	133.3
2018	12.2	19.5	39.0	54.7	10.0	2.3	0.7	0.0	1.0	139.5
2018	12.8	20.5	41.0	57.4	10.5	2.5	0.7	0.0	1.1	146.4

INDUSTRY: HOME CENTERS INDUSTRY (NAICS 44411)
PRODUCT LINE: TREATED LUMBER (Sub Category)

NAICS 44411: Home Centers. This industry comprises establishments
known as home centers primarily engaged in retailing a general line of
new home repair and improvement materials and supplies, such as
lumber, plumbing goods, electrical goods, tools, housewares, hardware,
and lawn and garden supplies, with no one merchandise line predominating.
The merchandise lines are normally arranged in separate departments.

5-YEAR TREND – ESTIMATED INDUSTRY SALES ($MILLIONS)

Year	Employee Size of Establishment									Total Industry Sales
	1-4 Emps.	5-9 Emps.	10-19 Emps.	20-49 Emps.	50-99 Emps.	100-249 Emps.	250-499 Emps.	500-999 Emps.	Unknown Emps.	
2015	7.5	14.8	38.6	77.1	56.6	3,705.2	327.7	6.1	2.6	4,236.3
2016	7.7	15.3	39.9	79.7	58.5	3,827.4	338.5	6.3	2.7	4,376.0
2017	8.0	15.8	41.1	82.1	60.3	3,942.2	348.7	6.5	2.8	4,507.3
2018	8.4	16.6	43.2	86.2	63.3	4,143.1	366.4	6.8	2.9	4,736.9
2018	8.8	17.5	45.5	90.8	66.7	4,363.1	385.9	7.1	3.0	4,988.5

INDUSTRY: HARDWARE STORES INDUSTRY (NAICS 44413)
PRODUCT LINE: TREATED LUMBER (Sub Category)

NAICS 44413: Hardware Stores. Establishments primarily engaged
in the retail sale of a number of basic hardware lines, such as tools,
builders' hardware, paint and glass, housewares and household appliances,
and cutlery.

5-YEAR TREND — ESTIMATED INDUSTRY SALES ($MILLIONS)

Year	Employee Size of Establishment									Total Industry Sales
	1-4 Emps.	5-9 Emps.	10-19 Emps.	20-49 Emps.	50-99 Emps.	100-249 Emps.	250-499 Emps.	500-999 Emps.	Unknown Emps.	
2015	7.2	11.6	23.3	32.6	6.0	1.4	0.4	0.0	0.6	83.1
2016	7.4	11.9	23.7	33.2	6.1	1.4	0.4	0.0	0.6	84.7
2017	7.5	12.0	24.1	33.7	6.2	1.4	0.4	0.0	0.6	86.1
2018	7.9	12.6	25.2	35.3	6.5	1.5	0.4	0.0	0.7	90.1
2018	8.2	13.2	26.5	37.0	6.8	1.6	0.4	0.0	0.7	94.5

INDUSTRY: HOME CENTERS INDUSTRY (NAICS 44411)
PRODUCT LINE: BUILDING BOARDS (Sub Category)

NAICS 44411: Home Centers. This industry comprises establishments
known as home centers primarily engaged in retailing a general line of
new home repair and improvement materials and supplies, such as
lumber, plumbing goods, electrical goods, tools, housewares, hardware,
and lawn and garden supplies, with no one merchandise line predominating.
The merchandise lines are normally arranged in separate departments.

5-YEAR TREND — ESTIMATED INDUSTRY SALES ($MILLIONS)

Year	Employee Size of Establishment									Total Industry Sales
	1-4 Emps.	5-9 Emps.	10-19 Emps.	20-49 Emps.	50-99 Emps.	100-249 Emps.	250-499 Emps.	500-999 Emps.	Unknown Emps.	
2015	3.0	5.9	15.3	30.5	22.4	1,463.1	129.4	2.4	1.0	1,672.8
2016	3.0	6.1	15.8	31.5	23.1	1,511.3	133.7	2.5	1.1	1,727.9
2017	3.1	6.2	16.2	32.4	23.8	1,556.6	137.7	2.5	1.1	1,779.8
2018	3.3	6.6	17.1	34.1	25.0	1,636.0	144.7	2.7	1.1	1,870.4
2018	3.5	6.9	18.0	35.9	26.3	1,722.8	152.4	2.8	1.2	1,969.8

INDUSTRY: HARDWARE STORES INDUSTRY (NAICS 44413)
PRODUCT LINE: BUILDING BOARDS (Sub Category)

NAICS 44413: Hardware Stores. Establishments primarily engaged
in the retail sale of a number of basic hardware lines, such as tools,
builders' hardware, paint and glass, housewares and household appliances,
and cutlery.

5-YEAR TREND – ESTIMATED INDUSTRY SALES ($MILLIONS)

Year	Employee Size of Establishment									Total Industry Sales
	1-4 Emps.	5-9 Emps.	10-19 Emps.	20-49 Emps.	50-99 Emps.	100-249 Emps.	250-499 Emps.	500-999 Emps.	Unknown Emps.	
2015	4.6	7.3	14.7	20.5	3.8	0.9	0.2	0.0	0.4	52.4
2016	4.7	7.5	14.9	20.9	3.8	0.9	0.3	0.0	0.4	53.4
2017	4.7	7.6	15.2	21.3	3.9	0.9	0.3	0.0	0.4	54.2
2018	5.0	7.9	15.9	22.2	4.1	1.0	0.3	0.0	0.4	56.8
2018	5.2	8.3	16.7	23.3	4.3	1.0	0.3	0.0	0.4	59.6

INDUSTRY: HOME CENTERS INDUSTRY (NAICS 44411)
PRODUCT LINE: GYPSUM & SPECIALTY BOARDS (Sub Category)

NAICS 44411: Home Centers. This industry comprises establishments
known as home centers primarily engaged in retailing a general line of
new home repair and improvement materials and supplies, such as
lumber, plumbing goods, electrical goods, tools, housewares, hardware,
and lawn and garden supplies, with no one merchandise line predominating.
The merchandise lines are normally arranged in separate departments.

5-YEAR TREND – ESTIMATED INDUSTRY SALES ($MILLIONS)

Year	Employee Size of Establishment									Total Industry Sales
	1-4 Emps.	5-9 Emps.	10-19 Emps.	20-49 Emps.	50-99 Emps.	100-249 Emps.	250-499 Emps.	500-999 Emps.	Unknown Emps.	
2015	5.4	10.7	28.0	55.8	41.0	2,681.2	237.1	4.4	1.9	3,065.5
2016	5.6	11.1	28.9	57.7	42.3	2,769.7	244.9	4.5	1.9	3,166.6
2017	5.8	11.4	29.7	59.4	43.6	2,852.7	252.3	4.7	2.0	3,261.6
2018	6.0	12.0	31.3	62.4	45.8	2,998.1	265.1	4.9	2.1	3,427.8
2018	6.4	12.6	32.9	65.7	48.3	3,157.3	279.2	5.2	2.2	3,609.8

INDUSTRY: HARDWARE STORES INDUSTRY (NAICS 44413)
PRODUCT LINE: GYPSUM & SPECIALTY BOARDS (Sub Category)

NAICS 44413: Hardware Stores. Establishments primarily engaged
in the retail sale of a number of basic hardware lines, such as tools,
builders' hardware, paint and glass, housewares and household appliances,
and cutlery.

5-Year Trend — Estimated Industry Sales ($Millions)

Year	Employee Size of Establishment									Total Industry Sales
	1-4 Emps.	5-9 Emps.	10-19 Emps.	20-49 Emps.	50-99 Emps.	100-249 Emps.	250-499 Emps.	500-999 Emps.	Unknown Emps.	
2015	4.0	6.4	12.8	17.9	3.3	0.8	0.2	0.0	0.3	45.7
2016	4.1	6.5	13.0	18.3	3.3	0.8	0.2	0.0	0.3	46.6
2017	4.1	6.6	13.3	18.6	3.4	0.8	0.2	0.0	0.3	47.3
2018	4.3	6.9	13.9	19.4	3.6	0.8	0.2	0.0	0.4	49.6
2018	4.5	7.3	14.6	20.4	3.7	0.9	0.2	0.0	0.4	52.0

INDUSTRY: HOME CENTERS INDUSTRY (NAICS 44411)
PRODUCT LINE: ENGINEERED WOOD PRODUCTS (Sub Category)

NAICS 44411: Home Centers. This industry comprises establishments
known as home centers primarily engaged in retailing a general line of
new home repair and improvement materials and supplies, such as
lumber, plumbing goods, electrical goods, tools, housewares, hardware,
and lawn and garden supplies, with no one merchandise line predominating.
The merchandise lines are normally arranged in separate departments.

5-Year Trend — Estimated Industry Sales ($Millions)

Year	Employee Size of Establishment									Total Industry Sales
	1-4 Emps.	5-9 Emps.	10-19 Emps.	20-49 Emps.	50-99 Emps.	100-249 Emps.	250-499 Emps.	500-999 Emps.	Unknown Emps.	
2015	0.6	1.2	3.2	6.4	4.7	307.5	27.2	0.5	0.2	351.5
2016	0.6	1.3	3.3	6.6	4.9	317.6	28.1	0.5	0.2	363.1
2017	0.7	1.3	3.4	6.8	5.0	327.1	28.9	0.5	0.2	374.0
2018	0.7	1.4	3.6	7.2	5.3	343.8	30.4	0.6	0.2	393.1
2018	0.7	1.5	3.8	7.5	5.5	362.1	32.0	0.6	0.3	414.0

INDUSTRY: HOME CENTERS INDUSTRY (NAICS 44411)
PRODUCT LINE: STRUCTURAL PANELS (Sub Category)

NAICS 44411: Home Centers. This industry comprises establishments known as home centers primarily engaged in retailing a general line of new home repair and improvement materials and supplies, such as lumber, plumbing goods, electrical goods, tools, housewares, hardware, and lawn and garden supplies, with no one merchandise line predominating. The merchandise lines are normally arranged in separate departments.

5-YEAR TREND — ESTIMATED INDUSTRY SALES ($MILLIONS)

Year	Employee Size of Establishment									Total
	1-4 Emps.	5-9 Emps.	10-19 Emps.	20-49 Emps.	50-99 Emps.	100-249 Emps.	250-499 Emps.	500-999 Emps.	Unknown Emps.	Industry Sales
2015	5.5	10.8	28.2	56.2	41.3	2,701.7	238.9	4.4	1.9	3,089.0
2016	5.6	11.2	29.1	58.1	42.7	2,790.8	246.8	4.6	1.9	3,190.8
2017	5.8	11.5	30.0	59.8	43.9	2,874.6	254.2	4.7	2.0	3,286.5
2018	6.1	12.1	31.5	62.9	46.2	3,021.0	267.2	4.9	2.1	3,454.0
2018	6.4	12.7	33.2	66.2	48.6	3,181.5	281.4	5.2	2.2	3,637.4

INDUSTRY: HARDWARE STORES INDUSTRY (NAICS 44413)
PRODUCT LINE: STRUCTURAL PANELS (Sub Category)

NAICS 44413: Hardware Stores. Establishments primarily engaged in the retail sale of a number of basic hardware lines, such as tools, builders' hardware, paint and glass, housewares and household appliances, and cutlery.

5-YEAR TREND — ESTIMATED INDUSTRY SALES ($MILLIONS)

Year	Employee Size of Establishment									Total
	1-4 Emps.	5-9 Emps.	10-19 Emps.	20-49 Emps.	50-99 Emps.	100-249 Emps.	250-499 Emps.	500-999 Emps.	Unknown Emps.	Industry Sales
2015	3.6	5.7	11.5	16.1	2.9	0.7	0.2	0.0	0.3	41.1
2016	3.6	5.9	11.7	16.4	3.0	0.7	0.2	0.0	0.3	41.8
2017	3.7	6.0	11.9	16.7	3.1	0.7	0.2	0.0	0.3	42.5
2018	3.9	6.2	12.5	17.4	3.2	0.7	0.2	0.0	0.3	44.5
2018	4.1	6.5	13.1	18.3	3.4	0.8	0.2	0.0	0.3	46.7

INDUSTRY: HOME CENTERS INDUSTRY (NAICS 44411)
PRODUCT LINE: OTHER PANEL PRODUCTS (Sub Category)

NAICS 44411: Home Centers. This industry comprises establishments
known as home centers primarily engaged in retailing a general line of
new home repair and improvement materials and supplies, such as
lumber, plumbing goods, electrical goods, tools, housewares, hardware,
and lawn and garden supplies, with no one merchandise line predominating.
The merchandise lines are normally arranged in separate departments.

5-YEAR TREND – ESTIMATED INDUSTRY SALES ($MILLIONS)

| Year | Employee Size of Establishment | | | | | | | | | Total |
	1-4 Emps.	5-9 Emps.	10-19 Emps.	20-49 Emps.	50-99 Emps.	100-249 Emps.	250-499 Emps.	500-999 Emps.	Unknown Emps.	Industry Sales
2015	5.3	10.5	27.2	54.3	39.9	2,610.6	230.9	4.3	1.8	2,984.8
2016	5.4	10.8	28.1	56.1	41.2	2,696.7	238.5	4.4	1.9	3,083.2
2017	5.6	11.1	29.0	57.8	42.5	2,777.6	245.6	4.5	1.9	3,175.7
2018	5.9	11.7	30.4	60.8	44.6	2,919.1	258.2	4.8	2.0	3,337.5
2018	6.2	12.3	32.0	64.0	47.0	3,074.1	271.9	5.0	2.1	3,514.7

INDUSTRY: HARDWARE STORES INDUSTRY (NAICS 44413)
PRODUCT LINE: OTHER PANEL PRODUCTS (Sub Category)

NAICS 44413: Hardware Stores. Establishments primarily engaged
in the retail sale of a number of basic hardware lines, such as tools,
builders' hardware, paint and glass, housewares and household appliances,
and cutlery.

5-YEAR TREND – ESTIMATED INDUSTRY SALES ($MILLIONS)

| Year | Employee Size of Establishment | | | | | | | | | Total |
	1-4 Emps.	5-9 Emps.	10-19 Emps.	20-49 Emps.	50-99 Emps.	100-249 Emps.	250-499 Emps.	500-999 Emps.	Unknown Emps.	Industry Sales
2015	4.0	6.5	13.0	18.1	3.3	0.8	0.2	0.0	0.3	46.3
2016	4.1	6.6	13.2	18.5	3.4	0.8	0.2	0.0	0.3	47.2
2017	4.2	6.7	13.4	18.8	3.4	0.8	0.2	0.0	0.4	47.9
2018	4.4	7.0	14.0	19.7	3.6	0.8	0.2	0.0	0.4	50.2
2018	4.6	7.4	14.7	20.6	3.8	0.9	0.2	0.0	0.4	52.7

INDUSTRY: HOME CENTERS INDUSTRY (NAICS 44411)
PRODUCT LINE: BUILDING COMPONENTS (Sub Category)

NAICS 44411: Home Centers. This industry comprises establishments known as home centers primarily engaged in retailing a general line of new home repair and improvement materials and supplies, such as lumber, plumbing goods, electrical goods, tools, housewares, hardware, and lawn and garden supplies, with no one merchandise line predominating. The merchandise lines are normally arranged in separate departments.

5-YEAR TREND — ESTIMATED INDUSTRY SALES ($MILLIONS)

Year	Employee Size of Establishment									Total
	1-4 Emps.	5-9 Emps.	10-19 Emps.	20-49 Emps.	50-99 Emps.	100-249 Emps.	250-499 Emps.	500-999 Emps.	Unknown Emps.	Industry Sales
2015	0.5	1.0	2.5	5.0	3.6	238.2	21.1	0.4	0.2	272.4
2016	0.5	1.0	2.6	5.1	3.8	246.1	21.8	0.4	0.2	281.4
2017	0.5	1.0	2.6	5.3	3.9	253.5	22.4	0.4	0.2	289.8
2018	0.5	1.1	2.8	5.5	4.1	266.4	23.6	0.4	0.2	304.6
2018	0.6	1.1	2.9	5.8	4.3	280.5	24.8	0.5	0.2	320.7

INDUSTRY: HOME CENTERS INDUSTRY (NAICS 44411)
PRODUCT LINE: CONNECTORS (Sub Category)

NAICS 44411: Home Centers. This industry comprises establishments known as home centers primarily engaged in retailing a general line of new home repair and improvement materials and supplies, such as lumber, plumbing goods, electrical goods, tools, housewares, hardware, and lawn and garden supplies, with no one merchandise line predominating. The merchandise lines are normally arranged in separate departments.

5-YEAR TREND — ESTIMATED INDUSTRY SALES ($MILLIONS)

Year	Employee Size of Establishment									Total
	1-4 Emps.	5-9 Emps.	10-19 Emps.	20-49 Emps.	50-99 Emps.	100-249 Emps.	250-499 Emps.	500-999 Emps.	Unknown Emps.	Industry Sales
2015	0.6	1.2	3.2	6.3	4.6	302.5	26.8	0.5	0.2	345.9
2016	0.6	1.3	3.3	6.5	4.8	312.5	27.6	0.5	0.2	357.3
2017	0.6	1.3	3.4	6.7	4.9	321.9	28.5	0.5	0.2	368.0
2018	0.7	1.4	3.5	7.0	5.2	338.3	29.9	0.6	0.2	386.7
2018	0.7	1.4	3.7	7.4	5.4	356.2	31.5	0.6	0.2	407.3

INDUSTRY: HARDWARE STORES INDUSTRY (NAICS 44413)

PRODUCT LINE: CONNECTORS (Sub Category)

NAICS 44413: Hardware Stores. Establishments primarily engaged
in the retail sale of a number of basic hardware lines, such as tools,
builders' hardware, paint and glass, housewares and household appliances,
and cutlery.

5-YEAR TREND – ESTIMATED INDUSTRY SALES ($MILLIONS)

Year	1-4 Emps.	5-9 Emps.	10-19 Emps.	20-49 Emps.	50-99 Emps.	100-249 Emps.	250-499 Emps.	500-999 Emps.	Unknown Emps.	Total Industry Sales
2015	2.8	4.4	8.8	12.4	2.3	0.5	0.1	0.0	0.2	31.6
2016	2.8	4.5	9.0	12.6	2.3	0.5	0.2	0.0	0.2	32.2
2017	2.9	4.6	9.2	12.8	2.3	0.6	0.2	0.0	0.2	32.7
2018	3.0	4.8	9.6	13.4	2.5	0.6	0.2	0.0	0.3	34.2
2018	3.1	5.0	10.1	14.1	2.6	0.6	0.2	0.0	0.3	35.9

INDUSTRY: HOME CENTERS INDUSTRY (NAICS 44411)

PRODUCT LINE: STEEL STUDS (Sub Category)

NAICS 44411: Home Centers. This industry comprises establishments
known as home centers primarily engaged in retailing a general line of
new home repair and improvement materials and supplies, such as
lumber, plumbing goods, electrical goods, tools, housewares, hardware,
and lawn and garden supplies, with no one merchandise line predominating.
The merchandise lines are normally arranged in separate departments.

5-YEAR TREND – ESTIMATED INDUSTRY SALES ($MILLIONS)

Year	1-4 Emps.	5-9 Emps.	10-19 Emps.	20-49 Emps.	50-99 Emps.	100-249 Emps.	250-499 Emps.	500-999 Emps.	Unknown Emps.	Total Industry Sales
2015	0.2	0.5	1.2	2.4	1.7	114.2	10.1	0.2	0.1	130.5
2016	0.2	0.5	1.2	2.5	1.8	117.9	10.4	0.2	0.1	134.8
2017	0.2	0.5	1.3	2.5	1.9	121.5	10.7	0.2	0.1	138.9
2018	0.3	0.5	1.3	2.7	2.0	127.7	11.3	0.2	0.1	145.9
2018	0.3	0.5	1.4	2.8	2.1	134.4	11.9	0.2	0.1	153.7

INDUSTRY: HOME CENTERS INDUSTRY (NAICS 44411)
PRODUCT LINE: DOORS & MOULDING (Sub Category)

NAICS 44411: Home Centers. This industry comprises establishments known as home centers primarily engaged in retailing a general line of new home repair and improvement materials and supplies, such as lumber, plumbing goods, electrical goods, tools, housewares, hardware, and lawn and garden supplies, with no one merchandise line predominating. The merchandise lines are normally arranged in separate departments.

5-YEAR TREND — ESTIMATED INDUSTRY SALES ($MILLIONS)

Year	Employee Size of Establishment									Total Industry Sales
	1-4 Emps.	5-9 Emps.	10-19 Emps.	20-49 Emps.	50-99 Emps.	100-249 Emps.	250-499 Emps.	500-999 Emps.	Unknown Emps.	
2015	13.5	26.7	69.5	138.8	101.9	6,666.5	589.6	10.9	4.7	7,622.0
2016	13.9	27.6	71.8	143.3	105.3	6,886.4	609.0	11.3	4.8	7,873.4
2017	14.3	28.4	73.9	147.6	108.4	7,093.0	627.3	11.6	4.9	8,109.6
2018	15.0	29.9	77.7	155.2	113.9	7,454.3	659.3	12.2	5.2	8,522.7
2018	15.8	31.4	81.8	163.4	120.0	7,850.2	694.3	12.8	5.5	8,975.3

INDUSTRY: HARDWARE STORES INDUSTRY (NAICS 44413)
PRODUCT LINE: DOORS & MOULDING (Sub Category)

NAICS 44413: Hardware Stores. Establishments primarily engaged in the retail sale of a number of basic hardware lines, such as tools, builders' hardware, paint and glass, housewares and household appliances, and cutlery.

5-YEAR TREND — ESTIMATED INDUSTRY SALES ($MILLIONS)

Year	Employee Size of Establishment									Total Industry Sales
	1-4 Emps.	5-9 Emps.	10-19 Emps.	20-49 Emps.	50-99 Emps.	100-249 Emps.	250-499 Emps.	500-999 Emps.	Unknown Emps.	
2015	8.5	13.6	27.3	38.2	7.0	1.6	0.5	0.0	0.7	97.4
2016	8.7	13.9	27.8	38.9	7.1	1.7	0.5	0.0	0.7	99.2
2017	8.8	14.1	28.2	39.5	7.2	1.7	0.5	0.0	0.7	100.8
2018	9.2	14.8	29.5	41.4	7.6	1.8	0.5	0.0	0.8	105.5
2018	9.7	15.5	31.0	43.4	7.9	1.9	0.5	0.0	0.8	110.7

INDUSTRY: HOME CENTERS INDUSTRY (NAICS 44411)
PRODUCT LINE: WINDOWS & SKYLIGHTS (Sub Category)

NAICS 44411: Home Centers. This industry comprises establishments
known as home centers primarily engaged in retailing a general line of
new home repair and improvement materials and supplies, such as
lumber, plumbing goods, electrical goods, tools, housewares, hardware,
and lawn and garden supplies, with no one merchandise line predominating.
The merchandise lines are normally arranged in separate departments.

5-YEAR TREND — ESTIMATED INDUSTRY SALES ($MILLIONS)

Year	Employee Size of Establishment									Total
	1-4 Emps.	5-9 Emps.	10-19 Emps.	20-49 Emps.	50-99 Emps.	100-249 Emps.	250-499 Emps.	500-999 Emps.	Unknown Emps.	Industry Sales
2015	7.9	15.6	40.7	81.3	59.7	3,905.3	345.4	6.4	2.7	4,465.0
2016	8.1	16.2	42.1	84.0	61.7	4,034.1	356.8	6.6	2.8	4,612.3
2017	8.4	16.6	43.3	86.5	63.5	4,155.1	367.5	6.8	2.9	4,750.6
2018	8.8	17.5	45.5	90.9	66.7	4,366.8	386.2	7.1	3.0	4,992.6
2018	9.3	18.4	47.9	95.7	70.3	4,598.7	406.7	7.5	3.2	5,257.8

INDUSTRY: HARDWARE STORES INDUSTRY (NAICS 44413)
PRODUCT LINE: WINDOWS & SKYLIGHTS (Sub Category)

NAICS 44413: Hardware Stores. Establishments primarily engaged
in the retail sale of a number of basic hardware lines, such as tools,
builders' hardware, paint and glass, housewares and household appliances,
and cutlery.

5-YEAR TREND — ESTIMATED INDUSTRY SALES ($MILLIONS)

Year	Employee Size of Establishment									Total
	1-4 Emps.	5-9 Emps.	10-19 Emps.	20-49 Emps.	50-99 Emps.	100-249 Emps.	250-499 Emps.	500-999 Emps.	Unknown Emps.	Industry Sales
2015	4.0	6.3	12.7	17.8	3.3	0.8	0.2	0.0	0.3	45.3
2016	4.0	6.5	12.9	18.1	3.3	0.8	0.2	0.0	0.3	46.2
2017	4.1	6.6	13.1	18.4	3.4	0.8	0.2	0.0	0.3	47.0
2018	4.3	6.9	13.8	19.3	3.5	0.8	0.2	0.0	0.4	49.1
2018	4.5	7.2	14.4	20.2	3.7	0.9	0.2	0.0	0.4	51.6

INDUSTRY: HOME CENTERS INDUSTRY (NAICS 44411)
PRODUCT LINE: WINDOWS & SKYLIGHTS (Sub Category)

NAICS 44411: Home Centers. This industry comprises establishments known as home centers primarily engaged in retailing a general line of new home repair and improvement materials and supplies, such as lumber, plumbing goods, electrical goods, tools, housewares, hardware, and lawn and garden supplies, with no one merchandise line predominating. The merchandise lines are normally arranged in separate departments.

5-Year Trend — Estimated Industry Sales ($Millions)

Year	Employee Size of Establishment									Total Industry Sales
	1-4 Emps.	5-9 Emps.	10-19 Emps.	20-49 Emps.	50-99 Emps.	100-249 Emps.	250-499 Emps.	500-999 Emps.	Unknown Emps.	
2015	0.4	0.8	2.2	4.4	3.2	211.0	18.7	0.3	0.1	241.3
2016	0.4	0.9	2.3	4.5	3.3	218.0	19.3	0.4	0.2	249.2
2017	0.5	0.9	2.3	4.7	3.4	224.5	19.9	0.4	0.2	256.7
2018	0.5	0.9	2.5	4.9	3.6	235.9	20.9	0.4	0.2	269.8
2018	0.5	1.0	2.6	5.2	3.8	248.5	22.0	0.4	0.2	284.1

INDUSTRY: HARDWARE STORES INDUSTRY (NAICS 44413)
PRODUCT LINE: WINDOWS & SKYLIGHTS (Sub Category)

NAICS 44413: Hardware Stores. Establishments primarily engaged in the retail sale of a number of basic hardware lines, such as tools, builders' hardware, paint and glass, housewares and household appliances, and cutlery.

5-Year Trend — Estimated Industry Sales ($Millions)

Year	Employee Size of Establishment									Total Industry Sales
	1-4 Emps.	5-9 Emps.	10-19 Emps.	20-49 Emps.	50-99 Emps.	100-249 Emps.	250-499 Emps.	500-999 Emps.	Unknown Emps.	
2015	7.5	12.0	24.0	33.6	6.1	1.4	0.4	0.0	0.6	85.6
2016	7.6	12.2	24.4	34.2	6.3	1.5	0.4	0.0	0.6	87.2
2017	7.7	12.4	24.8	34.8	6.4	1.5	0.4	0.0	0.7	88.7
2018	8.1	13.0	26.0	36.4	6.7	1.6	0.4	0.0	0.7	92.8
2018	8.5	13.6	27.3	38.2	7.0	1.6	0.5	0.0	0.7	97.4

INDUSTRY: HOME CENTERS INDUSTRY (NAICS 44411)
PRODUCT LINE: MASONRY SUPPLIES (Sub Category)

NAICS 44411: Home Centers. This industry comprises establishments known as home centers primarily engaged in retailing a general line of new home repair and improvement materials and supplies, such as lumber, plumbing goods, electrical goods, tools, housewares, hardware, and lawn and garden supplies, with no one merchandise line predominating. The merchandise lines are normally arranged in separate departments.

5-YEAR TREND – ESTIMATED INDUSTRY SALES ($MILLIONS)

Year	Employee Size of Establishment									Total Industry Sales
	1-4 Emps.	5-9 Emps.	10-19 Emps.	20-49 Emps.	50-99 Emps.	100-249 Emps.	250-499 Emps.	500-999 Emps.	Unknown Emps.	
2015	4.2	8.2	21.4	42.8	31.4	2,056.9	181.9	3.4	1.4	2,351.7
2016	4.3	8.5	22.1	44.2	32.5	2,124.7	187.9	3.5	1.5	2,429.3
2017	4.4	8.8	22.8	45.6	33.5	2,188.5	193.5	3.6	1.5	2,502.1
2018	4.6	9.2	24.0	47.9	35.2	2,300.0	203.4	3.8	1.6	2,629.6
2018	4.9	9.7	25.2	50.4	37.0	2,422.1	214.2	4.0	1.7	2,769.3

INDUSTRY: HARDWARE STORES INDUSTRY (NAICS 44413)
PRODUCT LINE: MASONRY SUPPLIES (Sub Category)

NAICS 44413: Hardware Stores. Establishments primarily engaged in the retail sale of a number of basic hardware lines, such as tools, builders' hardware, paint and glass, housewares and household appliances, and cutlery.

5-YEAR TREND – ESTIMATED INDUSTRY SALES ($MILLIONS)

Year	Employee Size of Establishment									Total Industry Sales
	1-4 Emps.	5-9 Emps.	10-19 Emps.	20-49 Emps.	50-99 Emps.	100-249 Emps.	250-499 Emps.	500-999 Emps.	Unknown Emps.	
2015	14.5	23.2	46.5	65.1	11.9	2.8	0.8	0.0	1.2	166.1
2016	14.8	23.7	47.4	66.3	12.1	2.8	0.8	0.0	1.2	169.2
2017	15.0	24.1	48.1	67.4	12.3	2.9	0.8	0.0	1.3	172.0
2018	15.7	25.2	50.4	70.6	12.9	3.0	0.9	0.0	1.3	180.0
2018	16.5	26.4	52.9	74.0	13.6	3.2	0.9	0.0	1.4	188.9

INDUSTRY: HOME CENTERS INDUSTRY (NAICS 44411)
PRODUCT LINE: INSULATION PRODUCTS (Sub Category)

NAICS 44411: Home Centers. This industry comprises establishments known as home centers primarily engaged in retailing a general line of new home repair and improvement materials and supplies, such as lumber, plumbing goods, electrical goods, tools, housewares, hardware, and lawn and garden supplies, with no one merchandise line predominating. The merchandise lines are normally arranged in separate departments.

5-YEAR TREND — ESTIMATED INDUSTRY SALES ($MILLIONS)

Year	Employee Size of Establishment									Total
	1-4 Emps.	5-9 Emps.	10-19 Emps.	20-49 Emps.	50-99 Emps.	100-249 Emps.	250-499 Emps.	500-999 Emps.	Unknown Emps.	Industry Sales
2015	2.1	4.2	10.9	21.7	16.0	1,044.7	92.4	1.7	0.7	1,194.4
2016	2.2	4.3	11.2	22.5	16.5	1,079.2	95.4	1.8	0.8	1,233.8
2017	2.2	4.5	11.6	23.1	17.0	1,111.5	98.3	1.8	0.8	1,270.8
2018	2.4	4.7	12.2	24.3	17.9	1,168.1	103.3	1.9	0.8	1,335.6
2018	2.5	4.9	12.8	25.6	18.8	1,230.2	108.8	2.0	0.9	1,406.5

INDUSTRY: HARDWARE STORES INDUSTRY (NAICS 44413)
PRODUCT LINE: INSULATION PRODUCTS (Sub Category)

NAICS 44413: Hardware Stores. Establishments primarily engaged in the retail sale of a number of basic hardware lines, such as tools, builders' hardware, paint and glass, housewares and household appliances, and cutlery.

5-YEAR TREND — ESTIMATED INDUSTRY SALES ($MILLIONS)

Year	Employee Size of Establishment									Total
	1-4 Emps.	5-9 Emps.	10-19 Emps.	20-49 Emps.	50-99 Emps.	100-249 Emps.	250-499 Emps.	500-999 Emps.	Unknown Emps.	Industry Sales
2015	5.0	8.1	16.2	22.7	4.1	1.0	0.3	0.0	0.4	57.8
2016	5.1	8.2	16.5	23.1	4.2	1.0	0.3	0.0	0.4	58.9
2017	5.2	8.4	16.8	23.5	4.3	1.0	0.3	0.0	0.4	59.9
2018	5.5	8.8	17.5	24.6	4.5	1.1	0.3	0.0	0.5	62.7
2018	5.7	9.2	18.4	25.8	4.7	1.1	0.3	0.0	0.5	65.8

INDUSTRY: HOME CENTERS INDUSTRY (NAICS 44411)
PRODUCT LINE: SIDING & EXTERIOR TRIM (Sub Category)

NAICS 44411: Home Centers. This industry comprises establishments known as home centers primarily engaged in retailing a general line of new home repair and improvement materials and supplies, such as lumber, plumbing goods, electrical goods, tools, housewares, hardware, and lawn and garden supplies, with no one merchandise line predominating. The merchandise lines are normally arranged in separate departments.

5-YEAR TREND — ESTIMATED INDUSTRY SALES ($MILLIONS)

Year	Employee Size of Establishment									Total
	1-4 Emps.	5-9 Emps.	10-19 Emps.	20-49 Emps.	50-99 Emps.	100-249 Emps.	250-499 Emps.	500-999 Emps.	Unknown Emps.	Industry Sales
2015	1.2	2.3	6.0	12.1	8.9	579.7	51.3	0.9	0.4	662.8
2016	1.2	2.4	6.2	12.5	9.2	598.8	53.0	1.0	0.4	684.7
2017	1.2	2.5	6.4	12.8	9.4	616.8	54.6	1.0	0.4	705.2
2018	1.3	2.6	6.8	13.5	9.9	648.2	57.3	1.1	0.5	741.1
2018	1.4	2.7	7.1	14.2	10.4	682.7	60.4	1.1	0.5	780.5

INDUSTRY: HARDWARE STORES INDUSTRY (NAICS 44413)
PRODUCT LINE: SIDING & EXTERIOR TRIM (Sub Category)

NAICS 44413: Hardware Stores. Establishments primarily engaged in the retail sale of a number of basic hardware lines, such as tools, builders' hardware, paint and glass, housewares and household appliances, and cutlery.

5-YEAR TREND — ESTIMATED INDUSTRY SALES ($MILLIONS)

Year	Employee Size of Establishment									Total
	1-4 Emps.	5-9 Emps.	10-19 Emps.	20-49 Emps.	50-99 Emps.	100-249 Emps.	250-499 Emps.	500-999 Emps.	Unknown Emps.	Industry Sales
2015	1.3	2.1	4.2	5.9	1.1	0.3	0.1	0.0	0.1	14.9
2016	1.3	2.1	4.3	6.0	1.1	0.3	0.1	0.0	0.1	15.2
2017	1.3	2.2	4.3	6.1	1.1	0.3	0.1	0.0	0.1	15.5
2018	1.4	2.3	4.5	6.3	1.2	0.3	0.1	0.0	0.1	16.2
2018	1.5	2.4	4.8	6.7	1.2	0.3	0.1	0.0	0.1	17.0

INDUSTRY: HOME CENTERS INDUSTRY (NAICS 44411)
PRODUCT LINE: ROOFING (Sub Category)

NAICS 44411: Home Centers. This industry comprises establishments known as home centers primarily engaged in retailing a general line of new home repair and improvement materials and supplies, such as lumber, plumbing goods, electrical goods, tools, housewares, hardware, and lawn and garden supplies, with no one merchandise line predominating. The merchandise lines are normally arranged in separate departments.

5-YEAR TREND – ESTIMATED INDUSTRY SALES ($MILLIONS)

Year	Employee Size of Establishment									Total Industry Sales
	1-4 Emps.	5-9 Emps.	10-19 Emps.	20-49 Emps.	50-99 Emps.	100-249 Emps.	250-499 Emps.	500-999 Emps.	Unknown Emps.	
2015	3.6	7.2	18.8	37.5	27.5	1,799.2	159.1	2.9	1.3	2,057.0
2016	3.7	7.4	19.4	38.7	28.4	1,858.5	164.4	3.0	1.3	2,124.9
2017	3.9	7.7	20.0	39.8	29.3	1,914.3	169.3	3.1	1.3	2,188.6
2018	4.1	8.1	21.0	41.9	30.8	2,011.8	177.9	3.3	1.4	2,300.1
2018	4.3	8.5	22.1	44.1	32.4	2,118.6	187.4	3.5	1.5	2,422.3

INDUSTRY: HARDWARE STORES INDUSTRY (NAICS 44413)
PRODUCT LINE: ROOFING (Sub Category)

NAICS 44413: Hardware Stores. Establishments primarily engaged in the retail sale of a number of basic hardware lines, such as tools, builders' hardware, paint and glass, housewares and household appliances, and cutlery.

5-YEAR TREND – ESTIMATED INDUSTRY SALES ($MILLIONS)

Year	Employee Size of Establishment									Total Industry Sales
	1-4 Emps.	5-9 Emps.	10-19 Emps.	20-49 Emps.	50-99 Emps.	100-249 Emps.	250-499 Emps.	500-999 Emps.	Unknown Emps.	
2015	5.2	8.4	16.8	23.6	4.3	1.0	0.3	0.0	0.4	60.1
2016	5.3	8.6	17.1	24.0	4.4	1.0	0.3	0.0	0.5	61.3
2017	5.4	8.7	17.4	24.4	4.5	1.0	0.3	0.0	0.5	62.3
2018	5.7	9.1	18.2	25.5	4.7	1.1	0.3	0.0	0.5	65.2
2018	6.0	9.6	19.1	26.8	4.9	1.2	0.3	0.0	0.5	68.4

INDUSTRY: HOME CENTERS INDUSTRY (NAICS 44411)
PRODUCT LINE: CEILINGS (Sub Category)

NAICS 44411: Home Centers. This industry comprises establishments known as home centers primarily engaged in retailing a general line of new home repair and improvement materials and supplies, such as lumber, plumbing goods, electrical goods, tools, housewares, hardware, and lawn and garden supplies, with no one merchandise line predominating. The merchandise lines are normally arranged in separate departments.

5-YEAR TREND — ESTIMATED INDUSTRY SALES ($MILLIONS)

Year	Employee Size of Establishment									Total
	1-4 Emps.	5-9 Emps.	10-19 Emps.	20-49 Emps.	50-99 Emps.	100-249 Emps.	250-499 Emps.	500-999 Emps.	Unknown Emps.	Industry Sales
2015	0.7	1.5	3.8	7.6	5.6	363.4	32.1	0.6	0.3	415.5
2016	0.8	1.5	3.9	7.8	5.7	375.4	33.2	0.6	0.3	429.2
2017	0.8	1.5	4.0	8.0	5.9	386.7	34.2	0.6	0.3	442.1
2018	0.8	1.6	4.2	8.5	6.2	406.4	35.9	0.7	0.3	464.6
2018	0.9	1.7	4.5	8.9	6.5	428.0	37.9	0.7	0.3	489.3

INDUSTRY: HARDWARE STORES INDUSTRY (NAICS 44413)
PRODUCT LINE: CEILINGS (Sub Category)

NAICS 44413: Hardware Stores. Establishments primarily engaged in the retail sale of a number of basic hardware lines, such as tools, builders' hardware, paint and glass, housewares and household appliances, and cutlery.

5-YEAR TREND — ESTIMATED INDUSTRY SALES ($MILLIONS)

Year	Employee Size of Establishment									Total
	1-4 Emps.	5-9 Emps.	10-19 Emps.	20-49 Emps.	50-99 Emps.	100-249 Emps.	250-499 Emps.	500-999 Emps.	Unknown Emps.	Industry Sales
2015	0.8	1.4	2.7	3.8	0.7	0.2	0.0	0.0	0.1	9.7
2016	0.9	1.4	2.8	3.9	0.7	0.2	0.0	0.0	0.1	9.8
2017	0.9	1.4	2.8	3.9	0.7	0.2	0.0	0.0	0.1	10.0
2018	0.9	1.5	2.9	4.1	0.8	0.2	0.0	0.0	0.1	10.5
2018	1.0	1.5	3.1	4.3	0.8	0.2	0.1	0.0	0.1	11.0

INDUSTRY: HOME CENTERS INDUSTRY (NAICS 44411)

PRODUCT LINE: KITCHENS & CABINETS (Sub Category)

NAICS 44411: Home Centers. This industry comprises establishments known as home centers primarily engaged in retailing a general line of new home repair and improvement materials and supplies, such as lumber, plumbing goods, electrical goods, tools, housewares, hardware, and lawn and garden supplies, with no one merchandise line predominating. The merchandise lines are normally arranged in separate departments.

5-YEAR TREND — ESTIMATED INDUSTRY SALES ($MILLIONS)

Year	Employee Size of Establishment									Total Industry Sales
	1-4 Emps.	5-9 Emps.	10-19 Emps.	20-49 Emps.	50-99 Emps.	100-249 Emps.	250-499 Emps.	500-999 Emps.	Unknown Emps.	
2015	15.0	29.7	77.3	154.4	113.4	7,418.0	656.0	12.1	5.2	8,481.2
2016	15.5	30.7	79.9	159.5	117.1	7,662.7	677.7	12.5	5.3	8,760.9
2017	15.9	31.6	82.3	164.3	120.6	7,892.5	698.0	12.9	5.5	9,023.7
2018	16.7	33.2	86.5	172.7	126.8	8,294.6	733.6	13.6	5.8	9,483.4
2018	17.6	35.0	91.1	181.8	133.5	8,735.1	772.5	14.3	6.1	9,987.0

INDUSTRY: HARDWARE STORES INDUSTRY (NAICS 44413)

PRODUCT LINE: KITCHENS & CABINETS (Sub Category)

NAICS 44413: Hardware Stores. Establishments primarily engaged in the retail sale of a number of basic hardware lines, such as tools, builders' hardware, paint and glass, housewares and household appliances, and cutlery.

5-YEAR TREND — ESTIMATED INDUSTRY SALES ($MILLIONS)

Year	Employee Size of Establishment									Total Industry Sales
	1-4 Emps.	5-9 Emps.	10-19 Emps.	20-49 Emps.	50-99 Emps.	100-249 Emps.	250-499 Emps.	500-999 Emps.	Unknown Emps.	
2015	10.7	17.1	34.2	47.9	8.8	2.1	0.6	0.0	0.9	122.1
2016	10.9	17.4	34.8	48.8	8.9	2.1	0.6	0.0	0.9	124.4
2017	11.0	17.7	35.4	49.6	9.1	2.1	0.6	0.0	0.9	126.4
2018	11.5	18.5	37.0	51.9	9.5	2.2	0.6	0.0	1.0	132.3
2018	12.1	19.4	38.9	54.4	10.0	2.3	0.7	0.0	1.0	138.9

INDUSTRY: HOME CENTERS INDUSTRY (NAICS 44411)
PRODUCT LINE: HEATING & HVAC UNITS (Sub Category)

NAICS 44411: Home Centers. This industry comprises establishments
known as home centers primarily engaged in retailing a general line of
new home repair and improvement materials and supplies, such as
lumber, plumbing goods, electrical goods, tools, housewares, hardware,
and lawn and garden supplies, with no one merchandise line predominating.
The merchandise lines are normally arranged in separate departments.

5-YEAR TREND — ESTIMATED INDUSTRY SALES ($MILLIONS)

Year	Employee Size of Establishment									Total
	1-4 Emps.	5-9 Emps.	10-19 Emps.	20-49 Emps.	50-99 Emps.	100-249 Emps.	250-499 Emps.	500-999 Emps.	Unknown Emps.	Industry Sales
2015	3.7	7.4	19.3	38.5	28.2	1,847.3	163.4	3.0	1.3	2,112.1
2016	3.9	7.6	19.9	39.7	29.2	1,908.3	168.8	3.1	1.3	2,181.8
2017	4.0	7.9	20.5	40.9	30.0	1,965.5	173.8	3.2	1.4	2,247.2
2018	4.2	8.3	21.5	43.0	31.6	2,065.6	182.7	3.4	1.4	2,361.7
2018	4.4	8.7	22.7	45.3	33.3	2,175.3	192.4	3.6	1.5	2,487.1

INDUSTRY: HARDWARE STORES INDUSTRY (NAICS 44413)
PRODUCT LINE: HEATING & HVAC UNITS (Sub Category)

NAICS 44413: Hardware Stores. Establishments primarily engaged
in the retail sale of a number of basic hardware lines, such as tools,
builders' hardware, paint and glass, housewares and household appliances,
and cutlery.

5-YEAR TREND — ESTIMATED INDUSTRY SALES ($MILLIONS)

Year	Employee Size of Establishment									Total
	1-4 Emps.	5-9 Emps.	10-19 Emps.	20-49 Emps.	50-99 Emps.	100-249 Emps.	250-499 Emps.	500-999 Emps.	Unknown Emps.	Industry Sales
2015	11.4	18.3	36.5	51.1	9.4	2.2	0.6	0.0	1.0	130.4
2016	11.6	18.6	37.2	52.1	9.5	2.2	0.6	0.0	1.0	132.8
2017	11.8	18.9	37.8	52.9	9.7	2.3	0.6	0.0	1.0	135.0
2018	12.3	19.8	39.6	55.4	10.1	2.4	0.7	0.0	1.0	141.3
2018	12.9	20.8	41.5	58.1	10.6	2.5	0.7	0.0	1.1	148.3

INDUSTRY: HARDWARE STORES INDUSTRY (NAICS 44413)
PRODUCT LINE: REFRIGERATION EQUIPMENT (Sub Category)

NAICS 44413: Hardware Stores. Establishments primarily engaged
in the retail sale of a number of basic hardware lines, such as tools,
builders' hardware, paint and glass, housewares and household appliances,
and cutlery.

5-YEAR TREND — ESTIMATED INDUSTRY SALES ($MILLIONS)

Year	Employee Size of Establishment									Total
	1-4 Emps.	5-9 Emps.	10-19 Emps.	20-49 Emps.	50-99 Emps.	100-249 Emps.	250-499 Emps.	500-999 Emps.	Unknown Emps.	Industry Sales
2015	1.2	1.9	3.8	5.3	1.0	0.2	0.1	0.0	0.1	13.5
2016	1.2	1.9	3.9	5.4	1.0	0.2	0.1	0.0	0.1	13.8
2017	1.2	2.0	3.9	5.5	1.0	0.2	0.1	0.0	0.1	14.0
2018	1.3	2.1	4.1	5.7	1.1	0.2	0.1	0.0	0.1	14.7
2018	1.3	2.2	4.3	6.0	1.1	0.3	0.1	0.0	0.1	15.4

INDUSTRY: HOME CENTERS INDUSTRY (NAICS 44411)
PRODUCT LINE: OTHER BUILDING MATERIALS (Sub Category)

NAICS 44411: Home Centers. This industry comprises establishments
known as home centers primarily engaged in retailing a general line of
new home repair and improvement materials and supplies, such as
lumber, plumbing goods, electrical goods, tools, housewares, hardware,
and lawn and garden supplies, with no one merchandise line predominating.
The merchandise lines are normally arranged in separate departments.

5-YEAR TREND — ESTIMATED INDUSTRY SALES ($MILLIONS)

Year	Employee Size of Establishment									Total
	1-4 Emps.	5-9 Emps.	10-19 Emps.	20-49 Emps.	50-99 Emps.	100-249 Emps.	250-499 Emps.	500-999 Emps.	Unknown Emps.	Industry Sales
2015	4.9	9.8	25.4	50.8	37.3	2,439.8	215.8	4.0	1.7	2,789.4
2016	5.1	10.1	26.3	52.5	38.5	2,520.2	222.9	4.1	1.8	2,881.4
2017	5.2	10.4	27.1	54.0	39.7	2,595.8	229.6	4.2	1.8	2,967.9
2018	5.5	10.9	28.4	56.8	41.7	2,728.1	241.3	4.5	1.9	3,119.1
2018	5.8	11.5	29.9	59.8	43.9	2,873.0	254.1	4.7	2.0	3,284.7

INDUSTRY: HARDWARE STORES INDUSTRY (NAICS 44413)
PRODUCT LINE: OTHER BUILDING MATERIALS (Sub Category)

NAICS 44413: Hardware Stores. Establishments primarily engaged
in the retail sale of a number of basic hardware lines, such as tools,
builders' hardware, paint and glass, housewares and household appliances,
and cutlery.

5-YEAR TREND — ESTIMATED INDUSTRY SALES ($MILLIONS)

Year	Employee Size of Establishment									Total Industry Sales
	1-4 Emps.	5-9 Emps.	10-19 Emps.	20-49 Emps.	50-99 Emps.	100-249 Emps.	250-499 Emps.	500-999 Emps.	Unknown Emps.	
2015	11.2	18.0	35.9	50.3	9.2	2.2	0.6	0.0	0.9	128.4
2016	11.4	18.3	36.6	51.3	9.4	2.2	0.6	0.0	1.0	130.8
2017	11.6	18.6	37.2	52.1	9.5	2.2	0.6	0.0	1.0	132.9
2018	12.1	19.5	38.9	54.5	10.0	2.3	0.7	0.0	1.0	139.1
2018	12.7	20.4	40.9	57.2	10.5	2.5	0.7	0.0	1.1	146.0

INDUSTRY: HOME CENTERS INDUSTRY (NAICS 44411)
PRODUCT LINE: PAINT & PAINTING SUPPLIES (Main Category)

NAICS 44411: Home Centers. This industry comprises establishments
known as home centers primarily engaged in retailing a general line of
new home repair and improvement materials and supplies, such as
lumber, plumbing goods, electrical goods, tools, housewares, hardware,
and lawn and garden supplies, with no one merchandise line predominating.
The merchandise lines are normally arranged in separate departments.

5-YEAR TREND — ESTIMATED INDUSTRY SALES ($MILLIONS)

Year	Employee Size of Establishment									Total Industry Sales
	1-4 Emps.	5-9 Emps.	10-19 Emps.	20-49 Emps.	50-99 Emps.	100-249 Emps.	250-499 Emps.	500-999 Emps.	Unknown Emps.	
2015	20.1	40.0	104.0	207.6	152.5	9,973.8	882.1	16.3	7.0	11,403.3
2016	20.8	41.3	107.4	214.5	157.5	10,302.8	911.2	16.9	7.2	11,779.4
2017	21.4	42.5	110.6	220.9	162.2	10,611.8	938.5	17.4	7.4	12,132.7
2018	22.5	44.7	116.3	232.2	170.5	11,152.4	986.3	18.3	7.8	12,750.8
2018	23.7	47.0	122.4	244.5	179.5	11,744.7	1,038.7	19.2	8.2	13,428.0

INDUSTRY: HARDWARE STORES (NAICS 44413)
PRODUCT LINE: PAINT & PAINTING SUPPLIES (Main Category)

NAICS 44413: Hardware Stores. Establishments primarily engaged
in the retail sale of a number of basic hardware lines, such as tools,
builders' hardware, paint and glass, housewares and household appliances,
and cutlery.

5-YEAR TREND — ESTIMATED INDUSTRY SALES ($MILLIONS)

Year	Employee Size of Establishment									Total
	1-4 Emps.	5-9 Emps.	10-19 Emps.	20-49 Emps.	50-99 Emps.	100-249 Emps.	250-499 Emps.	500-999 Emps.	Unknown Emps.	Industry Sales
2015	210.0	337.0	673.8	943.6	172.7	40.5	11.4	0.6	17.7	2,407.3
2016	214.0	343.3	686.5	961.4	176.0	41.2	11.6	0.6	18.1	2,452.7
2017	217.5	349.0	697.8	977.2	178.9	41.9	11.8	0.6	18.4	2,493.2
2018	227.6	365.3	730.4	1,022.8	187.2	43.9	12.3	0.6	19.2	2,609.4
2018	238.9	383.3	766.4	1,073.2	196.5	46.0	12.9	0.6	20.2	2,737.9

INDUSTRY: DEPARTMENT STORES INDUSTRY (NAICS 45211)
PRODUCT LINE: PAINT & PAINTING SUPPLIES (Main Category)

NAICS 45211: Department Stores Industry . this industry comprises
establishments known as department stores primarily engaged in retailing
a wide range of the following new products with no one merchandise line
predominating: apparel, furniture, appliances and home furnishings; and
selected additional items, such as paint, hardware, toiletries, cosmetics,
photographic equipment, jewelry, toys, and sporting goods. merchandise lines
are normally arranged in separate departments.

5-YEAR TREND — ESTIMATED INDUSTRY SALES ($MILLIONS)

Year	Employee Size of Establishment									Total
	1-4 Emps.	5-9 Emps.	10-19 Emps.	20-49 Emps.	50-99 Emps.	100-249 Emps.	250-499 Emps.	500-999 Emps.	Unknown Emps.	Industry Sales
2015	0.0	0.0	0.1	4.3	82.1	272.3	119.5	16.0	0.7	495.0
2016	0.0	0.0	0.1	4.4	83.2	275.8	121.0	16.2	0.7	501.4
2017	0.0	0.0	0.1	4.4	84.1	278.8	122.3	16.4	0.7	506.8
2018	0.0	0.0	0.1	4.4	84.4	280.1	122.9	16.5	0.7	509.1
2018	0.0	0.0	0.1	4.5	85.1	282.1	123.8	16.6	0.7	512.8

INDUSTRY: WAREHOUSE CLUBS & SUPERCENTERS (NAICS 45291)
PRODUCT LINE: PAINT & PAINTING SUPPLIES (Main Category)

NAICS 45291: Warehouse Clubs and Superstores This industry comprises establishments known as warehouse clubs, superstores or supercenters primarily engaged in retailing a general line of groceries in combination with general lines of new merchandise, such as apparel, furniture, and appliances.

5-YEAR TREND — ESTIMATED INDUSTRY SALES ($MILLIONS)

Year	1-4 Emps.	5-9 Emps.	10-19 Emps.	20-49 Emps.	50-99 Emps.	100-249 Emps.	250-499 Emps.	500-999 Emps.	Unknown Emps.	Total Industry Sales
2015	0.2	0.0	0.0	2.3	2.9	352.0	1,556.0	41.1	0.5	1,955.0
2016	0.3	0.0	0.0	2.3	3.0	364.8	1,612.9	42.6	0.5	2,026.4
2017	0.3	0.0	0.0	2.4	3.1	377.0	1,666.7	44.0	0.5	2,094.0
2018	0.3	0.0	0.0	2.6	3.3	409.5	1,810.2	47.8	0.6	2,274.3
2018	0.3	0.0	0.1	2.8	3.5	434.9	1,922.4	50.8	0.6	2,415.4

INDUSTRY: ELECTRONIC SHOPPING & MAIL-ORDER (NAICS 45411)
PRODUCT LINE: PAINT & PAINTING SUPPLIES (Main Category)

NAICS 45411: Electronic Shopping and Mail-Order Houses This industry comprises establishments primarily engaged in retailing all types of merchandise by means of mail or by electronic media, such as interactive television or computer. Included in this industry are establishments primarily engaged in retailing from catalogue showrooms of mail-order houses.

5-YEAR TREND — ESTIMATED INDUSTRY SALES ($MILLIONS)

Year	1-4 Emps.	5-9 Emps.	10-19 Emps.	20-49 Emps.	50-99 Emps.	100-249 Emps.	250-499 Emps.	500-999 Emps.	Unknown Emps.	Total Industry Sales
2015	1.8	1.0	1.4	2.3	1.7	3.2	4.7	6.0	0.3	22.4
2016	1.9	1.0	1.5	2.5	1.8	3.4	5.0	6.4	0.3	23.9
2017	2.0	1.1	1.6	2.6	1.9	3.7	5.4	6.8	0.3	25.3
2018	2.3	1.2	1.8	3.0	2.1	4.2	6.1	7.5	0.4	28.6
2018	2.6	1.4	2.0	3.3	2.4	4.6	6.8	8.2	0.4	31.7

INDUSTRY: HOME CENTERS INDUSTRY (NAICS 44411)
PRODUCT LINE: INTERIOR PAINT (Sub Category)

NAICS 44411: Home Centers. This industry comprises establishments known as home centers primarily engaged in retailing a general line of new home repair and improvement materials and supplies, such as lumber, plumbing goods, electrical goods, tools, housewares, hardware, and lawn and garden supplies, with no one merchandise line predominating. The merchandise lines are normally arranged in separate departments.

5-YEAR TREND – ESTIMATED INDUSTRY SALES ($MILLIONS)

Year	Employee Size of Establishment									Total Industry Sales
	1-4 Emps.	5-9 Emps.	10-19 Emps.	20-49 Emps.	50-99 Emps.	100-249 Emps.	250-499 Emps.	500-999 Emps.	Unknown Emps.	
2015	7.5	14.9	38.9	77.6	57.0	3,727.1	329.6	6.1	2.6	4,261.3
2016	7.8	15.4	40.1	80.1	58.8	3,850.1	340.5	6.3	2.7	4,401.9
2017	8.0	15.9	41.3	82.5	60.6	3,965.5	350.7	6.5	2.8	4,533.9
2018	8.4	16.7	43.4	86.8	63.7	4,167.6	368.6	6.8	2.9	4,764.9
2018	8.9	17.6	45.8	91.4	67.1	4,388.9	388.2	7.2	3.1	5,018.0

INDUSTRY: HARDWARE STORES INDUSTRY (NAICS 44413)
PRODUCT LINE: INTERIOR PAINT (Sub Category)

NAICS 44413: Hardware Stores. Establishments primarily engaged in the retail sale of a number of basic hardware lines, such as tools, builders' hardware, paint and glass, housewares and household appliances, and cutlery.

5-YEAR TREND – ESTIMATED INDUSTRY SALES ($MILLIONS)

Year	Employee Size of Establishment									Total Industry Sales
	1-4 Emps.	5-9 Emps.	10-19 Emps.	20-49 Emps.	50-99 Emps.	100-249 Emps.	250-499 Emps.	500-999 Emps.	Unknown Emps.	
2015	69.2	111.0	222.0	310.8	56.9	13.3	3.7	0.2	5.8	793.0
2016	70.5	113.1	226.1	316.7	58.0	13.6	3.8	0.2	6.0	807.9
2017	71.6	115.0	229.9	321.9	58.9	13.8	3.9	0.2	6.1	821.3
2018	75.0	120.3	240.6	336.9	61.7	14.5	4.1	0.2	6.3	859.6
2018	78.7	126.3	252.5	353.5	64.7	15.2	4.3	0.2	6.6	901.9

INDUSTRY: HOME CENTERS INDUSTRY (NAICS 44411)
PRODUCT LINE: EXTERIOR PAINT (Sub Category)

NAICS 44411: Home Centers. This industry comprises establishments known as home centers primarily engaged in retailing a general line of new home repair and improvement materials and supplies, such as lumber, plumbing goods, electrical goods, tools, housewares, hardware, and lawn and garden supplies, with no one merchandise line predominating. The merchandise lines are normally arranged in separate departments.

5-YEAR TREND — ESTIMATED INDUSTRY SALES ($MILLIONS)

Year	Employee Size of Establishment									Total
	1-4 Emps.	5-9 Emps.	10-19 Emps.	20-49 Emps.	50-99 Emps.	100-249 Emps.	250-499 Emps.	500-999 Emps.	Unknown Emps.	Industry Sales
2015	2.3	4.5	11.8	23.6	17.3	1,132.7	100.2	1.9	0.8	1,295.1
2016	2.4	4.7	12.2	24.4	17.9	1,170.1	103.5	1.9	0.8	1,337.8
2017	2.4	4.8	12.6	25.1	18.4	1,205.2	106.6	2.0	0.8	1,377.9
2018	2.6	5.1	13.2	26.4	19.4	1,266.6	112.0	2.1	0.9	1,448.1
2018	2.7	5.3	13.9	27.8	20.4	1,333.9	118.0	2.2	0.9	1,525.0

INDUSTRY: HARDWARE STORES INDUSTRY (NAICS 44413)
PRODUCT LINE: EXTERIOR PAINT (Sub Category)

NAICS 44413: Hardware Stores. Establishments primarily engaged in the retail sale of a number of basic hardware lines, such as tools, builders' hardware, paint and glass, housewares and household appliances, and cutlery.

5-YEAR TREND — ESTIMATED INDUSTRY SALES ($MILLIONS)

Year	Employee Size of Establishment									Total
	1-4 Emps.	5-9 Emps.	10-19 Emps.	20-49 Emps.	50-99 Emps.	100-249 Emps.	250-499 Emps.	500-999 Emps.	Unknown Emps.	Industry Sales
2015	44.6	71.6	143.2	200.6	36.7	8.6	2.4	0.1	3.8	511.7
2016	45.5	73.0	145.9	204.4	37.4	8.8	2.5	0.1	3.8	521.4
2017	46.2	74.2	148.3	207.7	38.0	8.9	2.5	0.1	3.9	530.0
2018	48.4	77.6	155.3	217.4	39.8	9.3	2.6	0.1	4.1	554.7
2018	50.8	81.5	162.9	228.1	41.8	9.8	2.7	0.1	4.3	582.0

INDUSTRY: HOME CENTERS INDUSTRY (NAICS 44411)
PRODUCT LINE: STAINS & VARNISHES (Sub Category)

NAICS 44411: Home Centers. This industry comprises establishments known as home centers primarily engaged in retailing a general line of new home repair and improvement materials and supplies, such as lumber, plumbing goods, electrical goods, tools, housewares, hardware, and lawn and garden supplies, with no one merchandise line predominating. The merchandise lines are normally arranged in separate departments.

5-YEAR TREND — ESTIMATED INDUSTRY SALES ($MILLIONS)

Year	Employee Size of Establishment									Total
	1-4 Emps.	5-9 Emps.	10-19 Emps.	20-49 Emps.	50-99 Emps.	100-249 Emps.	250-499 Emps.	500-999 Emps.	Unknown Emps.	Industry Sales
2015	1.9	3.8	9.9	19.8	14.5	950.1	84.0	1.6	0.7	1,086.2
2016	2.0	3.9	10.2	20.4	15.0	981.4	86.8	1.6	0.7	1,122.1
2017	2.0	4.0	10.5	21.0	15.5	1,010.8	89.4	1.7	0.7	1,155.7
2018	2.1	4.3	11.1	22.1	16.2	1,062.3	94.0	1.7	0.7	1,214.6
2018	2.3	4.5	11.7	23.3	17.1	1,118.8	98.9	1.8	0.8	1,279.1

INDUSTRY: HARDWARE STORES INDUSTRY (NAICS 44413)
PRODUCT LINE: STAINS & VARNISHES (Sub Category)

NAICS 44413: Hardware Stores. Establishments primarily engaged in the retail sale of a number of basic hardware lines, such as tools, builders' hardware, paint and glass, housewares and household appliances, and cutlery.

5-YEAR TREND — ESTIMATED INDUSTRY SALES ($MILLIONS)

Year	Employee Size of Establishment									Total
	1-4 Emps.	5-9 Emps.	10-19 Emps.	20-49 Emps.	50-99 Emps.	100-249 Emps.	250-499 Emps.	500-999 Emps.	Unknown Emps.	Industry Sales
2015	22.9	36.7	73.4	102.8	18.8	4.4	1.2	0.1	1.9	262.3
2016	23.3	37.4	74.8	104.8	19.2	4.5	1.3	0.1	2.0	267.3
2017	23.7	38.0	76.0	106.5	19.5	4.6	1.3	0.1	2.0	271.7
2018	24.8	39.8	79.6	111.5	20.4	4.8	1.3	0.1	2.1	284.3
2018	26.0	41.8	83.5	116.9	21.4	5.0	1.4	0.1	2.2	298.3

INDUSTRY: HOME CENTERS INDUSTRY (NAICS 44411)
PRODUCT LINE: PAINTING EQUIPMENT (Sub Category)

NAICS 44411: Home Centers. This industry comprises establishments known as home centers primarily engaged in retailing a general line of new home repair and improvement materials and supplies, such as lumber, plumbing goods, electrical goods, tools, housewares, hardware, and lawn and garden supplies, with no one merchandise line predominating. The merchandise lines are normally arranged in separate departments.

5-YEAR TREND – ESTIMATED INDUSTRY SALES ($MILLIONS)

Year	Employee Size of Establishment									Total Industry Sales
	1-4 Emps.	5-9 Emps.	10-19 Emps.	20-49 Emps.	50-99 Emps.	100-249 Emps.	250-499 Emps.	500-999 Emps.	Unknown Emps.	
2015	3.6	7.1	18.5	36.9	27.1	1,770.6	156.6	2.9	1.2	2,024.4
2016	3.7	7.3	19.1	38.1	28.0	1,829.0	161.8	3.0	1.3	2,091.1
2017	3.8	7.5	19.6	39.2	28.8	1,883.9	166.6	3.1	1.3	2,153.9
2018	4.0	7.9	20.6	41.2	30.3	1,979.8	175.1	3.2	1.4	2,263.6
2018	4.2	8.4	21.7	43.4	31.9	2,085.0	184.4	3.4	1.5	2,383.8

INDUSTRY: HARDWARE STORES INDUSTRY (NAICS 44413)
PRODUCT LINE: PAINTING EQUIPMENT (Sub Category)

NAICS 44413: Hardware Stores. Establishments primarily engaged in the retail sale of a number of basic hardware lines, such as tools, builders' hardware, paint and glass, housewares and household appliances, and cutlery.

5-YEAR TREND – ESTIMATED INDUSTRY SALES ($MILLIONS)

Year	Employee Size of Establishment									Total Industry Sales
	1-4 Emps.	5-9 Emps.	10-19 Emps.	20-49 Emps.	50-99 Emps.	100-249 Emps.	250-499 Emps.	500-999 Emps.	Unknown Emps.	
2015	44.1	70.8	141.6	198.3	36.3	8.5	2.4	0.1	3.7	505.8
2016	45.0	72.1	144.2	202.0	37.0	8.7	2.4	0.1	3.8	515.3
2017	45.7	73.3	146.6	205.3	37.6	8.8	2.5	0.1	3.9	523.8
2018	47.8	76.7	153.5	214.9	39.3	9.2	2.6	0.1	4.0	548.3
2018	50.2	80.5	161.0	225.5	41.3	9.7	2.7	0.1	4.2	575.3

INDUSTRY: HOME CENTERS INDUSTRY (NAICS 44411)
PRODUCT LINE: PAINTING SUPPLIES (Sub Category)

NAICS 44411: Home Centers. This industry comprises establishments known as home centers primarily engaged in retailing a general line of new home repair and improvement materials and supplies, such as lumber, plumbing goods, electrical goods, tools, housewares, hardware, and lawn and garden supplies, with no one merchandise line predominating. The merchandise lines are normally arranged in separate departments.

5-YEAR TREND – ESTIMATED INDUSTRY SALES ($MILLIONS)

Year	Employee Size of Establishment									Total Industry Sales
	1-4 Emps.	5-9 Emps.	10-19 Emps.	20-49 Emps.	50-99 Emps.	100-249 Emps.	250-499 Emps.	500-999 Emps.	Unknown Emps.	
2015	4.8	9.6	24.9	49.8	36.6	2,393.3	211.7	3.9	1.7	2,736.3
2016	5.0	9.9	25.8	51.5	37.8	2,472.2	218.6	4.0	1.7	2,826.5
2017	5.1	10.2	26.5	53.0	38.9	2,546.3	225.2	4.2	1.8	2,911.3
2018	5.4	10.7	27.9	55.7	40.9	2,676.1	236.7	4.4	1.9	3,059.6
2018	5.7	11.3	29.4	58.7	43.1	2,818.2	249.2	4.6	2.0	3,222.1

INDUSTRY: HARDWARE STORES INDUSTRY (NAICS 44413)
PRODUCT LINE: PAINTING SUPPLIES (Sub Category)

NAICS 44413: Hardware Stores. Establishments primarily engaged in the retail sale of a number of basic hardware lines, such as tools, builders' hardware, paint and glass, housewares and household appliances, and cutlery.

5-YEAR TREND – ESTIMATED INDUSTRY SALES ($MILLIONS)

Year	Employee Size of Establishment									Total Industry Sales
	1-4 Emps.	5-9 Emps.	10-19 Emps.	20-49 Emps.	50-99 Emps.	100-249 Emps.	250-499 Emps.	500-999 Emps.	Unknown Emps.	
2015	29.2	46.8	93.6	131.1	24.0	5.6	1.6	0.1	2.5	334.5
2016	29.7	47.7	95.4	133.6	24.5	5.7	1.6	0.1	2.5	340.8
2017	30.2	48.5	97.0	135.8	24.9	5.8	1.6	0.1	2.6	346.4
2018	31.6	50.8	101.5	142.1	26.0	6.1	1.7	0.1	2.7	362.6
2018	33.2	53.3	106.5	149.1	27.3	6.4	1.8	0.1	2.8	380.4

INDUSTRY: HOME CENTERS INDUSTRY (NAICS 44411)
PRODUCT LINE: GASOLINE & AUTOMOTIVE FUELS (Main Category)

NAICS 44411: Home Centers. This industry comprises establishments known as home centers primarily engaged in retailing a general line of new home repair and improvement materials and supplies, such as lumber, plumbing goods, electrical goods, tools, housewares, hardware, and lawn and garden supplies, with no one merchandise line predominating. The merchandise lines are normally arranged in separate departments.

5-YEAR TREND — ESTIMATED INDUSTRY SALES ($MILLIONS)

Year	Employee Size of Establishment									Total Industry Sales
	1-4 Emps.	5-9 Emps.	10-19 Emps.	20-49 Emps.	50-99 Emps.	100-249 Emps.	250-499 Emps.	500-999 Emps.	Unknown Emps.	
2015	0.0	0.0	0.0	0.0	0.0	1.8	0.2	0.0	0.0	2.0
2016	0.0	0.0	0.0	0.0	0.0	1.8	0.2	0.0	0.0	2.1
2017	0.0	0.0	0.0	0.0	0.0	1.9	0.2	0.0	0.0	2.2
2018	0.0	0.0	0.0	0.0	0.0	2.0	0.2	0.0	0.0	2.3
2018	0.0	0.0	0.0	0.0	0.0	2.1	0.2	0.0	0.0	2.4

INDUSTRY: HARDWARE STORES (NAICS 44413)
PRODUCT LINE: GASOLINE & AUTOMOTIVE FUELS (Main Category)

NAICS 44413: Hardware Stores. Establishments primarily engaged in the retail sale of a number of basic hardware lines, such as tools, builders' hardware, paint and glass, housewares and household appliances, and cutlery.

5-YEAR TREND — ESTIMATED INDUSTRY SALES ($MILLIONS)

Year	Employee Size of Establishment									Total Industry Sales
	1-4 Emps.	5-9 Emps.	10-19 Emps.	20-49 Emps.	50-99 Emps.	100-249 Emps.	250-499 Emps.	500-999 Emps.	Unknown Emps.	
2015	2.4	3.9	7.8	10.9	2.0	0.5	0.1	0.0	0.2	27.8
2016	2.5	4.0	7.9	11.1	2.0	0.5	0.1	0.0	0.2	28.3
2017	2.5	4.0	8.1	11.3	2.1	0.5	0.1	0.0	0.2	28.8
2018	2.6	4.2	8.4	11.8	2.2	0.5	0.1	0.0	0.2	30.1
2018	2.8	4.4	8.8	12.4	2.3	0.5	0.1	0.0	0.2	31.6

INDUSTRY: SUPERMARKETS INDUSTRY (NAICS 44511)
PRODUCT LINE: GASOLINE & AUTOMOTIVE FUELS (Main Category)

NAICS 44511: Grocery Stores Industry. this industry comprises establishments generally known as supermarkets and grocery stores primarily engaged in retailing a general line of food, such as canned and frozen foods; fresh fruits and vegetables; and fresh and prepared meats, fish, and poultry. Included in this industry are delicatessen-type establishments primarily engaged in retailing a general line of food.

5-YEAR TREND – ESTIMATED INDUSTRY SALES ($MILLIONS)

Year	Employee Size of Establishment									Total Industry Sales
	1-4 Emps.	5-9 Emps.	10-19 Emps.	20-49 Emps.	50-99 Emps.	100-249 Emps.	250-499 Emps.	500-999 Emps.	Unknown Emps.	
2015	48.0	35.9	91.0	297.4	721.4	1,645.1	474.2	65.4	9.1	3,387.5
2016	47.1	35.3	89.5	292.2	708.9	1,616.6	466.0	64.3	8.9	3,328.8
2017	46.2	34.6	87.7	286.5	694.9	1,584.7	456.8	63.0	8.7	3,263.2
2018	46.2	34.6	87.7	286.5	695.0	1,585.0	456.9	62.9	8.7	3,263.7
2018	46.3	34.7	87.9	287.1	696.5	1,588.3	457.9	63.0	8.8	3,270.4

INDUSTRY: BEER, WINE & LIQUOR STORES (NAICS 44531)
PRODUCT LINE: GASOLINE & AUTOMOTIVE FUELS (Main Category)

NAICS 44531: Beer & Wine & Liquor Stores. Establishments primarily engaged in the retail sale of packaged alcoholic beverages, such as ale, beer, wine, and liquor, for consumption off the premises. Stores selling prepared drinks for consumption on the premises are classified in SIC 5813.

5-YEAR TREND – ESTIMATED INDUSTRY SALES ($MILLIONS)

Year	Employee Size of Establishment									Total Industry Sales
	1-4 Emps.	5-9 Emps.	10-19 Emps.	20-49 Emps.	50-99 Emps.	100-249 Emps.	250-499 Emps.	500-999 Emps.	Unknown Emps.	
2015	29.7	28.9	24.2	17.6	2.3	1.7	0.0	0.9	1.7	107.0
2016	31.0	30.1	25.2	18.4	2.4	1.8	0.0	0.9	1.7	111.5
2017	32.2	31.2	26.2	19.1	2.5	1.8	0.0	1.0	1.8	115.8
2018	34.4	33.4	28.0	20.4	2.7	2.0	0.0	1.0	1.9	123.9
2018	36.9	35.9	30.0	21.9	2.9	2.1	0.0	1.1	2.1	132.9

INDUSTRY: GAS STATIONS W/CONVENIENCE STORES (NAICS 44711)
PRODUCT LINE: GASOLINE & AUTOMOTIVE FUELS (Main Category)

NAICS 44711: Gas Stations with Convenience Stores. this industry comprises establishments primarily engaged in selling gasoline and lubricating oils. These establishments frequently sell other merchandise, such as tires, batteries, and other automobile parts, or perform minor repair work. Gasoline stations combined with other activities, such as grocery stores, convenience stores, or carwashes, are classified according to the primary activity.

5-YEAR TREND – ESTIMATED INDUSTRY SALES ($MILLIONS)

Year	Employee Size of Establishment									Total
	1-4 Emps.	5-9 Emps.	10-19 Emps.	20-49 Emps.	50-99 Emps.	100-249 Emps.	250-499 Emps.	500-999 Emps.	Unknown Emps.	Industry Sales
2015	23,001.1	61,916.2	100,204.6	61,639.4	5,397.9	3,373.6	473.8	12.0	260.5	256,279.1
2016	24,746.1	66,613.6	107,806.9	66,315.8	5,807.5	3,629.5	509.7	12.9	280.2	275,722.3
2017	26,445.1	71,187.2	115,208.8	70,869.0	6,206.2	3,878.7	544.7	13.8	299.5	294,652.9
2018	28,845.1	77,647.6	125,664.1	77,300.4	6,769.4	4,230.7	594.1	14.8	326.6	321,392.9
2018	31,446.6	84,650.6	136,997.7	84,272.1	7,380.0	4,612.3	647.7	15.8	356.1	350,378.9

INDUSTRY: DEPARTMENT STORES INDUSTRY (NAICS 45211)
PRODUCT LINE: GASOLINE & AUTOMOTIVE FUELS (Main Category)

NAICS 45211: Department Stores Industry . this industry comprises establishments known as department stores primarily engaged in retailing a wide range of the following new products with no one merchandise line predominating: apparel, furniture, appliances and home furnishings; and selected additional items, such as paint, hardware, toiletries, cosmetics, photographic equipment, jewelry, toys, and sporting goods. merchandise lines are normally arranged in separate departments.

5-YEAR TREND – ESTIMATED INDUSTRY SALES ($MILLIONS)

Year	Employee Size of Establishment									Total
	1-4 Emps.	5-9 Emps.	10-19 Emps.	20-49 Emps.	50-99 Emps.	100-249 Emps.	250-499 Emps.	500-999 Emps.	Unknown Emps.	Industry Sales
2015	0.0	0.0	0.0	0.1	1.6	5.3	2.3	0.3	0.0	9.6
2016	0.0	0.0	0.0	0.1	1.6	5.4	2.4	0.3	0.0	9.8
2017	0.0	0.0	0.0	0.1	1.6	5.4	2.4	0.3	0.0	9.9
2018	0.0	0.0	0.0	0.1	1.6	5.5	2.4	0.3	0.0	9.9
2018	0.0	0.0	0.0	0.1	1.7	5.5	2.4	0.3	0.0	10.0

INDUSTRY: WAREHOUSE CLUBS & SUPERCENTERS (NAICS 45291)
PRODUCT LINE: GASOLINE & AUTOMOTIVE FUELS (Main Category)

NAICS 45291: Warehouse Clubs and Superstores This industry comprises establishments known as warehouse clubs, superstores or supercenters primarily engaged in retailing a general line of groceries in combination with general lines of new merchandise, such as apparel, furniture, and appliances.

5-YEAR TREND — ESTIMATED INDUSTRY SALES ($MILLIONS)

Year	Employee Size of Establishment									Total Industry Sales
	1-4 Emps.	5-9 Emps.	10-19 Emps.	20-49 Emps.	50-99 Emps.	100-249 Emps.	250-499 Emps.	500-999 Emps.	Unknown Emps.	
2015	0.0	0.0	0.0	0.4	0.5	57.0	251.9	6.7	0.1	316.5
2016	0.0	0.0	0.0	0.4	0.5	59.1	261.1	6.9	0.1	328.1
2017	0.0	0.0	0.0	0.4	0.5	61.0	269.8	7.1	0.1	339.0
2018	0.0	0.0	0.0	0.4	0.5	66.3	293.1	7.7	0.1	368.2
2018	0.0	0.0	0.0	0.5	0.6	70.4	311.3	8.2	0.1	391.1

INDUSTRY: GAS STATIONS W/CONVENIENCE STORES (NAICS 44711)
PRODUCT LINE: UNLEADED REGULAR GASOLINE (Sub Category)

NAICS 44711: Gas Stations with Convenience Stores. this industry comprises establishments primarily engaged in selling gasoline and lubricating oils. These establishments frequently sell other merchandise, such as tires, batteries, and other automobile parts, or perform minor repair work. Gasoline stations combined with other activities, such as grocery stores, convenience stores, or carwashes, are classified according to the primary activity.

5-YEAR TREND — ESTIMATED INDUSTRY SALES ($MILLIONS)

Year	Employee Size of Establishment									Total Industry Sales
	1-4 Emps.	5-9 Emps.	10-19 Emps.	20-49 Emps.	50-99 Emps.	100-249 Emps.	250-499 Emps.	500-999 Emps.	Unknown Emps.	
2015	15,702.1	42,268.3	68,406.7	42,079.4	3,685.0	2,303.0	323.4	8.2	177.8	174,953.9
2016	16,893.4	45,475.1	73,596.5	45,271.8	3,964.6	2,477.7	348.0	8.8	191.3	188,227.2
2017	18,053.3	48,597.4	78,649.5	48,380.1	4,236.8	2,647.9	371.9	9.4	204.4	201,150.6
2018	19,691.6	53,007.6	85,787.1	52,770.7	4,621.3	2,888.2	405.6	10.1	223.0	219,405.2
2018	21,467.6	57,788.4	93,524.2	57,530.0	5,038.1	3,148.6	442.2	10.8	243.1	239,193.1

INDUSTRY: GAS STATIONS W/CONVENIENCE STORES (NAICS 44711)
PRODUCT LINE: UNLEADED MID-GRADE GASOLINE (Sub Category)

NAICS 44711: Gas Stations with Convenience Stores. this industry comprises establishments primarily engaged in selling gasoline and lubricating oils. These establishments frequently sell other merchandise, such as tires, batteries, and other automobile parts, or perform minor repair work. Gasoline stations combined with other activities, such as grocery stores, convenience stores, or carwashes, are classified according to the primary activity.

5-YEAR TREND — ESTIMATED INDUSTRY SALES ($MILLIONS)

Year	Employee Size of Establishment									Total
	1-4 Emps.	5-9 Emps.	10-19 Emps.	20-49 Emps.	50-99 Emps.	100-249 Emps.	250-499 Emps.	500-999 Emps.	Unknown Emps.	Industry Sales
2015	3,303.4	8,892.3	14,391.3	8,852.6	775.2	484.5	68.0	1.7	37.4	36,806.5
2016	3,554.0	9,567.0	15,483.1	9,524.2	834.1	521.3	73.2	1.9	40.2	39,598.9
2017	3,798.0	10,223.8	16,546.1	10,178.1	891.3	557.1	78.2	2.0	43.0	42,317.7
2018	4,142.7	11,151.6	18,047.7	11,101.8	972.2	607.6	85.3	2.1	46.9	46,158.0
2018	4,516.3	12,157.4	19,675.4	12,103.1	1,059.9	662.4	93.0	2.3	51.1	50,321.0

INDUSTRY: GAS STATIONS W/CONVENIENCE STORES (NAICS 44711)
PRODUCT LINE: UNLEADED PREMIUM GASOLINE (Sub Category)

NAICS 44711: Gas Stations with Convenience Stores. this industry comprises establishments primarily engaged in selling gasoline and lubricating oils. These establishments frequently sell other merchandise, such as tires, batteries, and other automobile parts, or perform minor repair work. Gasoline stations combined with other activities, such as grocery stores, convenience stores, or carwashes, are classified according to the primary activity.

5-YEAR TREND — ESTIMATED INDUSTRY SALES ($MILLIONS)

Year	Employee Size of Establishment									Total
	1-4 Emps.	5-9 Emps.	10-19 Emps.	20-49 Emps.	50-99 Emps.	100-249 Emps.	250-499 Emps.	500-999 Emps.	Unknown Emps.	Industry Sales
2015	2,543.4	6,846.6	11,080.5	6,816.0	596.9	373.0	52.4	1.3	28.8	28,338.9
2016	2,736.4	7,366.0	11,921.1	7,333.1	642.2	401.3	56.4	1.4	31.0	30,488.9
2017	2,924.3	7,871.8	12,739.6	7,836.6	686.3	428.9	60.2	1.5	33.1	32,582.3
2018	3,189.6	8,586.2	13,895.7	8,547.8	748.6	467.8	65.7	1.6	36.1	35,539.1
2018	3,477.3	9,360.5	15,149.0	9,318.7	816.1	510.0	71.6	1.8	39.4	38,744.4

2017 U.S. Product & Retail Outlook

INDUSTRY: GAS STATIONS W/CONVENIENCE STORES (NAICS 44711)
PRODUCT LINE: LEADED GASOLINE (Sub Category)

NAICS 44711: Gas Stations with Convenience Stores. this industry comprises establishments primarily engaged in selling gasoline and lubricating oils. These establishments frequently sell other merchandise, such as tires, batteries, and other automobile parts, or perform minor repair work. Gasoline stations combined with other activities, such as grocery stores, convenience stores, or carwashes, are classified according to the primary activity.

5-Year Trend – Estimated Industry Sales ($Millions)

Year	Employee Size of Establishment									Total Industry Sales
	1-4 Emps.	5-9 Emps.	10-19 Emps.	20-49 Emps.	50-99 Emps.	100-249 Emps.	250-499 Emps.	500-999 Emps.	Unknown Emps.	
2015	49.2	132.5	214.5	131.9	11.6	7.2	1.0	0.0	0.6	548.5
2016	53.0	142.6	230.7	141.9	12.4	7.8	1.1	0.0	0.6	590.2
2017	56.6	152.4	246.6	151.7	13.3	8.3	1.2	0.0	0.6	630.7
2018	61.7	166.2	269.0	165.5	14.5	9.1	1.3	0.0	0.7	687.9
2018	67.3	181.2	293.2	180.4	15.8	9.9	1.4	0.0	0.8	750.0

INDUSTRY: GAS STATIONS W/CONVENIENCE STORES (NAICS 44711)
PRODUCT LINE: DIESEL FUEL (Sub Category)

NAICS 44711: Gas Stations with Convenience Stores. this industry comprises establishments primarily engaged in selling gasoline and lubricating oils. These establishments frequently sell other merchandise, such as tires, batteries, and other automobile parts, or perform minor repair work. Gasoline stations combined with other activities, such as grocery stores, convenience stores, or carwashes, are classified according to the primary activity.

5-Year Trend – Estimated Industry Sales ($Millions)

Year	Employee Size of Establishment									Total Industry Sales
	1-4 Emps.	5-9 Emps.	10-19 Emps.	20-49 Emps.	50-99 Emps.	100-249 Emps.	250-499 Emps.	500-999 Emps.	Unknown Emps.	
2015	1,282.1	3,451.3	5,585.5	3,435.8	300.9	188.0	26.4	0.7	14.5	14,285.3
2016	1,379.4	3,713.1	6,009.3	3,696.5	323.7	202.3	28.4	0.7	15.6	15,369.0
2017	1,474.1	3,968.0	6,421.9	3,950.3	345.9	216.2	30.4	0.8	16.7	16,424.3
2018	1,607.9	4,328.2	7,004.6	4,308.8	377.3	235.8	33.1	0.8	18.2	17,914.8
2018	1,752.9	4,718.5	7,636.4	4,697.4	411.4	257.1	36.1	0.9	19.8	19,530.5

INDUSTRY: GAS STATIONS W/CONVENIENCE STORES (NAICS 44711)
PRODUCT LINE: OTHER AUTOMOTIVE FUELS (Sub Category)

NAICS 44711: Gas Stations with Convenience Stores. this industry comprises establishments primarily engaged in selling gasoline and lubricating oils. These establishments frequently sell other merchandise, such as tires, batteries, and other automobile parts, or perform minor repair work. Gasoline stations combined with other activities, such as grocery stores, convenience stores, or carwashes, are classified according to the primary activity.

5-YEAR TREND – ESTIMATED INDUSTRY SALES ($MILLIONS)

Year	Employee Size of Establishment									Total Industry Sales
	1-4 Emps.	5-9 Emps.	10-19 Emps.	20-49 Emps.	50-99 Emps.	100-249 Emps.	250-499 Emps.	500-999 Emps.	Unknown Emps.	
2015	120.8	325.2	526.3	323.7	28.3	17.7	2.5	0.1	1.4	1,345.9
2016	130.0	349.8	566.2	348.3	30.5	19.1	2.7	0.1	1.5	1,448.0
2017	138.9	373.9	605.1	372.2	32.6	20.4	2.9	0.1	1.6	1,547.5
2018	151.5	407.8	660.0	406.0	35.6	22.2	3.1	0.1	1.7	1,687.9
2018	165.2	444.6	719.5	442.6	38.8	24.2	3.4	0.1	1.9	1,840.1

INDUSTRY: HOME CENTERS INDUSTRY (NAICS 44411)
PRODUCT LINE: AUTOMOTIVE TIRES & OTHER PARTS (Main Category)

NAICS 44411: Home Centers. This industry comprises establishments known as home centers primarily engaged in retailing a general line of new home repair and improvement materials and supplies, such as lumber, plumbing goods, electrical goods, tools, housewares, hardware, and lawn and garden supplies, with no one merchandise line predominating. The merchandise lines are normally arranged in separate departments.

5-YEAR TREND – ESTIMATED INDUSTRY SALES ($MILLIONS)

Year	Employee Size of Establishment									Total Industry Sales
	1-4 Emps.	5-9 Emps.	10-19 Emps.	20-49 Emps.	50-99 Emps.	100-249 Emps.	250-499 Emps.	500-999 Emps.	Unknown Emps.	
2015	0.2	0.5	1.3	2.5	1.8	120.4	10.6	0.2	0.1	137.6
2016	0.3	0.5	1.3	2.6	1.9	124.3	11.0	0.2	0.1	142.1
2017	0.3	0.5	1.3	2.7	2.0	128.1	11.3	0.2	0.1	146.4
2018	0.3	0.5	1.4	2.8	2.1	134.6	11.9	0.2	0.1	153.9
2018	0.3	0.6	1.5	3.0	2.2	141.7	12.5	0.2	0.1	162.0

INDUSTRY: HARDWARE STORES (NAICS 44413)
PRODUCT LINE: AUTOMOTIVE TIRES & OTHER PARTS (Main Category)

NAICS 44413: Hardware Stores. Establishments primarily engaged in the retail sale of a number of basic hardware lines, such as tools, builders' hardware, paint and glass, housewares and household appliances, and cutlery.

5-YEAR TREND — ESTIMATED INDUSTRY SALES ($MILLIONS)

Year	Employee Size of Establishment									Total Industry Sales
	1-4 Emps.	5-9 Emps.	10-19 Emps.	20-49 Emps.	50-99 Emps.	100-249 Emps.	250-499 Emps.	500-999 Emps.	Unknown Emps.	
2015	14.6	23.4	46.8	65.5	12.0	2.8	0.8	0.0	1.2	167.2
2016	14.9	23.8	47.7	66.8	12.2	2.9	0.8	0.0	1.3	170.3
2017	15.1	24.2	48.5	67.9	12.4	2.9	0.8	0.0	1.3	173.2
2018	15.8	25.4	50.7	71.0	13.0	3.0	0.9	0.0	1.3	181.2
2018	16.6	26.6	53.2	74.5	13.6	3.2	0.9	0.0	1.4	190.2

INDUSTRY: SUPERMARKETS INDUSTRY (NAICS 44511)
PRODUCT LINE: AUTOMOTIVE TIRES & OTHER PARTS (Main Category)

NAICS 44511: Grocery Stores Industry. this industry comprises establishments generally known as supermarkets and grocery stores primarily engaged in retailing a general line of food, such as canned and frozen foods; fresh fruits and vegetables; and fresh and prepared meats, fish, and poultry. Included in this industry are delicatessen-type establishments primarily engaged in retailing a general line of food.

5-YEAR TREND — ESTIMATED INDUSTRY SALES ($MILLIONS)

Year	Employee Size of Establishment									Total Industry Sales
	1-4 Emps.	5-9 Emps.	10-19 Emps.	20-49 Emps.	50-99 Emps.	100-249 Emps.	250-499 Emps.	500-999 Emps.	Unknown Emps.	
2015	0.6	0.4	1.1	3.4	8.3	19.0	5.5	0.8	0.1	39.1
2016	0.5	0.4	1.0	3.4	8.2	18.6	5.4	0.7	0.1	38.4
2017	0.5	0.4	1.0	3.3	8.0	18.3	5.3	0.7	0.1	37.6
2018	0.5	0.4	1.0	3.3	8.0	18.3	5.3	0.7	0.1	37.6
2018	0.5	0.4	1.0	3.3	8.0	18.3	5.3	0.7	0.1	37.7

INDUSTRY: PHARMACIES & DRUG STORES (NAICS 44611)
PRODUCT LINE: AUTOMOTIVE TIRES & OTHER PARTS (Main Category)

NAICS 44611 Pharmacies and Drug Stores – this industry comprises establishments known as pharmacies and drug stores engaged in retailing prescription or nonprescription drugs and medicines.

5-YEAR TREND – ESTIMATED INDUSTRY SALES ($MILLIONS)

Year	Employee Size of Establishment									Total
	1-4 Emps.	5-9 Emps.	10-19 Emps.	20-49 Emps.	50-99 Emps.	100-249 Emps.	250-499 Emps.	500-999 Emps.	Unknown Emps.	Industry Sales
2015	0.5	1.1	4.8	13.5	1.3	0.5	0.2	0.1	0.0	21.8
2016	0.5	1.2	5.0	14.2	1.3	0.5	0.2	0.1	0.0	23.0
2017	0.5	1.2	5.3	14.8	1.4	0.5	0.2	0.1	0.0	24.1
2018	0.5	1.3	5.6	16.0	1.5	0.6	0.2	0.1	0.0	25.9
2018	0.6	1.4	6.1	17.2	1.6	0.6	0.2	0.1	0.0	27.8

INDUSTRY: GAS STATIONS W/CONVENIENCE STORES (NAICS 44711)
PRODUCT LINE: AUTOMOTIVE TIRES & OTHER PARTS (Main Category)

NAICS 44711: Gas Stations with Convenience Stores. this industry comprises establishments primarily engaged in selling gasoline and lubricating oils. These establishments frequently sell other merchandise, such as tires, batteries, and other automobile parts, or perform minor repair work. Gasoline stations combined with other activities, such as grocery stores, convenience stores, or carwashes, are classified according to the primary activity.

5-YEAR TREND – ESTIMATED INDUSTRY SALES ($MILLIONS)

Year	Employee Size of Establishment									Total
	1-4 Emps.	5-9 Emps.	10-19 Emps.	20-49 Emps.	50-99 Emps.	100-249 Emps.	250-499 Emps.	500-999 Emps.	Unknown Emps.	Industry Sales
2015	180.5	485.8	786.2	483.6	42.4	26.5	3.7	0.1	2.0	2,010.8
2016	194.2	522.7	845.9	520.3	45.6	28.5	4.0	0.1	2.2	2,163.4
2017	207.5	558.5	903.9	556.0	48.7	30.4	4.3	0.1	2.3	2,311.9
2018	226.3	609.2	986.0	606.5	53.1	33.2	4.7	0.1	2.6	2,521.7
2018	246.7	664.2	1,074.9	661.2	57.9	36.2	5.1	0.1	2.8	2,749.1

INDUSTRY: DEPARTMENT STORES INDUSTRY (NAICS 45211)
PRODUCT LINE: AUTOMOTIVE TIRES & OTHER PARTS (Main Category)

NAICS 45211: Department Stores Industry . this industry comprises establishments known as department stores primarily engaged in retailing a wide range of the following new products with no one merchandise line predominating: apparel, furniture, appliances and home furnishings; and selected additional items, such as paint, hardware, toiletries, cosmetics, photographic equipment, jewelry, toys, and sporting goods. merchandise lines are normally arranged in separate departments.

5-YEAR TREND – ESTIMATED INDUSTRY SALES ($MILLIONS)

Year	Employee Size of Establishment									Total
	1-4 Emps.	5-9 Emps.	10-19 Emps.	20-49 Emps.	50-99 Emps.	100-249 Emps.	250-499 Emps.	500-999 Emps.	Unknown Emps.	Industry Sales
2015	0.1	0.0	0.1	11.0	208.3	690.9	303.1	40.6	1.8	1,255.9
2016	0.1	0.0	0.1	11.1	211.0	699.8	307.0	41.1	1.8	1,272.1
2017	0.1	0.0	0.1	11.2	213.3	707.4	310.3	41.6	1.8	1,285.8
2018	0.1	0.0	0.1	11.3	214.3	710.6	311.8	41.8	1.8	1,291.8
2018	0.1	0.0	0.1	11.4	215.8	715.7	314.0	42.1	1.8	1,301.1

INDUSTRY: WAREHOUSE CLUBS & SUPERCENTERS (NAICS 45291)
PRODUCT LINE: AUTOMOTIVE TIRES & OTHER PARTS (Main Category)

NAICS 45291: Warehouse Clubs and Superstores This industry comprises establishments known as warehouse clubs, superstores or supercenters primarily engaged in retailing a general line of groceries in combination with general lines of new merchandise, such as apparel, furniture, and appliances.

5-YEAR TREND – ESTIMATED INDUSTRY SALES ($MILLIONS)

Year	Employee Size of Establishment									Total
	1-4 Emps.	5-9 Emps.	10-19 Emps.	20-49 Emps.	50-99 Emps.	100-249 Emps.	250-499 Emps.	500-999 Emps.	Unknown Emps.	Industry Sales
2015	1.2	0.0	0.2	11.3	14.2	1,750.3	7,737.8	204.4	2.4	9,721.8
2016	1.3	0.0	0.2	11.7	14.7	1,814.3	8,020.7	211.9	2.5	10,077.3
2017	1.3	0.0	0.2	12.1	15.2	1,874.8	8,288.1	219.0	2.6	10,413.3
2018	1.4	0.0	0.2	13.1	16.5	2,036.2	9,002.0	237.8	2.8	11,310.1
2018	1.5	0.1	0.3	13.9	17.5	2,162.5	9,560.1	252.6	3.0	12,011.3

INDUSTRY: ELECTRONIC SHOPPING & MAIL-ORDER (NAICS 45411)
PRODUCT LINE: AUTOMOTIVE TIRES & OTHER PARTS (Main Category)

NAICS 45411: Electronic Shopping and Mail-Order Houses This industry comprises establishments primarily engaged in retailing all types of merchandise by means of mail or by electronic media, such as interactive television or computer. Included in this industry are establishments primarily engaged in retailing from catalogue showrooms of mail-order houses.

5-YEAR TREND – ESTIMATED INDUSTRY SALES ($MILLIONS)

Year	Employee Size of Establishment									Total
	1-4 Emps.	5-9 Emps.	10-19 Emps.	20-49 Emps.	50-99 Emps.	100-249 Emps.	250-499 Emps.	500-999 Emps.	Unknown Emps.	Industry Sales
2015	760.8	403.9	599.8	970.3	698.0	1,360.7	1,991.0	2,522.1	115.0	9,421.6
2016	811.5	430.9	639.8	1,035.1	744.5	1,451.5	2,123.8	2,690.3	122.7	10,050.1
2017	860.8	457.0	678.6	1,097.9	789.7	1,539.6	2,252.6	2,853.5	130.2	10,659.9
2018	979.5	520.0	772.2	1,249.3	898.6	1,751.9	2,563.3	3,167.5	148.1	12,050.5
2018	1,087.9	577.6	857.7	1,387.6	998.1	1,945.9	2,847.1	3,457.3	164.5	13,323.5

INDUSTRY: GAS STATIONS W/CONVENIENCE STORES (NAICS 44711)
PRODUCT LINE: AUTOMOTIVE TIRES & TUBES (Sub Category)

NAICS 44711: Gas Stations with Convenience Stores. this industry comprises establishments primarily engaged in selling gasoline and lubricating oils. These establishments frequently sell other merchandise, such as tires, batteries, and other automobile parts, or perform minor repair work. Gasoline stations combined with other activities, such as grocery stores, convenience stores, or carwashes, are classified according to the primary activity.

5-YEAR TREND – ESTIMATED INDUSTRY SALES ($MILLIONS)

Year	Employee Size of Establishment									Total
	1-4 Emps.	5-9 Emps.	10-19 Emps.	20-49 Emps.	50-99 Emps.	100-249 Emps.	250-499 Emps.	500-999 Emps.	Unknown Emps.	Industry Sales
2015	36.1	97.3	157.4	96.8	8.5	5.3	0.7	0.0	0.4	402.6
2016	38.9	104.6	169.3	104.2	9.1	5.7	0.8	0.0	0.4	433.1
2017	41.5	111.8	181.0	111.3	9.7	6.1	0.9	0.0	0.5	462.8
2018	45.3	122.0	197.4	121.4	10.6	6.6	0.9	0.0	0.5	504.8
2018	49.4	133.0	215.2	132.4	11.6	7.2	1.0	0.0	0.6	550.4

INDUSTRY: DEPARTMENT STORES INDUSTRY (NAICS 45211)
PRODUCT LINE: AUTOMOTIVE TIRES & TUBES (Sub Category)

NAICS 45211: Department Stores Industry . this industry comprises
establishments known as department stores primarily engaged in retailing
a wide range of the following new products with no one merchandise line
predominating: apparel, furniture, appliances and home furnishings; and
selected additional items, such as paint, hardware, toiletries, cosmetics,
photographic equipment, jewelry, toys, and sporting goods. merchandise lines
are normally arranged in separate departments.

5-YEAR TREND – ESTIMATED INDUSTRY SALES ($MILLIONS)

Year	1-4 Emps.	5-9 Emps.	10-19 Emps.	20-49 Emps.	50-99 Emps.	100-249 Emps.	250-499 Emps.	500-999 Emps.	Unknown Emps.	Total Industry Sales
2015	0.0	0.0	0.0	1.3	24.7	81.8	35.9	4.8	0.2	148.7
2016	0.0	0.0	0.0	1.3	25.0	82.9	36.4	4.9	0.2	150.6
2017	0.0	0.0	0.0	1.3	25.3	83.8	36.7	4.9	0.2	152.3
2018	0.0	0.0	0.0	1.3	25.4	84.1	36.9	4.9	0.2	153.0
2018	0.0	0.0	0.0	1.3	25.6	84.8	37.2	5.0	0.2	154.1

INDUSTRY: WAREHOUSE CLUBS & SUPERCENTERS (NAICS 45291)
PRODUCT LINE: AUTOMOTIVE TIRES & TUBES (Sub Category)

NAICS 45291: Warehouse Clubs and Superstores This industry
comprises establishments known as warehouse clubs, superstores or
supercenters primarily engaged in retailing a general line of groceries
in combination with general lines of new merchandise, such as apparel,
furniture, and appliances.

5-YEAR TREND – ESTIMATED INDUSTRY SALES ($MILLIONS)

Year	1-4 Emps.	5-9 Emps.	10-19 Emps.	20-49 Emps.	50-99 Emps.	100-249 Emps.	250-499 Emps.	500-999 Emps.	Unknown Emps.	Total Industry Sales
2015	0.5	0.0	0.1	4.7	5.9	732.6	3,238.6	85.6	1.0	4,069.0
2016	0.5	0.0	0.1	4.9	6.2	759.3	3,357.0	88.7	1.0	4,217.7
2017	0.5	0.0	0.1	5.0	6.4	784.7	3,468.9	91.7	1.1	4,358.4
2018	0.6	0.0	0.1	5.5	6.9	852.2	3,767.7	99.5	1.2	4,733.7
2018	0.6	0.0	0.1	5.8	7.3	905.1	4,001.3	105.7	1.2	5,027.2

INDUSTRY: DEPARTMENT STORES INDUSTRY (NAICS 45211)
PRODUCT LINE: AUTO PARTS & ACCESSORIES (Sub Category)

NAICS 45211: Department Stores Industry . this industry comprises establishments known as department stores primarily engaged in retailing a wide range of the following new products with no one merchandise line predominating: apparel, furniture, appliances and home furnishings; and selected additional items, such as paint, hardware, toiletries, cosmetics, photographic equipment, jewelry, toys, and sporting goods. merchandise lines are normally arranged in separate departments.

5-YEAR TREND – ESTIMATED INDUSTRY SALES ($MILLIONS)

Year	Employee Size of Establishment									Total Industry Sales
	1-4 Emps.	5-9 Emps.	10-19 Emps.	20-49 Emps.	50-99 Emps.	100-249 Emps.	250-499 Emps.	500-999 Emps.	Unknown Emps.	
2015	0.1	0.0	0.1	8.3	157.1	521.1	228.6	30.6	1.3	947.3
2016	0.1	0.0	0.1	8.4	159.2	527.9	231.6	31.0	1.3	959.5
2017	0.1	0.0	0.1	8.5	160.9	533.6	234.1	31.3	1.4	969.9
2018	0.1	0.0	0.1	8.5	161.6	536.0	235.2	31.5	1.4	974.4
2018	0.1	0.0	0.1	8.6	162.8	539.9	236.8	31.8	1.4	981.4

INDUSTRY: WAREHOUSE CLUB & SUPERCENTERS (NAICS 45291)
PRODUCT LINE: AUTO PARTS & ACCESSORIES (Sub Category)

NAICS 45291: Warehouse Clubs and Superstores This industry comprises establishments known as warehouse clubs, superstores or supercenters primarily engaged in retailing a general line of groceries in combination with general lines of new merchandise, such as apparel, furniture, and appliances.

5-YEAR TREND – ESTIMATED INDUSTRY SALES ($MILLIONS)

Year	Employee Size of Establishment									Total Industry Sales
	1-4 Emps.	5-9 Emps.	10-19 Emps.	20-49 Emps.	50-99 Emps.	100-249 Emps.	250-499 Emps.	500-999 Emps.	Unknown Emps.	
2015	0.5	0.0	0.1	4.9	6.2	762.1	3,369.0	89.0	1.0	4,232.8
2016	0.5	0.0	0.1	5.1	6.4	789.9	3,492.2	92.3	1.1	4,387.6
2017	0.6	0.0	0.1	5.2	6.6	816.3	3,608.6	95.3	1.1	4,533.9
2018	0.6	0.0	0.1	5.7	7.2	886.6	3,919.4	103.6	1.2	4,924.3
2018	0.6	0.0	0.1	6.1	7.6	941.5	4,162.4	110.0	1.3	5,229.6

INDUSTRY: GAS STATIONS W/CONVENIENCE STORES (NAICS 44711)
PRODUCT LINE: AUTO PARTS & ACCESSORIES (Sub Category)

NAICS 44711: Gas Stations with Convenience Stores. this industry comprises establishments primarily engaged in selling gasoline and lubricating oils. These establishments frequently sell other merchandise, such as tires, batteries, and other automobile parts, or perform minor repair work. Gasoline stations combined with other activities, such as grocery stores, convenience stores, or carwashes, are classified according to the primary activity.

5-YEAR TREND — ESTIMATED INDUSTRY SALES ($MILLIONS)

Year	Employee Size of Establishment									Total
	1-4 Emps.	5-9 Emps.	10-19 Emps.	20-49 Emps.	50-99 Emps.	100-249 Emps.	250-499 Emps.	500-999 Emps.	Unknown Emps.	Industry Sales
2015	75.3	202.8	328.2	201.9	17.7	11.0	1.6	0.0	0.9	839.4
2016	81.1	218.2	353.1	217.2	19.0	11.9	1.7	0.0	0.9	903.1
2017	86.6	233.2	377.3	232.1	20.3	12.7	1.8	0.0	1.0	965.1
2018	94.5	254.3	411.6	253.2	22.2	13.9	1.9	0.0	1.1	1,052.7
2018	103.0	277.3	448.7	276.0	24.2	15.1	2.1	0.1	1.2	1,147.6

INDUSTRY: GAS STATIONS W/CONVENIENCE STORES (NAICS 44711)
PRODUCT LINE: BATTERIES (Sub Category)

NAICS 44711: Gas Stations with Convenience Stores. this industry comprises establishments primarily engaged in selling gasoline and lubricating oils. These establishments frequently sell other merchandise, such as tires, batteries, and other automobile parts, or perform minor repair work. Gasoline stations combined with other activities, such as grocery stores, convenience stores, or carwashes, are classified according to the primary activity.

5-YEAR TREND — ESTIMATED INDUSTRY SALES ($MILLIONS)

Year	Employee Size of Establishment									Total
	1-4 Emps.	5-9 Emps.	10-19 Emps.	20-49 Emps.	50-99 Emps.	100-249 Emps.	250-499 Emps.	500-999 Emps.	Unknown Emps.	Industry Sales
2015	7.9	21.3	34.5	21.3	1.9	1.2	0.2	0.0	0.1	88.4
2016	8.5	23.0	37.2	22.9	2.0	1.3	0.2	0.0	0.1	95.1
2017	9.1	24.5	39.7	24.4	2.1	1.3	0.2	0.0	0.1	101.6
2018	9.9	26.8	43.3	26.7	2.3	1.5	0.2	0.0	0.1	110.8
2018	10.8	29.2	47.2	29.1	2.5	1.6	0.2	0.0	0.1	120.8

INDUSTRY: DEPARTMENT STORES INDUSTRY (NAICS 45211)
PRODUCT LINE: BATTERIES (Sub Category)

NAICS 45211: Department Stores Industry . this industry comprises establishments known as department stores primarily engaged in retailing a wide range of the following new products with no one merchandise line predominating: apparel, furniture, appliances and home furnishings; and selected additional items, such as paint, hardware, toiletries, cosmetics, photographic equipment, jewelry, toys, and sporting goods. merchandise lines are normally arranged in separate departments.

5-YEAR TREND — ESTIMATED INDUSTRY SALES ($MILLIONS)

Year	Employee Size of Establishment									Total
	1-4 Emps.	5-9 Emps.	10-19 Emps.	20-49 Emps.	50-99 Emps.	100-249 Emps.	250-499 Emps.	500-999 Emps.	Unknown Emps.	Industry Sales
2015	0.0	0.0	0.0	1.4	26.5	87.9	38.6	5.2	0.2	159.9
2016	0.0	0.0	0.0	1.4	26.9	89.1	39.1	5.2	0.2	161.9
2017	0.0	0.0	0.0	1.4	27.1	90.0	39.5	5.3	0.2	163.7
2018	0.0	0.0	0.0	1.4	27.3	90.5	39.7	5.3	0.2	164.4
2018	0.0	0.0	0.0	1.4	27.5	91.1	40.0	5.4	0.2	165.6

INDUSTRY: WAREHOUSE CLUBS & SUPERCENTERS (NAICS 45291)
PRODUCT LINE: BATTERIES (Sub Category)

NAICS 45291: Warehouse Clubs and Superstores This industry comprises establishments known as warehouse clubs, superstores or supercenters primarily engaged in retailing a general line of groceries in combination with general lines of new merchandise, such as apparel, furniture, and appliances.

5-YEAR TREND — ESTIMATED INDUSTRY SALES ($MILLIONS)

Year	Employee Size of Establishment									Total
	1-4 Emps.	5-9 Emps.	10-19 Emps.	20-49 Emps.	50-99 Emps.	100-249 Emps.	250-499 Emps.	500-999 Emps.	Unknown Emps.	Industry Sales
2015	0.2	0.0	0.0	1.6	2.1	255.7	1,130.3	29.9	0.4	1,420.1
2016	0.2	0.0	0.0	1.7	2.1	265.0	1,171.6	31.0	0.4	1,472.0
2017	0.2	0.0	0.0	1.8	2.2	273.8	1,210.6	32.0	0.4	1,521.1
2018	0.2	0.0	0.0	1.9	2.4	297.4	1,314.9	34.7	0.4	1,652.1
2018	0.2	0.0	0.0	2.0	2.6	315.9	1,396.4	36.9	0.4	1,754.5

INDUSTRY: GAS STATIONS W/CONVENIENCE STORES (NAICS 44711)
PRODUCT LINE: AUTO ACCESSORIES (Sub Category)

NAICS 44711: Gas Stations with Convenience Stores. this industry comprises establishments primarily engaged in selling gasoline and lubricating oils. These establishments frequently sell other merchandise, such as tires, batteries, and other automobile parts, or perform minor repair work. Gasoline stations combined with other activities, such as grocery stores, convenience stores, or carwashes, are classified according to the primary activity.

5-YEAR TREND – ESTIMATED INDUSTRY SALES ($MILLIONS)

Year	Employee Size of Establishment									Total Industry Sales
	1-4 Emps.	5-9 Emps.	10-19 Emps.	20-49 Emps.	50-99 Emps.	100-249 Emps.	250-499 Emps.	500-999 Emps.	Unknown Emps.	
2015	14.9	40.1	65.0	40.0	3.5	2.2	0.3	0.0	0.2	166.1
2016	16.0	43.2	69.9	43.0	3.8	2.4	0.3	0.0	0.2	178.7
2017	17.1	46.1	74.7	45.9	4.0	2.5	0.4	0.0	0.2	191.0
2018	18.7	50.3	81.5	50.1	4.4	2.7	0.4	0.0	0.2	208.3
2018	20.4	54.9	88.8	54.6	4.8	3.0	0.4	0.0	0.2	227.1

INDUSTRY: GAS STATIONS W/CONVENIENCE STORES (NAICS 44711)
PRODUCT LINE: OTHER AUTO SUPPLIES (Sub Category)

NAICS 44711: Gas Stations with Convenience Stores. this industry comprises establishments primarily engaged in selling gasoline and lubricating oils. These establishments frequently sell other merchandise, such as tires, batteries, and other automobile parts, or perform minor repair work. Gasoline stations combined with other activities, such as grocery stores, convenience stores, or carwashes, are classified according to the primary activity.

5-YEAR TREND – ESTIMATED INDUSTRY SALES ($MILLIONS)

Year	Employee Size of Establishment									Total Industry Sales
	1-4 Emps.	5-9 Emps.	10-19 Emps.	20-49 Emps.	50-99 Emps.	100-249 Emps.	250-499 Emps.	500-999 Emps.	Unknown Emps.	
2015	46.2	124.3	201.1	123.7	10.8	6.8	1.0	0.0	0.5	514.4
2016	49.7	133.7	216.4	133.1	11.7	7.3	1.0	0.0	0.6	553.4
2017	53.1	142.9	231.2	142.2	12.5	7.8	1.1	0.0	0.6	591.4
2018	57.9	155.8	252.2	155.1	13.6	8.5	1.2	0.0	0.7	645.0
2018	63.1	169.9	275.0	169.1	14.8	9.3	1.3	0.0	0.7	703.2

INDUSTRY: HOME CENTERS INDUSTRY (NAICS 44411)
PRODUCT LINE: PETS & PET FOODS & SUPPLIES (Main Category)

NAICS 44411: Home Centers. This industry comprises establishments known as home centers primarily engaged in retailing a general line of new home repair and improvement materials and supplies, such as lumber, plumbing goods, electrical goods, tools, housewares, hardware, and lawn and garden supplies, with no one merchandise line predominating. The merchandise lines are normally arranged in separate departments.

5-YEAR TREND — ESTIMATED INDUSTRY SALES ($MILLIONS)

Year	Employee Size of Establishment									Total Industry Sales
	1-4 Emps.	5-9 Emps.	10-19 Emps.	20-49 Emps.	50-99 Emps.	100-249 Emps.	250-499 Emps.	500-999 Emps.	Unknown Emps.	
2015	0.8	1.7	4.3	8.6	6.3	415.2	36.7	0.7	0.3	474.7
2016	0.9	1.7	4.5	8.9	6.6	428.9	37.9	0.7	0.3	490.3
2017	0.9	1.8	4.6	9.2	6.8	441.7	39.1	0.7	0.3	505.0
2018	0.9	1.9	4.8	9.7	7.1	464.2	41.1	0.8	0.3	530.8
2018	1.0	2.0	5.1	10.2	7.5	488.9	43.2	0.8	0.3	559.0

INDUSTRY: HARDWARE STORES (NAICS 44413)
PRODUCT LINE: PETS & PET FOODS & SUPPLIES (Main Category)

NAICS 44413: Hardware Stores. Establishments primarily engaged in the retail sale of a number of basic hardware lines, such as tools, builders' hardware, paint and glass, housewares and household appliances, and cutlery.

5-YEAR TREND — ESTIMATED INDUSTRY SALES ($MILLIONS)

Year	Employee Size of Establishment									Total Industry Sales
	1-4 Emps.	5-9 Emps.	10-19 Emps.	20-49 Emps.	50-99 Emps.	100-249 Emps.	250-499 Emps.	500-999 Emps.	Unknown Emps.	
2015	10.1	16.3	32.5	45.5	8.3	2.0	0.5	0.0	0.9	116.1
2016	10.3	16.6	33.1	46.4	8.5	2.0	0.6	0.0	0.9	118.3
2017	10.5	16.8	33.7	47.1	8.6	2.0	0.6	0.0	0.9	120.2
2018	11.0	17.6	35.2	49.3	9.0	2.1	0.6	0.0	0.9	125.8
2018	11.5	18.5	37.0	51.8	9.5	2.2	0.6	0.0	1.0	132.0

INDUSTRY: SUPERMARKETS INDUSTRY (NAICS 44511)
PRODUCT LINE: PETS & PET FOODS & SUPPLIES (Main Category)

NAICS 44511: Grocery Stores Industry. this industry comprises establishments generally known as supermarkets and grocery stores primarily engaged in retailing a general line of food, such as canned and frozen foods; fresh fruits and vegetables; and fresh and prepared meats, fish, and poultry. Included in this industry are delicatessen-type establishments primarily engaged in retailing a general line of food.

5-YEAR TREND — ESTIMATED INDUSTRY SALES ($MILLIONS)

Year	Employee Size of Establishment									Total Industry Sales
	1-4 Emps.	5-9 Emps.	10-19 Emps.	20-49 Emps.	50-99 Emps.	100-249 Emps.	250-499 Emps.	500-999 Emps.	Unknown Emps.	
2015	74.4	55.7	141.1	461.0	1,118.3	2,550.3	735.2	101.4	14.1	5,251.4
2016	73.1	54.7	138.7	453.0	1,098.9	2,506.0	722.4	99.6	13.8	5,160.3
2017	71.6	53.6	136.0	444.1	1,077.3	2,456.7	708.2	97.6	13.6	5,058.7
2018	71.7	53.6	136.0	444.2	1,077.4	2,457.0	708.3	97.6	13.6	5,059.4
2018	71.8	53.7	136.3	445.1	1,079.7	2,462.2	709.8	97.7	13.6	5,069.9

INDUSTRY: BEER, WINE & LIQUOR STORES (NAICS 44531)
PRODUCT LINE: PETS & PET FOODS & SUPPLIES (Main Category)

NAICS 44531: Beer & Wine & Liquor Stores. Establishments primarily engaged in the retail sale of packaged alcoholic beverages, such as ale, beer, wine, and liquor, for consumption off the premises. Stores selling prepared drinks for consumption on the premises are classified in SIC 5813.

5-YEAR TREND — ESTIMATED INDUSTRY SALES ($MILLIONS)

Year	Employee Size of Establishment									Total Industry Sales
	1-4 Emps.	5-9 Emps.	10-19 Emps.	20-49 Emps.	50-99 Emps.	100-249 Emps.	250-499 Emps.	500-999 Emps.	Unknown Emps.	
2015	2.5	2.4	2.0	1.5	0.2	0.1	0.0	0.1	0.1	9.0
2016	2.6	2.5	2.1	1.5	0.2	0.1	0.0	0.1	0.1	9.4
2017	2.7	2.6	2.2	1.6	0.2	0.2	0.0	0.1	0.2	9.7
2018	2.9	2.8	2.4	1.7	0.2	0.2	0.0	0.1	0.2	10.4
2018	3.1	3.0	2.5	1.8	0.2	0.2	0.0	0.1	0.2	11.2

INDUSTRY: PHARMACIES & DRUG STORES (NAICS 44611)
PRODUCT LINE: PETS & PET FOODS & SUPPLIES (Main Category)

NAICS 44611 Pharmacies and Drug Stores – this industry comprises establishments known as pharmacies and drug stores engaged in retailing prescription or nonprescription drugs and medicines.

5-YEAR TREND – ESTIMATED INDUSTRY SALES ($MILLIONS)

Year	Employee Size of Establishment									Total Industry Sales
	1-4 Emps.	5-9 Emps.	10-19 Emps.	20-49 Emps.	50-99 Emps.	100-249 Emps.	250-499 Emps.	500-999 Emps.	Unknown Emps.	
2015	4.3	10.7	45.2	127.7	12.0	4.7	1.5	0.6	0.4	207.0
2016	4.5	11.3	47.5	134.4	12.6	5.0	1.5	0.6	0.4	217.8
2017	4.7	11.8	49.8	140.8	13.2	5.2	1.6	0.6	0.4	228.2
2018	5.1	12.7	53.6	151.4	14.2	5.6	1.7	0.7	0.4	245.4
2018	5.5	13.7	57.7	163.0	15.3	6.0	1.9	0.7	0.5	264.1

INDUSTRY: GAS STATIONS W/CONVENIENCE STORES (NAICS 44711)
PRODUCT LINE: PETS & PET FOODS & SUPPLIES (Main Category)

NAICS 44711: Gas Stations with Convenience Stores. this industry comprises establishments primarily engaged in selling gasoline and lubricating oils. These establishments frequently sell other merchandise, such as tires, batteries, and other automobile parts, or perform minor repair work. Gasoline stations combined with other activities, such as grocery stores, convenience stores, or carwashes, are classified according to the primary activity.

5-YEAR TREND – ESTIMATED INDUSTRY SALES ($MILLIONS)

Year	Employee Size of Establishment									Total Industry Sales
	1-4 Emps.	5-9 Emps.	10-19 Emps.	20-49 Emps.	50-99 Emps.	100-249 Emps.	250-499 Emps.	500-999 Emps.	Unknown Emps.	
2015	24.9	67.0	108.4	66.7	5.8	3.6	0.5	0.0	0.3	277.2
2016	26.8	72.0	116.6	71.7	6.3	3.9	0.6	0.0	0.3	298.2
2017	28.6	77.0	124.6	76.7	6.7	4.2	0.6	0.0	0.3	318.7
2018	31.2	84.0	135.9	83.6	7.3	4.6	0.6	0.0	0.4	347.6
2018	34.0	91.6	148.2	91.1	8.0	5.0	0.7	0.0	0.4	379.0

INDUSTRY: DEPARTMENT STORES INDUSTRY (NAICS 45211)
PRODUCT LINE: PETS & PET FOODS & SUPPLIES (Main Category)

NAICS 45211: Department Stores Industry . this industry comprises establishments known as department stores primarily engaged in retailing a wide range of the following new products with no one merchandise line predominating: apparel, furniture, appliances and home furnishings; and selected additional items, such as paint, hardware, toiletries, cosmetics, photographic equipment, jewelry, toys, and sporting goods. merchandise lines are normally arranged in separate departments.

5-YEAR TREND – ESTIMATED INDUSTRY SALES ($MILLIONS)

Year	Employee Size of Establishment									Total
	1-4 Emps.	5-9 Emps.	10-19 Emps.	20-49 Emps.	50-99 Emps.	100-249 Emps.	250-499 Emps.	500-999 Emps.	Unknown Emps.	Industry Sales
2015	0.1	0.0	0.2	12.3	234.4	777.6	341.1	45.7	2.0	1,413.5
2016	0.1	0.0	0.2	12.5	237.5	787.6	345.5	46.3	2.0	1,431.8
2017	0.1	0.0	0.2	12.6	240.0	796.1	349.3	46.8	2.0	1,447.2
2018	0.1	0.0	0.2	12.7	241.1	799.8	350.9	47.0	2.0	1,453.9
2018	0.1	0.0	0.2	12.8	242.9	805.6	353.4	47.4	2.1	1,464.4

INDUSTRY: WAREHOUSE CLUBS & SUPERCENTERS (NAICS 45291)
PRODUCT LINE: PETS & PET FOODS & SUPPLIES (Main Category)

NAICS 45291: Warehouse Clubs and Superstores This industry comprises establishments known as warehouse clubs, superstores or supercenters primarily engaged in retailing a general line of groceries in combination with general lines of new merchandise, such as apparel, furniture, and appliances.

5-YEAR TREND – ESTIMATED INDUSTRY SALES ($MILLIONS)

Year	Employee Size of Establishment									Total
	1-4 Emps.	5-9 Emps.	10-19 Emps.	20-49 Emps.	50-99 Emps.	100-249 Emps.	250-499 Emps.	500-999 Emps.	Unknown Emps.	Industry Sales
2015	1.2	0.0	0.2	11.4	14.3	1,769.9	7,824.4	206.7	2.4	9,830.7
2016	1.3	0.0	0.2	11.8	14.9	1,834.6	8,110.5	214.3	2.5	10,190.1
2017	1.3	0.0	0.2	12.2	15.4	1,895.8	8,380.9	221.4	2.6	10,529.8
2018	1.4	0.0	0.2	13.2	16.7	2,059.0	9,102.7	240.5	2.8	11,436.7
2018	1.5	0.1	0.3	14.1	17.7	2,186.7	9,667.1	255.4	3.0	12,145.8

INDUSTRY: ELECTRONIC SHOPPING & MAIL-ORDER (NAICS 45411)
PRODUCT LINE: PETS & PET FOODS & SUPPLIES (Main Category)

NAICS 45411: Electronic Shopping and Mail-Order Houses This industry comprises establishments primarily engaged in retailing all types of merchandise by means of mail or by electronic media, such as interactive television or computer. Included in this industry are establishments primarily engaged in retailing from catalogue showrooms of mail-order houses.

5-YEAR TREND — ESTIMATED INDUSTRY SALES ($MILLIONS)

Year	Employee Size of Establishment									Total Industry Sales
	1-4 Emps.	5-9 Emps.	10-19 Emps.	20-49 Emps.	50-99 Emps.	100-249 Emps.	250-499 Emps.	500-999 Emps.	Unknown Emps.	
2015	119.2	63.3	94.0	152.1	109.4	213.3	312.0	395.3	18.0	1,476.5
2016	127.2	67.5	100.3	162.2	116.7	227.5	332.8	421.6	19.2	1,575.0
2017	134.9	71.6	106.4	172.1	123.8	241.3	353.0	447.2	20.4	1,670.6
2018	153.5	81.5	121.0	195.8	140.8	274.6	401.7	496.4	23.2	1,888.5
2018	170.5	90.5	134.4	217.5	156.4	305.0	446.2	541.8	25.8	2,088.0

INDUSTRY: BOOK STORES INDUSTRY (NAICS 451211)
PRODUCT LINE: PETS & PET FOODS & SUPPLIES (Main Category)

NAICS 451211: Book Stores. this industry comprises establishments primarily engaged in the retail sale of new books and magazines. Establishments primarily engaged in the retail sale of used books are classified in 5932.

5-YEAR TREND — ESTIMATED INDUSTRY SALES ($MILLIONS)

Year	Employee Size of Establishment									Total Industry Sales
	1-4 Emps.	5-9 Emps.	10-19 Emps.	20-49 Emps.	50-99 Emps.	100-249 Emps.	250-499 Emps.	500-999 Emps.	Unknown Emps.	
2015	0.0	0.1	0.1	0.3	0.1	0.1	0.0	0.0	0.0	0.7
2016	0.0	0.1	0.1	0.3	0.1	0.1	0.0	0.0	0.0	0.8
2017	0.0	0.1	0.1	0.3	0.1	0.1	0.0	0.0	0.0	0.8
2018	0.0	0.1	0.1	0.3	0.1	0.1	0.0	0.0	0.0	0.8
2018	0.0	0.1	0.1	0.3	0.1	0.1	0.0	0.0	0.0	0.8

INDUSTRY: SUPERMARKETS INDUSTRY (NAICS 44511)
PRODUCT LINE: STATIONERY PRODUCTS (Sub Category)

NAICS 44511: Grocery Stores Industry. this industry comprises establishments generally known as supermarkets and grocery stores primarily engaged in retailing a general line of food, such as canned and frozen foods; fresh fruits and vegetables; and fresh and prepared meats, fish, and poultry. Included in this industry are delicatessen-type establishments primarily engaged in retailing a general line of food.

5-YEAR TREND — ESTIMATED INDUSTRY SALES ($MILLIONS)

Year	Employee Size of Establishment									Total Industry Sales
	1-4 Emps.	5-9 Emps.	10-19 Emps.	20-49 Emps.	50-99 Emps.	100-249 Emps.	250-499 Emps.	500-999 Emps.	Unknown Emps.	
2015	3.6	2.7	6.9	22.5	54.5	124.2	35.8	4.9	0.7	255.7
2016	3.6	2.7	6.8	22.1	53.5	122.0	35.2	4.9	0.7	251.3
2017	3.5	2.6	6.6	21.6	52.5	119.6	34.5	4.8	0.7	246.4
2018	3.5	2.6	6.6	21.6	52.5	119.7	34.5	4.8	0.7	246.4
2018	3.5	2.6	6.6	21.7	52.6	119.9	34.6	4.8	0.7	246.9

INDUSTRY: PHARMACIES & DRUG STORES (NAICS 44611)
PRODUCT LINE: STATIONERY PRODUCTS (Sub Category)

NAICS 44611 Pharmacies and Drug Stores – this industry comprises establishments known as pharmacies and drug stores engaged in retailing prescription or nonprescription drugs and medicines.

5-YEAR TREND — ESTIMATED INDUSTRY SALES ($MILLIONS)

Year	Employee Size of Establishment									Total Industry Sales
	1-4 Emps.	5-9 Emps.	10-19 Emps.	20-49 Emps.	50-99 Emps.	100-249 Emps.	250-499 Emps.	500-999 Emps.	Unknown Emps.	
2015	6.6	16.5	69.7	196.9	18.5	7.3	2.3	0.9	0.6	319.2
2016	7.0	17.4	73.3	207.2	19.5	7.6	2.4	1.0	0.6	335.9
2017	7.3	18.2	76.8	217.1	20.4	8.0	2.5	1.0	0.6	351.9
2018	7.8	19.6	82.6	233.5	21.9	8.6	2.7	1.0	0.7	378.4
2018	8.4	21.1	88.9	251.3	23.6	9.3	2.9	1.1	0.7	407.3

INDUSTRY: DEPARTMENT STORES INDUSTRY (NAICS 45211)
PRODUCT LINE: STATIONERY PRODUCTS (Sub Category)

NAICS 45211: Department Stores Industry . this industry comprises establishments known as department stores primarily engaged in retailing a wide range of the following new products with no one merchandise line predominating: apparel, furniture, appliances and home furnishings; and selected additional items, such as paint, hardware, toiletries, cosmetics, photographic equipment, jewelry, toys, and sporting goods. merchandise lines are normally arranged in separate departments.

5-YEAR TREND – ESTIMATED INDUSTRY SALES ($MILLIONS)

Year	Employee Size of Establishment									Total
	1-4 Emps.	5-9 Emps.	10-19 Emps.	20-49 Emps.	50-99 Emps.	100-249 Emps.	250-499 Emps.	500-999 Emps.	Unknown Emps.	Industry Sales
2015	0.0	0.0	0.0	3.4	63.9	212.0	93.0	12.5	0.5	385.4
2016	0.0	0.0	0.0	3.4	64.8	214.8	94.2	12.6	0.5	390.4
2017	0.0	0.0	0.0	3.4	65.5	217.1	95.2	12.8	0.6	394.6
2018	0.0	0.0	0.0	3.5	65.8	218.1	95.7	12.8	0.6	396.5
2018	0.0	0.0	0.0	3.5	66.2	219.7	96.4	12.9	0.6	399.3

INDUSTRY: WAREHOUSE CLUBS & SUPERCENTERS (NAICS 45291)
PRODUCT LINE: STATIONERY PRODUCTS (Sub Category)

NAICS 45291: Warehouse Clubs and Superstores This industry comprises establishments known as warehouse clubs, superstores or supercenters primarily engaged in retailing a general line of groceries in combination with general lines of new merchandise, such as apparel, furniture, and appliances.

5-YEAR TREND – ESTIMATED INDUSTRY SALES ($MILLIONS)

Year	Employee Size of Establishment									Total
	1-4 Emps.	5-9 Emps.	10-19 Emps.	20-49 Emps.	50-99 Emps.	100-249 Emps.	250-499 Emps.	500-999 Emps.	Unknown Emps.	Industry Sales
2015	0.3	0.0	0.0	2.6	3.2	399.9	1,767.7	46.7	0.6	2,221.0
2016	0.3	0.0	0.0	2.7	3.4	414.5	1,832.3	48.4	0.6	2,302.2
2017	0.3	0.0	0.1	2.8	3.5	428.3	1,893.4	50.0	0.6	2,378.9
2018	0.3	0.0	0.1	3.0	3.8	465.2	2,056.5	54.3	0.6	2,583.8
2018	0.3	0.0	0.1	3.2	4.0	494.0	2,184.0	57.7	0.7	2,744.0

INDUSTRY: OFFICE SUPPLIES & STATIONERY STORES (NAICS 45321)
PRODUCT LINE: STATIONERY PRODUCTS (Sub Category)

NAICS 45321: Office Supplies and Stationery Stores . this industry comprises establishments primarily engaged in one or more of the following: (1) retailing new stationery, school supplies, and office supplies; (2) selling a combination of new office equipment, furniture, and supplies; and (3) selling new office equipment, furniture, and supplies in combination with selling new computers.

5-YEAR TREND – ESTIMATED INDUSTRY SALES ($MILLIONS)

Year	Employee Size of Establishment									Total
	1-4 Emps.	5-9 Emps.	10-19 Emps.	20-49 Emps.	50-99 Emps.	100-249 Emps.	250-499 Emps.	500-999 Emps.	Unknown Emps.	Industry Sales
2015	86.0	64.3	340.5	959.8	23.3	23.1	0.1	0.6	18.0	1,515.6
2016	86.0	64.3	340.7	960.5	23.3	23.2	0.1	0.6	18.0	1,516.7
2017	85.9	64.3	340.3	959.2	23.3	23.1	0.1	0.6	18.0	1,514.8
2018	84.0	62.8	332.6	937.5	22.8	22.6	0.1	0.6	17.6	1,480.4
2018	82.3	61.5	325.8	918.6	22.3	22.1	0.1	0.6	17.2	1,450.6

INDUSTRY: ELECTRONIC SHOPPING & MAIL-ORDER (NAICS 45411)
PRODUCT LINE: STATIONERY PRODUCTS (Sub Category)

NAICS 45411: Electronic Shopping and Mail-Order Houses This industry comprises establishments primarily engaged in retailing all types of merchandise by means of mail or by electronic media, such as interactive television or computer. Included in this industry are establishments primarily engaged in retailing from catalogue showrooms of mail-order houses.

5-YEAR TREND – ESTIMATED INDUSTRY SALES ($MILLIONS)

Year	Employee Size of Establishment									Total
	1-4 Emps.	5-9 Emps.	10-19 Emps.	20-49 Emps.	50-99 Emps.	100-249 Emps.	250-499 Emps.	500-999 Emps.	Unknown Emps.	Industry Sales
2015	300.0	159.3	236.5	382.6	275.2	536.6	785.1	994.5	45.4	3,715.1
2016	320.0	169.9	252.3	408.2	293.6	572.4	837.5	1,060.8	48.4	3,963.0
2017	339.4	180.2	267.6	432.9	311.4	607.1	888.3	1,125.2	51.3	4,203.4
2018	386.2	205.1	304.5	492.6	354.3	690.8	1,010.8	1,249.0	58.4	4,751.8
2018	429.0	227.8	338.2	547.2	393.6	767.3	1,122.7	1,363.3	64.9	5,253.7

| INDUSTRY: BOOK STORES INDUSTRY (NAICS 451211) |
| PRODUCT LINE: STATIONERY PRODUCTS (Sub Category) |

NAICS 451211: Book Stores. this industry comprises establishments primarily engaged in the retail sale of new books and magazines. Establishments primarily engaged in the retail sale of used books are classified in 5932.

5-YEAR TREND — ESTIMATED INDUSTRY SALES ($MILLIONS)

Year	Employee Size of Establishment									Total Industry Sales
	1-4 Emps.	5-9 Emps.	10-19 Emps.	20-49 Emps.	50-99 Emps.	100-249 Emps.	250-499 Emps.	500-999 Emps.	Unknown Emps.	
2015	2.7	4.2	8.6	22.6	10.2	4.0	0.7	2.7	1.4	57.3
2016	2.9	4.4	9.1	23.9	10.8	4.2	0.8	2.9	1.5	60.4
2017	3.0	4.6	9.6	25.1	11.3	4.5	0.8	3.0	1.6	63.4
2018	3.0	4.7	9.6	25.2	11.4	4.5	0.8	3.1	1.6	63.9
2018	3.1	4.7	9.7	25.4	11.5	4.5	0.8	3.2	1.6	64.5

| INDUSTRY: SUPERMARKETS INDUSTRY (NAICS 44511) |
| PRODUCT LINE: OFFICE PAPER (Sub Category) |

NAICS 44511: Grocery Stores Industry. this industry comprises establishments generally known as supermarkets and grocery stores primarily engaged in retailing a general line of food, such as canned and frozen foods; fresh fruits and vegetables; and fresh and prepared meats, fish, and poultry. Included in this industry are delicatessen-type establishments primarily engaged in retailing a general line of food.

5-YEAR TREND — ESTIMATED INDUSTRY SALES ($MILLIONS)

Year	Employee Size of Establishment									Total Industry Sales
	1-4 Emps.	5-9 Emps.	10-19 Emps.	20-49 Emps.	50-99 Emps.	100-249 Emps.	250-499 Emps.	500-999 Emps.	Unknown Emps.	
2015	0.8	0.6	1.6	5.1	12.5	28.5	8.2	1.1	0.2	58.7
2016	0.8	0.6	1.5	5.1	12.3	28.0	8.1	1.1	0.2	57.6
2017	0.8	0.6	1.5	5.0	12.0	27.4	7.9	1.1	0.2	56.5
2018	0.8	0.6	1.5	5.0	12.0	27.4	7.9	1.1	0.2	56.5
2018	0.8	0.6	1.5	5.0	12.1	27.5	7.9	1.1	0.2	56.6

INDUSTRY: PHARMACIES & DRUG STORES (NAICS 44611)
PRODUCT LINE: OFFICE PAPER (Sub Category)

NAICS 44611 Pharmacies and Drug Stores – this industry comprises establishments known as pharmacies and drug stores engaged in retailing prescription or nonprescription drugs and medicines.

5-YEAR TREND – ESTIMATED INDUSTRY SALES ($MILLIONS)

Year	Employee Size of Establishment									Total Industry Sales
	1-4 Emps.	5-9 Emps.	10-19 Emps.	20-49 Emps.	50-99 Emps.	100-249 Emps.	250-499 Emps.	500-999 Emps.	Unknown Emps.	
2015	2.0	5.1	21.4	60.6	5.7	2.2	0.7	0.3	0.2	98.2
2016	2.1	5.3	22.6	63.7	6.0	2.4	0.7	0.3	0.2	103.3
2017	2.2	5.6	23.6	66.8	6.3	2.5	0.8	0.3	0.2	108.2
2018	2.4	6.0	25.4	71.8	6.7	2.6	0.8	0.3	0.2	116.4
2018	2.6	6.5	27.4	77.3	7.3	2.9	0.9	0.3	0.2	125.3

INDUSTRY: DEPARTMENT STORES INDUSTRY (NAICS 45211)
PRODUCT LINE: OFFICE PAPER (Sub Category)

NAICS 45211: Department Stores Industry . this industry comprises establishments known as department stores primarily engaged in retailing a wide range of the following new products with no one merchandise line predominating: apparel, furniture, appliances and home furnishings; and selected additional items, such as paint, hardware, toiletries, cosmetics, photographic equipment, jewelry, toys, and sporting goods. merchandise lines are normally arranged in separate departments.

5-YEAR TREND – ESTIMATED INDUSTRY SALES ($MILLIONS)

Year	Employee Size of Establishment									Total Industry Sales
	1-4 Emps.	5-9 Emps.	10-19 Emps.	20-49 Emps.	50-99 Emps.	100-249 Emps.	250-499 Emps.	500-999 Emps.	Unknown Emps.	
2015	0.0	0.0	0.0	3.0	56.2	186.5	81.8	11.0	0.5	338.9
2016	0.0	0.0	0.0	3.0	56.9	188.9	82.9	11.1	0.5	343.3
2017	0.0	0.0	0.0	3.0	57.6	190.9	83.7	11.2	0.5	347.0
2018	0.0	0.0	0.0	3.0	57.8	191.8	84.1	11.3	0.5	348.6
2018	0.0	0.0	0.0	3.1	58.2	193.2	84.7	11.4	0.5	351.1

INDUSTRY: WAREHOUSE CLUBS & SUPERCENTERS (NAICS 45291)
PRODUCT LINE: OFFICE PAPER (Sub Category)

NAICS 45291: Warehouse Clubs and Superstores This industry comprises establishments known as warehouse clubs, superstores or supercenters primarily engaged in retailing a general line of groceries in combination with general lines of new merchandise, such as apparel, furniture, and appliances.

5-YEAR TREND – ESTIMATED INDUSTRY SALES ($MILLIONS)

Year	Employee Size of Establishment									Total Industry Sales
	1-4 Emps.	5-9 Emps.	10-19 Emps.	20-49 Emps.	50-99 Emps.	100-249 Emps.	250-499 Emps.	500-999 Emps.	Unknown Emps.	
2015	0.3	0.0	0.0	2.5	3.1	384.5	1,700.0	44.9	0.5	2,135.9
2016	0.3	0.0	0.0	2.6	3.2	398.6	1,762.2	46.6	0.5	2,214.0
2017	0.3	0.0	0.0	2.6	3.3	411.9	1,820.9	48.1	0.6	2,287.8
2018	0.3	0.0	0.1	2.9	3.6	447.4	1,977.8	52.3	0.6	2,484.9
2018	0.3	0.0	0.1	3.1	3.8	475.1	2,100.4	55.5	0.7	2,638.9

INDUSTRY: OFFICE SUPPLIES & STATIONERY STORES (NAICS 45321)
PRODUCT LINE: OFFICE PAPER (Sub Category)

NAICS 45321: Office Supplies and Stationery Stores . this industry comprises establishments primarily engaged in one or more of the following: (1) retailing new stationery, school supplies, and office supplies; (2) selling a combination of new office equipment, furniture, and supplies; and (3) selling new office equipment, furniture, and supplies in combination with selling new computers.

5-YEAR TREND – ESTIMATED INDUSTRY SALES ($MILLIONS)

Year	Employee Size of Establishment									Total Industry Sales
	1-4 Emps.	5-9 Emps.	10-19 Emps.	20-49 Emps.	50-99 Emps.	100-249 Emps.	250-499 Emps.	500-999 Emps.	Unknown Emps.	
2015	166.9	124.9	661.1	1,863.7	45.3	44.9	0.2	1.1	34.9	2,943.0
2016	167.0	124.9	661.6	1,865.0	45.3	45.0	0.2	1.2	34.9	2,945.2
2017	166.8	124.8	660.7	1,862.6	45.2	44.9	0.2	1.1	34.9	2,941.4
2018	163.0	122.0	645.8	1,820.4	44.2	43.9	0.2	1.1	34.1	2,874.6
2018	159.7	119.5	632.7	1,783.6	43.3	43.0	0.2	1.1	33.4	2,816.6

INDUSTRY: ELECTRONIC SHOPPING & MAIL-ORDER (NAICS 45411)
PRODUCT LINE: OFFICE PAPER (Sub Category)

NAICS 45411: Electronic Shopping and Mail-Order Houses This industry comprises establishments primarily engaged in retailing all types of merchandise by means of mail or by electronic media, such as interactive television or computer. Included in this industry are establishments primarily engaged in retailing from catalogue showrooms of mail-order houses.

5-YEAR TREND — ESTIMATED INDUSTRY SALES ($MILLIONS)

Year	Employee Size of Establishment									Total Industry Sales
	1-4 Emps.	5-9 Emps.	10-19 Emps.	20-49 Emps.	50-99 Emps.	100-249 Emps.	250-499 Emps.	500-999 Emps.	Unknown Emps.	
2015	263.4	139.8	207.6	335.9	241.6	471.1	689.2	873.1	39.8	3,261.5
2016	280.9	149.1	221.5	358.3	257.7	502.5	735.2	931.3	42.5	3,479.1
2017	298.0	158.2	234.9	380.1	273.4	533.0	779.8	987.8	45.1	3,690.2
2018	339.1	180.0	267.3	432.5	311.1	606.5	887.4	1,096.5	51.3	4,171.6
2018	376.6	199.9	296.9	480.3	345.5	673.6	985.6	1,196.8	57.0	4,612.3

INDUSTRY: BOOK STORES INDUSTRY (NAICS 451211)
PRODUCT LINE: OFFICE PAPER (Sub Category)

NAICS 451211: Book Stores. this industry comprises establishments primarily engaged in the retail sale of new books and magazines. Establishments primarily engaged in the retail sale of used books are classified in 5932.

5-YEAR TREND — ESTIMATED INDUSTRY SALES ($MILLIONS)

Year	Employee Size of Establishment									Total Industry Sales
	1-4 Emps.	5-9 Emps.	10-19 Emps.	20-49 Emps.	50-99 Emps.	100-249 Emps.	250-499 Emps.	500-999 Emps.	Unknown Emps.	
2015	0.9	1.4	2.9	7.6	3.4	1.4	0.2	0.9	0.5	19.3
2016	1.0	1.5	3.1	8.1	3.6	1.4	0.3	1.0	0.5	20.4
2017	1.0	1.6	3.2	8.5	3.8	1.5	0.3	1.0	0.5	21.4
2018	1.0	1.6	3.3	8.5	3.8	1.5	0.3	1.0	0.5	21.6
2018	1.0	1.6	3.3	8.6	3.9	1.5	0.3	1.1	0.5	21.8

INDUSTRY: SUPERMARKETS INDUSTRY (NAICS 44511)
PRODUCT LINE: OFFICE & SCHOOL SUPPLIES (Sub Category)

NAICS 44511: Grocery Stores Industry. this industry comprises establishments generally known as supermarkets and grocery stores primarily engaged in retailing a general line of food, such as canned and frozen foods; fresh fruits and vegetables; and fresh and prepared meats, fish, and poultry. Included in this industry are delicatessen-type establishments primarily engaged in retailing a general line of food.

5-YEAR TREND – ESTIMATED INDUSTRY SALES ($MILLIONS)

Year	Employee Size of Establishment									Total
	1-4 Emps.	5-9 Emps.	10-19 Emps.	20-49 Emps.	50-99 Emps.	100-249 Emps.	250-499 Emps.	500-999 Emps.	Unknown Emps.	Industry Sales
2015	6.8	5.1	12.8	41.9	101.7	231.9	66.9	9.2	1.3	477.6
2016	6.6	5.0	12.6	41.2	99.9	227.9	65.7	9.1	1.3	469.3
2017	6.5	4.9	12.4	40.4	98.0	223.4	64.4	8.9	1.2	460.0
2018	6.5	4.9	12.4	40.4	98.0	223.4	64.4	8.9	1.2	460.1
2018	6.5	4.9	12.4	40.5	98.2	223.9	64.5	8.9	1.2	461.0

INDUSTRY: PHARMACIES & DRUG STORES (NAICS 44611)
PRODUCT LINE: OFFICE & SCHOOL SUPPLIES (Sub Category)

NAICS 44611 Pharmacies and Drug Stores – this industry comprises establishments known as pharmacies and drug stores engaged in retailing prescription or nonprescription drugs and medicines.

5-YEAR TREND – ESTIMATED INDUSTRY SALES ($MILLIONS)

Year	Employee Size of Establishment									Total
	1-4 Emps.	5-9 Emps.	10-19 Emps.	20-49 Emps.	50-99 Emps.	100-249 Emps.	250-499 Emps.	500-999 Emps.	Unknown Emps.	Industry Sales
2015	12.1	30.2	127.7	360.9	33.9	13.3	4.1	1.7	1.0	585.0
2016	12.7	31.8	134.4	379.8	35.7	14.0	4.3	1.7	1.1	615.6
2017	13.4	33.3	140.8	398.0	37.4	14.7	4.6	1.8	1.1	645.1
2018	14.4	35.9	151.4	428.0	40.2	15.8	4.9	1.9	1.2	693.6
2018	15.5	38.6	163.0	460.7	43.3	17.0	5.3	2.0	1.3	746.6

INDUSTRY: DEPARTMENT STORES INDUSTRY (NAICS 45211)
PRODUCT LINE: OFFICE & SCHOOL SUPPLIES (Sub Category)

NAICS 45211: Department Stores Industry . this industry comprises establishments known as department stores primarily engaged in retailing a wide range of the following new products with no one merchandise line predominating: apparel, furniture, appliances and home furnishings; and selected additional items, such as paint, hardware, toiletries, cosmetics, photographic equipment, jewelry, toys, and sporting goods. merchandise lines are normally arranged in separate departments.

5-YEAR TREND – ESTIMATED INDUSTRY SALES ($MILLIONS)

Year	Employee Size of Establishment									Total Industry Sales
	1-4 Emps.	5-9 Emps.	10-19 Emps.	20-49 Emps.	50-99 Emps.	100-249 Emps.	250-499 Emps.	500-999 Emps.	Unknown Emps.	
2015	0.0	0.0	0.0	3.9	73.8	244.8	107.4	14.4	0.6	445.0
2016	0.0	0.0	0.0	3.9	74.8	247.9	108.8	14.6	0.6	450.7
2017	0.0	0.0	0.1	4.0	75.6	250.6	109.9	14.7	0.6	455.6
2018	0.0	0.0	0.1	4.0	75.9	251.8	110.5	14.8	0.6	457.7
2018	0.0	0.0	0.1	4.0	76.5	253.6	111.2	14.9	0.6	461.0

INDUSTRY: WAREHOUSE CLUBS & SUPERCENTERS (NAICS 45291)
PRODUCT LINE: OFFICE & SCHOOL SUPPLIES (Sub Category)

NAICS 45291: Warehouse Clubs and Superstores This industry comprises establishments known as warehouse clubs, superstores or supercenters primarily engaged in retailing a general line of groceries in combination with general lines of new merchandise, such as apparel, furniture, and appliances.

5-YEAR TREND – ESTIMATED INDUSTRY SALES ($MILLIONS)

Year	Employee Size of Establishment									Total Industry Sales
	1-4 Emps.	5-9 Emps.	10-19 Emps.	20-49 Emps.	50-99 Emps.	100-249 Emps.	250-499 Emps.	500-999 Emps.	Unknown Emps.	
2015	0.6	0.0	0.1	5.7	7.2	889.5	3,932.5	103.9	1.2	4,940.8
2016	0.6	0.0	0.1	5.9	7.5	922.1	4,076.3	107.7	1.3	5,121.5
2017	0.7	0.0	0.1	6.1	7.7	952.8	4,212.2	111.3	1.3	5,292.2
2018	0.7	0.0	0.1	6.7	8.4	1,034.9	4,575.0	120.9	1.4	5,748.0
2018	0.8	0.0	0.1	7.1	8.9	1,099.0	4,858.6	128.4	1.5	6,104.4

INDUSTRY: OFFICE SUPPLIES & STATIONERY STORES (NAICS 45321)
PRODUCT LINE: OFFICE & SCHOOL SUPPLIES (Sub Category)

NAICS 45321: Office Supplies and Stationery Stores . this industry comprises establishments primarily engaged in one or more of the following: (1) retailing new stationery, school supplies, and office supplies; (2) selling a combination of new office equipment, furniture, and supplies; and (3) selling new office equipment, furniture, and supplies in combination with selling new computers.

5-YEAR TREND – ESTIMATED INDUSTRY SALES ($MILLIONS)

Year	Employee Size of Establishment									Total
	1-4 Emps.	5-9 Emps.	10-19 Emps.	20-49 Emps.	50-99 Emps.	100-249 Emps.	250-499 Emps.	500-999 Emps.	Unknown Emps.	Industry Sales
2015	236.2	176.7	935.5	2,637.1	64.0	63.6	0.3	1.6	49.4	4,164.4
2016	236.4	176.8	936.2	2,639.0	64.1	63.6	0.3	1.6	49.4	4,167.4
2017	236.1	176.6	935.0	2,635.6	64.0	63.5	0.3	1.6	49.4	4,162.1
2018	230.7	172.6	913.7	2,575.8	62.5	62.1	0.3	1.6	48.3	4,067.6
2018	226.0	169.1	895.3	2,523.8	61.3	60.9	0.3	1.6	47.3	3,985.6

INDUSTRY: ELECTRONIC SHOPPING & MAIL-ORDER (NAICS 45411)
PRODUCT LINE: OFFICE & SCHOOL SUPPLIES (Sub Category)

NAICS 45411: Electronic Shopping and Mail-Order Houses This industry comprises establishments primarily engaged in retailing all types of merchandise by means of mail or by electronic media, such as interactive television or computer. Included in this industry are establishments primarily engaged in retailing from catalogue showrooms of mail-order houses.

5-YEAR TREND – ESTIMATED INDUSTRY SALES ($MILLIONS)

Year	Employee Size of Establishment									Total
	1-4 Emps.	5-9 Emps.	10-19 Emps.	20-49 Emps.	50-99 Emps.	100-249 Emps.	250-499 Emps.	500-999 Emps.	Unknown Emps.	Industry Sales
2015	1,015.0	538.9	800.2	1,294.6	931.2	1,815.5	2,656.3	3,364.9	153.5	12,570.1
2016	1,082.7	574.8	853.6	1,381.0	993.3	1,936.6	2,833.5	3,589.4	163.7	13,408.7
2017	1,148.4	609.7	905.4	1,464.8	1,053.6	2,054.1	3,005.4	3,807.2	173.7	14,222.3
2018	1,306.8	693.8	1,030.3	1,666.8	1,198.9	2,337.4	3,419.9	4,226.0	197.6	16,077.6
2018	1,451.4	770.6	1,144.3	1,851.3	1,331.6	2,596.1	3,798.5	4,612.7	219.5	17,776.1

INDUSTRY: BOOK STORES INDUSTRY (NAICS 451211)
PRODUCT LINE: OFFICE & SCHOOL SUPPLIES (Sub Category)

NAICS 451211: Book Stores. this industry comprises establishments primarily engaged in the retail sale of new books and magazines. Establishments primarily engaged in the retail sale of used books are classified in 5932.

5-YEAR TREND — ESTIMATED INDUSTRY SALES ($MILLIONS)

Year	Employee Size of Establishment									Total Industry Sales
	1-4 Emps.	5-9 Emps.	10-19 Emps.	20-49 Emps.	50-99 Emps.	100-249 Emps.	250-499 Emps.	500-999 Emps.	Unknown Emps.	
2015	5.4	8.3	17.1	44.9	20.3	8.0	1.5	5.4	2.8	113.5
2016	5.7	8.7	18.1	47.3	21.4	8.4	1.5	5.7	2.9	119.7
2017	6.0	9.2	19.0	49.7	22.4	8.8	1.6	5.9	3.1	125.7
2018	6.0	9.2	19.1	50.0	22.6	8.9	1.6	6.1	3.1	126.7
2018	6.1	9.3	19.3	50.4	22.8	9.0	1.6	6.3	3.1	127.8

INDUSTRY: DEPARTMENT STORES INDUSTRY (NAICS 45211)
PRODUCT LINE: OFFICE EQUIPMENT (Sub Category)

NAICS 45211: Department Stores Industry . this industry comprises establishments known as department stores primarily engaged in retailing a wide range of the following new products with no one merchandise line predominating: apparel, furniture, appliances and home furnishings; and selected additional items, such as paint, hardware, toiletries, cosmetics, photographic equipment, jewelry, toys, and sporting goods. merchandise lines are normally arranged in separate departments.

5-YEAR TREND — ESTIMATED INDUSTRY SALES ($MILLIONS)

Year	Employee Size of Establishment									Total Industry Sales
	1-4 Emps.	5-9 Emps.	10-19 Emps.	20-49 Emps.	50-99 Emps.	100-249 Emps.	250-499 Emps.	500-999 Emps.	Unknown Emps.	
2015	0.0	0.0	0.0	1.5	27.8	92.3	40.5	5.4	0.2	167.8
2016	0.0	0.0	0.0	1.5	28.2	93.5	41.0	5.5	0.2	170.0
2017	0.0	0.0	0.0	1.5	28.5	94.5	41.5	5.6	0.2	171.8
2018	0.0	0.0	0.0	1.5	28.6	95.0	41.7	5.6	0.2	172.6
2018	0.0	0.0	0.0	1.5	28.8	95.7	42.0	5.6	0.2	173.9

INDUSTRY: WAREHOUSE CLUBS & SUPERCENTERS (NAICS 45291)
PRODUCT LINE: OFFICE EQUIPMENT (Sub Category)

NAICS 45291: Warehouse Clubs and Superstores This industry comprises establishments known as warehouse clubs, superstores or supercenters primarily engaged in retailing a general line of groceries in combination with general lines of new merchandise, such as apparel, furniture, and appliances.

5-YEAR TREND – ESTIMATED INDUSTRY SALES ($MILLIONS)

Year	Employee Size of Establishment									Total Industry Sales
	1-4 Emps.	5-9 Emps.	10-19 Emps.	20-49 Emps.	50-99 Emps.	100-249 Emps.	250-499 Emps.	500-999 Emps.	Unknown Emps.	
2015	0.1	0.0	0.0	0.9	1.1	139.9	618.7	16.3	0.2	777.3
2016	0.1	0.0	0.0	0.9	1.2	145.1	641.3	16.9	0.2	805.7
2017	0.1	0.0	0.0	1.0	1.2	149.9	662.7	17.5	0.2	832.6
2018	0.1	0.0	0.0	1.0	1.3	162.8	719.8	19.0	0.2	904.3
2018	0.1	0.0	0.0	1.1	1.4	172.9	764.4	20.2	0.2	960.4

INDUSTRY: OFFICE SUPPLIES & STATIONERY STORES (NAICS 45321)
PRODUCT LINE: OFFICE EQUIPMENT (Sub Category)

NAICS 45321: Office Supplies and Stationery Stores . this industry comprises establishments primarily engaged in one or more of the following: (1) retailing new stationery, school supplies, and office supplies; (2) selling a combination of new office equipment, furniture, and supplies; and (3) selling new office equipment, furniture, and supplies in combination with selling new computers.

5-YEAR TREND – ESTIMATED INDUSTRY SALES ($MILLIONS)

Year	Employee Size of Establishment									Total Industry Sales
	1-4 Emps.	5-9 Emps.	10-19 Emps.	20-49 Emps.	50-99 Emps.	100-249 Emps.	250-499 Emps.	500-999 Emps.	Unknown Emps.	
2015	109.2	81.7	432.6	1,219.6	29.6	29.4	0.1	0.8	22.8	1,925.9
2016	109.3	81.8	432.9	1,220.4	29.6	29.4	0.1	0.8	22.9	1,927.3
2017	109.2	81.7	432.4	1,218.9	29.6	29.4	0.1	0.8	22.8	1,924.8
2018	106.7	79.8	422.6	1,191.2	28.9	28.7	0.1	0.7	22.3	1,881.1
2018	104.5	78.2	414.0	1,167.2	28.3	28.1	0.1	0.7	21.9	1,843.2

INDUSTRY: ELECTRONIC SHOPPING & MAIL-ORDER (NAICS 45411)
PRODUCT LINE: OFFICE EQUIPMENT (Sub Category)

NAICS 45411: Electronic Shopping and Mail-Order Houses This industry comprises establishments primarily engaged in retailing all types of merchandise by means of mail or by electronic media, such as interactive television or computer. Included in this industry are establishments primarily engaged in retailing from catalogue showrooms of mail-order houses.

5-YEAR TREND — ESTIMATED INDUSTRY SALES ($MILLIONS)

Year	Employee Size of Establishment									Total Industry Sales
	1-4 Emps.	5-9 Emps.	10-19 Emps.	20-49 Emps.	50-99 Emps.	100-249 Emps.	250-499 Emps.	500-999 Emps.	Unknown Emps.	
2015	186.4	99.0	147.0	237.8	171.0	333.4	487.9	618.0	28.2	2,308.6
2016	198.9	105.6	156.8	253.6	182.4	355.7	520.4	659.2	30.1	2,462.7
2017	210.9	112.0	166.3	269.0	193.5	377.3	552.0	699.2	31.9	2,612.1
2018	240.0	127.4	189.2	306.1	220.2	429.3	628.1	776.2	36.3	2,952.8
2018	266.6	141.5	210.2	340.0	244.6	476.8	697.6	847.2	40.3	3,264.8

INDUSTRY: SUPERMARKETS INDUSTRY (NAICS 44511)
PRODUCT LINE: GREETING CARDS (Sub Category)

NAICS 44511: Grocery Stores Industry. this industry comprises establishments generally known as supermarkets and grocery stores primarily engaged in retailing a general line of food, such as canned and frozen foods; fresh fruits and vegetables; and fresh and prepared meats, fish, and poultry. Included in this industry are delicatessen-type establishments primarily engaged in retailing a general line of food.

5-YEAR TREND — ESTIMATED INDUSTRY SALES ($MILLIONS)

Year	Employee Size of Establishment									Total Industry Sales
	1-4 Emps.	5-9 Emps.	10-19 Emps.	20-49 Emps.	50-99 Emps.	100-249 Emps.	250-499 Emps.	500-999 Emps.	Unknown Emps.	
2015	21.9	16.4	41.5	135.7	329.1	750.5	216.3	29.8	4.1	1,545.3
2016	21.5	16.1	40.8	133.3	323.4	737.5	212.6	29.3	4.1	1,518.5
2017	21.1	15.8	40.0	130.7	317.0	722.9	208.4	28.7	4.0	1,488.6
2018	21.1	15.8	40.0	130.7	317.1	723.0	208.4	28.7	4.0	1,488.8
2018	21.1	15.8	40.1	131.0	317.7	724.6	208.9	28.8	4.0	1,491.9

INDUSTRY: PHARMACIES & DRUG STORES (NAICS 44611)
PRODUCT LINE: GREETING CARDS (Sub Category)

NAICS 44611 Pharmacies and Drug Stores – this industry comprises establishments known as pharmacies and drug stores engaged in retailing prescription or nonprescription drugs and medicines.

5-YEAR TREND – ESTIMATED INDUSTRY SALES ($MILLIONS)

Year	Employee Size of Establishment									Total
	1-4 Emps.	5-9 Emps.	10-19 Emps.	20-49 Emps.	50-99 Emps.	100-249 Emps.	250-499 Emps.	500-999 Emps.	Unknown Emps.	Industry Sales
2015	34.7	86.5	365.5	1,032.9	97.0	38.1	11.8	4.8	2.9	1,674.3
2016	36.5	91.1	384.6	1,087.0	102.1	40.1	12.4	5.0	3.1	1,761.9
2017	38.2	95.4	403.0	1,139.0	107.0	42.0	13.0	5.2	3.2	1,846.2
2018	41.1	102.6	433.4	1,224.8	115.0	45.2	14.0	5.5	3.4	1,985.0
2018	44.2	110.5	466.5	1,318.4	123.8	48.6	15.1	5.7	3.7	2,136.6

INDUSTRY: DEPARTMENT STORES INDUSTRY (NAICS 45211)
PRODUCT LINE: GREETING CARDS (Sub Category)

NAICS 45211: Department Stores Industry . this industry comprises establishments known as department stores primarily engaged in retailing a wide range of the following new products with no one merchandise line predominating: apparel, furniture, appliances and home furnishings; and selected additional items, such as paint, hardware, toiletries, cosmetics, photographic equipment, jewelry, toys, and sporting goods. merchandise lines are normally arranged in separate departments.

5-YEAR TREND – ESTIMATED INDUSTRY SALES ($MILLIONS)

Year	Employee Size of Establishment									Total
	1-4 Emps.	5-9 Emps.	10-19 Emps.	20-49 Emps.	50-99 Emps.	100-249 Emps.	250-499 Emps.	500-999 Emps.	Unknown Emps.	Industry Sales
2015	0.0	0.0	0.1	5.8	110.7	367.0	161.0	21.6	0.9	667.2
2016	0.0	0.0	0.1	5.9	112.1	371.8	163.1	21.8	0.9	675.8
2017	0.1	0.0	0.1	6.0	113.3	375.8	164.8	22.1	1.0	683.1
2018	0.1	0.0	0.1	6.0	113.8	377.5	165.6	22.2	1.0	686.2
2018	0.1	0.0	0.1	6.0	114.6	380.2	166.8	22.4	1.0	691.2

INDUSTRY: WAREHOUSE CLUBS & SUPERCENTERS (NAICS 45291)
PRODUCT LINE: GREETING CARDS (Sub Category)

NAICS 45291: Warehouse Clubs and Superstores This industry comprises establishments known as warehouse clubs, superstores or supercenters primarily engaged in retailing a general line of groceries in combination with general lines of new merchandise, such as apparel, furniture, and appliances.

5-YEAR TREND — ESTIMATED INDUSTRY SALES ($MILLIONS)

Year	Employee Size of Establishment									Total
	1-4 Emps.	5-9 Emps.	10-19 Emps.	20-49 Emps.	50-99 Emps.	100-249 Emps.	250-499 Emps.	500-999 Emps.	Unknown Emps.	Industry Sales
2015	0.2	0.0	0.0	2.3	2.9	356.8	1,577.3	41.7	0.5	1,981.8
2016	0.3	0.0	0.0	2.4	3.0	369.8	1,635.0	43.2	0.5	2,054.2
2017	0.3	0.0	0.0	2.5	3.1	382.2	1,689.5	44.6	0.5	2,122.7
2018	0.3	0.0	0.0	2.7	3.4	415.1	1,835.0	48.5	0.6	2,305.6
2018	0.3	0.0	0.1	2.8	3.6	440.8	1,948.8	51.5	0.6	2,448.5

INDUSTRY: OFFICE SUPPLIES & STATIONERY STORES (NAICS 45321)
PRODUCT LINE: GREETING CARDS (Sub Category)

NAICS 45321: Office Supplies and Stationery Stores . this industry comprises establishments primarily engaged in one or more of the following: (1) retailing new stationery, school supplies, and office supplies; (2) selling a combination of new office equipment, furniture, and supplies; and (3) selling new office equipment, furniture, and supplies in combination with selling new computers.

5-YEAR TREND — ESTIMATED INDUSTRY SALES ($MILLIONS)

Year	Employee Size of Establishment									Total
	1-4 Emps.	5-9 Emps.	10-19 Emps.	20-49 Emps.	50-99 Emps.	100-249 Emps.	250-499 Emps.	500-999 Emps.	Unknown Emps.	Industry Sales
2015	2.2	1.6	8.7	24.5	0.6	0.6	0.0	0.0	0.5	38.7
2016	2.2	1.6	8.7	24.6	0.6	0.6	0.0	0.0	0.5	38.8
2017	2.2	1.6	8.7	24.5	0.6	0.6	0.0	0.0	0.5	38.7
2018	2.1	1.6	8.5	24.0	0.6	0.6	0.0	0.0	0.4	37.8
2018	2.1	1.6	8.3	23.5	0.6	0.6	0.0	0.0	0.4	37.1

INDUSTRY: ELECTRONIC SHOPPING & MAIL-ORDER (NAICS 45411)
PRODUCT LINE: GREETING CARDS (Sub Category)

NAICS 45411: Electronic Shopping and Mail-Order Houses This industry comprises establishments primarily engaged in retailing all types of merchandise by means of mail or by electronic media, such as interactive television or computer. Included in this industry are establishments primarily engaged in retailing from catalogue showrooms of mail-order houses.

5-YEAR TREND — ESTIMATED INDUSTRY SALES ($MILLIONS)

Year	Employee Size of Establishment									Total Industry Sales
	1-4 Emps.	5-9 Emps.	10-19 Emps.	20-49 Emps.	50-99 Emps.	100-249 Emps.	250-499 Emps.	500-999 Emps.	Unknown Emps.	
2015	25.4	13.5	20.0	32.4	23.3	45.4	66.4	84.2	3.8	314.4
2016	27.1	14.4	21.4	34.5	24.8	48.4	70.9	89.8	4.1	335.4
2017	28.7	15.3	22.6	36.6	26.4	51.4	75.2	95.2	4.3	355.7
2018	32.7	17.4	25.8	41.7	30.0	58.5	85.5	105.7	4.9	402.2
2018	36.3	19.3	28.6	46.3	33.3	64.9	95.0	115.4	5.5	444.6

INDUSTRY: BOOK STORES INDUSTRY (NAICS 451211)
PRODUCT LINE: GREETING CARDS (Sub Category)

NAICS 451211: Book Stores. this industry comprises establishments primarily engaged in the retail sale of new books and magazines. Establishments primarily engaged in the retail sale of used books are classified in 5932.

5-YEAR TREND — ESTIMATED INDUSTRY SALES ($MILLIONS)

Year	Employee Size of Establishment									Total Industry Sales
	1-4 Emps.	5-9 Emps.	10-19 Emps.	20-49 Emps.	50-99 Emps.	100-249 Emps.	250-499 Emps.	500-999 Emps.	Unknown Emps.	
2015	7.1	10.8	22.4	58.6	26.4	10.4	1.9	7.0	3.6	148.2
2016	7.5	11.4	23.6	61.7	27.9	11.0	2.0	7.4	3.8	156.2
2017	7.8	12.0	24.7	64.8	29.3	11.5	2.1	7.8	4.0	164.0
2018	7.9	12.0	24.9	65.3	29.5	11.6	2.1	8.0	4.0	165.3
2018	7.9	12.1	25.1	65.8	29.7	11.7	2.1	8.2	4.1	166.8

INDUSTRY: SUPERMARKETS INDUSTRY (NAICS 44511)
PRODUCT LINE: MAGAZINES & NEWSPAPERS (Sub Category)

NAICS 44511: Grocery Stores Industry. this industry comprises establishments generally known as supermarkets and grocery stores primarily engaged in retailing a general line of food, such as canned and frozen foods; fresh fruits and vegetables; and fresh and prepared meats, fish, and poultry. Included in this industry are delicatessen-type establishments primarily engaged in retailing a general line of food.

5-YEAR TREND — ESTIMATED INDUSTRY SALES ($MILLIONS)

Year	Employee Size of Establishment									Total Industry Sales
	1-4 Emps.	5-9 Emps.	10-19 Emps.	20-49 Emps.	50-99 Emps.	100-249 Emps.	250-499 Emps.	500-999 Emps.	Unknown Emps.	
2015	31.3	23.5	59.5	194.3	471.4	1,075.0	309.9	42.7	5.9	2,213.6
2016	30.8	23.1	58.5	191.0	463.2	1,056.3	304.5	42.0	5.8	2,175.2
2017	30.2	22.6	57.3	187.2	454.1	1,035.5	298.5	41.2	5.7	2,132.3
2018	30.2	22.6	57.3	187.2	454.2	1,035.7	298.6	41.1	5.7	2,132.6
2018	30.3	22.7	57.4	187.6	455.1	1,037.9	299.2	41.2	5.7	2,137.1

INDUSTRY: BEER, WINE & LIQUOR STORES (NAICS 44531)
PRODUCT LINE: MAGAZINES & NEWSPAPERS (Sub Category)

NAICS 44531: Beer & Wine & Liquor Stores. Establishments primarily engaged in the retail sale of packaged alcoholic beverages, such as ale, beer, wine, and liquor, for consumption off the premises. Stores selling prepared drinks for consumption on the premises are classified in SIC 5813.

5-YEAR TREND — ESTIMATED INDUSTRY SALES ($MILLIONS)

Year	Employee Size of Establishment									Total Industry Sales
	1-4 Emps.	5-9 Emps.	10-19 Emps.	20-49 Emps.	50-99 Emps.	100-249 Emps.	250-499 Emps.	500-999 Emps.	Unknown Emps.	
2015	14.3	13.9	11.6	8.5	1.1	0.8	0.0	0.4	0.8	51.4
2016	14.9	14.4	12.1	8.8	1.2	0.9	0.0	0.4	0.8	53.6
2017	15.4	15.0	12.6	9.2	1.2	0.9	0.0	0.5	0.9	55.6
2018	16.5	16.1	13.5	9.8	1.3	0.9	0.0	0.5	0.9	59.5
2018	17.7	17.2	14.4	10.5	1.4	1.0	0.0	0.5	1.0	63.8

INDUSTRY: PHARMACIES & DRUG STORES (NAICS 44611)
PRODUCT LINE: MAGAZINES & NEWSPAPERS (Sub Category)

NAICS 44611 Pharmacies and Drug Stores – this industry comprises establishments known as pharmacies and drug stores engaged in retailing prescription or nonprescription drugs and medicines.

5-YEAR TREND – ESTIMATED INDUSTRY SALES ($MILLIONS)

Year	Employee Size of Establishment									Total
	1-4 Emps.	5-9 Emps.	10-19 Emps.	20-49 Emps.	50-99 Emps.	100-249 Emps.	250-499 Emps.	500-999 Emps.	Unknown Emps.	Industr y Sales
2015	6.9	17.2	72.6	205.2	19.3	7.6	2.3	0.9	0.6	332.6
2016	7.2	18.1	76.4	215.9	20.3	8.0	2.5	1.0	0.6	350.0
2017	7.6	19.0	80.1	226.2	21.3	8.3	2.6	1.0	0.6	366.7
2018	8.2	20.4	86.1	243.3	22.9	9.0	2.8	1.1	0.7	394.3
2018	8.8	21.9	92.7	261.9	24.6	9.7	3.0	1.1	0.7	424.4

INDUSTRY: GAS STATIONS W/CONVENIENCE STORES (NAICS 44711)
PRODUCT LINE: MAGAZINES & NEWSPAPERS (Sub Category)

NAICS 44711: Gas Stations with Convenience Stores. this industry comprises establishments primarily engaged in selling gasoline and lubricating oils. These establishments frequently sell other merchandise, such as tires, batteries, and other automobile parts, or perform minor repair work. Gasoline stations combined with other activities, such as grocery stores, convenience stores, or carwashes, are classified according to the primary activity.

5-YEAR TREND – ESTIMATED INDUSTRY SALES ($MILLIONS)

Year	Employee Size of Establishment									Total
	1-4 Emps.	5-9 Emps.	10-19 Emps.	20-49 Emps.	50-99 Emps.	100-249 Emps.	250-499 Emps.	500-999 Emps.	Unknown Emps.	Industr y Sales
2015	147.1	396.0	640.9	394.3	34.5	21.6	3.0	0.1	1.7	1,639.2
2016	158.3	426.1	689.6	424.2	37.1	23.2	3.3	0.1	1.8	1,763.6
2017	169.1	455.3	736.9	453.3	39.7	24.8	3.5	0.1	1.9	1,884.7
2018	184.5	496.7	803.8	494.4	43.3	27.1	3.8	0.1	2.1	2,055.7
2018	201.1	541.4	876.3	539.0	47.2	29.5	4.1	0.1	2.3	2,241.1

INDUSTRY: PRERECORDED TAPES & CDs STORES (NAICS 45122)
PRODUCT LINE: MAGAZINES & NEWSPAPERS (Sub Category)

NAICS 45122: Prerecorded Tape, Compact Disc, and Record Stores .
This industry comprises establishments primarily engaged in retailing new
prerecorded audio and video tapes, compact discs (CDs), and phonograph
records.

5-YEAR TREND — ESTIMATED INDUSTRY SALES ($MILLIONS)

Year	Employee Size of Establishment									Total
	1-4 Emps.	5-9 Emps.	10-19 Emps.	20-49 Emps.	50-99 Emps.	100-249 Emps.	250-499 Emps.	500-999 Emps.	Unknown Emps.	Industry Sales
2015	2.5	4.9	12.8	25.6	18.8	1,228.2	108.6	2.0	0.9	1,404.2
2016	2.6	5.1	13.2	26.4	19.4	1,268.7	112.2	2.1	0.9	1,450.5
2017	2.6	5.2	13.6	27.2	20.0	1,306.7	115.6	2.1	0.9	1,494.0
2018	2.8	5.5	14.3	28.6	21.0	1,373.3	121.5	2.2	1.0	1,570.1
2018	2.9	5.8	15.1	30.1	22.1	1,446.2	127.9	2.4	1.0	1,653.5

INDUSTRY: DEPARTMENT STORES (NAICS 45211)
PRODUCT LINE: MAGAZINES & NEWSPAPERS (Sub Category)

NAICS 45211: Department Stores Industry . this industry comprises
establishments known as department stores primarily engaged in retailing
a wide range of the following new products with no one merchandise line
predominating: apparel, furniture, appliances and home furnishings; and
selected additional items, such as paint, hardware, toiletries, cosmetics,
photographic equipment, jewelry, toys, and sporting goods. merchandise lines
are normally arranged in separate departments.

5-YEAR TREND — ESTIMATED INDUSTRY SALES ($MILLIONS)

Year	Employee Size of Establishment									Total
	1-4 Emps.	5-9 Emps.	10-19 Emps.	20-49 Emps.	50-99 Emps.	100-249 Emps.	250-499 Emps.	500-999 Emps.	Unknown Emps.	Industry Sales
2015	0.0	0.0	0.0	2.6	48.7	161.4	70.8	9.5	0.4	293.4
2016	0.0	0.0	0.0	2.6	49.3	163.5	71.7	9.6	0.4	297.2
2017	0.0	0.0	0.0	2.6	49.8	165.3	72.5	9.7	0.4	300.4
2018	0.0	0.0	0.0	2.6	50.1	166.0	72.8	9.8	0.4	301.8
2018	0.0	0.0	0.0	2.7	50.4	167.2	73.4	9.8	0.4	304.0

INDUSTRY: WAREHOUSE CLUBS & SUPERCENTERS (NAICS 45291)
PRODUCT LINE: MAGAZINES & NEWSPAPERS (Sub Category)

NAICS 45291: Warehouse Clubs and Superstores This industry comprises establishments known as warehouse clubs, superstores or supercenters primarily engaged in retailing a general line of groceries in combination with general lines of new merchandise, such as apparel, furniture, and appliances.

5-YEAR TREND – ESTIMATED INDUSTRY SALES ($MILLIONS)

Year	Employee Size of Establishment									Total
	1-4 Emps.	5-9 Emps.	10-19 Emps.	20-49 Emps.	50-99 Emps.	100-249 Emps.	250-499 Emps.	500-999 Emps.	Unknown Emps.	Industry Sales
2015	0.2	0.0	0.0	1.4	1.8	223.5	988.0	26.1	0.3	1,241.3
2016	0.2	0.0	0.0	1.5	1.9	231.6	1,024.1	27.1	0.3	1,286.6
2017	0.2	0.0	0.0	1.5	1.9	239.4	1,058.2	28.0	0.3	1,329.5
2018	0.2	0.0	0.0	1.7	2.1	260.0	1,149.4	30.4	0.4	1,444.1
2018	0.2	0.0	0.0	1.8	2.2	276.1	1,220.6	32.2	0.4	1,533.6

INDUSTRY: ELECTRONIC SHOPPING & MAIL-ORDER (NAICS 45411)
PRODUCT LINE: MAGAZINES & NEWSPAPERS (Sub Category)

NAICS 45411: Electronic Shopping and Mail-Order Houses This industry comprises establishments primarily engaged in retailing all types of merchandise by means of mail or by electronic media, such as interactive television or computer. Included in this industry are establishments primarily engaged in retailing from catalogue showrooms of mail-order houses.

5-YEAR TREND – ESTIMATED INDUSTRY SALES ($MILLIONS)

Year	Employee Size of Establishment									Total
	1-4 Emps.	5-9 Emps.	10-19 Emps.	20-49 Emps.	50-99 Emps.	100-249 Emps.	250-499 Emps.	500-999 Emps.	Unknown Emps.	Industry Sales
2015	196.1	104.1	154.6	250.2	179.9	350.8	513.3	650.2	29.7	2,428.9
2016	209.2	111.1	164.9	266.8	191.9	374.2	547.5	693.6	31.6	2,591.0
2017	221.9	117.8	175.0	283.0	203.6	396.9	580.7	735.7	33.6	2,748.1
2018	252.5	134.1	199.1	322.1	231.7	451.7	660.8	816.6	38.2	3,106.6
2018	280.5	148.9	221.1	357.7	257.3	501.6	734.0	891.3	42.4	3,434.8

INDUSTRY: BOOK STORES INDUSTRY (NAICS 451211)
PRODUCT LINE: MAGAZINES & NEWSPAPERS (Sub Category)

NAICS 451211: Book Stores. this industry comprises establishments primarily engaged in the retail sale of new books and magazines. Establishments primarily engaged in the retail sale of used books are classified in 5932.

5-YEAR TREND — ESTIMATED INDUSTRY SALES ($MILLIONS)

Year	Employee Size of Establishment									Total Industry Sales
	1-4 Emps.	5-9 Emps.	10-19 Emps.	20-49 Emps.	50-99 Emps.	100-249 Emps.	250-499 Emps.	500-999 Emps.	Unknown Emps.	
2015	16.7	25.5	52.7	138.1	62.4	24.6	4.5	16.5	8.6	349.5
2016	17.6	26.9	55.6	145.6	65.7	25.9	4.7	17.4	9.0	368.5
2017	18.5	28.2	58.4	152.9	69.0	27.2	5.0	18.3	9.5	386.9
2018	18.6	28.4	58.8	154.0	69.5	27.4	5.0	18.8	9.5	390.0
2018	18.7	28.6	59.3	155.2	70.1	27.6	5.0	19.3	9.6	393.5

INDUSTRY: SUPERMARKETS INDUSTRY (NAICS 44511)
PRODUCT LINE: SOUVENIR & NOVELTY ITEMS (Main Category)

NAICS 44511: Grocery Stores Industry. this industry comprises establishments generally known as supermarkets and grocery stores primarily engaged in retailing a general line of food, such as canned and frozen foods; fresh fruits and vegetables; and fresh and prepared meats, fish, and poultry. Included in this industry are delicatessen-type establishments primarily engaged in retailing a general line of food.

5-YEAR TREND — ESTIMATED INDUSTRY SALES ($MILLIONS)

Year	Employee Size of Establishment									Total Industry Sales
	1-4 Emps.	5-9 Emps.	10-19 Emps.	20-49 Emps.	50-99 Emps.	100-249 Emps.	250-499 Emps.	500-999 Emps.	Unknown Emps.	
2015	7.4	5.5	14.0	45.8	111.1	253.3	73.0	10.1	1.4	521.5
2016	7.3	5.4	13.8	45.0	109.1	248.9	71.7	9.9	1.4	512.4
2017	7.1	5.3	13.5	44.1	107.0	244.0	70.3	9.7	1.3	502.4
2018	7.1	5.3	13.5	44.1	107.0	244.0	70.3	9.7	1.3	502.4
2018	7.1	5.3	13.5	44.2	107.2	244.5	70.5	9.7	1.3	503.5

INDUSTRY: BEER, WINE & LIQUOR STORES (NAICS 44531)
PRODUCT LINE: SOUVENIR & NOVELTY ITEMS (Main Category)

NAICS 44531: Beer & Wine & Liquor Stores. Establishments primarily engaged in the retail sale of packaged alcoholic beverages, such as ale, beer, wine, and liquor, for consumption off the premises. Stores selling prepared drinks for consumption on the premises are classified in SIC 5813.

5-YEAR TREND — ESTIMATED INDUSTRY SALES ($MILLIONS)

Year	Employee Size of Establishment									Total Industry Sales
	1-4 Emps.	5-9 Emps.	10-19 Emps.	20-49 Emps.	50-99 Emps.	100-249 Emps.	250-499 Emps.	500-999 Emps.	Unknown Emps.	
2015	6.6	6.4	5.4	3.9	0.5	0.4	0.0	0.2	0.4	23.9
2016	6.9	6.7	5.6	4.1	0.5	0.4	0.0	0.2	0.4	24.9
2017	7.2	7.0	5.8	4.3	0.6	0.4	0.0	0.2	0.4	25.8
2018	7.7	7.5	6.2	4.6	0.6	0.4	0.0	0.2	0.4	27.6
2018	8.2	8.0	6.7	4.9	0.6	0.5	0.0	0.2	0.5	29.6

INDUSTRY: PHARMACIES & DRUG STORES (NAICS 44611)
PRODUCT LINE: SOUVENIR & NOVELTY ITEMS (Main Category)

NAICS 44611 Pharmacies and Drug Stores – this industry comprises establishments known as pharmacies and drug stores engaged in retailing prescription or nonprescription drugs and medicines.

5-YEAR TREND — ESTIMATED INDUSTRY SALES ($MILLIONS)

Year	Employee Size of Establishment									Total Industry Sales
	1-4 Emps.	5-9 Emps.	10-19 Emps.	20-49 Emps.	50-99 Emps.	100-249 Emps.	250-499 Emps.	500-999 Emps.	Unknown Emps.	
2015	6.7	16.6	70.3	198.7	18.7	7.3	2.3	0.9	0.6	322.0
2016	7.0	17.5	74.0	209.1	19.6	7.7	2.4	1.0	0.6	338.8
2017	7.4	18.4	77.5	219.1	20.6	8.1	2.5	1.0	0.6	355.1
2018	7.9	19.7	83.3	235.6	22.1	8.7	2.7	1.1	0.7	381.8
2018	8.5	21.2	89.7	253.6	23.8	9.4	2.9	1.1	0.7	410.9

INDUSTRY: MEN'S CLOTHING STORES INDUSTRY (NAICS 44811)
PRODUCT LINE: SOUVENIR & NOVELTY ITEMS (Main Category)

NAICS 44811: Men's Clothing Stores. this industry comprises establishments primarily engaged in retailing a general line of new men's and boys' clothing. These establishments may provide basic alterations, such as hemming, taking in or letting out seams, or lengthening or shortening sleeves.

5-YEAR TREND – ESTIMATED INDUSTRY SALES ($MILLIONS)

Year	Employee Size of Establishment									Total Industry Sales
	1-4 Emps.	5-9 Emps.	10-19 Emps.	20-49 Emps.	50-99 Emps.	100-249 Emps.	250-499 Emps.	500-999 Emps.	Unknown Emps.	
2015	1.3	2.0	4.7	2.7	0.7	0.4	0.1	0.0	0.2	12.2
2016	1.4	2.1	4.9	2.9	0.7	0.4	0.2	0.0	0.2	12.8
2017	1.5	2.2	5.1	3.0	0.8	0.4	0.2	0.0	0.2	13.3
2018	1.5	2.3	5.3	3.1	0.8	0.4	0.2	0.0	0.3	13.8
2018	1.6	2.4	5.5	3.2	0.8	0.4	0.2	0.0	0.3	14.3

INDUSTRY: WOMEN'S CLOTHING STORES INDUSTRY (NAICS 44812)
PRODUCT LINE: SOUVENIR & NOVELTY ITEMS (Main Category)

NAICS 44812: Women's Clothing Stores . this industry comprises establishments primarily engaged in retailing a general line of new women's, misses' and juniors' clothing, including maternity wear. These establishments may provide basic alterations, such as hemming, taking in or letting out seams, or lengthening or shortening sleeves.

5-YEAR TREND – ESTIMATED INDUSTRY SALES ($MILLIONS)

Year	Employee Size of Establishment									Total Industry Sales
	1-4 Emps.	5-9 Emps.	10-19 Emps.	20-49 Emps.	50-99 Emps.	100-249 Emps.	250-499 Emps.	500-999 Emps.	Unknown Emps.	
2015	1.8	4.0	9.9	6.8	2.1	2.1	0.8	0.7	0.4	28.5
2016	1.8	4.2	10.2	7.0	2.2	2.1	0.8	0.7	0.4	29.6
2017	1.9	4.3	10.6	7.3	2.3	2.2	0.8	0.7	0.4	30.6
2018	2.0	4.6	11.3	7.7	2.4	2.3	0.9	0.8	0.5	32.5
2018	2.2	4.9	12.0	8.2	2.6	2.5	0.9	0.8	0.5	34.6

INDUSTRY: FAMILY CLOTHING STORES INDUSTRY (NAICS 44814)
PRODUCT LINE: SOUVENIR & NOVELTY ITEMS (Main Category)

NAICS 44814: Family Clothing Stores . this industry comprises establishments primarily engaged in retailing a general line of new clothing for men, women, and children, without specializing in sales for an individual gender or age group. These establishments may provide basic alterations, such as hemming, taking in or letting out seams, or lengthening or shortening sleeves.

5-YEAR TREND – ESTIMATED INDUSTRY SALES ($MILLIONS)

Year	Employee Size of Establishment									Total Industry Sales
	1-4 Emps.	5-9 Emps.	10-19 Emps.	20-49 Emps.	50-99 Emps.	100-249 Emps.	250-499 Emps.	500-999 Emps.	Unknown Emps.	
2015	3.8	6.8	29.1	89.1	93.4	23.3	23.0	9.1	1.0	278.6
2016	3.9	7.0	30.1	92.3	96.8	24.1	23.9	9.5	1.1	288.5
2017	4.0	7.2	31.1	95.3	99.9	24.9	24.6	9.8	1.1	297.9
2018	4.3	7.7	33.0	101.1	106.0	26.4	26.1	10.3	1.2	316.1
2018	4.5	8.1	35.0	107.4	112.7	28.1	27.8	11.0	1.2	335.9

INDUSTRY: DEPARTMENT STORES INDUSTRY (NAICS 45211)
PRODUCT LINE: SOUVENIR & NOVELTY ITEMS (Main Category)

NAICS 45211: Department Stores Industry . this industry comprises establishments known as department stores primarily engaged in retailing a wide range of the following new products with no one merchandise line predominating: apparel, furniture, appliances and home furnishings; and selected additional items, such as paint, hardware, toiletries, cosmetics, photographic equipment, jewelry, toys, and sporting goods. merchandise lines are normally arranged in separate departments.

5-YEAR TREND – ESTIMATED INDUSTRY SALES ($MILLIONS)

Year	Employee Size of Establishment									Total Industry Sales
	1-4 Emps.	5-9 Emps.	10-19 Emps.	20-49 Emps.	50-99 Emps.	100-249 Emps.	250-499 Emps.	500-999 Emps.	Unknown Emps.	
2015	0.0	0.0	0.1	4.1	78.4	260.2	114.1	15.3	0.7	472.9
2016	0.0	0.0	0.1	4.2	79.5	263.5	115.6	15.5	0.7	479.0
2017	0.0	0.0	0.1	4.2	80.3	266.4	116.9	15.6	0.7	484.2
2018	0.0	0.0	0.1	4.2	80.7	267.6	117.4	15.7	0.7	486.4
2018	0.0	0.0	0.1	4.3	81.3	269.5	118.2	15.9	0.7	489.9

INDUSTRY: WAREHOUSE CLUBS & SUPERCENTERS (NAICS 45291)
PRODUCT LINE: SOUVENIR & NOVELTY ITEMS (Main Category)

NAICS 45291: Warehouse Clubs and Superstores This industry comprises establishments known as warehouse clubs, superstores or supercenters primarily engaged in retailing a general line of groceries in combination with general lines of new merchandise, such as apparel, furniture, and appliances.

5-YEAR TREND — ESTIMATED INDUSTRY SALES ($MILLIONS)

Year	1-4 Emps.	5-9 Emps.	10-19 Emps.	20-49 Emps.	50-99 Emps.	100-249 Emps.	250-499 Emps.	500-999 Emps.	Unknown Emps.	Total Industry Sales
2015	0.1	0.0	0.0	1.0	1.2	152.7	674.9	17.8	0.2	848.0
2016	0.1	0.0	0.0	1.0	1.3	158.3	699.6	18.5	0.2	879.0
2017	0.1	0.0	0.0	1.1	1.3	163.5	722.9	19.1	0.2	908.3
2018	0.1	0.0	0.0	1.1	1.4	177.6	785.2	20.7	0.2	986.5
2018	0.1	0.0	0.0	1.2	1.5	188.6	833.9	22.0	0.3	1,047.7

INDUSTRY: OFFICE SUPPLIES & STATIONERY STORES (NAICS 45321)
PRODUCT LINE: SOUVENIR & NOVELTY ITEMS (Main Category)

NAICS 45321: Office Supplies and Stationery Stores . this industry comprises establishments primarily engaged in one or more of the following: (1) retailing new stationery, school supplies, and office supplies; (2) selling a combination of new office equipment, furniture, and supplies; and (3) selling new office equipment, furniture, and supplies in combination with selling new computers.

5-YEAR TREND — ESTIMATED INDUSTRY SALES ($MILLIONS)

Year	1-4 Emps.	5-9 Emps.	10-19 Emps.	20-49 Emps.	50-99 Emps.	100-249 Emps.	250-499 Emps.	500-999 Emps.	Unknown Emps.	Total Industry Sales
2015	0.8	0.6	3.3	9.3	0.2	0.2	0.0	0.0	0.2	14.7
2016	0.8	0.6	3.3	9.3	0.2	0.2	0.0	0.0	0.2	14.7
2017	0.8	0.6	3.3	9.3	0.2	0.2	0.0	0.0	0.2	14.7
2018	0.8	0.6	3.2	9.1	0.2	0.2	0.0	0.0	0.2	14.3
2018	0.8	0.6	3.2	8.9	0.2	0.2	0.0	0.0	0.2	14.1

INDUSTRY: ELECTRONIC SHOPPING & MAIL-ORDER (NAICS 45411)
PRODUCT LINE: SOUVENIR & NOVELTY ITEMS (Main Category)

NAICS 45411: Electronic Shopping and Mail-Order Houses This industry comprises establishments primarily engaged in retailing all types of merchandise by means of mail or by electronic media, such as interactive television or computer. Included in this industry are establishments primarily engaged in retailing from catalogue showrooms of mail-order houses.

5-YEAR TREND — ESTIMATED INDUSTRY SALES ($MILLIONS)

Year	Employee Size of Establishment									Total Industry Sales
	1-4 Emps.	5-9 Emps.	10-19 Emps.	20-49 Emps.	50-99 Emps.	100-249 Emps.	250-499 Emps.	500-999 Emps.	Unknown Emps.	
2015	410.3	217.8	323.5	523.4	376.4	733.9	1,073.8	1,360.3	62.1	5,081.5
2016	437.7	232.4	345.1	558.3	401.6	782.9	1,145.5	1,451.0	66.2	5,420.6
2017	464.2	246.5	366.0	592.1	425.9	830.4	1,215.0	1,539.1	70.2	5,749.4
2018	528.3	280.5	416.5	673.8	484.7	944.9	1,382.5	1,708.4	79.9	6,499.4
2018	586.8	311.5	462.6	748.4	538.3	1,049.5	1,535.6	1,864.7	88.7	7,186.1

INDUSTRY: BOOK STORE INDUSTRY (NAICS 451211)
PRODUCT LINE: SOUVENIR & NOVELTY ITEMS (Main Category)

NAICS 451211: Book Stores. this industry comprises establishments primarily engaged in the retail sale of new books and magazines. Establishments primarily engaged in the retail sale of used books are classified in 5932.

5-YEAR TREND — ESTIMATED INDUSTRY SALES ($MILLIONS)

Year	Employee Size of Establishment									Total Industry Sales
	1-4 Emps.	5-9 Emps.	10-19 Emps.	20-49 Emps.	50-99 Emps.	100-249 Emps.	250-499 Emps.	500-999 Emps.	Unknown Emps.	
2015	13.2	20.1	41.7	109.1	49.3	19.4	3.5	13.0	6.8	276.1
2016	13.9	21.2	43.9	115.1	51.9	20.5	3.7	13.8	7.1	291.1
2017	14.6	22.3	46.1	120.8	54.5	21.5	3.9	14.4	7.5	305.6
2018	14.7	22.4	46.4	121.6	54.9	21.6	3.9	14.8	7.5	308.1
2018	14.8	22.6	46.8	122.6	55.4	21.8	4.0	15.2	7.6	310.9

DEFINITIONS, METHODOLOGY AND TERMS

Methodology

Barnes Reports' Product Lines reports provide estimates of the sales of product lines in the largest retail industries. These estimates are produced by a proprietary economic model that is based on a number of sources and factors:

-The size and characteristics of the largest U.S. industries (based on the U.S. Bureau of the Census statistics, inflation rates and industry trends).
-The sales of product lines by industry. Main category and sub category product lines weights are a proportion of the U.S. total product lines sales.
-U.S. States statistics are based on industry breakdown and product lines weights are applied by size of firm.

NAICS codes (North American Classification System codes) are used in each industry definition in order to aid report users in clarifying and standardizing the definitions of each industry.
Product lines codes are available through the U.S. Bureau of the Census.

Number of Establishments

General Definition

An establishment is a single physical location at which business is conducted and/or services are provided. It is not necessarily identical with a company or enterprise, which may consist of one establishment or more. Economic census figures represent a summary of reports for individual establishments rather than companies. For cases where a census report was received, separate information was obtained for each location where business was conducted. When administrative records of other Federal agencies were used instead of a census report, no information was available on the number of locations operated. Each economic census establishment was tabulated according to the physical location at which the business was conducted.

When two activities or more were carried on at a single location under a single ownership, all activities generally were grouped together as a single establishment. The entire establishment was classified on the basis of its major activity and all data for it were included in that classification. However, when distinct and separate economic activities (for which different industry classification codes were appropriate) were conducted at a single location under a single ownership, separate establishment reports for each of the different activities were obtained in the census.

Sector-Specific Information

Construction sector. Establishments are defined as a relatively permanent office or other place of business where the usual business activities related to construction are conducted. Establishments do not represent each project or construction site. Includes all establishments that were in business at any time during the year. It covers all full-year and part-year operations. Construction establishments which were inactive or idle for the entire year were not included. Establishments are based on a survey which included all large employers and a sample of the smaller ones.

Information; Professional, Scientific, and Technical Services; Administrative and Support and Waste Management and Remediation Services; Educational Services; Health Care and Social Assistance; Arts, Entertainment, and Recreation; and Other Services (Except Public Administration) sectors. An establishment is included in the census if it is an employer, the establishment has $1,000 in payroll, and was in operation at any time during 1997. Leased service departments (separately owned businesses operated as departments or concessions of other service establishments or of retail businesses, such as a separately owned shoeshine parlor in a barber shop, or a beauty shop in a department store) are treated as separate service establishments for census purposes. Leased retail departments located in service establishments (e.g., a gift shop located in a hotel) are considered separate retail establishments. Manufacturing sector. Includes all manufacturing establishments (plants) with one employee or more and establishments in operation at any time during the year.

Mining sector. Includes all mineral establishments with one employee or more and establishments in operation at any time during the year. Establishments in the crude petroleum and natural gas and support activities for mining represent statewide operations rather than those at a single physical location.

Real Estate and Rental and Leasing sector. Data for individual properties leased or managed by property lessors or property managers are not normally considered separate establishments, but rather the permanent offices from which the properties are leased or managed are considered establishments. Data for separate automotive rental offices or concessions (e.g., airport locations) in the same metropolitan area for which a common fleet of cars is maintained are merged together and not considered as separate establishments.

Retail Trade sector. Leased departments are treated as separate establishments and are classified according to the kind of business they conduct. For example, a leased department selling shoes within a department store would be considered a separate retail establishment under the "shoe stores" classification.

Accommodation and Foodservices sector. Leased departments are treated as separate establishments and are classified according to the kind of business they conduct. For example, a leased department selling gifts/souvenirs within a hotel would be considered a separate retail establishment under the "gift, novelty, and souvenir stores" classification.

Auxiliaries sector. In the Standard Industrial Classification (SIC) system, auxiliary establishments (i.e., those establishments primarily serving other establishments of the same enterprise) were classified in the industry of the establishments served. In the North American Industry Classification System (NAICS), auxiliary establishments are classified according to the services performed rather than the industry served.

Sales, Shipments, Receipts, Revenue, or Business Done

General Definition

Includes the total sales, shipments, receipts, revenue, or business done by establishments within the scope of the economic census. The definition of each of these items is included in the information provided below.

Sector-Specific Information

Construction sector - Includes the value of construction work and other business receipts for work done by establishments during the year. Included is new construction, additions and alterations or reconstruction, and maintenance and repair construction work. Also included is the value of any construction work done by the reporting establishments for themselves.

Speculative builders were instructed to include the value of buildings and other structures built or being built for sale in the current year but not sold. They were to include the costs of such construction plus normal profit. Also included is the cost of construction work done on buildings for rent or lease.

Establishments engaged in the sale and installation of such construction components as plumbing, heating, and central air-conditioning supplies and equipment; lumber and building materials; paint, glass, and wallpaper; electrical and wiring supplies; and elevators or escalators were instructed to include both the value for the installation and the receipts covering the price of the items installed.

Excluded was the cost of industrial and other specialized machinery and equipment, which are not an integral part of a structure.

Finance and Insurance sector - Includes revenue from all business activities whether or not payment was received in the census year, including commissions and fees from all sources, rents, net investment income, interest, dividends, royalties, and net insurance premiums earned. Revenue from leasing property marketed under operating leases is included, as well as interest earned from property marketed in the census year under capital, finance, or full payout leases. Revenue also includes the total value of service contracts and amounts received for work subcontracted to others.

Revenue does not include sales and other taxes collected from customers and remitted directly by the firm to a local, state, or Federal tax agency.

Information sector - Includes receipts from customers or clients for services rendered, from the use of facilities, and from merchandise sold, whether or not payment was received. Receipts include royalties, license fees, and other payments from the marketing of intangible products (e.g., licensing the use of or granting reproduction rights for software, musical compositions, and other intellectual property). Receipts also include the rental and leasing of vehicles, equipment, instruments, tools, etc.; total value of service contracts; market value of compensation received in lieu of cash; amounts received for work subcontracted to others; dues and assessments for members and affiliates; this establishment's share of receipts from departments, concessions, and vending and amusement machines operated by others. Receipts from services provided to foreign customers from U.S. locations, including services preformed for foreign parent firms, subsidiaries, and branches are included. For public broadcast stations and libraries, include receipts from contributions, gifts, grants, and income from interest, rental of real estate, and dividends.

Receipts DO NOT include sales and other taxes collected directly from customers or clients and paid directly to a local, state, or Federal tax agency. Also excluded are gross receipts collected on behalf of others; gross receipts or departments or concessions operated by others; sales of used equipment previously rented or leased to customers; proceeds from the sale of real estate (land and buildings), investments, or other assets (except inventory held for resale); contributions, gifts, grants, and income from interest, rental of real estate, and dividends EXCEPT for public broadcast stations and libraries; domestic intracompany transfers; receipts of foreign subsidiaries; and other nonoperating income.

Management of Companies and Enterprises sector- For holding companies, revenue includes revenue of only the holding company establishment, including net investment income, interest, and dividends.

Manufacturing sector - Covers the received or receivable net selling values, f.o.b. plant (exclusive of freight and taxes), of all products shipped, both primary and secondary, as well as all miscellaneous receipts, such as receipts for contract work performed for others, installation and repair, sales of scrap, and sales of products bought and resold without further processing. Included are all items made by or for the establishments from materials owned by it, whether sold, transferred to other plants of the same company, or shipped on consignment. The net selling value of products made in one plant on a contract basis from materials owned by another was reported by the plant providing the materials.

In the case of multiunit companies, the manufacturer was requested to report the value of products transferred to other establishments of the same company at full economic or commercial value, including not only the direct cost of production but also a reasonable proportion of "all other costs" (including company overhead) and profit.

Mining sector - Includes the net selling values, f.o.b. mine or plant after discounts and allowances, excluding freight charges and excise taxes. Shipments includes all products physically shipped from the establishment during the year, including material withdrawn from stockpiles and products shipped on consignment, whether or not sold in the current year. Prepared material or concentrates includes preparation from ores mined at the same establishment, purchased, received from other operations of the same company, or received for milling on a custom or toll basis. For products transferred to other establishments of the same company or prepared on a custom basis, companies were requested to report the estimated value, not merely the cost of producing the items. Multiestablishment companies were asked to report value information for each establishment as if it were a separate economic unit. They were instructed to report the value of all products transferred to other plants of the company at their full economic value; to include, in addition to direct cost of production, a reasonable proportion of company overhead and profits. For all establishments classified in an industry, value of shipments and receipts includes (1) the value of all primary products of the industry; (2) the value of secondary products which are primary to other industries; (3) the receipts for contract work done for others, except custom milling; and (4) the value of products purchased and resold without further processing. Receipts for custom milling are not included to avoid duplication with the value of custom milled ores included in an industry's primary and secondary products. Some duplication exists in industry and industry group totals because of the inclusion of materials transferred from one establishment to another for mineral preparation or resale.

Professional, Scientific, and Technical Services; Administrative and Support and Waste Management and Remediation Services; Educational Services; Health Care and Social Assistance; Arts, Entertainment, and Recreation; and Other Services (Except Public Administration) sectors - TAXABLE ESTABLISHMENTS: Includes receipts from customers or clients for services rendered, from the use of facilities, and from merchandise sold whether or not payment was received. For advertising agencies, travel industries, and other service establishments operating on a commission basis, receipts include commissions, fees, and other operating income, NOT gross billings and sales. Excise taxes on gasoline, liquor, tobacco, etc., which are paid by the manufacturer or wholesaler and passed on in the cost of goods purchased by the service establishment are also included. The establishments share of receipts from departments, concessions, and vending and amusement machines operated by others are included as part of receipts. Receipts also include the total value of service contracts, market value of compensation received in lieu of cash, amounts received for work subcontracted to others, and dues and assessments from members and affiliates. Receipts from services provided to foreign customers from U.S. locations, including services preformed for foreign parent firms, subsidiaries, and branches are included.

Receipts are net after deductions for refunds and allowances for merchandise returned by customers. Receipts DO NOT include sales, occupancy, admissions, or other taxes collected from customers and remitted directly by the firm to a local, state, or Federal tax agency, nor do they include income from such sources as contributions, gifts, and grants; dividends, interest, and investments; or sale or rental of real estate. Also excluded are receipts (gross) of departments and concessions which are operated by others; sales of used equipment rented or leased to customers; domestic intracompany transfers; receipts of foreign subsidiaries; and other nonoperating income, such as royalties, franchise fees, etc. Receipts DO NOT include service receipts of manufacturers, wholesalers, retail establishments, or other businesses whose primary activity is other than service. They do, however, include receipts other than from services rendered (e.g., sale of merchandise to individuals or other businesses) by establishments primarily engaged in performing services and classified in the service industries.

TAX EXEMPT ESTABLISHMENTS: Includes revenue from customers or clients for services rendered and merchandise, whether or not payment was received, and gross sales of merchandise, minus returns and allowances. Also included are income from interest, dividends, gross rents (including display space rentals and share of receipts from departments operated by other companies), gross contributions, gifts, grants (whether or not restricted for use in operations), royalties, dues and assessments from members and affiliates, commissions earned from the sale of merchandise owned by others (including commissions from vending machine operators), and gross receipts from fundraising activities. Receipts from taxable business activities of firms exempt from Federal income tax (unrelated business income) are also included in revenue. Revenue DOES NOT include sales, admissions, or other taxes collected by the organization from customers or clients and paid directly to a local, state, or Federal tax agency; income from the sale of real estate, investments, or other assets (except inventory held for resale); gross receipts of departments, concessions, etc., that are operated by others; and amounts transferred to operating funds from capital or reserve funds.

Real Estate and Rental and Leasing sector - Includes revenue from all business activities whether or not payment was received in the census year, including commissions and fees from all sources, rents, net investment income, interest, dividends, and royalties. Revenue from leasing property marketed under operating leases is included. Revenue also includes the total value of service contracts, amounts received for work subcontracted to others, and rents from real property sublet to others.

Revenue does not include sales and other taxes collected from customers and remitted directly by the firm to a local, state, or Federal tax agency.

Retail Trade sector - Includes merchandise sold for cash or credit at retail and wholesale by establishments primarily engaged in retail trade; amounts received from customers for layaway purchases; receipts from rental of vehicles, equipment, instruments, tools, etc.; receipts for delivery, installation, maintenance, repair, alteration, storage, and other services; the total value of service contracts; and gasoline, liquor, tobacco, and other excise taxes which are paid by the manufacturer or wholesaler and passed on to the retailer. Sales are net after deductions for refunds and allowances for merchandise returned by customers. Trade-in allowances are not deducted from sales. Sales do not include carrying or other credit charges; sales (or other) taxes collected from customers and forwarded to taxing authorities; gross sales and receipts of departments or concessions operated by other companies; and commissions or receipts from the sale of government lottery tickets.

Sales do not include retail sales made by manufacturers, wholesalers, service establishments, or other businesses whose primary activity is other than retail trade. They do include receipts other than from the sale of merchandise at retail, e.g., service receipts, sales to industrial users, and sales to other retailers, by establishments primarily engaged in retail trade.

Transportation and Warehousing sector - Includes revenue from all business activities whether or not payment was received in the census year, including commissions and fees for arranging the transportation of freight. Revenue does not include sales and other taxes collected from customers and remitted directly by the firm